Encyclopaedia of
Architectural Terms

BY THE SAME AUTHOR

European Cities and Society. The Influence of Political Climate on Town Design. Leonard Hill Books, London, 1970 and 1972.

The Victorian Celebration of Death. David & Charles (Publishers) Ltd, Newton Abbot, 1972.

City of London Pubs (with Timothy Richards). David & Charles (Holdings) Ltd, Newton Abbot, 1973.

Victorian Architecture: Its Practical Aspects. David & Charles (Holdings) Ltd, Newton Abbot, 1973.

The Cemeteries and Burial Grounds of Glasgow. City of Glasgow Parks Department, Glasgow, 1975.

The Erosion of Oxford. Oxford Illustrated Press Ltd, Oxford, 1977.

English Architecture: An Illustrated Glossary. David & Charles (Publishers) Ltd, Newton Abbot, 1977. Second edition, 1987.

Mausolea in Ulster. Ulster Architectural Heritage Society, Belfast, 1978.

Moneymore and Draperstown. The Architecture and Planning of the Ulster Estates of the Drapers' Company. Ulster Architectural Heritage Society, Belfast, 1979.

A Celebration of Death. An Introduction to Some of the Buildings, Monuments, and Settings of Funerary Architecture in the Western European Tradition. Constable & Co. Ltd, London, 1980. American edition published by Scribners, New York, 1980.

Classical Churches in Ulster. Ulster Architectural Heritage Society, Belfast, 1980.

The History, Architecture, and Planning of the Estates of the Fishmongers' Company in Ulster. Ulster Architectural Heritage Society, Belfast, 1981.

The Egyptian Revival. An Introductory Study of a Recurring Theme in the History of Taste. George Allen & Unwin (Publishers) Ltd, London, 1982.

The Life and Work of Henry Roberts (1803–76), Architect. Phillimore & Co. Ltd, Chichester, 1983.

Winchester Walks. Paul Cave Publications Ltd, Southampton, 1983.

The Londonderry Plantation 1609–1914. The History, Architecture, and Planning of the Estates of the City of London and its Livery Companies in Ulster. Phillimore & Co. Ltd, Chichester, 1986.

Victorian Architecture. David & Charles Publishers plc, Newton Abbot, 1990.

The Art and Architecture of Freemasonry. B. T. Batsford Ltd, London, 1991.

Classical Architecture. An Introduction to its Vocabulary and Essentials. B. T. Batsford Ltd, London, 1992.

Encyclopaedia of Architectural Terms

JAMES STEVENS CURL

with illustrations
by the author
and
John J. Sambrook

DONHEAD

© James Stevens Curl 1992
Line drawings © James Stevens Curl and John Sambrook 1992

The moral right of the author has been asserted

First published in the United Kingdom
in 1993, and reprinted in 2003 by
Donhead Publishing Ltd
Lower Coombe
Donhead St Mary
Shaftesbury
Dorset SP7 9LY
Tel: +44 (0) 1747 828422
www.donhead.com

The paperback reprinted edition published
in 1997 and reprinted in 2003 by Donhead Publishing Ltd.
ISBN 1 873394 25 X (paperback)
ISBN 1 873394 04 7 (hardback)

A CIP catalogue for this book is available from the British Library.

Typeset by Keyboard Services, Luton
Printed in Great Britain at the Alden Press,
Osney Mead, Oxford

For
my daughters,
Astrid James and Ingrid Curl,
who accompanied me on expeditions
to many of the buildings illustrated
in this book, and who made
the gathering of material a pleasure,
this volume is inscribed
with gratitude and love

The more closely, constantly, and carefully we study [the native architecture of our own country, and that of our forefathers], the more entirely shall we be convinced that our love and admiration cannot exceed what is due to its intrinsic excellencies.

SIR GEORGE GILBERT SCOTT (1811–78)

[The English cathedrals] are more than buildings, more than art, something intangible was built into them with their stones and burnt into the glass. The work of a man, a man may understand; but these are the works of ages, of nations. They are serene, masterly, non-personal, like works of nature – indeed they are such, natural manifestations of the minds of men working under the impulse of a noble idea.

WILLIAM RICHARD LETHABY (1857–1931)

One of the most sad wastes of power to which men of good will are subject is vain strife about words, especially when pairs of words have been allowed to come into opposition – such as faith and works, or art and science. There is really no opposition between art and science. Show me your art, as St James might have said, and I will show you your science. The most of art is science in operation, and a large part of science is reflection on art.

WILLIAM RICHARD LETHABY (1857–1931)

Preface

Architecture aims at Eternity; and therefore is the only Thing uncapable of Modes and Fashions in its Principals, the *Orders*.

CHRISTOPHER WREN
Tracts on Architecture I, quoted
in Stephen Wren's *Parentalia, or
Memoirs of the Family of Wrens*, 1750
Reprinted in *The Wren Society*,
Vol. 19, p. 126, Oxford, 1942.

This book is intended to provide an introduction to the vocabulary used to describe our built heritage so that the basic architectural elements can be identified. I have therefore compiled a list of historical terms, illustrated where appropriate, and accompanied with succinct explanations. I rejected the notion of including potted biographies of British architects: Howard M. Colvin has provided the definitive work in his *A Biographical Dictionary of British Architects 1600–1840*, published in 1978, which should be consulted by those interested in the personalities of that period. *A Biographical Dictionary of Architects in Ireland 1600–1720*, by Rolf Loeber (1981), *Dictionary of Land Surveyors and Local Cartographers of Great Britain and Ireland*, edited by Peter Eden (1979), and *The Penguin Dictionary of Design and Designers*, by Simon Jervis (1984), are also useful. My work is mostly my own compilation, but owes debts to *An Encyclopaedia of Architecture, Historical, Theoretical, and Practical*, by Joseph Gwilt, revised by Wyatt Papworth (1903), to *A Glossary of Terms used in Grecian, Roman, Italian, and Gothic Architecture*, published by John Parker (1850), to *An Architectural and Engineering Dictionary, Containing Correct Nomenclature and Derivation of the Terms Employed by Architects, Builders, and Workmen*, by Peter Nicholson

(1835), to *A Treatise on the Decorative Part of Civil Architecture*, by Sir William Chambers (in the Gwilt edition of 1825), to *The Architectural Director: Being a Guide to Builders, Draughtsmen, Students, and Workmen* by John Billington (1848), and to many other sources listed in the Select Bibliography. For those who wish to know something of the sculptors who created so many monuments in churches, on buildings, in graveyards, and in public places, the *Dictionary of British Sculptors 1660–1851*, by Rupert Gunnis, is indispensable. Journals such as *The Builder, The Journal of the Royal Institute of British Architects*, and *The Architect and Building News*, provide information concerning later architects and their works for those disposed to ferret out the details. John Claudius Loudon's *An Encyclopaedia of Cottage, Farm, and Villa Architecture and Furniture* (1834) is also useful, as are many of Loudon's other publications.

Included in the book are some Scots terms, many of which are encountered in the northern counties of England, and I make no apology for including them: many were collected during the three very interesting years when I was Architectural Adviser to the Scottish Committee for European Architectural Heritage Year, 1975, and many others can be found in 'A Scottish Building Glossary: Survival of Craft Terms' by Ralph E. Bullock, published in *The Builder* of 20 June 1952. Glen L. Pride's *Glossary of Scottish Building*, published in 1975, is recommended to readers who wish to pursue a study of Scots terms.

I have tried to be as comprehensive as possible, but I have rejected Japanese, Chinese, and many other foreign terms unless they are appropriate to European architecture. Some readers may wonder why so many terms from Graeco-Roman Antiquity and from other non-British architecture are included: the reason is that historical architecture is often eclectic, especially in the nineteenth century, and includes not only Classical and Neoclassical examples, but work owing much to Moorish, Islamic, Indian, Spanish, and other sources.

As many unhackneyed pictures are included as was possible, often from my own collection, but I am also indebted to the staffs of the libraries and collections acknowledged with each illustration where it has not been possible to provide my own photographs. All drawings are my own (*JSC*), or are by John J. Sambrook (*JJS*). I am indebted to the staffs of the Shropshire County Council Record Office, of the Hereford City Library, the library of the Royal Borough of Kensington and Chelsea, the RIBA British Architectural Library, the Guildhall Library, City of London, the Royal Archives at Windsor Castle, and of the Greater London Photograph Library for help. I am also grateful to all the vicars and other clergy, and to the various cathedral authorities, for permission to photograph.

My long-suffering family accompanied me in search of examples for this book, and I am indebted to them for their patience and understanding: they often spent a great deal of time in cathedrals and churches while I made notes and took photographs. My old friend, Mr Rodney C. Roach, who has collaborated with me for many years, enlarged the pictures and processed my film in his usual expert fashion: I acknowledge a large debt to his kindness and efficiency. Miss Iona Cruickshank also very kindly helped with many of the illustrations. Mr Robert Blow and Mr Ian Leith of the Architectural Section of the Royal Commission on the Historical Monuments of England (RCHME) were helpful beyond all duty, while Miss Kitty Cruft of the National Monuments Record of Scotland (the Royal Commission on the Ancient and Historical Monuments of Scotland (RCAHMS)) and Mr Chris Denvir of the Greater London Photograph Library rendered courteous assistance.

The source of each drawing and photograph is acknowledged in its caption.

I am also grateful to Mr Anthony F. Kersting of London for providing me with material, and to Mr John J. Sambrook for revising many of his drawings and for making many helpful suggestions. Miss Hermione Hobhouse, General Editor of the *Survey of London*, was most kind, while Professor Peter G. Swallow, Head of the Department of Building Surveying, School of the Built Environment, De Montfort University, Leicester, gave invaluable help and advice. He and Dr David Watkin, Head of the Department of History of Art, University of Cambridge, read the drafts and made kind and helpful comments: their advice is most warmly acknowledged. Others who rendered assistance were the late Mr A. H. Buck, the late Mr Terence Davis, Mr Joseph Kilner, Miss Helen I. Logan, Mr Denis F. McCoy, the late Mr Kit Norbury, and the late Mr A. W. Pullan. Mrs Pamela Walker assisted in the preparation of the material for this book and I record here my thanks to her for her suggestions and help, especially in relation to the arduous task of typing the manuscript.

The British Academy made a Personal Research Grant towards the costs of providing the illustrations: this is acknowledged with thanks. Practical help was also given by The Worshipful Company of Carpenters, by The Worshipful Company of Tylers and Bricklayers, by The Building Centre Trust, and by The Interbuild Trust, to which bodies grateful thanks is given.

Finally, Professor Swallow and Mr Sambrook very kindly read the proofs and made helpful suggestions for corrections and improvements: their help is warmly appreciated.

It is my earnest hope that this encyclopaedia will give pleasure to those who use it, that it will indeed be useful, and that it will stimulate a greater understanding of the unique riches to be found among the buildings of Europe.

JAMES STEVENS CURL
Burley-on-the-Hill
Rutland
1992

TEXTUAL NOTE

All cross-references are indicated by the symbol ▷.

A

Aaron's rod [1] A winged olive staff entwined with ▷leaves, or with ▷serpents coiled around it; also called the *caduceus* or *Wand of Hermes*.

Abaciscus Synonymous with ▷abacus, but more properly a square compartment enclosing part of a design of a ▷mosaic ▷pavement. A ▷tessalla or ▷*tessera* in mosaic work, also called an *abaculus*. A small abacus.

Abaculus ▷Abaciscus.

Abacus The ▷slab at the top of a ▷capital, crowning the ▷column and supporting the ▷entablature. Vitruvius confined the term *abacus* to ▷Ionic and ▷Corinthian capitals, and called the ▷Doric abacus *plinthus*, which corresponds to the ▷plinth ▷block under many later column ▷bases of other ▷Orders. The ▷Tuscan abacus, in the versions of Palladio and Serlio, is square on plan, with flat, plain, unmoulded sides, but in the versions of Scamozzi and Vignola it has a plain crowning ▷fillet with ▷cavetto moulding (▷mould) under it. The ▷Greek Doric abacus is a simple square block, unmoulded and unchamfered; the ▷Roman Doric abacus, while also square on plan, has plain sides surmounted by a ▷*cyma reversa* (▷Lesbian cymatium) moulding (plain or

[1] AARON'S ROD Also known as the *caduceus*. (*JSC*)

enriched) over which is a fillet. The Greek Ionic abacus is very thin, with an ▷ovolo edge, and is sometimes enriched; in some cases (Cockerell's version of the Temple of Apollo Epicurius at Bassae) it is deeper, with concave sides on plan; usually, however, it has straight sides on plan, although, in the case of ▷corner-capitals with ▷volutes at 45°, it follows the shape of the capital. Roman Ionic abaci usually have fillets over cyma reversa mouldings (the latter plain or enriched), although the ovolo–fillet–cavetto section also occurs. Usually the Corinthian (both Greek and Roman) and ▷Composite abacus has four concave faces segmental on plan, joining in points, or, more often, ▷chamfered where the concave sides meet. The four-concave-sided abacus o plan is also found in the Roman Ionic Order where there are eight volutes present instead of the usual four (▷angular capital and ▷Scamozzi Order). In the centres of each of the four faces of the Corinthian abacus is a floral or other ▷ornament (▷fleuron), and the vertical section consists of an ovolo, fillet, and cavetto moulding, plain or ornamented. In the Tower of the Winds, Athens, also known as the *Horologium* of Andronikus Cyrrhestes, the capitals have one row of ▷acanthus leaves and a row of pointed forms resembling ▷palm ▷leaves (▷Corinthian Order); the abacus, unusually for the Corinthian type, is square on plan, although in vertical section it still has the ovolo, fillet, and cavetto moulds. Abaci, according to Newton's *Vitruvius*, can mean flat tabulated surfaces (▷tabulate), and can be applied to the ▷panels of ▷walls formed of ▷stucco, or to the walls above a ▷dado or ▷podium which would be decorated (▷Order and under the names of Orders). The ▷Egyptian abacus is thick, sometimes ▷bell-shaped, sometimes a square block of considerable thickness, and sometimes elaborated in the form of a ▷shrine. ▷Saxon abaci are generally unmoulded and flat. ▷Norman or ▷Romanesque abaci are found square,

1

circular, octagonal, and frequently moulded and decorated. During the Middle Ages the abacus varied greatly, and was sometimes vestigial. In some instances, where the capitals consist of clusters of mouldings, the abacus is difficult to define.

Abamurus A ▷buttress or a ▷wall erected against a wall in order to reinforce that wall.

Abat-jour An opening with ▷splayed ▷jambs, ▷head, and ▷sill, to admit more light to the interior from a relatively small ▷window: that is, the interior opening is bigger than the exterior.

Abat-vent A sloping ▷louvre which allows light and air to enter, but which restricts the entry of wind. It is usually placed in the ▷belfry ▷stages of ▷church ▷towers.

Abat-voix A sound-reflecting ▷canopy behind or over a ▷pulpit, also called a ▷tester.

Abated Cut away or beaten down to create a pattern in low ▷relief.

Abaton A building, the entrance to which is forbidden to everybody. It was named after a structure in Rhodes erected by Artemisia. A ▷sanctuary, a Holy of Holies.

Abattoir A public slaughter-house, from the French *abattre*, to knock down.

Abbey [2] A ▷monastery of religious persons secluded wholly or partially from the world, and under vows of celibacy, poverty, and obedience, consisting of monks under an abbot, or of nuns under an abbess. It was the jurisdiction or benefice of an abbot, the religious establishment, and the monastic buildings. In the sense of structure, the term means the ▷church and buildings of a monastic establishment, the superior of which was an abbot. The monastic ▷architecture of mediaeval times evolved in the sixth century, and was a response to the rules established by St Benedict at

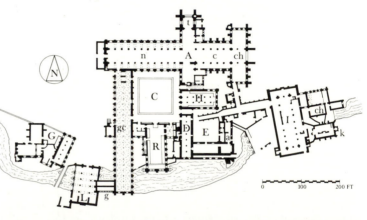

(a)

[2] ABBEY (*a*) Plan of Fountains Abbey, Yorkshire. **A** abbey church, **C** cloister, **H** chapter-house, **E** cells, **R** refectory, **D** undercroft of dormitory, **I** infirmary, **L** lay infirmary, **G** guest-houses, **ch** chapels, **n** nave, **c** choir, **k** kitchen, **a** abbot's house, **g** garderobe or reredorter, **t** tower, **gc** Great Cellar. (*JJS*) (*b*) The Great Cellar at Fountains Abbey, Yorkshire. Note that the vaulting runs from the piers without capitals, and springs from corbels on the walls. This beautiful vaulted room, virtually intact, dates from the latter half of the twelfth and the first decades of the thirteenth century. The floor has risen somewhat since the Great Cellar was built. (*JSC*)

(b)

Monte Cassino, although other orders subsequently established monasteries, notably the Cistercians. In the later Middle Ages monasteries became highly complex developments: they consisted of ▷church, ▷cloisters, ▷chapter-house, ▷refectory, ▷guest-hall, ▷locutory, ▷dormitory, ▷almonry, ▷library, ▷cells, and sometimes a ▷prison for offenders. Often there were ▷granges, ▷schools with accommodation, ▷common-rooms, ▷mints, ▷treasuries and ▷sanatoria. All abbeys had graveyards (▷grave), ▷gardens, and ▷bakehouses. ▷Kitchens, ▷brewhouses, corn-mills (▷mill), ▷stables, ▷byres, ▷piggeries, ▷workshops, ▷smithies and stores completed the complex. Abbeys were self-contained communities and played a positive part in economic, spiritual, and intellectual life. They frequently vied with each other as places of pilgrimage and were often richly endowed with relics and magnificent furnishings to attract the faithful. There were, of course, several religious orders with specializations of their own. Many abbeys developed great traditions of musical performance, and the singing-schools of several were world famous. Traditional plainchant, and later polyphony, were living parts of the great religious services. It is chiefly to the abbeys that we are indebted for the cultivation of architecture and painting during the Middle Ages.

Abditorium A secret place for records, associated with the ▷columns of Solomon's ▷Temple, which were supposed to be hollow, and therefore were considered to hold within them the eternal secrets of the world.

Aberdeen granite A grey ▷granite, extremely hard and durable, used in buildings and ▷monuments, especially in the ▷Victorian period. It is capable of taking a high polish.

Ablaq ▷Masonry laid and partly coloured.

Abreuvoir, abrevoir, abbreuvoir In ▷masonry, the interstice, or joint, between two stones to be filled with ▷mortar.

Absidiole ▷Apse.

Absis ▷Apse.

Abuse A term applied to practices in ▷architecture which corrupt the best forms. Palladio wrote copiously on the subject, and identified four main abuses: the introduction of ▷brackets, ▷modillions, or ▷consoles to support a weight; the practice of breaking ▷pediments to leave the central part open; excessive ▷projections of ▷cornices; and practices of rusticating (▷rustic) ▷columns. Gwilt added the following: allowing ▷pilasters and columns to join, especially at an ▷angle; coupling columns (▷couple), as in the east front of the

▷Louvre; the enlarging of the ▷metopes of the ▷Doric Order to accommodate wider ▷intercolumniations; omitting the inferior part of the ▷tailloir or ▷abacus of the ▷Ionic ▷capital; ▷Giant Orders instead of ▷Orders for each floor; joining the ▷plinth of a column to the cornice of a ▷pedestal by means of an inverted ▷cavetto; the use of ▷architrave cornices; and breaking an ▷entablature over a column.

All these 'abuses' have really passed into the realms of a rich architectural language of ▷Classicism through the deliberate distortions of inventive architects such as Michelangelo (columns on consoles) and Perrault (paired columns).

Abutment [3] The solid part of a ▷pier from which an ▷arch springs, or the extremities of a ▷bridge. Abutments can be artificial, of stone (▷masonry), ▷bricks, or ▷concrete, to counteract the lateral thrust of an arch, but the term can also be applied to solid rock which receives the ▷foot of an arch. Abutments must be strong enough to resist the natural tendency of an arch or an ▷arcade to collapse by opening outwards. Any solid structure which receives the thrust of an arch or a ▷vault. An abutment is also an intersection between a ▷roof and a ▷wall, and an *abutment-piece* is a ▷sill or a

[3] ABUTMENT The arcade in Leominster Priory church, showing a typical Romanesque arrangement of nave-arcade, tribune over, and clerestory lights above. Note the massive abutments and piers. (*JSC*)

▷sole-▷plate. *Abutting tenons* are two tenons entering a piece of timber from opposite sides and meeting in the centre of a ▷mortise.

Abuttals   The buttings or boundings of land.

Acaina, akaina   An Ancient ▷Greek measurement roughly equivalent to 30.86 metres. It may relate to a ▷pole measure (5.5 ▷yards).

Acanthus [4]   A genus of herbaceous plants, especially the species *acanthus spinosus*, *Bear's Breech*, or *Brank-Ursine*, native to the shores of the Mediterranean and prized among the ▷Greeks and ▷Romans for the elegance of its ▷leaves. A stylized version of the thick leaf of this spiny plant, said to have been modelled first by Callimachus, is used to decorate the lower part of ▷capitals of the ▷Corinthian and ▷Composite Orders, but the disposition of the leaves is different for each of these Orders. The acanthus is also found as a decorative feature elsewhere in ▷Classical architecture. In some instances (the ▷triumphal arches of Titus and Septimius Severus in Rome, for example), the leaves of the Composite Order resemble parsley, while those of the Temple of Vesta in Rome look more like the leaves of the ▷laurel. The acanthus seems to have been used in important ▷architecture for the first time on the ▷acroteria of the ▷Parthenon and in the decorations of the ▷Erechtheion in Athens.

Access   An ▷approach. An ▷access for maintenance is a ▷panel in a ▷chase, ▷conduit, or ▷duct. A ▷passage of communication to various ▷apartments of a building.

Accidental point   In ▷perspective, it is the point in the horizontal line where lines parallel to each other, not perpendicular in the picture, meet. A *vanishing* point.

Accolade   An ▷ornamental arrangement over an opening which consists of two ▷ogee curves meeting in the middle above or in an ▷arch.

Accompaniment   An ▷ornament added to another ornament for the greater ▷embellishment of the work.

Accouplement   An arrangement of paired ▷columns or ▷pilasters, as on the east ▷front of the ▷Louvre or the west front of St Paul's Cathedral.

[4] ACANTHUS LEAF. (*JJS*)

[5] ACORN Used as a finial or decorative device on top of a gate-pier or pedestal, the acorn is often a substitute for the pine-cone, pineapple, or urn. (*JSC*)

Acerra   An ▷altar erected in ▷Antiquity near the bed of a deceased person and on which offerings were made until the funeral. The term was also applied to a small jar in which incense and perfumes were kept until they were burned on altars before the dead.

Achievement of Arms   An ▷escutcheon or ▷ensign armorial, granted in memory of some achievement or distinguished feat. The term is contracted as ▷hatchment, to signify Arms, as hung up in a ▷church. An Achievement is the Arms of gentlemen, well marshalled with the ▷supporters, ▷helmet, ▷wreath, and crests (▷cress).

Acorn [5]   An ▷ornament in the form of an acorn used as a ▷finial or a ▷terminating feature on a ▷pier, on a ▷pediment, or on some other architectural element.

Acoustics   The science of sound, especially applicable to buildings. *Acoustic jars*, also known as *acoustic resonators* or *Golosniki*, were clay pots built into the ▷domes or the upper parts of ▷walls: they were arranged with their mouths towards the interior of the building but ▷flush with the wall surface. They are fire-proof and light, and so hollow clay ▷blocks were often used in the construction of ceilings, notably by Soane. Resonators give a rich acoustical effect, and they occur in ▷Byzantine and Greek and Russian Orthodox ▷churches. *Acoustic plaster* is wall- and ceiling-plaster with high sound absorption: this is created by the ▷honeycombed structure caused by the addition of aluminium powder which reacts with the mixing water to produce a gas.

Acroaterion   A ▷hall or place for lectures.

Acrobaticon   ▷Scaffolding in ▷Antiquity.

Acrolinthon   A colossal statue.

Acrolithi   Statues of which the face, hands, and feet only were of ▷marble, the remaining parts being of wood, which were usually covered with drapery.

Acropodium A raised ▷podium, ▷pedestal, or ▷plinth on which a statue is placed.

Acropolis Literally a 'high city', the fortress (▷fort) on a high eminence of a ▷Greek city-state, on which the finest buildings stood.

Acrostolium An ▷ornament on the ▷prow of a ship, usually circular or spiral, with a ▷buckler, helm, or animal: the extremities or business-end of a prow or ▷ram, as on a *Rostral column*.

Acroteria ▷Pedestals or ▷plinths at the ▷apex and lower extremities of ▷pediments: they can support statuary or ▷ornaments or can be quite unadorned. Acroteria or *acroters* can also refer, incorrectly, to the statues or ornaments on the plinths, while the singular (*acroterium*, *acroterion*) is applied to the ▷ridge of a building (▷[6]), and is also erroneously used to describe the pieces of ▷wall between pedestals and ▷balusters. *Acroterium* can be interchangeable with ▷*fastigium* in the sense of the ▷blocks. The blocks at the lower extremities of the pediment are called *acroteria angularia*.

According to Vitruvius (Book III, Chapter v, No. 12), the lower acroteria should be half the height of the ▷tympanum, and the acroterion at the apex should be an eighth higher than those at the corners to make it more visible. The term was sometimes used to denote ▷pinnacles. Acroteria are also found at the apices of ▷gables in ▷Gothic ▷achitecture, especially in ▷canopies (▷[234]).

Actus A ▷Roman measurement of land 120 *pedes* long. An *actus minimus* was 120 Roman feet long by 4 wide, and the *actus quadratus* was 120 Roman feet square. The Roman foot (*pes*) was divided into 12 *uniciae*. A Roman foot was about 0.97 English feet, or approximately 11.65 inches, so an *actus* was about 35.5 metres in length.

Acuminated Ending in a point, or finished as such, as in a ▷Gothic ▷roof or ▷vault.

[6] ACROTERION The ornament is set on a block (one of the *acroteria angularia*) at the end of the raking tops of the pediment. The example is based on that of the Temple of Aphaia at Aegina. (*JSC*)

Acute Something terminating in a sharp point or edge. Less than a right-angle. An *obtuse angle* is the opposite of *acute*, and is greater than 90°. Very acute angles in plans, ▷sections, materials, or ▷architecture are fundamentally weak, difficult to construct, impossible to maintain, and should be avoided. An *acute arch* is a sharply pointed *two-centred arch* with the radii greater than the ▷span of the arch (▷arch).

Adam style An architectural style derived from the work of Robert Adam (1728–92) and his brothers which dominated British taste from 1760 to 1780, and which influenced interior and furniture design. It was a phase of ▷Neoclassicism and was characterized by clarity of form, beautiful and subtle detail, and by unified schemes of clear colouring, mostly of great refinement. While influenced by ▷Antiquity, especially ▷Greek and ▷Pompeian precedents, it was never as severe as the Greek and ▷Egyptian ▷Revivals.

Adam's cement The Adam brothers used ▷stucco at the Adelphi development in London. This stucco consisted of a mixture of stone-lime and bone-ash in equal quantities with seven measures of clean sand mixed with lime-water. It was a quick-setting material.

Additive An admixture, or a substance added to something to improve performance, or for some other purpose, e.g. colour or strength.

Additus maximus The main entrance to a ▷Roman amphitheatre (▷amphi).

Addorsed Timbers or other elements placed back to back (▷affronted).

Adit, aditus The approach or entrance to a building. ▷Doors on ▷stairs.

Adjacent angle An ▷angle contiguous to another. Adjacent angles are those formed by one straight line standing on another.

Adobe Unburned, sunbaked ▷bricks or ▷blocks containing straw, used for building, known as *clay bats*, common in parts of Cambridgeshire. The term is sometimes confused with *cob*, or with *pisé de terre*, but these terms are quite distinct and have different meanings: *cob*, for example, is mud walling built up layer by layer, requiring neither ▷form-work nor ramming, while *pisé de terre* needs both ramming and form-work.

Advice stone A ▷lintel or other stone with lettering carved on it, otherwise known as a *marriage-lintel* or *-stone*.

Adytum The secret ▷chamber or inner ▷sanctuary of

a ▷Greek ▷temple from which oracles were delivered. It was usually without natural lighting. In Ancient Egypt it was known as the ▷Secos.

Adze A carpenter's tool like an axe with the blade set at right angles to the handle, and curving inwards towards it. It is used for cutting or slicing away the surface of pieces of timber. To adze is therefore to cut or ▷dress with an adze.

Aedes, aedis In ▷Antiquity, a ▷chapel, shrine, or ▷temple, not consecrated by the Augurs, or any small temple or chapel.

(b)

[7] AEDICULE (a) Aediculated and pedimented window-opening. **p** pulvinated frieze, **d** die. (*JJS*) (b) Aediculated doorway from Kirby Hall, Northamptonshire. An early Renaissance example. (*JSC*)

Aedicule [7] A ▷shrine or opening framed (▷frame) by two ▷columns or ▷pilasters supporting an ▷entablature and ▷pediment (segmental or triangular), usually containing a statue. It is also used as a term signifying the framing of a ▷door, ▷window, or ▷niche, with two columns, pilasters, or ▷piers, carrying a ▷gable, entablature, and pediment, or a single ▷lintel. An opening framed in such a manner could be said to be *aediculated*. An *aedicula* in ▷Antiquity, also known as ▷*sacellum*, signified a small ▷temple, an inner part of a temple in which the ▷altar and cult-statue were enshrined, or a niche in which a statue could be placed. *Aediculus* was the deity who presided over the construction and conservation of buildings.

Aegicrane In ▷Classical ▷architecture, a ▷frieze is often decorated with a ▷relief ▷sculpture of an animal's head or ▷skull, often ▷garlanded. The most usual is an ox-skull (▷*bucranium*), frequently used to decorate the ▷metopes of the ▷Roman Doric frieze (▷Doric Order). If a ram's or goat's head or skull is sculpted instead, it is termed an *aegicrane*.

Aegis A ▷shield or a goat-skin, usually associated with the left arm or shoulder or both, and subsequently meaning a protective breastplate (hence *under the aegis*). It signifies protection, and as a goat-skin was used to identify the wearer with Zeus/▷Jupiter.

Aenum, ahenum A system for making hot water in ▷Roman ▷thermae involving three ▷copper vessels: the largest was over the furnace, while the smallest, at the highest level, received the cold water from the ▷cistern. As hot water was drawn from the lowest vessel, it was topped up with water from the middle vessel, which had already received some heat from the furnace. This system helped to conserve fuel.

Aeolic [8] A very early form of the ▷Ionic ▷capital, probably of Semitic origin. The Aeolic capital had a long ▷abacus carried on two ▷volutes with palmettes (▷palm) filling the space between them. Unlike the fully developed Ionic capital (▷Ionic Order), the Aeolic volutes seemed to grow from the ▷shaft.

Aerarium The public ▷treasury in Rome.

Aes A blend of ▷copper and ▷tin, making ▷bronze.

Aesthetics That science in the fine arts which has its first principles in the effect that objects have on the mind and sensibilities. It is the sciences of the states and conditions of sensual perception. In the early nineteenth century, the term came to mean the philosophy of taste or the perception of the ▷Beautiful. The *Aesthetic Movement* in Britain from the 1860s was associated with the ▷Arts-and-Crafts Movement, the

(a)

(b)

[8] AEOLIC (*a*) Capital from Larissa in Aeolis. Note the volute motifs that resemble stylized Egyptian paintings of the lotus. (*JSC*) (*b*) Capital from Neandria. Note the fan-like palmette motif between the volutes. These Aeolic capitals may be the origins of the Ionic Order, but their ancestors are clearly Asiatic and Egyptian types. The palmette pattern was borrowed by Minoan Cretans from Egypt, and Greeks of the seventh and sixth centuries BC appear also to have derived it afresh from Egyptian sources. Many designs from Cyprus and elsewhere feature paintings of capitals of the Aeolic type, with strong Egyptian influences. Note that the volutes appear to grow from the 'stem' rather than lie on top of it like a rolled bolster, as in true Ionic. (*JSC*)

▷Queen Anne ▷Revival, and an appreciation of Japanese and ▷Chinese artefacts (▷Japonaiserie). ▷Picturesque, ▷Sublime.

Aethousa A ▷portico on the sunlit side of the ▷court of a ▷Greek house, or the place where house-guests slept: a stranger's room.

Aetiaioi The ▷slabs forming the ▷face of a ▷tympanum.

Aetoma, aetos The ▷tympanum of a ▷pediment. It is derived from the custom of decorating the ▷apex or ▷ridge of the ▷roof with ▷sculpture, and the name first applied to the ridge was transferred to the pediment (▷[234a]).

Affronted A term applied to two figures, often animals, facing each other in a symmetrical composition, often found on ▷capitals. If, on the other hand, the figures are arranged with their backs opposite each other, they are termed *addorsed*.

African architects An eighteenth-century ▷Freemasonic research society in Prussia, founded by King Friedrich II (the Great) (1712–86).

Agalma Any artefact dedicated to a deity in Ancient Greece, such a cult-statue or an ▷altar.

Agger ▷Foundations of ▷Roman roads. The earthworks of ▷forts. Any mound made of stone, earth, or other substance. It was also a mound raised by an attacking army around a besieged town and which was increased until it equalled or overtopped the defensive ▷walls, enabling the attackers to gain advantage. An *agger murorum* is an embankment on top of which the fortifications of a Roman city were erected. An *agger viae* is the central ▷cambered convex carriageway of a Roman road paved with large stones embedded in ▷mortar and laid on ▷hardcore.

Aggregate Material added to ▷lime or ▷cement to make ▷concrete. It is usually composed of a fine aggregate, such as sand, and a coarser aggregate such as gravel or broken stones. It should be carefully chosen, for if it is to be exposed by washing or hammering it will affect the colour of the finish.

Agiasterium That part of a ▷basilican ▷church in which the ▷altar is sited (▷apse).

Agnus Dei A representation of a ▷lamb with a ▷halo, and supporting a banner or the ▷Cross or both. An ▷emblem of Christ.

Agora The open space in a ▷Greek city which doubled as market-place and general rendezvous: it was usually surrounded by ▷colonnades.

Agrafe, agraffe A keystone (▷key) decorated with a carved ▷cartouche or mask.

Agricultural Order [9] A variety of the ▷Corinthian Order ▷embellished with agricultural produce, animal heads, etc.

Aguilla An ▷obelisk, a ▷spire, or any tall, thin, tapering feature.

[9] AGRICULTURAL ORDER A variety of the Corinthian Order. This version was designed by W. J. Donthorn, and adorns the monument to Thomas William Coke, Earl of Leicester, at Holkham in Norfolk. It was erected in 1845. Note the bulls instead of volutes, the sheaf of corn on top, the rope moulding between the shaft and the capital, and the mangelwurzel and turnip leaves instead of acanthus. (*JSC*)

Agyci ▷Obelisks in ▷Antiquity placed in the ▷vestibules of houses.

Agyieus A representation of ▷Apollo or an ▷altar dedicated to Apollo in the guise of the Guardian of Public Places, often situated at the street-door of ▷Greek houses.

Aileron Half a ▷gabled or ▷pedimented arrangement, hiding the end of a ▷lean-to ▷roof of an ▷aisle.

Ailure ▷Alura.

Air brick A ▷perforated ▷brick built into a ▷wall to allow air to enter a space. *Air drains* are dry areas, or ▷cavities between the external walls of a building and the earth, as in a ▷basement, to prevent the penetration of damp. *Air holes* are holes for the admission of air, as between the timbers of ▷floors, to prevent fungal decay.

An *air trap* prevents foul gases from rising from drains: it comprises a U-shaped bend which retains water and thus seals the curved part of the U.

Airie A building where farm labourers lodge together. ▷Bothy.

Aisle [10]   A lateral portion of a ▷basilican building or a ▷church parallel to the ▷nave, ▷choir and ▷chancel, and separated from the central portion of the building by ▷arcades or ▷colonnades carrying the ▷clerestorey. The aisles are usually much lower in height than the central, main body of the edifice. The usual arrangement is a central clerestoreyed nave with ▷lean-to aisles on either side, but in Germany the aisles are often the same height as the nave (*hall-church*). The Constantinian basilica of St Peter's in Rome had a clerestoreyed nave with two lower aisles on either side. In some instances (e.g. north transept of Westminster Abbey) the aisles are carried round on both sides of the transepts, while in others (Salisbury Cathedral) the aisles can be found on one side of the transepts only (▷[36], [66], [134]). Also a passageway between rows of seats in an ▷auditorium. An *aisle-*▷*post* is the equivalent

[10] AISLE The south aisle of Wells Cathedral showing the Early English or First-Pointed style of Gothic. (*JSC*)

of a pier in ▷framed work, and is part of a row separating the nave from the aisle. An aisle also means an enclosed and covered burial-place adjoining a church, a ▷mausoleum, or ▷mortuary ▷chapel attached to a church.

Aïsywas The top of a house ▷wall, or the part of a wall adjacent to the ▷eaves.

Aitheran Cross-ropes over ▷thatch woven into other securing ropes to hold the thatch in place.

Aithousa ▷Aethousa.

Ajaraca ▷Ornament constructed of patterned brickwork (usually half a ▷brick deep), and found in Spanish architecture.

Ajimez A ▷window of two arched ▷lights separated by a ▷colonnette or a ▷mullion, found in ▷Moorish architecture in Spain.

Ajour, ajouré ▷Perforated decorative patterns as in a flat ▷slab or panel, letting light through.

Ajutage A tube through which water in a ▷fountain is played.

Akaina ▷Acaina.

Ala (pl. **alae**) [11]   *Cellae* (▷cell) on either side of the central *cella* of a ▷Tuscan ▷temple, so that there were one large central and two smaller compartments set behind a ▷portico. The term can also be applied to ▷apartments, ▷alcoves, or recesses on either side of a ▷vestibule, or to an opening off an ▷atrium.

Alabaster A semi-translucent variety of ▷gypsum, white and brown in colour, much used for decorative ▷sculpture in ▷churches. It is very common in ▷Victorian work, and is easily carved. It is frequently found in ▷reredos ▷panels, ▷pulpits, and especially in monumental or funerary ▷sculpture. It is usually found inside a building.

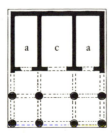

[11] ALA Etruscan temple after Vitruvius. **a** ala, **c** cella. (*JSC*)

Alameda A public walk or ▷promenade shaded by trees or by a ▷canopy.

Alatorium, alatoria A covered walk, a ▷corridor, or the ▷flank of a building: a *pentice* or ▷appentice.

Albanega A ▷spandrel created by a rectangular ▷frame (or ▷alfiz) placed around a horseshoe arch (▷arch) in ▷Islamic architecture.

Albani stone A brownish stone used in ▷Roman architecture prior to the widespread use of ▷marble ▷cladding.

Albarium *Opus albarium* or *tectorium* was the coating of *stucco* applied to sun-dried ▷brick, coarse stone, or other roughly finished ▷walls. The finest stucco was made of burned powdered ▷marble, and *opus albarium* could be polished once it had set. Also a coating of pure ▷lime not intended to be painted afterwards (▷opus).

Album A ▷plaque of ▷plaster on a ▷Roman building on which ▷inscriptions were placed.

Alcala A Moorish ▷citadel. The term is related to *alcazaba* and *alcazar*, meaning a Spanish ▷castle or fortress (▷fort).

Alcoran A ▷minaret (▷alkoranes).

Alcove A portion of a room set aside for a ▷bed, often raised above the level of the ▷floor, and separated from the rest of the room by a balustrade (▷baluster) with ▷doors. The term is also used to denote small ▷ornamental buildings with seats in ▷gardens, or to suggest large ▷niches.

Aleaceria A ▷castle or a ▷palace.

Aleatorium A room in which dice were thrown in ▷Roman ▷Antiquity.

Aleipterion, alipterion, alipterium A room in ▷Roman ▷thermae in which bathers could apply ointments to themselves or to each other.

Aleois Loopholes (▷loop) in military ▷architecture, or ▷balistraria.

Alette A ▷wing of a building, a ▷jamb of a ▷door, a ▷pilaster which is partly visible, or the exposed parts of a ▷pier on either side of an ▷engaged ▷column.

Alexandrian work ▷Mosaic-work composed of large pieces of stone or ▷marble ▷dressed and laid in geometrical (▷geometry) patterns, also called *opus Alexandrinum* (▷opus). The usual type is composed of black and red *tesserae* (▷tessella) laid in a white ground, and includes ▷guilloche designs, therefore embracing *opus sectile*.

Alfarje A timber framework supporting a ▷roof, and decoratively treated with ▷laceria, or geometrical (▷geometry) patterns made of ▷intersecting straight lines, found in ▷Islamic architecture.

Alfiz The rectangular ▷frame surrounding the ▷albanegas or ▷spandrels above a horseshoe ▷arch in ▷Islamic architecture.

Alhambra The palace of the Moorish kings at Granada, Spain. Any building derived from the style of the Alhambra, hence *Alhambresque*.

Alicatado A ▷finish on the outside and inside of buildings consisting of brightly coloured patterned glazed ▷tiles, favoured in the Iberian peninsula and in Latin America. The tiles are called ▷azulejos.

Aliform Shaped like a ▷wing, or having extensions like wings.

Alignment Theoretical or imaginary lines establishing the position of a building or parts of a building.

Alinda A ▷veranda(h).

Alipterion ▷Aleipterion.

Alkoranes ▷Minarets, or tall ▷towers attached to ▷mosques from which calls to prayer are made.

Allars A ▷garden-walk or alleys like garden-walks (▷alura, ▷allée).

Allée, alley A walk regularly planted with trees on each side, the trees being twice the width of the ▷promenade in height. An enclosed walk in a ▷garden. A wide spacious ▷avenue planted with trees. An alley is also a mean ▷passage between houses or ▷walls. An ▷aisle.

Allege A section of ▷wall that is much thinner than the rest of it, as under a ▷window ▷sill.

Allegory A representation of something in which the meaning is alluded to, and represents something it itself is not. An ▷emblem.

Allering The highest part of a building, or the part of the ▷wall on which the ▷roof is built. A ▷parapet wall, *aloring*, or a crenellation (▷crenel). A parapet walk. A ▷gutter or ▷channel behind a parapet. A ▷clerestorey ▷gallery, as at Ely Cathedral. Also *allaring, alrine, alura*.

Alley ▷Allée.

Alligatoring Crazing giving a pattern like the skin of an alligator, also called *crocodiling*.

Allover A repetitive decorative pattern covering an entire surface.

Almariol A storage-place for vestments, or an ▷aumbry.

Almemar, almemor A ▷bema. A desk in a ▷synagogue on which the *Torah* is placed.

Almena An indented trapezoidal arrangement on merlons. A ▷merlon with notched sides, usually associated with Moresque styles.

Almeny ▷Aumbry.

Almery ▷Aumbry.

Almonry A ▷closet for the reception of victuals for the poor. It also came to signify the building near a ▷church in ▷abbeys provided with offices for the distribution of alms, and with accommodation for the almoner.

Almorie ▷Aumbry.

Almorrefa Brickwork laid with ▷azulejos used in decorative ▷floor patterns in the Iberian peninsula.

Almshouse A house devoted to the shelter of poor or old persons and endowed for this use. Almshouses usually consist of more than one building, and often comprise groups of houses associated with communal buildings such as a ▷chapel or a ▷hall. Almshouses were endowed by private charities, and although there were mediaeval ▷'hospitals', such as Browne's in Stamford, completed 1475–76, many surviving almshouses date from after the Dissolution of the ▷monasteries in England, for they were designed to fill the huge void left by the Dissolution for the dispensing of alms and hospitality. Many almshouses were ▷Elizabethan or ▷Jacobean foundations, and were memorials to the beneficence of their founders. Almshouses often take the form of ranges of houses around a courtyard, with a hall and chapel (like Browne's Hospital or the ▷Victorian Beauchamp Almshouses at Newland, Worcestershire), but they may also only consist of a humble row of cottages.

Aloring ▷Allering, ▷alura.

Alorium ▷Alatorium, ▷appentice, or ▷alura.

Altar [12]   An elevated ▷table or ▷podium on which to place or sacrifice offerings to deities. The term signifies a table raised on a substructure, and is associated only with celestial or superior deities. An ▷ara, on the other hand, stood on the ground, and was associated with more earth-bound deities. Altars to infernal gods were set up in excavations, and were called *scrobiculi*. In Christian ▷churches, altars were of stone from the sixth century onwards, until the Reformation encouraged the use of wooden ▷Communion tables. The Christian altar was consecrated for the celebration of the ▷Sacrament. Such altars were usually built of solid ▷masonry, and the ▷slab forming the top was sometimes partially carried on ▷columns or ▷brackets. Altars were found

(*a*)

[12] ALTAR The high altar and reredos of the Church of St Francis of Assisi, Pottery Lane, Kensington, by John Francis Bentley, constructed in 1863 of alabaster, richly inlaid with marble and mosaic. The altar-frontal has short marble colonnettes with ornate capitals and cushions that support the slab itself. The central panel is painted, while on either side are panels much enriched with inlays. The first super-altar is inlaid with triangular patterns of dark and light marbles, and the second super-altar has circular recessed panels separated from each other by inlays of black foliate patterns of proto-Art-Nouveau style. The reredos itself is surmounted by a leaf cornice, and has four panels of eight-pointed star shapes each containing a painted figure. A corbel carries a throne above with a Vesica Piscis panel inlaid with mosaics. The pelican in piety surmounts the gilded canopy over the throne. In the centre of the altar is a tabernacle set behind an aediculated front, with a brass door enriched with enamels and precious coloured stones. (*Greater London Photographic Library 70/11/80*)

(*b*)

[13] ALTAR TOMB (*a*) Altar-tomb of cast iron in the church-yard of St Michael, Madeley, Shropshire. (*JSC*) (*b*) A fine, late Elizabethan altar-tomb of Edmund Walter (*d.*1594) and his wife (*d.*1583). Note the aediculated arrangement with an Order of coarse Corinthian with exaggerated entasis, the ribbon-work in the spandrels, and the cartouche held in strapwork above the entablature. Two short obelisks flank the strapwork attic. There is strapwork at the back of the arch too. The alabaster effigies lie on a tomb-chest with kneeling figures in the panels between the colonnettes, and the wrought ironwork with the iron flags is contemporary. Church of St Laurence, Ludlow, Shropshire. (*JSC*)

at the east end of the church and in ▷side-▷chapels, each named after a particular saint. The principal altar was termed the ▷high altar, and stood at the east end of the ▷chancel. From the period in which stone altars were introduced it was usual to enclose relics in the altar-slab. Altars have ▷sides or ▷horns termed ▷Epistle (south) and ▷Gospel (north). In England there was much destruction of altars in and around 1550, although some restoration took place under Queen Mary I. Further desecration occurred under Queen Elizabeth I and more under the Puritans in the seventeenth century. An *altar-frontal* (▷front) is the finish or covering for the front of an altar, often of elaborately woven fabric, or of metal. It is called an *antependium, altar-front,* or *altar-facing.* An *altar-piece* is the decoration of an altar. An *altar-pyx* is a pyx (▷pix) or a box in which consecrated Elements are placed. An *altar-rail* is the ▷rail separating the *sacrarium* from the rest of the chancel. Many early seventeenth-century timber altar-rails survive in English churches, dating from the time of Archbishop Laud (▷Laudian rails), who sought to restore the beauty of church furnishings. An *altar of repose* is a side-altar or a ▷niche where the Host is kept from Maundy Thursday to Good Friday. An *altar-screen* or *altar-wall* is the wall behind an altar, separating the ▷choir from the east (usually ▷Lady) chapel. It is often of the richest carved work, as in Winchester Cathedral or New College, Oxford. An *altar-slab* is the slab of stone on top of an altar in a church, usually carved with five ▷crosses indicating the Five Wounds of Christ, and with a relic inlaid in the centre. An *altar-stair* is one leading to the raised part of which an altar stands. An *altar-tomb* (▷[13]) is a tomb-chest or ▷memorial resembling an altar. Such tombs often have recumbent ▷effigies on top, and always have solid sides. They were not used as altars.

Alto rilievo High ▷relief in which the figures project more than half their full forms.

Alura, alure, ailure A ▷passage or gangway, ▷gallery, or garden-walk. It may also be a covered ▷pavement. The ▷clerestorey gallery in the ▷nave at Ely Cathedral is referred to in the Sacristy Rolls as an *alura: Pro sexdecim fenestris factis de novo in superioribus alluris ecclesiae.* The term may also be used to denote the passages on the ▷roof of a building along the ▷gutters, the galleries behind the crenellations (▷crenel) of a ▷castle or city-wall ▷parapet, the passage in a ▷cloister, or other building.

Alveus A ▷bath sunk in the ▷floor of a room, the upper part appearing above the surface of the floor, found in ▷thermae or ▷Roman houses.

Amaille ▷Enamel.

Amalyeit ▷Enamelled.

Ambitus A space round a ▷tomb. A ▷loculus for a body in a ▷catacomb, or a ▷niche for an ▷urn or cinerary (▷cinerarium) chest in a ▷columbarium. The funerary *ambitus* was often decorated, and usually sealed in with ▷slabs on which were inscribed the names of the dead. The term was also given to consecrated ground around a ▷church, so it also had a funerary significance in that sense.

Ambivium A ▷Roman street that surrounded a site, leaving it an island.

Ambo An elevated ▷lectern or ▷pulpit in the ▷nave, before the steps of the ▷chancel, and sometimes associated with the balustrade (▷baluster) dividing the chancel from the nave. *Ambones* usually had two ascents, and were sometimes isolated. Where they are associated with the ▷choir, they are twinned, the one on the south side being used for the reading of the ▷Epistle, and the other, on the north, acting as a ▷platform for the reading of the ▷Gospel. Ambones were important features in ▷Italian ▷churches, and fine examples may still be seen there, notably in San Clemente in Rome. From the fourteenth century they became less important, but were revived in the nineteenth century.

Ambre ▷Aumbry.

Ambrices In ▷Roman architecture, the ▷laths on the ▷rafters carrying the ▷tiles.

Ambrie ▷Aumbry.

Ambry ▷Aumbry.

Ambulacrum A ▷promenade shaded with formally planted trees, or an open ▷court in front of a ▷basilica, also called an ▷atrium.

Ambulatio The space between the ▷wall of a temple *cella* (▷cell) and the ▷columns of the ▷peristyle, also called ▷*pteroma.* Any ▷promenade, open or covered.

Ambulatory A covered place in which to walk, such as a ▷cloister. The term is also used to denote the semicircular, right-angled, or polygonal ▷aisle enclosing a ▷sanctuary, and joining the two ▷chancel-aisles behind the ▷high altar (▷[66]). An *ambulatory church* is one with the latter arrangement.

American bond Brickwork with all ▷bricks laid as ▷stretchers except for a header (▷head) ▷course each fifth, sixth, or seventh course. Also called *English garden-wall bond,* or *USA common bond* (▷brick).

American Order A type of ▷Corinthian ▷capital featuring ▷corn-ears and tobacco-leaves instead of ▷acanthus.

[14] AMMONITE ORDER An example from the Old Kent Road, London, of *c.* 1820. (*JSC*)

Amertree A timber ▷beam or iron ▷bar built into a ▷chimney recess over a fire from which chains are suspended for pots. Also *emmertree, crooktree, galley-baulk*, and *railtree*. The term ▷tree in this sense means any structural beam.

Ammonite Order [14] A variety of Ionic (▷Ionic Order) in which the ▷capital ▷volutes are modelled on the fossil genus of Cephalopods, consisting of whorled chambered shells, also called snake-stones. This ▷Order is peculiarly English, and most examples occur in Kent and Sussex. It was often used in designs by Amon Wilds (*c.* 1762–1833), possibly as a type of 'signature', and may have been suggested by designs of Piranesi.

Amorino A diminutive of Amor, the god of ▷love, also identified with Eros. *Amorini* were often depicted as *cupids* or ▷cherubs. They must not be confused with the wingless *putti* (▷putto).

Amortizement A sloping top of, for example, a ▷buttress, or the top of a ▷pier. Any canted top.

Amphi A prefix, suggesting the same architectural features on both sides of a centre-line. *Amphi-antis* is a ▷portico arrangement of ▷columns ▷*in antis* (▷anta) at both ends of a ▷temple. *Amphiprostyle* means a ▷Classical building with a ▷prostyle portico at each end, but with no columns along the sides. In compounds such as *amphiprostyle* or *amphidistyle* the *amphi* means that the same architectural features occur at the front and back (▷[234]). *Amphistylar* thus suggests a Classical temple with columns at both ends. *Amphithalamos* is a ▷chamber in a ▷Roman house placed across a ▷corridor from the main bedroom. An *amphitheatre* (▷theatre) was elliptical on plan (like the Colosseum (▷Coliseum) in Rome), and was essentially two ▷theatres with the stages joined together to form an ▷arena or ▷pit. Amphitheatres had no ▷Greek precedent: they were used by the Romans for large-scale spectacles and gladiatorial combat. The term *amphithura* means a veil or curtain dividing the ▷chancel from the body of the ▷church, and opening in the centre, like folding ▷doors.

Amussis A ▷table of ▷marble used to establish a plane that was absolutely level and flat, used by ▷Roman craftsmen.

Amygdalatum A variety of *opus reticulatum* (▷opus).

Anabathra ▷Steps leading to a raised ▷area such as a ▷platform, a ▷dais, or even a ▷pulpit or ▷ambo.

Anacampteria Lodgings of persons seeking ▷sanctuary in ▷Antiquity.

Anactoron A sacred building or a sacred part of a building, used chiefly in connection with the Mysteries.

Anaglypha Adorned with ▷sculptures in *basso rilievo* (▷relief). *Anaglyphic* means ▷embossing, while *Anaglyphice* or *Anaglyptice* is a species of ▷sculpture where the figures are raised or ▷embossed. *Anaglypta* is a patent embossed decorative paper for use on ▷walls, ▷dados, ▷ceilings, etc., commonly used in the late-▷Victorian period.

Anaimaktos ▷Altars on which flowers or fruit were offered in ▷Greek ▷Antiquity, without blood or fire.

Analemma A retaining ▷wall, or any ▷pier, ▷buttress, ▷foundation; or wall strengthening another wall.

Analogion, analogium A reading-desk, ▷lectern, or ▷ambo.

Anamorphosis In ▷perspective, a drawing which presents a confused and distorted image, or even an image of something quite different, which, when seen from a particular point, or in a reflection, recovers its proportions and is recognizable.

Anathyrosis A system of close fitting of the ▷drums of a ▷Classical ▷column at the edges only. Within the edge-ring was a rough surface, then a shallow circular depression with a deep hole in the centre for the reception of the ▷empolia, or wooden blocks which contained the *poloi*, or timber ▷dowels that connected the ▷drums. Anathyrosis was also employed in the vertical and horizontal joints of the stones of which ▷walls were built.

Ancaster stone A creamy-brown limestone (▷lime), durable in non-polluted atmospheres, with a fine even texture allowing free working, from Ancaster in Lincolnshire.

Anchor An ▷ornament like an ▷anchor or an arrow-head, used with an egg design to ▷enrich certain mouldings, usually the ▷echinus or ▷ovolo. This anchor, with its concomitants, is generally carved on the echinus of the Ionic ▷capital (▷Ionic Order), and on the ovolo of the richer ▷Orders. It is also known as a *dart*. It is not used in ▷Greek ▷Doric Orders, but it is employed in the capitals of the Trajan and ▷Antonine columns in Rome (▷[110]). An anchor is also any means by which a building is secured, such as a ▷bolt or other piece of metal ▷grouted into the ▷wall, or held by expansion within a recess. An *anchor-block* is a timber fixing-brick built into a wall. An *anchor-iron* is a metal ▷tie used to fix a ▷beam to a wall or to tie a ▷floor to a wall. An *anchor-plate* is a cast-iron ▷plate used as a flooring tile: it is bedded in a ▷screed and held in position by downward-pointing lugs. An anchor is the ▷attribute of Hope, usually depicted as a female figure with her anchor. It is also a piece of metal fixed to the end of a tie and exposed on a wall to prevent bulging.

Anchorage, anchoridge A room over a ▷vestry on the north side of a ▷chancel, sometimes occupied by an anchorite, who was a person who has withdrawn from the world for religious reasons, or by a hermit or a recluse. An *anchorite* ▷*cell* was where an anchorite lived, sometimes in caves or in huts, but sometimes in parts of a ▷church, and even in the church ▷roof. Occasionally anchorites chose to be walled up, leaving only a small ▷window through which food and water could be passed, or through which persons could converse with the anchorite.

Ancillary Buildings having a secondary use to the main building grouped with them.

Ancon (pl. **ancones**) The ▷console ▷ornament cut on the *keystone* (▷key, ▷arch) of an arch, and supporting a bust or other feature. On a keystone the ancon is wedge-shaped, that is narrower at the bottom than at the top. The term is also used to denote a *truss*, *console*, *shouldering-piece* (▷shoulder), or *crossette* employed in the dressings (▷dressed) or *antepagmenta* of ▷apertures, serving as apparent supports for the ▷cornice above at the topmost corners of the aperture. In this sense an ▷Antique ancon was often not in contact with the ▷flanks of the ▷architrave, but placed at a small distance from the sides of the architrave, and was frequently wider at the top than at the bottom, like an ancon on a keystone: indeed the term *ancon* seems most properly to apply to this tapering type of form, as opposed to a cros-sette or a console, which usually would have parallel sides. Vitruvius called ancones *prothyrides*. An ancon is also the corner of a ▷quoin of a ▷wall. It can also be used to describe a projecting ▷boss on a ▷drum of a ▷column, or a ▷cramp used to fasten stones together.

Ander, andor A ▷porch or ▷vestibule, a ▷lobby. A ▷shelf above a ▷door. Storage space between the top of a ▷wall and the ▷angle of a ▷roof.

Andirons Firedogs. An andiron is an iron ▷bar held at one end by an upright support (often ▷ornamented) and at the other by a short ▷foot. A pair of andirons was placed, one at each side of the ▷hearth or fireplace (▷fire), with the ornaments to the front, to support the burning wood. In a ▷kitchen fireplace the upright support carrying a rack on the front for the spit to rotate was also termed an andiron.

Andron, andronitis An ▷apartment reserved for men, especially a dining-room, in a ▷Greek house. The ▷passage in a ▷Roman house beside the ▷tablinum.

Angel light A small triangular ▷light between the arches of Second- and Third-▷Pointed ▷tracery.

Angiportus A narrow lane between two rows of houses in ▷Antiquity, often ending at a private house, so therefore an angiportus was a *cul-de-sac* (▷cul).

Angle The mutual inclination of two lines meeting at a point, called the *angular point, vertex*, or *point of concourse*. Angles are measured in ▷degrees, based on a ▷circle divided into 360 wedges, each called a degree. An *angle-*▷*bar* is an upright at the angles of a polygonal or canted ▷window, or ▷bay. It effects the join at each angle of the glazing. An *angle-bead* is a vertical ▷bead of wood fixed to an angle and flush with the surface of the intended ▷plaster on either side to secure the angle against accident and also to serve as a guide for floating the plaster. This was a common detail in houses of the ▷Victorian period. The term is now applied to a moulding (▷mould) of metal made for the plasterer to work to at corners, as a permanent form of ▷screed or fixing: it is usually made of ▷galvanized steel. An *angle-*▷*block* is a right-angled triangular prism of timber glued and pinned at the junction of two timber components to stiffen it, e.g. under a ▷stair between ▷tread and ▷riser.

An *angle-▷brace* is a tie-bar fixed across an angle to secure it: a ▷bracket projecting from a ▷wall in order to support a ▷projection, such as a ▷shelf. An *angle-buttress* is one at the corner of a building usually associated with another ▷buttress at an angle of 90°. In the ▷Ionic Order, the corner ▷capitals often have the corner ▷volutes only placed at an angle of 135° with the planes of the front and returning ▷entablatures: this is called an *angle-capital* and should not be confused with the ▷angular capital or ▷Scamozzi Order. An *angle-▷chimney* is one placed in the corner of a room An *angle-closer* is a ▷brick cut to complete the ▷bond near the corner of a wall. An *angle-▷column* is one set at the corner of a building. In the ▷Ionic Order it requires a special capital. An *angle-drafted ▷margin* is one round two faces of a stone at a corner. An *angle-iron* is a plate of iron rolled into an L-shape: angle-irons are now usually made of mild steel. A joint between two pieces of timber at a corner is known as an *angle-joint*. An *angle-leaf* is a carved ▷claw, ▷spur, or ▷leaf in ▷mediaeval architecture which projects from the ▷torus of the ▷base of the ▷column or ▷pier and covers one of the corners of the ▷plinth on which the column or pier rests. There are usually four angle-leaves in such instances. An *angle-▷modillion* occurs at the ▷mitring of a ▷cornice, and is generally regarded as an ▷abuse of ▷Classical detail, although it occurs in the remains of Diocletian's palace at Spalato, in the *vestibulum*, and in the ruins at Palmyra and Baalbek. An *angle-▷niche* occurs in the corner of building, inside or outside. In ▷timber-framed construction, the ▷post at the corner of a ▷frame is called the *angle-post*. In ▷perspective, the angle under which the objects are seen, and upon which their apparent sites depend is called the *angle of vision*, and should not exceed 60°. A timber in a hipped ▷roof on the line of the junction of the two inclined planes is called an *angle-▷rafter*, or, more often, a ▷hip-rafter or *angle-▷ridge*. A plain round moulding, or ▷bowtell, is called an *angle-▷roll*. An *angle-▷shaft* is a ▷colonnette set in the right-angled recesses of ▷Romanesque ▷door- and ▷window-▷jambs: a decorative roll or colonnette at an external corner of a building. An *angle-shaft* or *angle-bead* is also termed an *angle-staff*. An *angle-stone* is a ▷quoin. A small piece of timber tying two timbers at an angle to each other is called an *angle-▷tie*. It is a horizontal timber carrying one end of the ▷dragon beam and tying the wall-plates (▷wall) together at the corner of the building. It is also called a *dragon-tie* (▷dragon-beam) or an *angle-▷brace*. A plain ▷tile moulded to a right-angle for covering a ▷hip or a ▷ridge, or when employed in a tile-hanging, to cover a corner, is known as an *angle-tile*, also called ▷*arris-tile* or an *angular hip-tile*. ▷Dressed stone with the tool-marks running diagonally is known as *angle-tooled* or *angle-droved*. A ▷stair in which flights are set at an angle of other than 180° to each other, with ▷landings between them, is an *angled stair*.

[15] ANGLO-SAXON Two stages of the west tower of the Church of St John the Baptist at Barnack, Soke of Peterborough, of the early eleventh century. Note the long-and-short quoins, the thin lesenes or pilaster strips, and the triangular- and semi-circular-headed openings (the latter not true arches, but lintels cut to look like arches). The rubble was probably rendered, the rendering stopping at the lesenes and quoins. The belfry stage is of early thirteenth-century date. (*JSC*)

Anglet A groove, usually a V-joint, in rusticated (▷rustic) ▷ashlar work.

Anglo-Saxon architecture [15] ▷Architecture in England in the centuries immediately preceding the ▷Norman Conquest in 1066. ▷Saxon.

Angular capital The Scamozzian or 'modern' ▷Ionic ▷capital (also called ▷Scamozzi Order), which is formed alike on all four faces, so as to return at the ▷angles of the building, as in the Temple of Saturn in Rome. It has eight ▷volutes, and so no special *angle-capital* is required at the corners. Some sources hold that this type was invented by Vincenzo Scamozzi (1552–1616), and that it was employed until the eighteenth century when it was rejected as inauthentic, but it was a ▷Roman invention, and has authentic ▷Antique ancestry. It recurs in nineteenth- and twentieth-century ▷Classical ▷architecture. It should not be confused with the angle-capital.

Angularis Timber ▷ties to strengthen timber ▷angles, as between the ▷rafters and the horizontal ceiling-▷joists, also called ▷oxter pieces.

Animal black Black pigment made by calcining bone or ivory, also called *drop black*, *bone black* and *ivory black*. *Animal glue*, also known as ▷Scotch glue is made from the bones, horns, sinews and hides of animals, and sold in cake or grain form. It is prepared by soaking the glue overnight and then heating (not boiling) it. Such glue is not water resistant. *Fish glue* has similar properties.

Ankh A ▷cross surmounted by a circle (☥) used in Ancient ▷Egyptian ▷hieroglyphs, and later identified with the ▷nimbus and ▷Cross of the ▷Crucifixion.

Annular That which relates to any figure generated by the revolution of a plane figure round an ▷axis in this plane at a given distance from it: the ▷channels under the ▷echinus of the ▷Greek ▷Doric Order are ▷annulets. All mouldings (▷mould) of ▷columns which have circular horizontal sections are annular. Tree-rings are annular. An *annular* ▷vault is a vaulted ▷roof over an annular space between two concentric ▷walls circular on plan, as in the church of St Costanza in Rome. When a ▷column or ▷pier is surrounded by clusters of slender ▷shafts, usually of ▷Purbeck marble, and attached to it by means of ▷bands of stone or metal, it is called *annulated*. It is a feature that recurs in ▷Early English or First-▷Pointed ▷mediaeval architecture.

Annulet A small flat ▷fillet encircling a ▷column. It is used under the ▷echinus of a Greek Doric ▷capital several times (▷Doric Order). It is also called a *shaft-ring* (▷shaft). The term has also been applied to the fillets separating ▷flutes in columns, and has been called a ▷*list* or a *listella* (▷[89], [144]). It is more commonly any horizontal ring around a column, or a ▷band set into the column, as of ▷bronze or gilt-bronze.

Anse de panier ▷Arch.

Anston stone A deep cream-coloured Magnesian limestone (▷lime) from the West Riding of Yorkshire.

Anta A species of ▷pilaster used in ▷Classical ▷architecture to terminate the side ▷walls of ▷temples. The anta ▷capital (and usually the ▷base, though not always) differs from the capitals of the ▷columns with which it is associated. When the ▷pronaos or ▷porch in front of the

▷cell is formed by the ▷projection of the ▷walls, terminated by *antae* with columns between the antae, the ▷portico is said to be ▷*in antis*: the columns in an *in antis* arrangement, therefore, do not stand in front of the outer ▷face of the antae (▷[234b]). Antae may be said to correspond to the ▷responds of ▷mediaeval architecture. The term also means a ▷jamb. Unlike pilasters, antae do not have ▷entasis.

Antechamber, anteroom An ▷apartment through which access is obtained to a main room beyond it. An *antechapel* is the part of a ▷chapel between the western ▷wall and the choir-screen (▷choir). An *antechoir* is the space between the inner and outer ▷arches of a deep stone choir-screen or ▷pulpitum. An *antechurch*, also called the *forechurch*, is a deep ▷narthex or ▷porch to the west of a ▷church, several ▷bays deep, consisting of a ▷nave and ▷aisles. An *antecourt* is the ▷approach to the principal ▷court of a house. It often served for communication with the ▷kitchens, etc., and frequently took the form of an entrance-court or outer court situated in front of the main court. A narthex or porch at the west end of the nave is termed an *antenave*.

Antefixa [16] An ▷ornamental vertical element fixed at regular intervals above the ▷cornice of a ▷Classical building at the end of each ▷ridge of tiling, concealing the ends of the *harmi*, or joint-▷tiles (▷harmus). *Antefixae* are usually ornamented with the ▷anthemion or with other ▷motifs. The term is also applied to ornamental heads, below the ▷eaves, through the mouths of which water is cast away: it is also given to ▷terracotta ornament fixed to the ▷entablatures of ▷Etruscan or early ▷Roman ▷temples.

Antemural(e) An outwork or outer defensive ▷wall around a ▷castle or fortress.

Antepagmenta Moulded (▷mould) ▷architraves around an opening. More accurately, the antepagmenta are the ▷jambs of a ▷door- or ▷window-opening, moulded like an architrave, while the top part of the architrave (or ▷lintel), returning at the ends (and with similar mouldings to those of the jambs) and bearing upon the antepagmenta, is called the *supercilium* (▷super). The singular is *antepagment* or *antepagmentum*. An antepagmentum can also mean an ▷anta or a ▷pilaster. An *antepagmentum superius* is a ▷lintel.

[16] ANTEFIXA (*JSC*)

Anteparabema A ▷chapel attached to a ▷Byzantine or ▷Early Christian ▷church, and balanced by another chapel on the opposite side of the ▷nave, giving an impression of a false ▷bema or ▷transept.

Antependium The frontal (▷front) of an ▷altar.

Antepodium A seat in the ▷choir of a ▷church for the clergy.

Anteport An outer portal (▷porta) or gateway (▷gate). A ▷porch or ▷portico in front of a main portico is known as an *anteportico*.

Anterides ▷Buttresses for the support of a ▷wall. They are also called *counter-forts* (▷counter), *antes*, and *crismae*, and in ▷Classical ▷architecture are a variety of ▷pilaster or ▷anta. The Italians called them ▷*speroni*, or ▷spurs. Any structures strengthening other structures, such as buttresses in subterranean construction.

Antevanna A boarded ▷lean-to ▷roof over a ▷Roman ▷window or ▷door, also known as an *auvanna*.

Anthemion [17] The ▷honeysuckle or palmette (▷palm) ▷ornament, found above ▷acroteria, on ▷cornices, on ▷antefixae, on the neckings (▷neck) of some ▷Ionic ▷capitals, and elsewhere in ▷Classical ▷architecture (▷Ionic Order). It is associated with the ▷fleuron design.

Antic A figure or figures of men of beasts used as ▷ornaments, grouped or figured with fantastic incongruity, ▷Grotesque in composition or shape, often mingling with floral forms, incongruously running into each other. Bizarre ornament featuring flora, fauna, and objects treated monstrously. A ▷caryatide or other human figure, represented in a distorted and Grotesque position. A representation of a face, such as is used in ▷gargoyles, with features distorted, grinning, or leering.

Anticlastic When a surface is composed of convex and concave curves running in different directions through a point, it is termed anticlastic, as in a ▷hyperbolic paraboloid ▷roof.

Anticum A ▷porch to a front ▷door. The space between the ▷columns of a ▷portico and the ▷wall of the

[17] ANTHEMION The honeysuckle or anthemion alternating with palmette ornament. Note the linking scrolls. (*JJS*)

cella (▷cell). It is sometimes incorrectly used to describe the ▷anta, but can also describe the ▷front of a ▷Classical building.

Antinoüs The lover and favourite of the Emperor Hadrian, who was elevated, after his death, to the status of a god. His statues include Egyptianizing (▷Egyptian) figures with kilt, ▷*Nemes* headdress, left foot placed before right, and arms held rigidly with clenched fists. Figures of Antinoüs occur as cult-statues, as *telamones* (▷Telamon), and identified with other deities in ▷Antiquity. After the *Villa Adriana* Antinoüs and telamones were rediscovered in ▷Renaissance times, the image became a popular ▷motif, especially during the Neoclassical (▷Neoclassicism) period, when it occurs as statues, statuettes, garden ornaments, and even repeated in ▷relief as a ▷frieze on Boullée's 'Cenotaph for a National Military Hero', which is in the form of a gigantic ▷sarcophagus (*Bibliothèque Nationale, HA 57, No. 27*).

Antiportico A ▷vestibule or ▷porch at the entrance to a building.

Antiquarium An ▷apartment in which ▷Antique ▷monuments were displayed.

Antiquary A student of Antiquities (▷Antiquity), ▷ruins, ▷sculptures, statues, books, and archaeological remains, or anything that will help in the understanding of the ▷Antique cultures. *Antiquarian* was the phase in taste from around 1750 to 1840 when themes, ▷motifs, and precedents were sought in Graeco-Roman and even ▷Egyptian ▷Antiquty, as well as from the Middle Ages: it was manifest in the Neoclassical (▷Neoclassicism) period, and in the ▷Greek, ▷Gothic, and Egyptian ▷Revivals.

Antique The term denotes something that is ancient, but is used in an architectural sense to denote work of Graeco-Roman ▷Antiquity.

Antique crown A ▷heraldic ▷crown consisting of a headband with projecting spikes rising from it.

Antiquing ▷Broken-colour work, a method of treating wet paint to reveal parts of the undercoat as in ▷combing, ▷graining, or marbling (▷marble).

Antiquity The word refers to the ▷Classical civilizations of the Graeco-Roman world. *Antiquities* means objects from Antiquity.

Antiquo-modern An archaic term meaning the ▷Pointed style of ▷architecture, or ▷Gothic.

Antis, In ▷Anta.

Antithema The backing of ▷steps, ▷architrave, and ▷frieze, usually separate ▷blocks to those of the facing.

Antlia A machine for raising water; a pump.

Antonine column The ▷Tuscan-▷Doric ▷column erected to the memory of Emperor Antoninus. It contained a circular staircase, and the ▷sculpture was similar to that of Trajan's column, arranged in a spiral around the ▷shaft.

Antrum An ▷Early-Christian place of worship situated in ▷hypogea, ▷catacombs, or caves.

Anubis The ▷Egyptian god with the head of a dog or jackal, identified with Hermes and ▷Mercury.

Apartment A part of a house, consisting of a set of one or more rooms which are self-contained. In ▷Victorian times the term became misused and was corrupted to mean a single room, so that phrases such as *suite of apartments* became common. In Scots usage, an apartment still means one room.

Aperture An opening in a ▷wall. Two sides are usually perpendicular to the horizon, and a third is parallel to it. The verticals are called ▷*jambs*, the lower level side is called the ▷*sill*, and the upper part the ▷*head* (which can be flat or curved). Apertures are made for the admission of light and air, as entrances, for ▷ornament (as ▷niches, etc.), or for defence. ▷Greek and ▷Roman apertures often had jambs that inclined (had ▷batters) towards each other at the tops, producing battered-sided apertures (▷Vitruvian opening). Apertures can be covered at the tops by means of ▷lintels or ▷arches of various kinds.

Apex The highest point, peak, or top of a structure, especially one of triangular form, like a ▷pediment or a ▷gable. An *apex stone* is the uppermost stone in a gable or pediment, also called the *saddle-stone* (▷saddle).

Apiary A place for keeping beehives.

Apis bull The sacred Ancient ▷Egyptian bull, associated with Osiris/Serapis/▷Jupiter. A recurrent theme in ▷Classical and ▷Renaissance art.

Apodyterium A place where a person took off his clothes in preparation for a bath or for gymnastic exercises.

Apogeum, apogoeum Same as ▷hypogeum.

Apolline decoration Classical and ▷Renaissance ▷*décor* featuring Apollo and his ▷attributes such as the ▷sun, the ▷lyre, the head of Apollo surrounded by sun-rays or a sunburst, and the chariot. It was favoured during the reign of King Louis XIV, and was revived in the nineteenth century.

Apollo The ▷Greek sun god, patron of poetry, music, medicine, archery, etc., his ▷attributes being the bow and the ▷lyre, while the bay tree was sacred to him. He is depicted as a handsome and muscular young man, and may be seen with chariot, horses, and sunbursts.

Aponsa A shed ▷roof with ▷rafters that were built in at one end or rested on a ▷wall: a ▷lean-to roof, or a *pentice* (▷appentice).

Apophyge [18] The concave curve given to the top and bottom of the ▷shaft of a ▷Classical ▷column, where it expands to meet the edge of the ▷fillet above the ▷base, and beneath the ▷astragal under the ▷capital: it is also known as the *apothesis* and the *apophysis*. The apophyge is called *congé* (▷conge) in French, or ▷*scape* (▷[144]). The term is also given to the ▷hollow or ▷scotia beneath the ▷echinus of archaic ▷Doric capitals.

Apostolaeum, apostolium A ▷church named after an Apostle.

Apotheca A store for wine, oil, and spices.

Apothesis ▷Apophyge.

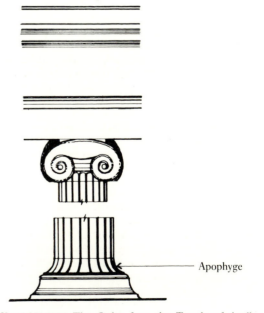

[18] APOPHYGE The Order from the Temple of Apollo Epicurius at Bassae, showing the 'Bassae Order' of Ionic. (*JSC*)

Appareille The slope or steps to the ▷dais of a ▷basilica or the top of a bastion.

Appartement A lodging consisting of a suite of rooms: a ▷flat.

Appentice, pent, penthice A structure erected against the sides of another building as a ▷lean-to, that is with a monopitched ▷roof. A covered walkway against a larger building or buildings. A *pentice* (▷penthouse).

Appleton stone A blue-brown, hard ▷sandstone from Shepley, Yorkshire.

Appley Bridge Blue A very hard grey-blue ▷sandstone from Wigan, Lancashire.

Applied column An ▷engaged ▷column, that is one attached to a wall.

Applied moulding Any moulding (▷mould) ▷planted on. An *applied* ▷*trim* is separate decorative strips or mouldings planted on to the ▷face and ▷sides of any ▷frame, and often gilded.

Appliqué The term suggests one material ▷planted on or fixed to another, such as a decorative feature on a piece of ▷furniture or a ▷panel.

Approach A road leading to a building.

Appuy A support, a ▷buttress, a rest.

Apron Also known as a *pitching-piece* (▷pitch), or *apron-piece*, it is a horizontal timber ▷beam, fixed to a ▷wall, and projecting outwards, which supports the ▷carriage-pieces ▷rough-▷strings, and ▷joists of the ▷landings of ▷stairs. The top covering is called an *apron-landing*. An apron is also a ▷panel below a ▷sill, or vertical ▷asphalte on a ▷fascia or an overhang of a ▷roof. In ▷plumbing, it is the same as ▷flashing, and a plumber's *apron-piece* is flashing at the lower side of a ▷chimney-stack. It is also a sill, a ▷platform, a ▷saddle, or a ▷plank against which ▷gates, ▷windows, or ▷doors can shut. A ▷spandrel in a multi-storeyed building, or a vertical infilling between a window-sill and the window-head below, or any opaque panel in ▷curtain-walling is called an *apron-wall*. *Apron-work* is therefore any covering, as with ▷lead. An apron is a strip of lead which conducts the ▷drip of a wall into a ▷gutter, or acts as a flashing. It can also be lead flashing under a sill and connecting with the ▷water-bar, behind tile-hanging (▷tile) to prevent water penetration. Any flashing.

Apse A semicircular or polygonal ▷domed recess, usually found at the end of a ▷nave of a ▷basilican building. Apses are frequently covered with a half-dome, and are found at the east ends of ▷choirs or ▷chancels, and sometimes in chancel-▷aisles or even as ▷chapels on the east sides of ▷transepts (as at Lincoln Cathedral). Early ▷churches sometimes had apses at the west ends. Chapels radiating from a ▷chevet were frequently of the apsed type. The term *apsidal* means shaped like an apse. An apse is also called an *absis* or *apsis*, and is that part of a church where the clergy were seated or the ▷altar was placed. An *apsis gradata* was raised, and was called an ▷*exedra* or a ▷*tribune* if the site of a bishop's throne (▷[36]). An *apse-aisle* is an ▷aisle or ▷ambulatory around an apse or a chevet. An *apse-chapel* is a chapel, usually one of several, radiating from the curved apsidal end of a ▷Romanesque or ▷Gothic cathedral. A subsidiary apse, or a small apsidal chapel, is called an *apsidiole*, such as those at the east of a transept (as in Lincoln Cathedral), or the radiating chapels of a chevet.

Apteral A ▷Classical building of a ▷temple form without ▷columns at the sides, but with a columnar ▷portico.

Apyroi ▷Altars on which unburned sacrifices were offered. The word is in contradistinction to *empyroi*.

Aquaminarium A ▷stoup for holy water.

Aquarium A case containing fresh or sea water, in which living aquatic flora and fauna could be kept.

Aqueduct A ▷channel for conveying water, often elevated on ▷brick or stone ▷piers carrying ▷arches. ▷Roman aqueducts were of great size and magnificence, with long ▷arcades above which the ▷duct (usually enclosed to protect the water from evaporation or pollution) was constructed.

Aquila A carved ▷tympanum named after the ▷eagles depicted on archaic ▷Classical ▷temple ▷pediments.

Ara An ▷altar, usually commemorative or funerary, or an altar in a private house. The term is applied to the funeral pyre as well as to *arae* raised in honour or for worship of people before or after death. It seems to have been a term associated with the idea of protection, possibly to appease the dead, or to secure a house or an area as a safe refuge. An *ara turicrema* was one on which frankincense was burned. The *Ara Pacis* is a large altar erected in 13 BC under Augustus in Rome, to celebrate the end of strife and the consolidation of imperial power. It is adorned with two processional ▷friezes.

Arabesque [19] Capricious ▷ornament found in ▷Classical ▷architecture, usually involving the combination of flowing lines of branches, ▷leaves and scroll-work (▷scroll), fancifully intertwined. The term

[19] ARABESQUE Design by John Francis Bentley for the altar of the Dominican Convent, Portobello Road, London. (*JJS*)

does not necessarily derive from ▷Arabian or ▷Saracenic examples, for the ▷Greeks and ▷Romans used Arabesque or capricious ornament, while the illuminations of the mediaeval period are often ▷enriched with Arabesque decoration. It does not contain human or animal figures, and is therefore not to be confused with Grotesque ornament, and is sometimes called *Moresque* (▷Moorish architecture).

Arabian architecture *Moresque* (▷Moorish architecture), ▷Saracenic, or ▷Arabian ▷architecture was occasionally the model for some late eighteenth- and nineteenth-century designs, but was not very common.

Arabic arch A horseshoe-shaped ▷arch.

Arabo-tedesco A curious and antiquated term referring to the mixing of ▷Romanesque and ▷Gothic, as in the ▷Baptistery in Pisa.

Araeostyle ▷Colonnade, ▷intercolumniation.

Arbalestine, arbalisteria ▷Balistraria, or narrow ▷apertures in mediaeval fortress ▷walls through which bowmen discharged their *balistae* or arrows.

Arbor, arbour A structure formed of closely planted trees, arranged in ▷*espalier* fashion, or twined together, or partly supported on a ▷lattice ▷frame to create a leafy place like a building or a built enclosure. A ▷garden of herbs or flowers, a flower-garden, a garden of fruit trees, or a shady retreat of which the sides and ▷roof are formed of trees and shrubs closely planted or inter-

twined, or a shaded alley or walk. It can also mean a place covered in grass. An arbor is also the main support of a ▷beam or a machine (as in crane or windmill), and is referred to as a ▷tree (e.g. *manteltree* (▷mantel)). It is also an axle or a spindle. The term was therefore used to describe ▷beams used in construction, as over a fireplace or some other opening. An *arbor Judae* is the Judas Tree (*Cercis Siliquastrum*).

Arboretum A ▷garden where trees are cultivated for show, study, or propagation. A botanical garden devoted to the growth and exhibition of trees, rare or otherwise.

Arc A portion of a circle or other curved line. An *arc-boutant* is an arch-formed ▷buttress, commonly called a *flying buttress* (▷buttress). For *arc doubleau*, ▷arch. An *arc formeret* is a ▷wall-arch or ▷wall-rib, or the ▷rib coming next to the ▷nave-▷arcade in ▷Gothic ▷vaulting. An *arc de triomphe* is a ▷triumphal arch, such as the arches on the ▷axis of the *Champs-Élysées* in Paris.

Arca A ▷chest or ▷coffer; a ▷coffin. An *arca custodiae* is a ▷cell for the confinement of prisoners.

Arcade [20] A series of ▷arches carried on ▷columns, ▷piers, or ▷pilasters, either free-standing or attached to a ▷wall to form a decorative rhythmic pattern: in the latter case it is referred to as a ▷*blind arcade*. The term is applied to the arches on piers or columns that divide a ▷nave from an ▷aisle, in which case the ensemble is referred to as a *nave-arcade* (▷[134]). The ▷Victorian *shopping arcade* illuminated from above derives from another meaning of the term signifying a continued arch, a ▷passage, a walk formed by a number of arches, or an ▷avenue of trees. An arcade in the sense of a covered avenue with shops on one or both sides dates from around 1731. Arcades are also the lines of vertical ▷posts on either side of a ▷timber-framed building. An *arcade-▷plate* is a timber running over the tops of vertical posts in timber-framed buildings in the position of a wall-plate, and within the building. Arcade-plates support the common ▷rafters of the ▷roof. An *arcade-post* is one of a series of uprights in timber-framed walls.

Arcady *Arcadia* in Greece: a district, the inhabitants of which were simple, innocent, ▷pastoral, and given to music and dancing in perfect, unspoilt surroundings. It was the rustic ideal, representing lost contentment.

Arcae The ▷gutters of the ▷*cavaedium*, or a timber ▷beam with a groove or ▷channel in it.

Arcature Arcading, or a miniature ▷arcade, or a decorative ▷blind arcade.

Arcella A room for storing cheese.

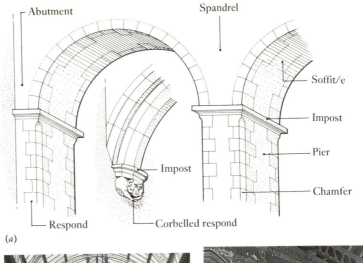

Abutment

Spandrel

Soffit/e

Impost

Pier

Chamfer

Impost

Respond

Corbelled respond

(a)

(b)

(c)

[20] ARCADE (*a*) Romanesque north arcade and (inset) thirteenth-century south arcade in St James's Church, Ewhurst, Sussex. (*JJS*) (*b*) The Central Arcade, Newcastle-upon-Tyne, by J. Oswald & Sons, of 1906, a fine Edwardian shopping arcade. (*JSC*) (*c*) Arcade in the Church of St Leonard at the Beauchamp Almshouses, Newland, Worcestershire, by P. C. Hardwick of 1862–64. The style is a vigorous French Gothic Revival. (*JSC*) (*d*) Part of the chapel of Ludlow Castle, Shropshire, showing blind, or blank, arcading in the circular nave of *c*.1140, with typical Romanesque work including scallop capitals and zigzag or chevron mouldings. (*JSC*)

(d)

Arceps ▷*Archarium*.

Arch [21] A construction of ▷blocks of material, disposed in a curve or curves and supporting one another by mutual pressure: an arch so formed over an opening is capable of carrying a superimposed load. Each block is called a ▷*voussoir* (usually in the shape of a truncated wedge), and the block in the centre is called the *keystone* (▷key). The solid extremities on or against which the arch rests are called ▷*abutments* (▷[20]). The lower or under-curve of each stone is called the *intrados*, and the upper curve the *extrados*. The distance between the ▷piers or abutments (that is, a line extending from the *springing line* on one side to the springing line on the other) is known as the ▷*chord* or ▷*span* of the arch, and the vertical distance between the level line of the springing to the intrados is the *height* or *rise* of the arch. The *springing, rein,* or ▷*impost* is the point at which an arch unites with its support, but *impost* usually implies a solid ▷block or ▷capital. The *vertex* or ▷*crown* of the arch is the most remote part of the intrados from the springing line. Each of the curved parts on the top of the section between the crown and each extremity of the spanning line is called the ▷*haunch* or ▷*flank* of the arch. The vertical plane figure contained by the span and the intrados is called the *section* of the cavity of the arch. The simplest arches are the *semicircular* and *segmental* arches, the former with its centre on the springing line and the latter with its centre below the springing line. In the ▷Saxon and ▷Norman periods, when semicircular arches were commonly used, the centre is often above the springing line, giving the arch an elongated, or ▷*stilted*, or sometimes *horseshoe* shape. The elongated arch is called a stilted arch, which is properly one with its springing line elevated by means of vertical piers above the impost. Occasionally, elongated ▷pointed arches are found, and when pointed arches have prolonged curves which narrow the arch at impost level, the effect is predominantly *Moresque* (▷Moorish architecture). The proportions of a pointed arch are governed by the position of the two centre points from which its curved sides are struck. An arch formed of two curves each with a radius equal to the span is called an ▷*equilateral* or a *two-centred* arch. When the centres of the curves forming the sides of the arch lie far apart, the radius is longer than the span, and so the height is increased: this is called a ▷*lancet* arch. In a case where the centres lie within this arch, the height is lessened, and the result is known as a ▷*drop* arch, (that is, with a span longer than the radius). ▷*Foil*, *foliated*, or *cusped* arches are found in Moresque architecture (▷Moorish architecture) and in mediaeval ▷Gothic work. Simple pointed or ▷*ogive* arches were used in all the periods of ▷Gothic architecture. The *lancet arch* is a characteristic of the ▷*Early English*, or First-▷*Pointed* period, while *drop* and *equilateral* arches are common in both *Early English* and *Decorated* (*Second-Pointed*) buildings (▷Decorated style). ▷*Perpendicular* (*Third-Pointed*) Gothic often has both drop and equilateral arches, but the characteristic form of later Perpendicular Gothic is the *four-centred arch*, also known as the ▷*Tudor*, although the Tudor is slightly different, being one in which the ▷shanks start as quarter-circles (with centres on the springing line) which continue as straight lines to the ▷apex. A true four-centred arch does not have straight lines, but upper central segments of arcs with centres *below* the springing line, and two lower outer arcs with centres *on* the springing line. The Tudor arch is a very ▷depressed arch, and is sometimes found in a single stone ▷lintel. During the Decorated (Second-Pointed) period, the ▷ogee arch was introduced, and is commonly found in ▷tomb-▷canopies, small ▷doorways, and ▷windows. Where arches are combined with *columnar* and *trabeated* systems, as in the Colosseum or in a ▷Roman ▷triumphal arch, the ▷intercolumniation was far greater than it would be if the arch were not there at all. The presence of the arch, however, gives a degree of strength and visual stability to the wide interval between the ▷columns, so that a balance is achieved.

Other arches are the *anse de panier*, with a curve like the handle of a basket, known also as a *basket* arch, formed by a segment of a circle joined to two other segments with smaller radii: it is also called, therefore, a *three-centred* arch. A *catenary* arch is an inverted catenary: the *common catenary* is the curve formed by a chain or rope of uniform thickness suspended from two points on a horizontal line not on the same vertical line. The catenary has long been recognized as one of the most beautiful gradated natural curves, and if it is fixed, as with ▷plaster, and reversed, it becomes the shape of a catenary arch. A ▷*compound* arch consists of a number of concentric arches successively placed within and behind each other, also referred to as a *recessed* arch or *order* arch. A ▷*corbel* arch is constructed by ▷cantilevering horizontal blocks cut from both sides of an opening until that opening is closed at the top: sometimes the opening is shaped at the top as though it is an arch, but it is still a *false, corbel,* or *pseudo-*arch. A ▷*diminished* arch is one lower or less than a semicircle, also known as a *segmental* arch. A ▷*discharging* arch is also called a *relieving* arch, and is built into a ▷wall above an opening such as a ▷door or ▷window in order to divert the load away from the lintel and to transfer it downwards on either side through the piers that flank the opening. An ▷*elliptical* arch is half an elliptical form with its ▷axis on the springing line. A *flat* arch is one with a level ▷soffite, also known as a ▷*soldier* arch. A ▷*Florentine* arch is one with intrados and extrados constructed on different centres. The voussoirs increase in length towards the top of the arch because the circle formed by the wider, top parts of the wedges has a different centre from that formed by the lower, narrower parts of

ELEVATION   **SECTION**

[21] ARCH (*a*) Parts of an arch. **X** extrados, **N** intrados. (*b*) Flat arch showing setting out of voussoirs. Note keystone. (*c*) Relieving arch over lintel. (*d*) Shouldered or false arch with corbels. (*e*) Venetian arch. (*f*) Florentine arch from the Palazzo Strozzi. (*g*) Florentine arch from Palazzo Pandolfini. (*h*) Elevation and section of a semicircular arch showing the parts. **a** archivolt, **s** springing line, **c** centre, **k** keystone, **v** voussoir, **e** extrados, **in** intrados, **so** soffite, **i** impost or springing line, **A** abutment, **r** radius. Note the height and span of the arch. Types of arch. (*i*) Segmental. (*j*) Semicircular or round-headed. (*k*) Horseshoe. (*l*) Equilateral. (*m*) Ogee. (*n*) Trefoil. (*o*) Cinquefoil. (*p*) Four-centred. (*q*) Lancet. (*a*–*g*, *i*–*q*, *JJS*; *h*, *JSC*)

the wedges. A ▷*gauged* arch is one with voussoirs radiating to a centre, with cut ▷bricks finely rubbed (known as *rubbers*) or stones precisely cut: they are laid with ▷lime mortar without ▷cement or sand (a pure lime ▷putty) to ensure extremely fine joints. ▷*Interlacing* arches are semicircular arches in an arcade, commonly found in Romanesque work in ▷blind arcading: the ▷intersecting or interlacing arches form pointed arches where the semicircular arches overlap in an intersecting arcade. An *inverted* arch is an arch turned upside-down, and is used in ▷foundations to resist the thrust of earth- or water-pressure, and to prevent the movement of the bases of piers or walls. An inverted arch also helps to spread the concentrated loads from piers to the more lightly loaded ▷foundation supporting the ▷spandrel ▷panels of brickwork in between, and thus it reduces the likelihood of differential settlement. A *jack* arch is a segmental brick arch which springs from and spans between iron beams, and was used in conjunction with ▷lime-▷concrete spread over the arch to form fire-proof floors in nineteenth-century factories and mills. A ▷*keel* arch is the same as an *ogee* arch, that is a pointed arch composed of four arcs with two centres *inside* the arch and two *outside*, producing two S-shaped curves: it was a common type from the beginning of the fourteenth century, and was characteristic of Decorated (Second-Pointed) Gothic architecture. A ▷*mitre* arch consists of two flat ▷slabs leaning together at the apex, joined in a mitre, thus forming a triangular head to the opening: it is not a true arch, and is found in ▷Anglo-Saxon work. An *obtuse-angled* arch is pointed, formed of circle-arcs with centres on either side of the centre-line of the arch. A *raking* arch has one impost at a higher level than the other, and is also termed a *rampant* arch. A *rear* arch is one spanning an opening on the inside of a wall, as when there is, say, a lintel on the outside, but a splayed ▷reveal requiring an arch over the top on the inside of the wall. A *rowlock* arch has voussoirs arranged in separate concentric rings. A *scheme* or *skene* arch is a segmental arch. A *secondary* arch is one placed over an opening to form a larger one, often serving as a *relieving* or *discharging* arch. It is also termed a *rear* arch or an *arrière voussure* or a *back* arch, the main characteristic of which is that the interior appearance is very different from the exterior. A *shouldered* arch is really a lintel carried on ▷corbels which have quadrants hollowed out of the outermost corners above which are vertical sides rising up to the underside of the lintel: a shouldered arch is therefore not an arch at all, but a lintel on corbels, and so is a false arch. A ▷*skew* arch has ▷jambs which are not at 90° to its face: a *skewback* is the part of the abutment which supports the arch (▷Dutch). The term *skew* indicates a slope, as in the skew of the abutment of a gauged-brick *straight* arch, which is essentially a lintel of voussoirs of rubbers based on the principle of the arch but with a flat or

slightly cambered intrados, and common in ▷Georgian ▷architecture. A ▷*soldier* arch is a *flat* arch of uncut bricks laid on end, which, because it is not a true arch, has to be supported on a metal angle or by some other means. A ▷*strainer* arch is one built into a space to prevent walls or piers from leaning inwards: they are used to separate walls or piers that show signs of moving towards each other. A ▷*surbased* arch rises to a height which is less than half its span. A ▷*surmounted* arch is one which rises higher than half its span. A ▷*transverse* arch is one which divides a compartment of a *vault* from another: it therefore spans from wall to wall or from wall to pier, and therefore creates a series of powerful subdivisions in the ▷ceiling that correspond to the rhythms of ▷bays or other architectural elements. A ▷*triumphal* arch is one erected to celebrate a person or event, usually a military victory, and often surmounted by a ▷*quadriga*. A triumphal arch is an important precedent for in it the ▷arcuated and columnar and trabeated forms are mixed: the wide ▷intercolumniation would look very weak without the arched forms behind. In addition, the mighty ▷Attic storeys of triumphal arches gave a greater *gravitas* to the composition. The importance of triumphal arches in Classical composition, especially in Renaissance times and during the eighteenth century, cannot be too strongly stressed. A ▷*Venetian* arch is a form of arched opening, either void or ▷blind, consisting of a pointed or semicircular arch within which are two semi-circular-headed openings separated by a ▷colonnette. Above the colonnette is a ▷roundel or a foiled opening, so the roundel or foiled opening is placed in the centre of the space between the tops of the smaller arches and the intrados of the larger main arch. A ▷*Welsh* arch comprises a ▷stretcher cut to the shape of a wedge and resting on two corbelled bricks or stones also cut to accommodate the stretcher: it is used to drain rain-water through a ▷parapet to a rainwater heads. An *arch ▷band* is part of the soffite of an arch or a vault, usually in the form of a band or raised strip projecting below the surface, in much the same relation to the arch or vault as a ▷pilaster is to a wall: arch bands are also called *arcs doubleaux*, and are used to stiffen ▷groin- or ▷barrel-vaults, or any arch. An *arch-bar* is a steel or iron bar of rectangular section set under a brick flat arch or *soldier arch* to hold the voussoirs in place, often used in fireplace openings. An *arch-▷beam* is a curved beam or a collar-brace. An *arch-brace* is a curved timber brace used in ▷roof construction: arch braces are found in pairs, and suggest the shape of an arch (▷[212k, l]. An *arch-▷brick* is a wedge-shaped brick for building an arch or lining a wall that is curved on plan, also called a ▷*compass-brick*, a *feather-edge brick*, or a *voussoir*. A *radial brick, radiating brick,* or *radius brick* is a curved brick used for constructing ▷culverts, etc. An *arch buttant* is a flying ▷buttress. An *arch-buttress* is also a flying buttress or *arc-boutant*, that is a buttress shaped like an arch and springing from a pier in arched form to the wall (▷buttress). An *arch centre* is ▷formwork to support the voussoirs of an arch when it is being built. An *arch corner bead* is a curved bead which is used to reinforce the curved part of an arched opening. *Arch mouldings* are a series of mouldings around an arch. In ▷Roman architecture, an arched opening framed by ▷engaged ▷columns and an ▷entablature, so mixing *arcuated* and *columnar and trabeated* work, as in a triumphal arch, is called an *arch Order*. It can also refer to successive planes of arches and colonnettes set within each other. In ▷Romanesque vaulting, a transverse ▷rib crossing a ▷nave or an ▷aisle at right-angles to the axis is called an *arch-rib*. It is also the main load-bearing part of a ribbed arch. An *arch-ring* is the curved part of an arched structure that carries the load, that is the arch of voussoirs. An *arch-stone* is a voussoir. An *arch-▷truss* is a truss with an arched upper member, the lower side of which is concave, and a horizontal lower member with vertical members linking them.

Archarium In ▷Antiquity, a building where the state archives were kept, also called an *archeion, archibus, archivum, archivium, arcibum,* or *tabularium.*

Arched An arched barrel roof is a ▷barrel-▷vault. A ▷beam with the upper surface curved, or a ▷collar-▷brace carried on a ▷hammer-beam at the lower extremity, is called an *arched beam.* An *arched ▷butment* is a flying buttress, also termed an *arched buttress* (▷buttress). Building using ▷arches, or carrying loads on arches instead of on ▷lintels or beams is termed *arched construction*, or ▷*arcuated* as opposed to *trabeated*. In ▷Early Christian and ▷Romanesque ▷architecture, a length of small arches carried on ▷corbels running between the tops of buttresses, and giving a decorative ▷frame to the top of a ▷wall-▷panel, is called an *arched corbel ▷table.* A ▷tomb-▷chest set within an arched recess is termed an *arched tomb.*

Archeion ▷Archarium.

Archeria An opening in a mediaeval fortified ▷wall through which an archer fired arrows. Also ▷balistraria.

Archibus ▷Archarium.

Archiepiscopal Cross A ▷cross with two arms, the longer one placed near the centre of the upright member, also called a *Patriarchal Cross* (▷cross).

Architect A person competent to design and superintend the execution of any building. A masterbuilder. A skilled professor of the art of building, who prepares designs for edifices, and oversees the erection of the structure from those plans. An architect is one who designs and frames any complex structure: he or she is a creator, even *The* Creator, who arranges elementary forms in a comprehensive plan. In the United Kingdom, the title *Architect* is protected by an Act of Parliament which requires a person to pass professional examinations and to receive practical training and experience before being admitted to the Register of Architects of the Architects' Registration Council of the United Kingdom. Sir John Soane (1753–1837) wrote that the 'business of the Architect is to make the designs and estimates, to direct the works, and to measure and value the different parts; he is the intermediate agent between the employer, whose honour and interest he is to study, and the mechanic, whose rights he is to defend. His position implies great trust; he is responsible for the mistakes, negligences, and ignorance of those he employs; and above all, he is to take care that the workmen's bills do not exceed his own estimates. If these are the duties of an Architect, with what propriety can his situation, and that of the builder or the contractor be united?' Contrary to popular belief, at present an architect in Britain does not have to be a member of the Royal Institute of British Architects to be entitled to call himself an architect: the only legal requirement is that he be registered with ARCUK.

Architecture The description of ancient buildings is termed *architectographia*, while *architectonic* is anything which relates to architecture or conforms with its principles. A ▷fountain producing ornamental jets which look as though they have a three-dimensional form is termed an *architectural fountain.* A burned clay element used in the decoration or construction of a building, often moulded with architectural features, and glazed or unglazed, is called *architectural ▷terracotta.* The art of designing and building according to rules and ▷proportions regulated by nature and taste, so that the resultant edifices arouse a response by virtue of their qualities of beauty, ▷geometry, emotional power, ▷Picturesque virtues, intellectual content, or ▷Sublime essence, is called *Architecture*, a term which suggests something far more significant, sophisticated, and intellectually complex than a mere building, although it must also involve sound construction, convenient planning, and durable materials. Ruskin, in the *Seven Lamps* (i.§I.7 [1849]), proposed that architecture was the 'art which so disposes and adorns the edifices raised by man . . . that the sight of them contributes to his mental health, power, and pleasure', a definition that suggests something far more than utilitarianism, and indicates a spiritual, aesthetic, and beneficial content. Architecture implies a sense of order, an organization, a geometry, and an aesthetic experience of a far higher degree than that in a mere building. Sir Henry Wotton's declaration that 'well building hath three conditions: Commodity, Firmness, and Delight' is derived from Vitruvius, who said that architecture depends on order, arrangement, eurythmy, ▷symmetry, propriety, and economy. By eurythmy (▷eurithmy) he seems to have meant ▷harmony of proportion, or some kind of rhythmical order of elements: central to that concept is beauty and fitness of the elements of a building, involving relationships of height to breadth, breadth to length, and symmetrical balance. Vitruvius also states that works of architecture should be realized with due reference to durability, convenience, and beauty: durability depends on ▷foundations and a wise choice of materials; convenience on the arrangement and usability of ▷apartments and on ▷orientation and exposure to the sun and air; and beauty on the appearance of the finished work and on the proportion of the various parts in relation to each other and to the whole. Usefulness, spaciousness, sound construction, and strength are indeed qualities to be expected in good buildings, but the addition of delight, uplifting of the spirits, and aesthetic aspects suggest that architecture is something more than building (see *Vitruvius*, Book i, Ch. i, 1, and Book i, Ch. iii, 2). Sir Christopher Wren stated (*Tracts on Architecture I. On Architecture; and Observations on Antique Temples, . . .* In the *Appendix* to *Parentalia*, published by the Wren Society, Vol. 19, Oxford, 1942, p. 126) that the principles of architecture were, in his time, 'rather the Study of Antiquity than Fancy', and that the main principles were 'Beauty, Firmness, and Convenience', the first two depending on the geometrical factors of 'Opticks and Staticks', while the third made the variety in a work of architecture.

Architrave The lowest of the divisions of an ▷entablature that rests directly on the *abaci* (▷abacus) of ▷columns. The term also refers to the ▷lintels, ▷jambs, and mouldings (▷mould) surrounding a ▷window, ▷door, ▷panel, or ▷niche. If an architrave around an opening springs out at 90°, rises vertically, then returns horizontally as the lintel, forming a ▷shoulder in the process, it is called a *shouldered architrave*, or an *eared* (▷ear) or *lugged architrave*. The term *architrave* can also be applied to the ornamental mouldings round the exterior curve of an ▷arch. Architraves in the ▷Doric Order are plain, but in the more elaborate ▷Orders are often divided into three ▷*fasciae*. In the simplest form the architraves as structural ▷beams resting on columns are called ▷*trabes compactiles*. Also the ▷trim planted to cover a joint between the ▷frame in an opening and the wall finish, usually at a door, window, or niche (▷[104], [105], and under the various ▷Orders). A ▷block at the foot of a door-, window-, or niche-architrave, which stops both architrave and skirting (▷skirt), also called a *plinth block* (▷plinth) or *skirting block*, is termed an *architrave block*. An entablature with no ▷frieze is called an *architrave* ▷*cornice*.

Archivium As ▷archarium.

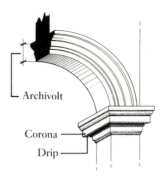

[22] ARCHIVOLT Archivolt springing from cornice with corona and drip. (*JJS*)

Archivolt [22] A group of concentric mouldings (▷mould) with which the face of a ▷Classical ▷arch is decorated: an ▷architrave that is curved to frame an arched opening. The term was originally used to designate a ▷vault, and is sometimes erroneously given to the ▷soffite of an arch.

Archivoltum An arched ▷sewer or ▷cesspit.

Archivum As archarium.

Archway A ▷passage under an ▷arch.

Arcosolium An arched recess or sepulchral ▷*loculus* in an ▷Antique ▷*hypogeum* or ▷catacomb.

Arcs doubleaux ▷Arch.

Arcuated A building dependent on the ▷arch principle, as opposed to the *trabeated* form of construction. ▷Roman arched structures, such as ▷aqueducts or ▷bridges, are called *arcuatio*.

Arcus In ▷Roman ▷architecture, an ▷arch. *Arcus choralis* is the ▷lattice or ▷screen separating the ▷choir from the ▷nave in a ▷basilica, also called *arcus toralis*. *Arcus ecclesiae* is the arch dividing the nave of a ▷church from the ▷chancel or choir. Roman plastered ▷tiles laid on straight or curved metal (usually iron) bars, and often plastered, required a methodology known as *arcus ferreus*. The arch over the ▷tribune marking the beginnings of its recess in a church was known as the *arcus presbyterii*. A ▷triumphal arch was the *arcus triumphalis*.

Area A ▷court or place, often sunk below the ground, allowing light into a ▷basement storey, frequently found in England. It is also used to denote a small courtyard, even when level with the ground. The term also means the superficial content of a figure in

▷geometry and the measurement of the superficies of a horizontal section. It is also applied to open spaces for recreation, or to the open space in front of a house or a ▷temple, or to that in front of a ▷Roman ▷cemetery where the ▷*bustrum* or ▷*ustrinum* on which cremations took place was situated.

Arena The central space of an amphitheatre (▷amphi) where gladiators fought, or any building where public contests were held. A type of ▷theatre with no ▷proscenium. An *arena* ▷*vomitory* was an access for actors to the arena ▷stage. A Roman amphitheatre, ▷cemetery, ▷crypt, ▷grave, or sandpit was known as *arenarium*.

Arenatum Used by Vitruvius to denote a type of ▷plaster. ▷Mortar consisting of ▷lime and sand.

Areola A small ▷area.

Argei Sites in Rome with small ▷temples or ▷chapels consecrated for religious rites.

Argent ▷Heraldic term for silver.

Ark A ▷chest. Repository for scrolls in a ▷synagogue.

Armariolum A place in a ▷cathedral or monastic ▷church where vestments were kept.

Armarium ▷Aumbry.

Armature Iron framework used in the construction of slender ▷columns or for supporting ▷canopies, ▷bosses, and ▷tracery.

(a)

(b)

[23] ART DECO (*a*) The Hoover factory, Great West Road, London, 1931–32, by Wallis, Gilbert, & Partners. Note the *loculus*-like windows on the left, the canted arched tall window (straight from the late eighteenth-century 'Egyptian' design), the battered form of the front (again a simplified Egyptianizing form), and the stepped centrepiece, recalling Piranesi's designs in *Diverse maniere.... (JSC)* (*b*) The foyer of the Strand Palace Hotel of 1930 by Oliver Bernard. Note the stepped and canted form of the display-case, and the stepped form of the illuminated upstand to the stair. Both these elements derive ultimately from Piranesi. (*Victoria and Albert Museum GX1637*)

Armoury A place where weapons are stored, military training takes place, or arms are made. An *armory* is a register of armorial bearings.

Aronade ▷Embattled, with ▷arches in the middle of each raised part.

Arrectarium A load-bearing ▷pier, ▷column, or ▷post in ▷Roman construction.

Arrière voussure ▷Arch.

Arris A sharp edge at the junction of two surfaces. An edge of a ▷brick or other element. The sharp edge between the ▷flutes of a ▷Greek ▷Doric ▷column. A triangular piece of timber used to raise ▷slates against ▷chimney-stacks, or against a ▷wall that cuts obliquely across a ▷roof, and in forming ▷gutters at the upper ends and sides of ▷skylights which have their planes coinciding with those of the roof, is called an *arris ▷fillet*. When the arris fillet is used to raise the slates at the ▷eaves of a building it is called the *eaves-board*, *eaves-lath*, or *eaves-catch*. An *arris-▷gutter* is a V-shaped timber gutter, also called a *Yankee gutter*. A triangular fence-▷rail made by cutting a square-sectioned piece of timber across the diagonal is known as an *arris-rail*. It is ▷mortised into the ▷posts, and is set with the diagonal side vertical, or sometimes at the ▷base. Any angular ▷tile, or one which covers a corner, is an *arris-tile*. Diagonal laying of bricks, slates, or tiles, or sawing of timber diagonally, is referred to as *arris-wise* or *arris-ways*, also known as ▷*herringbone*.

Arrow loop A loophole or ▷aperture with ▷splays on the inside of a fortification or ▷wall through which archers could fire arrows.

Arsenal A public store for arms and ammunition, or a place where they are manufactured.

Art Deco [23] A style fashionable in the 1920s and 1930s, taking its name from the *Exposition des Arts Décoratifs et Industriels Modernes* in Paris in 1925. Its sources derive from the rectilinear forms which were explored in a reaction to the curvilinear shapes of ▷*Art Nouveau*. It is associated with stepped forms, the ▷chevron, bright primary colours, and rich materials. It was strongly influenced by Ancient ▷Egyptian design, prompted by the discovery of Tutankhamun's tomb in 1922, and incorporated not only *echt*-Egyptian elements, but forms and ▷motifs that were *associated* with what Europeans *thought* Egyptian design included, notably the stepped ▷corbel and the stepped ▷gable (both of which suggest the ▷pyramidal form), and the canted 'arch', most of which can be found in the designs by Piranesi in *Diverse maniere d'adornare i cammini*. There was also a Mexican/Aztec influence, and it was known as *Style Moderne*.

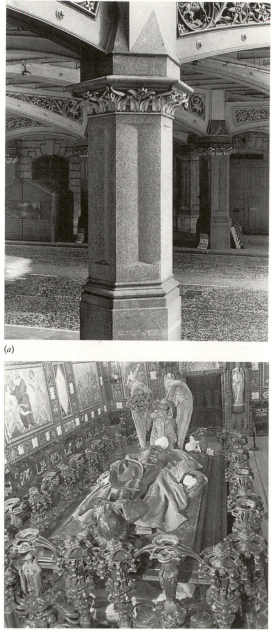

(a)

(b)

[24] ART NOUVEAU (*a*) Capital of a pier at Holborn Viaduct heralding Art-Nouveau forms. William Haywood, Chief Engineer. (*JCS*) (*b*) Tomb of Albert Victor Christian Edward, Duke of Clarence and Avondale (*d.* 1892) by Alfred Gilbert, almost completed 1898, and finished in 1926. It stands in the Albert Memorial Chapel (formerly the Lady Chapel of St George's Chapel, Windsor). The details of the metalwork grille are in the Art-Nouveau style. (*By permission of the Dean and Canons of Windsor*)

Art Nouveau [24] A style named after a shop in Paris of 1895 which sold modern, non-period, non-reproduction objects, including oriental artefacts. It was characterized by flowing, sinuous, vegetal lines, not entirely unlike ▷Rococo or ▷Auricular ▷ornament. It began as a branch of late ▷Gothic ▷Revival. The ▷capitals of Blackfriars Railway Bridge (1862–64) show pronounced ▷proto-Art-Nouveau ▷motifs, while those of Holborn Viaduct are even more clearly proto-Art-Nouveau. Art-Nouveau swaying ▷tendril-like lines appeared in quantity in the works of many designers, including Mackmurdo, and there are early pre-echoes of Art Nouveau in the works of William Morris and other members of the ▷Arts-and-Crafts Movement. Émile Gallé's glass, produced in Nancy in the 1880s, exploited sinuous flowing forms. Undulating, wave-like marine plants or flowing hair were motifs that recurred with increasing frequency, reaching remarkable virtuoso expression in the works of Guimard in Paris and Horta in Brussels. The drawings of Aubrey Beardsley, the ▷furniture of Majorelle and Mackintosh, the posters of Mucha, and the architecture of Olbrich, Hoffmann, and Gaudí all include distinctive Art-Nouveau elements. The style was promoted by journals such as *The Studio, Pan, Art Décoratif,* and *Kunst und Kunsthandwerk.* In Germany the style became known as ▷*Jugendstil* from the magazine *Jugend,* and in Italy the ▷*Stile Liberty* from Liberty's shop in London which sold Art-Nouveau artefacts. The style was most popular from the 1880s to around 1905, but lingered on in the tiles of Neatby, and in the designs of jewellery, stained glass, and picture-frames almost until the First World War. It was also associated with the Vienna ▷*Sezession,* and in Spain it was called ▷*Modernismo.*

Artemis Diana, the goddess of light by night, identified with all possible goddesses of the moon and night. She was a huntress, so her ▷attributes are the ▷crescent moon, the ▷bow, and the horns of animals. Artemis of Ephesus was celebrated in cult-statues that featured many horned animals in the wrappings of her body, a ▷nimbus around her head, and necklaces of testicles of sacrificed animals (formerly thought to be breasts [*multimammiam*]). This figure was an important ▷motif in ▷Antique and ▷Neoclassical art. A ▷temple or ▷shrine dedicated to Artemis, such as the great temple of Artemis in Ephesus, was called an *Artemision.*

Artificer A person who designs, as an ▷architect, and a cut above the ▷artisan, whose knowledge is limited to his trade only.

Artificial aggregates Lightweight ▷aggregates such as slag and clinker. ▷*Scagliola* or *Marezzo* ▷marble, made with ▷gypsum ▷plaster and coloured, is *artificial marble. Artificial stone* is a material resembling stone, but made with a mix of materials, and fired or unfired.

Artisan A tradesman or craftsman. The use of ▷Classical ▷motifs in a way not like their original dispositions, evolved by craftsmen rather than ▷architects, is known as *Artisan* ▷*Mannerism.*

Arts-and-Crafts [25] An English social and ▷aesthetic movement in the latter part of the nineteenth century which grew from a dissatisfaction with the quality of design in manufactured artefacts, especially after the Great Exhibition of 1851. It had its origins in an admiration for traditional art and craftsmanship,

[25] ARTS-AND-CRAFTS The Black Friar, 174 Queen Victoria Street, London, of 1905, designed by H. Fuller Clark and Henry Poole. A sumptuous Arts-and-Crafts interior, with certain Art-Nouveau features as well, notably the capitals of the square columns. (*Eric de Maré by permission the Editor, the Architectural Review*)

and in a romantic longing to recapture the supposed ideal of the mediaeval craft-guilds: these notions can be traced to the theories of Rousseau (who advocated the teaching of manual processes to persons of all classes and conditions), to the writings of Pugin, and to the polemics of Ruskin. The key figure of the Arts-and-Crafts Movement was William Morris (1834–96), who first built and designed the furnishings for his own house, then founded the firm of Morris, Marshall, and Faulkner in 1861, which produced wallpapers, the ornamental parts of ▷stained-glass ▷windows, chintzes, and other printed textiles, carpets, ▷tapestries, woven furnishing materials, books, and ▷furniture. The firm thus recreated hand-crafted industry in a machine age. The Movement influenced young ▷architects and designers, crusaded to make towns beautiful, sought to reform society so that ugliness would be abolished, and argued for the preservation and protection of old buildings. The philosophy of doing the minimum to conserve buildings without altering their character was developed, largely in response to the drastic '▷restorations' of ▷churches carried out by certain ▷Victorian architects who favoured virtual rebuilds in a ▷revival of mediaeval styles rather than sensitive ▷conservation of old ▷fabric. The Movement was responsible for the founding of the Society for the Protection of Ancient Buildings. The Arts-and-Crafts Movement had a profound influence on designers such as Walter Crane, W. R. Lethaby, and C. R. Ashbee, and its chief legacies were the founding of the Guild and School of Arts and Crafts and the Art Workers' Guild, both in 1888. The Arts and Crafts Exhibition Society held several important exhibitions in the 1890s, and the Movement influenced design in Germany, Belgium, the Netherlands, Scandinavia and Austria. In ▷architecture, its chief legacy was the revival of ▷vernacular architecture and the movement we now call the ▷Domestic Revival, from the conscious derivations from ordinary buildings as opposed to grand architecture. The Movement was in a sense an offspring of the ▷Gothic Revival, and it had an enormous effect on the design of model housing, notably at Bournville, Port Sunlight, and Letchworth. Its first manifestation in a suburb was at Bedford Park, which influenced the design of domestic architecture until 1939.

Arula A diminutive form of ▷*ara*, an ▷altar.

Arx A ▷citadel in a city containing ▷temples. It is the equivalent of an ▷*acropolis*.

Asarotum A variety of painted ▷pavement used by the ▷Romans as an alternative to ▷mosaic. It often involved a kind of *trompe l'oeil* (▷trompe), as when the painting suggested crumbs, so that the viewer would think the ▷floor had not been swept.

Asbestine An extender.

Asbestos A mineral crystal consisting of ▷fibres, which can resist heat. ▷Cement reinforced with asbestos fibre to make cheap fire-resistant sheets for roof-and ▷wall ▷cladding and ▷flue-pipes is known as *asbestos cement*. ▷Slates made of this material can be laid like ordinary slates, but must be drilled rather than punched.

Ascendant ▷Chambranle.

Asclepius The god of medicine in the Graeco-Roman world. He could resurrect the dead, and is associated with healing springs, with groves in woods, and with ▷fountains. Cures were effected in his ▷shrines, usually by 'incubation', when patients were required to sleep in the sacred buildings: these cures were associated with fasting, sleep, dreams, and the drinking of pure water. Asclepius is associated with the ▷serpent, the ▷symbol of rejuvenation, healing, prophecy, and wisdom, and he is recognized as Osiris/Serapis/Horus. His usual ▷attribute is a staff with a serpent coiled around it, known as *caduceus*.

Ashburton stone A Devonshire ▷marble of a dark-grey colour, verging on black, with bright red-and-white veins, and fossils, from Newton Abbot.

Ashlar Cut stone, worked to even ▷faces and right-angled edges, or ▷arrises, used on the ▷front of a building, and laid in horizontal ▷courses with vertical joints. When the work is smooth and ▷rubbed, so as to remove the marks of the tools by which the stone was cut, it is called *plain (or plane) ashlar*. When the surface is cut in a regular fashion, with parallel incisions like miniature fluting placed perpendicular in the wall, it is called *tooled ashlar*. Other finishes are ▷*random tooling*, or irregular texturing using a broad implement without care or regularity; *chiselling* (▷chiselled) or *boasting* (▷boast), created with a fine, narrow tool; and ▷*pointed*, if the surface is finished with a very narrow tool. When the face of the ashlar projects beyond the joints, the finish is known as *rustication* (▷rustic), and the faces can have smooth or broken surfaces. The ▷Romans called ashlar ▷*opus quadratum*, from the regular squared forms of the ▷blocks (▷[163], [215]). In the United States the term *ashlar* also includes any blocks of burnt clay bigger than standard ▷bricks, so would embrace ▷terracotta or ▷faience. An *ashlar brick*, also known as ▷*rock-faced brick*, is brickwork with a hacked facing which looks like roughly ▷dressed stone. An *ashlar-line* is a horizontal line on the outside face of a ▷masonry ▷wall, also a *string-*▷*course*. *Ashlar masonry* is masonry of rectangular blocks of stone or burned clay, bigger than ordinary bricks, and bonded, with sawn squared dressed ▷beds, jointed with ▷mortar. For *ashlar-piece*

[26] ASIATIC BASE (IONIC) (*JSC*)

or *ashlering*, ▷roof. *Ashlaring* also means the setting of ashlars.

Ashpit A space under a fireplace grating for ashes. It often contains an ashpan which can be removed to empty the débris.

Asiatic base [26] An ▷Ionic ▷base with a lower disc with horizontal fluting or reeding above which is a ▷torus, also reeded (▷flute, ▷reed). It may rest on a ▷plinth, and is associated with the Ionic ▷temples of Asia Minor. It is contrasted with the ▷Attic base.

Asidua The place in a ▷church where the altar stands, also *assidua*.

Aspaticum A room joined to or near a ▷church where the clergy received visitors for business, ceremonial, or devotional purposes. Also called a ▷*salutorium*.

Aspect The direction in which a building faces.

Aspersorium The ▷stoup, or holy-water basin.

Asphalt(e) A bituminous substance, impervious to damp. Asphalte roofing is roofing with ▷mastic asphalte laid in two or three coats. *Asphaltum* is natural asphalte.

Assemblage of the Orders The placing of the Orders of architecture above one another in ranges of ▷colonnades, with the axes of ▷columns in continuous vertical lines.

Asser (pl. **asseres**) *Trabiculae* are the main ▷beams resting on the *mutuli* of a ▷temple. On top of the *trabiculae* are the *asseres* laid over the main beams and spanning over them at right angles. Asseres were therefore a variety of substantial ▷laths, and from the projections the denticulated ▷cornice is supposed to have originated. Asseres were not disposed horizontally, but laid according to the ▷pitch of the ▷roof. Therefore Vitruvius did not recommend ▷dentils in ▷pediments, but only along the horizontal courses of ▷entablatures. Asseres were also ▷ribs or ▷brackets of an arched ceiling.

Assis A flat ▷board of timber in ▷Roman work.

Assize A ▷drum forming part of a stone ▷column, or any ▷course of ▷masonry.

Assommoir A ▷platform above a ▷door or a ▷passage in a fortress from which the defenders could rain missiles on the attackers.

Assula A splinter, or any small sliver of wood or stone. Also *astula, asula*.

Astler As *ashlar*.

Astragal A small moulding (▷mould) with a semi-circular profile, a ▷bead, sometimes called a ▷*roundel*, a *baguette* (▷bagnette), or a ▷*chaplet*. It is properly applied only to the ring that separates the ▷capital from the ▷shaft of a ▷Classical ▷column, and may be ▷ornamented with a bead or a reel or both (▷bead). It may also denote the bead that separates the ▷fasciae of ▷architraves, and in such a position is usually ornamented with ▷bead-and-reel. The name, meaning 'knuckle-bones', however, implies enrichment with bead-and-reel. It can also be applied to the member fixed to one of a pair of ▷doors or ▷casement windows to cover the joint between the ▷stiles. *Astragals* is a use of the term (especially in Scotland) to denote glazing-bars (▷glass). An *astragal-joint* is one used in a ▷lead rainwater-▷pipe where the socket has mouldings that are bead-like astragals.

Astreated ▷Embellished with ▷stars or star-like ▷ornament.

Astula ▷Assula.

Astylar Without ▷columns or ▷pilasters.

Asylum A ▷temple, ▷altar, grove, or statue with the privilege of protection; a ▷sanctuary, secure place, refuge, or retreat; a benevolent institution affording shelter and support to the afflicted and destitute.

Ataracea Coloured ▷inlaid wood, like ▷marquetry.

Ataurique Architectural decoration which features ▷leaves and flowers in ▷plaster, found in ▷Moorish work.

Atelier A ▷studio or ▷workshop in which arts and crafts are produced.

Athenaeum A ▷school founded by Emperor Hadrian for the teaching of literature, science, and other subjects. It was a kind of university, and was named after Athens, which had the reputation as the centre of intellectual endeavour in the Graeco-Roman world: it was therefore dedicated to Athene.

Atkinson's cement A quick-setting patent ▷cement or ▷stucco, made from nodules found near Whitby in

Yorkshire, which were broken and burned in a ▷kiln, and reduced to powder. Two measures of water to five of the powder made ▷*tarras*, and ▷lime and sand could be added. Nearly all patent cements were similar in composition, including ▷*Parker's cement*, which was reddish-brown in colour. The Adam brothers used a variety of stucco at their great development known as the Adelphi (▷Adam's cement). Most of the stucco finishes in use in the first half of the nineteenth century were quick-setting.

Atlantes, Atlantides   Heroic male figures used instead of ▷columns, ▷pilasters, or ▷brackets to support an ▷entablature, and usually shown straining against the superimposed load. ▷*Telamon* appears to have been an alternative name for *Atlas*, and so *Atlantes* are also named *telamoni* or *telamones* (▷Telamon), but these are usually straight male figures used instead of columns, and not shown in an attitude of vigorous struggle (▷canephora, ▷caryatide).

Atlas   ▷Atlantes.

Atramentum   Any black colouring substance.

Atriolum   A small ▷atrium, or a second atrium in large ▷Roman houses. Also an ▷antechamber to a ▷sepulchre.

Atrium   An open ▷court, usually surrounded by a covered ▷area or a walk, ▷colonnaded, found in ▷Roman domestic ▷architecture and in front of ▷Early Christian ▷churches. It was roofed to leave a large opening (*compluvium*) in the centre to admit light and rain: the latter was received in a ▷cistern (*impluvium*) formed in the ▷pavement. It was also called *cavum aedium* or ▷*cavaedium*. The term *atrium* has been revived to describe large top-lit spaces rising through several ▷floors in modern buildings. Where an atrium was placed at the west end of a ▷basilican church it usually had a ▷fountain in the centre where pilgrims could wash: the open space was much larger than in domestic examples, and was the precedent for the mediaeval ▷cloister. An *atrium Corinthium* is an atrium with more than four ▷columns associated with the cavaedium, and of great magnificence. An *atrium* ▷*displuviatum* is one with the ▷roof sloping outwards away from the opening, so that rainwater was collected in ▷gutters rather than pouring directly into the impluvium. A *displuviate* atrium permitted a better natural illumination of the rooms surrounding the atrium, and indeed of the atrium itself. An *atrium testudinatum* was one with no compluvium covered with a ▷testudo, or arched ▷vault of plastered wood. An *atrium tetrastylum* is an atrium with the beams around the compluvium carried on four columns. An *atrium Tuscanicum* is very small and simple with the opening in

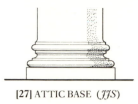

[27] ATTIC BASE (*JJS*)

the roof formed only by means of two large ▷beams spanning from ▷wall to wall and with two shorter beams trimming (▷trim) the opening and spanning from beam to beam: there were no columns.

Attached column   An ▷engaged ▷column, that is one attached to a ▷wall, with various proportions exposed.

Attic   A low ▷storey over the main ▷entablature, not to be confused with a ▷garret. An attic has ▷ceilings square with the side ▷walls, and is quite distinct from a roof-space. The term also applies to *Attica* in Greece. An *Attic base* (▷[27]) is the base of a ▷Classical ▷column consisting of two torus (large convex) rings separated by a ▷scotia (concave) with ▷fillets (i.e. two large convex mouldings between which is a concave moulding plus two flat elements). This is found with all Orders except the ▷Greek ▷Doric and the ▷Tuscan. It seems first to have evolved as part of the ▷Ionic Order, and is by far the most commonly used Classical base. An *Attic Order* is one consisting of low ▷pilasters placed over some other Order of columns or ▷pilasters. An *Attic storey* is one above the main entablature in Classical ▷architecture in which the arrangement of pilasters, etc., relates to the arrangement below that entablature (▷[129]): ▷triumphal arches have attic storeys. The term *Atticurges* refers to the Attic base or to a type of Doric ▷doorway with ▷*fasciae* all round the ▷architrave, but with the opening wider at the bottom than at the top (that is the opening is ▷battered, and the ▷jambs incline towards the top).

Attributes   Symbols or ▷motifs associated with mythological or legendary figures, and used decoratively. Hercules is indicated by a ▷club, Neptune by a ▷trident, and Pallas by a ▷spear. For attributes given to saints, ▷symbols.

Auditorium   A room or ▷hall for an audience to listen and view, as in a ▷theatre or a concert-hall. In ▷Antiquity it was a place where orators and others could recite to an audience. The section of an ancient ▷church where the congregation stood to hear the ▷Gospel was called the *auditory*, or the ▷nave of a church. An auditory suggests belonging to an auditorium of a theatre, and is a lecture-room, a place for an audience, as in a theatre, or a place for hearing or listening. An *auditory plan* is one specially constructed for its ▷acoustic properties, where all members of the audience can hear clearly: it also means a plan for congregational as opposed to liturgical worship.

Aufklärung The ▷Enlightenment in German-speaking lands.

Auger A tool for boring holes.

Augusteum A ▷temple dedicated to Augustus, first Roman emperor.

Aula A ▷court or ▷hall, and especially an open court associated with a house. An *aula regia* was the central part of the ▷scene (▷scaena, ▷schema) in ▷theatres in ▷Antiquity, and represented a grave and handsome building.

Aulaeum In ▷Antiquity it was a curtain, usually decorated with some pictorial matter, which was lowered as a kind of backdrop for a play or other performance. The term was also given to a curtain hung in a ▷temple to veil the statue of a deity. Any hanging in a house, such as a ▷tapestry or a ▷canopy. A ▷blind outside a house to protect a ▷balcony or a ▷gallery. A hanging over ▷colonnades to protect people underneath, like an ▷awning or a tent.

Auleolum A small ▷chapel or a tiny ▷church.

Aumbry Also known as *almeny*, *almery*, *almorie*, *ambre*, *ambrie*, *ambry*, *armarium*, *aumbrye*, or *aumery*, it was a recess by the side of an ▷altar built into a ▷wall to receive the sacred vessels. Ornate ▷doors were provided, and often the stonework around aumbries was finely carved. The term also applies to a ▷cupboard, a ▷larder, or a ▷niche in which precious objects, including arms, clothes, and books were stored. The term *armarium* meant a division in a ▷Roman ▷library.

Aureole A ▷framed, circular, elliptical, rectangular, or almond-shaped ▷halo (the latter created by two segmental ▷arcs interlocking), surrounding the figure of Christ, the Virgin, or saints (▷Mandala, Vesica Piscis). It is also called a *glory*, and is surrounded by radiating gilt beams. When a circular halo surrounds the head only, it is termed a *nimbus*.

Auricular ▷Ornament in a seventeenth-century style, so called because it is like the curved and melting forms found in the human ear. It is associated with ▷Mannerism, with the flaccid forms of much design of the period, and with ▷antic and ▷Grotesque ornament. It anticipates ▷Rococo and ▷Art-Nouveau design.

Aurrie A ▷passage in a ▷church, or an ▷aisle.

Auvanna ▷Antevanna.

Avant-corps Part of a structure that projects from the main ▷block, such as a ▷porch, or a ▷pavilion.

Aventurine ▷Glass or glazed materials containing spangles of ▷fabric not made of glass. It is brown in colour with gold spangles, and was made in Murano. Any colouring to resemble aventurine.

Avenue A wide thoroughfare or street, usually straight, and planted formally with trees. It is also an ▷approach or an ▷access to a building, or even a broad path in the country lined by trees.

Aviary A place for the keeping and breeding of birds.

Awning A covering to screen persons or parts of buildings from the sun or rain. An awning-▷pole, also called a ▷*malus*, is a ▷pole or a ▷beam supporting an awning.

Axed ▷Dressed. A finish to hard stone after the ▷face has been reduced with a punch (Scots). The term can also mean a stone surface struck with a bush hammer or an axe. If a surface is once-axed it is rough, but if fine-axed it is smooth. Axed ▷bricks are bricks cut to shape with an axe or a bolster, as opposed to ▷rubbed bricks, and therefore the joints are less fine than in ▷gauged work.

Axial A building planned on an ▷axis, or longitudinal on an axis, as opposed to a centrally planned structure. An *axial* ▷*tower* is a round tower, circular on plan.

Axicia An upright ▷axis on which a ▷door turned, also known as *assis*. A plank.

Axis In ▷architecture, the straight line about which the parts of a building are symmetrically arranged.

Axle pulley A ▷sash-pulley in a ▷window-▷frame.

Axonometric projection A drawing showing a building in three dimensions with verticals and horizontals to scale: it is projected from a plan which is drawn at an angle or 60° and 30° to the usual horizontal ▷axis.

Aya Sophia Holy wisdom, of *Hagia Sophia*, the dedication of the great ▷Byzantine ▷church in Istanbul (Constantinople).

Azotea, azothea A ▷roof-▷terrace on a Spanish house.

Aztec architecture ▷Architecture derived from the

Toltec civilizations of what is now Mexico from the fourteenth century. Its most impressive structures were the stepped ▷pyramids supporting ▷platforms on which ▷temples were built. It had an influence on the ▷*Art Deco* Movement, and its affinities with ▷Egyptian design were exploited in artefacts in the 1920s and 1930s, in the *Style Moderne*.

Azulejo A Spanish ▷tile with a metallic lustre.

Azure ▷Heraldic term for blue.

B

Baccha A ▷Roman lighthouse.

Bacchic ornament Decoration with ▷attributes of Bacchus or Dionysus, alluding to wine and honey. ▷Motifs include ass, bay, ▷dolphins, ▷grapevines, ▷ivy, ▷laurel, panthers, ▷rams, ▷serpents and ▷tigers. While Bacchic decoration appears in ▷Antiquity, it is very common in ▷Renaissance work, often to suggest the sensual life as opposed to reason, which was alluded to by means of Apollonian attributes. Bacchus is often represented as a youth with a drunken smile, and he is accompanied by dancing female figures. Faces crowned with grapes and ▷vine ▷leaves are also Bacchic.

Back The rear, reverse, or hidden part of a structure. The support for a visible part. The top, exposed, or visible side of a ▷slate or ▷tile as opposed to the ▷bed. The ▷ridge or top of a straight member such as a ▷roof, a ▷rafter or a ▷joist, as opposed to a ▷face. A main rafter. The *extrados* of an ▷arch. When a piece of timber is placed in an inclined position, the top side is the *back* and the lower the *breast*: the upper part of a handrail, for example, is the back, a principle that is also applied to ▷ribs of ▷ceilings or ▷vaults or to rafters. *Back arch*, ▷arch. A *back-boiler* is one fitted at the back of a fireplace. *Back-boxing* is the back-▷lining of a ▷sash-▷frame, or that parallel to the pulley-piece. A *back of a chimney* is the recessed face of it facing the room; the *back* of a ▷hip or *rafter* is the upper side. A *back* ▷*choir* is a ▷retrochoir. A *backdrop* is a curtain or canvas hung at the rear of a ▷stage to screen the backstage area, or a connection at a ▷manhole where an incoming branch-drain enters at a higher level than the manhole bottom. A *back-*▷*fillet* is the return of a ▷jamb or a ▷groin projecting beyond a ▷wall: it is the return to the ▷face of a wall of the ▷margin of a projecting ▷quoin, as in a plain ▷architrave to an opening. *Backfilling* or *backfill* is material used to refill

an excavation (as in ▷foundations), or rough ▷masonry behind a facing or between two faces of finished work, or brickwork between structural timbers, also known as *nogging* (▷nog). A *back-flap* ▷*hinge* resembles a ▷butt hinge, but is much wider and is fixed to the face of a counter-flap where the knuckle of a butt hinge would stand proud of the counter-top. *Background, backing* or *base* is the surface on which a first coat of ▷stucco is laid. *Background heating* is the cheapest form of heating for rooms, supplemented when necessary by other appliances. A *back* ▷*gutter* is one on a sloping ▷roof where a chimney breaks through it, at the upper part, diverting the water around the chimney. A *back* ▷*hearth* or *inner hearth* is the part of the ▷floor within the fireplace. A *back-*▷*lintel* is a lintel supporting the backing of a wall, not visible on the face. *Back-puttying* is the placing of the ▷putty in the rebate (▷rabbet) of a sash-▷bar on the inside so that the ▷glass can be bedded properly before the fillet is formed. *Back-*▷*shutters* are folds of a shutter which do not appear on the face, and are folded in the *boxing*. The *back of a stone* is the side opposite the face, and is generally rough. The *back of a* ▷*wall* is the inner face. The *back of a* ▷*window* is the ▷frame between the lower part of the sash-frame and the ▷floor: it is bounded to the right and left by the ▷elbows of the window. *Backing* is a ▷bevel on a hip-rafter, *firring* on joists for making them level for floor-▷boards or ▷laths, the shaping of ▷linings so that they lie flat against a wall, the opposite of the *facing* of a wall, unexposed or unfinished inner face of a wall, coursed ▷masonry over the extrados of an arch, or stone in random-▷rubble walls. The term is also applied to a *backing* ▷*brick*, which is a poor-quality brick behind masonry or facing bricks. A *backjoint* is a rebate (▷rabbet), such as that on the inner side of a decorative feature like a chimney-piece into which a tongue can be placed. A *back-to-back* is a house with a ▷party wall at the rear as well as the sides: it is not to

35

be confused with ▷terrace-houses with ▷areas and alleys behind. A *back-coat* is any coat other than a finishing coat. *Backset* is stone cut back so that ▷rendering over it is ▷flush with the rest of the face.

Backsteingotik Mediaeval ▷brick ▷architecture in northern Germany. It is simplified ▷Gothic, such as the brick ▷town-halls of Lübeck and Stralsund, or the great Gothic brick churches of Wismar, Lübeck, and Schwerin.

Badger A large timber plane for cutting rebates (▷rabbet).

Badigeon A mixture of ▷plaster and ▷freestone, ground, and used to repair statuary or carvings. The term is also applied to a mixture of sawdust and strong ▷glue used to repair blemishes in timber: sometimes ▷whiting and glue, or ▷putty and chalk, are used for this purpose.

Bagnette, baguet, baguette A moulding (▷mould) like a ▷bead or ▷astragal, or a ▷chaplet (when ▷ornaments were cut on it).

Bagnio A ▷bath, usually a Turkish bath. The term also came to signify a brothel or 'stew' in the seventeenth century. A Turkish ▷prison for slaves, where baths could be had, among other things.

Bague An ▷annular moulding (▷mould) anywhere around a ▷shaft, hence *baguette* (▷bagnette).

Bahut The rounded upper ▷course or coping (▷cope) of a ▷masonry ▷wall or ▷parapet, or a low wall over a ▷cornice carrying the ▷roof.

Baignoire A ▷theatre-▷box in the lowest tier of boxes.

Bail, bailey, ballium The space between the circuits of the ▷walls of a ▷castle and the ▷keep, also called a ▷*ward*. The outer ▷court of a castle or any court within its walls. The term seems to have meant originally the walls around a castle. There can be an outer bailey and an inner bailey

Bakehouse A place fitted up with troughs and ovens where bread is made.

Bakelite An early brown plastic used for electrical fittings, radio cases, and ▷door-▷knobs.

Balanced construction Plywood with an equal thickness of wood in both directions of the grain, with an odd number of plies, and symmetrical about its centre-line.

Balanced flue A ▷flue for a gas-heating appliance

with the air inlet next to the exhaust gas outlet in a windproof casing fixed to the outside ▷wall.

Balanced sash A ▷sash-▷window in which the opening ▷lights are balanced by weights on cords or spring-balances. They slide vertically.

Balanced winders Also known as *dancing steps* or *dancing winders*, they are ▷steps in a curved part of a ▷stair, or a turn in a stair, the narrow ends of which are the same width as that of the ▷treads of the straight ▷flight adjacent. They are much more comfortable to use than when the ▷nosings radiate from a common point.

Balaneion A ▷Greek ▷bath.

Balconet A fake ▷balcony, or low railing in front of a ▷window, projecting a small amount in front of the ▷sill.

Balcony A ▷platform ▷projecting from the surface of a ▷wall of a building carried on ▷brackets, ▷consoles or ▷columns, or ▷cantilevered. It is usually placed before ▷windows or openings, and is protected by a ▷railing or a balustrade (▷baluster). It is also a ▷gallery projecting in an ▷auditorium with seats, or an elevated platform in a permanent stage-set. A *balcon* is a circular row of seats projecting beyond the tier of ▷boxes above the ▷pit. A *balcony stage* is a balcony used for performance, as in an Elizabethan ▷theatre.

Baldacchino, baldachin, baldachino, baldaquin [28] A ▷canopy over an ▷altar, ▷tomb, or ▷throne, carried on ▷columns, supported on ▷brackets, or suspended. A *ciborium*, which is sometimes used synonymously with *baldacchino*, is properly a ▷cupola or domed structure supported on four columns and set over an altar.

Bale tack A *tingle* or strip of flexible metal used for holding pipes or wires, or securing ▷patent glazing, or to support a long line used by bricklayers.

Bale tomb A type of ▷table- or ▷altar-▷tomb found in the Cotswolds on which is a semicylindrical top carved with ▷scallop-▷shell ends, resembling woollen bales or perhaps representing a corpse wrapped in a woollen shroud.

Balection ▷Bolection

Balinea Also ▷*balnea*, plural of *balneum*, they were private ▷Roman bathing establishments, as opposed to the larger, public ▷thermae. Also called *balnearium*.

Balistraria [29] The narrow ▷aperture in a mediaeval fortress ▷wall through which the bowmen or *arbalasters*

[28] BALDACCHINO The Albert Memorial, London, of 1863–72: George Gilbert Scott's High-Victorian monument. The canopy is based on Italian Gothic exemplars of the thirteenth century. Precedents were the Scaliger tombs in Verona, and various canopies over altars, reliquaries, and the like. (*Greater London Photographic Library 70/10351 45.5ALB*)

discharged their arrows. It was often ▷cruciform, and came into general use in the thirteenth century. It is also known by the terms *arbalestina* or *arbalisteria*. A balistraria is also a room in which arbalests or crossbows were kept.

Balk, baulk A piece of fir, rough-squared, or the upper ▷tie between ▷rafters. It is also a ridge of earth marking a boundary. A *balk-tie* joins the timbers of a ▷roof, thus preventing it from spreading.

Ballast Unscreened gravel containing sand, grit and small stones.

Ballaster A ▷baluster.

(a)   (b)

[29] BALISTRARIA Also called a loophole. (*a*) From Tattershall Castle, Lincolnshire. (*JJS*) (*b*) Cruciform balistraria at the Micklegate Bar, York. Note the shouldered arched that once led to the wall-walks of the barbican (demolished), and note the fourteenth-century bartisans with crenellations. (*JSC*)

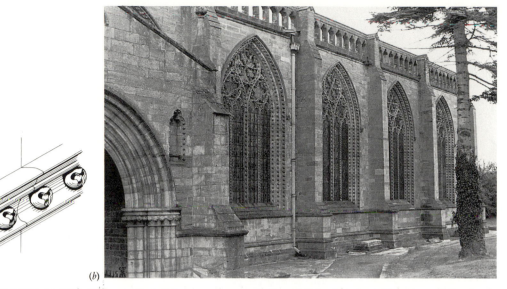

[30] BALL-FLOWER (*a*) (*JJS*). (*b*) Spectacular ball-flower ornament on the Second-Pointed windows of Leominster Priory church, Herefordshire. (*JSC*)

Ball-and-bar Rows of spaced ▷beads on chair-backs and other timber uprights found in eighteenth-century work in eastern England.

Ball-and-claw A type of ▷foot or termination for ▷furniture featuring a ▷claw or ▷talon clutching a ▷ball which provides the ▷base for furniture and metalwork.

Ball-catch A ▷door-fastening in which a spring-loaded ball, projecting from a ▷plate and set in a ▷mortise in the ▷door, engages with a circular hole cut in a *striking-plate* fixed to the ▷frame.

Ball-flower [30] An ▷ornament like a ▷ball enclosed within ▷petals and usually placed in a hollow moulding (▷mould). It is usually regarded as a characteristic ▷ornament of the ▷*Decorated* or *Second-*▷*Pointed* ▷*Style* of ▷Gothic ▷architecture of the fourteenth century.

Ball-valve Also known as a *ball-cock*, it is a valve closed by a floating, air-filled ball fixed to a lever.

Ballistraria ▷Balistraria.

Ballium ▷Bailey.

Balloon A globe or *ballon* set on a ▷column or ▷pier, or the ▷ball on top of a ▷dome. *Balloon-framing* or ▷*-frame* is a type of ▷timber-framed construction in which all the vertical structural elements of the ▷walls and ▷partitions are single ▷studs rising from the ▷sole-plate to the ▷roof-plate past the ▷floor-▷joists which are nailed to them.

Balteus The wide ▷step in ▷theatres or amphitheatres which allowed people to walk without disturbing those seated, and which divided the theatres horizontally into upper and lower zones. The term is also used to describe the 'strap' which appears to bind the ▷volutes, ▷cushion or ▷*coussinet* of the Ionic ▷capital (▷Ionic Order): it is applied both to the ▷band in the centre of the cushion and to the band joining the volutes.

Baluster A small ▷colonnette or ▷post forming part of a balustrade and supporting the handrail or ▷coping (▷[190]). Balusters are also known as ▷*columellae*. They can be square, polygonal, or circular on plan, and their ▷profile can be elaborate: because of their columnar form, balusters can be treated according to the conventions of the ▷Orders, and many ▷pattern-books recommend certain types of baluster for use with certain Orders but not with others. A *baluster-*▷*shaft* is a small colonnette with pear-shaped ▷entasis dividing an opening in ▷Anglo-Saxon architecture: baluster-shafts are also the short, thick colonnettes in Italian ▷*campanili*, also known as *baluster-*▷*columns*. A baluster is also the ▷roll forming the side of an Ionic ▷capital, like a baluster on its side, also called a *pulvinus* (▷pulvin), ▷*bolster*, ▷*cushion*, or *baluster side*, which joins the ▷volutes (▷Ionic Order). The fat part of a baluster is termed the *belly*, and the thin part the *sleeve*. A *balustrade* is the entire ensemble, as on a ▷parapet, a ▷balcony, or a ▷stair, and

38

includes a ▷top rail, balusters, sometimes a bottom rail, and sometimes ▷pedestals. *Banister* is commonly used instead of baluster, while the plural, *banisters*, signifies a balustrade.

Balustrum A ▷chancel-▷screen or ▷-rail.

Bamboo The stems of bamboo plants are found in *Chinoiserie* work, simulated in chair-legs and -backs, beading, and even a cast-iron balustrade at the Royal Pavilion in Brighton (▷Chinese). The fashion for Japanese artefacts created a new craze for bamboo in the late nineteenth century (▷Japonaiserie). Bamboo ▷foliage was frequently used in wallpapers and other decorations.

Band A flat ▷face or square horizontal moulding (▷mould) encircling a building or running across its ▷façade and projecting slightly from the ▷wall-▷plane: it usually marks a division in the ▷wall, or coincides with ▷sills, ▷floors or some other feature. It is also termed a *band moulding*, a ▷*string-course*, or a ▷*band-course*. It can also be a continuous series of ▷ornaments, such as a band of ▷foliage, ▷quatrefoils, or ▷bricks, arranged within horizontal mouldings. In Scots usage, a *band* is a *bond*, where *inband* and *outband* will occur. It is also a ▷fascia on the ▷architrave of an ▷entablature, and the term can also be applied to a ▷fillet or a ▷list. The strips from which ▷modillions or ▷dentils project are therefore termed *modillion-* or *dentil-bands*. A *band of a* ▷*shaft* (▷[31]) is a moulding or series of mouldings encircling ▷piers and ▷shafts in ▷Gothic architecture, usually of the ▷Early English or First-▷Pointed period: they are also known as *shaft-rings, bandelets, bandlets*, or *annulets*. A *bandelet* is any narrow flat moulding such as the ▷taenia between the ▷Doric ▷frieze and ▷architrave (▷Doric Order). A *banderol, banderole* or *bannerol* is a carved representation of a ▷ribbon or a continuous ▷scroll, often decorated, and frequently bearing an ▷inscription, and is simply an ornamented band or string-course. *Banding*, also known as *railing*, or *lipping*, or *edging*, is inlays or strips of wood to cover the edges of ▷veneer and protect them. *Bandwork* is a development of the lines in ▷Arabesque ▷ornament, and is used to ▷frame decorations. C-scrolls and flowery scrolls mixed with flat bands are found in ▷*parterre* ▷gardens, and reached their apogee in the borders and frames of the

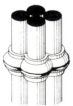

[31] BAND OF A SHAFT Band of a shaft and a clustered column. (*JJS*)

▷Rococo style. A *band-and-hook* ▷*hinge*, also called a ▷*strap-hinge*, a *band-and-*▷*gudgeon hinge*, or a *hook-and-ride hinge*, is a ▷gate-hinge made of a heavy ▷wrought-iron ▷strap or band fixed to the ▷gate which is then dropped onto a ▷pin fixed to a ▷post or a ▷wall.

Bandage A ring or chain of iron at the corner of a stone ▷wall or around the circumference of a ▷tower or a ▷drum which acts as a ▷tie to keep the walls together.

Banded A term meaning interrupted by plain ▷blocks. A *banded* ▷*architrave* is one broken at intervals by smooth projecting blocks between which the moulded conventional ▷architrave appears as normal: it is like a ▷Gibbs surround. A *banded* ▷*column*, also known as a ▷*ringed column* or *rusticated column* (▷rustic), is a column with the ▷shaft broken by larger plain or rusticated blocks which can either be circular or square on plan. A *banded* ▷*impost* is one with the section of the arch-moulding identical to that of the ▷pier below, found in ▷mediaeval ▷architecture. A *banded* ▷*pilaster* is one with the shaft broken by means of rectangular blocks at intervals, plain or rusticated, and usually responding to banded columns. *Banded rustication* is smooth ▷ashlar alternating with rusticated ▷bands projecting beyond its ▷face.

Banister ▷Baluster.

Banker-mark A mark cut in dressed stone found in mediaeval work, which identifies the mason. A mason's mark. *Banker*, in this sense, means the bench on which masons prepared stone: it is also a ▷board on which ▷concrete, ▷mortar, or ▷plaster is mixed. A *banker-mason* is one working at a banker.

Bannerol ▷Band.

Banner-stave cupboard A place where the ▷poles from which banners are suspended are stored.

Banner-vane Also known as a *banneret*, it is a ▷weather-vane having the shape of a banner of flag, which is counterbalanced by an ▷ornament on the other side of the upright.

Banquet, banquette A footway on a ▷bridge set above the carriageway, or a ledge or footpath along a ▷canal, ▷sewer, ▷tunnel, ▷aqueduct, or ditch. A bench-like seat. A raised footpath beside a road.

Baptisterium A cold ▷bath in a ▷Roman ▷*frigidarium*, often consisting of a sunken circular pool in a circular building. It was the model for ▷baptisteries in Christian ▷churches.

Baptistery, baptistry [32] Part of a ▷church (often

apsidal (▷apse)) or a separate building (often circular or polygonal) used for the rite of Baptism, and therefore containing the ▷font. Early baptisteries had large pools for total immersion, but later custom involved symbolic baptism with water from a font.

Bar   A piece of wood or iron used to fasten ▷doors or ▷windows. A place in ▷courts of justice where counsel have their places to plead. It is also the bar at which prisoners are placed to be tried. It is any ▷*counter* across which refreshments are served, but the term has come also to be applied to a building or room in which alcohol is served as well as to the actual counter. A bar is also a ▷*ledge*, as in a ledged door, so a *barred door* is a *ledged door*. A ▷*bolt* used to secure an opening. A *gateway*, as in the ▷walls of a city such as York, or Temple Bar in London. A *bar of a* ▷*sash* is the light piece of timber or metal dividing a ▷window-▷sash into compartments for the ▷glass, also known as a *glazing-bar*. The *angle-bars* of a sash are those at the intersection of two vertical planes (▷[217]). *Bar-iron* is iron made of cast metal: the *sows* or *pigs*, as the shapes of the castings are called, pass through forges and *chaufery*, where, having gone

through further heats, they are formed into bars. *Bar-▷posts* are posts driven into the ground and forming the sides for field-gates: they are ▷mortised to allow horizontal bars to be inserted or taken out. *Bar* ▷*tracery* is completely developed ▷Gothic window tracery, so-called from its resemblance to bars of iron wrought into the fanciful shapes: the bars are moulded, as opposed to flat ▷*plate tracery* (▷tracery).

Baraban   A ▷drum.

Barbacan, barbican   A watch-▷tower. An outwork or defence before a ▷gate, or a fortified gate to a ▷castle, fortress, or town. It is also a ▷loop-hole or ▷balistraria.

Bareface tenon   A ▷tenon with a ▷shoulder cut on one side only, found in ▷door rails which are thinner than the ▷stiles containing the ▷mortises.

Bares   Parts of an ▷image which represent bare flesh.

Barge-boards [33]   The inclined projecting ▷boards placed at the ▷gable of a building, covering the ends of the horizontal timbers (▷purlins and ▷ridge-piece) of the ▷roof, and set under ▷tiles or ▷slates. They are frequently ▷ornamented and carved. In Scots usage, a *barge* is a stone ▷drip at the base of a ▷chimney-stack, a shaped timber-drip at the bottom rail of a ▷door, or an ▷apron of ▷lead or ▷copper. It is also spelled *berge*, and can also be applied to barge-boards, as in England. Barge-boards are also called ▷*gable-boards* or ▷*verge-boards*. A *barge-couple* is one of two timbers supporting that part of the roof projecting beyond the gable wall: barge couples are also ▷beams ▷mortised and ▷tenoned together for the purpose of increasing the strength of a structure, or the rafters serving as ▷grounds for the barge-boards, and helping to support the plastered or boarded ▷soffites, and are therefore called *barge-rafters*. A *barge-*▷*course* is that part of the tiled roof which projects beyond the principal rafters beyond the gable, and is made good with ▷mortar or parging (▷parge work): a barge-course is also the coping of a

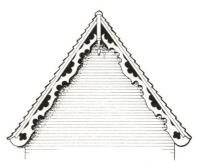

[33] BARGE-BOARDS Barge-boards from London Road, Isleworth, Middlesex (*c.* 1870). (*JJS*)

(a)   (b)

[34] BAROQUE. (a) Monument to Thomas Foley by Rysbrack in the Church of St Michael, Great Witley, Worcestershire, completed c. 1740. Note the fat obelisk in the background, the large urn, the Arms and cartouche, and the attitudes of the figures. (*JSC*) (b) The remarkable south porch of the Church of St Mary in Oxford, by Nicholas Stone, of 1637. Note the Solomonic twisted or barley-sugar columns, the broken scrolled segmental pediment, and the Mannerist aedicule crashing through the entablature. (*JSC*)

gable formed of bricks-on-edge or tumbled (▷tumbling course) brickwork. A *barge-stone* is one of the stones forming the raked top of a gable.

Barley-sugar column A ▷Classical ▷column twisted like a stick of barley-sugar, also known as a *Solomonic* (from its use in the Temple of Solomon in Jerusalem), or ▷*twisted*, or a ▷*spiral column* (▷Salomónica).

Barmkin A defensive enclosure around a ▷tower.

Barn A covered building for storing grain, hay, or straw. Many fine mediaeval barns exist throughout England. A *barn-door hanger* is a steel rail-and-pulley system over a heavy ▷door designed to carry it horizontally along the ▷rail.

Baroque [34] A florid form of ▷Classical ▷architecture prevalent during the seventeenth and eighteenth centuries. It is characterized by exuberance, movement, curvaceous forms, theatrical illusionist effects, and by cunningly contrived and complex spatial inter-relationships often involving centralized planning,

syncopation of elliptical plans, and startling use of colour and modelling, so that sometimes it is difficult to see where three-dimensional architectural detail ends and painted illusion begins. The Baroque styles originate with ▷Mannerism, and in their late phase become ▷Rococo. There was a Baroque ▷Revival (▷[35]) which reached its peak around 1900.

Barrack(s) A building for the housing of troops. A *barrack-room* is a long room for the accommodation of a number of personnel in cases where individual rooms do not exist.

Barred A *barred* ▷*gate* or ▷*door* is one with one or more horizontal timber ▷ledges, while a *barred-and-braced* gate is one with a diagonal timber to support the horizontals and prevent the gate from sagging. A *barred opening* is one protected by means of iron bars.

Barrel A *barrel-*▷*arch* or *barrel-*▷*vault* is a continuous elongated ▷arch forming a curved ▷plate or ▷slab, contrasted with one broken up by means of ▷ribs or a series of arches. A *barrel-*▷*bolt or a* ▷*tower-bolt*

41

(a)

(b)

[35] BAROQUE REVIVAL (a) The Roman Baroque façade of the Brompton Oratory, London, of 1892–5, by Herbert Gribble. (*JSC*) (b) Belfast City Hall of 1898–1906 by Sir Alfred Brumwell Thomas. A sumptuous late-Victorian Baroque composition in which the corner towers and the central cupola are much influenced by the work of Sir Christopher Wren, notably at St Paul's Cathedral in London. (*JSC*)

is a ▷*door-bolt* in a cylindrical sleeve. A *barrel ceiling* is like a barrel-vault, that is a ceiling that is in effect a half-cylinder. A *barrel-drain* is one in the form of a hollow cylinder. A *barrel-*▷*light* is one with curved ▷glass set in glazing-bars. *Barrel-roof*, *barrel-shell roof*, *barrel-vault*, ▷*cradle-vault*, ▷*tunnel-vault*, *wagon-head vault*,

and ▷*wagon-vault* are all vaults or ▷roofs of plain semicircular cross-section carried on parallel ▷walls, ▷colonnades, or ▷arcades, with no ▷groins or ribs (▷vault).

Barrow A sepulchral ▷monument in the form of an elongated mound or ▷*tumulus* over a *chambered* ▷*tomb* or ▷*passage-*▷*grave*.

Barstones Upright stones on either side of a fire-place to carry the ends of the metal ▷bar.

Bartisan, bartizan A ▷turret ▷projecting from the ▷angle or corner of the top of a ▷tower, ▷castle, house, or ▷wall. In Scotland the term is also applied to the ▷embattled ▷parapet of a tower, but a true bartisan is ▷corbelled out, is placed at a corner, and pierced with ▷loopholes or ▷windows. It is circular on plan.

Barycae, barycephalae An *araeostyle* ▷temple (▷colonnade, ▷intercolumnication).

Bascule A structure, such as a ▷bridge, which rotates about an ▷axis and is ▷cantilevered with a counterweight beyond its axis so that it can be raised to enable ships to pass underneath.

Base The base of a ▷column is that part of it between the ▷shaft and the ▷pavement or the ▷pedestal. The ▷*Greek* ▷*Doric Order* has no base; the ▷*Tuscan* base has only a single ▷*torus* with a ▷fillet above it; the ▷*Roman Doric* base has a torus, an ▷astragal. and a fillet; the ▷*Ionic* base has a single large torus over two slender ▷*scotiae* separated by two astragals; the ▷*Corinthians* base has two tori, two scotiae, and two astragals; the ▷*Composite* base has a double astragal in the middle. The commonest type of base, however, is the ▷*Attic base*, consisting of two tori and a scotia, the top torus being smaller than the bottom, and the tori separated from the scotia by a fillet on the top of one and the bottom of the other. The Attic base can be used on all ▷Orders except the Greek Doric and the Tuscan, and even then it occasionally occurs on impure Tuscan Orders. *Base* ▷*blocks* are ▷plinth blocks. Bases can also be built-up skirtings with plain ▷bands and separate mouldings (▷mould) above. A *base* ▷*course* is also called a plinth. A base means a *basis*, a *support*, or a ▷*pedestal*. The circular Ionic and Corinthian column-base is called ▷*spira*, and can be confined to a single torus moulding, but can also be extended to include the square plinth under the base proper, or the base of an ▷*anta*, or its continuation as a ▷wall-base or skirting. Greek Ionic bases can be extremely elaborate, with many horizontal ▷flutes called ▷reeds, torus and scotia mouldings, and fillets. Bases of ▷pilasters usually correspond to those of columns, but those of antae can be different. Bases of mediaeval ▷piers and columns are often of great complexity. There is usually some sort of plain plinth or block, square, polygonal, or circular, over which sundry mouldings rise. The term *base* is the lowest and often the widest visible part of a building, often ▷battered or rusticated (▷rustic), and is applied to a low, thickened part of a wall. A *base* ▷*court or basse-cour* is the outer court or ▷yard of a ▷castle, a service-yard, or a lesser courtyard. A *base moulding* is the ▷trim moulding at the top of a skirting or base-board, also called a *base-*▷*cap*. A *base-*▷*shoe*, *base-shoe moulding*, ▷*floor moulding*, or *shoe moulding* is a moulding next to the floor on a skirting-board (▷skirt). A *base-*▷*table* is the lower part of the wall, and a *base-*▷*tile* is the lowest course of tiles on a tiled wall.

Basement The lowest ▷storey of a building, whether above or wholly below ground (▷[129]).

Basilica [36] A building divided into a ▷nave and two or more ▷aisles, the former being wider and taller than the latter and lit by means of a ▷clerestorey. The basilican form is that used in ▷church plans, and originally had an ▷apse at one end of the nave: it is the model for ▷Early Christian church designs, and the origin of mediaeval church design. In large basilicas there were often ▷transepts, apsidal ends to the aisles, a large ▷vestibule or ▷narthex at the west end, and a cloistered ▷court with ▷atrium to the west of the narthex. Clerestorey walls were carried on ▷colonnades or ▷arcades. In ▷Roman times a basilica was a large ▷hall of justice, and the term originally referred to the building-type rather than to its form. The Constantinian basilica of St Peter's in Rome was the important prototype for church design for the next millennium and a half.

Basilisk A mythical creature, also called a *cockatrice*, with the body of a snake and the crested head and claws of a cock. It is commonly found in mediaeval decoration.

Basis ▷Base.

Basket capital A ▷capital with ▷interlacing decoration like ▷basket-weave found in ▷Byzantine and ▷Romanesque ▷architecture.

Basket-handle arch ▷Arch.

Basket of fruit and flowers Also known as a ▷*corbeil*, it is a common type of ▷ornament, often combined with ▷festoons, but also free-standing, as on ▷gate-▷piers.

Basket weave A ▷chequer-board pattern of ▷bricks formed by three bricks laid on end, and three laid normally, the pattern repeated to form squares. The term is also applied to patterns imitating interwoven rushes, canes, or straw found in metalwork and ▷ceramics, commonly found in the eighteenth century.

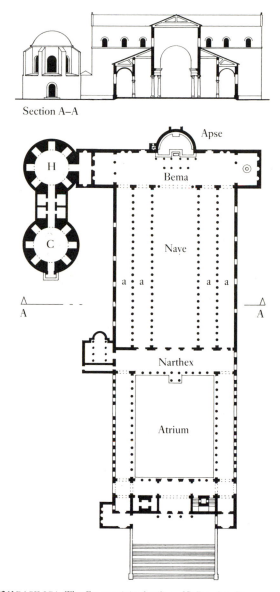

Section A–A

[36] BASILICA The Constantinian basilica of St Peter's in Rome showing the double lean-to aisles (**a**), the clerestoreyed nave, the apse, the cruciform arrangement, and the connected mausolea later called Santa Petronilla (**H**) and Santa Maria della Febbre (**C**). This arrangement was the model for later mediaeval Cathedrals, with the transepts and the polygonal chapter-houses attached to the transepts. The atrium was moved to the north or south sides, and became the cloisters. (*JJS*)

Bas-relief, basso rilievo ▷Relief.

Bastard ashlar This is stone cut in thin ▷blocks used to ▷face a ▷brick or ▷rubble ▷wall and looking like structural ▷masonry. It is also applied to stones for

▷ashlar work not fully ▷dressed when they leave the quarry. The use of the term *bastard* suggests something that is imitation, or not genuine, as in *bastard* ▷*tuck-pointing*, which is not true tuck-pointing.

Bastide A mediaeval fortified planned town built for colonization or pacification of an area, such as Flint or Montpazier. The term is also given to small country houses in France.

Bastille A fortification used as a ▷prison, or a ▷tower or ▷bulwark in the fortifications of a town. A *bastel*, *bastille*, or *bastle* house is a partly fortified house, the lowest storey of which is ▷vaulted.

Bastion A ▷projection at an ▷angle of a fortress or ▷wall which enables the ground in front of the ▷ramparts to be seen and defended.

Baston Also *baton* or *batoon*, it is a ▷torus, or a ▷batten.

Bat A piece of ▷brick less than half the length of a whole brick. A metal ▷cramp or a ▷lead wedge. Part of a ▷hinge built into a ▷wall. To caulk (▷caulking). *Bat insulation* is an insulating blanket placed between the ▷studs of external walls. A *bat-*▷*bolt* is a ▷*rag-bolt*. A bat is also the winged mammal which is associated with sleep and ▷death.

Batch One mix of ▷plaster, ▷concrete, or ▷mortar. A *batch-*▷*box* is a box with four sides and no bottom, placed on a *banker* in which stones or sand are measured before mixing with ▷cement and water to make concrete.

Batement light A ▷window-light with the lower part fitting the shape of an ▷arch below, as found in mediaeval ▷tracery.

Bath A tub used for washing. The room containing the tub or pool. A large establishment in ▷Antiquity with hot, warm, and cold baths, sweating rooms, and athletic and other facilities. ▷Balnea.

Bath stone Limestone (▷lime) obtainable in the vicinity of Bath, used for general building purposes. It varies in colour from white to light cream or ochre, has a fine grain, and is easily worked.

Baton ▷Batten.

Bâtons rompus The short, straight mouldings (▷mould) in ▷Romanesque ▷chevron or ▷zigzag.

Batoon ▷Batten.

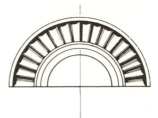

[37] BATSWING Typical batswing pattern in recess at Suffolk Place, Haymarket, London, by John Nash. (*JSC*)

Batswing [37] A ▷motif composed of radiating ▷flutes, also called a *fluted* ▷*patera*, rather like a ▷fan, and found in semicircular-headed openings such as ▷niches, and over ▷doors and ▷windows in ▷architecture and ▷furniture of the late eighteenth and early nineteenth centuries. ▷Fanlight.

Batted Batted work, or *broad-tooled work* is a hand-▷dressed stone surface with parallel indentations, usually vertical, cut in a smooth surface, and traversing the full height of the stone ▷face. The resulting pattern is of a series of small ▷flutes in the face, also called *batting*, ▷*droving*, or *angle-dunting*.

Batten A ▷scantling or small rectangular piece of timber used to provide fixings for ▷tiles or ▷slates, or in order to receive ▷laths for plasterwork. A batten is also a ▷cover-slip concealing the joint between two ▷boards, or a strip of timber fixed across two or more parallel boards to join them together. A *batten* ▷*door* is a ledged or unframed door without ▷stiles, constructed of vertical boards fixed by means of horizontal battens or ▷ledges. A *battened* ▷*column* is one of two long ▷shafts joined together. A *battened* ▷*wall*, also called a *strapped wall*, is a wall to which battens have been fixed. *Battening* is the fixing of battens or the battens in the state of being fixed. A *batten seam* is a join in a metal ▷roof formed over a wooden strip or ▷roll.

Batter An inclined plane. A ▷wall that is sloping, thicker at the bottom than at the top, with a ▷face that inclines or rakes, is said to be battered.

Battlement [38] A ▷parapet that is notched or indented consisting of rising parts called ▷merlons or ▷cops separated by spaces called *crenelles* (▷crenel), ▷*embrasures*, or ▷*loops*, also called *embattlement* (▷embattled). To say that a wall is *crenellated* means that it has battlements. *Guelphic crenellations* have merlons that have V-shaped notches with curved sides at the tops, giving them a horned effect: they were common in mediaeval ▷Italian ▷architecture, and are also called ▷*swallowtail merlons*. Battlements are found in ▷church furnishings, on the ▷transomes of late-▷Gothic

(a)

(b)

(c)

[38] BATTLEMENT (*a*) Crenellation with machicolations. **c** coping, **co** corbel carrying the arches supporting the parapet & between the parapet and the walkway are gaps called machicolations through which missiles could be fired, **e** embrasure, crenelle, or loop, **m** merlon or cop. (*JJS*) (*b*) Battlement cresting from the Church of Sts Peter and Paul at Lavenham, Suffolk. Note the transomed four-light window with crenellations on the transom. The buttresses have traceried panels featuring ogee arches with crocketed pinnacles. The merlons of the parapets are pierced and filled with large Tudor flowers. Here the main theme is Perpendicular, although there are late-Decorated elements. (*JJS*) (*c*) Guelphic crenellations on the Templeton Factory, Glasgow Green, of 1889, by William Leiper. It is an essay in the Paduan Gothic, and is constructed of hard, impervious materials. (*RCAHMS GW/4761*)

45

▷tracery, on ▷pier-▷capitals of the Third-▷Pointed (▷Perpendicular) period, and even in ▷chimney-pots. They are often purely decorative, as on church parapets, and are often pierced or otherwise ▷ornamented with ▷quatrefoils and other decorations. If the merlon has notched sides it is termed ▷almena.

Baulk ▷Balk.

Bawn A fortified enclosure attached to a ▷castle or ▷manor-house, protected at the corners by circular or polygonal *flankers* or ▷towers (▷flank). Many fine bawns associated with the colonization of Ulster were built in the seventeenth century.

Bay The principal compartment or division in the architectural arrangement of a building, marked by ▷buttresses or ▷pilasters, or by the main ▷vaults or ▷rafters of the roof (▷Gothic). It could be a space enclosed by four ▷columns and two ▷beams. Bays are regular and uniform, and are essentially structural divisions. It would not be correct to describe an ▷astylar ▷Classical ▷façade of a house as of seven bays wide: it would be appropriate to describe it as seven ▷windows wide. ▷Churches are usually divided into distinct bays. A bay is also a batch of ▷concrete poured, or an ▷area of ▷plaster laid, at one time. It is the free or light space between the main openings of a ▷sash-window. It is a recess or ▷alcove formed by planting. A *bay* ▷*stall* is the seat in a bay window, and the latter is a window forming a bay or recess in a room, projecting out from the ▷wall on a rectangular, polygonal, semicircular or segmental plan [▷40]. On an upper floor only, ▷cantilevered or ▷corbelled out, it is called an ▷*oriel*. A *segmental bay* is sometimes called a ▷*bow*, and is particularly associated with the ▷architecture of the ▷Regency period.

Bay-leaf garland [39] A ▷torus moulding (▷mould) enriched with bound ▷garlands of bay ▷leaves.

Bead A small cylindrical or partly cylindrical mould-ing (▷mould) often enriched with ▷beads-and-reels. It is any small moulding with a curved section. *Bead-and-* ▷*butt* refers to frames in which the ▷panels are ▷flush with the ▷frame, with beads ▷struck or ▷run upon the two edges with the grain, the ends being left plain. *Bead, butt, and square work* is similar to bead-and-butt, but having the panels flush on the beaded side only, with

[39] BAY-LEAF GARLAND Bay-leaf garland on a torus mould-ing. (*JJS*)

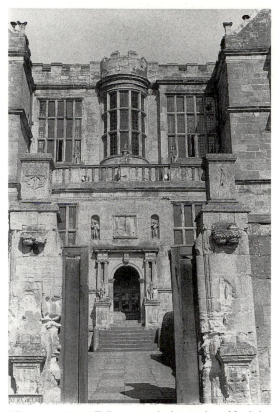

[40] BAY WINDOW Tall, semicircular bay window of five lights with two transomes at Fountains Hall, Yorkshire, built *c.* 1611. On either side are two two-transomed, five-light windows. Note the central doorway flanked by coupled Ionic columns, the crenellation above, the balustrade with statues on the pedestals, and the niches with statues. (*JSC*)

square ▷reveals on the other. *Bead-and-flush work* is a piece of framed work with beads run on each edge of the panel enclosed, that is with a bead all round the edges of each panel. *Bead, flush, and square work* is framing with bead-and-flush on one side, and square on the other, used chiefly in ▷doors. *Bead-and-quirk* refers to a bead stuck on the edge of a piece of wood, flush with its surface, with only one ▷quirk (a furrow parallel to a bead and terminating it), or without being returned on the other surface. A *bead-moulding* of convex profile, of semicircular or greater section, is also called a *half-round*, a ▷*roundel*, or a *baguette* (▷bagnette). *Beading* or *beadwork* is a word signifying the bead mould-ings, but *beading* or *pearling* is an ▷enrichment consisting of a continuous row of small beads, originally found in ▷Romanesque work, but revived in the eighteenth century, especially in plasterwork, ▷ceramics, and silverware. A *bead-moulding*, unlike an ▷*astragal*, does not project in front of adjoining surfaces; several parallel

bead-moulds are called reeding (▷reed). ▷*Angle-beading*, also known as *angle-staff* or *corner-bead*, is a moulding, once a roundel, but now of ▷galvanized steel, fixed at corners, and plastered over, as a permanent ▷screed. A *guard-bead*, also known as a ▷*sash-stop* or a ▷*window-bead*, is a moulding ▷mitred round the inner frame of a sash-window to prevent the sliding sash from falling into the room. A *quirk-bead* is a semicircular bead with a quirk at one side to frame an edge of a ▷board: a *double-quirk bead* has quirks on each side. A *staff-bead* is a moulded external angle usually run in ▷Keene's plaster: it is also another name for a *sash-stop*, *window-bead* or *guard-bead* or *stop-bead*. A *bead-house* (or *bede house*) is a dwelling for poor religious persons, located near the ▷church where the founder of the ▷chantry was buried, and for whose soul the bedesmen or women would pray.

Bead-and-reel [41] ▷Enrichment of an ▷astragal, resembling a string of ▷beads and reels.

Bead-and spindle Circular ▷beads (usually three) alternating with long ▷spindles were mouldings (▷mould) common in seventeenth-century interiors and ▷furniture, and were revived in the latter part of the nineteenth century.

Beak A hanging ▷fillet left on the edge of a ▷larmier, sometimes formed by a groove recessed on the ▷soffite of the larmier (▷[172]).

Beak-head [42] An ornamental moulding (▷mould) resembling a ▷beak or head with a beak, found in ▷Romanesque ▷doorways, sometimes (when the beaks are shorter and more like cones) called *catshead*. The

beak or ▷tongue is wrapped around the ▷roll mouldings below.

Beak moulding A moulding which forms an ▷ovolo or ▷ogee with or without a ▷fillet under it, followed by a hollow. It is found on the ▷capital of an ▷anta of the ▷Doric Order.

Beam A principal horizontal load-bearing structural member of a building, spanning from ▷wall to wall. A structural member carrying joists. A *beam-*▷*anchor*, *beam-iron*, ▷*joist-anchor*, or *wall-anchor* is a metal ▷tie used to anchor a beam or joist to a wall. A *beam-ceiling* is one where the joists and beams are exposed, with the ▷panels between showing the ▷floor-▷boards, or finished off with ▷plaster. *Beam-fill* or *beam-filling* is ▷brick or plaster infill between joists or beams to improve fire-resistance. It can also be the filling of the space from the top of the wall-▷plate to the underside of the ▷slates. A *beam-hanger* is a *stirrup-strap*.

Bearer A support carrying something, such as a ▷gutter, and on which loads are spread.

Bearing The length of a ▷beam or ▷joist carried on a ▷wall or other support. A *bearing* ▷*bar* is a steel bar on brickwork to provide a level support for the joists: it is used instead of a wall-plate. A *bearing* ▷*plate* is a plate in a wall carrying a beam or ▷column, spreading the load on the wall. A *bearing wall* is a load-bearing wall.

Beaumontage A resin, ▷beeswax, and ▷shellac mixture to fill faults in timber.

Beautiful With the ▷Picturesque and the ▷Sublime, an ▷aesthetic category defined in the eighteenth century. ▷Architecture as an ideal, with systems of ▷proportion based on anthropometric perfection was defined as the Beautiful. *The Beautiful* was a term given to a general notion formed in the mind of the assembly of qualities constituting beauty: it is also defined as the result of a working of something by Man in accordance with certain principles of the Beautiful found in Nature.

Beaux Arts A method of teaching art, ▷architecture, and planning based on the composition of felicitously proportioned elements as part of an harmoniously proportioned ▷Classical whole. It was developed in the *École des Beaux-Arts* in Paris in the nineteenth and early twentieth centuries. *Beaux Arts* town planning favoured regularly laid out geometrical forms, with ▷axes terminating at focal points, and helped to promote a ▷revival of ▷Baroque and Neoclassical styles (▷Neoclassicism). The *École*, as transformed from 1793 to 1815, became a major centre for the teaching of Classical ▷architecture, and Classicism was its main subject until 1968 when it succumbed to fashionable

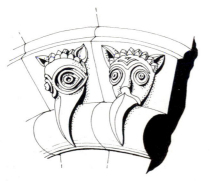

anarchy. Other schools based on the Parisian model were founded in America but there was no equivalent in Britain.

Bed The horizontal surface on which stones, ▷bricks, etc., lie: the under-surface of bricks, stones, or ▷tiles. A *bed-chamber* (▷chamber) is a room holding a bed. A *bed-▷dowel* is a dowel in the centre of the bed of a stone. A *bed-joint* is a horizontal joint in ▷masonry or brickwork, and includes the *voussoir* joints of an ▷arch. A *bed moulding* (▷mould) is the moulding under a ▷corona between it and the ▷frieze, or any moulding under any ▷projection. It is also the lowest member of a ▷band of mouldings, or a moulding under a ▷projection, as between the ▷eaves and the ▷walls. *Bed-▷putty* or *back-putty* is glazier's putty under the ▷glass in which the latter is bedded.

Bee A symbol of industry and of order, particularly associated with Napoleonic and ▷Freemasonic ▷emblems, but also with Pope Urban VIII. Beehives often occur in architectural decoration.

Beehive structure A circular stone building with ▷courses decreasing in diameter as the height is increased, thus forming a pseudo-domed structure. It is termed a *tholos* (▷thole).

Beeswax The wax obtained from honeybees, used in stains, stoppings, matt ▷varnishes, and polish.

Beetle A *maul, mall,* or heavy *mallet.* Wood-boring beetles are a problem in timber structure. The most important are *death-watch (Xestobium Rufovillosum), common furniture (Anobium Punctatum),* and *Lyctus powder-post (Lyctidae).* Death-watch attacks mature ▷hardwood in old buildings: eggs are laid in fissures in the wood, and the larvae bore into the wood for one-and-a-half or more years, causing the destruction by means of tunnels about 3 mm in diameter. The common furniture beetle attacks hardwoods and ▷softwoods, and the diameter of the bored holes is about 1.5 mm. Grubs of the Lyctus powder-post cause immense damage to the sapwood of newly or partially seasoned hardwoods, but softwoods are immune. Holes can be around 2 mm in diameter.

Beggin, begging A dwelling slightly bigger than a cottage: a house, especially one roofed with turf.

Belection ▷Bolection.

Belfast truss Also called a ▷*bowstring truss*, it is a timber truss for spans of up to about fifteen metres with a segmental section at the top, and a horizontal ▷tie called the *string* joined by inclined ▷*lattice-members* to the *top* ▷*chord*.

Belfry [43] Properly, the upper part of a ▷tower where bells are hung, or the ▷timber framing by which bells are supported, but now applied to the whole tower.

Belgian block Paving of stones with battered sides, like the base of a pyramid.

Bell The 'bell' of a ▷capital of Ancient ▷Egyptian ▷architecture, or the solid form of a ▷Corinthian or ▷Composite capital from which the ▷leaves and ▷scrolls have been removed, also called the *vase* or the *basket.* A *bell-▷arch* is an arch carried on shaped ▷corbels, giving the opening the shape of a bell. The *bell-▷cage* is the ▷timber framework carrying the bells in a ▷belfry or a *bell-▷chamber.* A *bell-▷canopy* is a gabled ▷roof protecting a bell. A *bell-cote, bell-▷gable* (▷[44]) or

[43] BELFRY The Decorated Gothic chapels at Oakham Cemetery, Rutland, designed by Bellamy and Hardy of Lincoln, completed in 1860. The belfry stands over the arched entrance. (*JSC*)

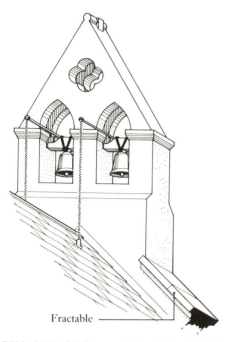

Fractable

[44] BELL-COTE A bell-cote or bell-gable from Little Coxwell, Berkshire, of the thirteenth century, set on the east gable. Note the *fractable*. (*JJS*)

bell-▷*turret* is a small turret or gable in which bells are hung: sometimes a bell-cote may be found on the gable of the eastern end of the nave, above the ▷chancel-arch, and in such a position is called a ▷*sancte-cote* for the *sanctus bell*. A *bell-*▷*roof* is one with a cross-section shaped like a bell. A *bell-*▷*tower* is a tall structure, free-standing or attached to a building, housing one or more bells, and known as a ▷*campanile* in ▷Italian. Bells are often associated with *Chinoiserie* (▷Chinese) ▷ornament, hanging from the many ▷eaves of ▷pagodas. Bells are also the ▷guttae of the ▷Doric Order. *Bell-and-*▷*baluster* is a turned bell-shape on a slender baluster.

Bellcast eaves ▷Eaves with ▷sprockets, ▷cocking-pieces, or short ▷boards nailed to each common ▷rafter at the ▷eaves to give the eaves overhang a flatter slope than the rest of the ▷roof, also called *sprocketed eaves* (▷sprocket). A *bellcast piece* is a treatment at the ▷base of a roughcast or harled ▷wall by which the ▷harling is brought out to form a ▷drip over a plain base, usually with a ▷fillet.

Bellflower [45] A ▷husk or stylized bud-like ▷motif common in the eighteenth century, nearly always found in a ▷string instead of ▷festoons.

Belt course A ▷*string-*▷*course* or ▷*sill-course* or a horizontal string or ▷band around a building.

[45] BELLFLOWERS Also called husks. (*JSC*)

Belting Plugged ▷bearers, or hat-and-coat ▷rails.

Belvedere A ▷turret, ▷lantern, or room built above a ▷roof or on an eminence for the enjoyment of an agreeable view. A ▷*gazebo*, *mirador*, or *summer-house*.

Bema A transverse space in a ▷church, usually slightly raised above the ▷floor of the ▷nave and ▷aisles, between them and the ▷apse or apses. It is the prototype of the ▷transept. In a ▷synagogue it is the raised ▷platform from which the *Torah* is read. It means the ▷sanctuary or ▷chancel of a church. A *bematis* is a place where the vessels used in the Eucharist are kept.

Benatura The holy-water vessel at the entrance to a ▷church, generally on the right of the ▷porch.

Bench end The end of a ▷pew, often carved with ▷poppy-heads and other decorations.

Bench-table A low stone seat on the inside of ▷walls and sometimes round the ▷bases of ▷piers, ▷porches, ▷cloisters, etc. A projecting course of ▷masonry associated with a pier and the base of an interior wall.

Bend [46] An oblique ▷band across a ▷shield.

Bénitier A ▷stoup for holy water, placed at the entrance to a ▷church.

Bent approach An arrangement of two ▷gate- or ▷doorways not in line, for privacy or defence.

Bent ribbon Patterns in late eighteenth-century cast-iron work showing flat ▷ribbon-like patterns.

Bequest board A painted, lettered ▷board hung in a ▷church giving information about bequests.

[46] BEND (*JJS*)

49

Berliner Large pieces of marble set in ▷terrazzo matrix in which are smaller pieces of marble. Also called *Palladiana*.

Berm The area between a ▷moat and a fortified ▷rampart slope. A bank of earth against a ▷wall. A piece of ground supporting ▷beams, etc.

Besant, bezant, byzant An ▷ornament like a disc, repeated, as a gold ▷roundel in heraldry.

Bestiarium The place where wild animals were kept before they entered a ▷Roman amphitheatre.

Bestiary Carved or painted beasts (often mythical) in a mediaeval ▷church. A source-book for animal ▷ornament, illustrated, and often very fanciful.

Bethel A place of worship, usually Non-conformist.

Béton ▷Concrete made of cement, ▷lime, sand, and gravel. *Béton brut* is concrete left in its natural state from the ▷formwork.

Bevel A sloped or canted surface. A *bevel-checked joint* is *bevel halving*, which is a halving-joint in which the parts touching are raked to make a stronger joint. *Bevel siding* is ▷*clapboard*, applied horizontally and overlapped, thicker at the lower edge, also known as ▷*lap-siding* or *bevelled siding*. A *bevelled closer* is a ▷brick cut along its length and vertically, from the middle of one end to a far corner.

Bible box A ▷box with a hinged lid to hold a Bible, usually of seventeenth-century date.

Bibliotheca A ▷library.

Bicoca A watch-tower or a ▷turret.

Bicorporate A mythical animal with two bodies and one head resembling ▷lions, ▷sphinxes, ▷stags, bulls, birds, lizards, and goats found in ▷Classical and ▷Romanesque work.

Bidental A ▷Roman ▷shrine with a ▷peristyle around an ▷altar built on a spot struck by lightning.

Biedermeier A style of interior decoration and ▷furniture design associated with Vienna and Munich after the Napoleonic Wars until about 1860: it was often robust, comfortable, and unshowy, and was influenced by ▷Empire and ▷Regency styles. The dominant flavour was Neoclassical (▷Neoclassicism).

Bier A portable carriage for a dead body.

Biforis, biforus ▷Doors or ▷windows opening in two ▷leaves, like a ▷French window.

Bifrons An ▷ornament with two heads back to back, looking in opposite directions, like a double ▷herm, also called *bifronted or Janus-headed*.

Biga, biriga An economy version of a ▷quadriga, with two ▷horses instead of four.

Bilection ▷Bolection.

Bilgate A timber fixing-▷slip, for ▷joinery, built into a ▷wall.

Billet [47] An ▷ornament used in ▷Norman work, formed by cutting a moulding (▷mould) in notches so that the parts left resemble short wooden billets or cylindrical ▷dowels, placed sometimes in hollow mouldings. The billets are arranged in several ▷bands and placed are regular intervals. Sometimes the billets are square or rectangular instead of cylindrical.

Bin, binn A subdivision in a ▷cellar for wine bottles.

Binder A stone bonding ▷masonry together, called ▷*perpend* or *binding stone*. A *binding* ▷*beam* is a ▷joist supporting ▷bridging joists above and ceiling-joists below. A *binding* ▷*rafter* is a longitudinal timber carrying the rafters between the ▷ridge and the ▷eaves, and is therefore a ▷purlin.

Bipeda A ▷Roman ▷brick two Roman feet long, one

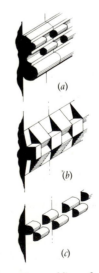

[47] BILLET Romanesque mouldings from: (*a*) Binham in Norfolk, (*b*) Winchester Cathedral, and (*c*) Chichester Cathedral. (*JJS*)

[48] BIRD'S BEAK Bird's-beak moulding. (*JJS*)

wide, and one third thick. *Bipedales* were used in bonding ▷courses.

Bird's-beak [48]   A moulding (▷mould) which in section forms an ▷ogee or ▷ovolo with a ▷fillet under.

Bird's-eye   Also known as ▷*peacock's eye*, it is a figure formed by depressions in the ▷annular rings of timber, and shows up when cut on a lathe by means of rotary cutting, particularly with maple-wood.

Bird's-mouth [49]   An interior ▷angle cut on the end of a timber to obtain a firm fixing upon the exterior angle of another piece.

Biriga   ▷Biga.

Bisellium   A ▷Roman seat of honour or state throne.

Bisomus   A ▷sarcophagus with spaces for two bodies.

Biss   A ▷stall division in a ▷byre.

Bivium   A junction of two ▷Roman roads meeting at an angle, often fitted with a ▷fountain.

Blackamoor   Negro heads occur in ▷Classical and ▷Renaissance ▷cameos, and Ducerceau published designs for *termes nègres*. A taste for exoticism, and the Slave Trade, created a fashion for black figures in ▷ornament, frequently crouching as foot-stools or supporting trays or ▷brackets. The blackamoor became fashionable again during the 1920s and 1930s.

Blade   A principal ▷rafter or ▷back of a ▷roof.

Blaes, blaze   Poor bituminous ▷sandstone.

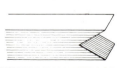

[49] BIRD'S MOUTH (*JJS*)

Blank arcade   A ▷blind ▷arcade. A *blank door* is a recess that looks like a door, or a sealed door. A *blank, blind,* or *dead* ▷*wall* is a wall the surface of which is unbroken by ▷window, door, or any other opening. *Blind* or *blank windows* are also simulated windows or sealed windows.

Blind   A draw-down covering for ▷windows. The term also means forms of wood or metal, covered with opaque material, to cover the whole or part of a window to protect it from the sun. *Blind* also means *blank*. A *blind* ▷*arcade* is a row of ▷arches attached to a ▷wall, or ▷engaged. A *blind-* ▷*box* holds a blind when it is not pulled down, secreting the roller on which the blind is carried. A *blind joint* is an invisible joint. A *blind pocket* is set in a window-head to hold a ▷Venetian blind when it is raised. A *blind* ▷*storey* is a ▷tribune, a fake storey or a heightened ▷parapet wall which is there for visual effect, and usually conceals a ▷roof behind it. *Blind* ▷*tracery* is decorative, and is applied to walls without glazing or openings, so is like ▷engaged artefacts (▷[134]).

Block   A walling unit larger than a ▷brick. A *block* ▷*capital* is a ▷cushion capital. A *block* ▷*cornice* is a type of ▷Italian cornice consisting of a ▷bed moulding (▷mould), a row of plain block ▷corbels or ▷modillions, and a ▷corona or cornice. *Block flooring* consists of a ▷floor finish of wooden blocks tongued and grooved and glued to the ▷concrete ▷screed under. Many types are found, from small cubes to ▷parquet blocks. A *block plan* is a plan showing broad outlines in a simplified form of buildings and layouts. A *main block* is the chief and largest building in a composition such as a ▷Palladian house with ▷wings. A *block* is also any plain piece of ▷ashlar or wood, against which a skirting or skirt mould might stop, such as at the ▷base of a ▷door-▷architrave.

Blocking   A piece of wood fixed to the ▷back of a timber for additional strength or for some other purpose: blockings would normally occur in the plural. A *blocking* ▷*course* is the plain course of stone which surmounts a ▷cornice at the top of a ▷Classical building and acts as a counterbalance to the ▷cantilevered sections of stone; it is also the ▷projecting course without mouldings (▷mould) at the ▷base of a building, or it is a ▷string-course. *Blocking out* is a term in ▷masonry referring to boasting(▷boast), and a term in ▷joinery referring to rough ▷grounds or fir ▷battens.

Blue brick   ▷Staffordshire blue ▷bricks have a high strength and are relatively impervious to water, so are used for ▷plinths and for engineering works.

Blue mortar   A dark blue ▷mortar used with blue or other dark ▷bricks. The colour is obtained by mixing ashes, clinkers, or old broken blue bricks in with the mortar.

Blue stain Also known as *sap stain*, it is a blue fungal discolouration of sapwood.

Board A piece of timber more than 10 centimetres wide and not more than 5 centimetres thick. Trapezoidal sections are called ▷*feather-edged boards*, and wider boards are called ▷*planks*. Boards for ▷valleys, or *valley boards*, are boards fixed to the valley-▷rafters for the ▷lead guttering. A *boarding-▷joist* is one to which boards are fixed. *Boarding for* ▷*pugging*, or ▷*sound-boarding* is an arrangement of short boards between joists of ▷floors fixed to ▷fillets, with a substance (usually ▷plaster) placed between them to prevent sound transmission. The plaster is known as *pugging*.

Boast To *boast* a piece of stone or wood is to shape it into the simple form approaching its ultimate appearance when carved. Often stone carvings or ▷capitals are boasted and built into position, to be carved at leisure. Boasted work may frequently be seen, the carving never having been completed. To *boast* is also to pare stone irregularly with a broad chisel: an alternative term is *droved*. A *boaster* is a *boasting chisel* or a ▷*bolster*. Any ▷projection left rough for the purpose of later ▷enrichment is referred to as *boasted* or *bossage* (▷*boss*).

Bobache, bobeche The ▷collar of a chandelier from which ▷glass ▷ornaments were suspended.

Body of a church The ▷nave.

Boiled oil Linseed oil heated for a short period at a temperature of about 260°C with soluble ▷lead or manganese ▷driers. Paint made with the oxidized oil dries more quickly than with raw linseed oil. Pale boiled oil is a linseed oil heated to a lower temperature (about 150°C), through which air has been blown: it contains a small amount of driers, and is used for hard gloss paints.

Boiserie ▷Wainscoting. The term is commonly applied to seventeenth- and eighteenth-century ▷panelling elaborately decorated with shallow-▷relief carvings.

Bolection Also *balection, belection, bellexion, bilection, bolexion*. A moulding (▷mould) which projects beyond the face of a ▷panel or ▷frame, usually found in panelling or in ▷doors. It is used to cover the joint between the members with different surface levels (▷[187]).

Bollard A low ▷post set in ▷pavements as a barrier to vehicles.

Bolster The return side of an ▷Ionic ▷capital resembling a ▷baluster on its side, also called *pulvinus* (▷pulvin) or *pillow* (▷[144]). *Bolster-work* is rusticated

(▷rustic) ▷masonry, with the corners bowed out like ▷cushions. A broad *chisel* (▷boast). A timber ▷plate.

Bolt A short section of timber cut from a tree trunk, or a short log from which ▷veneer is peeled or shaved. A device for securing shut a ▷door or ▷window, but, unlike a ▷lock, is not operated by a ▷key.

Boltel ▷Bowtell.

Bombé Swelling out in convex shapes.

Bomon A ▷Greek ▷altar.

Bond Bond timbers were formerly built into ▷walls to ▷tie them and allow fixings for the finishes. *Bondstones* or *bonders* are those placed to run through the full thickness of a wall to help to stabilize it. Bond is essentially an arrangement of units in brickwork or ▷masonry to give strength, stability and aesthetic quality through the pattern of overlapping units on the face. *Bond header* is a *bondstone* extending through the full width of the wall, also known as a ▷*throughstone* (▷brick).

Bone house A ▷charnel-house or ▷ossuary in which bones disinterred from a churchyard or ▷cemetery are stored so that the ground never fills.

Boneing *Judging* or marking a surface level. *Boneing* or *boning in* means locating and driving pegs into the ground so that their tops line up to mark a surface, gradient, slope, or level. A *boning rod* is used for this purpose in conjunction with ▷profile boards or sight-rails.

Bonnet A ▷chimney-cap. A *bonnet-hip tile* or a *cone tile* is a ▷tile resembling a woman's bonnet used on the ▷hip of a ▷roof. A *bonnet-top* is a *scrolled* ▷*pediment*.

Book matching Also known as ▷*herringbone matching*, it is an arrangement of wood ▷veneers from the same ▷flitch with the sheets arranged alternately ▷face up or face down. In *figured work* the effect is like an open book, with the adjoining veneers appearing as symmetrical mirror-images on either side of the junction between the veneers.

Booth Any temporary structure for shade or shelter.

Border A piece of wood or other stuff round the edges or along the upper edge of any artefact.

Bordure A ▷border round a ▷heraldic ▷shield.

Borrowed light A glazed ▷frame in an interior ▷wall which permits light from one interior space to enter another, also applied to the light transmitted through such an opening.

[50] BOSS A mid-thirteenth-century example from Westminster Abbey. (*JJS*)

Bosket Also *bosquet*, it is a grove, thicket, or small plantation of trees in a ▷garden or park.

Boss [50] An ▷enriched ornamental projecting ▷block at the intersection of the ▷ribs of a ▷vault, ▷beam-junctions, or ▷terminations of mouldings (▷mould) (▷[245h]). It is also a roughly shaped stone left for carving *in situ*, also known as *boasted* (▷boast). *Bossage* means *rusticated* (▷rustic) work with the ▷faces of the stones projecting beyond the ▷mortar-joint, or projecting stones laid in a ▷wall to be carved later. A *boss-head* is a ▷box-▷staple for a ▷bolt or ▷lock. *Bossing* is a recess in a wall on the inside under a ▷window, but the term is more usually applied to the shaping of metal, especially ▷lead, so that it will fit the surface to which it is applied. A *bossing-mallet* is the mallet used to beat the metal during bossing, and a *bossing-stick* is an implement used for shaping sheet lead.

Botanic garden A ▷garden containing varieties of plants grown for study, propagation, instruction, and display, and usually containing ▷palm-houses, ▷hot-houses, and the like.

Bothy Also *bothie*, a small cottage or hut, or a dwelling for employees on a farm.

Botras, botrasse, botress, boteresse ▷Buttress.

Bottle A ▷bowtell. *Bottled* means rounded. *Bottle-*▷*nosing* is rounded nosing.

Bottoming ▷Hardcore or filling.

Boudoir A room for the use of the lady of the house as a sitting-room for privacy and informal purposes.

Boulder wall A ▷wall constructed of round stones, often without ▷mortar.

Bouleuterion A place of assembly or a council-▷chamber in Ancient Greece.

Boulevard A large thoroughfare, often planted with trees to separate the carriageway from the ▷pavements.

Boultine, boltel, boultell ▷Bowtell, ▷[209].

Bound ▷Framed. *Bound* ▷*masonry* is bonded stone-work.

Bovile As *bubile*, or a structure housing cattle.

Bow The curvature of a ▷bar, ▷rod, timber, or similar. Also an archway or a flying ▷buttress. The term is more often applied to a ▷projecting part of a building, semicircular or segmental on plan. Bows on polygonal plans are called *canted bows* or *canted* ▷*bays*. A *bow room* is one having a bow on one or more sides. A *bow-saw* is one with a blade which can be removed from a ▷frame which is tightened by twisting a string or a bolt. It is used for sawing around curves. A *bow-*▷*window* is the same as a *bay window*: that is, it projects from the face of a ▷wall on a plan which is a segment of a circle: it is also called a ▷*compass window*. An ▷attribute of the ▷hunt, and especially of ▷Artemis – Diana.

Bower A sheltered recess in a ▷garden, or a covered room or ▷gazebo in a garden, often of deliberately 'rustic' and ▷Picturesque appearance. Synonymous with ▷boudoir.

Bowl capital A ▷capital without ▷ornament resembling a bowl.

Bowlers Also known as *bolders* or *boulders*, they are pebbles 15–23 centimetres deep used for paving.

Bow-shaped A double-bellied ▷baluster shaped like two ▷bows, back to back: that is, with the ▷profile identical above and below the waist, like a longbow.

Bowstring A ▷beam, ▷girder or ▷truss, with a segmental member the shape of a ▷bow at the top and a straight or cambered member below tying together the two ends of the bow. Also called a ▷*Belfast truss*.

Bowtell A round convex moulding (▷mould) or ▷bead, or the small ▷shafts of clustered ▷piers, ▷window-▷jambs, or ▷mullions. It is also a term meaning an ▷astragal, and its section is a segment of a circle. It is also called a ▷*torus*, ▷*round moulding*, ▷*roll moulding*, ▷*quarter-round*, or ▷*ovolo*. It is also called *bolted*, ▷*bowtell*, or ▷*edge roll* (▷[209]).

Box A small dwelling. A private seating area in a ▷theatre ▷auditorium, also known as a *box of a theatre*, which is essentially a partitioned-off compartment, usually on either side of the ▷proscenium, in tiers, where parties can attend the play. A *box-beam* is a hollow ▷beam. A *box-bolt* is a sliding ▷bolt of rectangular section used to fasten a ▷door. *Box-casing* is the ▷lining of the cased ▷frame of a ▷window, often constructed to hold the folded ▷shutters. A *box-▷column* is a hollow column. A *box-▷cornice*, also known as a *boxed cornice* or a *closed cornice*, is a hollow cornice built up of ▷boards and mouldings (▷mould), with the ▷gutter and ▷roof-covering above: the ▷fascia-board stands in front, the ▷soffite-boards below, and the ▷wall of the building behind. A *box-frame* is a structure where the loads are taken on the cross-walls, usually only suitable for ▷flats or ▷hotel apartments, also known as *cross-wall construction*. In ▷timber-framed construction a box-frame is a structural frame of ▷cells side by side and in vertical tiers, and the cross-walls or frames carry the loads. A *box-gutter*, also known as a *trough-gutter* or *parallel gutters*, is a timber gutter lined with metal, ▷asphalte, or ▷felt, used in ▷valleys or behind ▷parapets. A *box-head window* is one made so that the ▷sashes can slide vertically above the ▷head so leaving the entire opening free. A *box-▷lewis* is a tapered metal element which, when fitted into a downward-flared recess cut into a stone, lifts it. A *box-▷pew* is a ▷Georgian pew with high wooden ▷partitions around it, usually large enough for one family. A *box-▷stair* is a *closed stair* made with a ▷close-string on both sides, and is usually enclosed by ▷partitions. A *box-▷stall* is an individual compartment in a ▷barn or a ▷stable where an animal has the freedom to move about or lie down. A *box-▷staple* is a ▷socket to receive the end of a ▷bolt. *Boxing* is any box-like enclosure or recess, a cased frame, or the mixing of paint by pouring. *Boxed heart*, also known as *boxed pith*, is timber sawn so that the pith is cut out. *Boxed ▷shutters* are folding shutters which fit into the boxings on either side of a window-opening.

Bracciale A ▷bracket with a ▷socket and ring to hold a ▷torch or a flag-pole, found on ▷Renaissance ▷*palazzi*, especially in Florence and Siena.

Brace An inclined piece of timber used to stiffen ▷roofs, ▷partitions and the like. When a brace supports a ▷rafter, it is called a ▷*strut*. A *braced ▷frame* is one with widely spaced corner-▷posts into which ▷binders are placed: the ▷studs between the posts do not carry loads, unlike ▷*balloon framing*. The corner-posts rise to the roof, framed into each ▷floor as they pass.

Bracket A ▷projection from the ▷face of a ▷wall, frequently ornamented, to support a statue, ▷colonnette, or other weight. Brackets may also be termed ▷*corbels*. Simple brackets of wood or metal can support shelves, seats, or other objects. A bracket is also a decorative detail like a ▷modillion attached to the ▷string of a ▷stair under the projecting edges of the ▷treads. A *bracket moulding* (▷mould) is a ▷Gothic ▷ornament of two ▷ogees with joined faces. A *bracketed ▷cornice* is one with a wooden ▷frame to support a large overhang, where the modillions become transmogrified into large brackets, usually found in early nineteenth-century work. A *bracketed stair* is one with decorative mouldings on the strings and under the return ▷nosings of the treads. *Bracketing* is any system of brackets. Brackets are also *braggers* or *corbels*.

Brad A ▷nail of constant breadth but tapering width, with a square head, used for fixing ▷floor-▷boards.

Braid pattern ▷Guilloche.

Branch A rib of a ▷Gothic ▷vault rising up from the tops of ▷piers to the ▷apex of the vault. *Branch ▷tracery* has branches like those of trees.

Brandering Battening to give better fixing to ▷laths for ▷plaster ceilings. *Branders* are thus ▷battens. Also known as *cross-firring*, or *counter-lathing*.

Brandreth, brandrith A ▷fence around a ▷well.

Brash Timber which breaks easily with little splintering, usually known as *short-grain*, and often due to fungal decay.

Brass Monumental ▷plate of brass (an alloy of ▷copper and ▷zinc), but more usually of ▷bronze or ▷latten (alloys of copper and ▷tin), laid on or in stone ▷slabs in the ▷pavements of ▷churches or on the tops of ▷altar-▷tombs, ▷incised with figures and lettering to celebrate the dead. The ▷incised work is filled with black resin, ▷mastic and ▷enamel. English sepulchral brasses offer a rich field of study, and beautiful mediaeval examples may still be found in abundance.

Brattice A corruption of *bretessé* or *bretêche*, meaning the top of a ▷tower or a partially ▷cantilevered construction on top of a fortification.

Brattishing [51] Also known as *brandishing, bretizment, bretaysing, bretise, bretisement*, it is a mediaeval ▷ornamental cresting (▷cress) above a ▷parapet, ▷screen or ▷cornice, usually composed of ▷foliate decoration, ▷battlements, or other ▷enrichment. The term is also applied to carved ▷open-work over ▷shrines.

Bread room A room with shelves and bins for flour, bread, biscuits and products, usually part of the ▷buttery, or part of the ▷pantry, or the pantry itself.

[51] BRATTISHING Cresting or brattishing on the screen in the Church of St Andrew, Cullompton, Devon. At the top is a form of Tudor flower, then three bands of elaborate foliage and repeating scrolled motifs, then at the bottom, inverted Tudor flowers. (*JSC*)

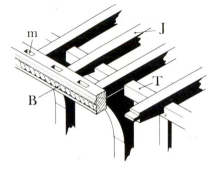

[52] BREASTSUMMER **B** bressumer or breastsummer, **T** top-plate, **J** common joist, **m** mortise for the first-floor studs. The projection of the first-floor joists tenoned into the bressumer is called a jetty. (*JJS*)

Break   The change of direction of a plane, usually of a ▷wall. A *break-in* is an ▷aperture in a wall (usually of ▷masonry or ▷brick) for the insertion of a timber. A *break-joint* is an arrangement of masonry ▷blocks or brickwork so that the vertical joints are not in a vertical line.

Breast   The portion of a ▷chimney projecting into a room. The *breast of a* ▷*window* is the solid part under the ▷sill. A *breast-*▷*lining* or *breast-moulding* is therefore the panelling between a *window-board* and the *skirting* of a room. *Breast* can also mean a ▷*riser*, or the underside of a handrail, ▷beam or ▷rafter. A *breast* ▷*beam* is a ▷*breastsummer*. A *breast* ▷*wall* is a retaining wall, or a ▷parapet which is breast-high. *Breastwork* is a parapet, masonry work for a ▷chimney-breast, or a defensive wall.

Breastsummer, bressummer, breastsommer [52]   The ▷beam supporting the ▷front of a building, rather like a massive ▷lintel, over an opening on an external ▷wall: it carries the whole of a ▷superstructure

as opposed to only a small portion over a ▷window or ▷door, and has the first-floor ▷joists ▷tenoned into it. It is not to be confused with a ▷fascia-▷board planted on normal ▷jetty construction.

Breccia   Where angular fragments of stone are found in a finer ▷ground, as in ▷*terrazzo* or some kinds of ▷marble, the appearance is called *brecciation*.

Breeze-block   A ▷block of ▷concrete with coke- and furnace-clinker used as ▷aggregate. A *breeze-*▷*brick* is brick made of ▷Portland ▷cement and breeze. A *breezeway* is a covered ▷passage open at the sides linking two or more buildings.

Bretasche   A defensive timber ▷gallery on top of a fortification, usually ▷cantilevered and roofed. *Bretexed* means *crenellated* (▷crenel) or ▷*embattled*.

Brewhouse   A building for the manufacture of malt liquors.

Brick [53], [54]   A walling unit made of clay, sand and ▷lime, or ▷concrete, moulded into a rectangular shape while plastic, and capable of being picked up and laid with one hand. Clay bricks may be sun-dried or burnt in a ▷kiln after moulding or cutting. Fine clay bricks have widely differing colours and textures depending upon the types of constituents and the manufacturing process. A *header* (▷head) is a brick laid so that only its short ▷face appears at the surface of the ▷wall. A *snapped header* is a brick broken in half and laid so that only its short face appears at the surface of the wall, used on work only half a brick thick, to create the appearance of a wall at least one brick thick. A ▷*vitrified header*, or *flare*, is one where the surface is glazed by very high temperatures in the kiln, is usually a dark blue or black colour, and is laid in patterns in a wall. A ▷*stretcher* is a brick laid so that its longest face appears at the surface

[53] BRICKWORK (*a*) Dutch bond variant. Note the closer near the quoin. (*b*) Dutch bond with each stretching course beginning with a three-quarter brick, and each alternate course has a header placed next to the quoin three-quarter brick. (*c*) English bond. It consists of alternate rows of headers and stretchers, with closers next to the quoins to keep the bond. (*d*) English cross-bond. Alternate rows of stretchers and headers, with queen-closers next to the quoin headers. Each alternate stretching course has a header placed next to the quoin stretcher, causing the stretchers to break joint with every alternate course. (*e*) English garden-wall bond. One course of headers to three or five stretchers. A queen-closer is introduced next to the quoin-header in the heading course. (*f*) Flemish bond. Header–stretcher–header in each course, with closers next to the quoins to keep the bond. (*g*) Flemish garden-wall bond, also known as Sussex and Scotch bond. It has three or five stretchers to one header in every alternate course, and a header is laid over the middle of each central stretcher. (*h*) Flemish stretcher bond. Three rows of stretchers then a row of stretcher–header–stretcher repeated. (*i*) Header bond, requiring three-quarter bricks at the quoins. (*j*) Monk bond. Each course consists of a series comprising a header and two stretchers, the header falling centrally over a joint between a pair of stretchers. Note the closer. (*k*) Raking stretcher bond. (*l*) Stretcher bond. (*m*) Dearne's bond, consisting of headers laid normally, then stretchers laid on edge in alternate courses. (*n*) Mixed garden-wall bond. Note that headers are not directly above each other, and this object is obtained by quarter-bricks as shown. (*o*) Silverlock's bond, also known as rat-trap bond. All bricks laid on edge, arranged to give the appearance of Flemish bond. An alternative would be to start each alternate course with a bat and header. (*p*) Herringbone bond. (*q*) Basket-weave bond. (*r*) Stack bond. (*s*) Struck joint. (*t*) Recessed joint. (*u*) Flush joint. (*v*) Keyed or bucket-handed joint. (*w*) Overhand struck joint. (*x*) Tuck pointing. (*JSC*)

of the wall. *Brick-▷bats* are cut bricks less than half the full length of a whole brick, so that cuts are made across the width of the brick: cut bricks can be half, three-quarter, or bevelled. A *closer* is a brick at the end of a horizontal length of wall, which is smaller than other full-size bricks, and is used to close the ▷course of bricks and keep the ▷bond. Closers are parts of bricks with the cut made lengthways, and leaving one uncut stretcher face: a ▷*queen-closer* is usually placed next to the first brick in a header course; a ▷*king-closer* is formed by removing a corner, leaving half-header and half-stretcher faces. A *bevelled closer* has a stretcher face bevelled, leaving half-header and whole-header faces. A *mitred closer* has an end bevelled so that adjacent bricks can be joined at an ▷angle, as in a canted ▷bay. Other bricks are *specials* or *purpose-mades*, and include the ▷*bull-nose*, used for copings (▷cope) or on vulnerable positions where sharp ▷arrises are to be avoided: they are single with one

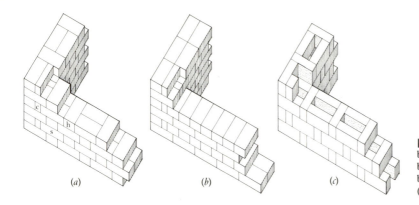

rounded edge, and a double is one with two rounded edges. A ▷*cow-nose* is a normal brick, semicircular at one end only. Special bricks, including *internal returns* (to achieve a mitring of a horizontal and vertical opening with a bull-nosed edge), *external returns* (to achieve the same when the bull-nose is on the outside or frame of a wall), and *stops*, including double-stops (to achieve a smooth transition between a bull-nose and a square arris) are also useful. A ▷*pistol brick* is used to form a circular or coved angle between a ▷*wall* and a ▷*floor*. A ▷*splay* is a brick with a bevelled top, used for the tops of ▷plinths or for ▷sills. A *dog-leg* or *angle-brick* is used to ensure a good bond at ▷quoins which are not right angles, and are neater than mitred closers. An *arris* is an edge of a brick, the ▷*bed* is the lower surface, the ▷*face* is the surface to be exposed, the ▷*frog* or *kick* is an indentation formed on the bed or the uppermost surface or both: bricks with only one frog should be laid with it on top to ensure it is filled with ▷mortar. A ▷*course* is a complete layer of bricks: a *heading course* is one of headers, while a *stretching course* is one of stretchers. A *brick-on-edge* course is one with bricks laid on their sides, while a *brick-on-end* or ▷*soldier* course is one with bricks laid on the smaller face. *Bed-joints* are mortar joints parallel to the beds of the bricks, and horizontal. A ▷*lap* is the horizontal distance by which one brick projects beyond a vertical joint in the course above or below it. *Nogging* (▷*nog*) is brick infill between timber ▷posts in a ▷timber-framed construction. ▷*Perpends* are imaginary vertical lines which include vertical joints that are plumb: that is, they line up. A ▷*quoin* is a corner or external angle of a wall. ▷ *Racking back* is a stepped arrangement formed during the construction of a wall when one portion is built to a greater height than that adjoining: no part of a wall should rise more than one metre above another if unequal settlement is to be avoided. A *stopped* or *closed* end is a square end to a wall the thickness of the wall, as opposed to a wall that continues in an L-shape around a corner. If each alternate course at the end of a wall projects in order to provide a proper bond if the wall is continued at a later

date, this notched effect is called *toothing*. Where toothing has not been provided it is necessary to provide *sinking* or *indentation* in each alternate course.

Brick bonds (▷[53], [54]) are of great complexity and variety. Early brickwork often shows no definable bond (which is the interlacement of bricks produced when they lap those immediately above and below them). An unbonded wall with continuous vertical joints has very little strength or stability. ▷*English bond* consists of alternate courses of headers and stretchers, and includes variations with one course of headers with three or five courses of stretchers before the next header course: in each heading course a queen-closer is placed next to the quoin-header. *Flemish bond* consists of alternate headers and stretchers in each course: variants of Flemish bond may have three or five stretchers to each header, but in true Flemish bond the headers are in line. *Double Flemish bond* shows the bond on both the external and internal faces of a wall. In Flemish bond each header is set vertically over the centre of a stretcher, and, unlike English bond, no header comes over a vertical face joint, although Flemish bond is not so strong because of the large number of continuous vertical joints occurring. In ▷*Dutch bond*, the courses are again alternate headers and stretchers in each course but the headers are superimposed, and lap half a header on each course, giving a ▷zigzag effect. A variation of Dutch bond is where one course of headers alternates with a course of stretchers, but the vertical joint of one row of stretchers comes under the centre of a header and under the centre of the stretcher above and below the header course. *Header bond*, or *bastard bond*, with only headers showing, is used for building curved walls, but also seems to have been used for display, as indicative of wealth. ▷*English cross-bond* consists of alternate courses of headers and stretchers and therefore is like English bond except that although the joints of the header courses line up, those of the alternate stretchers do not, so that the joints of one stretcher course are over the centres of each header one course above or below: it is similar to a Dutch bond variant.

English garden-wall bond has one course of headers, three courses of stretchers, then another of headers, so it is a variant of English bond. *Flemish garden wall bond* consists of courses of three or five stretchers, a header, then three or five more stretchers laid so that the header is always over the central of the three or five stretchers on the course above and below. It is also known as ▷*Sussex* or *Scotch* ▷*bond*. *Monk bond* is a variant of Flemish garden-wall bond, with each course comprising a header, two stretchers, then another header, the header being placed over a joint between the pairs of stretchers. *Flemish stretcher bond* consists of a course of alternate headers and stretchers, three courses of stretchers, then another of alternate headers and stretchers. *Raking stretcher bond* consists of alternate courses of stretchers, with the laps only one-quarter the length of each stretcher, rather than half. *Stretcher bond* consists of stretchers only showing, each lap being half a stretcher. *Rat-trap bond* (also called *Silverlock's* or *Chinese bond*) has outer and inner leaves of bricks laid on edge with a ▷cavity in between: the header bricks, also laid on edge, run through the wall as bonders. It consists, therefore, of courses of alternate headers and stretchers laid on edge, the headers-on-edge being placed directly under the centre of each stretcher-on-edge, so it is a variant on Flemish bond. While this bond saved one brick in three compared with an ordinary solid wall one full brick in width, it was always ▷rendered on the outside to make it more watertight if used for dwellings. Its great advantage is that all the hollows are connected, and so could be heated. Silverlock's bond was therefore ideal for walls of ▷gardens against which fruit trees might be grown, for the hollows could act as ▷flues through which heated air could pass to a chimney. *Dearne's bond* is a variation on *English bond* in which the stretcher courses are laid on edge with a cavity between them, but the header courses which bind the ▷leaves together are laid normally: this bond economizes on bricks by a gain in height for each alternate course of stretchers. Dearne's bond is quite clearly described thus in early nineteenth-century sources, but in twentieth-century books is confused with *Silverlock's bond*: the true distinction is as described here. Dearne (or Dearn) also designed a variant on his bond using one course of headers, then a course of stretchers halved longitudinally so that the wall looked like an ordinary English bond, but there were continuous cavities between the stretchers. Dearne also proposed that his cavity walls could be heated for use in ▷conservatories, vineries, and so on. *Facing bond* was used when thin fine bricks were employed to face a thicker wall of ordinary common bricks: care had to be taken with the bonding.

Brick patterns are achieved by laying the bricks in different ways. *Stack*, for example, is simply brick laid or bedded so that the perpend joints line through unbroken, with no attempt to bond, but the bricks can be laid vertically or horizontally. ▷*Herringbone* is an assembly of bricks in diagonal zigzag fashion, with the bricks laid at right-angles to each other. ▷*Basket-weave* is where three soldiers alternate with three stretchers in squares with no bonding. Brick walls as they increase in thickness increase in transverse strength, but become weaker in a longitudinal direction because stretchers are not placed in the interior of the wall. This problem traditionally was remedied by using raking courses at regular intervals (from four to eight courses), with the joints not coinciding with the joints of ordinary courses above and below. Raking bonds, usually herringbone and diagonal, are laid in alternate courses in different directions, and are 'faced' with ordinary brickwork. *Vitrified headers* can be used to form ▷*chequer-board*, *diaper*, *lettered*, or *numerical* patterns. Many vitrified headers may in fact be *snapped*, so the wall may only be half a brick thick. *Moulded* and *gauged* brickwork is also found, but the finest decorative brickwork is *rubbed* and *gauged* work, where the brick is extremely finely textured and soft, and can take very fine joints of lime ▷*putty*. *Brick rubbers* or *cutters* are chiefly soft red, white, or buff-coloured bricks, made of washed loamy clay containing a large proportion of sand, and are hand-made in a box-mould, and baked rather than burnt: they can easily be cut, rubbed, and carved, and are used for gauged arches, quoins, and jambs.

Where alternate headers project to carry a projecting course the effect is called *dentilation*. Where bricks are laid diagonally and project to carry courses over they are called *dog-teeth*.

Glazed bricks are usually made of fireclay or shale, and are true to shape with fine, straight arrises: they are impervious to water, and are either *salt-glazed* or *enamelled*. Salt is thrown on the fires of the kiln when the bricks are about 1200°C, forming a vitreous brown glassy surface suitable for dados, plinths, and other positions. *Dry-dipped enamelled bricks* are known as *biscuitware*, and are moulded, dried, burnt, cooled, coloured, glazed, and reburnt. The colouring, or *bodying*, is applied as follows: the *slip*, *engobe*, or *body*, consisting of a slurry of china clay, crushed burnt flint, ball clay, and water, is applied first, usually by dipping the brick; then a second mixture, similar to the first, but with added metallic oxides (such as manganese for brown, chromium for pink, antimony for yellow, copper for green, cobalt for blue, and a mixture of cobalt and manganese for black) to provide colour, is applied; then a third mixture of china clay, felspar (silicate of alumina with varying proportions of sodium, potassium, etc.), ▷whiting (calcium carbonate pigment), and water provides the glaze. The wet-dipped process involves the application of the slip, colouring solution, and glaze to the bricks after they have been moulded and dried. This is cheaper than the dry-dipped method as it requires just one burning, but the bricks are only suitable for interior work, and a large proportion is damaged during handling.

▷*Air bricks* have regular perforations through them and are used to allow air to pass through a wall, as in positions under timber floors, etc., or for other ventilation purposes. The perforations have to be well formed and regular as they are visible on the surface. Air bricks, however, are not the same as ▷*perforated bricks* which have cylinders of clay removed from the centre, leaving the faces untouched. Such bricks save clay, are less heavy for transport or handling, and can allow reinforcement rods to pass through vertically.

Brindle or *brindled bricks* are bricks discoloured with stripes, unsuitable for facings but otherwise perfect. ▷*Engineering bricks* are exceptionally strong and durable, and are used for ▷piers, ▷bridges, ▷sewers, and engineering purposes: the most usual are *Accringtons* (pressed, smooth, and bright red), *Southwaters* (pressed and wire-cut), *Staffordshire Blues* (wire-cut and hand-made), and *Hunzikers* (made of crushed ▷flints and ▷lime). *Hollow bricks* are clay walling units offering speed of erection and good insulation. *Multi-coloured bricks*, known as *multis*, are bricks, the faces of which have varying shades of bright red, dark red, blue, and other colours, often used for facing work, and looking best with a white pointing.

Sand-faced bricks are made by sprinkling sand on the clay band as it is being extruded, or by sanding the internal faces of the mould before it is charged. A *stock brick* originally denoted a hand-made brick moulded on a *stock-board*, but the term is now applied loosely, and generally means common ▷*wire-cut bricks*. *London stocks* are the yellow-brown bricks made of clay containing silica and alumina to which chalk is added to prevent excessive shrinkage in drying and burning: they may also contain clinker. *Sand-lime* bricks are made of a mixture of sand, lime, and water, pressed into moulds and hardened in an autoclave kiln.

Glass bricks can be solid or hollow, and are bedded in mortar: they are square and are unlike normal bricks.

Bridge A construction with one or more open intervals under it to span a river or other space. It can be constructed of rope, wood, iron, stone, ▷brick, or ▷concrete, or a combination of these. A *bridge-over* is a piece of timber fixed over parallel timbers, such as ▷rafters over ▷purlins.

Bridgeboard A ▷board into which the ends of the ▷steps of wooden ▷stairs are fixed: it supports the ▷treads and ▷risers, and is also called a ▷string, which may be an *open-* or *cut-stringer*.

Bridgestone Stone laid from the ▷pavement to the front ▷door of a house over a sunken ▷area, usually supported by an ▷arch or a portion of a ▷vault.

Bridging The term means the spanning of a gap with ▷common ▷joists, or spanning any gap. It also means

the *stiffening* of adjacent common joists, by-passing a ▷damp-proof course, or creating a cold bridge across a gap. A *bridging* ▷*floor* is one carried on common joists only. A *bridging joist* is a principal ▷joist spanning between ▷walls and into which common joists are ▷tenoned, but the term also seems to mean, in modern usage, any common joist. *Bridging-pieces* are timbers placed between ▷beams or joists to prevent bending towards each other. *Bridging to floors* is ▷*herringbone strutting* between floor-joists, acting in the same way as bridging-pieces.

Bridle A *trimmer-*▷*joist*. A *bridle-joint* is one where the ▷tenoned member is a ▷post with a central ▷tongue set into a ▷mortise in the upper member or horizontal piece. A bridle in the sense of a trimmer- or trimming-joist is also called a *bridling-joist*.

Brig, briggs A division or divisions between ▷flues, also known as a ▷*withe* or *withes*.

Brise-soleil A sunshade outside a building, usually composed of fins or ▷louvres, fixed or moveable, to prevent direct sunlight from penetrating a room.

Britannia An heroic ▷Classical female figure representing Great Britain: her helmet is like that of ▷Minerva, her ▷shield is decorated with the Union Flag, and she carries a ▷trident to show her naval power. The figure often appears on commercial buildings, railway stations, docks, and ▷monuments. The *Britannic Order* (▷[55]) is a Classical ▷Order invented by Robert Adam which is based on the ▷Corinthian, but which incorporates the ▷lion and ▷unicorn instead of the ▷volutes and includes the Crown and other devices: it is also known as the *German Order* because it included Hanoverian ▷motifs.

Broach To finish a ▷masonry surface (known as *broached work*) with broad parallel grooves, cut diagonally with a broach, or mason's pointed chisel. To free ▷blocks of stone from a ledge by cutting between the

[55] BRITANNIC ORDER After Robert Adam in his *Works in Architecture* of 1773–79. (*JSC*)

▷blocks of stone from a ledge by cutting between the holes drilled in the stone. An old English word for a ▷spire, but it is now applied to the pyramidal form set above the corners of a square ▷tower that effects the transition between the square tower (without ▷parapets) and an octagonal spire. It also seems to mean a spire rising from a tower without parapets, but in such a case the pyramidal broaches are nearly always present. It also means any pointed, terminating, ornamental structure. A *broach-* or *broached spire* is an octagonal spire with broaches (▷spire).

Broadstone ▷Freestone or ▷ashlar.

Broccoli Decoration resembling the acanthus or parsley.

Broken A *broken ▷arch* is a type of segmental arch where the centre of the arch is replaced by a carved decorative feature. *Broken ▷ashlar*, also called ▷*random-work, random range ashlar*, or *random range work* is random ▷masonry not laid in regular courses. *Broken-colour work* is the same as ▷*antiquing*, or handling wet paint to expose the undercoat, thereby creating ▷*graining* or *marbling*. For *broken pediment*, ▷pediment. *Broken rangework* is masonry laid in horizontal ▷courses of differing heights, that is, with the horizontal joints broken. A *broken ▷column* signifies life cut off in its prime, and is found in funerary ▷architecture.

Bronze An alloy of ▷copper and ▷tin. It is found in funerary ▷monuments, ▷sculpture, commemorative ▷plaques, and in first-class ▷metalwork, especially ▷doors, ▷grilles, and ▷window-▷frames. A *bronze ▷cramp* is a ▷bar used for holding ▷ashlars together or to fix stone facings to a ▷wall behind. It has an advantage over iron or steel in that it does not rust.

Brotch A piece of green tree-branch bent to a U-shape to fasten ▷thatch to ▷roofs, also called a *buckle* or a ▷*spar*.

Brutalism A term invented in the 1950s to describe the style of Le Corbusier at the time of his *Unité* at Marseilles and his government buildings at Chandigarh: that style involves copious use of ▷concrete left raw and exposed, on which the impressions of the ▷formwork are left. The term seems to derive from the French ▷*béton brut*, but it may also have connections with the nickname of Peter Smithson as 'Brutus': *New Brutalism* was intended to draw attention to work designed by the Smithsons and their circle, all firmly within the Corbusian camp, but the term also cocked a snook at the 'New Humanism' and 'New Empiricism' of the time. Curiously, the ▷architecture that first emerged as New Brutalism owed more to Mies van der Rohe than to Le Corbusier (as in the Smithsons' school

[56] BUCRANIUM The ox-skull is hung with garlands of bell-flowers or husks. (*JSC*)

at Hunstanton, Norfolk of 1949–54, where steel, ▷brick, pipe-runs, and electrical ▷conduits were all exposed to view), but the movement rapidly became associated with a ruthless 'honesty' in expressing function, spaces, inter-relationships, and materials.

Bubile As ▷bovile.

Buckle As ▷brotch.

Buckler A circular or ▷lozenge-shaped ▷ornament on ▷friezes. A small round ▷shield.

Bucrane, bucranium [56] A ▷garlanded ox-▷skull used on ▷Classical ▷friezes, or as ▷ornament elsewhere. ▷Aegicrane.

Bud An element set at the point from which the helices (▷helix) or ▷volutes in a Corinthian capital spring.

Buhl *Buhl, boule* or *boulle work* consists of one or more metals (usually including ▷brass) inlaid on a ▷ground of tortoiseshell.

Built dooks Fixing-▷pads or ▷hardwood ▷plugs.

Built steps Built into or on support-▷walls.

Bulb Bulbous decoration on late sixteenth- and early seventeenth-century wooden uprights, often consisting of a shape like a melon or like a cup with a cover, frequently ▷enriched with ▷gadrooning, ▷foliage, and other ▷ornament. It is associated with ▷Elizabethan and ▷Jacobean work.

Bulker A ▷beam or a ▷rafter.

Bulkhead A roofed structure on top of a ▷roof to enclose a water tank, lift shaft, or similar, often unsightly excrescence. Any structure to give headroom. A structure to retain earth and prevent it from moving into an ▷area. An inclined or horizontal ▷door or trap to give access from the outside to a ▷cellar, as outside public houses and the like. The part of a door-▷frame forming the base for a side-▷light adjacent to a door.

Bulla A circular metal ▷boss usually found in the centres of ▷doors as a ▷knob-like ▷ornament.

Bullen, boleyn nail A ▷nail with round head and short shank, turned and ▷lacquered, used to secure the hangings of rooms.

Bullion A ▷*bull's eye*. The piece of ▷glass cut from the centre of a 'table' of ▷crown glass where the glass was attached to the glass-blower's *pontil*. It was either rejected or used to glaze windows in unimportant positions.

Bull-nosed Anything with a rounded end, or rounded ▷arris, as a ▷brick or a ▷step: the section is usually a half- or quarter-circle. A *bull-nosed step* is also one which has the ▷tread rounded to a semicircle projecting beyond the ▷string, and returning to the string around the ▷newel.

Bull's eye A small circular or elliptical ▷aperture for the admission of light and air: it is open, ▷louvred, or glazed, and is also called an ▷*oculus* or an ▷*oeil-de-boeuf*. The term also is used to describe the ▷frame of such an aperture with its mouldings (▷mould): it may consist of a double-arched frame with two or four ▷key-▷voussoirs. It is therefore an ▷ornament of concentric ▷bands. It is also applied to the thickening of a ▷pane of ▷glass produced by the ▷crown-glass method (▷bullion). A *bull's head* is also a *bucranium*, but is with flesh and hide rather than depicted as a ▷skull; like the ▷*bucrane*, though, it usually has ▷garlands suspended from the horns.

Bulwark A defensive structure, usually quite low, offering protection to those returning fire.

Bundle pier In ▷Gothic ▷architecture, a ▷pier with a plan of complex form, suggesting a densely packed bundle of ▷colonnettes, but quite distinct from the ▷compound pier.

Bungalow Derived from the Hindu term for a thatched house, it has come to mean a single-storey dwelling.

Bush hammering A technique to obtain an even textured surface on ▷concrete: the work is carried out using a power-operated bush-hammer with a serrated head containing pyramidal points, so that the smooth surface is chipped away to expose the ▷aggregate. It is time-consuming and expensive.

Bustum The ground or ▷platform on which funeral pyres were built and bodies were cremated in Ancient Rome. It was usually an enclosed ▷area or platform beside the ▷tomb where the ashes were placed.

Butment As ▷abutment. *Butment* ▷*checks* are two solid pieces on either side of a ▷mortise.

Butt A square or fitted end, or heading-joint. A *butt end* is that part of a timber which was nearest the root of the tree, but the term is also applied to the thicker end of a timber, handle, or other object. A *butt* ▷*hinge* is one consisting of two metal ▷plates joined by a ▷pin, and is fastened to butting surfaces such as a ▷door-▷frame and a door: the two halves of the hinge close against each other as opposed to ▷strap hinges. *Rising butt* hinges cause a door to rise as it opens. A *butting joint* is one formed by two pieces of wood, which do not overlap, but are end-to-end or at right angles to each other.

Butterfly Anything with the appearance of a butterfly, such as a *butterfly* ▷*hinge* where the ▷plates are shaped like wings. The butterfly is often found in *Chinoiserie* schemes of decoration, and represents immortality and metamorphosis (▷Chinese).

Buttery A store for provisions, usually on the north side of a building. The term has come to be applied to places where food is served. A ▷pantry or a ▷wine-cellar. A *buttery-hatch* is one in a ▷screen between the buttery and the dining-hall.

Button A small piece of wood or metal, fixed on a ▷pin or a screw, used to fasten a ▷door, ▷window, or drawer.

Buttress [57] A ▷projection from a ▷wall and bonded to the wall to create additional strength and support. ▷*Anglo-Saxon* and *Romanesque* buttresses are often wide but of small projection, and are commonly not divided into ▷stages: in fact they do little more than define ▷bays or ▷panels of wall, and are more like ▷pilaster strips or ▷lesenes than true buttresses. ▷*Early English* or *First-*▷*Pointed* buttresses are usually of considerable depth, but are often less wide than Romanesque work, and are often staged, with reductions in their width and projection: each stage is marked by ▷offsets, and the buttresses are capped with sloping stones or with triangular ▷gables or ▷pediments. Buttresses at the ▷angle of a building usually consist of a pair meeting at an angle of 90° at the corner (*angle-buttress*); or of a large square buttress encasing the corner (*clasping buttress*) in the First-Pointed period. ▷*Decorated* or *Second-Pointed* buttresses are almost invariably worked in stages, and are usually ▷ornamented with ▷niches, crocketed ▷canopies, and other carved decorations, and they frequently terminate in crocketed ▷pinnacles rather than in triangular gablets. With the introduction of the Decorated style, buttresses were often set diagonally at corners, forming 135° angles with the walls. During the ▷*Perpendicular* or *Third-Pointed* period, buttresses were often panelled. Other types of buttress include the *flying buttress*, which transmits the thrust of a ▷vault or a ▷roof

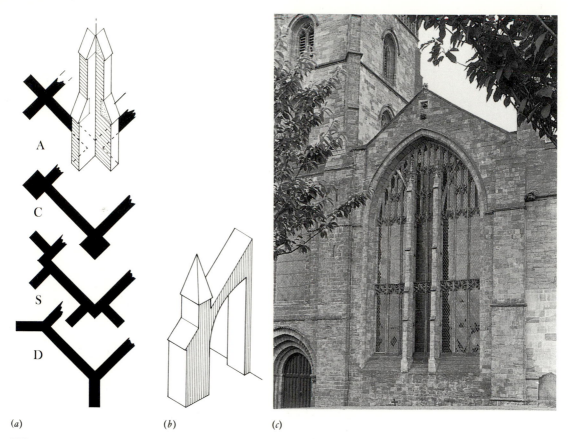

(a) (b) (c)

[57] BUTTRESS (a) A angle-buttress, C clasping buttress, S setback buttress, D diagonal buttress. (*JJS*) (b) A flying buttress. (*JJS*)
(c) Priory of Sts Peter and Paul, Leominster, west window with buttresses instead of mullions; it is Third-Pointed or Perpendicular in style. (*JSC*)

from the top of a ▷wall to an outer support by means of an ▷arch or part of an arch, known as an *arch-buttress* or *arc-boutant*: a flying buttress springs, therefore, from a solid mass of ▷masonry and abuts against the springing of another arch which rises from the upper points of ▷abutment of the first: it acts as a counterthrust to the weight of nave vaulting. A *hanging buttress* is a free-standing vertical buttress, ▷pier, ▷colonnette, or ▷rib supported from a ▷corbel. A *lateral buttress* is set at the corner of a building on the ▷axis of one of the walls. A *pier-buttress* is an external pier which counters the outward thrust of a vault or arch: spectacular pier buttresses occur at ▷chapter-houses of ▷cathedrals. A pier buttress is a term also given to that part of a buttress which rises above the point of thrust of a vault. A *setback buttress* is like an angle-buttress but is set back from the corner on the face of the wall so that it does not join its counterpart, but leaves the corner of the angle of the building freely expressed. A *buttress* ▷*tower* is one which flanks an arched opening and appears to act as a buttress.

Byewood flushing Planing or sanding down the joints of boarded ▷floors.

Byre A place where cattle are housed.

Byzantine A style of ▷architecture and of ▷ornament which developed in the eastern Roman Empire from the foundation of Constantinople to AD 1453. It combined the highest achievements of late ▷Roman and ▷Hellenistic work, but differs greatly from ▷Classical architecture in that the ▷Orders were abandoned, although Classical forms can just be discerned, transmogrified. Christian iconography replaced pagan decorative ▷motifs, and Roman structural techniques were evolved even further using ▷brick, ▷concrete, and ▷arched and ▷vaulted systems. Decorations, often of ▷mosaic, were usually rich and glowingly coloured. The Byzantine style was one of the bases for ▷Romanesque decoration. Scholarly publications of Byzantine buildings in the nineteenth century prompted a Byzantine

[58] BYZANTINE REVIVAL
Westminster Cathedral by John
Francis Bentley, begun in 1894. Note
the Diocletian windows in the
clerestorey. (*RCHME CC73/1951*)

▷Revival (▷[58]), especially in Germany, and in England one of the great monuments of the Revival was the Roman Catholic cathedral at Westminster of 1894–1903 by John Francis Bentley.

C

C The Roman symbol for 100; CC = 200; CD = 400.

Cabin A hut or cottage; ▷primitive hut. A *cabin hook* is a hooked ▷bar on a ▷window-▷frame or ▷cupboard-▷door which drops into a *screw* ▷*eye* to hold the door shut.

Cabinet A ▷chamber set aside for study, private converse, or the display of treasures, or a suite of rooms for the same. A *cabinet* ▷*window* is a ▷projecting window or ▷bay window used for shop-fronts in the early nineteenth century. *Cabinet-work* is fine quality ▷joinery.

Cable A convex moulding (▷mould) set in the ▷flutes of ▷columns or ▷pilasters in ▷Classical ▷architecture, nearly filling up the hollow flute to less than one-third the total height of the ▷shaft (▷[195]), also called *cabled fluting, cabling, ribbed fluting,* or *stopped flute*. Cabling is not known in the Ancient ▷Greek ▷Orders. A *cable moulding*, on the other hand, is an ▷ornament formed like a cable, and resembling twisted cord or rope, also known as ▷*rope moulding*, found in ▷Romanesque work, especially around ▷arches.

Cabochon A small convex ▷cartouche with carved ▷frame, especially on the knee of a ▷cabriole leg. Also a raised elliptical or circular ▷ornament in carving, especially in the centres of ▷guilloche or other repetitive ornament, or in ▷strapwork, where it usually alternates with a ▷lozenge.

Cabriole An ▷ornamental leg based on animal ▷*monopodia* from ▷Classical ▷Antiquity, revived during the seventeenth and eighteenth centuries. It often has feet carved to resemble ▷claws, ▷paws, or hooves.

Cabriole knees are often ornamented with ▷scallop shells or ▷cartouches.

Caduceus A winged baton around which ▷serpents are entwined: it is an ▷attribute of Hermes or ▷Mercury (who invented the alphabet in mythology), and is used in the decorations of printing-presses, post-offices, libraries, and writing-desks. With the ▷cornucopia it is associated with commerce.

Caementicium ▷Opus.

Caen stone Limestone (▷lime) from Caen in Normandy, often found in early mediaeval work in the south of England.

Caernarvon A ▷Welsh ▷arch, or a ▷lintel carried on ▷corbels.

Cage An outer work of timber surrounding another. A ▷screen around a ▷chantry-▷chapel or similar.

Cairn A ▷monument or pile of stones for marking or memorial purposes. A ▷tumulus.

Caisson A structure driven down to a firm ▷foundation used to facilitate building below water level. The term also refers to the sunken ▷panels in ceilings (▷ceil), ▷vaults, ▷cupolas, and ▷soffites generally.

Calathus The bell-shaped core of a ▷Corinthian ▷capital, also known as a *campana*.

Calcareous Composed of or containing chalk or ▷lime.

Caldarium, calidarium A room in ▷Roman ▷ther-

64

mae where perspiration was induced by steam, hot water, or heated air: a vapour bath or hot plunge.

Calefactory A heated room in a ▷monastery.

Calendar Decorations emblematic of the months of the year.

Calf's tongue A series of ▷tongue-like mouldings pointing in the same direction (as under ▷eaves) or towards a centre when ▷enriching an ▷arch.

Caliduct A hot-air ▷flue of ▷brick, ▷terracotta, or ▷tile in a ▷Roman system of heating.

Calotte A semicircular ▷dome on a circular ▷base sitting directly on ▷pendentives or ▷squinches with no ▷drum intervening.

Calvary Rock-work on which three ▷crosses are erected, or a sculptured and architectural representation of the ▷Crucifixion. A ▷*Calvary Cross* is one erected on three steps representing Faith, Hope, and Charity.

Calyon ▷Flint or ▷pebble ▷panels in ▷walls.

Calyx ▷Classical ▷ornament resembling the ▷calyx of a plant, often found in the work of the Adam brothers, and in the ▷Corinthian ▷capital.

Camara, camera A ▷roof or ceiling (▷ceil) of ▷brick, stone, or ▷concrete of ▷vaulted construction, or a vaulted room. *Camerated* means having an ▷arched or vaulted appearance. A *camera vitrea* is a vaulted ceiling with its ▷soffite lined with sheets of ▷glass.

Camber A curve in the form of a very shallow, almost flat ▷arch. A *camber-*▷*beam* has a slight curve so that its centre is higher than its ends, thus avoiding a sagging effect: cambers are therefore used for arches or beams for optical correction. Cambers are also found on road-sections. A *camber-piece* or *camber-slip* is the wooden ▷board used to construct a flat arch with an upward curve in the *intrados*. A *camber-*▷*window* is one arched at the top.

Camboge A ▷concrete unit with decorative openings for the admission of air and the exclusion of sunlight, a variant of the ▷*brise-soleil.*

Came Slender H-sections of cast or extruded ▷lead used to hold pieces of ▷glass in position in ▷stained-glass windows or other ▷leaded lights.

Camel Any creature with a hump, used in representations of the Magi, and also in ▷misericords to symbolize Christ's humility. It is used to suggest Asia in schemes of decoration representing the ▷continents,

and also in connection with trade with the East. It is also found in Grotesque ▷ornament.

Cameo A decorative device using stratified stone in which the top layer is partially cut away to leave the design in ▷relief on the darker ▷ground.

Camp ceiling One with a sagging inward curve, also known as ▷*coom* or ▷*comb* ceiling (▷ceil). It is also a ceiling with ▷canted sides sloped to follow the lines of the ▷rafters, as in a ▷garret. *Camp-sheeting* or *camp-shot* is the ▷sill or ▷capping of a wharf ▷wall.

Campanile A ▷bell-tower, generally attached to a ▷church, but sometimes unconnected with it. A *campana* is the bell-shaped body of a ▷capital; and *campaniform* means bell-shaped, as does *campanulated*. *Campanulae* are bells, small bells, or the ▷guttae of the ▷Doric Order.

Canal A ▷duct for carrying liquid. The fluting (▷flute) of a ▷column or ▷pilaster, or the hollows between the ▷fillets or ▷reeds of the volutes of an ▷Ionic ▷capital, or between the ▷echinus and ▷abacus of the capital, also known as *canalis* meaning a wide shallow concave ▷channel edged by small mouldings (▷mould). The ▷channels in a ▷triglyph. A ▷passage or alley. A ▷pipe or ▷gutter. Part of a ▷Roman ▷forum. A *canaliculus* is the groove on a triglyph or any small channel or groove.

Cancelli ▷Lattice ▷windows. Barred ▷screens separating the ▷sanctuary from the ▷nave in a ▷basilica, or the ▷balusters or railings around an ▷altar. Any barred ▷gates, as in a ▷prison or a starting-▷stall. A *cancello* is a screen separating the ▷chancel from a nave.

Candelabrum A stand for the support of lamps, consisting of a central upright and branches. *Candelabra* forms were also used to decorate ▷panels and are especially associated with ▷Grotesque ▷ornament.

Candle-beam A ▷beam in a ▷church on which are ▷prickets with trays for candles, associated with the ▷rood-▷screen or the entrance to a ▷choir or ▷chapel.

Canephora A figure of a young person with a ▷basket of offerings on the head used instead of ▷caryatides or ▷columns. *Canephorae* are used both as supports or as free-standing ▷ornaments or statues, and do not have ▷capitals with ▷abaci over.

Cannon A component of ▷trophies and ▷panoplies of ▷military decoration, often associated with ramrods, powder kegs, and cannonballs. Cannon barrels are occasionally used instead of ▷columns, and are common as ▷bollards.

Canonnière An opening in a ▷retaining wall to allow water to drain.

Canopic jar or vase An egg-shaped jar with a stopper in the form of a head, used to hold the viscera of the dead in Ancient Egypt. The form using a humanoid head was adopted in late eighteenth- and early nineteenth-century Egyptianizing ▷ornament.

Canopy The ▷tester and curtains of a ▷bed, or any covering or ▷hood over an ▷altar, statue, ▷pulpit, or ▷tomb (▷[59]). A *canopy of honour* is a decorative panelled ceiling over an altar, tomb, ▷chantry-▷chapel, or similar, known as a ▷*ceilure, cellure,* or *celure.*

Cant An external ▷angle of a building, or the cutting off of an angle of a square. Any part of a building on a polygonal plan is said to be *canted,* as a ▷bay ▷window. A *canted* ▷*column* is one that is polygonal on plan. The term also means a tilt, and can signify stone laid with its natural ▷bed vertical and showing on the ▷face. A *canted moulding* is a raking or a bevelled moulding.

Canterius The principal ▷rafter of a wooden ▷roof in ▷Antiquity. *Canthers* or *canterii* are the rafters of a roof the ends of which may be represented by the ▷mutules or even by the ▷triglyphs of the ▷Doric ▷Order. Also *cantherius.*

Cantharus A ▷fountain or pool in the ▷atrium of an ancient ▷church where worshippers washed before entering the building. The holy-water ▷stoup is a vestigial survival of the *cantharus.*

Cantilever A ▷bracket built into a ▷wall to support ▷eaves, ▷cornices, ▷balconies, or ▷canopies. It is essentially any ▷projecting member supported by a downward force on the far side of a ▷fulcrum.

Canton A corner of a building embellished with a ▷pilaster or a ▷projecting ▷course of ▷masonry.

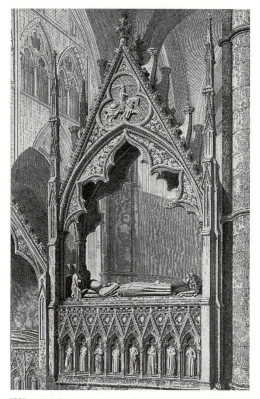

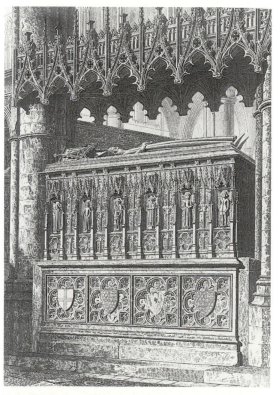

[59] CANOPIED TOMB (*a*) Canopied tomb of Aymer de Valence, Earl of Pembroke, in Westminster Abbey, drawn and engraved by Blore. This fourteenth-century example has a large Second-Pointed canopy with a cinquefoiled arch and crocketed gable set over the tomb-chest enriched with gabled niches containing weepers. (*JSC Collection*) (*b*) Tomb of Edward III in Westminster Abbey. The base is enriched with square panels of cusped quatrefoils containing heraldic shields. The altar-tomb is of marble, and has niches on each side under vaulted canopies enriched with tabernacle-work. In the niches are beautifully wrought figures (weepers) of gilt latten, and under each niche is a quatrefoil. Between the niches are blind panels of tracery surmounted by crocketed gables, and flanking each niche are buttresses capped by crocketed finials. Over the tomb is a wooden canopy or tester. Drawn and engraved by Blore. (*JSC Collection*)

Cantoned therefore means ▷ornamented at the corner with rusticated (▷rustic) ▷quoins, or some other projections. A *cantoned* ▷*pier* is a ▷Gothic pier or *pilier cantonné* consisting of a core with four ▷colonnettes responding to the ▷nave-▷arcade, the ▷aisle ▷vaults, and the nave-vaults.

Cantoria A choir ▷gallery. *Cantoris* refers to the *cantor* or *precentor* and to the *cantoris* side of the ▷choir, that is, the north.

Cap A ▷capital, ▷cornice, or uppermost crowning member. A coping (▷cope), ▷lintel, upper member of a ▷column, ▷pilaster, cornice, etc. A *cap-house* is the upper covering of a ▷stair leading to a ▷parapet or ▷gallery. A *cap moulding* is one on top of a ▷dado, at the ▷head of a ▷window or ▷door, or above anything.

Capillary groove A groove or space between surfaces to prevent capillary entry of water.

Capital [60] The upper part or ▷head of a ▷column or ▷pilaster set over the ▷shaft. Each of the ▷Orders has a distinctive capital. The ▷*Aeolic* capital is an early form of the ▷Ionic capital (▷Aeolic). Capitals of the ▷*Tuscan* and ▷*Roman* ▷*Doric Orders* are similar, and consist of an ▷abacus, ▷ovolo, ▷neck, and ▷astragal: the Roman Doric Order has more elaboration of the mouldings, and the necks are sometimes enriched with rosettes; the ▷*Greek Doric* capital has a plain abacus, a ▷cushion-like ▷echinus under which are ▷annulets, and a groove called the ▷hypotrachelium below; the ▷*Ionic* capital has coiled or scrolled elements known as ▷volutes, sometimes placed between the abacus and the ovolo moulding, and sometimes springing separately from the ovolo (front and side faces of volutes normally are not the same, except when four volutes are set diagonally (i.e. 135° to the plane of the ▷entablature), or when angle-volutes are used at corners); the ▷*Corinthian* capital (about one-and-one-sixth diameters high) is a ▷bell-shaped object with two rows of eight ▷acanthus ▷leaves (*acanthus spinosus* in Greek work and *acanthus mollis* in Roman) rising above the astragal: from between the leaves of the upper row rise eight ▷stalks or *caulicoli* (▷caulcoles) each surmounted by a ▷calyx from which emerge volutes or *helices* (▷helix) carrying the 'corners' of the concave-sided abacus and the central ▷ornaments (a variation has one row of acanthus leaves with ▷palm leaves above, no caulicoli or volutes, and a moulded abacus, square on plan, as at the Tower of the Winds in Athens); and the ▷*Composite* capital (a Roman Order) has two rows of acanthus leaves over an astragal with, instead of the caulicoli, eight Ionic volutes set at the corners (i.e. at 135° to the plane of the entablature), and ▷egg-and-dart and ▷bead-and-reel between them. The Composite Order is a late-Roman form, is not described by Vitruvius, was identified by Alberti, and

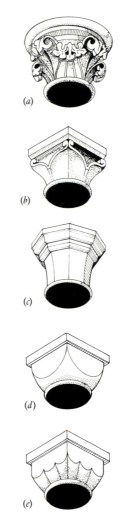

[60] CAPITAL (*a*) Stiff-leaf (First-Pointed) capital. (*b*) Water-leaf (Transitional) capital. (*c*) Moulded Perpendicular capital. (*d*) Romanesque cushion capital. (*e*) Romanesque scallop capital. (*JJS*)

designated by Serlio as the fifth and grandest of all the Orders. The *bell-capital* has a bell-like form, reversed, found in ▷Egyptian ▷architecture and as the basis of the Corinthian capital. The ▷*crocket capital* is a ▷Gothic capital with rolled leaves resembling ▷Classical volutes. The ▷*cushion capital* is a ▷Romanesque capital, basically cubic in form, but with the lower parts rounded to fit the circular shaft: the flat ▷faces remaining are referred to as ▷lunettes from their half-moon forms. The ▷*scallop capital* is similar to the ▷cushion, but with the curved portion carved with part-cones as ▷enrichment (▷moulded capital, ▷Orders).

Capitellum, capitolium The ▷chapter-house of a ▷monastery. The Roman Capitol.

Capping Any member serving as a ▷cap or a coping (▷cope). A *capping-piece* is a piece of timber covering the ▷head of an upright.

Capreolus A ▷strut or ▷brace, a ▷tie-▷beam, or a ▷king-post. A ▷rafter in a ▷roof.

Capriccio A free composition, or an invention. A picture combining real and imaginary buildings in a townscape where existing buildings are placed in an entirely new context.

Caprice A decorative ▷vignette featuring architectural ▷ruins inhabited by figures of the ▷seasons or the Ages of Man, and surrounded by ▷Rococo ▷scroll-work.

Capstone A stone in a coping (▷cope) or a ▷cap to an upright.

Caput ecclesiae The *caput*, or ▷head, of a ▷church is usually the east end.

Caracol, caracole A ▷spiral staircase.

Caramanian A type of decoration featuring ▷topographical scenes, such as views of ▷abbeys, ▷country seats, cities, or even ▷Egyptian Antiquities, usually in a sepia ▷monochrome.

Carcase, carcass The shell of a building. Similarly, *carcass flooring* or *roofing* refers to the ▷frame of timber that carries ▷boards. The loadbearing part of a structure without finishes.

Carcer A ▷prison, starting-▷stall for a race, or a den for a beast.

Card cut A type of ▷fret ▷ornament not pierced but carved in low ▷relief, often used to enrich ▷friezes, and associated with *Chinoiserie* (▷Chinese) or eighteenth-century *Gothick* (▷Gothic).

Cardinal Cardinal faces are those facing north, south, east or west. The *cardinal* ▷*virtues* are ▷justice, prudence, temperance, and fortitude, often represented as figures. ▷Ecclesiastical hat.

Cardo A ▷hinge or a pivot. The main north–south ▷axis of a ▷Roman camp, fortress, or town, or the axis of a building.

Carillon A set of bells in a ▷tower: the term is also sometimes given to a ▷bell-tower.

Carnel An ▷embrasure of crenellation (▷crenel).

Carol, carrel, carrol A ▷closet or enclosure in which to study. A small ▷bay ▷window or ▷niche in a ▷cloister, or any small ▷area partitioned off.

Carolean Of the time of King Charles I (1625–49) or II (1660–85), also *Caroline*.

Carolingian Associated with the period of Emperor Charlemagne (768–814).

Carolitic A ▷column with branches and ▷leaves, or with a foliated ▷shaft.

Carpentry A structure of timber, distinguished from ▷joinery in that it is constructed using the simple tools of axe, adze, saw, and chisel, whereas joinery implies the use of a plane and more sophistication in the design. The term is also applied to the trade of carpentry. *Carpenter's* ▷*Gothic* is a term given to ▷pattern-book *Gothick* derived from the publications of people such as Batty Langley in the mid-eighteenth century, and later applied to timber-built structures in America. It is essentially a whimsical and unversed type of Gothick.

Carpet-strip A strip or ▷step below a ▷door, the thickness of the carpet, now usually a metal strip to trim the edge of the carpet.

Carquois A ▷quiver for arrows in decoration.

Carrara marble A white Tuscan ▷marble commonly used for mantelpieces (▷mantel) and for monumental ▷sculpture. It is an unsuitable material for use out of doors in Britain because it quickly dissolves in the polluted acidic rain.

Carraraware A matt-glazed ▷stoneware made by Doulton to resemble ▷Carrara marble. It was used at the Savoy Hotel, and, from the late 1880s the range was gradually increased to add further choices apart from the original ivory-white colour.

Carreau A square or ▷lozenge-shaped piece of ▷glass or ▷tile.

Carrefour A space from which several streets radiate, or a crossroads, or any public square from which roads lead.

Carrelage Decorative tiling.

Carriage The timber frame on which ▷steps of a ▷stair are supported. A *carriage-piece*, ▷*rough-*▷*string*, ▷*bearer*, or *stair-horse* is a ▷bearer between two strings to support the stairs in the middle of each ▷tread. A *carriage-▷bolt* is a *coach-bolt*. A *carriageway* is part of a road for vehicular traffic, or the traffic-lane. A *carriage-▷porch* is a roofed structure over a drive at the entrance to a building to protect those entering the building and leaving a vehicle.

Cartibulum A ▷slab of ▷marble on a ▷bracket or support used as a ▷table.

Carton pierre A variety of *papier maché* made of paper-pulp, chalk, ▷glue, and ▷whiting, used to make architectural ▷enrichments.

Cartoon A full-scale drawing of a decoration or a painting.

Cartouch, cartouche [61] A ▷modillion, usually internal, or those under the ▷eaves of a building, as opposed to the modillions of a standard ▷Classical ▷cornice. The term is more usually applied to a decorative framed ▷tablet for ▷inscriptions in the form of a ▷scroll or curving piece of parchment. Any ▷frame around an inscription.

Carved work, carving Hand-cut ▷embellishment.

[61] CARTOUCHE Cartouche of 1691 with typical Rococo S- and C-curves around it, from the Mico Almshouses, Stepney, London. (*JSC*)

Carvel A ▷flush-joint between two ▷planks.

Caryatid(e) [62] A female figure used instead of a ▷column for the support of an ▷entablature, with ▷astragal, ▷ovolo (usually enriched with ▷egg-and-dart and ▷bead-and-reel), and ▷abacus on top of the ▷head. The term is also given to any support carved in the form of a human figure, but it is not, strictly speaking, correct. Male figures, usually heroic in scale and proportion, and 'bent' under the weight of what they are carrying, are called ▷*atlantes*: if the male figures are un-bowed and straight, they are called *telamoni* or *telamones* (▷*telemon*). Figures of young persons with baskets on their heads instead of astragal, ovolo, and abacus, also used instead of columns, are called ▷*canephorae*. ▷*Herms* are portions of figures on ▷pedestals, whether carrying a weight or not, while ▷*terms* are actually pedestals (often inverted ▷obelisks or parts of obelisks) which merge into the torsos and busts of humanoid or other figures. The term *caryatides* derives from the belief by Vitruvius that the female figures of the ▷Erechtheion represent Carian prisoners.

Case bay A piece of ▷floor or ▷roof between two ▷girders. ▷Joists framed between girders. When the ends of flooring-joists are let into a ▷wall and the other into a girder, they are called *tail-bays*.

Cased Facing to a building. The term signifies that the outside of a building is covered with materials of superior quality to those used in its construction. A *cased ▷beam* is one encased with finished work of uniform ▷profile or with other ▷embellishment. *Cased ▷glass*, otherwise known as *case-*, *flashed*, or *overlay-glass*, is glass formed of two fused layers, usually a colour on plain glass, so that when the top layer is cut the under-layer is exposed, as in Victorian 'brilliants' of plain stars set in a coloured surround. A *case of a ▷door* is a wooden ▷frame in which a door is hung: the term *door-case* is also applied to the whole of an elaborate ▷Classical frame to a doorway. The *case of a ▷stair* is the ▷well around a staircase. *Casing* is ▷lining, or the exposed ▷trim around an opening, or the finished work covering or encasing a structural member such as a ▷post or a beam. A *casing-▷bead* is one providing a stop or covering a join between two different materials or surfaces. A *cased ▷sash-frame* is one with the interior verticals hollow for the weights to balance the sashes.

Casemate A vaulted ▷chamber in the thickness of fortified ▷ramparts, with ▷embrasures. The term is also used to signify a ▷barrack or a battery. In archaic usage it also meant a hollow moulding (▷mould), such as the ▷cavetto. *Casemated ▷wall* means provided with case-mates, or strongly fortified. A *casemate ▷wall* is a fortified enclosure consisting of an inner and outer wall braced

SOUBASSEMENT CARYATIDE ET ENTABLEMENT
du Temple de Pandrose à Athènes.

Planche LV.

[62] CARYATIDE ORDER
The Caryatide Order from the Erechtheion in Athens. On the left are the details of the plinth on which the Order stands. Note that there is no frieze, and that the dentils of the bed mouldings of the cornice sit directly on the top fascia of the architrave. (*Normand*)

by strong *cross-walls* dividing the space between them into ▷chambers.

Casement [63]   A ▷frame enclosing part of the glazing of a ▷window, with ▷hinges to open and shut it. A *casement window* is a metal or timber window in which the opening lights are hung on hinges as opposed to being sliding ▷sashes or pivot-hung. The term was also used to describe the deep hollow moulding, similar to the ▷cavetto or ▷scotia, in ▷Gothic ▷architecture in ▷cornices, and in ▷door- and window-▷jambs. It was often ▷enriched.

Casino   A small country house, or a ▷lodge in a park.

The term was formerly applied to a defence-post, but later came to mean a ▷*summer-house* or decorative ▷lodge. It also means any public room for social meetings, especially a public music- or dancing-saloon, but is now used to describe a room or building used for gambling.

Cassoon   As ▷caisson, in the sense of coffers.

Cast   Anything poured into a ▷mould and then set, like cast iron or artificial stone. In ▷joinery, *casting* means *warping* or *bending*: in ▷metalwork it means the pouring of molten metal into a ▷mould, or the result of such a pouring when set, such as a ▷gulley-grating

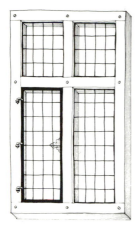

[63] CASEMENT A seventeenth-century cross-casement of oak, with opening light of wrought iron and glass set in lead cames, from the brewhouse at Crostwight Hall, Norfolk. (*JJS*)

or a ▷bell. A *cast-iron* ▷*front* is a ▷façade of pre-fabricated kits-of-parts, often found in ▷Victorian commercial buildings. A *cast-staff* is a shape, made in a mould, and then fixed in place in ▷plaster decorations.

Castella, castelle, castellum A receptacle for the collection of water for distribution, often a large ▷chamber with vaulted rooms or ▷cisterns. A *castellum* was also a small fortified town. A *castellum aquae* was a ▷reservoir at the end of an ▷aqueduct from which water

was distributed: it was often ▷embellished with ▷ornament.

Castellated With ▷battlements, or ▷ornamented with crenellations (▷crenel).

Castle [64] A building fortified for defence. It is also a habitation with ▷towers, surrounding ▷walls, and ▷moats. The chief parts of a castle are the *valla* or embankments, *fossae* or ditches, walls with ▷battlements, ▷bastions at angles or at intervals along the wall, and the central tower or ▷*keep*. The fosse or moat had a ▷bridge that could be raised, leading to the ▷gates which were protected by descending metal-reinforced ▷grilles called ▷*portcullises*. The *barbican* (or ▷barbacan) was in advance of the castle and defended the entrance, being constructed on a mound or tower principle with ▷terraces facing the castle. The *gatehouse* (▷gate) was flanked by towers and crowned with projecting ▷machicolations. Inside the castle was the *outer bailey* (▷bail) or wall and gatehouse, and usually containing ▷stables and offices. The *inner bailey* was the innermost defence, in the corner or centre of which was the *keep* or ▷*donjon*, a tower-stronghold containing the state apartments, a ▷well, a ▷chapel, and other important rooms. A *castrum* was a castle, fortress, or fortified town. The *Castle Style* is found in ▷follies, gateways, sham ▷ruins, and ▷Picturesque cottages in the eighteenth century. Its characteristics were *crenellations*, *loopholes* (often false), ▷*drawbridges*, and ▷*turrets*, and it was used by many ▷architects including Robert Adam, and was applied to regular ▷Classical plans as well as to asymmetrical compositions.

[64] CASTLE Stokesay Castle, Shropshire. One of the earliest fortified houses in England, built in the latter part of the thirteenth century. On the left is a timber-framed gatehouse largely of the sixteenth century. (*JSC*)

Cat A moveable structure to protect besiegers, or a double ▷tripod with six legs. A *cat-face* is a depression or blemish in a finished coat of ▷plaster. A *cat-head* is a notched wedge placed between two members meeting at an oblique angle. A *cat-ladder* is a ▷plank with strips of wood fixed across it to give a footing for workers repairing a ▷roof. A *cat's eye* is a small, elongated knot in timber. A *cat's head* is an ▷ornament like the ▷Romanesque ▷beak-head, but with the animal mask resembling the head of a cat. A *catslide* is a long sloping roof, especially one where the main roof-slope on a two-storey building is continued down to cover a single-storey *outshot*. A *cat's* ▷step is the same as a *crow-step* (▷corbel). A *catwalk* is a narrow fixed walkway in a roof-space, around a fly-tower, or in some other position to gain access to otherwise inaccessible parts.

Catabasis, catabasion A place under an ▷altar where Relics are placed.

Catacomb [65] An underground public ▷cemetery, usually hollowed out of the solid rock to form ▷*loculi* or

[65] CATACOMBS Catacombs under the Anglican chapel at the General Cemetery of All Souls, Kensal Green, London, designed by John Griffith, and built 1837. Note the coffins on shelves (*loculi*), the groin-vaults of brick, and the cast-iron grilles. (*Greater London Photographic Library 70/12201*)

places to deposit corpses on either side of ▷galleries or passageways (▷passage). A type of ▷basement built rather than hollowed out, used for the depositing of ▷coffins in cemeteries, usually associated with ▷mortuary ▷chapels. Many ▷Victorian cemeteries were furnished with catacombs, and the disused stone-quarries of Montparnasse in Paris were used to deposit the bones removed from the closed churchyards. A *catacumba* appears to relate either to the ▷atrium or courtyard in front of a ▷basilican ▷church (associated with burial of the dead in the atrium or *porticus*).

Catafalco, catafalque A temporary structure, decorated and usually draped, representing a ▷tomb or ▷cenotaph, and used in funeral ceremonies to support the ▷coffin. Some permanent catafalques may be found in ▷mortuary ▷chapels, in ▷cemeteries and ▷crematoria. In both ▷Victorian mortuary chapels and later crematoria, catafalques often have mechanisms so that the coffins can be carried downwards to the ▷vaults or furnaces below.

Catch A device for fastening a ▷door, usually opened from one side. A *catch-basin* is a ▷reservoir for catching surface water so that the sediment can settle in it. A *catch-drain* is one on the side of a large open ▷canal to take the surplus water, or one along sloping ground to catch the surface-water.

Catenary ▷Arch. *Catenated* means ▷ornamented with chain-like forms, or ▷festoons of ▷chains.

Cathedra A bishop's chair or throne, originally placed in the ▷apse behind the ▷high altar, but in ▷Gothic ▷architecture usually found in ▷cathedrals associated with the ▷choir-▷stalls.

Cathedral [66] The principal ▷church of a Diocese in which the ▷*cathedra* is placed. The *Cathedral Style* means the phase of the ▷Gothic ▷Revival from about 1810 to 1840 which involved the use of Gothic ▷motifs without the archaeological and scholarly rigour of the post-Pugin Revival.

Catherii ▷Rafters in ▷Roman construction.

Catherine-wheel window Also called a ▷*marigold window*, it is a geometrically patterned window with radiating divisions or spokes, also called a ▷*wheel window* (▷rose window).

Cathetus The ▷axis of a cylinder. The axis of the ▷eye of an ▷Ionic ▷volute.

Caulcoles, caulicolae, caulicoli In the ▷Corinthian ▷capital, the ▷stalks that spring from the greater stalks. The ▷volutes of the capital are carried by stalks from

Chapels — Ambulatory

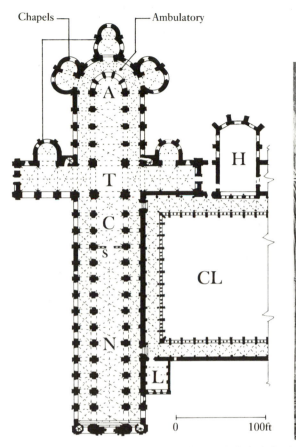

[66] CATHEDRAL (*a*) An idealized plan of Norwich Cathedral with *chevet* arrangement at the east end, and semicircular ambulatory behind the high altar, with radiating chapels. Note the chapels on the eastern sides of the transepts. **A** altar, **C** choir, **T** crossing with tower over, **CL** cloister with garth in the centre, **H** chapter-house, **N** nave, **L** locutory, **s** screen. (*JJS*) (*b*) The Cathedral of Sts Mary and Peter, Exeter, Devon, looking east towards the pulpitum with organ-case above. The building is largely Second-Pointed work of the fourteenth century, and the screen is 1318–25. The organ-case is seventeenth-century. (*JSC*)

which the *caulicoli* arise (▷Composite and ▷Corinthian Orders). A *caulis* is one of the main stalks springing from between the second row of ▷acanthus ▷leaves.

Caulking, cocking The mode of fixing the ▷tie-▷beam of a ▷roof or the binding ▷joists of a ▷floor to the ▷wall-▷plates. The term also means the stopping-up of crevices.

Causeway A raised ▷dam or bank across a marsh and carrying a road. It also means any paved road, a paving of ▷setts, or of squared stones.

Cavaedium The *cavum aedium*, or main room of a ▷Roman house, also called the ▷atrium, and partly open to the sky by means of the *compluvium*, with an ▷*impluvium* or tank for water in the centre.

Cavetto A hollow moulding (▷mould) with its ▷profile a quadrant of a circle, principally used in ▷cornices. It is also called a ▷*gorge*, ▷*hollow*, ▷*chamfer*, ▷*throat*, or ▷*trochilus*. A *cavetto cornice* is the characteristic ▷*Egyptian gorge* or cornice of most Ancient Egyptian buildings, sometimes plain and sometimes decorated with vertical ▷leaves. It usually has a ▷torus moulding below it.

Cavity wall A ▷wall with an inner and outer ▷leaf separated by a continuous space, but tied together with metal ▷ties: it gives improved thermal insulation and less possibilities for penetration by damp.

Cavo rilievo Also known as a *sunk* ▷*relief* or ▷*intaglio rilevato*, it is relief which does not project before the general surface in which it is carved.

Cavum aedium ▷Cavaedium.

Ceele, seele A ▷canopy.

Ceil To place a ceiling over, or to line with a ▷wainscot. A ceiling is the overhead surface of a room which hides the structure above. A *ceiling-▷cornice* is a concave or ▷cavetto moulding (▷mould) between ceiling and ▷wall. A *ceiling-▷joist* is a small ▷beam fixed to the binding joists for the attachment of lathing (▷lath) to take the ▷plaster on a ceiling.

Ceilure, cellure, celure A panelled and painted ▷roof or ceiling over an ▷altar, ▷chancel, or ▷rood. A ▷canopy.

Celature ▷Embossed, engraved, or ▷chased decorations on metal.

Cell A small ▷closet in which to sit or read, especially the bedsitting-room of a monastic establishment. Part of a ▷temple enclosed within the ▷walls, otherwise the *cella* (▷cell) or ▷*naos* containing the statue (▷[234]). A compartment of a ▷groined or ▷ribbed ▷vault. A ▷chamber in which a prisoner is confined. A small cavity surrounded by walls. A small room in a ▷dormitory or an ▷inn. A chamber containing conveniences for bathing in ▷thermae.

Cellar The lowest ▷storey of a building, wholly or partly underground, used for storage. A store-room, usually underground.

Cellarium Monastic buildings with stores and ▷cellars on the west side of the ▷cloisters.

Cellular beam A ▷beam of iron plates with ▷cells at the top of the ▷web.

Celtic Celtic art developed from around the fifth century BC in the Rhineland, then in Central Europe, and by 250 BC was established in the British Isles. It was to absorb influences from ▷Greek, ▷Etruscan, ▷Oriental, ▷Early Christian, and ▷Byzantine decoration. Typical ▷motifs are ▷knots, spirals, ▷interlacing ▷ribbons, stylized fauna, and abstract patterns. Many themes found their way into ▷Anglo-Saxon, ▷Romanesque, and ▷Hiberno-Romanesque ▷ornament.

Celtic cross [67] A ▷cross with a tall vertical ▷shaft and short horizontal arms, with a circlet linking them with its centre at the intersection of the arms. It is elaborately ▷ornamented, and usually capped by a ▷shrine-like ▷sculpture. The ▷*Celtic* ▷*Revival* was A nineteenth-century movement associated with ▷ Hiberno-Romanesque, and then with the ▷Arts-and-Crafts styles, and played no small part in aspects of ▷Art-Nouveau decorations.

[67] CELTIC CROSS The great Cross of Abbot Muiredach at Monasterboice, Co. Louth, of the tenth century. (*JSC*)

Cement An adhesive composed of a powdered substance made into a paste with water, which hardens on drying to bind ▷bricks or stones together. ▷*Portland cement* is cement made from limestone (▷lime) and clay.

Cemetery [68] Any place where the dead are interred or deposited. The term is usually associated with large public burial-grounds, as opposed to the churchyards attached to ▷churches. Cemeteries are often landscaped, contain ▷mortuary ▷chapels, ranges of ▷*loculi*, and ▷mausolea set within the grounds. A *cemetery beacon* was a lighthouse placed in mediaeval graveyards on the Continent, often associated with an ▷altar.

Cenotaph A ▷monument that celebrates the memory of a person or persons buried elsewhere. An empty ▷tomb.

Centaur A creature in ▷Greek mythology with the head, trunk, and arms of a man, and the legs and body of a horse, often armed with bow and arrows. Centaurs

[68] CEMETERY Design for the General Cemetery of All Souls, Kensal Green, probably by John Griffith. (*Museum of London*)

are associated with sensuality and occur in ▷Bacchic ornament.

Centering Wooden framework used in ▷arch or ▷vault construction, and ▷struck or removed when the arch or vault is completed or the ▷mortar has set. In some early vaults, constructed of rough-hewn stone, the centering was covered with a thick layer of mortar so that when it was struck the impression of the wooden structure was left.

Centrepiece An ▷ornament in the middle of something, as on a ▷wall or ceiling.

Centrie garth A ▷cemetery in the centre of a ▷cloister or walled enclosure.

Ceramic A product made of clay and burnt, such as ▷stoneware or ▷terracotta. A *ceramic ▷veneer* has vitreous or glazed surfaces, usually formed of a compound of metal oxides and clays, burnt at high temperatures.

Ceres The goddess of agriculture, also known as Demeter, with the ▷attributes of ▷wheat, corn-sheaf, ▷poppy, ▷cornucopia, and ▷scythe, and sometimes holding a ▷torch. With two torches she represents the Church, holding the New and Old Testaments, but more often she is found in ▷Bacchic ornament or on corn exchanges and the like.

Cerquate An arrangement of ▷oak ▷leaves and ▷acorns in ▷Renaissance decoration.

Certosa A Carthusian ▷monastery (▷Charterhouse).

Cesspit A pit for the collection of human waste.

Cesspool A ▷well, usually lead-lined, sunk below the level of a ▷parapet or ▷valley-▷gutter, to receive rainwater before it enters the drainpipe.

Chafer house An ale-house.

Chain bond ▷Masonry bounded with iron ▷bars or chains. A *chain ▷course* is one of stones ▷cramped together.

Chaînes Vertical strips of rusticated (▷rustic) ▷masonry dividing ▷walls into ▷panels, common in the seventeenth century. The ▷blocks may be of alternating width like ▷quoins, but may also be the same width.

Chains ▷Symbols of enslavement, either physical or spiritual, and so are associated with the ▷Vices. Carved chains on ▷masonry occur on buildings associated with the navy or with maritime trade, and with punishment, as on ▷prisons. A *chain moulding* (▷mould) is a moulding resembling a chain, usually on a ▷band. A *chain trailing*, otherwise known as *trailed decoration*, *trailing*, or *threading*, is a type of decoration used on ▷glass in which molten threads of glass are applied, often in a chain-like form.

Chair-rail A ▷dado-▷rail or moulding (▷mould) around a room to prevent the backs of chairs from damaging the plasterwork. It conforms to the ▷cornice of a ▷pedestal.

Chalcidicum A building for the administration of justice. A ▷portico or ▷hall supported by ▷columns, or an addition to a ▷basilica. A ▷narthex. A *chalcidium* was a meeting-room attached to a basilica.

Châlet A timber house with exposed timbers, ▷balconies, and ▷stairs and a ▷jettied upper ▷floor. A small timber house.

Chamber A room for private functions, or a room of importance such as a senate-chamber or an audience-chamber. A *great chamber* was contiguous to the ▷hall, and was the equivalent of a ▷drawing-room. The term *camera* is used to signify a suite of rooms or an ▷apartment: the camera of an Abbot, for example, was a suite of lodgings, also known as *chalmer*. *Chambers* means a suite of rooms for living or professional use, especially by the legal profession. A chamber-▷storey is a storey for bedrooms. A *chamber-▷tomb* is a space reached by a long ▷passage and set within an artificial mound.

Chambranle An ▷ornamental and structural ▷border on the sides and tops of ▷doors, ▷windows, ▷niches, and fireplaces: the part across the top is ▷*transverse*, and the upright sides are *ascendants*. The same as ▷architrave. It is joiner's or mason's work, and conforms to the architrave section used elsewhere in the building.

Chamfer An ▷arris or ▷angle which is shaved off is said to be *chamfered*. A chamfer resembles a ▷splay, but is smaller. A *hollow chamfer* is concave. A ▷bevel or ▷cant. A groove or furrow. A *swelled chamfer* is the same as a ▷wave moulding, or ▷Vitruvian scroll. A *chamfer-stop* is any ▷ornamentation which terminates a chamfer, usually on a timber ▷beam, but also on splayed ▷jambs, etc. *Chamfered rustication* (▷rustic) is where the stone ▷face is bevelled at the joints so that V-shaped lines are created. A *chamfret* or *chamferet* is a hollow chamfer, ▷channel, or ▷gutter.

Champ, champe The field or ▷ground on which ▷relief carving is raised.

Chancel The ▷choir and ▷sanctuary in the liturgical eastern part of a ▷church appropriated for the use of those who officiate during services. The term was originally applied only to that part of the church where the ▷altar was placed (▷[77]). A *chancel-▷aisle* is one to the side of a chancel: in larger churches it passes round behind the ▷high altar, forming an ▷ambulatory. A *chancel-▷arch* is one marking the separation between the chancel and the ▷nave: it usually supports a ▷gable ▷wall (frequently decorated with the ▷Last ▷Judgement) often with a ▷*Sancte-cote* on top, so that the chancel can have a higher or a lower ▷roof than that of the nave. A *chancel-▷rail* is the barrier separating the chancel from the nave: a *chancel-▷screen* divides the chancel from the nave, often has a ▷gallery on top of it, and may carry a ▷rood.

Chancellery An office for a chancellor or the office of an envoy.

Chancery A building housing a law court, archives, secretariats, or a chancellery.

Chandelle Infill of the lower part of ▷flutes of ▷columns, etc., with beading (▷bead) or ▷foliate forms, like ▷enriched cabling (▷cable).

Chandlery, chandry A room for storing candles, lamps, and oil.

Channel A ▷gutter sunk below a surface to collect water. A decorative groove. *Channelling* is a series of rebates (▷rabbet) in ▷ashlar to form rustication (▷rustic), or a series of grooves in any architectural member, such as a ▷column. Also *canalis* (▷canal).

Chantlate A piece of timber fixed to the ends of ▷rafters at the ▷eaves and projecting beyond a ▷wall to support the ▷roof-covering and throw rainwater off.

Chantry, chauntry An endowment to provide for the chanting of masses or the saying of prayers for the dead. A *chantry-▷chapel* (▷[69]) was a chapel devoted to the chanting of prayers for the dead: most such chapels were in ▷abbeys, ▷cathedrals, or the grander ▷churches in which it was considered a privilege to be buried, and these were often attached to or over the ▷grave or ▷vault of the person or persons providing the endowment. Chantry-chapels, such as those in Winchester Cathedral, have fine stone ▷screens around them, and contain elaborate ▷tomb-▷chests on which are ▷effigies. Chantries tended to be provided only by the wealthy, so craftsmen and merchants banded together to endow their own chapel, keep an ▷altar, and pay for

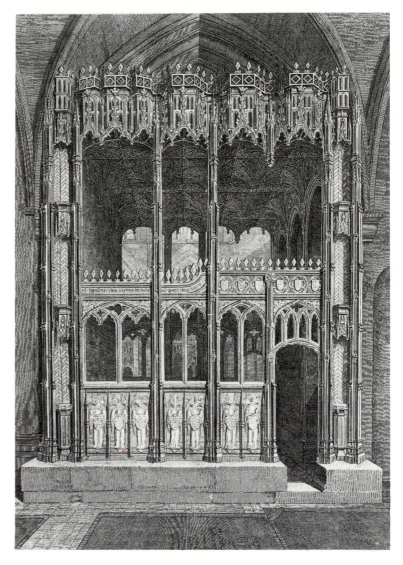

[69] CHANTRY-CHAPEL
Chantry-chapel of Isabel, Countess
of Warwick (*d.* 1439) at Tewkesbury,
drawn by Carter. Note the elaborately
vaulted roof. (*JSC Collection*)

the services of priests: one of the main reasons for the formation of mediaeval guilds or *Mysteries*, such as the London Livery Companies, was the desire to endow a chantry. In the reign of King Edward VI, when Purgatory was denounced as a 'vain opinion', all chantries in England were dissolved, and the endowments seized by the Crown, but many fine chantry-chapels survive. A *chantry-chamber* was the room used by the priests attached to a chantry.

Chapel A small building or part of a building set aside for prayer, veneration, contemplation, or worship, and dedicated separately. Before the Reformation all great houses, ▷castles, and ▷granges had chapels attached to them. The parish ▷churches and ▷cathedrals had numbers of chapels (small areas within or attached to the larger building), usually to the east of the ▷high altar, at the east sides of the ▷transepts, and in the ▷aisles. The largest and most magnificent of these chapels attached to a church or cathedral was usually for the veneration of Our Lady. The term *chapel* generally signifies a building endowed with fewer privileges than churches, and in which the ▷sacrament of baptism could not be administered. Free-standing chapels generally had no burial ground attached. A *chapel-of-ease* was a church built in a large parish for the convenience of parishioners living too far from the parish church. For a *chantry-chapel*, ▷chantry. A *chapel royal* is the chapel of a royal palace or royal castle. *Chapel* also signifies a building used for forms of worship practised by

Dissenting or Non-conformist sects, while in Ireland *chapel* means a Roman Catholic church, probably because mass was said in chapels attached to other buildings during the Penal Times (▷[66]).

Chapiter, chaptrel   ▷Capital.

Chaplet   A moulding (▷mould) carved with ▷beads, ▷olives, etc., or any ▷astragal or bead moulding.

Chapter-house [70]   The building attached to a ▷cathedral or collegiate ▷church or ▷abbey where the dean and prebendaries or monks and canons met for the transaction of business. Chapter-houses are often polygonal on plan (as at Lincoln, Salisbury, Southwell, Wells, Worcester and York Cathedrals). The position of the chapter-house in relation to the church owes its origin to the Constantinian ▷basilica of St Peter's in Rome, and its attached ▷mausolea (▷basilica).

Chaptrel   An ▷impost, or a small ▷capital, usually associated with ▷vaulting.

[70] CHAPTER-HOUSE Wells Cathedral chapter-house. Thirty-six ribs spring from the central pier, *c.* 1290–1315, and the building is early Decorated or Second-Pointed in style. Note the carved bosses and capital. (*JSC*)

Char, chare   To hew or work.

Charette, charrette   An exercise in solving an architectural problem.

Charged   A ▷frieze is *charged* with the ▷ornament on it, so the term means the dependence of one part of a work of ▷architecture upon another. The term also means filled, as when a ▷kiln is filled or charged with ▷bricks for burning.

Charnel-house   A building where the disinterred bones of the dead are stored: the charnel-house ensured that churchyards never filled and that the ground could be used over and over again. Hythe in Kent and Rothwell in Northamptonshire have charnel-houses within the fabric of the ▷church, but often they were free-standing structures. Post-Reformation concepts of ownership of ▷graves and permanent burial-places heralded the end of charnel-houses, although they can still be found on the Continent.

Charterhouse   A Carthusian ▷monastery, ▷*Certosa*, or *Chartreuse*.

Chase   An indent in a ▷wall for a pipe or for the bonding with another wall. A *chase-*▷*mortise* is one in a pair of parallel timbers for the insertion of one end of a transverse or bridging member.

Chasse   A container for the relics of a saint.

Château [71]   A ▷castle or country house in France, or a building in the style of such, especially that of ▷François I. A *château d'eau* is a ▷reservoir, usually given an architectural treatment, at the end of an ▷aqueduct.

Chatri   A parasol-shaped, ▷dome-like form over a flat, supported on a vertical ▷post or *chattrayashti*. A *chattravali* has three parasols on the same ▷pole, like a triple parasol. Also *chattra*. A *chatri* can also be carried on ▷colonnettes, and is found in exotic ▷architecture based on ▷Indian precedent. A *chavada* is an Indian ▷pavilion-like form, often with a *chatri* on top. These are found on Indian ▷Revival buildings.

Check   A rebate (▷rabbet). A *check* ▷*fillet* is one on a ▷roof to direct the flow of rainwater. A *check* ▷*throat* is a groove under a ▷cill or ▷step to prevent water reaching the ▷wall: a ▷drip. A ▷sneck.

Checky   Divided into ▷heraldic ▷squares or ▷chequers.

Cheek   An upright ▷face forming the end or side of an opening or a structure, such as the sides of a dormer window or a doorway. The cheeks of a ▷mortise are the solid pieces of timber on either side of the mortise itself.

[71] CHÂTEAU STYLE Royal Holloway College, Egham, Surrey, by W. H. Crossland, of 1879–87, an essay in the French château style of the Loire Valley. (*RCHME BB84/3110*)

Chemin-de-ronde A continuous walkway behind a ▷parapet along a fortified ▷wall.

Cheneau An ▷ornamented ▷gutter at the ▷eaves of a ▷roof, an ornamented crest (▷cress), or a ▷cornice.

Chequer A ▷square in a chequer-pattern contrasted with its neighbours by colour or texture. *Chequer-work* is a decorative treatment of pavings or ▷walls involving squares of contrasting colours or materials in a chess-board pattern. A pattern of chequers repeated over a large surface on a rectangular or diagonal grid is also called ▷*diaper-work.*

Cherub Christian *Cherubim* are in the first hierarchy of angels, represent Divine Wisdom, and are ▷personified as winged adult figures with two or four wings, and holding books. The term *cherub* usually means a winged male child, or even a winged child's head, also known as ▷*Cupids* from the iconographical similarity to a winged ▷*Love* or ▷*Amorino* found in ▷Antique and ▷Renaissance ▷ornament. Cherubs are common in ▷Baroque architectural decoration, especially on funerary ▷monuments, on the ▷eyes of ▷capitals, supports for ▷consoles, or ▷spandrels. Cherubs with puffed cheeks represented the ▷winds, while cherubs with crossed wings appeared in funerary art. The ▷skull with ▷bats' wings was a funerary variant on the winged cherubic head. Cherubs are not to be confused with unwinged ▷*putti* (boys).

Chest A receptacle. In ▷churches, special chests are found for the storage of vestments, vessels, and linens. The term is also used to denote a ▷coffin, or to suggest a treasure or ▷treasury.

Cheval-de-frise A series of ▷nails or spikes set into the top of a ▷wall.

Chevet The east end of a ▷church built in the ▷French style, with apsidal form and ▷ambulatory, usually with radiating ▷chapels (▷[66]).

Chevron [72] A ▷zigzag ornament found in ▷Romanesque work, usually on the ▷archivolt, but also on ▷string-courses, also called ▷*dancette* or *zigzag*. Any

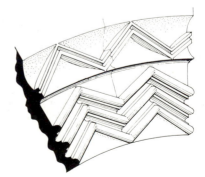

[72] CHEVRON Chevron from Chichester Cathedral. (*JJS*)

[73] CHIEF (*JJS*)

V-shaped stripe pointing up or down, used singly or in groups, commonly in the ▷Art-Deco style, but also found in ▷Roman ▷mosaic and in *Bargello* ▷ornament.

Chien-assis A small unglazed dormer (▷dormant) opening, lighting a roof-space and set in a sloping ▷roof, usually with a ▷foiled opening and a pitched roof, like a dog kennel in a roof.

Chief [73] The upper third of an ▷heraldic ▷shield.

Child Heads and full figures of children (usually male) are often used in ▷ornament, and are known as *putti*, represented as chubby, knowing little boys. A ▷*putto* is wingless, and should not be confused with an ▷*amorino* or a ▷*cherub*.

Chimera A mythical creature with the head, mane, and legs of a ▷lion, tail of a dragon, body of a goat, and wings of an ▷eagle, found in ▷Pompeian and ▷Classical decorations and ▷Grotesque ▷ornament.

Chimney A fireplace, but the term now includes the ▷flue and the structure above a ▷roof. In early mediaeval times chimney-shafts appear to have been rare. In domestic buildings chimneys are often found as massive stacks of ▷brick or stone in the core of the house, and sometimes at the ▷gable-ends. The opening into a room is called the *fireplace*, and the ▷floor of the fireplace is the ▷*hearth*. The part of the ▷flue that contracts as it ascends is called the *gathering*. That part of the chimney-stack containing the chimneys and the flues, often projecting into a room, is called a *chimney-*▷*breast*, while the breast is supported above the opening by a *chimney-*▷*bar*, a ▷*mantel-tree* (or horizontal ▷beam supported on ▷jambs of the fireplace), or a *chimney-*▷*arch*. A *chimney-back*, also the *fireback*, is the back ▷wall of the fireplace, often with a cast-iron plate. A *chimney-*▷*cheek* is the side of a fireplace opening, supporting the mantel-tree. A *chimney-corner*. ▷*inglenook*, or *roofed ingle* is a volume adjacent to the hearth or the stack, usually with seating, and often with a ▷window: it is often a volume with a ceiling lower than that of the room adjacent. A *chimney-*▷*crane* is a pivoted metal arm from which pots are hung over a fire. A *chimney-cricket* is a small roof built over the main roof behind a chimney to help to stop water penetration. A *chimney-crook* or *-hook* is an adjustable chimney-crane with a hook for pots. A *chimney-*▷*head* is the top of a chimney. A *chimney-*▷*hood* is a metal or other

hood above a fireplace which helps to draw the smoke upwards. A *chimney-piece*, also called the *mantelpiece*, is the decorative architectural surround of a fireplace, usually with a ▷shelf over. A *chimney-pot* or *-can* is a square or cylindrical pipe of ▷brick, metal, or burnt clay on top of a stack to increase the draught from the flues. A *chimney-*▷*shaft* is a *stack* with one flue only. The *chimney-*▷*throat* or *-waist* is the narrowest part of the flue between the gathering and the flue proper, where the damper is placed. A *chimney-wing* is a side or cheek of the gathering above a fireplace which helps to contract the jamb towards the throat.

Chinbeak A moulding (▷mould) with a convex and concave section, with or without a ▷fillet between, like an ▷ogee.

Chinese [74], [75] Chinese-▷fret or ▷-lattice was used on balustrades (▷baluster), railings (▷rail), ▷gates, and ▷furniture during the fashion for *Chinoiserie* in the eighteenth and early nineteenth centuries. It is composed of square-sectioned wood arranged in squares and rectangles vertically and diagonally. *Chinoiserie* was a style of ▷architecture and decoration that evoked Cathay. It first appeared in the seventeenth, but reached its finest flowering in the eighteenth century. Furniture and decorations in the Chinese taste rivalled the ▷Rococo style for delicacy and ingenuity. ▷Pagodas, tea-houses, ▷bridges, and ▷pavilions were erected in the Chinese style, but it was never regarded as a serious architectural style.

Chip carving A simple method of ▷ornamenting woodwork with a chisel or gouge. It results in indentations forming geometrical patterns, frequently circular.

Chi-Rho ▷Chrismon.

[74] CHINESE FRET (CHINOISERIE) The drawing shows all the characteristics of the fret. There are variations, but these all consist of simple square bars forming rigid patterns, often with diagonals.(*JSC*)

[75] CHINOISERIE The pagoda in the Chinese style at Kew Gardens by Sir William Chambers of 1763. (*JSC*)

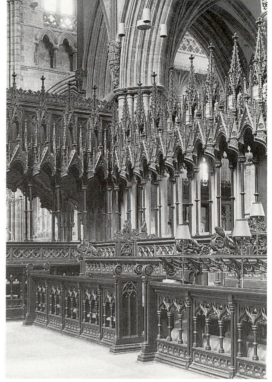

[76] CHOIR-STALLS Exeter Cathedral choir-stalls, originally dating from 1309–10, these are now the work of Sir George Gilbert Scott of the 1870s, in the Second-Pointed style. (*JSC*)

Chiselled work The finish given to the surface of stones by means of a chisel. A *chisel-drafted ▷margin* is a margin made by chiselling around a stone ▷face so that a ▷frame of fine lines is formed around the main face.

Choir, quire Strictly speaking, it is that part of a ▷church with ▷stalls for singers, but it has come to mean the entire space, including the ▷choir and ▷presbytery, used for the performance of services. In cruciform churches it is therefore the eastern limb. It is the part of the church east of the ▷nave reserved for singers and clergy. A *choir-▷aisle* is one parallel to the choir, often continuing behind the ▷high altar to form an ▷*ambulatory*. A *choir-▷loft* is a ▷balcony in the choir. A *choir-▷rail* is one separating the choir from the nave. A *choir-▷screen* or *-enclosure* is a screen-wall or ▷partition dividing the choir and presbytery from the side aisles, and also means the screen between the chancel (or choir) and the nave. A *choir-stall* (▷[76]) is an elevated seat in the choir of a church: it is fixed, enclosed wholly or partially at the backs and sides, and forms part of a range of choir-stalls which, in ▷cathedrals, was enclosed at the back with ▷panelling (often set against stone walls), surmounted by overhanging ▷canopies of ▷open-work, and formed part of serried rows. The open canopies were enriched with ▷pinnacles, ▷crockets, ▷tracery, and other ▷ornament. The choir-stall seats, if hinged, frequently had carvings on the underside (▷misericord). A *choir-▷wall* is a wall between ▷piers and under an ▷arcade separating the choir from the choir-aisles.

Choragic monument A commemorative structure in Ancient Greece erected by the winner of a competition featuring choral dances in Dionysian festivals. The ▷monuments (of which the most celebrated are those of Lysicrates and Thrasyllus) supported the ▷bronze ▷tripod given as the prize. A *choragium* was the space behind the ▷stage of an ▷Antique ▷theatre where rehearsals took place. A *choraula* was a rehearsal-room in a ▷church for a choir.

Chord The ▷span of an ▷arch. The main member of a ▷truss spanning from one side to the other, or the line between two points on a curve.

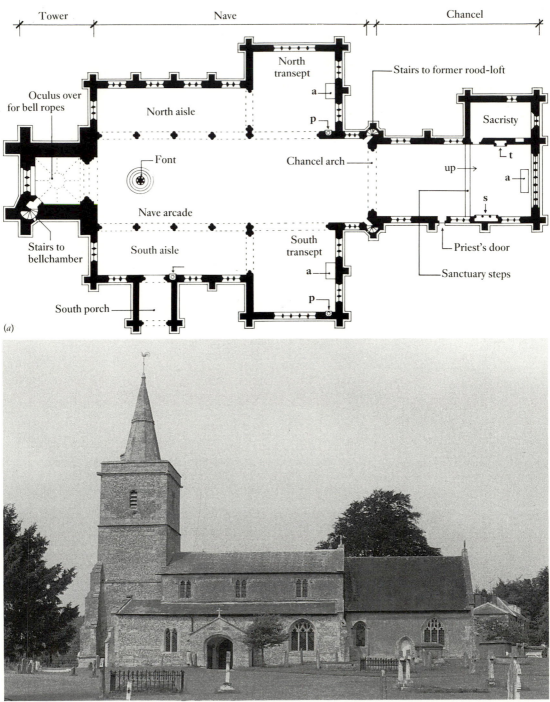

North transept

a

p

Stairs to former rood-loft

Sacristy

t

Oculus over for bell ropes

North aisle

Font

Chancel arch

up →

a

Stairs to bellchamber

Nave arcade

s

South aisle

South transept

a

p

Priest's door

Sanctuary steps

South porch

(a)

(b)

[77] CHURCH (a) Plan of the Parish Church of St Andrew, Heckington, Lincolnshire. **a** site of altar, **p** piscina, **s** sedilia, **t** tomb recess. (*JJS*) (b) All Saints' Church, Fittleton, Wiltshire. This is a typical mediaeval parish church, built of flint and stone dressings, with a fourteenth-century, three-stage west tower, and short spire set behind a parapet. The other parts of the church are clearly shown. There is a clerestoreyed nave with lean-to south aisle, south porch, and chancel. (*JSC*)

82

Chrismatory A recess like a ▷piscina near the site of a ▷font which contained *chrism*, or holy oil.

Chrismon A ▷symbol composed, of the first two ▷Greek letters of the Greek word for Christ, the *Chi* and the *Rho* (X and P), also known as a *Christogram*, arranged as ☧. Christian symbols include the Greek letters *Alpha* and *Omega* (the Beginning and the End); INRI (*Iesus Nazarenus Rex Iudaeorum*; IHS, variously explained as an abbreviation of *Iesus Hominum Salvator, In Hoc Signo*, and *In Hac Salus*; and the ▷fish, which is a symbol of baptism as it cannot live without water (▷symbol).

Christian door A ▷door in which the central frame forms a ▷cross.

Chryselephantine Made of gold and ivory, or coloured to resemble ivory, with ▷gold ▷leaf.

Church [77] A building for public Christian worship. In its simplest form it consists of an area for the congregation known as the ▷nave, and a smaller part (usually divided from the nave by an ▷arch) known as the ▷chancel. More elaborate churches have ▷aisles, ▷transepts, and ▷chapels (▷abbey, ▷aisle, ▷cathedral, ▷chancel, ▷chapel, ▷choir, ▷nave, ▷sanctuary, ▷tabernacle, etc.). A *church stile* is a ▷pulpit. A *churchyard* is land adjacent to the church used for burial, and consecrated for that purpose: historically it was regarded as part of the church, and burial in it was continuous, bones being disinterred and placed in ▷charnel-houses to make way for new burials. A *churchyard cross* was a stone ▷cross on a ▷shaft set on a ▷base (usually of steps) as a sign of consecration.

Churrigueresque A lavish eighteenth-century Spanish ▷Baroque style of ▷ornament found in Spain and Latin America, involving the contortion of ▷Classical ▷motifs almost beyond recognition.

Chymol A ▷hinge. Also ▷*gemel, gimmer, jimmer*, meaning two elements constituting a pair, such as paired ▷columns or the twin flaps of a hinge.

Ciborium A permanent domed ▷canopy over a ▷high altar or similar. The term comes from the lidded vessel in which the ▷Sacrament was preserved: this was suspended from a canopy carried on four ▷columns over the ▷altar, so the canopy itself is called the *ciborium*, as is the lidded vessel standing on the altar.

Ciele A ▷canopy.

Cilery Drapes or ▷foliage carved on a ▷capital.

Cill, sill, sole, sule The horizontal piece of timber, stone, or metal forming the bottom of a ▷window-opening, doorway (▷door), or other ▷aperture, usually and properly designed to throw off water.

Cimbia A ▷fillet, ▷string-▷course, or ▷cornice, more usually applied to a ▷fillet around the ▷shaft of a ▷column.

Cimborio A ▷cupola or ▷lantern over a ▷high altar, or any raised lantern over a ▷roof through which light is admitted.

Cincture A ring at the top or bottom of a ▷column that divides the ▷shaft from the ▷capital or ▷base. Also a ▷fillet round a ▷post. It is also called a ▷*girdle*.

Cinerarium A depository for ▷chests or ▷urns containing cremated remains. A *cinerarium lid* was a type of ▷capping for ▷gate-▷posts, funerary ▷monuments, and ▷parapet ▷ornament during the ▷Neoclassical period.

Cinquecento ▷Italian ▷High Renaissance art and ▷architecture dating from the sixteenth century. A nineteenth-century ▷revival of the style.

Cinquefoil An ▷ornamental ▷foliation in ▷tracery or ▷panels in the ▷Gothic style arranged so that the intervals between them resemble five ▷petals or ▷leaves. A *cinquefoil* ▷arch is one with five foliations on the *intrados*.

Cippus A small low ▷column, often with no ▷base or ▷capital, and frequently bearing an ▷inscription. It was used for milestones, markers, and funerary ▷monuments.

Circle An arrangement of stones, such as at Avebury or Stonehenge. A *circle-on-circle* ▷*face* is a face in ▷joinery or ▷masonry worked to a convex hemispherical shape, while *circle-on-circle sunk face* has a concave outline on plan and ▷section. A *circular* ▷*stair* is a ▷spiral stair or a cylindrical staircase.

Circumvallate To surround with a ▷wall or ▷ramparts.

Circumvolution A turn in the spiral of a ▷volute.

Circus A long, narrow building with a central barrier, curved ends, and tiered seating, used by the Romans for chariot races. Also a group of buildings around a circular space, as in Bath or at Oxford Circus.

Cist A ▷tomb-▷chamber consisting of stone ▷slabs on end with a covering slab, like a box, and covered with a mound.

Cistercian A strict monastic order adhering to the rule of St Benedict: ▷monastery buildings were austere, and the monks wore white habits. The greatest Cistercian monasteries in England were Rievaulx, Furness, and Fountains. ▷Abbey.

Cistern A ▷reservoir or tank for water. A dungeon.

Citadel A fortress situated in a fortified town or city, or near them.

Civery Also *severy* (▷severey). A *ciborium*, or a ▷bay in a ▷vaulted ceiling, or other ▷domed or ▷vaulted structure.

Civic crown, civic wreath A ▷garland of ▷acorns and ▷oak ▷leaves used in architectural ▷ornament.

Cladding An external ▷face or skin of a building. Rough beading or *cleading*.

Claircolle Also *clairecolle* or *clearcole*, it is a primer of ▷glue, water, and white lead, or a clear coating for the application of ▷gold ▷leaf.

Clamp In brick-making, a clamp was a large mass of green ▷bricks stacked with intermediate layers of breeze on a ▷foundation of old bricks, and preceded ▷kiln-burning. Clamp-fired bricks are not uniformly burnt and so have interesting varieties of colour.

Clapboard An external facing of overlapping timber ▷boards, with the grain horizontal, and the boards thicker at the lower edge than the top. Also called ▷*bevel-siding* or ▷*lap-siding*.

Clapper bridge A ▷bridge of stone formed of ▷piers with ▷slabs bridging across them.

Clasp nail A ▷nail with a wedge shape cut from a sheet, also called a *cut nail*, with a sheared blunt point.

Clasping buttress ▷Buttress.

Classical The term is applied to ▷architecture, ▷enrichment, and ▷motifs based on the precedents of Graeco-Roman ▷Antiquity. During the ▷Renaissance period, theories of architecture were evolved based on the treatises of Vitruvius which had been rediscovered in the fifteenth century, and the Renaissance theorists elaborated these, especially in regard to the canonical nature of the ▷Orders. In the eighteenth century, a scholarly return to ▷Antique principles was led by William Kent, Lord Burlington, and Colen Campbell, who revered the works of Palladio and Inigo Jones: this movement was known as ▷*Palladianism*

and dominated significant architecture for most of the century. Palladianism, in a sense, was a purifying of style after the 'excesses' of ▷Baroque, although Baroque architecture is firmly rooted in the Classical language of architecture, and indeed there were ▷Roman parallels with Baroque during the Empire, notably in the second century of our era. Studies of the buildings of Antiquity, especially those of Rome, Greece, Spalato, Palmyra, Herculaneum, and Pompeii, led to the *Neoclassical* (▷Neoclassicism) movement, of which the ▷Greek ▷Revival was an important element. Neoclassicism, in short, sought to recapture the full vocabulary of Antiquity, based not on 'corrupt' Renaissance precedent, but on originals, and ultimately led to a synthesis of Graeco-Roman and ▷Egyptian elements, with a strong dash of stereometrically pure forms. By the middle of the nineteenth century the purity of Classical sources was again obscured, and taste moved towards Renaissance opulence until by the end of the century there was a full-blown Baroque Revival which, as before, gave way to a twentieth-century Neoclassical Revival that sought a severe, stripped language, free of excess (▷the various Classical Orders).

Clathri A ▷lattice of ▷bars, arranged in a pattern, as a grating for a ▷window.

Claustra Geometrical pattern on early ▷reinforced-concrete work.

Clausura Part of a ▷monastery not open to the public. *Claustral* means pertaining to a ▷cloister or a monastery.

Clavel, clavis, clavy A keystone or a ▷mantelpiece.

Clavicula A quarter-circle ▷rampart preventing direct entry to a ▷Roman town or camp.

Claw A mason's chisel with a serrated end to work across furrows and prevent the formation of holes. A *claw* was also used as a foot for ▷Antique furniture. ▷Ball-and-claw feet are common features of ▷Classical, ▷Renaissance, ▷Baroque, and ▷Neoclassical design.

Cleam To ▷glue.

Clean Wrought timber, or timber free from ▷knots.

Cleat A small ▷block or strip fixed so as to support a member in place, such as a ▷shelf.

Cleithral As *clithral*, meaning with a ▷roof forming a complete covering of a ▷Greek ▷temple, distinguished from ▷hypaethral, meaning one open, or partly open, to the sky.

Clepsydra A water-clock.

Clerestorey Also *clearstory*, *clearstorey*, or *clerestory*. Any ▷window, row of windows, or openings in the upper part of a building. Also known as an ▷*overstorey*, it is usually applied to the upper part of the ▷nave, ▷choir, or ▷transepts of a ▷church in which windows are formed in the ▷walls above the ▷arcades and above the ▷lean-to ▷roofs of the ▷aisles (▷[134]).

Cling To shrink.

Clink A ▷gaol or a ▷welt.

Clipeus An ▷ornamental disc (or *clypeus*) like a ▷shield suspended in the ▷intercolumniations of the ▷atria of ▷Roman houses, or fixed to the ▷frieze. Also a metal stopper at the top of the ▷*caldarium* of a ▷Roman ▷bath to allow hot air and vapour to escape.

Clipped gable A hipped ▷gable.

Clipsham A Jurassic limestone (▷lime) from Rutland of the Lower Oölitic series, pale cream in colour but with a tendency to blue patches.

Cloaca A large ▷conduit or ▷sewer in ▷Antiquity.

Clochan A beehive-shaped dwelling constructed of ▷corbelled pseudo-▷vaults.

Clocharium, clochier A ▷bell-▷tower or ▷*campanile*.

Clock-jack A figure on a clock-▷tower which strikes a ▷bell on the hour.

Cloisonné A geometrical pattern of surface decoration in which coloured ▷bricks ▷frame stone ▷blocks. ▷Polychrome decoration with the colour in the materials used. Also decoration involving coloured ▷enamels separated by ▷fillets.

Cloister [78] A covered ▷ambulatory forming part of a monastic or collegiate establishment, arranged around three or four sides of a quadrangular ▷area known as a ▷*garth*. The ambulatory was roofed, sometimes with timber as at New College, Oxford, and sometimes with stone vaulting as at Norwich. The ▷arches which admitted light from the garth often had fine ▷tracery, and sometimes were glazed or partially glazed. Cloisters gave covered access to several buildings or ▷apartments. They often contained carrels or places for study, and frequently had lavatories or places to wash. There were benches and ▷niches, and often ▷memorials, for cloisters were sometimes used for sepulture (as in the *Campo Santo* in Pisa). The ▷*sides* of the cloister were its ▷*panes* (▷[2], [66]). A *cloistered* ▷arch or ▷vault is a *coved vault*.

[78] CLOISTER The cloisters at Wells Cathedral, rebuilt in the fifteenth century. Note the springing of the vaults, like fans, that become lierne-vaults with bosses. Note the elegant tracery. (*JSC*)

Close An enclosed ▷area, especially that around a great ▷church or ▷cathedral. A narrow lane or ▷passage leading from a street. A *close-end* is the stopped end of an ▷eaves ▷gutter. For *close-▷string*, see ▷stair. A *closed ▷cornice* is a ▷*box-cornice*, or one built up of ▷boards and mouldings (▷mould), and hollow: it is also a wooden cornice with no ▷soffite, but with a ▷frieze-▷board and a crowning moulding. *Closed eaves* are those in which the ▷rafters, etc. are concealed. A *closed* ▷newel is the solid ▷wall built through the shaft of a stair. For *closer*, ▷brick. A *closing* ▷ring is one fixed to a ▷door by which it is pulled shut.

Closet A small room to communicate with a ▷chamber.

Clour Hack- or ▷hammer-▷dressed stonework.

Cloven foot A ▷*hoof-foot* or ▷*pied-de-biche* of a goat or ▷ram used to terminate the legs of ▷Antique and ▷Neoclassical ▷furniture, often associated with ram- or goat-heads or ▷satyr masks at the tops of the ▷cabriole legs.

Club An ▷attribute of Hercules, and used with schemes of ▷military decoration. Also a building reserved for the members with similar interests, such as the Reform Club or Travellers' Club.

Club skew A ▷springer or ▷spur-stone.

Clunch Hard chalk. It weathers badly, and has to be protected by means of wide overhanging ▷roofs and/or skins of ▷lime-wash applied regularly.

Cluniac The Cluniac monastic order developed the double ▷transept, so this arrangement is known as a *Cluniac transept.*

Clustered column [31] Several ▷columns or ▷shafts grouped together and connected so that together they act as one vertical support (▷banding (band of a shaft)). A *clustered* ▷*pier* has a massive central core to which various separate shafts are attached by means of *bands of a shaft*, and not to be confused with the ▷*bundle pier.*

Coade stone Artificial cast stone made from ball-clay, water, grog (pre-fired clay ▷stoneware ground to powder), crushed ▷flint, fine sand, and crushed soda-lime-silica ▷glass, fired at 1100–1150°C, which has a ▷vitrified nature, and was very hard and resistant to weathering. It was called by Mrs Coade *Lithodipyra* (stone twice-fired), which accounted for why the shrinkage was very small, and why the material looked very like a fine real stone. It was used from the second half of the eighteenth century for decorative keystones, ▷quoins, statuary, and architectural ▷ornament.

Coakel A *cockle* or ▷*spiral stair.*

Coaming A ▷frame round an opening in a ▷roof and raised to stop water penetration.

Coarse stuff Lime and sand ▷mortar used for first and second coats of ▷plaster. It hardens slowly, so is often ▷gauged with ▷gypsum ▷plaster or ▷cement.

Coat of arms ▷Heraldic insignia developed from the *surcoat* worn over armour for identification purposes. The coat of arms refers to what is borne on the ▷shield, but nowadays seems to include the ▷helmet above it and the crest (▷cress) over the ▷helmet.

Coatwork A covering, such as a thatched ▷roof, or a finish.

Cob A mix of straw, gravel, and clay used for making *cob* ▷*walls*. The mixture is prepared by the addition of water and kneaded to a glue-like consistency. Cob walls are raised layer by layer without the use of ▷form-work, and must not be confused with either ▷*adobe* or ▷*pisé de terre.*

Cochlea A tower for a ▷spiral staircase or the ▷stair

itself. *Cochleated* means helically twisted, as in such a stair.

Cock bead One not ▷flush with the adjoining surface, but raised, used for edging drawers or ▷panels. Several *cock beads* laid parallel to each other resemble reeding (▷reed). A cock in ▷Classical ▷ornament is associated with the chariot of ▷Mercury, with dawn, the rising sun, ▷Apollo, and ▷Louis XIV, and it is an ▷emblem of the denial of Christ by St Peter. It is also an emblem of the ▷French Revolution and of ▷Liberty.

Cockatrice A ▷basilisk.

Cocking ▷Caulking. Also the ▷mortising of a ▷wall-plate and the underside of a ▷beam so that the latter drops into the wall-plate. Also known as or *cogging* or *corking.* ▷Hinges fixed so that the ▷door rises when it opens are said to be cocked. A *cocking-piece* is a ▷board nailed to a ▷rafter at the ▷eaves to give the ▷roof a flatter slope, also known as a ▷*sprocket-piece.*

Cockle Something that winds, like a ▷spiral stair.

Cockloft A ▷garret over the highest part of the ceiling.

Coctilis *Coctile*, or burnt, as opposed to hardening in the sun, as with ▷bricks. Also *coctus.*

Coddings The ▷base or footings for ▷chimneys. ▷Pad-stones or ▷templates.

Coelanaglyphic Carving in ▷relief where no part of the ▷sculpture projects in front of the plane in which it is set.

Coffer A ▷chest. A sunken ▷panel in a ceiling or ▷dome. A ▷*caisson* or *lacunar* (▷lacuna). Coffering is the formation of recessed ▷ornamental ▷panels in a ceiling. To say that something is coffered means it is ornamented with sunken panels. A *coffer-*▷*dam* is a watertight piled dam constructed enable ▷piers or ▷walls to be built in water.

Coffin A ▷chest or ▷coffer to enclose a dead body. In the mediaeval period coffins of the wealthy were often of stone, with shaped and carved lids that sometimes formed part of the ▷floor of a ▷church. The body of the coffin had a circular cavity to receive the head, and there were holes in the bottom to allow liquids to drain off. ▷Lead coffins were also common, especially when burial took place in churches or in ▷vaults. A stone coffin is often called a ▷*sarcophagus* (*flesh-eater*), but most coffins were of plain wood, often elm. The subject of coffin-▷furniture is vast, and beyond the scope of this book (▷Charnel-house). A *coffin-end* is a type of ▷finial resembling a coffin-shape.

[79] COIN MOULDING (*JSC*)

Cogging Cocking.

Coign, coillon, coin, coyning ▷Quoin.

Coin moulding [79] Also called a ▷*money-pattern*, it is a repeating pattern of overlapping discs used horizontally and vertically resembling ▷guilloche or ▷scale-patterns.

Colarin, Colarino Collarino.

Coliseum, colosseum A large ▷Roman amphitheatre, but especially the huge Flavian structure in Rome. Any large sports ▷arena, open or roofed, or a large ▷theatre or ▷music-hall.

Collar A horizontal ▷tie connecting a pair of ▷rafters at any point below the ▷ridge and above the ▷wall-▷plate. Also *collar-*▷*beam*, ▷*span-piece*, ▷*spar-piece*, ▷*top-beam*, or ▷*wind-beam*. A *collar-beam* ▷*roof* or *collar-roof* is one constructed thus. A *collar-*▷*brace* is a structural member which strengthens a roof ▷truss, also known as an *arch-brace* (▷[212]). A *collar* ▷*purlin*, more correctly known as *collar* ▷*plate*, is a horizontal timber above a ▷crown-▷post that ties together the collars of the trusses.

Collarino The cylindrical part of the ▷capital of the ▷Tuscan and ▷Roman ▷Doric Orders which lies between the ▷annulets under the ▷ovolo and the ▷astragal, also called the ▷*neck* or ▷*hypotrachelium* (▷[106]). Also the astragal itself.

College In origin, a self-governing, self-recruiting, property-owning corporation, it is today generally associated with establishments for education in the higher branches of learning. The traditional college in England consists of one or more ▷quadrangles around which the rooms are disposed. It will contain a ▷library, a ▷chapel, a ▷refectory, ▷common-rooms, ▷kitchens, etc. *Collegiate* ▷*Gothic* a secular version of Gothic, like that found in Oxford and Cambridge colleges, occurring in nineteenth-century institutional buildings such as ▷schools, often with a pronounced ▷Tudor flavour.

Colliciae, colliquiae ▷Tile ▷gutters under the ▷eaves of ▷Roman houses to carry water to the ▷*impluvium*.

Colluviarium A ventilator in an ▷aqueduct.

Collyweston A fissile limestone (▷lime) used for stone ▷slating from the area around Collyweston on the Northamptonshire–Rutland border.

Colombage ▷Timber-framed construction.

Colonial A style of ▷architecture that developed in the colonies. American Colonial is a type of ▷Queen Anne or ▷Georgian ▷architecture, often quite distinct from the native British variety. ▷Dutch Colonial (as in South Africa) and Spanish Colonial (as in Latin America) were equally distinctive, and virtually became separate styles. *Colonial casing* is a decorative ▷trim-moulding. *Colonial* ▷*Revival* was a type of twentieth-century version of American Colonial architecture used by Lutyens at Hampstead Garden Suburb, and by Louis de Soissons at Welwyn Garden City. *Colonial siding* is ▷weatherboarding the same thickness, laid with overlaps, and with a ▷roll moulding on the bottom edge. A *colonia* or *colonica* was a ▷Roman farmhouse or farm.

Colonnade [80] A row of ▷columns with ▷entablature. If four, the range is called *tetrastyle*; if six, *hexastyle*; if eight, *octastyle*; if ten, *decastyle*, etc. When a colonnade stands before a building it is called a ▷*portico*, and if it surrounds a building it is called a *peristyle*. Colonnades are further described in terms of the spaces between columns: ▷*intercolumniation* is the distance between columns measured from the lower parts of the ▷shafts in multiples of the diameter of a column. The main types of intercolumniation as defined by Vitruvius are: *pycnostyle*, where columns are one-and-a-half diameters apart; *systyle* where they are two diameters apart; *eustyle* where they are two-and-a-quarter diameters apart; *distyle* where they are three diameters apart; and *araeostyle* where they are greater than three diameters apart (up to a maximum of five), the latter only used with the ▷Tuscan Order, but occasionally is found in ▷Hellenistic ▷architecture where the taste for wider spacing to enhance lightness and elegance developed.

In ▷Classical architecture, two columns between ▷*antae* would be described as *distyle in antis*; a front portico of four columns standing before the antae is *prostyle tetrastyle*; and a building with four columns standing before the antae at the front and rear is described as *amphiprostyle tetrastyle*. A circular building with columns all round it is *peripteral circular*, while the term *peripteral octastyle* means a rectangular building surrounded by columns, with eight at each end forming porticoes. *Pseudo-peripteral* means that columns are joined (▷engaged) to the ▷walls and are not free-standing. To say that a colonnade is ▷*dipteral* means that there are double rows of columns, so *dipteral octastyle* means a building surrounded by two rows of columns, with two porticoes of sixteen columns at each end, eight columns wide (▷[234]).

Colonnette A small ▷column, or a thin circular ▷shaft giving a vertical emphasis, or an element in a ▷clustered or ▷compound ▷pier.

Colossal Order An ▷Order where the ▷columns or ▷pilasters rise from the ground or ▷plinth more than one ▷storey, also known as a ▷*Giant Order.*

Columbarium A ▷dovecote, or building with holes or ▷niches on the inside of the ▷walls, such as a structure for the storage of ▷urns or ash-chests containing cremated remains, called a *columbarium* from its resemblance to the niches for pigeons or doves. A ▷putlog hole.

Columbeion A ▷fountain in the ▷atrium of a ▷basilica.

Columbethra A ▷piscina. A pool in a ▷baptistry.

Columella As ▷colonnette. *Columellae* are ▷balusters.

Columen The ▷ridge-▷beam, or *culmen*, of a ▷gabled ▷roof resting in front on the ▷tympanum of the primitive ▷Tuscan Order. It was therefore supported on a ▷wall or on other timbers resting on the ▷*trabes compactiles* or ▷architraves supported on the widely spaced ▷columns, and was ▷cantilevered out over the line of the ▷colonnade to the same ▷projection as the *mutuli*, or secondary beams. The ▷rafters, or *cantherii*, were supported on the columen and on the mutuli at the sides, producing a very deep ▷pedimented space with over-hanging roof at the ends.

Column An upright, usually circular on plan, but also polygonal or square, supporting a ▷lintel. A structural member in compression, supporting a load acting near the direction of its main ▷axis. It consists of a ▷base, ▷shaft, and ▷capital, except the ▷Greek ▷Doric ▷Order, which has no base. It must not be confused with a ▷pier, which is more massive, and must never be described as a ▷pillar. *Columniation* means an arrangement of columns (▷annular, ▷barley-sugar, ▷bundle, ▷carolitic, ▷cippus, ▷clustered, ▷colonnade, ▷engaged, ▷grouped, ▷intercolumniation, ▷Orders). A *columna bellica* was a short column in the ▷Roman ▷forum from which the consul declared war by hurling a spear towards the territory of the enemy. A *columna caelata* had a decorated shaft. A *columna cochlis* had a ▷spiral staircase inside it, and the spiral form was echoed on the outside as a continuous ▷sculpture, as on Trajan's column. A

columna rostrata (▷[81]) or *rostral column*, was one set on a ▷pedestal and decorated with the ▷bows of warships to celebrate naval victories: it was a Roman form, and was revived in seventeenth- and eighteenth-century decoration. A *column baseplate* is a horizontal ▷plate under a column which distributes the load.

Combing A method of suggesting wood grain or ▷marble by manipulating a wet coat of paint over a ▷ground by means of combs or brushes. The process is also known as ▷*graining* or ▷*feathering.*

Comedy ▷Masks of ▷Comedy and ▷Tragedy are ▷emblems of drama, and occur in the ▷ornament of ▷theatres and concert-halls.

Comitium An assembly building.

Commissure A joint between ▷ashlars, doors, etc.

Commode step One at the foot of a flight of ▷stairs with curved ends projecting beyond the ▷string and sweeping back around the ▷newel.

Common A term used to imply the usual or the communal. *Common* ▷*ashlar* is pick- or hammer-dressed stone; *common* ▷*bond*, also called ▷*American bond*, is one where every fifth or sixth ▷course consists of headers (▷brick); a *common-house* is a room in a ▷monastery where there was always a fire in winter – it was also called the *common-room*, and was the prototype of the university common-room; a *common* ▷*joist* is one in a ▷floor which runs uninterrupted by openings for staircases from ▷wall to wall to which boards are fixed; a *common* ▷*rafter* is one to which boards or ▷laths for ▷roofs are fixed, is at right-angles to the wall-▷plate, and extends from that plate to the ▷ridge-piece (▷[212]); a *common roof* is one consisting of common rafters only, sometimes bridging over ▷purlins; a *common round* is a ▷*roll moulding* (▷mould).

Communion table A wooden ▷table for the bread and wine in Protestant ▷churches, replacing the stone ▷altar.

Compactilis A term meaning fastened together, as ▷*trabes compactiles* or ▷rafters.

Compartment ceiling A ▷panelled or ▷coffered ceiling.

Compass Anything which used circular forms or is associated with a curve in its overall design. A *compass* ▷*brick* is a ▷voussoir; a *compass-headed* ▷*arch* is semi-circular; a *compass* ▷*rafter* is curved on one or both sides; a *compass* ▷*roof* has a ▷ridge in the centre as opposed to

a ▷lean-to or 'flat' roof, and is also one having curved ▷rafters or ▷ties, or where the components of the structure form an arch on the underside; a *compass* ▷*window* is a ▷bay, ▷bow-, or ▷oriel window. *Compasses* or *dividers* are found in schemes of ▷marine decoration and as ▷attributes of Astronomy, Freemasonry, Geometry, and Justice.

Compitum A junction of two or more ▷Roman roads, often associated with ▷altars and ▷shrines to the ▷*lares compitales*, or deities of the crossroads. It was distinct from the *carrefour* (an open space, usually in a town), or a ▷*trivium*, which was only applied to a street-junction in a built-up area.

Compluvium ▷Cavaedium.

Composite Order [82], [83] A ▷Roman ▷Order, mixing features of ▷Ionic and ▷Corinthian Orders. It is the grandest of all the Orders. It resembles the Corinthian Order except that the ▷capitals have Ionic ▷volutes and ▷*echini* instead of the Corinthian *caulicoli* and ▷scrolls.

Composite arch An ▷arch struck from four centres.

Compound For *compound arch*, ▷arch. A *Compound Order* is a ▷Composite Order. A *compound* ▷*pier* is one with several ▷shafts attached to it or clustered about it, also called a ▷*clustered pier*. A *compound* ▷*vault* is any vault other than the simplest type, such as a ▷groined or ▷fan-▷vault.

Concameration An ▷arch or ▷vault. A ▷chamber.

Conch, concha The hemi-▷dome over an ▷apse or a ▷niche, sometimes also applied to a ▷pendentive or even to a whole niche with such a feature over it. A ▷shell is sometimes carved in the hemi-dome.

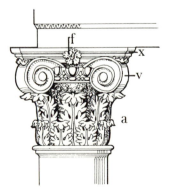

[82] COMPOSITE ORDER Composite capital, showing the mixture of Ionic and Corinthian Orders. f fleuron, x abacus, v volute, a two rows of acanthus leaves. (*JJS*)

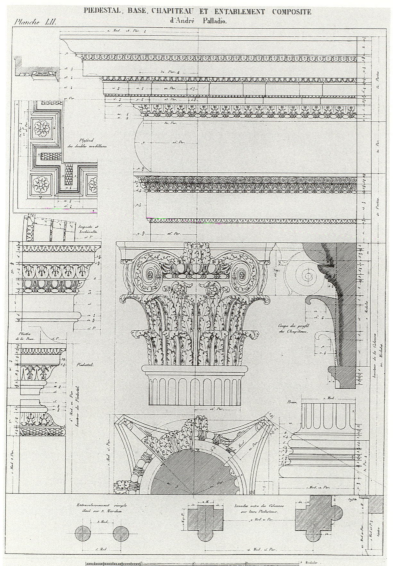

PIEDESTAL, BASE, CHAPITEAU ET ENTABLEMENT COMPOSITE
d'André Palladio.

Planche LII.

[83] COMPOSITE ORDER
Composite Order after Palladio. Note the pulvinated frieze and the treatment of the pedestal. (*Normand*)

Conclavium A rectangular room, usually for meetings or dining.

Concourse A place where several roads meet, or a large space in a building, such as in an air-terminal or railway-station.

Concrete A mixture of water, fine and coarse ▷aggregates (usually sand and stone gravel), and a ▷binder, which is usually ▷Portland ▷cement today. ▷Lime, aggregates, and ▷brick-dust or similar were formerly used. *Structura cementicia, caementicium* and ▷*opus structile* were names for ▷Roman concrete. Broken stones or bricks were laid in ▷courses and each course, when laid, was filled with liquid ▷mortar made from lime and volcanic dust. The Romans used types of concrete in ▷vaults and ▷domes very extensively, often in association with brick or stone reinforcing. The discovery of Portland cement enabled the technology of concrete to develop: concrete is strong in compression, and, reinforced with steel, which is strong in tension, has revolutionized building construction, for the material can be used for ▷beams as well as ▷columns, and for many other functions.

Conditorium An underground ▷vault in which the entire uncremated dead body was placed in the Graeco-Roman world. A *conditory* is any store.

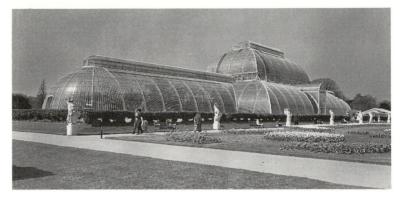

[84] CONSERVATORY The palm-house of 1844–48 at Kew Gardens, a spectacular example of an iron-and-glass structure, by Decimus Burton and Richard Turner. (*A. F. Kersting*)

Conductor A rainwater ▷pipe or a means by which electricity is transmitted, e.g. ▷lightning conductor.

Conduit A ▷reservoir for water. A ▷canal or a ▷pipe. A tube or pipe in which electric cables are laid.

Cone tile A ▷bonnet-hip ▷tile.

Confessio A recess for holding relics, the ▷tomb of a martyr, the ▷altar and the subterranean ▷chamber holding the relics. When a ▷church was specifically erected over a chamber containing such relics, the building was known as *confessio*. A *confessional* is a recess, ▷booth, ▷box, or seat where a priest (concealed from view) sits to hear confession.

Conge The ▷echinus or ▷quarter-round, and the ▷cavetto. The former is the *swelling conge* and the latter is the *hollow conge*. *Congé* is an ▷apophyge, that is with an outward swelling formed of a ▷cove terminating in a ▷fillet, usually formed at the junction of a ▷wall and ▷floor, also called a *sanitary shoe*.

Congelated Rustication (▷rustic) resembling icicles found on ▷fountains and ▷grottoes.

Conical vault A ▷vault shaped like half a cone on its side.

Conservation The technique and means by which a building is retained, properly avoiding drastic changes to its character or architectural detail.

Conservatory [84] A building for conserving plants, a grander version of a ▷greenhouse. The finest conservatories date from the nineteenth century when iron-and-glass construction reached its zenith in terms of invention and elegance. Conservatories are heated and kept humid by large tanks of water. The word is also

given to establishments where music and drama are taught, practised, and perfected.

Consistory, consistorium The meeting-place of the College of Cardinals, where an ecclesiastical court sits, or where a privy council met in ▷Antiquity.

Console [85] An S-shaped ▷bracket or ▷corbel, ▷ornamented, with a greater height than projection in the vertical position (called also ▷*ancones*, ▷*trusses*, or ▷*crossettes*). Consoles can be placed vertically, with the smaller ▷scroll at the base, and can support a bust or ▷urn, or, if placed on either side of a doorcase, the superimposed ▷cornice. If laid horizontally (the larger scroll nearer the ▷wall or vertical ▷face) it becomes the expression of a ▷cantilever to carry a ▷balcony: such horizontal consoles under cornices are called ▷*modillions*. Consoles also occur as keystones, in which case they are definitely called *acones*. A console is also known as ▷*parotis*. A *console* ▷*table* is one fixed to a wall and carried on consoles.

Constructivism An anti-aesthetic leftist ideology which evolved in the USSR from 1920, and was preached through the Dessall *Bauhaus*. It held that expression of construction using machine-made parts was the basis of architecture.

[85] CONSOLE (*JJS*)

Contignatio, contignation A framework of ▷beams.

Continent From the ▷Renaissance period ▷sculpture of female figures representing the four continents often replaced ▷emblems of the four winds. Europe appears with a bull, the arts and sciences, and ▷symbols of authority and war; Asia features ▷camels, turbans and censers; Africa is accompanied by ▷elephants, ▷cornucopia, scorpion, ▷snake, and ▷lion, with the occasional ▷obelisk or ▷crocodile; and America is a female Red Indian with feathered headdress, alligator, armadillo, and buffalo.

Continuous impost This occurs where the mouldings of a ▷Gothic arch or ▷vault are carried down to the ▷base of a ▷pier without any ▷capital or horizontal mouldings (▷mould) to mark the ▷impost.

Contractura The ▷diminution or tapering of the ▷shaft of a ▷column with its height, usually associated with ▷entasis.

Contramure A ▷wall in front of another wall to strengthen it.

Contrasted arch An ▷ogee.

Contre-imbrication ▷Ornamental pattern achieved by overlapping elements set behind the plane of the surface. In imbrication (▷imbrex) the elements project before the plane, like overlapping ▷tiles.

Convenance Seemliness, fitness, propriety, and decorum in ▷Classical ▷architecture.

Convent An order of religious persons, or the building occupied by such an order. A *conventual* ▷*church* is one attached to a convent.

Conventicle A room used for secret worship, and therefore, by association, a place of Non-conformist worship, or a *conventiculum*.

Coom, comb A sloping ▷soffite or ceiling.

Cop A rising part of ▷battlements, also known as ▷*merlon* (▷[38]).

Copal A natural resin used in ▷varnish to give gloss and hardness. *Copal-varnish* a is a high-gloss variety made with linseed oil and copal.

Cope, coping [86] The covering ▷course of a ▷wall, ▷parapet, or ▷chimney, designed to throw off water, also called ▷*capping*. Coping thinner on one side is called ▷*feather-edged coping*, while that with a ▷ridge is called ▷*saddle-back coping*. It is most effective if it projects

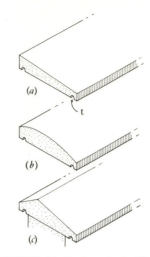

[86] COPE, COPING (*a*) Feather-edged. (*b*) Segmented. (*c*) Saddle-backed. **t** throating or drip. (*JJS*)

beyond the wall-▷face and is cut on the underside with a ▷drip. A ▷*copstone, copestone,* or *coping stone* is any stone forming part of a coping. A *coped* ▷*tomb* is one with a top sloping on either side of a ridge. A *cope* is also the top of a ▷pipe-▷box or ▷stair-▷string, or a timber edge to the top of a sink. A *coped joint* is one where a moulding (▷mould) is fitted over another moulding without a ▷mitre by cutting the first with a ▷profile of the second, also called *scribed* (▷scribing).

Copper A reddish metal, both ductile and malleable, with a high tensile strength, which is a good electrical and thermal conductor. It is widely used for ▷gutters, ▷pipes, ▷flashings, and ▷roofing. When used in exposed positions, as for the covering of ▷domes, it gradually becomes a light green colour. It is also widely used for ▷cramps, ▷nails, etc.

Coquillage Decoration involving ▷shells, or in the form of shells, particularly associated with ▷*rocaille* patterns.

Coquina Porous limestone (▷lime) with a very coarse texture in which shells and shell fragments occur.

Corbeil, corbeille A carved basket with sculptured flowers and fruit. The term is also given to the ▷bell of a ▷Corinthian capital (▷*calathus*) or to the baskets on the heads of ▷*canephorae*.

Corbel [87] A ▷projecting ▷cantilevered ▷block supporting elements over it such as a ▷parapet or a ▷beam, or terminating an ▷arcade (▷[20], [38]). In ▷masonry, corbels can project over each other, anchored back in a ▷wall. For *corbel* ▷*arch*. A *corbel* ▷*course* is any corbelled

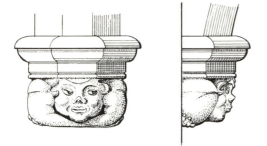

[87] CORBEL From the nave-arcade in the Church of St James, Ewhurst, Sussex. (*JJS*)

corbelled masonry course, such as a ▷string-course. A *corbel, crow* or *corbie* ▷*gable* (▷[88]) is a term for a *crow-stepped gable*; a *corbie-, crow-* or *corbel-*▷*step* is one of the steps in such a gable, and a *crow-stone* is the *top stone*. A *corbel-piece* is the same as ▷*bolster-work*. A *corbel* ▷*table* is a range of corbels carrying a ▷parapet or ▷battlement, running just below the ▷eaves (▷[38]). A *corbel* ▷*vault* is constructed on the same principle as a *corbel arch* (▷arch). *Corbelling* is courses built out over corbels below.

Corbie steps   ▷Corbel.

Cordon   The stone moulding (▷mould) below a ▷parapet. A ▷*string-course* or a ▷*belt-course*.

Corinthian Order [89]   A lavish ▷Order of ▷architecture used by the Greeks and Romans, and the most festive of the ▷Greek Orders, associated with beauty, and first used by Ictinus in the three ▷columns at the south end of the ▷naos of the ▷temple of Apollo Epicurius at Bassae (*c.*429–*c.*400 BC). The distinctive feature is the ▷capital, which is about one-and-one-sixth diameters high, and very ornate, with two rows of ▷acanthus ▷leaves, and *caulicoli* (each of which is

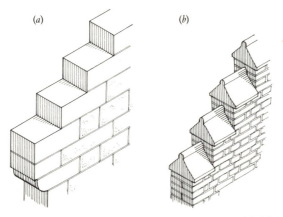

[88] CORBEL, CROW, CORBIE, OR CROW-STEPPED GABLE Examples with plain (*a*) or saddle-backed (*b*) copings. (*JJS*)

surmounted by a ▷calyx from which emerge ▷volutes or ▷helices supporting the ▷abacus and the central foliate ▷ornaments (the ▷fleurons) on each ▷face of the abacus). Originally only the capital differentiated the Corinthian from the ▷Ionic Order, but in ▷Roman work the Corinthian ▷entablature became rich in carved ornament. The ▷architrave, for example, had many decorated mouldings, while the ▷frieze was enriched with acanthus ▷scroll and figured ornament. ▷Cornices had sculptured ▷coffers on the ▷soffites, and elaborate moulded ▷modillions. Much ▷egg-and-dart, ▷bead-and-reel, ▷dentil, and florid decoration was in evidence. ▷Shafts were ▷fluted or plain, but in the Greek version of the Order they were fluted. Abaci have moulded concave faces, meeting at points, or with ▷chamfered 'corners' over the volutes. A simpler form of the capital (and one often used in the late eighteenth century), found at the Tower of the Winds in Athens, has one row of acanthus leaves over which is a row of ▷palm leaves, but with this version the abacus is square on plan. The beautiful Order on the ▷Choragic Monument of Lysicrates has a capital that is taller than most: the flutes terminate in plain leaves, like ▷tongues, above which is a ▷channel that may have been intended for a bronze ▷collar; then there is a row of ▷lotus-like leaves, then a single row of very elegant acanthus leaves between each pair of which is an eight-petalled flower resembling a lotus, and above, the arrangement of volutes differs from the usual pattern, the volutes springing from single acanthus leaves. Instead of the fleuron there is an elegant ▷anthemion. ▷Atrium.

Corkscrew   A ▷spiral stair.

Corncob   A feature used as a ▷finial in nineteenth-century ▷ironwork and ▷furniture, and also occurring in the ▷American Order, a variety of ▷Corinthian incorporating corncobs and tobacco ▷leaves, used by Benjamin Latrobe in the Capitol in Washington DC.

Corner   A *corner-*▷*bead* is one forming the ▷arris of ▷plastered walls, or one terminating the ends of ▷boards in ▷cladding, in which case it is more usually called a *corner-*▷*board*. A *corner-*▷*capital* is an angle-capital. A *corner-*▷*post* is that at the corner of a ▷timber-framed structure. A *corner-stone* is a ▷foundation stone or one forming a corner or ▷angle: *corners* are ▷*quoins* in ▷masonry.

Cornice   A moulded (▷mould) ▷projection crowning an ▷entablature, moulding, ▷pedestal, ▷wall, or opening; it is the top division of an entablature. It is also the ▷ornamental moulding around the top of a wall below the ceiling, also called a *crown moulding*, or the external moulding where the ▷roof meets the wall. A cornice return is the continuation of a cornice in a different direction (▷figures associated with the various Orders).

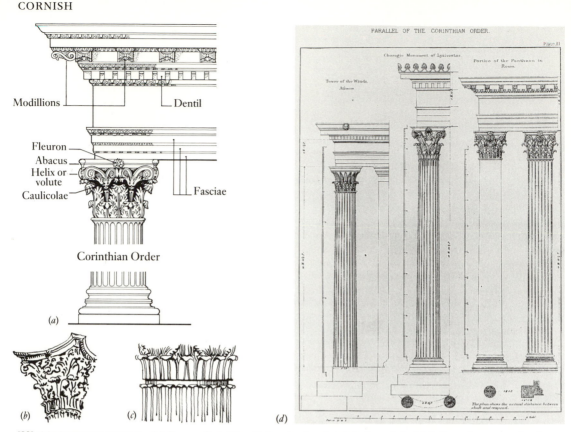

Modillions — ⌐ — Dentil

Fleuron —
Abacus —
Helix or volute —
Caulicolae — — Fasciae

Corinthian Order

(a)

(b)   (c)   (d)

[89] CORINTHIAN ORDER   (*a*) Roman Corinthian Order showing fluted shaft, capital with helices, fleuron on the abacus, and elaborate entablature with modillions. (*JJS*) (*b*) The capital of the Corinthian Order from the Choragic Monument of Lysicrates in Athens. (*JSC*) (*c*) Detail of the Corinthian capital from the Choragic Monument of Lysicrates in Athens. The flutes are unusual in that they terminate in upright leaves, suggesting the *uraeus* frieze of upright cobra heads facing outwards. The foliage above consists of sixteen small lotus leaves over which is a single row of acanthus leaves between which are eight-petalled flowers like the Egyptian lotus. Palmettes were placed in the centre of each convex abacus. The recessed band probably contained a bronze collar. (*JSC*) (*d*) Parallel of the Corinthian Order. On the left is the Order from the Tower of the Winds in Athens, an unusual type with one row of acanthus leaves, a row of palm-like leaves, and a square abacus. Note that the shaft has no base, and note that the *anta* differs

If a cornice occurs on a pedestal it is called the ▷*cap of a pedestal*. An *encased cornice* was one faced with ▷terracotta, which implies an earlier timber model. A *cornicione* is a very large elaborate crowning cornice of an ▷Italian ▷*palazzo*, used by Barry on his Italianate buildings, and usually associated with ▷astylar ▷façades. Vignola invented a type of cornice fusing elements of ▷Doric and ▷Corinthian, in which channelled vertical ▷consoles line up with horizontal Corinthian consoles, with square panels of ▷sculpture between. This massive cornice was used on the Castello Farnese, and was published in his *Regola*.

Cornish   Cornish ▷granite from Bodmin is a muscovite-biotite light greenish-grey in colour and medium grained. Cornish ▷slates are called *Delabole*, and are grey-green in colour.

Cornucopia   A goat's ▷horn overflowing with flowers and fruit, also called a *Horn of Plenty*, and used as an ▷attribute of ▷Ceres, Bacchus, ▷Peace, and ▷Plenty. It is a common ▷ornament in ▷Classical ▷architecture, and with the ▷*caduceus*, adorns commercial buildings such as banks, ▷exchanges, and markets.

Corona   The flat, vertical, square part of a ▷Classical ▷cornice, more usually called the ▷*drip* or ▷*larmier*, situated between the ▷bed mouldings below and the *cymatium* (▷cyma) above, used to shed water from the building, and to protect the ▷frieze. It has a vertical ▷face. In Latin usage the term *corona* seems to have meant the whole cornice, but now it means part of the ▷projecting member (▷[22]). A *corona lucis* is quite different: it is a ▷crown or circlet suspended from a ▷roof of a ▷dome or ▷vault, and carries candles or other

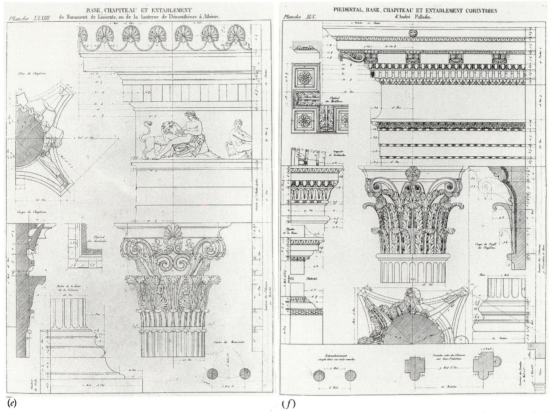

BASE, CHAPITEAU ET ENTABLEMENT
du Monument de Lisicrate, ou de la lanterne de Démosthènes à Athènes.

PIEDESTAL, BASE, CHAPITEAU ET ENTABLEMENT CORINTHIEN
d'André Palladio.

(e)   (f)

from the column. In the centre is the Order from the Choragic Monument of Lysicrates in Athens in which the flutes terminate in leaf-like forms, then there is a small circle of plain leaves, then a row of acanthus, then very tall and elegant helices. Note the antefixae above the entablature. On the right is the Roman Corinthian Order from the Pantheon in Rome with its modillioned cornice. (*Spiers*) (*e*) Greek Corinthian Order from the Choragic Monument of Lysicrates in Athens. The beauty of this capital, with its two distinct rows of differing leaves, its height, and the forms of its flowing helices should be noted. The dentils and antefixae are also shown. The abacus has concave sides. (*Normand*) (*f*) Palladio's version of the Corinthian Order. Note the extreme elaboration of the entablature, with dentils, egg-and-dart, bead-and-reel, etc., and the modillions. Coffers are enriched with rosettes. (*Normand*)

lights. It is a form of chandelier. *Coronarium* is ▷stucco applied to a cornice or other projecting moulding on which decorations could be applied. A *coronet* is a ▷pediment or other ▷embellishment in ▷relief over a ▷window or ▷door, often of limited projection: in an ▷Achievement of ▷Arms the coronet (anciently with an arrangement of ▷*fleurs-de-lys* but now more usually, in British heraldry, decorated with ▷pearls and strawberry leaves), is placed below the crest (▷cress). Coronets are often found decorating the tops of picture-frames and chairs, or set on ▷sarcophagi, as an indication of rank.

Corps de logis The central or main ▷block of a building, as opposed to the ▷wings.

Corpse-gate A lych-gate (▷lich-gate).

Corridor A ▷gallery or ▷passage round a ▷quadrangle, or any ▷passage in a building giving access to rooms.

Corsa A ▷fascia, ▷platband, or square fascia with a height greater than its ▷projection: a plain ▷string-▷course. *Corsae* are the mouldings (▷mould) on a ▷door-▷architrave .

Corsham Down A light cream, fine-grained, free-working limestone (▷lime) from Wiltshire.

Cortile [90] An open courtyard in the centre of a building. A ▷court surrounded by the ▷apartments of a large house, usually with ▷arcades or ▷colonnades, and of several ▷storeys, associated with ▷*palazzi*. Also *cortis*.

[90] CORTILE The central saloon or *cortile* of Barry's Reform Club in London, showing superimposed Orders (Ionic on the lower storey and Corinthian above). In an Italian *palazzo* the top of the *cortile* would be open to the sky, but Barry adapted the form to a London Club, roofing the space in and lighting it from above. (*RCHME BB86/8419*)

Cosmati work ▷Inlaid geometrical decorative patterns of ▷marble, ▷mosaic, and coloured stones, particularly associated with ▷Italian ▷Romanesque design.

Cosse de pois ▷Peapod ▷ornament, mixing ▷Arabesque patterns and floral decoration, with sprays of dots resembling peas.

Cot, cote A small house or other building, such as a ▷dove-cote. A *cottage* is a small house for artisans. A *cottage orné*, also called *ferme ornée*, is a small ▷villa or house in a rural setting, used to ▷ornament parks and to house labourers, or as retreats for the gentry: ▷Picturesque effects were achieved by the use of ▷thatch, fretwork, ▷barge-boards, and rough wooden ▷colonnades formed of tree-trunks, and the type was much favoured at the end of the eighteenth and beginning of the nineteenth centuries.

Cotswold A light brown limestone (▷lime) with traces of blue and cream from Oxfordshire, but found throughout the Cotswolds. Cotswold stone ▷slating is a fissile limestone capable of being split along its natural ▷bed: the best slates came from Stonesfield.

Coulisse, cullis A ▷channel in which a ▷frame or ▷gate slides.

Counter The term suggests opposition, as a counter of a ▷bar or a shop separating customers and staff. A *counter-*▷*apse* is an apse opposite another. A *counter-*▷*arch* is one that counteracts the thrust of another, as in a flying ▷buttress. A *counter-*▷*batten* is one fixed across the ▷backs of several ▷boards to join them, as on drawing-boards, but the term is also used to describe battens parallel to the ▷rafters and nailed over them on a boarded and felted ▷roof so that the slating or tiling battens are then nailed at right-angles to them. Counter-battens allow moisture to run down over the ▷felt. A *counter-change* consists of interlocking patterns of identical shapes, the simplest of which is the ▷chequer-board. A *counter-▷check* is a rebated meeting-▷rail of a ▷folding door. A *counter-▷floor* is the lower of two sets of floor-boards, often laid diagonally, to carry ▷parquet or other finishes. Sometimes when the floor gets worn, boards are fixed at right-angles over them, which may give a false impression of the direction in which the ▷joists run. A *counterfort* is a ▷buttress, ▷spur-▷wall, ▷pier, or other ▷projection to oppose the thrust of a structure. *Counter-imbrication* is as ▷*contre-imbrication*. A *counterlight* is a ▷window opposite another. A *countermure* is a wall behind another, as ▷*contramure*, to strengthen it, or as a second line of defence. A *counterscarp* is an exterior slope of a ditch, or the area between a ▷parapet and the ▷glacis on a fortification. To *countersink* is to make a conical sinking to receive a screw-head. A *countervault* is an inverted ▷arch.

Countess   A size of ▷slate 20 × 10 inches.

Country seat   A rural residence of the landed gentry or aristocracy.

Couple   A ▷rafter. *Couples* signify rafters framed together in pairs with ▷ties above their feet to form triangles, creating a *close-couple*, double-pitched ▷roof: an ordinary *couple-roof* only has rafters carried on the ▷wall-▷plates and pitched together at the ▷ridge, so it is less stable than a close-couple. *Coupled* ▷*columns* are those set as close pairs, either in line with the ▷colonnade or ▷arcade or at right-angles to them. *Coupled*, in this sense, is used to signify pairs, as in ▷pilasters or ▷windows.

Cour d'honneur   A monumental forecourt to a building, usually embraced by ▷colonnades and ▷wings.

Course   A continuous level range of stones or ▷bricks of the same height. *Coursed* ▷*rubble*, for example, is rough stone walling laid in courses, as opposed to *random rubble*. Any continuous layer of material, such as ▷tiles, etc. *Coursed* ▷*masonry* implies rows of ▷blocks the same height, but each row can be of a different height (▷masonry).

Court   An uncovered ▷area before, behind or in the centre of a building, or an open area in densely built-up parts of cities. It is also a building where law is administered, or the residence of royalty. A courtyard is an open area partly or fully enclosed by buildings or ▷walls.

Coussinet, cushion   A ▷block placed on the ▷impost of a ▷pier for receiving the first ▷voussoir of an ▷arch, or that part of an ▷Ionic ▷capital between the ▷abacus and ▷echinus, with ▷volutes.

Cove   A concave ▷corner of a room or a moulding

(▷mould), especially between ▷wall and ceiling: *coving* is that concave moulding. A *cove*, or *coved*, *ceiling* is one with a large concave section around the walls, joining them to a flat or ▷coffered centre. A *coved* ▷*vault*, also known as a ▷*cloistered* ▷*arch* or *vault*, is one formed of four quarter-cylinders joining in a point on a square plan, with ▷diminishing ▷courses ▷corbelled out. A *cove moulding* is any ▷cavetto. *Cove bracketing* is the framing for a cove, as of a coved ceiling. ▷Rood-▷screens often had covings under the rood-▷loft. *Coving* is also the outward curve of an exterior wall, as in *coved* ▷*eaves*, or the ▷jambs of a fireplace narrowing at the ▷back.

Covent   A ▷convent or ▷monastery, as in Covent Garden.

Cover   A *cover-▷fillet* is a moulding (▷mould) or strip covering a joint, also called *cover moulding* or *cover-strip*. A *cover-▷flashing* is flashing overlapping the lead ▷soakers, or lead ▷slates, or the turn-up at the edge of a flat ▷roof.

Cow-nose   A ▷brick with a semicircular end, used for the ▷jambs of ▷walls only half a brick thick.

Cowl   A covering of metal, stone, or pottery, over a ▷chimney.

Coyn   ▷Quoin.

Cradle   A *cradle-▷roof* or ▷*-vault* is the same as a ▷*barrel-vault*. *Cradling* is ▷framing for ceilings or shop-fronts. Any ▷timber framing supporting ▷lath and ▷plaster, or the timber framing erected during the construction of a ▷masonry ▷vault.

Crail work   ▷Ornamental ▷ironwork.

Cramp   Metal bent to fasten stones together. Iron rusts, and so, when used for cramping, has often caused problems, such as staining and splitting, so ▷copper, ▷bronze, or stainless steel cramps are used instead. *Crampets* are cramps, ▷wall-hooks, ▷holdfasts, and ▷gutter-▷brackets.

Crane   A representation of the bird suggesting vigilance, often shown holding a stone in a raised ▷claw. It is frequently found as a ▷motif in *Chinoiserie* decoration (▷Chinese).

Crapaudine   ▷Doors on pivots rather than ▷hinges.

Crease   *Creasing* is a row of ▷tiles ▷corbelled out over ▷walls to throw off rainwater, and held in place with a coping (▷cope). Tile-creasing is also found at the ▷verges of ▷roofs, or at ▷eaves.

Credence A small ▷shelf or ▷table to the ▷side of an ▷altar, where cruets containing wine and water are placed before consecration. The term ▷*prothesis* is also used. The word also signified a buffet-table where food was tasted as a safeguard against poison.

Creeper A ▷brick in a ▷wall adjacent to an ▷arch and cut to conform to the shape of the arch. *Creepers* are also the same as ▷*crockets*.

Crematory, crematorium A place or building where bodies are burnt. Modern crematoria contain a hall, transfer-room, and furnace-room where bodies are consumed in gas-fired or electric furnaces at temperatures around 1000°C. There are ancillary rooms for the grinding of the incinerated bones, the storage of ashes, and various offices.

Cremone, cremorne bolt A locking device for ▷French ▷windows consisting of an ornate rotating handle which moves two ▷rods, one upwards and one downwards, which slide ▷bolts into ▷sockets in the ▷frame. ▷Espagnolette.

Crenel, crenelle A ▷battlement, but more properly the term refers to the ▷embrasures or ▷loopholes. Crenellated mouldings (▷mould) are those which resemble battlements. A crenelle is also called a *kernel*, or the open space between ▷cops or ▷merlons (▷[38]). A *crenelet* is a small embrasure, whether real or decorative, or an ▷arrow-loop. To say something is *crenellated* means it has battlements or is patterned with repeated indentations like battlements.

Crepido A ▷projecting ▷ornament or ▷cornice. A raised ▷base to carry something, or a raised footpath. A *crepidoma* is the stepped ▷platform of a ▷Greek ▷temple, usually of three ▷steps, also called *crepis* or *crepido*. These steps were usually too high to be used as a ▷stair, so ▷ramps or intermediate steps were introduced on main ▷axes for use. The topmost step on which the temple was built is called the ▷*stylobate*.

Crescent [91] Buildings planned on an ▷arc, partial ellipse, or segment. A *crescent arch* is a *horseshoe* ▷*arch*. A crescent is the ▷symbol of the moon, and therefore an ▷attribute of ▷Artemis–Diana–Isis: it appears to have suggested the segmental ▷pediment, unknown in ▷Classical ▷architecture before the first century of our era, and was particularly associated with Isiac ▷temples and ▷shrines in the Graeco-Roman world.

Cress, crest, creste An ▷ornamental finish to a ▷wall, ▷ridge, ▷canopy, or other part of a building. *Crest-*▷*tiles* cover the ▷ridge of a ▷roof, and may be of stone, clay or ▷lead: in ▷Victorian times cast-iron cresting was popular, cheap, and decorative. The term also means a ▷finial. A *crest-*▷*table* is a coping ▷course (▷cope). A *crest* in heraldry is a device fixed to the top of a knight's ▷helmet to identify the wearer. The *coronet* is fixed below the crest .

Cresset stone A ▷block with cup-shaped holes to contain oil or candles for use in the lighting of ▷churches.

Crinkle-crankle A ▷wall that is serpentine on plan, that is, with a plan of continuous elongated S-shaped curves. This form stiffens the wall and removes the necessity for ▷buttresses. Such walls were commonly used as ▷garden walls.

Cripple window A dormer ▷window (▷dormant).

Crocket ▷Projecting hook-shaped ▷knobs of ▷leaves, flowers, or bunches of ▷foliage used in ▷Gothic ▷ornament, and regularly spaced along sloping mouldings (▷mould) such as those on ▷gables, ▷pinnacles, or ▷spires (▷[198]). A ▷*crocket* ▷*arch* is one with ▷foils on the *intrados*. For *crocket capital*, ▷capital.

[91] CRESCENT Royal Crescent, Norland Estate, North Kensington, by Robert Cantwell, 1839. A grand essay in the manner of Nash. (*Royal Borough of Kensington and Chelsea Public Library*)

Crocodile A ▷motif found on ▷Regency ▷furniture and artefacts associated with the ▷Egyptian ▷Revival and Nelson's victory at the Battle of the Nile in 1798. It occurs in representations of Africa, while the alligator is associated with America. *Crocodiling* is the same as ▷*alligatoring.*

Croft ▷Crypt.

Croisée A ▷French ▷window.

Croisette ▷Crossette.

Cromlech Three or more upright stones capped by a large flat stone to form a ▷chamber: it was covered with a mound, and is also known as a ▷*dolmen.*

Crook A ▷post with cross-▷beam and ▷strut.

Crop, crope A bunch of sculptured ▷leaves terminating a ▷spire, ▷finial, or other decorative member, also called a ▷*pommel* (▷finial, ▷pinnacle).

Cross The ▷symbol of Christianity, used often as an architectural ▷ornament to crown ▷gables and to enrich ▷altars. The basic form is a vertical member with a shorter one across it at right-angles. The commonest crosses are the ▷Latin, with the three topmost arms the same length, but the bottom one longer; the ▷*Greek*, with the arms of equal length; the ▷*Saltire* or *X-cross*; and the

Patriarchal, with a smaller secondary cross-beam. Crosses were set up in churchyards to show that the ground was consecrated, and smaller crosses were used to mark ▷graves or boundaries. Large crosses were set up in market-places, often associated with buildings and large decorative crosses were erected to commemorate events, such as those erected after the funeral of Queen Eleanor, of which three fine examples survive (▷[93]). *Consecration crosses*, twelve in number, were painted or carved on the ▷walls of ▷churches to show where the bishop was to anoint them with chrism. Several fine consecration crosses survive in the church of St Mary of Ottery in Devon. A *cross-*▷*aisle* is a ▷transept, a way between ▷pews, or a way parallel to rows of seats connecting with exits. *Cross-banded* means placing ▷veneers on a handrail with the grain running across the length. A *cross-*▷*beam* is one going from wall to wall, one holding walls together, or any transverse beam. For *Calvary Cross*, ▷Calvary. A *cross-church* is a ▷cruciform church. *Cross-cut* is cut at right-angles to the

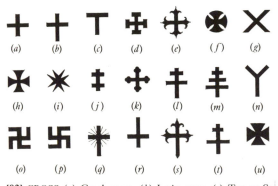

[92] CROSS (*a*) Greek cross. (*b*) Latin cross. (*c*) Tau or St Anthony cross. (*d*) Potent cross. (*e*) Fleury or Fleurée cross. If the centre leaf of each arm is missing, the cross is known as Moline. (*f*) Alisée patée or Pattée cross. (*g*) Saltire or St Andrew cross. (*h*) Patée cross or iron cross (*Eisenkreuz*) of Prussia. (*i*) Maltese cross. (*j*) Double cross. (*k*) Clover-leaf or bottonée cross. (*l*) Patriarchal cross. (*m*) Papal cross. If the bottom arm is set diagonally it is a Russian Orthodox cross. (*n*) Forked cross. (*o*) Fylfot or Swastika. Sometimes the arms are treated as human legs. (*p*) Potent rebated cross or *Hackenkreuz* of National Socialists in Germany (both (*o*) and (*p*) are related to Greek key, fret, or labyrinth, and to the potent cross). (*q*) Glory cross. (*r*) St Peter Cross. (*s*) St James Cross. (*t*) Cross of Lorraine. (*u*) Patée Formée cross. (*JSC*)

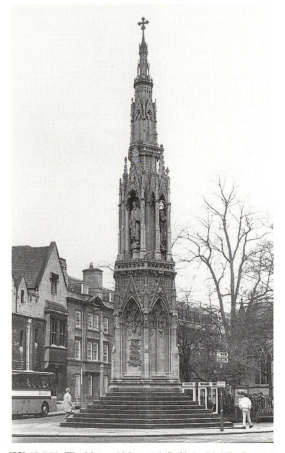

[93] CROSS The Martyrs' Memorial, Oxford, a Middle-Pointed essay by Sir George Gilbert Scott of 1841–43, recalling the precedents of the mediaeval Eleanor crosses. (*JSC*)

grain, and a *cross-cut* saw is one adapted for cutting across the grain. A *cross-▷gable* is one parallel to the main ▷roof-▷ridge. *Cross-▷garnet* is a T-shaped ▷hinge, with the tail fastened to the ▷door and the top of the T fixed to the ▷frame. *Cross-▷quarters* refers to a row of ▷quatrefoil openings with each quatrefoil arranged so that the ▷lobes are arranged diagonally: the effect is like a row of saltires. A *cross-▷rib* is a transverse rib. A *cross-▷springer* is a diagonal ▷arch of a ribbed ▷groin-▷vault. A *cross-tailed hinge* is the same as a cross-garnet or T-hinge. A *cross-vault* is one formed by the intersection of two barrel-vaults (▷vault). A *cross-▷window* is one with the ▷mullion and ▷transome forming a cross (▷[63]).

Crossette A ▷projection, known as ▷*console, crosette, crossette,* or ▷*truss* at the junctions of ▷jambs and ▷lintels, on the ▷flanks of the ▷architrave and set under the ▷cornice: they are also called ▷*ancones,* ▷*ears,* ▷*elbows, hawksbills,* ▷*knees, lugs,* or *prothyrides.* They are called ears or lugs by their resemblance to the ▷volutes of human ears, and because of their position on the architraves or casings of ▷door-, ▷window-, or ▷niche-openings on the flanks. The term is also given to a type of architrave, the *supercilium* of which projects beyond the ▷*antepagmenta,* forming ears. It also signifies a ledged projection in the ▷voussoirs of a built-up architrave or a flat ▷arch (or a segmental arch) which rests within a corresponding recess in the adjoining voussoir, thus strengthening the construction: it also means a ledged voussoir resting on other voussoirs, as in ▷ashlar, especially rusticated (▷rustic) work over an arch.

Crossing The junction of ▷nave, ▷chancel, and ▷transepts of a ▷church, often crowned with a ▷tower.

Crotchet As ▷crocket.

Croud, croude, crowd, crowde ▷Crypt.

Crow-footed Having *crow-steps* (▷corbel).

Crow-gable ▷Corbel.

Crow-steps ▷Corbel.

Crown The upper part of any building or part of a building, such as a terminal feature, the top of an ▷arch (including the keystone) or a ▷vault, or the ▷corona of a ▷cornice including anything above it. The *crown of an arch* is also called the *extrados,* but is more properly the highest point. Crown ▷glass was fine window-glass produced as follows: a globe was blown and attached to an iron rod by means of a blob of molten glass opposite the entry-point of the blow-pipe, which was then broken free; the incomplete globe was then spun rapidly in a furnace until the glass had softened, at which point the

globular shape flattened into a disc from which crown glass was cut. The point at which the glass was attached to the rod was a ▷bull's-eye or ▷bullion, and was never used in good work. Crown glass is slightly uneven, and is often faintly tinted, with a brilliant, fire-finish lustre, which gives it pleasing properties. *Crown moulding* is any moulding (▷mould) finishing off a structure, such as a corona or cornice. A *crown-▷plate* is a ▷*bolster,* or a ▷*ridge-▷beam.* A *crown-▷post* is the ▷*king-* or ▷*joggle-▷post* of a roof rising from the ▷tie-beams and supporting the ▷*principal rafters* and ▷*collar-plate* (▷[212]) A *crown-▷steeple* is a terminating feature of a ▷tower or a ▷turret, with flying ▷buttresses and the like, looking like a crown. A *crown-▷tile* is a ridge-tile or ridge-cresting. A crown is also a very ancient ▷symbol of sovereignty, honour, or achievement, and is found in both secular and religious contexts. A crown with the cruciform top raised to hold the orb and cross signifies a higher authority (emperor) than that of king (which has the cruciform centre sunk).

Crozier An ▷ornamented pastoral staff with a crook-shaped head (associated with the Tree of Life and with the ▷*caduceus*) which is the ▷symbol of authority carried by a bishop. It is often found carved on ▷tombs.

Crucifixion Crucifixion groups were set up on ▷rood-▷beams and usually showed Christ on the Rood (Cross) with Sts Mary and John.

Cruciform Cross-shaped, as a ▷church with ▷transepts.

Cruck [94] A pair of large curved timbers which rise from ground-level or the top of a ▷wall to join together at the ▷apex of an inverted V, so forming a primitive structural ▷truss, often tied together. Each part of a cruck or crutch is called a ▷*blade.*

Crypt A ▷vault beneath a building, wholly or partly underground, also known as a croft, croud, croude,

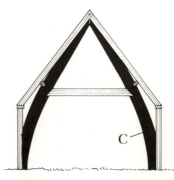

[94] CRUCK Each member of the cruck (in black) is called a *blade* (C). (*JJS*)

crowd, crowde, shroud, or ▷undercroft. Crypts are usually found only under ▷chancels and chancel-▷aisles, and were often fitted with ▷altars. Many crypts had natural lighting, were divided into ▷chapels, and often contained burials. Many ▷Georgian ▷churches had crypts that were specifically intended for the depositing of bodies in lead ▷coffins. Large crypts exist in Canterbury and other cathedrals. The ▷Roman *crypta* was essentially a place for storage, but the term was also used to describe a long ▷gallery at ground level, often with ▷colonnades, or to indicate ▷stables or coach-houses.

Crypto-porticus An enclosed ▷gallery with ▷walls instead of ▷columns, or an enclosed gallery, also known as *crypta* (▷crypt).

Crystal Palace A large exhibition-building of iron and glass erected for the Great Exhibition of 1851, or any similar building.

C-scroll The C- and S-scrolls were the commonest type in ▷Rococo ▷ornament, especially ▷frames to ▷cartouches.

Cubicle A small enclosed space or a *carrel*. A *cubiculum* is a small ▷chamber, a bedchamber, a tent, a ▷mortuary ▷chapel attached to a ▷church, a burial-chamber fitted with ▷niches or *loculi* for the reception of the remains of the dead, or an elevated ▷box for spectators in a ▷theatre or amphitheatre.

Cubiform A ▷*cushion* ▷*capital*, or anything shaped like a cube.

Cubism A movement in twentieth-century art in which quasi-geometrical shapes predominated, and a new ▷perspective of superimposed and interlocking partly transparent planes was introduced. The irregular geometric forms were used by ▷Art-Deco and ▷Modernist designers, and were most successfully applied to flat surfaces, although in ▷achitecture the work of Chochol in Czechoslovakia and that of the De Stijl group in the Netherlands experimented with Cubist ideas.

Cubit A unit of linear measurement based on a sixteenth of the level by which the Nile rose in flood, and subsequently based on the distance from the elbow to the middle fingertip. The ▷Egyptian cubit was about 52.42 cm, while the ▷Roman *cubitus* was about 44.19 cm.

Cul A *cul-de-four* is a half-▷dome, as over a ▷niche or an ▷apse. A *cul-de-lampe* is a pendent ▷ornament in the shape of a ▷pyramid or cone, but often ▷embellished: it is also a half-cone, ornamented, used as a ▷corbel from

which an ▷arch or ▷vault springs. A *cul-de-sac* is an alley, lane, ▷passage, or street closed at one end.

Culina A ▷Roman ▷kitchen.

Cullis A groove or ▷channel.

Cullot Also *culot*, meaning a ▷string, ▷margent, or ▷festoon of ▷husks or ▷bellflowers.

Culvert An arched ▷channel for conveying water.

Culvertail A ▷dovetail.

Cuneiform Wedge-shaped. A *cuneus* is a wedge-shaped section of the seating of a ▷theatre bounded by ▷stairs and ▷passages. Also a ▷voussoir.

Cup and cover The bulbous thickening on ▷Elizabethan and ▷Jacobean ▷furniture-legs or ▷table-▷tombs, or other turned and carved ▷ornament.

Cupboard Originally a sideboard, but now a recess or a piece of furniture with ▷shelves.

Cupid The god of ▷love, or a winged male child (▷cherub). Not to be confused with ▷*putto*.

[95] CUPOLA Robert Adam's square towers at the former Church of St Mary, Mistley, Essex, built in 1776. Note the Tuscan Order, medallions on the frieze, simple Attic storey, and surmounting drum with engaged Ionic Order, with domed top. The upper circular part with the domed top is known as a cupola. (*JSC*)

Cupola [95] A ▷drum or polygonal space on top of a ▷dome, also called a ▷lantern. A ▷roof or ▷vault over a circular, elliptical, or polygonal plan: a concave ceiling over such plans. A vaulted or domed roof of a building or part of a building, or a diminutive domed form.

Curb A ▷nosing to protect the edge of ▷steps, or the edge of a raised footpath, also called ▷kerb or curb-stone. A *curb-▷plate* is the wall-plate of a ▷dome or a circular ▷skylight. A *curb-▷roof* is a *▷mansard roof* or one with two ▷battered sides carrying a ▷pitched roof over.

Curia A council-house, usually a rectangular ▷hall with a ▷niche or ▷apse at one end opposite the ▷door.

Curstable A ▷course of stones forming a ▷string-course, often moulded (▷mould).

Curtail The first ▷step of a ▷stair with a curved ▷scroll at the point furthest from the ▷wall, or any scroll-like ▷termination of any architectural member. A *curtail-step* or *scroll-step* can also have scrolls at both ends projecting beyond and often around the ▷newels.

Curtain wall A ▷wall between two ▷towers, ▷bastions, or ▷pavilions. The term is sometimes applied to the side-wall between ▷buttresses in ▷churches. In modern usage it is any non-load-bearing wall placed as a weatherproof membrane round a structure, and usually made of ▷glass and metal.

Curtilage The ground adjacent to a building.

Curvilinear The late, flowing style of ▷Decorated or Second-▷Pointed ▷Gothic, characterized by the ▷ogee curves of ▷tracery, dating from the second half of the fourteenth century (▷[241]).

Cushion Any architectural element resembling a ▷bolster, ▷cushion, ▷pad, or *pulvinus* (▷pulvin), with convex profiles. The term also refers to a ▷corbel for roofing, or a padstone. For *cushion capital*, ▷capital, (▷[60]). A *cushion-▷course* is a ▷torus or a *pulvinated* or *cushioned* ▷frieze.

Cusp A point formed by the meeting of two curves thus the term is applied to the points formed by the meeting of small ▷arches or ▷foils in ▷Gothic ▷tracery, often ▷ornamented. A *cusped arch* is one with cusps on the intrados, while *cuspidation* means a system of ornament featuring cusps (▷tracery).

Cussome *Cussomes* are very large heavy stone ▷slates bedded in ▷mortar and slightly inclined, used to form the under-▷eaves course.

Cut *Cut ▷brackets* are those moulded on the edges. A *cut ▷roof* is a truncated roof with the part above the ▷collar-▷beams flattened off. A *cut ▷splay* refers to oblique cutting of ▷bricks at ▷door reveals, etc. *Cut-string ▷stairs* are ▷strings cut to the profiles of the ▷steps, also known as *open-string* stairs (▷stair). A cut-▷nail is a machine-made nail. A *cutwater* (▷[96]) is the V-shaped point of the ▷pier of a ▷bridge, also called a *▷starling*. (▷[96])

Cyclopean ▷Masonry constructed of huge stones with no ▷mortar, sometimes polygonal in form. Also masonry ▷dressed to look as though the surface is naturally rough, and straight from the quarry, 'undressed'

[96] CUTWATER Seventeenth-century bridge at Bradford-on-Avon, Wiltshire, with the lock-up corbelled out above one of the cutwater piers. (*JSC*)

(but actually carved to look so). It is also called ▷*rock-faced* work.

Cyclostyle   A circular ▷colonnade around an open centre.

Cylindrical vault   A ▷*wagon-head*, ▷*barrel-*, or ▷*cradle-*▷*vault* springing from parallel ▷walls (▷[245]). It may also refer to segmental vaults or ceilings.

Cyma [97]   A moulding (▷mould) which is hollow in its open part, and ▷cushioned or swelling out below, so called from its resemblance to a wave. Its section consists of a concave and convex line, like an elongated S. An ▷ogee. A *cyma recta* or *Doric cyma* is an S-shaped moulding at the top of a ▷cornice, with the concave part uppermost, while a *cyma reversa* is similar but reversed

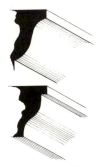

[97] CYMA Above is the cyma recta, and below is the cyma reversa, Lesbian cymatium, or reverse ogee. (*JJS*)

(i.e. with the convex upper and concave lower part), and is also known as the ▷*Lesbian cymatium* or *reverse ogee*. A *cymatium* is the top member of a group of ▷Classical mouldings, usually the cornice, often in the form of a cyma, but may also be an ▷ovolo or a ▷cavetto moulding.

Cymbals   These occur, usually with drums and tambourines, in ▷Bacchic decoration, and in ▷trophies associated with ▷music, opera, or dance.

Cymbia   ▷Cimbia.

Cypher   An initial interlocked with another to form linear designs. Cyphers are often reversed so that symmetrical designs can be achieved: cyphers were common from the fourteenth century, and were revived as architectural decoration during the reign of King Louis xiv. ▷Gothic ▷Revival cyphers often involved complex patterns.

Cyphering   The making of ▷cyphers, but the term is more usually given to *chamfering* (▷chamfer).

Cypress   An evergreen tree associated with ▷death, mourning, and immortality, which often appears in funerary art.

Cyrtostyle   A ▷projecting curved ▷portico on a semicircular plan.

Cyzicene   A dining-room in a ▷Greek house with a view of a ▷garden, the equivalent of the ▷*triclinium*.

D

D The Roman symbol for 500; MD = 1500.

Dabbed, dabbled, daubed, pitched Stone tooled with a sharp point to form a series of minute indentations.

Dado The solid ▷block or cube forming the body of a ▷pedestal or ▷plinth in ▷Classical ▷architecture, between the ▷base and the ▷cornice, also called a ▷*die* (▷[190]). Interiors are also found decorated with a base, dado-▷course, and cornice, resembling an elongated continuous pedestal all around the ▷walls: in such a sense the cornice becomes the ▷chair rail, the plinth the skirting (▷skirt), and the dado the surface between the chair-rail and the skirting.

Dagger A form found in ▷Decorated ▷tracery resembling a ▷dagger (or ▷*mouchette*) contained within a fish-like shape. The dagger-shape consists of two small ▷ogee ▷arches separated by ▷cusping (▷[241]).

Dairy A building or a room for the preservation of milk and the manufacture of butter, cheese, or other dairy produce.

Dais A raised ▷table in a ▷hall where distinguished guests sat during feasts. The term is also applied to the ▷platform on which the high table was placed, or to any raised platform, known also as a *footpace, halpace,* or ▷*estrade.* Another meaning is that of a ▷canopy or ▷tester over a seat or throne.

Dalle A ▷slab or large piece of stone, burnt clay, etc. with the surface ▷incised or ▷ornamented, such as an incised or sepulchral slab.

Dam A barrier to confine water.

Damascene To ▷ornament with designs ▷incised in the surface and filled with another metal, usually gold or silver.

Damp-proof course A ▷course of impermeable material to prevent damp rising from the earth and penetrating a ▷wall.

Dancer A ▷stair or a step.

Dancette A ▷chevron or ▷zigzag moulding (▷mould) (▷[72]).

Dancing steps ▷Balanced winders.

Danish knot The *Runic Knot,* or ▷interlacing twisted ▷ornament found in ▷Anglo-Saxon and ▷Celtic decoration.

Dantesque A nineteenth-century ▷revival of mediaeval styles current in Italy from around 1300.

Darley Dale A ▷sandstone, also known as Stancliffe, from Derbyshire: it is light brown or honey-coloured, and is very strong and durable.

Dart ▷Egg-and-dart or ▷anchor.

Daub To coat roughly with clay, ▷plaster, or mud, as in ▷wattle-and-▷daub.

David's shield The six-pointed Star of David, or *Mogen David,* composed of two equilateral triangles superimposed.

Day The ▷light of a ▷window, i.e. the space framed by ▷mullions, ▷transomes, or ▷tracery: one division in a window. Day is ▷personified by Aurora or Eos, and attributes include the cock, fire, and the sun, so ▷Apolline ornament is invoked.

Dead bolt, dead lock A type of ▷lock with a square ▷bolt operated by a ▷key or turn-piece.

Deadlight A fixed ▷light, or one which does not open. Also *dead ▷window* or blank (filled) window.

Dead wall A blank ▷wall, or one unpierced.

Deafening ▷Pugging or ▷sound-boarding.

Deal Small thicknesses of timber. The term now refers to any kind of ▷softwood.

Dealbatus Covered with white ▷stucco, or ▷*opus albarium*, so that the rough brickwork is concealed.

Deambulatory An ▷ambulatory, or ▷aisle extending around the ▷apse of a ▷church behind the ▷high altar. The ambulatory of a ▷cloister.

Dearn, dern A ▷door-▷post or a ▷threshold.

Death The subject has spawned a huge iconography. Death is ▷personified as a hunter, a warrior, a ▷lion, a skeleton, or a figure with a ▷scythe and hour-glass. ▷Symbols of mortality include shrouded figures, bones and ▷skulls, broken ▷columns, clocks, ▷urns (shrouded or not), female mourners, ▷cypress trees, ▷weeping willows, mattocks, pick-axes, ▷coffins, ▷obelisks, ▷pyramids, angels, ▷*putti* with inverted ▷torches, ▷labyrinths, ▷mourners or ▷weepers, ▷bells, and rotting bodies. ▷Cherubs on pillows, skulls with bats' wings, ▷ivy, evergreen plants, lighted lamps, and flaming urns all appear in funerary art, with ▷effigies, ▷altar-and ▷table-▷tombs, ▷crosses, headstones, ▷lilies, forget-me-nots, and a profusion of Egyptianesque ▷ornament. Setting suns, ▷anchors (hope), ▷hearts, clasped hands, padlocks, ▷roses, ▷feathers, ▷wreaths, and ▷serpents eating their tails are also found. *Death-watch ▷beetle* is one which causes destruction in timber, notably the sapwood of ▷oak: the damage is done by the larvae which bore labyrinthine ▷tunnels and weaken the timber.

Debir The Holy of Holies in Solomon's ▷Temple where the ▷Ark was kept.

Decalogue A ▷board or ▷panel on which the Ten Commandments are painted or cut, usually on the ▷reredos.

Decanicum A ▷prison for ecclesiastical offenders.

Decani side The south side of a ▷church.

Decastyle A ▷colonnade or ▷portico of ten ▷columns in line; ▷colonnade.

Decempada A rod or measurement of ten ▷Roman feet (*pedes*).

Declination The ▷angle which the planes of the ▷wall and the ▷soffites of the ▷mutules of the ▷Doric Order make with each other. All ▷Greek Doric mutules are inclined.

Décor The combination of materials, furnishings, and artefacts arranged according to a scheme to produce a style of interior decoration.

Decorated style [98] A term that is given to English ▷mediaeval architecture as it developed from the late thirteenth century until the second half of the fourteenth century. As the term implies, its chief characteristics were the use of decoration covering surfaces, especially ▷diaper-work and ▷crocketing. The ▷ball-flower and ▷four-leafed flower largely replaced the ▷*Early English* or *First-Pointed* ▷dog-tooth and ▷nail-head ▷enrichment. *Decorated* work is characterized by a ▷naturalistic treatment of floral decoration, and characteristic forms include ▷ogees, the ▷*Vesica Piscis* or ▷*mandala*, ▷*mouchettes, crockets*, and ▷star-▷*vaulting*. The style developed the ogee or S-shaped curve in ▷tracery of remarkable richness and flowing lines. ▷Foliage began as stylized but became more naturalistic. ▷Clerestoreys were often very large, while the ▷triforium (now known as ▷tribune) went into decline. Vaulting became complex, and intermediate and ▷*lierne* ribs formed star-shaped patterns. The use of intermediate and ▷ridge-ribs in the ▷nave-vault at Exeter Cathedral is a *tour de force* of Decorated design. Decorated is also referred to as *Second-* or ▷*Middle-Pointed*. The earliest Second-Pointed tracery tends to be of the geometrical (▷geometry) type, while the later phase is ▷curvilinear or ▷flowing, related to the ▷*Flamboyant* or flame-like forms of the Continent (▷[134], [241]).

Decumanus The main east–west street of a ▷Roman military camp, fortress or planned town.

Dedication cross A consecration ▷cross. The dedication of a ▷church is to Almighty God only, usually in commemoration of a saint: it is incorrect to say that a church or ▷chapel is dedicated to a saint, for it is only dedicated or consecrated to God because in Christianity saints were not gods. The naming of a church or chapel after a saint was as an honour to that saint: but in common usage, churches are said to be dedicated to St Mary or some other saint.

Dégagement Disengagement, as when ▷columns are free-standing rather than ▷engaged into a ▷wall.

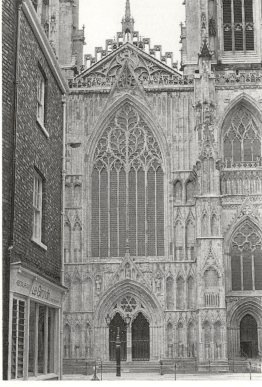

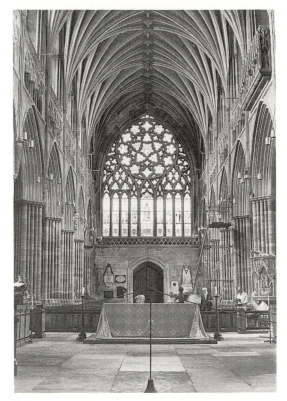

(a) *(b)*

[98] DECORATED STYLE (*a*) The west front of York Minster. This is a mixture of First-Pointed and Second-Pointed styles of Gothic. Note the screen-like effect of the four tiers of gabled niches which extend around the buttresses. The façade is dominated by the huge Decorated window of 1338 with its flowing tracery, with *mouchettes* and other flame-like lights. The tracery under the south tower on the right is also Decorated work. Note also the panel-like effects of the treatment of the wall above the gabled niches and on either side of the great west window, the flowing blind tracery of the gable, and the open crenellations with central pinnacle. (*JSC*) (*b*) The west window of the Cathedral of St Peter in Exeter, largely Decorated work of the fourteenth century. (*JSC*)

Degree   A ▷step or a ▷stair.

Delabole   A Cornish ▷slate.

De Lanc   A silver-grey ▷granite from Bodmin in Cornwall, medium-grained.

Della Robbia   ▷Plaques of tin-glazed ▷earthenware in the manner of those of Luca della Robbia (fifteenth-century Florentine artist), featuring ▷polychrome ▷tiles or figures on a light blue ▷ground, used in architectural decoration, notably in the nineteenth century.

Delphin   A ▷dolphin. *Delphinorum columnae* refers to ▷columns on which carvings of stylized dolphins were placed.

Delubrum   A ▷sanctuary. A part of a ▷Classical ▷temple containing the statue of the deity. A ▷church with a ▷font, or the font itself.

Demicolumn   A half-▷column or ▷engaged column, distinct from a ▷pilaster.

Demilune   A triangular or ▷crescent-shaped outwork to a fortress, also known as a ▷*ravelin*. Demilunes were suited to swivelling guns on tracks.

Demimetope   A half-▷metope on a ▷Doric ▷frieze.

Demi rilievo, demi-relievo   Anything in half-▷relief.

Dentil   An ▷ornament like a small rectangular or cubic ▷projection used in series in the ▷bed-mouldings (▷mould) of the ▷cornices of the ▷Ionic, ▷Corinthian, and ▷Composite ▷Orders, and occasionally in the

▷Roman ▷Doric Order. Their width should be half their height, and the spaces between them should be two-thirds of their width. *Dentilated* or *denticulated* is a term signifying cornices with dentils in the bed mouldings. A dentil is *denticulus* in Latin. It seems originally to have signified the ▷cantilevered ends of ▷beams supporting projecting upper ▷storeys, like ▷jetties in mediaeval ▷timber-framed work. A *dentil-▷band* is a band in the position in a cornice normally occupied by a row of dentils.

Dependency A subsidiary structure or ▷wing attached to or near a main building.

Depressed arch A ▷drop ▷arch or a flat-headed opening with ▷angles rounded.

Design To prepare plans of a building. The architectural concept indicated by the plans, ▷elevations, ▷sections, and ▷perspectives.

Destina An ▷aisle or a small ▷cell in a ▷church. A ▷pier or other support.

Detached A *detached ▷column* is an ▷*insulated column* or one that is not ▷engaged: a column that can be viewed all round it.

Device A ▷cypher, ▷emblem, ▷heraldic decoration, ▷*impresa*, or ▷*rebus*.

Devil A representation of the Devil, usually an animal-like form, the ▷personification of evil, a goat-like figure with tail, hair, horns, and claws, or as a devouring monster in ▷Doom paintings. The domain of the Devil is a region of chaos, fire, and cruelty. Devils are common in ▷mediaeval ▷architecture, in ▷gargoyles and other ▷sculptures. A *devil's ▷door* is the north door of a ▷church, probably because the north side of the churchyard was at one time used by non-Christians when Christianity and the pagan religions were competing for supremacy.

Dexter The right-hand side of an ▷heraldic device (left-hand when viewed from the front).

Diaconicum The place in, contiguous to, or near ancient ▷churches where sacred vessels, vestments, and ▷ornaments were kept. It was also used as a ▷treasury and ▷library. It is the equivalent of the modern ▷sacristy.

Diaglyph An ▷incised carving, known as ▷*intaglio*, the opposite of *relief*.

Diagonal buttress One set at 135° to the ▷walls of the corner to which it is built.

Diagonal jointing ▷Bricks or ▷tiles set obliquely in respect of a vertical or horizontal ▷axis.

Diagonal rib A ▷rib crossing a ▷bay or compartment of a ▷vault diagonally (▷[245j]).

Diagonal slating or tiling A method of laying ▷slates or ▷tiles so that the diagonal of each piece is horizontal giving a saw-toothed effect.

Diamicton A ▷Roman method of ▷wall-building consisting of ▷ashlar ▷faces with ▷rubble between, similar to ▷*emplecton*, but without binding-stones.

Diamond *Diamond-▷fret*, also called ▷*lozenge-fret*, is a continuous moulding (▷mould) of ▷intersecting ▷fillets or ▷roundels forming ▷diamonds or rhomboid shapes. *Diamond-matching*, or *four-piece ▷butt-matching*, is a method of laying four adjacent squares of wood-▷veneer so that a diamond pattern is formed in the centre. *Diamond-▷panes* are ▷lozenge-shaped panes of ▷glass in wooden glazing-bars or ▷lead ▷cames. A *diamond ▷pavement* is one with the ▷slabs or ▷tiles laid in lozenge patterns. For *diamond-pointed rustication*, ▷rustic. *Diamond ▷slate* is an ▷asbestos-▷cement ▷shingle or slate, square in shape, with corners cut off, laid so that the diagonal of each slate is horizontal. *Diamond-work* is ▷masonry construction in which diamond patterns are formed on the ▷face of the ▷wall.

Diana ▷Crescent, ▷Artemis.

Diaper-work [99] Surface decoration consisting of repetitive patterns of ▷diamonds or squares, often enriched with stylized flowers or other ▷ornaments, and either carved or painted. It is found extensively in buildings of the ▷Gothic style on ▷walls and in the ▷spandrels of ▷arcades. It is also any repetitive design in a ▷panel or on a wall.

Diaphragm A *diaphragm ▷vault* is an ▷arch across a space and carrying ▷masonry walls dividing the timber ▷roofs above into sections: the idea is similar to that of a ▷party wall, and helps to minimize the spread of fire.

Diastyle ▷Colonnade.

Diatoni Binding- or through-stones.

Diazoma The wide ▷passage between the lower and upper tiers of seats of an ancient ▷theatre. Also *diozomata*.

Dicasterium A tribunal or ▷hall of justice.

Dictyotheton ▷Masonry worked to resemble the meshes of a net, or an arrangement of square-cut stones

[99] DIAPER-WORK Diaper patterns in flared or vitrified headers from Ranworth Old Hall in Norfolk. (*JJS*)

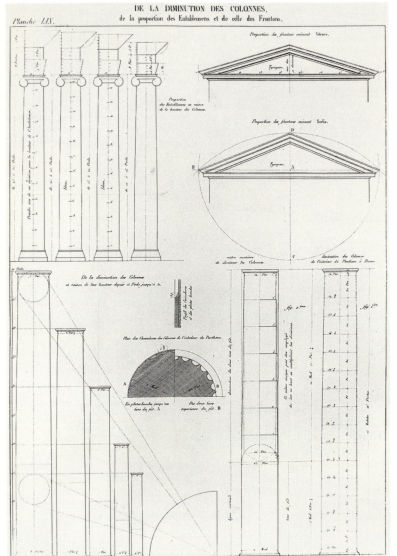

[100] DIMINUTION Methods of setting out the diminution of shafts of columns. The easiest method is to start the diminution about a third of the way up, narrowing each section of the remaining ten parts, as on the right. (*Normand*)

108

laid diagonally, similar to ▷*opus reticulatum*. Also open ▷lattice-work to admit light and air.

Dideron A ▷Roman ▷brick about 30.5 cm long by 15.2 cm wide.

Die A cube, or the body of a ▷pedestal between the ▷plinth and the ▷cornice, also called the ▷dado. A die is also a term used instead of ▷abacus. In a pedestal it often has half-▷balusters ▷engaged with it if it is part of a balustrade (▷[190]). It is also a pattern through which metal can be ▷drawn.

Diglyph A ▷projecting ▷face with two vertical ▷channels or grooves cut into it, without the two half-grooves as on the ▷triglyph. It is found in late-▷Renaissance versions of the ▷Doric Order.

Dihl's cement Otherwise *Dahl* or *Dehl*, it was a ▷stucco ▷rendering, patented in 1815 and 1816, and consisted of linseed oil rendered dry by boiling with litharge mixed with porcelain clay in fine powder, and coloured with ground ▷bricks or pottery. The addition of oil of turpentine to the ▷cement aided the adhesion to the background. *Hamelin's cement* was fifty parts siliceous sand, fifty measures ▷lime wash, and of litharge ground with linseed oil. The application of these oil ▷mastics involved the brushing of the background with linseed oil, which makes repairs difficult, and involves the use of ▷emulsions to ensure adhesion.

Dike, dyke A ▷dry-stone ▷wall.

Dimension stone Selected stone, ▷dressed, and used as a marker, ▷block, ▷flag, ▷kerb, or fine building-stone.

Diminished arch A segmental ▷arch, i.e. one less than a semicircle in ▷elevation.

Diminished bar or **sash** One thinner on the edge facing the interior of a building.

Diminishing *Diminishing* or *graduated* ▷*courses* are rows of roofing ▷slates which diminish in size and ▷gauge from the ▷eaves to the ▷ridge. A *diminishing* ▷*stile*, called a *gunstock* ▷*stile*, is one which has different widths above and below the ▷middle or ▷lock ▷rail of a glazed ▷door.

Diminution [100] The term expressing the decrease of diameter in the upper part of a ▷column: the continuing contraction of the diameter with height in order to give it the appearance of strength and elegance. A *diminishing rule* is a ▷board cut with a concave edge to establish the ▷profile of a column. From the eighteenth century the diminution was *de rigueur* from about one-third of the height of the column, but in

[101] DIOCLETIAN WINDOW This example is in the tomb of Julius Beer, Highgate Cemetery, designed by John Oldrid Scott and H. Hugh Armstead, 1877–78. Note the stepped pyramidal roof based on that of the Mausoleum at Halicarnassus. (*JSC*)

▷Greek ▷Antique ▷architecture the diminution began from the bottom of the ▷shaft immediately above the ▷apophyge. It is also termed ▷*contractura*.

Diocletian window [101] A semicircular ▷window divided into three ▷lights by two ▷mullions, also known as a *thermal window* from its use in the Baths (▷thermae) of Diocletian in Rome. It was revived by Palladio, and recurs in eighteenth-century ▷architecture.

Diorama A large painting, or series of paintings, exhibited in a darkened room, and giving an appearance of realism; also the building in which such displays are shown.

Dioscuri Castor, the horse-tamer, and Pollux, the boxer, sons of Zeus, models of brotherly love, later identified with Sts Cosmas and Damian, who practised medicine in Cilicia.

Diplinthius ▷Roman work two ▷bricks thick.

Dipteral A ▷Classical building, such as a ▷temple, with two rows of ▷columns surrounding the ▷*cella* (▷colonnade, ▷[234f]). Dipteral arrangements meant that the ▷porticoes at either end were at least ▷*octastyle*.

Dipylon With two ▷gates side by side.

Directoire The style prevalent in France in the 1790s, before the ▷*Empire* style. It was stripped and severe ▷Neoclassicism, based on ▷Antiquity, but the spare ▷ornament often included the ▷Phrygian cap and clasped hands. Later *Directoire* work often has ▷Egyptian motifs such as the ▷lotus and the ▷sphinx, prompted by Napoleon's Egyptian campaigns and by the publication of Denon's *Voyage . . .* The *American Directory* style is based on French *Directoire* designs, and is a phase of the so-called ▷*Federal* ▷*Style* in the United States from 1776 until around 1830. American Directory lasted from around 1805 to 1830.

Diretta The ▷cyma recta.

Disc moulding A ▷Romanesque ▷ornament of flat adjacent disc-like forms, but not overlapping as in ▷*coin mouldings*.

Discharging arch Also called a *relieving* ▷*arch* or a *safety arch*, it is usually segmental and is ▷blind, built ▷flush with the ▷wall-surface over a ▷lintel to relieve it from the weight of ▷masonry above, and to discharge the forces away from the lintel (▷[21]).

Discontinuous impost One in which the mouldings (▷mould) of the ▷arch stop at the ▷impost, or are different from those of the ▷pier from which the arch springs.

Dishing out Cradling of framing.

Displuviatum An arrangement of the *cavum aedium* by which the roof was sloped away from the *compluvium*, permitting a better natural illumination of an ▷atrium (▷cavaedium).

Distemper ▷Whiting mixed with ▷size and water.

Distribution The laying-out, disposition, or arrangement of rooms, as in a plan.

Distyle ▷Colonnade, ▷[234d]. As two ▷columns are minimal as far as buildings are concerned (although there are a few examples of one between ▷*antae*, as in the case of the ▷Choragic Monument of Thrasyllus in Athens), the distyle arrangement is usually ▷*in antis*, or set between the antae of the ends of ▷walls.

Ditriglyph A space between two ▷columns with two ▷triglyphs in the ▷entablature above instead of the more usual single triglyph in Greek Doric.

Ditterling ▷Elizabethan.

Divan A smoking-room, as in a public restaurant.

Doctors of the Church *St Ambrose* (with scourge or beehive), *St Gregory* (cross and dove), *St Jerome* (with lion and ink-horn), and *St Augustine* (with heart). Ambrose is usually shown as a bishop, Gregory as a pope, Jerome as a cardinal, and Augustine as a doctor.

Dodecastyle A ▷colonnade of twelve ▷columns in a line.

Dog An attribute of fidelity and watchfulness and of the sense of smell. It occurs on funerary ▷monuments to represent marital fidelity, and hounds appear on schemes of ▷ornament to suggest the ▷hunt. A *dog-ear* is a ▷box-like external corner of a roof made by folding a metal sheet between a roof-sheet and two ▷intersecting uprights, also called a ▷*gusset-piece* or a *pig-lug*. A *dog-leg* ▷*stair* is one with no ▷well, the ▷face of one ▷string being set over another (▷[227c]. ▷Stairs). *Dog-nose*, also known as ▷*pied-de-biche*, *split-end*, *trifid*, ▷*trefid*, or ▷*trefoil*, is a tripartite ▷lobed ▷splay, often with small triangular projections between the ▷foils (suggestive of a ▷paw), used for the feet of pieces of ▷furniture in the eighteenth century. *Dog-tooth* (▷[102]) is a type of *First-*▷*Pointed* or ▷*Early English* repetitive ▷ornament set in ▷cavetto mouldings: it is like a small ▷pyramid with triangular notches taken out of each side at the ▷base, giving it a spiky, rasping appearance. Sometimes the diagonal parts are treated as ▷leaves or ▷petals radiating from the raised point. The term is also given to a ▷brick laid diagonally so that its corner projects from the ▷wall: *dog-tooth* ▷*course* is therefore a ▷string-course of bricks laid diagonally to give a serrated effect.

Dolmen ▷Cromlech. Also known as a ▷*table-stone*.

Dolomitic Dolomitic limestone (▷lime) is one in which magnesium carbonate and calcium carbonate are

[102] DOG-TOOTH (*JJS*)

present in equal proportions, such as Anston or Park Nook stone, also known as *dolomites* or *magnesian limestones*. A magnesian stone with a large proportion of silica is called a *calcareous*, *dolomitic*, or *magnesian* ▷*sandstone*, such as *White Mansfield*.

Dolphin A stylized ▷motif featuring the aquatic mammal, appearing on ▷Classical and ▷Early Christian ▷sarcophagi. A dolphin and ▷anchor is the Church guided by Christ. Dolphins suggest the Saviour by the idea of the bearer of souls over the waters, but they also occur with ▷tritons and ▷nereids to suggest the sea, and marine ▷attributes. Dolphins are found with the ▷head used as a ▷base and the tail arranged as a ▷scroll supporting an upright. Dolphins are often found ornamenting ▷bridges, embankments, ▷fountains, ▷well-heads, ▷fish-markets, and naval establishments.

Dome A ▷vault over a circular, elliptical, or polygonal plan: it is semicircular, segmental, pointed, or bulb-

[103] DOMESTIC REVIVAL (*a*) Leys Wood, Sussex, by R. N. Shaw, 1868. In this design vernacular elements are introduced, including mullions and transomes, timber-framed gables, barge-boards, and tall chimneys. Note the asymmetrical composition. (*Eastlake*). (*b*) Gabled half-timbered cottages, with elaborate pargeting in the gables and panels, in Park Road, Port Sunlight, Wirral, by William and Segar Owen. A use of forms derived from Cheshire vernacular architecture, and a mature example of the Domestic Revival. (*JSC*)

shaped in section. Domes are often found over a square substructure, and if so the corners must be built up so that the dome, on its circular or polygonal plan, can sit comfortably: ▷pendentives or ▷squinch ▷arches are used to accomplish this purpose. A *domical vault* is a dome rising directly on a square or polygonal base, the surface being framed by ▷groins: it is known also as a ▷*cloister vault* (▷vault).

Domestic Revival [103]   The Domestic Revival, or ▷Old English style, involved ▷Picturesque compositions using elements from ▷vernacular ▷architecture. Tall ▷chimneys, ▷gables, ▷tile-hanging, ▷mullioned, and ▷transomed ▷windows, ▷timber-framed elements, and leaded ▷lights were combined in a ▷revival of native English domestic forms. The Domestic Revival was born of the ▷Gothic ▷Revival.

Dominicans   An order of friars named after St Dominic, an Augustinian canon, who wear a black mantle over the white habit, and so are called Black Friars.

Domus   A ▷Roman house, often of considerable size.

Donjon, dungeon   The main and strongest ▷tower of a ▷castle, also called the ▷*keep*. A ▷chamber in the keep, usually in the base. A dark ▷cell or ▷prison, often underground or partly so.

Dooking   Plugging. A *dook* is a wooden ▷brick used for fixing.

Doom   A large mediaeval ▷wall-painting showing the ▷Last Judgement, usually above the ▷chancel-▷arch. Viewed from the ▷nave, Christ is shown in the centre, with Hell on the right (His left), and the Blessed on the left (His right).

Door, doorway [104], [105]   The entrance to a building, ▷apartment, or any enclosure. Doorways are usually rectangular, but are often ▷arched. The mouldings (▷mould) round a doorway are called the ▷architrave, and there are often mouldings in addition on top carried on ▷ancones or ▷consoles. A door itself is a barrier which swings, slides, tilts, or folds in order to close the doorway. Doors may be of wood, metal, stone, or ▷glass, or a combination of these, and may be mounted on ▷hinges or pivots, or slide vertically or horizontally on tracks or in recesses. Doorways are often significant architectural features, and are ▷ornamented in appropriate ways to give them a hierarchy of importance. ▷Saxon doorways are often plain, with ▷heads formed of two stone ▷slabs leaning together so that the opening has a triangular head, or sometimes with semicircular arches. ▷Romanesque doorways are more ornamental and usually with semicircular arches,

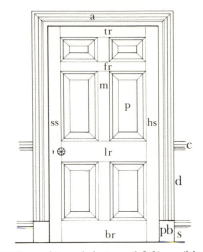

[104] DOOR **a** architrave, **br** bottom rail, **fr** frieze rail, **hs** hanging stile, **lr** lock-rail, **m** muntin, **p** panel, shown as raised and fielded, **ss** shutting stile, **tr** top rail, **c** chair-rail, **d** die or dado, **s** skirting, **pb** plinth block. (*JJS*)

often layered, with several ▷Orders of ▷colonnettes and mouldings. ▷Gothic doorways often have a ▷*trumeau* or vertical ▷post dividing the opening into two parts, with elaborate ▷sculpture of a religious nature in the ▷tympanum. ▷Classical doorways often have ▷battered sides, eared architraves, and ▷cornices over, and may be framed with ▷pilasters, ▷columns, and ▷pediments: such doorcases became very elaborate during the seventeenth and eighteenth centuries. A *door-*▷*cheek* is a *door-*▷*jamb* or *door-post*; a *door-head* is the upper part of a *door-*▷*frame* or the horizontal projection over a door; a *door-*▷*knocker* is the ▷bar, ▷knob, lever, or ring fixed to the outside of a door, and hinged so that it can be banged on a ▷plate fixed to the door; a *door-*▷*mullion* is the central vertical structural member of a door, also called ▷*muntin*; a *door* ▷*rail* is a horizontal structural member of a door, usually divided into ▷*top* ▷*rail*, ▷*frieze rail*, ▷*lock rail* or ▷*middle rail*, and *bottom rail* – door rails are fixed at either side of the ▷*shutting* ▷*stile* and *hanging stile* (vertical structural members on either side), and may be exposed as in *panelled doors*, or concealed, as in ▷*flush doors*; and a *door* ▷*stop* is the ▷slip of wood against which a door stops in its frame. A *door-*▷*sill* or *door-*▷*saddle* is a piece of timber or similar covering a floor-joint at the ▷threshold of a doorway. A *door-stone* is a ▷step at the threshold, or a stone sill. The *door-*▷*tree* is the jamb of a doorway. A *door* ▷*window* is a ▷*French window*.

The following are the main types of door encountered in traditional buildings: a ledged and battened door consisting of vertical ▷boards or ▷battens fixed to horizontal ▷ledges to which the ▷ironmongery is fixed; a *ledged, braced, and battened* door is as above, but with ▷struts or

▷braces added to prevent the door dropping at the nose, a defect common in the simpler type – these braces *must* incline upwards from the hanging side; a *framed, ledged, braced and battened* door is superior to the above types, and consists of a top, middle and bottom rail ▷mortised and ▷tenoned into the two vertical stiles, with the braces housed in the corners or into the ▷rails; and a *panelled door* is one with a ▷frame and one or more ▷panels.

Doric Order [106] The Doric Order exists in its ▷Greek and ▷Roman forms. In the *Greek version* it consists of a ▷stylobate supporting a baseless ▷column (usually ▷fluted with sharp ▷arrises between the flutes, but sometimes unfluted) with a pronounced ▷entasis; a distinctive ▷capital with ▷annulets or horizontal ▷fillets (from three to five in number) stopping the vertical lines of the arrises and flutes of the ▷shaft, an ▷echinus or ▷cushion over them, and a plain square ▷abacus; and an ▷entablature (usually one quarter the height of the ▷Order) with plain ▷architrave or principal ▷beam over which are the ▷frieze and ▷cornice. Greek Doric architraves may project slightly in front of the ▷faces of the tops of the columns below, but, because of the pronounced entasis, do not project beyond the faces of the columns at the bases. The frieze is separated from the cornice by a plain moulding called the ▷*taenia* under which, at intervals under each ▷triglyph, is a narrow ▷band with six ▷*guttae* called the ▷*regulus*. The Doric frieze is composed of alternate ▷*metopes* (often ornamented with ▷sculpture) and ▷triglyphs (vertical elements with two V-shaped incised channels and two half-V ▷channels at the edges producing three flat verticals and a flat band across the top). Above is the *crowning cornice* consisting of a ▷*cyma recta* with ▷mutules and guttae on the ▷soffites of the ▷corona under the *cymatium*. Greek Doric mutules are placed over triglyphs and metopes, slope downwards with the soffite, and project beneath it. They do not always occur under the raking cornices (▷rake) of ▷pediments.

The ▷*Roman Doric Order* nearly always has a ▷base, while the Greek version never has one. In the Roman version the triglyphs at the corners of the building are set on the centre-line of the columns, leaving a portion of metope at the corner, but in the Greek Doric Order the triglyphs join at the corner of the frieze, with the result that the corner-columns of the Greek version are closer to their neighbours than elsewhere in the ▷colonnade, so the corners of Greek buildings appear to be more solidly proportioned. Roman Doric often has ▷*bucrania* or ▷*paterae* in the metopes, and moulded *abaci*, rosettes (▷rose) or other ▷ornaments in the ▷neck of the capital between the capital proper and the ▷astragal, so the Order is quite distinct from the Greek version. Channels at the tops of Greek triglyphs are rounded, but in the Roman versions they are rectangular. Roman Doric mutules, usually set over triglyphs only, are very slightly inclined, and do not project beneath the soffite

except in the so-called mutule Order of Vignola, also used by Chambers. Roman Doric Orders often feature ▷dentils, but in Greek Doric these never appear, except in the very occasional ▷Hellenistic example. The ornaments of the Roman Doric soffite between the mutules do not drop lower than the soffite, and are usually shallowly cut, with ▷thunderbolts, rosettes, ▷lozenges, and other patterns, while guttae, correctly conical, are often carved as truncated ▷pyramids. Greek Doric mutules occur over metopes as well as triglyphs, so the spaces between the mutules are usually too small for any ornamentation, except at the corners of buildings, where ▷anthemion or other ornaments may sometimes be found on the soffites. Roman architraves do not project beyond the faces of the columns below. A *Doric cyma* is a cyma recta, and *Doric* ▷*drops* are guttae.

Dormant A *dormant* ▷*tree* or main ▷beam carrying smaller beams.

Dormant or **dormer window** A window inserted vertically in a sloping ▷roof and with its own roof and ▷sides (which are known as *dormer* ▷*cheeks*). If the ▷gable over it is low-pitched and is formed into a ▷pediment, it is called a *dormer head*. A *dormer window* is placed vertically on the ▷rafters and is *not* over the ▷wall of the main ▷façade below. If the windows over the main ▷cornice are constructed perpendicularly over the ▷naked or surface of the main façade below the ▷entablature they are called *lutherns* or ▷*lucarnes* (▷[2121]).

Dormitory A sleeping-▷apartment, usually for large numbers of people, arranged with or without separate ▷cubicles. A resting-place. A college hostel in the USA. A dormitory town or suburb is one where most residents work elsewhere.

Dorse A ▷canopy or ▷tester.

Dorter, dortour A ▷dormitory.

Dorsel, dossal, dossel A ▷reredos, or a hanging at the back of an ▷altar or at the sides of a ▷chancel. A *dossel* is also a hanging in ▷sedilia, usually of ▷tapestry, silk, or carpet-work.

Dosseret A ▷block set above an ▷abacus and placed between it and the springing of an ▷arch above. An ▷*impost block*. It is also called a ▷*super-abacus*.

Dot A spot of ▷plaster on a surface or a temporary ▷nail to assist in levelling the surface of plaster. A soldered dot is a fixing for ▷lead on a steep surface: a lead dot is also poured lead which forms a ▷rivet-like section into a stone or other ▷base to secure lead coverings.

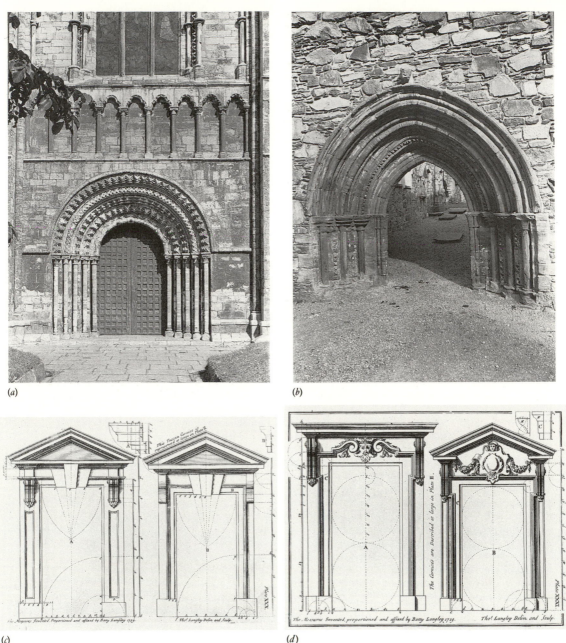

(a)   (b)

(c)   (d)

[105] DOOR, DOORWAY (*a*) Romanesque doorway from Selby Abbey, Yorkshire. Note the zigzag or chevrons running on the faces and at right-angles to them. Note also the crossed chevrons. The five Orders of shafts have water-leaf capitals, pointing to a late date, that is late twelfth century. Over the portal is a blind arcade of trefoil arches decorated with pellets. The capitals of the arcade are mixed water-leaf and scrolled. Above the arcade is mature Early English work, with dog-tooth ornament. (*JSC*) (*b*) The west door of Grey Abbey, Co. Down. An Early English or First-Pointed example. Note the four Orders with shafts and bell-capitals, dog-tooth enrichment, and roll mouldings in the arch itself, *c.* 1220. (*JSC*) (*c*) Pedimented doorways with keystones set through the architraves. Both with plinth blocks and consoles. (*Langley*) (*d*) Doorways with ĕared architraves, consoles, plinth blocks, and dentilled bed mouldings. Note the open-bed pediment on the right with cartouche and swags or festoons. (*Langley*). (*e*) Door-case at 14 Fournier Street, Spitalfields, London, of 1726, showing the aediculated arrangement with two fluted engaged Ionic columns and open-bed segmental pediment. Note the ancon over the fanlight. (*JSC*) (*f*) Early eighteenth-century door-case from 37 Stepney Green, London, with scallop-shell canopy and large consoles or crossettes. (*JSC*) (*g*) Door-cases by Vignola. Note the eared architraves and the treatment of the crossettes. (*Normand*). (*h*) Door-cases. That on the left has a Gibbs surround, or a variety of it, while that on the right has chamfered rustication with a decorative ancon. (*Langley*)

114

(e)

(f)

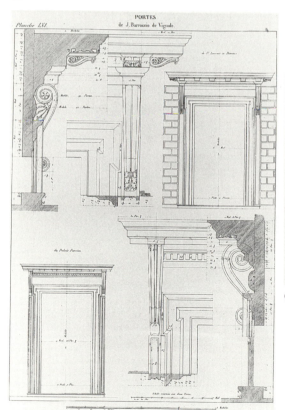

(g)

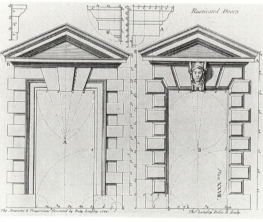

(h)

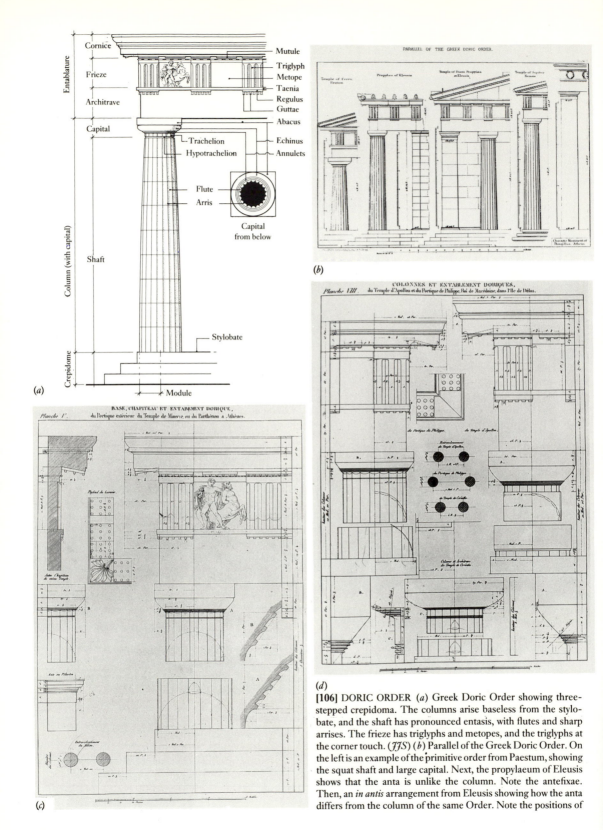

(a)

(b)

(c)

(d)

[106] DORIC ORDER (*a*) Greek Doric Order showing three-stepped crepidoma. The columns arise baseless from the stylobate, and the shaft has pronounced entasis, with flutes and sharp arrises. The frieze has triglyphs and metopes, and the triglyphs at the corner touch. (*JJS*) (*b*) Parallel of the Greek Doric Order. On the left is an example of the primitive order from Paestum, showing the squat shaft and large capital. Next, the propylaeum of Eleusis shows that the anta is unlike the column. Note the antefixae. Then, an *in antis* arrangement from Eleusis showing how the anta differs from the column of the same Order. Note the positions of

116

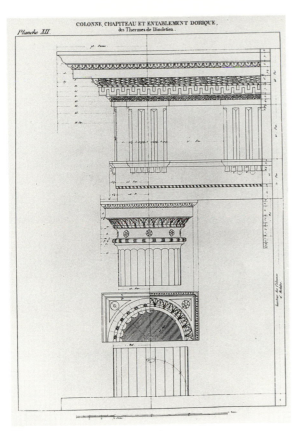

(e)

(f)

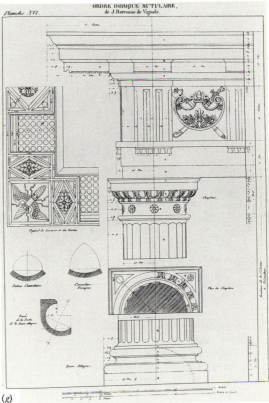

(g)

the triglyphs in relation to the centre-lines of columns, but that the condition does not obtain at the corner of the frieze where triglyphs join. On the extreme right is a detail from the Choragic Monument of Thrasyllus, showing the square anta, continuous row of guttae under the frieze, and the wreaths on the frieze itself: this Order was favoured by Schinkel. (*Spiers*) (*c*) Greek Doric Order from the Parthenon in Athens. Note the three steps of the crepidoma, the fluted shaft with arrises, the annulets under the cushion-like echinus, the plain abacus, the plain architrave, the taenia with the regulus and guttae, then the frieze of metopes and triglyphs, then the cornice on the underside of which are mutules with guttae. Note the treatment of the soffit at the corner, with the anthemion motif. (*d*) Two other versions of the Greek Doric Order. Note the relationships of the mutules to the cornice. On the right is a detail from the Temple of Apollo at Delos, with flutes and arrises showing only at the top and bottom of an otherwise plain shaft. At the bottom is a primitive type of Doric capital with very wide capital and strong entasis. (*e*) Roman Doric Order from the Thermae of Diocletian in Rome. Note the flutes with arrises, no base, the distinctive 'un-Greek' capital, with rosettes on the neck, and the position of the triglyph on the centre-line of the column, even at the corner. (*f*) Palladio's version of the Roman Doric Order. There are flutes with arrises, but the Attic base is used, while the mutules slope, and there are bucrania in the metopes. (*g*) Vignola's version of Roman Doric, with arrises, flutes, Attic base, and a thunderbolt in the corner of the soffit. Note the mutules are clearly visible. (*c–g*, *Normand*)

117

Double The term suggests a mirror-image, as in *double-bellied*, which describes a ▷baluster the ▷profile of which is identical on either side of its middle. *Double-boarded* ▷*floors* are floors laid in two thicknesses: the first ▷boards are laid diagonally across the ▷joists, and the final boards are laid at right-angles to the joists: such floors are very strong, and are representative of first-class work. A *double* ▷*church* is one of two ▷storeys, either for two services, or so that two congregations can hear the same service. A *double-cone* moulding is one with cones placed base-to-base and ▷apex-to-apex, found in ▷Romanesque work. A *double* ▷*floor* is one with binding- and ▷bridging-▷joists. A *double-framed* ▷*roof* is one with ▷purlins and a ▷ridge-piece, usually with ▷principal ▷rafters and smaller ▷common rafters. A *double* ▷*hammer-beam* is a type of timber ▷truss with four hammer-beams to stiffen the ▷principals and transmit the loads to the ▷walls. *Double-hung* ▷*sashes* describes a ▷window with two sashes, one to go up and the other to come down, both set in the same ▷frame. A *double* ▷*lancet* is a window with a ▷mullion between two lancet-▷lights, usually with a small light over the mullion. A *double-margin* ▷*door* is a wide single door designed to look like a pair of doors. A *double* ▷*monastery* is where two monasteries share the same church and are under the same superior. A *double-pile house* is an English seventeenth-century type consisting of a rectangular ▷block two rooms deep, the rooms separated by a ▷passage running the full depth. A *double-raised* ▷*panel* is a ▷fielded panel, that is, with the central portion thicker than the edges, and exposed on both sides of a door. A *double-return* ▷*stair* is one starting in one ▷flight and returning in two, but the whole rising in one ▷well. A *double* ▷*Roman* ▷*tile* is a ▷single-lap British roofing tile 42 × 36 × 1.3–1.6 cm with 7.6 cm side-lap, two waterways, two nail-holes and no nibs. It differs from the *single* ▷*Roman tile* in that it has a ▷roll in the centre, and differs from Poole's tile (41 × 34 × 1 cm) which has a central ridge only half-way up. *Double-sunk* refers to recessed ▷steps in a panel below the surface of a larger panel. A *double* ▷*vault* is where an inner structural vault is separated from an outer shell or covering. A *double window* is one with two lights framed to form a single architectural unit. *Doubling* means ▷eaves-boards or tilting-▷fillets.

Doucine A ▷cyma.

Douglas fir A strong ▷softwood used for constructional timber and plywood, also called *Oregon pine* or *red fir*.

Doultonware Coloured, salt-glazed, ▷stoneware for ▷tiles, or modelled for architectural details in a variety of colours, made at the works of John Doulton (1793–1873) and his successors, especially the type used for decorating architectural ▷façades: it is also known as ▷sgraffito-ware. The factory produced three types:

Doultonware (which was as described above); *Lambeth* ▷*faience* (coloured structural ▷blocks finished with a transparent ▷glaze); and ▷*impasto* (thickly coloured ▷earthenware, also glazed).

Dove An ▷attribute of ▷Venus and ▷Love, often found in decorations with ▷amorini and ▷cupids. The dove is also representative of the Holy Spirit, innocence and baptism. With an ▷olive branch it is ▷Peace.

Dovecot A building, square, polygonal, or circular on plan, for keeping pigeons or doves, usually with small ▷niches called ▷*columbaria* around the ▷walls. In Scotland it is called a *doocot*.

Dovetail A joint formed in the shape of a spreading pigeon's tail. A *dovetail moulding*, also known as the *triangular fret*, is an ▷ornament of ▷running bands of fretwork, in the form of interlocked triangles or *dovetails*.

Dowel A ▷pin or peg of wood or metal, to pin stones or other members together.

Downcomer A rainwater ▷pipe or any vertical pipe. A *downpipe, downspout, downcomer,* ▷*conductor, leader,* or *rainwater pipe*, often treated with great architectural verve and decoration.

Dracontine ▷Ornament featuring ▷dragons and sinuous, weaving interlocked forms.

Draft A narrow, ▷dressed ▷border around the ▷face of an ▷ashlar, the width of a chisel, also called a *drafted* ▷*margin* or a *margin draft*. Each margin is tooled separately.

Dragged An exposed surface of stone over which a metal drag has been scraped to give a textured surface or ▷face.

Dragging Tooling soft stone with a steel comb. A *dragging-*▷*beam* is a ▷*dragon-beam* or *dragging-* or *dragon-piece*.

Dragon Creatures with a ▷serpent's body, fierce head, and ▷claws. They symbolize evil, the ▷Devil, and destruction, but may be guardians of knowledge, treasure, and women. They are also ▷symbols of power or chiefdom, and in such a sense are benevolent, full of wisdom, strength, and supernatural forces. The *dragon-style* is ▷ornament derived from ▷Viking art; it influenced the ▷Celtic Revival and ▷Art Nouveau design.

Dragon-beam A horizontal ▷beam laid diagonally, supporting the ▷corner-▷post where a building ▷jetties on two adjacent sides. Also a short timber or dragon-piece bisecting the ▷angle above the ▷wall-▷plate, supporting the foot of the ▷hip-▷rafter at one end and tied by a dragon-▷tie at the other. The *dragon-tie* is an ▷angle-▷brace (▷[237]).

Drapery panel A timber ▷panel decorated with ▷linenfold carving. In ▷Classical decoration, ▷swags of drapery are found instead of ▷festoons of flowers or ▷fruit hanging from the horns of ▷bucrania, and they may be wrapped round ▷masks. Drapery was treated with great verve in ▷Baroque decoration, being carved on ▷frames, funerary ▷monuments, ▷chimney-pieces, and much else.

Drawbolt A ▷barrel-▷bolt.

Drawbridge A ▷bridge which can be raised and lowered.

Drawing-room A room to which company withdraws after dinner.

Drawn A finish for metal drawn through a ▷die or dies, as in drawn rainwater ▷pipes.

Draw-pinned A draw-pinned slot ▷mortise-and-▷tenon joint was used for large ▷frames, and involved a mortise continued to the end of the ▷head with ▷dowels through the ▷cheeks and the tenon.

Dressed The term indicates a finish: planed timber, or ▷masonry that has been worked to a finish. *Dressings* of a ▷door, ▷window, or other opening are the finishes, mouldings (▷mould), and ▷ornaments that surround them. The term is also used to describe stone used in such positions, usually in conjunction with ▷walls of another material: to say a building is constructed of ▷brick with stone dressings means that worked stone frames the corners and openings.

Drier Essentially a compound of ▷lead, cobalt, manganese, etc. to encourage the oxidization of drying oil in a paint, but really any other drier.

Drip The ▷projecting edge of a moulding (▷mould), ▷channelled, or ▷throated beneath, so that rain will be thrown off. A *dripbox* is a ▷cesspool in a ▷lead ▷flat or ▷gutter. A *drip* is also called a ▷*head mould*, ▷*hood mould*, ▷*label*, *throating*, or ▷*weather-moulding*. A *drip-▷cap* is a horizontal moulding, fixed above a doorway or ▷window-opening to divert the water and cause it to drip on either side of that opening. A *drip-▷channel* is the ▷throat under the drip-mould. A *drip-▷course* is a continuous horizontal drip moulding on a ▷wall, also called a *dripstone-course*. A *drip-▷mould* and *drip moulding* is any moulding or ▷hood functioning as a drip. *Dripping ▷eaves* refers to eaves projecting beyond a wall,

and *not* provided with gutters, so that water drips directly to the ground. A *dripstone* is any ▷*label*, ▷*weather-moulding*, or *hood mould* which ▷enriches and defines the opening (▷[172a]).

Dromos A long entrance-▷passage, partly within a mound, leading to a ▷tomb-▷chamber.

Drop A *drop ▷arch* is a pointed ▷arch of less height than ▷span, that is, one ▷struck from two centres that are closer together than the width of the arch: it is also called a *▷depressed arch*. The term is also applied to the lower ▷projecting end of a ▷newel-▷post. *Drops* are the conical shapes known as ▷guttae (also known as *droplets*, *campanulae*, or *lachrymae*) under the ▷triglyphs and ▷mutules of the ▷Doric Order, or any pendent ▷ornament. *Drop moulding* is a ▷panel moulding set below the surface of the ▷frame. *Drop ornament* is a pendent form like a drop or a tear, found in ▷Gothic work on the borders of pendants on the *intrados* of arches, like cusping, but treated with greater freedom. *Drop-point slating* is a method of laying ▷slates with the diagonal of each slate running horizontally, also called ▷*diagonal slating*. *Drop ▷tracery* is pendent tracery on the ▷soffite of a Gothic arch. A *drop* is also an outlet to an ▷eaves-▷gutter.

Droving Chiselled ▷ashlar. *Droving* and *boasting* (▷boast) is finishing stone with a fine texture of parallel lines.

Drum A circular or polygonal structure supporting a ▷dome or ▷cupola. The term is also given to the ▷shaft-▷blocks of a ▷column-shaft or to the ▷bell of a ▷Corinthian ▷capital.

Drum panelling A form of ▷door-construction in which the ▷panelling is ▷flush on each side and covered with cloth or leather.

Dry A *dry ▷area* is a space between the ▷basement of a building and the surrounding earth, to keep the building dry. *Dry ▷masonry* implies stone laid without ▷mortar. *Dry ▷rubble*, for example, has no mortar, also called *dry-stone walling*. *Dry rot* is decay in seasoned timber caused by a fungus in warm, damp, badly ventilated positions: it is extremely infectious, and the fungus, usually *Merulius* or *Serpula Lachrymans*, produces droplets of water (hence *lachrymans*). The fungus attacks the fibres of the wood and breaks down the timber, making it friable and dry.

Dubbing out The filling of an uneven surface with pieces of ▷tile or ▷daubs of ▷mortar before ▷plastering to an even surface.

Duchess A size of ▷slate 24 × 12 inches.

Duck foot A three-toed foot on eighteenth-century ▷furniture, etc.

Duck's nest A cast-iron grate made of curved bars at the bottom and front, with a decorated hob on either side.

Duct Any casing, ▷chase, crawl-way, or subway to carry anything, such as cables or pipes.

Dumb waiter A mechanism for raising or lowering a tray or small ▷box within a building, as when food is brought up from a ▷kitchen to a dining-room.

Dungeon Donjon.

Dutch A *Dutch* or ▷*French* ▷*arch* is a flat 'arch' in which only the central bricks are wedge-shaped, but the rest do not have radial joints. A *Dutch barn* is an open-sided, ▷timber-framed barn with a ▷roof that can be raised or dropped. The sides are open or partly closed. For *Dutch bond*, ▷brick, ▷brickwork. A *Dutch brick* is a small brick 17.9 × 7.5 × 3.75 cm approximately. *Dutch* ▷*Colonial* is a style of ▷architecture in South Africa and in parts of North America, dating from the seventeenth century. It employs stepped ▷gables, ▷gambrel ▷roofs, overhanging ▷eaves, and fine brickwork. *Dutch diaper bond* is similar to ▷English cross-bond. A *Dutch* ▷*door* is one with two separate hinged ▷leaves, one above the other, which can open independently or together. A *Dutch gable* has curved sides, often with ▷volutes, and is surmounted by a ▷pediment. *Dutch* ▷*lap* is a method for fixing ▷shingles or ▷tiles with laps below and on the side. *Dutch* ▷*stoep* or *Dutch stoop* is a small timber ▷porch protected by a roof with seats on either side of a door.

Dwang ▷Bridging or ▷herringbone strutting, or nogging (▷nog) of ▷partitions or ▷floors.

Dwarf A *dwarf* ▷*gallery* is a ▷passage on the outside of a ▷wall which is protected by an ▷arcade constructed on a small and delicate scale. *Dwarf wainscoting* (▷wainscot) is a ▷dado. *Dwarf walls* are low walls used as the supports for the ▷joists of a ground ▷floor.

Dyke A dry-stone ▷wall.

E

Eachea A resonating jar under the seats of ▷Antique ▷theatres to improve the ▷acoustics.

Eagle A ▷pediment or more properly a ▷tympanum. A ▷symbol of St John the Evangelist, and therefore an important ▷motif in the design of ▷lecterns, and also a symbol of strength and watchfulness. It is frequently found in ▷French ▷*Empire* designs.

Ear A projecting member, decorative or structural. ▷Crossette.

Early Christian A style of ▷architecture developed in the ▷Roman Empire from the fourth to the sixth centuries AD, primarily associated with ▷church buildings, usually of ▷brick, and often on the ▷basilica plan, with ▷semicircular-headed openings. Early Christian churches frequently incorporated ▷arcaded or ▷colonnaded ▷naves, the ▷columns and ▷entablatures of which were looted from earlier buildings, and they usually had apsidal (▷apse) ends. The style was revived in the nineteenth century, notably in Germany, and there are examples in England (Holy Redeemer, Exmouth Market, London, for example).

Early English [107] The first of the ▷Pointed or ▷Gothic styles of ▷architecture in general use in England from the end of the twelfth to the end of the thirteenth century. It succeeded the ▷Romanesque (or ▷Norman) style, although there was a brief period when early Gothic work was distinctively ▷French in manner, due to the Burgundian sources of ▷Cistercian architecture. The ▷rib vaulting (▷vault) of Durham Cathedral is the earliest in England, and possibly in all Europe, but the first complete Gothic building in England is the east end of Canterbury Cathedral, begun by William of Sens in 1175 in an almost completely French style. The first example of an Early English (*First-Pointed*) Gothic that has a distinctly native flavour is probably Wells Cathedral, closely followed by Lincoln, both dating from the end of the twelfth century. Early English mouldings (▷mould) consist largely of contrasted concave and convex ▷rolls, sometimes with ▷fillets, producing a strong effect of light and shade. The most common Early English ▷ornaments, associated with the horizontal mouldings, are the ▷nail-head, which consists of a repetitive row of small pyramidal forms, often found on ▷capitals, very frequently of the ▷bell type. The larger, spikier moulding known as ▷dog-tooth is also commonly found in Early English work. ▷Foliage ornament was deeply carved, vigorous, and stylized, often with ▷trefoil leaves. ▷Bases of ▷columns or ▷piers had ▷torus mouldings, sometimes with cylinders and sometimes with ▷cavettos, and clearly owed something to ▷Classical precedent, just as in the capitals the foliate and bell forms also have a Classical ancestry. Openings have pointed arches, and ▷windows are of the ▷lancet type, either with very sharp points, or with equilateral arches. Trefoil and ▷cinquefoil arches are found in smaller openings, while large doorways are often divided into two by a single ▷shaft known as a ▷*trumeau*, with a ▷quatrefoil or a ▷*Vesica Piscis* set above, often associated with elaborate sculpture in the ▷tympanum of west ▷doors, which can be elaborated with numerous ▷Orders and dog-tooth enrichment. ▷Head mouldings add emphasis, while clusters of ▷shafts, often detached, and of black or dark grey ▷Purbeck marble, further ornament, emphasize, and enrich the architecture. Circular windows are found, and simple geometrical ▷cusped openings suggest the beginnings of ▷tracery. Ribbed vaulting came into common use, with ▷bosses at the ▷intersections: the problems of vaulting rectangular or even square spaces

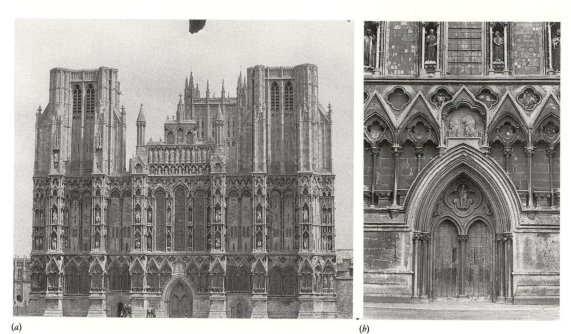

(a)

(b)

(c)

[107] EARLY ENGLISH OR FIRST-POINTED GOTHIC (*a*) The west front of Wells Cathedral, Somerset, a screen of niches with statuary, and fine shafts. It dates from the first half of the thirteenth century, and is divided into five parts by six large buttresses. The west towers were built later; the southern tower dates from after 1386, and that on the north (left) from after 1424. (*JSC*) (*b*) The west door of Wells Cathedral, showing the trumeau with quatrefoil over. The stiff-leaf capitals should also be noted. In the quatrefoil is the Virgin, with the remains of angels right and left. The gabled arches, the quatrefoils, and the detached shafts are all typical of the thirteenth century in England. (*JSC*) (*c*) Ely Cathedral. The east end of the church and the Lady chapel (on the right). The fenestration of the retrochoir on the left consists of three tall lancets, shafted and enriched with dog-tooth, with two tiers of five stepped lancets above. On the left, at the lower level, is a Perpendicular window, while balancing it, on the right, is a Decorated window. We are looking, therefore, at a thirteenth-century scheme with fourteenth-century additions. To the right of the retrochoir is part of the Romanesque transept, and then, on the extreme right, is the perfect Lady chapel, completed in 1353 in the Second-Pointed style, with characteristic crocketed pinnacles and elaborate tracery. (*JSC*)

122

with the semicircular arch (involving stilts, segments, and bodged junctions) were overcome by the use of the pointed arch, which, by being 'hinged', as it were, at the ▷apex, enabled complicated plans to be vaulted with elegance, while the finer ▷ribs could be gathered together over ▷abaci without an aesthetic disaster. Tracery itself, if it were used, started as flat ▷masonry panels pierced with ▷lights, known as ▷plate tracery, but during the thirteenth century geometrical patterns of ▷bar tracery were evolved, which consisted of moulded ▷mullions intersecting at the window-head which featured circles and ▷foils: this type is called ▷geometrical tracery. Columns and piers are often composed of large piers with clusters of contrasting ▷marble shafts around, held at intervals by means of ▷bands. In country ▷churches, piers are usually simple, either circular or polygonal on plan (although in some cases, as at Whissendine in Rutland, the clustered piers are as elaborate as could be found anywhere), with plain moulded capitals or foliage ▷enrichment. ▷Buttresses are prominent, are used to carry the thrusts of ▷vaults and ▷arches, and are terminated in ▷gables or stepped arrangements. ▷Pinnacles only came into general use towards the end of the style, but Early English pinnacles are found, often treated as ▷bundle piers, or even plainer. ▷Roofs, like ▷Norman structures, were steeply pitched (▷[210]). It is incorrect to refer to Gothic architecture of the period everywhere as Early English: First-▷Pointed is the term applied.

Earth table A ▷plinth of a ▷wall, or the lowest ▷course of ▷projecting stones above the ground, also called ▷*ground* ▷*table*.

Earthenware Any artefact made of clay and other matter obtained from the ground, moulded or modelled, and burnt in a ▷kiln.

East The east end of a ▷church is where the ▷altar is placed. Where churches are not orientated with the ▷sanctuary at the east, the ▷orientation is referred to as *liturgical east*. For *eastern crown*, ▷Antique crown.

Easter sepulchre A recess under an ▷arch or ▷canopy associated with a ▷tomb-▷chest, situated on the north side of a ▷chancel, used for the sacred elements, including an ▷effigy of Christ, placed there from Maundy Thursday to Easter Day.

Eastlake A style of ▷Gothic using heavy oversized elements and rich ▷ornament named after C. L. Eastlake (1836–1906), a pioneer of the ▷Domestic Revival of cottage or ▷vernacular late-▷mediaeval architecture: it is also called the ▷*Stick Style*, and is characterized by very bold elements, angularity, expression of ▷frames, and a general toughness not usually associated with the ▷Arts-and-Crafts move-

ment. Eastlake himself was an important figure in the link between the Gothic ▷Revival and the Arts-and-Crafts concerns.

Eaves The lower edge of a sloping ▷roof which overhangs the ▷face of the ▷wall. An *eaves* ▷*channel* is a small ▷gutter along the top of a wall to take water to the ▷gargoyles. An *eaves-gutter* is one at the eaves to collect the water from the roof, fixed to the ▷fascia-▷board, to the ▷rafter-ends, or to the top of the wall.

Echea As ▷eachea.

Ecclesiastical hat The wide-brimmed cardinal's hat with ▷tassels: fifteen tassels denotes a cardinal, ten an archbishop, six a bishop, and three an abbot. It is used in statuary, heraldry, and decoration.

Ecclesiology The study of ▷churches and their furnishings.

Échauguette A ▷bartisan.

Echelon Parallel lines of varying length.

Echinus An ▷ovolo moulding below the ▷abacus of a ▷Doric or ▷Ionic ▷capital. In ▷Greek Doric it is plain, rather like a ▷cushion, but in Ionic it is carved with ▷egg-and-dart ▷enrichment. An ▷*echinus-and-*▷*astragal* is a horizontal moulding (▷mould) with egg-and-dart above and ▷bead-and-reel below.

Eclecticism [108] Design involving disparate elements from various styles put together coherently. Drawing from many sources in design. Eclectic designs fostered the notion of an appropriate style for a building type, and also mixed styles in various rooms as well as in the one building.

Ecphora The ▷projection of something beyond the moulding (▷mould) or the ▷face below.

Ectype An ▷embossed image, or one in any ▷relief.

Edge bedding Stone laid so that the natural ▷bed is vertical and at right-angles to the ▷wall-▷face. Stone so laid is used for ▷projecting features such as ▷string-▷courses and ▷cornices. ▷Voussoirs are laid with the natural bed parallel to the radius of the curve of the ▷arch of which they are part.

Edge hinge A ▷butt ▷hinge.

Edge roll A rounded or convex moulding (▷mould) a ▷torus, ▷ovolo, ▷roll, or ▷bowtell.

Edge shaft ▷Shafts, from which ▷arches spring,

[108] ECLECTICISM A group of buildings at Devonport, Plymouth, of 1824 designed by John Foulston. It includes a terrace of houses with a Giant Order of Corinthian columns, a prostyle tetrastyle Greek Doric town-hall, a commemorative Greek Doric column on a high stepped pedestal, a chapel in the 'Indian' style, an exotic offshoot of Gothick, and, on the right, a library in the Egyptian taste with torus mouldings, battered pylon shapes and fantastic patterns of glazing-bars. (*Lithograph by T. J. Ricauti, printed by G. Lee*)

▷engaged with a ▷pier or ▷wall, commonly found in ▷*Romanesque* and First-▷*Pointed* work.

Edwardian ▷Architecture and art of the period of the reign of King Edward VII (1901–10), characterized by ebullience, or by ▷Baroque or ▷Neoclassical ▷Revivals.

Effigy [109] A representation of a figure in ▷sculpture, as on funerary ▷monuments.

Efflorescence A powdery deposit of white salts on a surface after drying: it can be unsightly, but it can also lift paint or even ▷plaster.

Egg-and-dart [110] Also called *egg-and-*▷*anchor* or *egg-and-*▷*tongue*, it is an ▷enrichment found on ▷ovolo or ▷echinus mouldings (▷mould), and consisting of upright egg-like ▷motifs with the tops truncated between which are arrow-like elements, repeated alternately. Egg-and-dart is best confined to the late sharp arrow-head or spiked forms, which were narrower and spikier than the earlier tongue-like shapes of

[109] EFFIGY Effigies of Lord and Lady Leverhulme in the narthex of Christ Church, Port Sunlight, Wirral. Sir William Goscombe John, Sculptor. (*JSC*)

[110] EGG-AND-DART (*JJS*)

▷leaves. *Nut-and-*▷*husk* is another term for egg-and-dart.

Eggshell A smooth, matt face to building stone, or a type of gloss finish in paintwork that is only partly with sheen.

Egyptian [111] An *Egyptian* ▷*gorge* is a large ▷cavetto ▷cornice with a ▷torus below. An *Egyptian* ▷*hall* is a large room with an internal ▷peristyle with a smaller superimposed peristyle above the ▷entablature, but is Vitruvian and ▷Palladian, and has no connection with Egyptian ▷architecture. The *Egyptian* ▷*Revival* (▷[112]) is a term used to describe the use of design ▷motifs from Ancient Egypt in European and American

▷architecture. Features peculiar to Ancient Egyptian architecture included ▷pyramids, ▷obelisks, ▷sphinxes, steeply ▷battered ▷walls, huge cavetto cornices, massive blank ▷walls, ▷pylon shapes, large ▷lotus- or ▷papyrus-headed ▷columns, and ▷hieroglyphs. Elements from such architecture were found in ▷Antiquity, especially after Egypt was incorporated within the ▷Roman Empire under Augustus, and the Egyptian deities were absorbed into Roman religious life. Many obelisks were brought to Rome and set up there, where they were seen throughout the centuries, and were studied during the ▷Renaissance period. Obelisks, of course, occur as common features of sixteenth- and seventeenth-century architecture, especially ▷monuments, but in ▷Antiquity many objects were made in Italy in the Egyptian style, so during Renaissance excavations in Rome and elsewhere many artefacts in that style were rediscovered and became familiar to antiquarians and designers.

During the second half of the eighteenth century Egyptian design began to have a considerable influence

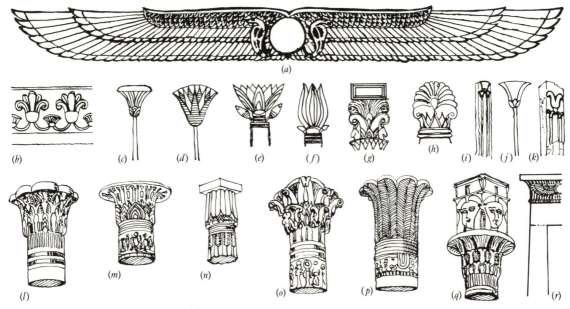

[111] EGYPTIAN MOTIFS (*a*) Winged solar globe or disc, with *uraei*, or rearing cobras. The motif is usually found in the cavetto or 'gorge' moulding that crowned pylons, walls, or door-cases in Egyptian architecture. (*b*) Egyptian lotus and papyrus decoration. Note the resemblance between the stylized lotus palmette and the Aeolic type of capital. (*c*) Egyptian painted papyrus decoration resembling a bell-capital. (*d*) Egyptian painted lotus flower decoration resembling the fan form or the palmette. (*e*) Egyptian lotus flower painted decoration. (*f*) Egyptian lotus bud painted decoration. (*g*) Egyptian wall-painting that shows a capital-like arrangement with volutes and stylized lotus flower. (*h*) Palmette design with vestigial floral and volute decorations of bronze, from Cyprus. The anthemion of Greek decorative schemes usually featured a variant on the lotus or palmette, (*i*) Egyptian pier at Karnak decorated with papyrus heads. (*j*) Egyptian stylized painted papyrus. (*k*) Egyptian pier at Karnak decorated with stylized lotus flowers, giving a volute-like effect. (*l*) Papyrus capital from Philae. (*m*) Egyptian bell-capital from Thebes showing lotus flowers and papyrus stalks and buds combined. The shape of the capital itself is like a stylized papyrus. (*n*) Egyptian bud-capital, based on the lotus. (*o*) Egyptian volute-capital from Philae, similar in general form to the Corinthian capital of Classical architecture: it consists of rings of lotus flowers and volutes, the latter themselves derived from the lotus. (*p*) Egyptian palm-capital from Edfu. (*q*) Hathor-headed capital from Philae, with bell-capital under the Hathor-heads of the abacus decorated with stylized lotus forms. (*r*) Typical Egyptian pylon-form, halved, with opening, and cornice with gorge and roll. Note the position of the winged solar globe. (*JSC*)

125

(a)

(b)

[112] EGYPTIAN REVIVAL (a) Freemasons' Hall, Mainridge, Boston, Lincolnshire, of 1860–63. Of stock brick with stone dressings, this pylon-like front with a distyle *in antis* arrangement of palm leaf capitals has an inscription in hieroglyphs which states when it was built. Note the winged disc with *uraei*. Although it is based on published sources such as Denon's *Voyage . . .* , with Dendera, Edfu and Philae in evidence, the palm capitals have extra non-Egyptian ornament. (*JSC*) (b) The Temple Mills, Leeds, by Joseph Bonomi Jr and James Combe of 1842. Note the battered sides, the torus mouldings around the edges, and the winged discs with *uraei* in the coved cornice. Capitals are of the papyrus type. (*JSC*)

on Western art and architecture, largely through publications such as those of Montfaucon and the Comte de Caylus, but a significant part of these works dealt with artefacts in the Egyptian style rather than *echt*-Egyptian examples (although these were included as well). An important publication which interpreted and used some of these Egyptianizing elements was G. B. Piranesi's *Diverse maniere d'adornare i cammini* of 1769: apart from 'Egyptian' figures (which owed much to the Villa Adriana ▷*telamoni* and the celebrated ▷Antinoüs), bogus hieroglyphs, ▷Apis bulls, ▷crocodiles, and so forth, Piranesi introduced stepped ▷corbelled pseudo-▷arches and canted 'arches' there and in his inventions of vast ▷prison scenes. Both the canted and corbelled pseudo-arches therefore were adopted as 'Egyptian', but were in fact derived entirely from Piranesi's work. In addition to this aspect, many designers, especially in France, sought to strip architecture to its bare essentials, and sought a 'primitive' quality in stereometrically pure forms such as the cone, pyramid, sphere, obelisk, cube, etc. Egyptian elements thus began to re-enter the ▷Neoclassical vocabulary through the post-Laugier concerns for honesty, simplicity, and essentials.

So stereometrically pure forms, Piranesian interpretations of ▷Antique Egyptian, Egyptianizing, and pseudo-Egyptian inventions mingled to produce a distinctive flavour in Western Neoclassicism, but gradually a concern for antiquarianism and archaeological correctness encouraged the use of real Egyptian

motifs in design, first in furniture, but a scholarly plundering of Egyptian elements began in earnest with the Napoleonic surveys of Egyptian antiquities published by Denon in 1802 and later by the Commission des Monuments d'Égypte from 1809: these were to the Egyptian Revival what Stuart and Revett's work was to the ▷*Greek Revival*, and both revivals were aspects of Neoclassicism. *Echt*-Egyptian motifs became an important part of ▷*Empire* taste, and were adopted in ▷Regency work in Britain. In England, the style became popular for ▷tombs and ▷cemetery buildings (by the association with death and permanence), while certain factories and utility buildings were neo-Egyptian in manner, partly because of association, and partly for advertising and novelty reasons. There was also a ▷Freemasonic connection in the use of Egyptian motifs between the legends of the Craft and the Ancient Mysteries, so many Masonic buildings and furnishings have a pronounced Egyptianizing flavour.

The commonest elements of the Revival are pylon-shaped ▷chimney-pots, lotus decorations, obelisks, sphinxes, and pyramids. The Metronome is a fat, stumpy obelisk, and pylon-forms were used for suspension ▷bridges, ▷retaining walls, and ▷dams because of their ▷battered profiles. Many cinemas and factories were built in the Egyptian-Revival style in the 1920s, prompted by the Tutankhamun discoveries of 1922; ▷Art Deco contains much that is Egyptianizing in form.

(a)

(b)

(c)

(d)

(e)

[113] ELIZABETHAN (*a*) Kirby Hall, Northamptonshire, commenced in 1570. Note the immense bay-windows, the elaborate gables, and the importance of chimneys. Such bays are more characteristic of the 1620s. (*b*) Giant Order of pilasters derived from De l'Orme's St Maur of 1541. The curious three-storey porch is of the 1570s except for the central window, which is later. Note the large mullioned and transomed windows, typical of Elizabethan work. (*c*) Condover Hall, Shropshire, probably by Walter Hancock, of the 1590s. The E-plan is clearly discernible in the entrance-front. Note the typical mullioned and transomed windows, the gables, and the chimneys. (*d*) Burghley House, Stamford, Soke of Peterborough. One of the grandest of all Elizabethan houses, with its elaborate showy façades, large mullioned and transomed windows, and intricate silhouette. The west front of *c.* 1577 and after. (*e*) Mentmore Towers, Buckinghamshire, of 1851–54, by Sir Joseph Paxton and G. H. Stokes. An example of the Elizabethan Revival applied to a large country house. (*a–d, JSC; e, RCHME BB76/3683*)

Eke piece A length of timber used to make up to a required size.

Elbow The upright side flanking ▷panelling, or vertical ▷linings of ▷windows, under ▷shutters. ▷Crossette.

Electrum An alloy of gold and silver.

Elements ▷Fire, ▷water, earth, and air, usually ▷personified by Vulcan, ▷Neptune, ▷Ceres, and Juno, or female figures with a flaming head, ▷thunderbolt, or ▷phoenix (fire), ▷dolphins (water), scorpion or ▷castellated ▷crown (earth), and chameleon (air). In the eighteenth century, when Masonic themes were popular, the elements were common themes of decoration.

Elephant Often used in decoration to suggest ▷war (elephant and castle), chastity, kingship, India, Africa, and industry. An elephant with an ▷obelisk on its back derives from an illustration in *Hypnerotomachia Poliphili* of 1499, and was repeated by Bernini and others. It was an important element in European exotic tastes, and recurs in the so-called ▷Indian style. The elephant and castle may be a corruption of the *Infanta de Castile*.

Elevation A geometrical ▷projection on a vertical plane perpendicular to the horizon to show any one ▷face of a building, inside or out, although it can also mean an external ▷façade (▷[202]).

Elizabethan [113] A style which prevailed during the reign of Queen Elizabeth I (1558–1603). It was based on Continental ▷Mannerism imported from the Low Countries and through books of ▷ornament. Characteristic elements are ▷strapwork, elaborate ▷finials and pendants, ▷Grotesque ornament, the use of ▷obelisks (upright and inverted), often with ▷herms, and superimposed ▷engaged ▷Orders. Dominant influences came from France (especially ▷Fontainebleau), ▷Flemish ▷Renaissance and ▷Mannerist design, and interpretations of *echt*-▷Italian Renaissance publications. The main influences were the publications of Vredeman de Vries and Wendel Dietterlein: the so-called *ditterling* type of ornament was a strong element in Elizabethan design, but it was mixed with items derived from the ▷Gothic traditions, such as ▷mullioned and ▷transomed ▷windows, nailhead mouldings, returned ▷labels over openings, ▷pendants (from late-Gothic work), and the E-shaped plan. Silhouettes of houses were often elaborate, and seemed to continue aspects of mediaevalism in their complexity and the surprising use of ▷spires (as at Burghley House) with an otherwise ▷Classical ensemble of ▷chimneys and obelisks. Elizabethan design was often exuberant, especially in the treatment of frontispieces, chimney-pieces, and funerary ▷monuments (where the colour was structural, that is, in the materials). The *Elizabethan* ▷*Revival* was associated with the search for a national style in the nineteenth century, and especially with another female monarch: Victoria, the 'Second Elizabeth'. It was seen as a separate entity, with the rise of national maritime and imperial power, and quite distinct from the ▷Tudor period with its lack of respectability (the priapic Henry VIII) and its dodgy theology. During the 1830s, Elizabethan was seen as being as important as Gothic, and it had the advantage in a Protestant nation of being free from any taint of Papistry. However, the Catholic Revival, Tractarianism, and ▷Ecclesiology ensured the success of Gothic, but Elizabethan was used very widely. Harlaxton in Lincolnshire and Mentmore in Buckinghamshire are two spectacular houses in the style, and it was very common in ▷furniture and in furnishings. There was another revival in the 1920s and 1930s, especially in house furnishing and in the design of public houses.

Ell A ▷wing at right-angles to the main ▷block.

Elliptical An ▷arch in the form of a half-ellipse is called an *elliptical arch*, and an elliptical ▷stair is one in an elliptical ▷well or with an elliptical ▷newel-post.

Elysium The abode of the blessed dead: a delightful, elegiac landscape. A landscaped ▷cemetery adorned with funerary ▷urns and incorporating aspects of the ▷Picturesque.

Emarginated With a notched ▷margin.

Embattled Crenellated (▷crenel), or with ▷battlements. Notched with ▷embrasures (▷[38]). An embattled moulding (▷mould) is a horizontal crenellated moulding, as on a *Third-*▷*Pointed* (▷Perpendicular) transom.

Embedded Something partly built into a ▷wall, as an ▷engaged ▷column.

Embellishment Any ▷ornamentation or ▷enrichment or completion for aesthetic reasons.

Emblem ▷Symbolic designs with ▷mottoes, fashionable during the late sixteenth and seventeenth centuries, which were often associated with alchemy, lost knowledge, and ▷hieroglyphs. Emblem-books were important sources for decorations and ▷motifs, but fell from favour by the end of the seventeenth century.

Emblemata Geometrical designs of ▷inlaid work using ▷squares, ▷lozenges, ▷stars, etc.

Emboss To raise a pattern or a surface or to indent it, often using patterned rollers: the raising or forming in *rilievo* of any sort of design, chiselled, carved, pressed, or moulded.

Embow With an ▷arch, ▷vault, or ▷bay. Embowed means with a bay window or a ▷bow-front.

Embrasure An interval between a ▷merlon or ▷cop in a ▷battlement, or a ▷splay of a ▷window so that the opening is bigger on one side of a ▷wall than on the other (▷[38]).

Empire A ▷Neoclassical style evolved during the Napoleonic period which incorporated severe forms, ▷Classical ▷motifs such as the ▷anthemion, ▷monopodia, winged ▷lions and ▷sphinxes, ▷eagles, ▷wreaths, ▷*fasces*, the letter N, ▷hieroglyphs, ▷scarabs, and the like. It was essentially a blend of ▷Etruscan, ▷Roman, ▷Pompeian, ▷Greek, ▷Egyptian, and the primitive, frequently with gilded ▷ornament set on fine rich woods. The chief designers of the style were Percier and Fontaine, Krafft, Beauvallet, and Normand. *Empire* had a profound effect on taste in ▷Regency Britain, in Prussia, in Russia, and in the United States of America, where Duncan Phyfe was one of the chief exponents.

Emplecton A method of constructing ▷walls in which the outside skins were formed of ▷dressed stone and the interior was filled with ▷rubble: binding-stones joined the two skins.

Empolia The wooden ▷blocks containing the ▷dowels, or *poloi*, connecting the ▷drums of ▷Greek ▷columns, and associated with the system of closely fitting each drum at the outer edge only (▷*anathyrosis*).

Empress A size of ▷slate 26 × 16 inches.

Emporium In Ancient Rome, a building where imported goods were stored until they were distributed to retailers, but more recently any large shop.

Empyroi ▷Apyroi.

Emulsion Paint based on polyvinyl acetate which dries quickly by evaporation of water giving a matt finish. Such paint is unsuitable for wet or steamy conditions. An emulsion is essentially a mixture of liquids insoluble in one another, but in which one is suspended in the other in the form of tiny globules or particles.

Enamel A hard gloss paint with a high proportion of ▷varnish and low pigment content: it requires good ▷undercoats as it is not opaque. *Vitreous enamel* is a ▷glass surface fixed by firing to cast-iron or other metal objects. It chips very easily, but is very hard and easy to clean: it is used for baths, basins, and the like. An enamelled ▷brick is *biscuit ware*, dry-dipped or wet-dipped, and has hard glazed surfaces.

Encarpus A ▷festoon of ▷fruit, flowers, and ▷leaves used to decorate a ▷frieze.

Encastré As ▷embedded or ▷engaged.

Encaustic A method of decoration where painted surfaces were waxed over after completion, or where the decorations were applied using tints mixed with hot wax. *Encaustic* implies colouring, glazing and setting with heat: the term is also applied to ▷bricks, ▷glass, or porcelain which are similarly coloured, glazed, and burnt. An *Encaustic* ▷tile is a decorative tile for ▷floors or ▷walls in which the pattern is laid in clay of one colour inset on a ▷ground of clay of another colour (often yellow or red), glazed, and burnt. Encaustic tiles were much used in mediaeval and ▷Victorian times for ▷church floors.

Enceinte The main centre of a fortress, protected by ▷walls, earthworks, and ditches; also the wall itself, or an enclosed ▷area within it.

Enchased Metal in which the pattern in ▷relief is made by beating down the depressed portions of the pattern over a ▷mould.

Endive Also known as ▷seaweed ▷scroll, it is a type of decoration loosely based on Moresque designs, and occurs in woodwork. It also occurs on the ▷foliage of Second-▷Pointed ▷crockets and ▷capitals.

Enfilade In ▷Baroque planning, the system of aligning internal ▷doors connecting rooms in ▷palaces on an ▷axis so that long vistas through the rooms are achieved.

Engaged Something attached to a ▷wall and partly buried or concealed within the wall, or apparently so, as with an *engaged* ▷*column*, also known as an ▷*applied*, ▷*attached*, or ▷*inserted* column. The term *engaged* also means framed in or fitting within. An engaged column must not be confused with a ▷pilaster. True engaged columns have between half and three-quarters of the ▷shafts exposed. The geometry of the ▷entasis makes the junction of the shaft and the wall extremely difficult to construct if more or less than half the shaft is to be exposed, especially if the shaft is ▷fluted.

Engine bed A solid ▷foundation to which an engine is fixed.

Engine-turned Patterns on metal or clay made with a machine-lathe, usually ▷fluted, ▷chequered, ▷basket-weave, ▷chevroned, curved, or geometrical.

Engineering brick A very hard ▷brick of high crushing-resistance and very low absorption, so it is useful for ▷damp-proof courses or for work underground, as in ▷manholes.

Enlightenment ▷*Aufklärung.* The spirit and aims of eighteenth-century intellectuals in imparting and receiving spiritual light through reason, the acquisition of wisdom, and the study of and respect for Nature. It was associated with a belief in the perfectability of Mankind.

English bond ▷Brick, ▷brickwork.

English cottage A style of ▷Picturesque rural ▷architecture, also called the *cottage orné* (▷cot).

English cross-bond Also called the ▷*saltire* or ▷*St Andrew's Cross* bond, it is like ▷English bond except that each alternating course has a header (▷head) placed next to the ▷quoin ▷stretcher, which causes the stretchers to break joint in alternate courses; ▷brick.

Engrailed Edged with a series of concave curves, or ▷scalloped.

Enneastyle With nine ▷columns in a row.

Enriched Embellished with further ▷ornament. Enrichment is any elaboration of mouldings (▷mould): ▷egg-and-dart on ▷ovolo mouldings, ▷bead-and-reel on ▷astragals, and ▷anthemion or ▷palmette on ▷cyma recta mouldings are examples of enrichment.

Ensign A sign or a characteristic mark. A badge of dignity or office, or ▷heraldic arms or bearings. A military standard, banner, or flag.

Entablature In ▷Classical ▷architecture, the superstructure of the ▷Order above the ▷abacus, consisting of ▷architrave, ▷frieze, and ▷cornice. Entablatures vary with the Order, and they also occur at the top of a ▷wall, inside and out.

Entablement The part above the ▷dado of a ▷pedestal.

Entail Elaborate portions of carving, or a term meaning sculptured ▷ornaments. It also refers to ▷*intaglio,* or ▷incised carving.

Entasis In ▷Classical ▷architecture ▷columns are wider at the ▷base than under the ▷capital: the transition from the base to the top is not a straight line, but a curve, and the ▷diminution usually begins from a point about a third of the height from the base. It was employed to prevent the columns from appearing concave, and the curve of the ▷shaft is called entasis. The pronounced entasis of the 'primitive' ▷Doric shafts at Paestum, with much narrower ▷necks than bases, seems to have been intended as an emphatic statement, rather than a subtle optical correction. In the ▷Elizabethan and ▷Jacobean periods, and in the free ▷Renaissance ▷Revival of the 1880s and 1890s, entasis was often grossly exaggerated, giving columns a squat and distorted appearance.

Enterclose A ▷passage between two rooms in a house, or leading from the ▷door to the ▷hall.

Entrelac ▷Interlacing ▷ornament, as in ▷Celtic, ▷Viking, and ▷Art-Nouveau designs. As ▷guilloche.

Entresol When a ▷floor can be introduced to a tall space with a high ceiling, the intermediate floor is the *entresol* or ▷*mezzanine.*

Envelope The outside of a building that contains the interior space, including the ▷roof: the skin or waterproof covering of the structure.

Eopyla A ▷church with an ▷apse at the east. *Eothola* is one with the apse at the west.

Épi A ▷termination of a point, ▷angle, or ▷hips of a ▷roof.

Epicranitis Crowning mouldings (▷mould) and ▷enrichment along the outer ▷walls of a ▷*cella* resembling the ▷capitals of the ▷*antae.* A moulding around the top of a wall or an interior ▷cornice. ▷Tiles forming the cymatium (▷cyma) or upper part of the ▷cornice.

Epinaos The open ▷vestibule within the ▷portico of a ▷Classical ▷temple at the rear of the ▷*naos.*

Episcenium The upper ▷Order of the ▷scene (▷scaena) in an ▷Antique ▷theatre.

Epistle side The south side of a ▷church.

Epistylium Also *epistyle,* it is the ▷architrave of an ▷entablature.

Epithedes Upper mouldings (▷mould) of a ▷cornice, or the cymatium (▷cyma).

Epiurus A wooden peg or ▷dowel.

Épure A full-size scale drawing.

Equilateral ▷Arch. An equilateral ▷roof is one with 60° ▷pitches forming an equilateral triangle in section.

Erased In heraldry, with a torn off part, leaving a ragged edge.

Erechtheion A major building in Athens representing the ▷Greek ▷Ionic style. It was an important model during the Greek ▷Revival, for its ▷motifs included a very beautiful ▷Order with a ▷neck of ▷anthemion and ▷palmette ▷ornament, a ▷caryatide ▷porch, and a doorway with moulded ▷architrave and ▷crossettes.

Ergastulum A private ▷prison where slaves worked in ▷chains.

Escallop A ▷scallop ▷shell.

Escape That part of the ▷shaft of a ▷column where it curves out from the ▷base mouldings, also called the ▷*apophyge*.

Escarp, escarpment The bank in front of and below the ▷ramparts of a ▷fort, or a similar arrangement in a ▷garden.

Escoinson Also *enconson*, ▷*sconcheon, scuncheon.* The interior edge of a ▷jamb, often ▷ornamented with a ▷pilaster or ▷shaft.

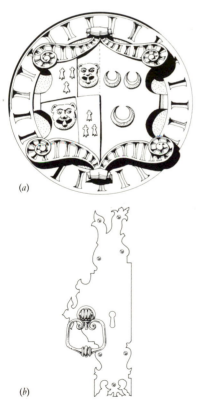

(a)

(b)

[114] ESCUTCHEON (a) Escutcheon from the spandrel of an arch on the gatehouse to Waxham Hall, Norfolk. (b) Finger-plate or escutcheon from Hornton Street, Kensington. (*JJS*)

Escutcheon [114] Also ▷*scutcheon*, it is a ▷plate for protecting the keyhole of a ▷door, or a plate to which a handle is attached. Also a ▷shield for armorial bearings.

Esonarthex A secondary ▷narthex when there are two.

Espagnolette As ▷cremone or cremorne bolt. It is also a female ▷mask with ruff under chin and around the head (often in the form of a ▷scallop ▷shell).

Espalier An arrangement of ▷trellis-work in which the branches of trees are encouraged to grow horizontally, or trees so arranged without the trellis.

Esplanade A level ▷promenade, often of generous proportions, for walking or driving, usually by the sea, and always affording a fine view.

Esquisse A sketch-design.

Estípite A ▷pilaster or a square ▷column wider at the top or bottom, like an inverted ▷obelisk, occurring in ▷Mannerist, ▷Elizabethan, and ▷Jacobean ▷architecture, and their ▷revivals. It generally consists of ▷panels ornamented with elaborate ▷cartouches and ▷sculpture, often separated by subsidiary ▷capitals: it was a feature of *ditterling* (▷Elizabethan) ▷ornament.

Estoil An ▷heraldic ▷star with six wavy points.

Estrade A ▷platform or ▷dais for a ▷bed or throne. A level space or a public road, as ▷espalanade.

Etruscan Referring to Etruria in northern Italy, now called Tuscany. In ▷architecture the main materials were wood and clay, and the Etruscans favoured unfluted short ▷columns carrying wooden ▷beams, so the ▷intercolumniation was very wide, and the ▷entablatures were ▷enriched with ▷terracotta ▷blocks. During the eighteenth century many ▷Antique ▷vases we now know to be ▷Greek were thought of as Etruscan, and these black-and-red objects provided the basis for the so-called *Etruscan Style* of furnishings and interior decoration. This style incorporated ▷motifs such as ▷griffins, ▷harpies, ▷lions, and ▷sphinxes, and it first appeared in the 1760s in France before being adopted by Robert Adam, whose Etruscan Room at Osterley House incorporates ▷Pompeian motifs such as ▷medallions with delicate ▷festoons and ▷husks, ▷tripods, ▷urns, ▷chimeras, and figures. The arrival in London of Sir William Hamilton's collection of vases from southern Italy gave further stimulus to the style, and Josiah Wedgwood produced *black basalt* and *rosso antico* Etruscan ware from 1769, providing exemplars for the potteries at Naples and Sèvres to follow. Black, red, and white were the predominant colours of the Etruscan Style, which also had pronounced Pompeian influences.

Eucharistic window   A ▷squint.

Euripus   A pond or ▷canal in the ▷garden of a ▷Roman ▷villa, often surrounded with ▷colonnades and statuary as at the Villa Adriana. The term is also given to the ditch around an ▷arena to prevent wild animals from escaping.

Eurithmy, eurythmy   Regular, just, and symmetrical measures resulting from ▷harmony in the proportions of a building or ▷Order.

Eustyle   ▷Colonnade, ▷intercolumniation.

Euthynteria   A levelling-▷course of a ▷Greek ▷temple, connecting the buried ▷foundation to the visible ▷superstructure forming the *crepis* or *crepidoma* (▷crepido).

Evangelists   Sts Matthew, Mark, Luke, and John, often represented by winged creatures: man (Matthew), lion (Mark), ox (Luke), and eagle (John), the wings representing the Divine Mission. They are also connected to the fixed signs of the ▷zodiac: Matthew – Aquarius/air; Mark – Leo/fire; Luke – Taurus/earth; John – Scorpio/water.

Evasé   Opened out or flared.

Ewery   A place where ewers were kept: a ▷scullery.

Exastyle   As ▷hexastyle.

Exchange   A building for the meeting and resort of merchants for business.

Exchequer   With a ▷chequered pattern.

Excubitorium   A ▷gallery in a ▷church where watch was kept all night, as on the eve of a feast-day, or from where an eye could be kept on a ▷shrine, as at the Abbey Church of St Alban in Hertfordshire. It was also an ▷apartment from which the monks could be called to prayer.

Exedra   An ▷apse or a large recess or semicircular ▷niche, often containing stone seats, roofed or open. It *can* be rectangular on plan, but the term means an open recess in which persons may sit. It is also a large apsidal element in a ▷church on one of the ▷axes, an ▷alcove off any building, a room for conversation, or a permanent public seat on a semicircular plan with a back.

Exonarthex   The outer of two ▷narthexes.

Exostes   A ▷loggia with ▷balcony, or a ▷cantilevered covered balcony.

Expanding vault   A ▷conical vault.

Expiatory chapel   A ▷chapel built in penance, in an attempt to expiate a crime: the *Chapelle Expiatoire* in Paris was erected in 1815–26 to designs by Percier and Fontaine. It was built as an act of atonement for the murder of the king and queen of France on the site of the burial-ground where their bodies were dumped.

Expletive   A filling, as of a cavity.

Exposed face   A fair ▷face. Exposed ▷masonry implies a ▷finish to the surface.

Extension   A ▷wing or an addition to an existing building. An extension ▷hinge, also called an *H-hinge*, *parliament hinge*, or *shutter-hinge*, has two long T-shaped flaps on either side of the joint: thus the ▷knuckle formed by the cross-bar of the H-shape projects beyond the face of the closed ▷shutter, ▷window, or ▷door so that the opening part can clear the ▷architrave and be fixed flat against the ▷wall when it is fully opened. It is particularly useful for shutters.

External dormer   One that projects from a sloping ▷roof.

Extrados   ▷Arch. An *extradosed* arch is one with the extrados indicated clearly, as with an ▷archivolt.

Eye   The centre of any part: the *eye of a* ▷*pediment* is a circular ▷window in its centre; that of a ▷volute is the circle or near-circle in the centre of an ▷Ionic volute; that of ▷tracery is one of the small openings between the ▷bars; and that of a ▷dome is the ▷*oculus* at the top. A ▷*bull's eye* or ▷*oeil-de-boeuf* window is a circular or elliptical opening. Eyes are also rings fixed to a surface into which hooks fit, as for fastening ▷doors or lids, or into which ▷stair-rods are slotted. Decorative eyes, based on Ancient ▷Egyptian protective amulets, occur in Egyptianizing ▷ornament, while the eye in a triangle is the All-Seeing, representing the Trinity in Christian iconography, and also occurring in ▷Freemasonic emblems as a symbol of enlightenment.

Eyebrow   A ▷fillet. A very low dormer (▷dormant) on a pitched ▷roof with no sides, the covering of the roof being carried over the top in a curve, so creating an eyebrow-like effect, is called an *eyebrow dormer*. An *eyebrow* ▷*window* is one with the opening ▷light hinged at the bottom, usually in a semicircular-headed opening, or a window set in an eyebrow dormer.

Eyecatcher A decorative feature in a landscape as the terminating focus of a vista. Eyecatchers were often described as ▷*follies*, and were frequently built as sham ▷ruins or as ▷Classical ▷temples in eighteenth-century parks. They could be entirely decorative or could be buildings used for pleasure.

Eyelet A small opening for light or air, or for defence, as a miniature loophole (▷loop). Any small ▷aperture in a ▷wall.

F

Fable Decoration based on the fables of Aesop and La Fontaine was not unusual during the seventeenth and eighteenth centuries, and was common in ▷Rococo work.

Fabric The elements of a building: the built reality.

Façade Any exterior ▷face or ▷front of a building, but more especially the main front, or that with architectural pretensions.

Face This implies the outer, visible part. A *face-mould* is a pattern for marking material out of which profiles are cut: it is a ▷template used to establish depth. A *face* ▷*string* is the outer string of a stair, finished to a higher standard than the ▷*rough-string* it covers. A *face wall* is a ▷retaining wall or the ▷front wall of a building. *Face-work*, also called *facing*, is any finishing applied to the exterior of a building, such as a skin of ▷ashlar, ▷faience, ▷stucco, or the like. Facing is also called ▷*revetment*, and can imply a facing on an *embankment*. It is also a term for a *moulding* or an ▷*architrave*. *Face-bedded* means stone laid so that the natural ▷bed is vertical with laminal planes parallel to the wall-face: this is poor practice as the *laminae* tend to flake away but ▷*voussoirs* have laminates coincident with radii.

Facet, facette A surface of a polyhedron, or a flat ▷fillet between ▷flutes. *Faceted* ▷*ornament* is ▷*jewelled* ▷*strapwork*, or ▷*lozenge ornament* in which diamond-shaped bosses are applied to strapwork.

Factabling Coping (▷cope).

Faïence Glazed ▷earthenware, or ▷terracotta, fired once without glaze, and once with. It is usually in large ▷blocks, and used structurally.

Fair *Fair-cutting* is the cutting of facing brickwork, measured by length. *Fair-faced brickwork* is finished with crafted pointing giving a neat appearance (▷brick).

Faldstool A portable seat made so as to fold up, also known as a *folding stool* or a *faldstory*. It is also synonymous with the ▷*cathedra*.

Fall A *fall-*▷*bar* is a wooden bar pivoted on a primitive ▷door moved by inserting a finger through a hole in the door. It is also the metal bar used in the thumb-▷latch, which drops into a ▷catch fitted to the door-▷frame. A *fall of land* is a measurement of area equivalent to 36 square ▷yards. A *fall-*▷*pipe* is a downspout or rainwater pipe. A *falling* ▷*mould* does in ▷elevation what the face-mould does in plan, so it is a ▷template. A *falling* ▷*stile* is the ▷shutting-stile of a door.

False A *false* ▷*arch* is not of arch construction: it is therefore a ▷*corbel arch* or a *pseudo-arch*. A *false* ▷*attic* is one without ▷pilasters, ▷windows, or balustrades (▷baluster): it is essentially a ▷wall concealing the ▷roof, but does not enclose rooms. A *false ceiling*, also called a *counter-ceiling*, *drop ceiling*, or *suspended ceiling*, is one hung below the ▷soffite of the ▷floor construction above to permit space for services, or for some other purpose. A *false* ▷*door* is a ▷blind door, as a *false* ▷*window* is also blind or blank, being used for architectural effects such as ▷symmetry. A *false* or *flying* ▷*front* is a ▷façade which extends beyond the side walls and/or roof of the building to make it more magnificent. A *false roof* is one between the ceiling of the upper floor and the covering of the roof. A *false* ▷*tenon* is an *inserted tenon*, that is, one made of stronger wood where the tenon of the timber to be jointed would not be strong enough.

Fame ▷Personified as a winged female figure, often

(a)

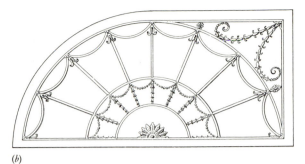

(b)

(c)

(d)

(e)

[115] FANLIGHTS (a) Gothick fanlight of c. 1740 of timber.
(b) Fan design typical of c. 1780–1800 of metal. (c) Large
'batswing' fanlight of c. 1820 with hexagonal gas lantern and rings
of amber-coloured glass. (d) Regency 'teardrop' with gilt and
black-bordered house number. (e) Fanlight and door-case with
margin-lights in Armagh. (a–d, JJS; e, JSC)

on the ▷spandrels of ▷triumphal arches, carrying a trumpet and a ▷palm, and often standing on a ▷globe, Fame is frequently found with ▷Mars in schemes of decoration alluding to battles or to victories.

Family pew A compartment in a ▷church, usually of timber, reserved for a family, also called a ▷*box-*▷*pew*.

Fan *Fan-groining* is the same as *fan-vaulting*. A *fan-light* (▷[115]) is a decorative ▷window, often semi-circular and over a ▷door, found in buildings of the eighteenth and nineteenth centuries, and so-called because the radiating glazing-bars suggest the shape of an opened fan. Early glazing-bars (1720–60) in fanlights, and those in rural areas, were often of timber, but from about 1750 metals, chiefly ▷brass and ▷wrought iron, were introduced in the interests of creating more elaborate designs. In about 1770 Francis Underwood, a plumber from Ampthill, Bedfordshire, devised a compound glazing-bar consisting of a web of iron or brass to which a moulded ▷rib of ▷lead was soldered, and this proved such a versatile medium that nearly all the urban fanlights produced between 1775 and the decline of the fashion in the 1840s were manufactured to Underwood's patent. During the last quarter of the eighteenth century most fanlights were semicircular fans decorated with ▷ornaments in cast lead in the style of Robert Adam. When gas lighting was introduced in London in the 1790s, some fanlights were fitted with hexagonal lanterns, illuminating both ▷hall and steps outside the door. After 1800 the fashion for applied decoration gradually gave way to the elegant ▷batswing and teardrop designs which predominate in the urban ▷terraces of the 1820s and 1830s. Although later there was a resurgence of variety in design, this development was cut short when glazing bars, and with them fanlights, were rendered obsolete by the introduction of polished sheet-▷glass in the 1830s. A fanlight is also called a *sunburst* ▷*light*. The term *fanlight* has come to be applied to any glazed opening over doors, whether in the form of a fan or not, and it is also applied to any upper window or part of a window that is hinged to open. A *fantail* is any feature resembling the construction of a fan, that is with radiating members. *Fan* ▷*tracery* or *fanwork* is tracery of the ▷soffite of a ▷vault with ▷ribs radiating like those of a fan. *Fan-vaulting* (▷[116]) is a system of vaulting used in the ▷Perpendicular period of English ▷Gothic in which all the ribs that rise from the springing of the ▷vault have the same curve and diverge equally in every direction, producing an effect of an opened fan. Essentially, the fan shape is formed by the intersecting of the main ribs, the ▷tiercerons, and the ▷liernes, and it was often used decoratively in ▷plaster ceilings in the Gothick style of the eighteenth and early nineteenth centuries. Fan-vaulting was frequently

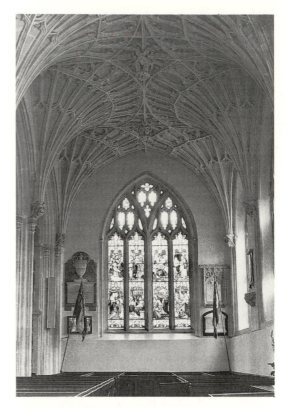

[116] FAN-VAULTING The Lane aisle of the early sixteenth century in the Church of St Andrew, Cullompton, Devon. (*JSC*)

used over ▷tombs, ▷chantry-▷chapels, and other small enclosures in ▷churches. Fine large-scale examples survive at King's College Chapel, Cambridge, and at St Andrew's Church, Cullompton, Devon (▷[245*n*]).

Fanum Ground consecrated to a deity in Ancient Rome, or a ▷temple on such ground, hence *fane*.

Farrarium A ▷Roman ▷barn.

Fartura Rubble between two skins of an outer ▷wall.

Fasces [117] An axe, the handle of which is surrounded with a bundle of bound rods: fasces were the ▷symbol of authority in Ancient Rome, and recur in ▷Renaissance and ▷Neoclassical ▷architecture, often in military and legal decorative schemes. Fasces were commonly found in ▷*Empire* designs, and are often used as a ▷motif in ▷Edwardian Classical architecture. Fasces became a symbol for the Fascists in Italy, but they continued in use in a somewhat angular form in architectural ▷enrichment during the 1920s and 1930s throughout Western Europe and America.

[117] FASCES (*JSC*)

Fascia A broad ▷fillet, ▷band, ▷face, or ▷platband, used in ▷Classical architecture, often in conjunction with other mouldings (▷mould). ▷Architraves are usually divided into two or three fasciae, each of which projects beyond the face of that below. The term is also applied to the name-board above traditional shop-fronts, as it is derived from Classical prototypes which included *fasciae*, and is given to any ▷board mounted in an elevated position to appear as a band or a stripe. *Fasciated* means composed of bands of fasciae, as in an ▷Ionic architrave, or even bands of colour.

Fastigium A ▷pediment, the ▷apex of a pediment, or a ▷ridge. It can also mean an ▷*acroterium* in the sense of the ▷blocks.

Fates Three old women, one spinning, one measuring the thread, and the other cutting it.

Father Time An old man, usually almost naked, and sometimes winged, with ▷scythe and hour-glass, often with ▷attributes of crutch, scales, and ▷serpent eating its tail.

Fathom Six feet.

Faucet end A socketed end. A *faucet* ▷*ear* is a projection from a ▷pipe by which it is fixed to a ▷wall.

Faux A ▷passage or ▷vestibule between the ▷atrium and the *peristylium*. The plural, *fauces*, refers to a vestibule between the front ▷door in the street and the atrium. If the door were to be set back from the line of the front ▷wall, the space outside the door is called *vestibulum* and that inside *prothyra*. *Fauces* implies a narrow space through which many pass to larger spaces.

Favissa A ▷Roman ▷crypt or ▷cellar.

Favus An hexagonal ▷tile or piece of ▷marble which, when used with other hexagonal forms, produces a ▷honeycomb pattern.

Feather A ▷projection, *spline*, or ▷tongue on the edge of the ▷board which fits into a groove of the board next to it, hence *tongued-and-grooved* boarding. The term is also given to the pendulum ▷slip separating the ▷sash-weights in a ▷window. *Feather-boarding* is that with the edge of one board overlapping part of the board below. *Feather curl* is a figure like an ostrich feather obtained from timber below a crotch or fork or the stump of a tree: it is often exploited in mahogany and rock-maple ▷veneers. *Feather-edged boarding* is that with boards tapered in section, used for weather-boarding or close-boarding, also called ▷clap-boarding, so it means a board of trapezoidal section, or thicker on one side than the other. Therefore a *feather-edge* ▷*brick* is a ▷voussoir. *Feather-edged coping* (▷cope), also called a *splayed coping* or *wedge-coping*, is that which slopes in one direction only. A *feather joint* is one in which two boards are butted against each other with a groove cut along the length of each into which a cross-tongue is fixed. A *feather tongue* is a cross-tongue, or strong piece of timber giving greater strength in the joint between two ▷tenoned members. Feather joints are also called ▷plough-and-tongue joints. *Feathers* as representations, in threes, are associated with the Prince of Wales, and are used as cresting ▷ornament in ▷Neoclassical work. Feathers are also found in a variety of ▷Corinthian ▷capital instead of ▷acanthus leaves, and they appear as head-dresses in representations of America: upright feathers arranged in a pyramidal shape growing from a circlet are called a ▷*panache*, and are part of Neoclassical decoration in which reference is made to the noble savage or primitive Man. A head-ornament of jewels arranged like a feather, or with feathers rising in a bunch, is called an *aigrette*. *Feathered decoration* is ▷zigzag, ▷festooned, or feathery patterning, while *feather ornament* is a decoration on the edge of seventeenth-century ▷furniture which resembles a feather.

Feathering An arrangement of small ▷arcs or ▷foils separated by ▷cusps, also called *foliation*.

Federal style An American style dominant from 1776 to the early decades of the nineteenth century, influenced by the ▷Adam style and by ▷French taste: it is therefore predominantly ▷Neoclassical. From 1805 the French ▷*Directoire* and ▷*Empire* styles exercised strong influences on the Federal style, which enjoyed a ▷revival in the present century.

Feeder A ▷channel by which water is conveyed.

Felt An unwoven fabric of fibres from asbestos, flax, wood, glass, etc. matted under pressure. *Felting-down* is rubbing a dry painted surface with a wet abrasive pad to reduce the gloss. *Felt-* or *flat-grain* is timber grain revealed by cutting more or less parallel to the growth-rings, as opposed to ▷quarter-grain which is achieved by cutting the piece at right-angles. *Felting* is the splitting of timber by the felt grain. *Bituminous felt* is used for roofing, and *inodorous felt* is used as an *underlay* beneath *flexible metal* ▷roof-covering.

Femerall, femerell, fomerell, fumerell A ▷lantern, ▷louvre, or cover placed over a ▷hall for ventilation or to allow smoke to escape without admitting rain when there was no ▷chimney.

Femme-fleur Also known as the *dream maiden*, it is a figure of a young woman with long flowing hair, often becoming her drapery, and associated with long sinuous wavy stems and elongated flowers, found in ▷Art-Nouveau decoration.

Femur Each face of a ▷triglyph between the grooves, ▷channels, or ▷glyphs.

Fence Any construction to enclose land, including banks, ditches, hedges, ▷walls, palings, etc, now usually applied to a timber or metal barrier.

Fender A ▷dwarf ▷wall in a ▷basement, to carry the front of the ▷hearth or fireplace. It is also a barrier of ▷brick, ▷marble, metal, or stone that rests on the outer extremity of a hearth to prevent burning material from falling out over the ▷floor. Fine decorative fenders were produced, especially in the eighteenth and nineteenth centuries. *Fender* ▷*piles* are driven into the ground to protect buildings and especially corners from damage.

Fenestella A ▷niche at the side of an ▷altar containing the ▷piscina or the ▷credence ▷table or both, nearly always set in the south ▷wall. A small ▷window or ▷aperture in a ▷shrine or altar to reveal the Relics.

Fenestra A loophole (▷loop) in a fortification, or a ▷window. *Fenestra* ▷*biforis* is an old form of ▷French window. *Fenestral* is a window-▷blind or a ▷casement closed with paper or cloth rather than ▷glass: it is a term also given to the ▷shutters or ▷leaves which closed the ▷lights, rather than glass, which was expensive in the past. Such shutters were very simple, hung on ▷hinges and fastened with ▷bolts, but they were sometimes ▷fretted or ▷panelled, and became highly decorated. Sometimes windows closed with such shutters are termed *fenestrals*, which can also mean small windows. *Fenestration* is the arrangement of windows in a ▷façade.

Fengite Translucent ▷alabaster or ▷marble used instead of ▷glass to admit light.

Fereter A ▷bier, ▷catafalque, ▷coffin, ▷tomb, or ▷shrine. It refers to a fixed shrine or tomb in which

relics were deposited, and was also a portable shrine containing the relics of saints. A *feretory* was the enclosure or ▷chapel within which a fereter stood.

Ferme ornée A *cottage orné* (▷cot).

Fern A common ▷Victorian ▷enrichment, frequently found in ▷capitals, cast-iron artefacts, and ▷ceramics.

Ferronnerie ▷Scrolled patterns of ▷arabesques and ▷volutes based on ▷wrought-iron ▷grilles or ▷gates, often found in ▷ceramic ▷tiles or ▷faience.

Ferruginous A term given to red ▷sandstone, such as Red Runcorn from Cheshire, in which the binding material contains iron oxides.

Ferrule A metal ▷band round a piece of timber at one end to protect it.

Fesse A horizontal ▷band across the centre of an ▷heraldic ▷shield. A *fesse-point* is the central point of an heraldic device.

Festoon A decorative design, composed of flowers, drapes, ▷fruit, and ▷foliage, suspended in ▷swags on ▷walls, ▷friezes, ▷altars, tablets, and other situations, and commonly found in ▷Classical ▷architecture. The swags are represented as tied, so they are narrow at one extremity, and thickest at the centre of the hanging part. They are often shown suspended from ▷*bucrania*.

Fête galante A ▷Rococo theme showing men and women in a ▷Romantic–Classical landscape.

Fibre *Fibre-*▷*board* is built up by felting from wood or vegetable fibre, and includes insulating boards (not compressed) and hardboards (compressed). *Fibreglass* is used to reinforce ▷precast or spray-moulded ▷concrete units for ▷cladding, ▷ducts, ▷pipes and street-furniture, hence *glass-reinforced concrete*, or *GRC*.

Fibrous plaster Casts of ▷plaster of Paris made in ▷moulds, and reinforced with canvas and wood, or wire netting and tow.

Fielded A term applied to ▷panels with the central part raised (▷[187a]).

Fig A fig leaf refers to the Fall. It is also used on ▷Classical figures to conceal the genitalia.

Figure The natural marking of timber grain and colour, hence *figuring*, meaning such patterns.

Fillet A narrow ▷band used between mouldings (▷mould) in order to separate and define them, found in ▷cornices and ▷bases. It is not always flat, but is often found cut into two or more narrow ▷faces with sharp edges between. If it is a narrow flat band it is also called a ▷*list*, ▷*listel*, or ▷*annulet*. The small bands between the ▷flutes of ▷columns are also called fillets. It is best used to give firmness or emphasis to a moulding such as a crowning cornice. In ▷carpentry, a fillet is any small timber ▷scantling equal to or less than a ▷batten, although it can sometimes indicate a batten used for tiling. A *fillet* ▷*gutter* is one on a slope, as against a ▷chimney. A *tilting fillet* is a wedge-shaped piece used to create a slope or an appropriate ▷angle. The term can also mean a carving representing a ▷ribbon ▷Flanch.

Filigree ▷Ornamental metallic ▷lacework, usually of gold and silver, twisted into elaborate forms, or any delicate metal structure like it.

Fillister A rebate (▷rabbet) in a glazing-bar to receive the ▷glass and ▷putty.

Fine stuff ▷Plaster used for ▷walls and ceilings, composed of slaked ▷lime sifted with a fine sieve and mixed with fine sand and hair. Any material for the finishing coat.

Finger A *finger-guard* is a strip of material fixed to the edges of ▷jambs to reduce injury to fingers should a ▷door close on them. A *finger-joint* is a longitudinal glued joint between two timbers, and consists of ▷interlacing ▷projections like fingers on the ends of the jointed members. A *finger-*▷*plate* or *push-plate* is one fixed to the ▷lock-▷stile of a door to protect the surface from dirt and damage. *Finger* is another term for a ▷*gadroon*.

Finial [118] An ▷ornament terminating ▷pinnacles, ▷canopies, ▷pediments, ▷gables, ▷spires, or the tops of ▷bench-ends. The term used to be applied to the whole pinnacle. The mediaeval term for a finial was a ▷*crop, crope*, or a ▷*pommel* (▷[198]).

Finish Fixed joinery, or the appearance of a final coat of paint. *Finishing* implies completion, or a last

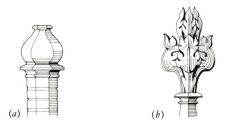

[118] FINIAL (*a*) Jacobean example, *c.* 1620. (*b*) Perpendicular finial of *c.* 1450. (*JJS*)

coat of anything, or joinery such as ▷panelling or ▷architraves.

Fir Fir in bond denotes ▷lintels or other timbers built into ▷walls. *Fir-framed* is rough-framed timber. *Fir-wrought* is planed ▷softwood. *Firring*, or *furring*, is the fixing of thin ▷scantlings of timber on the edges of other timbers to bring a surface up to a level. The timbers themselves are called *firrings* or ▷*shreddings*. A *fir-cone* or *pine-cone*, also known as fir-apple or ▷*pine-apple*, occurs on ▷finials and ▷pendants.

Fire Shown as flames, as a ▷thunderbolt (Zeus/▷Jupiter), or as a male figure with ▷hammer and anvil (Hephaestos/Vulcan), it appears as an ▷ornament on fire-backs, fireplaces, fire-▷dogs, ▷stoves, etc. Fire is also represented by ▷dragons, ▷griffins, ▷phoenixes, ▷salamanders, and by ▷Apolline decoration. A *fire-back*, also called the ▷*chimney-back*, is the back ▷wall of a fireplace, made of heat-resisting materials, or a decorative cast-iron ▷panel which also radiates heat. A *fireplace* is the opening at the base of a chimney-stack. From the twelfth century, the grander ▷castles and ▷monasteries had large fireplaces, recessed, with ▷arched or trabeated openings, and occasionally ▷hoods. ▷Perpendicular fireplaces survive in numbers, and from the later mediaeval period ▷enrichment of fireplaces became usual. ▷Renaissance and ▷Classical fireplaces became highly decorative foci for rooms, and were treated with ▷Orders, ▷architraves, and a whole range of Classical architectural features (▷chimney). *Fireplace* ▷*cheeks* are the ▷splayed sides.

First A *first coat* is ▷plaster on ▷laths, or first ▷rendering on brickwork. When it is the first coat on laths it is called ▷*pricking-up*, and when on ▷bricks it is *roughing-in*. First-fixings are ▷grounds, ▷plugs, structural timbers (such as ▷joists), etc. The *first* ▷*floor* is the term used in the UK to denote the floor above the floor at ground-level. The *first* ▷*storey* is the volume between the first and second floor.

Fish To fish is to secure a piece of timber by fastening another piece above or below it, and sometimes both, to strengthen it. The fish as a representation of the aquatic animal is a sacred ▷symbol of Christ, Christianity, and baptism, and an ▷attribute of St Peter, the Fisher of Men. When two circles overlap, a figure is formed consisting of two pointed ▷arches, or an almond shape, known as the ▷*Vesica Piscis*. Three fishes arranged in a triangle represent the Trinity. A fish also represents Pisces in signs of the ▷Zodiac, and fish appear in decorative schemes to suggest water. They also occur in ▷grottoes. Fishing nets and implements are found in ▷Rococo ▷ornament, especially in *Chinoiserie* (▷Chinese) decorations. A *fish-*▷*beam* is a made-up timber beam of two beams placed end to end and secured by fish-▷plates covering the joint on each side and bolted to the beams. *Fish-bellied* implies a ▷truss with the bottom ▷flange curving downwards into the room. A *fish-bladder* is an opening in ▷curvilinear ▷tracery, also called a *mouchette* or *dagger*. *Fish-▷glue* is made from the remains of fish. A *fish-tail* is a split and twisted end of a metal ▷bar in order to give a secure fixing when it is inserted and ▷mortared into ▷masonry.

Fistuca A ▷pile-driving weight raised on ropes by a system of pulleys, sometimes called a ▷*monkey*.

Fistula A lead or ▷earthenware ▷pipe.

Fitch A long-handled brush for painting almost inaccessible details. A small flat fitch with a slanting edge is called a *liner* or *lining tool*. A fitch is also a ▷veneer, or a bundle of veneers.

Fitzhugh pattern A type of *Chinoiserie* (▷Chinese) pattern of ▷trellis-work, ▷butterflies, ▷fruit, flowers, and ▷keys or ▷frets, usually in blue, with some green

and red. It is usually found on ▷ceramics, but also occurs on decorative schemes.

Five-centred arch One struck from five centres with ▷foils and ▷cusps, also called a ▷cinquefoil.

Fixed light A ▷window that does not open, also called a ▷*deadlight*.

Flabelliform Shaped like a ▷fan, palmette (▷palm), or similar.

Flag, flagg A stone used for paving. A ▷standard.

Flambé A glaze on ▷ceramics which contains ▷copper, and has a varied colour.

Flambeau [119] A ▷torch, the ▷symbol of life: if reversed, it symbolises ▷death. It is found on ▷tombs and ▷memorials and in schemes of ▷Neoclassical decoration. The flaming torch is also an ▷attribute of Eros, of Hymen, and of ▷Venus. The flambeau occurs

[119] FLAMBEAU Cast-iron reversed flambeau (a symbol of death) on a gate-pier at Nunhead Cemetery, London, designed by J. B. Bunning, 1840. On the Attic storey is a serpent eating its tail, a symbol of immortality. (*JSC*)

[120] FLAMBOYANT Mausoleum of Emperor Napoleon III, Empress Eugénie, and the Prince Imperial at Farnborough in Hampshire, designed by Destailleur in the French *Flamboyant* Gothic style. (*JSC*)

as a ▷finial, as a repeated element, as chair-legs, and, with ▷wings, as a symbol of knowledge.

Flamboyant [120] A *flamboyant finish* is achieved by applying transparent ▷varnishes or coloured ▷lacquers on a polished metal ▷base. The *Flamboyant style* is the last phase of Continental (especially ▷French) ▷Gothic, the name deriving from the flame-like forms of the ▷tracery. It is a derivative of Second-▷Pointed or ▷Curvilinear work, and first occurs in the 1370s. It reached its most extraordinary phase in the Holy Roman Empire, especially in Bohemia, and in parts of what is now Germany and Poland. *Flamboyant ▷Revival* can be found in England, as in the ▷Mausoleum of Napoleon III at Farnborough in Hampshire. Flamboyant ▷crockets and other ▷ornaments are often very like ▷Art-Nouveau designs, and may have been the inspiration for some aspects of the decorative effects of that style.

Flame A ▷symbol of ▷fire, of ▷day, of ▷love, and of ardour. A flaming ▷torch is life and love (inverted it is ▷death), a flaming ▷heart is religious zeal, and a flaming ▷urn signifies funerary rites. ▷Tracery like flames is called ▷*Flamboyant*.

Flanch, flaunch A widening and slanting of the top of a ▷chimney-stack so that water is thrown away from the ▷flue. A ▷cement-▷mortar ▷fillet around the top of a chimney-stack around the pot.

Flange A projection round a ▷pipe or other article of metal to permit its fixing. L-shaped pieces of metal are termed *flanges* when used for fixing.

Flank The side of a ▷bastion, or that part of a building which forms a side. A *flanker* is a circular or polygonal or square projecting ▷tower at the corner of a fortified enclosure, or ▷bawn. The ▷party walls of a ▷terrace of houses are called *flanks*. A ▷valley. A *flanking ▷window* is a side-light or framed area of fixed ▷glass alongside a ▷door- or ▷window-opening: it is also called a ▷*margin-, side-*, or *wing-*▷*light*.

Flanning The internal ▷splay of a ▷window-▷jamb.

Flashing A piece of metal, usually of ▷lead, ▷copper, or ▷zinc, let into the joints of brickwork to lap over ▷gutters, or set along the ▷slates of a ▷roof, to prevent water from penetrating at the junctions. To *flash* is to make a weather-tight joint. A flash is also a colour variation, as on the surface of a ▷brick, by means of surface fusion or vitrification.

Flat A horizontal covering of a building, a level ▷platform, a ▷floor of a multi-▷storey building, or a dwelling in a large building. Matt paint. For *flat arch*,

▷arch. A *flat coat* is a coat of filler. A *flat* ▷*roof* is one with a slope of less than ten degrees to the horizontal. *Flat-sawn* timber is a log sawn with parallel cuts. A *flat* ▷*tile* is a ▷*tegula*, meaning a common flat tile, the joints of which were covered with an ▷*imbrex* or covering tile in ▷Antiquity. *Flatting* is rubbing down or sanding to prepare a surface for painting. A *flat* ▷*varnish* is one with the gloss reduced.

Flèche A slender ▷spire on the ▷ridge of a ▷roof, often used instead of a ▷tower over the ▷crossing of a ▷church, and usually constructed of wood and metal.

Flemish bond ▷Brick.

Flemish bricks A species of hard Dutch or Belgian ▷brick used for paving.

Flemish Mannerism The north-European variety of ▷High Renaissance styles in which ▷Italian ▷Mannerism and aspects of ▷French ▷Renaissance derived from the School of ▷Fontainebleau were mixed with late ▷*Flamboyant* ▷Gothic. The style made liberal use of ▷cartouches, ▷caryatides, ▷herms, ▷banded ▷pilasters, ▷obelisks, ▷strapwork, and much ▷Grotesque ▷ornament, and was widely used in England, notably in ▷chimney-pieces, ▷door-cases, and funerary ▷monuments. Sources for Flemish Mannerism included the ▷pattern-books published in Antwerp, e.g. those of Vredeman de Vries.

Flemish Revival A variation of Flemish ▷Renaissance ▷architecture fashionable in the 1870s and 1880s, making much use of ▷panels of ▷rubbed brickwork, elaborate ▷gables, ▷Grotesques, and ▷strapwork. It was particularly associated with Belgium and the Netherlands, but was also found in England, where its most successful protagonist was Sir Ernest George in the Kensington and Knightsbridge areas of London. It is also called *Pont-Street Dutch*.

Fletton Named after Fletton, near Peterborough, it is a ▷brick made from Knotts clay containing silica, alumina, lime, iron, carbonaceous matter, magnesia, potash, soda, and oil, which permits a partially self-fuelling *clamp*.

Fleur-de-lys Also known as *fleur-de-lis*, or *flower-de-luce*, it is a ▷lily-like ▷flower with three ▷petals, often used as a ▷finial. It is a ▷symbol of the Virgin Mary, and is a common element in late ▷Gothic work, appearing on ▷tiles, with ▷trefoils, or as ▷poppy-head ▷bench-ends.

Fleur-de-pêche A rich purple ▷marble, mottled with white, from Italy.

Fleuron A decorative carved or painted stylized

floral pattern, square in shape, used in ▷Gothic ▷architecture on cresting (▷cress), ▷tiles, ▷crockets, and on ▷cavetto mouldings (▷mould). The fleuron is also known as *flos, printer's flower, Röslein,* or *vignette de font,* and was used to make decorative ▷borders or to ▷embellish ▷frames. The fleuron is also, especially, the small flower in the centre of each face of the ▷Corinthian ▷abacus.

Flier Also *flyer.* Any ▷step in a straight ▷flight of ▷stairs, each ▷tread of which is of uniform width. A *flight* is a series of steps from one ▷landing to another.

Flight A series of ▷steps in a straight line in a ▷stair from ▷landing to landing, ▷floor to floor, or floor to landing.

Flint A hard, dense, fine-grained stone occurring as irregular nodules, grey, black, or brown in colour within, but white or cream on the outside. Flint is a form of silica, and occurs where chalk abounds. Flints are used for building either whole (where they appear as whitish round nodules in the wall surface), or broken (▷knapped), where they appear as irregular black or dark grey irregular squares. Flint always needs to be used with ▷freestone or ▷brick ▷quoins, ▷dressings, copings (▷cope), and ▷plinths, so is best used in ▷panels because of the difficulties of obtaining a clear straight quoin or ▷jambs at openings. Where panels of knapped flint are used with freestone ▷frames in ▷Gothic patterns, the result is called *flushwork* (▷flush), and is a common feature in East Anglia.

Flitch A steel or iron ▷plate bolted between two timber ▷joists to strengthen them: the result is called a *flitched* ▷*beam.* A pile of veneers, stacked in order as cut.

Float A flat, rectangular board or plate with handle used to produce a small plaster finish. *Floated* ▷*lath-and-*▷*plaster* is three-coat plaster on laths, the first called ▷*pricking up,* the second *floating,* and the last (the ▷setting-coat), is known as ▷*fine stuff.* A *floating* ▷*floor* is one with the light ▷slabs supported on insulation ▷pads fixed to the subfloor to improve sound insulation.

Floor The ▷pavement or boarded lower horizontal surface of any room. It may be of earth, ▷brick, stone, ▷tile, wood, or other materials. The term is also applied to a ▷storey of a building. A *sunken floor* is the ▷basement, the next is the ▷principal or ▷ground, the next the ▷first, and so on. The expression ▷*one pair* implies a storey above the first flight of ▷stairs from the ground. *Floor cloth* is stout canvas covered with oil paint and then printed with a pattern: it was used in ▷Victorian times, but only rare examples survived, as it was superseded by linoleum and by other coverings. *Floor-*▷*joists* are joists supporting the floor surface

(▷bridging joist). A *single floor* has one set of ▷common or bridging joists; a ▷*double floor* has additional and larger joists called ▷*binders* which support the bridging joists; and *triple* or ▷*framed floors* have three sets of joists: bridging, and binders framed into and supported by larger joists called ▷*girders.* *Floor-*▷*boards* are of many types: the most usual are shot, ▷butt-jointed, or plain-edged, usually only used in double-boarded floors; *rebated-joint* boards with a ▷tongue fitting into a rebate in the adjacent board; *tongued-and-grooved* or *feathered-and-grooved* (t & g or f & g), with a tongue or ▷feather along one edge and a groove on the other, usual in better quality work; *rebated, tongued, and grooved* (usual with concealed nails); *splayed, rebated, tongued, and grooved;* and *ploughed and tongued.*

Floral ornament Any decorative scheme involving representations of flowers, whether naturalistic or stylized.

Florentine Appertaining to Florence in Tuscany. For *Florentine arch,* ▷arch. A *Florentine* ▷*lily* is a variety of ▷*fleur-de-lys* or *giglio.* A *Florentine* ▷*mosaic* is one made of precious and semi-precious stones, ▷inlaid in a surface of white or black ▷marble in floral patterns.

Floreated, floriated Decorated with floral patterns, or carved in imitation of flowers. A *floriated* ▷*merlon* is when the solid upright section of a ▷battlement is pierced and decorated with a floriated form.

Flory-counter-flory An ▷heraldic ▷tressure with ▷*fleurs-de-lys* pointing alternately in and out.

Flowing An obsolete term for later ▷Curvilinear Second-▷Pointed or ▷Flamboyant ▷Gothic ▷tracery, also called ▷*undulating.* It consists largely of continuous curved ▷ogees.

Flue The hollow part of a ▷chimney through which smoke passes. It was formerly ▷parged, or lined with ▷plaster, but today's practice is to provide a flue-liner to ensure the smoke is contained. *Fluing* means ▷*splaying.*

Flush On the same plane. In ▷masonry and brickwork, flushing signifies the splintering of stones or ▷bricks from pressure at the joints, also termed *spaultering.* A *flush* ▷*bead moulding* is a bead set in a ▷channel so that its outer projection is flush with the ▷wall or ▷panel. A *flush* ▷*bolt* is one let into the surface so that its head does not project. *Flush* is also a term used to denote the bedding of stones or bricks in ▷mortar leaving no vacant space. *Flush-pointing* is where the mortar is brought out to the ▷face of the brickwork. *Flushwork* (▷[121]) is the use of ▷knapped

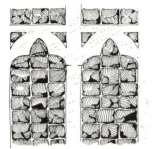

(*a*)

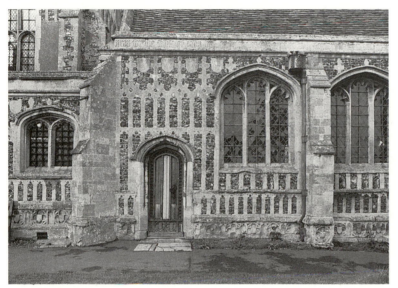

(*b*)

[121] FLUSHWORK (*a*) An example of squared flint and limestone tracery from the gatehouse of St Osyth's Priory, Essex. (*JJS*) (*b*) Church of the Holy Trinity, Long Melford, Suffolk: the Lady chapel of 1496, showing the flushwork and the Perpendicular windows with flattened arched heads. Around the parapet is an inscription inviting the reader to 'pray for ye soule of John Hyll' and many others named. (*JSC*)

▷flint in ▷panels of ▷freestone to form patterns, the split side set flush with the face of the wall.

Flute A hollow ▷channel or groove. Flutes are found in the ▷shafts of ▷Classical ▷columns, cut perpendicularly, and are used in all ▷Orders save the ▷Tuscan, and are semicircular or segmental in section. Flutes in the ▷Greek ▷Doric Order are segmental, separated by sharp ▷arrises, and there are usually twenty flutes. There are usually twenty-four in the ▷Ionic, ▷Corinthian, and ▷Composite Orders, deeper in section, separated not by arrises but by small ▷fillets. Except in the Greek Doric Order, flutes are sometimes filled with a convex moulding or ▷bead to one-third the height of the ▷shaft, called *cabling* (▷cable) (▷figures associated with the various Orders). Flutes usually terminate in quarter-spherical forms, but in the Doric Order they are stopped by ▷annulets. The horizontal fluting of the ▷torus of a Greek Ionic ▷base is called *reeding* (▷reed). Flutes also occur in numerous other architectural features, including ▷chimneys and ▷pilasters. *Fluting* means a series of flutes and may form spirals around a column.

Fly A *fly*- or *flying* ▷*rafter* carries the ▷roof projecting over a ▷gable, often protected by a ▷barge-board. A *fly-tower* is the space over the ▷proscenium of a ▷theatre from which the scenes, etc., are controlled. A *fly-screen* is a perforated metal sheet over a ▷larder ▷window.

Flying buttress ▷Buttress.

Flying front ▷False.

Foil [122] A small ▷arc or ▷lobe in ▷Gothic ▷tracery, separated from the next ▷foil by a ▷cusp: the number of foils is indicated by a prefix, e.g. ▷trefoil, ▷quatrefoil, ▷cinquefoil. Similarly, an ▷arch with foils and cusps is called a *foil arch,* and *foiled* means decorated with foils.

143

Foldage A ▷frieze of ▷scrolled ▷foliage.

Folding *Folding* ▷*doors* are made to meet each other from the opposite ▷jambs, are ▷hinged, and often tracked. When closed they appear to be a panelled ▷wall or one door. A *folding* or *folded* ▷*floor* is one in which the ▷boards are laid so that their joints are not continuous but in ▷bays or folds of 3, 4, 5, or more boards each, as opposed to straight-joint floors. A *folding wedge* is a pair of wedges used to ensure a tight ▷centring under the construction of an ▷arch.

Folding shutter ▷Box.

Foliage *Bocage*, or ▷leaves used as a background for figures. Also ▷leaf ▷ornament. The term *foliated* signifies sculptured leaves as ornaments, or the use of ▷arcs and ▷cusps in the formation of ▷tracery or in openings. A *foliate* ▷*mask* is a human face surrounded by foliage, and often with leaves growing from the mouth and nostrils, also called a *masque feuillu*, or ▷*Green Man*, found in ▷Antiquity, in the Middle Ages, and in the ▷Renaissance period.

Folly A building erected for a whimsical purpose, often as an ▷eyecatcher. Many had no practical use, and were often built as ▷ruins, or as ▷Gothic or ▷Classical remains, while others served as vantage-points for the appreciation of views.

Fons A ▷fountain.

Font [123] The vessel which contains the consecrated water for baptism. The body of the font was usually a large ▷block of stone hollowed out

and carried on a short ▷column or ▷pier or a clustered ▷shaft, and usually elevated on a ▷plinth or a series of ▷steps. The basin was usually lined with ▷lead. Fonts were covered, and many fine late-▷Gothic ▷canopies carried on pulleys survive. Lavish ▷ornament was applied to both basin and canopied covers.

Fontainebleau A style of decoration evolved at the ▷*château* by the Italian, French, and Flemish artists who worked there for ▷François I from 1528. It was essentially ▷High Renaissance and ▷Mannerist, and incorporated ▷strapwork, ▷cartouches, ▷caryatides, ▷Grotesques, ▷scrolls, and much ▷symbolism and ▷allegory. Among the ▷architects working there were Vignola and Serlio, and many of the decorations were published in Antwerp, so the style influenced ▷Flemish Mannerism and ▷Elizabethan work.

Foot That part on which anything stands; a base; a termination of a leg in ▷furniture. A measure of 12 inches. A *footing* is a foundation to a wall. A *foot-*▷*base* is a moulding (▷mould) above a ▷plinth. A *footing* ▷*beam* is a tie-beam. The *footing of a* ▷*wall* consists of the ▷courses at the base of a wall which project beyond the ▷face, or the lowest parts of a ▷foundation. A *footpace* is a ▷dais, ▷landing, broad ▷step, or ▷hearth-stone. A *footstall* is a plinth or base carrying a ▷pier or ▷column, or a ▷pedestal supporting something. A *footstone* is a ▷kneeler or ▷gable-▷springer, or an upright stone at the foot of a ▷grave.

Foramen Another word for ▷*fenestella*.

Fore Standing before, as *fore-*▷*choir* (antechoir), *fore-*▷*church* (consecrated extension to the liturgical west), *forecourt* (▷court forming an entrance, such as a ▷*cour*

(a) (b)

[123] FONT (a) The sumptuous Romanesque font in the Church of St Mary the Blessed Virgin, Stottesdon, Shropshire, of *c.* 1160, with much interlacing ornament. (*Salop County Council Record Office SRO 770/Large Box 1 No 9*) (b) Font in the nave of the Church of St Mary, Ottery St Mary, Devon, by William Butterfield, of 1850, an example of that architect's polychrome work, using inlaid marbles. (*JSC*)

d'honneur).

Foreyn A ▷cesspool or drain.

Foris One of two ▷leaves (*fores*) of a ▷door to a ▷Classical building.

Formeret An ▷arch-▷rib in ▷Gothic work lying next to the ▷wall, therefore called wall-rib. It is less wide than the other ribs dividing the vaulted ceiling (▷[245l]).

Form-pieces The stones forming the ▷tracery of a ▷window.

Formwork A structure of wood or metal which forms the ▷mould for wet ▷concrete. ▷Shuttering.

Forniciform Shaped like a ▷vaulted ▷roof or ceiling. *Fornix* is an ▷arch or a vault, vaulted opening, archway, arched ▷door, or an arch erected as a ▷monument.

Fort A fortified place for an army, often a fortified camp. A *fortress* is a ▷castle or a military structure constructed for defence, and comprises ▷walls, earthworks, ▷ramparts, bunkers, etc.: it is of much more monumental character than a fort.

Forum An open space in a Roman town serving as a market-place and general place of rendezvous. It often was surrounded by ▷porticoes and ▷colonnades. It was like the ▷Greek ▷*agora*, but was more formally planned as a series of civic spaces.

Foss, fosse A ditch, either wet or dry, for defence. A *fosse communale* was a common ▷grave.

Foundation The ground prepared for the footings (▷foot) of a ▷wall. The ▷concrete and footings are now called foundations, together with piling (▷pile). Also *founds*. A *foundation stone* is a ▷corner-stone or one inscribed. A foundation is the *fundamentum* or buried substructure of a building. The ▷Greeks called it ▷*euthynteria* as a levelling ▷course joining the foundation to the *crepidoma* (▷crepido).

Foundry An establishment where metals are cast in ▷moulds.

Fountain A natural or artificial ▷aperture from which water springs. In natural fountains the effect is produced by the pressure of the water-head, while in artificial fountains a head must be provided either by placing the source above the aperture or by the installation of a pump. Fountains have often given considerable scope for architectural ▷enrichment.

Four-centred arch ▷Arch.

Fourches patibulaires ▷Gallows for many victims, consisting of ▷piers with ▷beams between.

Four-leaf flower A ▷Gothic square ▷ornament in ▷cavetto mouldings (▷mould), also called ▷*fleuron*. The term is sometimes given to ▷ball-flower ornament.

Four-piece butt match ▷Diamond matching.

Fox Commonly found in illustrations of the ▷Fables, and often on ▷misericords (the fox dressed as a friar preaching to geese, for example). A *fox-*▷*bolt* is a bolt with a split end to receive a *foxtail wedge*: the latter is used to secure the split end of a ▷tenon in a ▷mortise, the split end of a fox bolt, or similar, by spreading the end as the wedge is driven home. Thus, a *foxtail tenon* employs this principle.

Foyer The entrance-▷hall of a ▷theatre, or any transitional space between the exterior and the main body of the interior of a public building.

Fractable Coping (▷cope) on a ▷gable, called *fractabling*. The term is used especially when the gable is stepped or has ▷ornamental ▷scrolled ends in layers (▷[44], [126]).

Frame The timber structure of a building, or any wooden structure which encloses volume. A *framed building* is any structure carried on a frame, whether timber, ▷concrete, or steel, as opposed to load-bearing ▷walls. ▷*Box-frame construction* involves setting up ▷posts on a ▷ground-▷beam, connecting them at the top by ▷wall-▷plates in one direction and ▷tie-beams in the other: the spaces between the posts are filled by ▷studs and ▷rails which are in turn filled by ▷brick-nogging (▷nog) or ▷wattle-and-▷daub. A ▷*cruck-frame* consists of two curved cruck-▷blades meeting at the ▷apex and resting on either stone or ▷brick ▷bases or on ground-beams. The cruck-frames were made on the ground and then raised in position. They were 'closed' by means of tie-beams which were ▷cantilevered out to hold the wall-plates, and carried ▷purlins and ▷ridge-pieces. The subject of ▷timber-framing is very complex, and readers are referred to the works of Maurice Barley, Ronald Brunskill, F. W. B. Charles, Cecil Hewett, and other authors. For *framed doors*, ▷door. A *frame saw* is one with multiple vertical or horizontal blades held in a frame and driven by machinery, or a heavy bow-saw. A frame is also something which surrounds a ▷panel or other feature, so

might be an ▷architrave or ▷trim, enclosing something, like a ▷border.

Franche-botrass A stone ▷buttress.

François I Also known as the *Premier style* it was the style of ▷High Renaissance and ▷Mannerist ▷architecture that appeared in France during the reign of Francois I (1515–47), and is associated with the ▷*Fontainebleau style*. It was revived during the nineteenth century (as ▷Elizabethan architecture was revived in England), and was also known as the ▷*Château style*. It mixed late ▷Gothic and early ▷Renaissance and Mannerist elements, and incorporated portrait-heads of the king, the ▷salamander (his ▷emblem), ▷Grotesques, half-figures, etc.

Franklin stove A closed cast-iron ▷stove with doors, invented by Benjamin Franklin in 1776.

Frater, fratery, fraterhouse A ▷refectory in a monastic establishment.

Free *Free Classicism* is a late nineteenth-century style in which various ▷Classical, ▷Mannerist, ▷Renaissance (▷[124]) and ▷Baroque elements were used in compositions, sometimes giving a very overloaded appearance. *Free style* (▷[125]) refers to a late nineteenth-century style in which the revival of ▷vernacular and ▷Queen Anne forms merged with a greater freedom of expression in which various elements were freely used, often with echoes of ▷Gothic, ▷Domestic Revival, and ▷Classical themes.

Freedstool, fridstool, frithstool A seat or chair near the ▷altar which was literally the seat of peace where those who claimed ▷sanctuary sat. Violation of a frithstool brought severe punishment.

Freemason A stonecutter who worked with ▷freestone. A craftsman who could hew and set freestones with ▷lime-▷mortar. One 'free' of a guild or company of masons, or, conversely, one *not* under the control of a local guild. An emancipated skilled craftsman in stone. A member of the Craft of Freemasonry, not necessarily connected with the building trade.

Freestone Any stone that can be easily worked.

French A *French arch* is a *Dutch arch* (▷arch). A *French* ▷*door*, also known as a *casement-door, door-*▷*window*, or *French window*, is a door with top and bottom ▷rails and ▷stiles, glazed for most of its length, usually arranged in two ▷leaves to give access to a ▷balcony or ▷garden. A *French* ▷*flier* or *flyer* is a flier of a three-quarter turn ▷stair arranged around an open ▷well. A *French* ▷*Order* is a ▷Classical Order in which the cock and ▷*fleur-de-*

(a)

(b)   (c)

[124] FREE RENAISSANCE STYLE (a) The Imperial Institute in South Kensington of 1887–93 by T. E. Colcutt. It incorporates Renaissance elements from Dutch, Spanish, French, German, and Flemish prototypes. (*RCHME BB71/11530*) (b)The Alliance Assurance Offices, St James's Street, London, 1881–88, by R. N. Shaw. A free-Renaissance hybrid with scrolled gables, mullioned and transomed windows, and other northern European features. (*JSC*) (c) The Grand Opera House, Belfast, of 1894–95, by Frank Matcham, an extraordinary concoction of freely treated Renaissance forms. (*JSC*)

147

[125] FREE STYLE Clouds, East Knoyle, Wiltshire, by Philip Webb, of 1879–91, a free mix of stylistic features, including Gothic, Queen Anne, vernacular elements, and Picturesque composition. (*RCHME BB69/2560 B. T. Batsford Ltd*)

lys decorate a variety of ▷Corinthian ▷capital. Philibert de l'Orme invented five French Orders with the ▷shaft banded with ▷leaves to conceal the joints between the ▷drums: the design of the ▷bands varied with each Order. Ribart de Chamoust's *l'Ordre François* of 1783 had plants twined around the shafts of the ▷columns (suggesting the ▷Solomonic or ▷spiral column) and the columns were arranged on a triangular plan, so there were three columns for each vertical support, an overtly Masonic device. *French Polish* is ▷shellac dissolved in methylated spirits, giving a high gloss. A *French* ▷*roof* is a tall roof, the sides of which are almost vertical, often with elaborate windows and cresting, and which contains one or more storeys (▷Mansard). The *French Second Empire* style of 1852–70 was eclectic, and drew on the styles of ▷François I, on the ▷Baroque of the ▷Louis Quatorze style, and on the ▷Neoclassical elements of ▷Louis Seize interiors: Napoleonic ▷motifs of the ▷*Empire* style re-emerged. The style is best seen in the Paris ▷boulevards, where tall French roofs with cresting (▷cress), ▷*oeil-de-boeuf* windows, and high ▷chimneys are very much in evidence, and where a wide range of architectural ▷enrichment occurs on the ▷façades. *French stuc* is imitation stone made of ▷plaster. A *French* ▷*tile* is a type of interlocking tile, often hexagonal.

Fresco ▷Wall or ceiling decoration where the colours are applied before the ▷lime-▷plaster is dry. Finishes are applied *a* ▷*secco*, or when the plaster is dry. *Buon fresco* is fresco painted on wet plaster, while *fresco secco*, or simply *secco*, is a ▷mural on a dry wall surface, and has a limited life as the colours are fugitive.

Fret, frette, fretwork ▷Ornaments of ▷fillets meeting at right-angles, arranged in ▷bands of angular ▷key-patterns, also called ▷*Greek key* (▷[137]) or ▷*meander*. Fret patterns can also occur as ▷diapers or as compartments, and are incised, pierced, ▷relief, or painted. Elaborate fretwork ▷trellises are known, and types of fretwork, are called ▷*Chinese paling*, ▷*interlacing, angular* ▷*guilloche*, or ▷*lattice*. It can be arranged as contrasting patterns of light and dark. Where some of the fillets are set at angles, the effect is oriental, and was popular in eighteenth-century ▷Rococo *Chinoiserie* (▷Chinese) designs.

Friary A religious establishment or ▷convent of friars. The friars were mostly brethren of four mendicant orders: the Franciscans, Minorites, or Grey Friars; the Augustines or Austin Friars; the Dominicans, Friars Preachers, or Black Friars; and the Carmelites, or White Friars.

Frieze The middle division of an ▷entablature lying between the ▷cornice and the ▷architrave. The ▷Tuscan frieze is plain, but the ▷Doric is subdivided along its length by ▷triglyphs and ▷metopes. ▷Ionic, ▷Corinthian, and ▷Composite friezes are often embellished with continuous ▷sculpture, but can be plain. Sometimes friezes are pulvinated (▷pulvin), convex, or cushioned, usually in the Ionic and Composite Orders. The frieze of a ▷capital is called the ▷*hypotrachelium*, as in a species of ▷Ionic from the ▷Erechtheion. A *frieze* ▷*panel* is the upper panel of a six-panelled door, while a *frieze-*▷*rail* is the upper rail but one of such a door. Friezes are also found at the top of interior walls below the cornice. Any strip of decoration (▷hypotrachelium, figures associated with the Classical Orders).

Frigidarium The room with the cold-water basin in an ancient ▷bath.

Frithstool ▷Freedstool.

Frog An indentation on a ▷bed-▷face or faces of a ▷brick to save clay: it is usually a V-shaped indentation, and is normally laid *frog-down* or *frog-empty*, but if the frog is uppermost, it should be filled with mortar. There is no structural advantage either way, but frog-down saves mortar and makes the wall less heavy.

Front Any ▷façade of a building, but usually the main ▷elevation. The ▷garden-front would be the elevation facing the gardens. A *frontal* is the hanging or ▷antependium in front of an ▷altar. A *frontis-piece* is the ▷face of a building, its decorated entrance, its main façade, an entrance embellished with architectural ▷motifs, or an ▷ornamented ▷bay of an elevation. A *fronton* is a small ▷pediment over a ▷niche, ▷door, or ▷window, sometimes called a *frontal*.

Frosted A type of rustication (▷rustic) in ▷masonry like icicles or ▷stalactites. Frosted ▷glass is roughened glass, made opaque by acid-etching or sand-blasting, and matt.

Fruit Often used in ▷ornament, in ▷festoons or ▷swags, and bursting forth from a ▷cornucopia. ▷Baskets with ▷fruit are found on ▷gate-▷piers, while fruit and flowers occur in decorative schemes concerned with the ▷seasons.

Fulcrum A support about which rotation can occur.

Fumarium A ▷*femerell* or *fumerell*.

Functionalism A twentieth-century dogma that holds that the form of a building should follow its function, ignoring the fact that ▷architecture must function as architecture, i.e. work well, be sound in structure, and give delight and aesthetic pleasure.

Furniture Fittings to ▷doors and ▷windows, including ▷knobs, levers, ▷hinges, ▷bolts, and ▷locks. Any finishings or fittings other than the structure.

Furring ▷Fir.

Fusarole A member with a semicircular section, or a ▷bead, found under the ▷echinus of the ▷Doric, ▷Ionic, and ▷Corinthian-▷Orders.

Fust The ▷shaft of a ▷column or the trunk of a ▷pilaster. The ▷ridge of a ▷roof.

Fylfot A ▷swastika-like form with bent human legs terminating in feet.

G

Gabbart scaffold A ▷scaffold of squared bolted timbers.

Gable, gavel [126] The end ▷wall of a building, the top of which conforms to the slope of the ▷roof which abuts against it. In contemporary usage, the term is applied only to the upper part of such a wall above ▷eaves-level, and the entire wall is called a *gable-end*. In

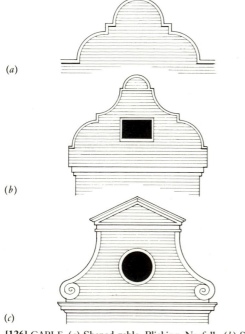

(*a*)

(*b*)

(*c*)

[126] GABLE (*a*) Shaped gable, Blicking, Norfolk. (*b*) Shaped gable, Knodishall, Suffolk. (*c*) Dutch gable, Raynham, Norfolk. (*JJS*)

some instances the large end-▷window of a building was referred to as a *gable window*. ▷*Romanesque gables* reflecting the ▷pitch of the roof were very steep, while *First-*▷*Pointed gables* were at first steep then nearly equilateral triangles. Later mediaeval gables were much lower, and were ▷coped and crenellated (▷crenel). When the roof was carried over the gable it terminated in ▷ornamental ▷barge-▷boards. During the sixteenth and seventeenth centuries gables were varied, stepped, curved, or angled, reflecting a north-European influence. A *gable-*▷*cross* is one used as a terminating feature at the ▷apex of a gable. A *Dutch gable* is one with curved or ▷scrolled sides crowned by a ▷pediment or an ▷arch. In ▷Classical architecture the low triangular gable, framed by the low pitches of the roof, is called a *pediment*. A *gabled* ▷*tower* is one finished with gables on two or four sides. A *gable-*▷*post* is the upright at the apex of a gable against which the barge-boards join. A *gable-roof* is one with gables at each end. A *gable-*▷*shoulder* is brickwork or ▷masonry carrying the foot of the gable, also called *gable-*▷*springer*. ▷*skew-block*, *skew-*▷*butt*, or ▷*kneeler*, which projects. A *gablet* is a small ornamental gable over a ▷niche, ▷buttress, or some other feature. Other gables include the *crow-stepped* or *corbie-stepped* (▷corbel) type with stepped sides; the *hipped gable* in which the top part slopes back with ▷hips; and the *shaped gable* with multi-curved sides. The tops of ▷brick gables often have *tumbled* (▷tumbling course) brickwork (▷barge-boards, ▷corbel, ▷roof).

Gadroon, godroon [127] One of a set of convex mouldings (▷mould) joined at their extremities to form an ▷enrichment: *gadrooning* is found on the upper surface of convex mouldings, similar to fingers. *Gadrooned* means enriched with convex ▷rods. It is also called *lobed decoration* (▷lobe), *knulled decoration* (▷knulling), or *thumb-moulding*.

150

[127] GADROONS (*JSC*)

Gaine A decorative ▷pedestal. A ▷herm.

Galilee A ▷porch or ▷chapel at the west end of a ▷church. The term is sometimes applied to the western portion of a ▷nave. A galilee is also called a ▷*narthex* or a ▷*paradise*. There is a fine galilee at Durham Cathedral. Galilees were often reserved for women, or were places where monks could meet female relations. The dead could be buried in galilees. A *galilee porch* is a ▷vestibule to the church, and connects directly with the exterior.

Galleon A common ▷motif in ▷Elizabethan ▷Revival and ▷Arts-and-Crafts work.

Gallery A room of great length in proportion to width used as a ▷passage or as a place for the display of pictures and sculpture, commonly found in grander ▷Elizabethan and ▷Jacobean houses. An upper ▷floor or ▷loft to accommodate musicians or spectators. ▷Screens in ▷churches often had galleries for the ▷rood-loft or for the placing of the organ. The ▷triforium or ▷tribune above the ▷aisles opening to the ▷nave is sometimes called a gallery. In post-Reformation times, galleries or ▷scaffolds were erected above aisles and at the west end of the nave to accommodate more people, often to the detriment of the ▷architecture. The whole or a portion of the upper ▷storey of ▷theatre-seating is called a gallery. A gallery is also a room, often top-lit, for the display of works of art, or a building in which such rooms are situated. The term is also given to an ▷arcade, in the sense of a covered walk, a shopping arcade, or a connection between buildings or parts of buildings. A *gallery* ▷*grave* has a burial-▷chamber and ▷passage forming a long stone-lined gallery. An arcade on a façade.

Gallet [128] A small stone chip or spall placed in wide ▷mortar joints for decorative purposes or to reduce the amounts of mortar used. The technique is called *galleting*, *garreting*, or *garnetting*.

[128] GALLETING Galleted joints in basalt rubble walls with dressed stone quoins with chamfered joints from the parish church at Waringstown, Co. Down. (*JSC*)

Gallows A ▷beam carried on two uprights from which persons were hanged. The term was sometimes synonymous with the ▷*Cross*. A *gallows* ▷*bracket* is a triangular bracket formed of an L-shape with ▷brace.

Galvanizing The coating of steel or iron with ▷zinc to prevent rusting.

Gambrel A hipped ▷roof with a small gable (▷gable) at the ▷apex, or a ▷Mansard roof (▷[212]).

Ganister A dark ▷sandstone containing up to 10 per cent of clay. It is ground and ▷lime is added as a binding agent. The ▷bricks are then made in powerful presses and burnt. Ganister bricks can withstand temperatures of 1800°C, so are useful for lining fireplaces or furnaces.

Gaol A ▷prison.

Garden A piece of ground, usually defined and often enclosed, wholly or partially, on which flowers, shrubs,

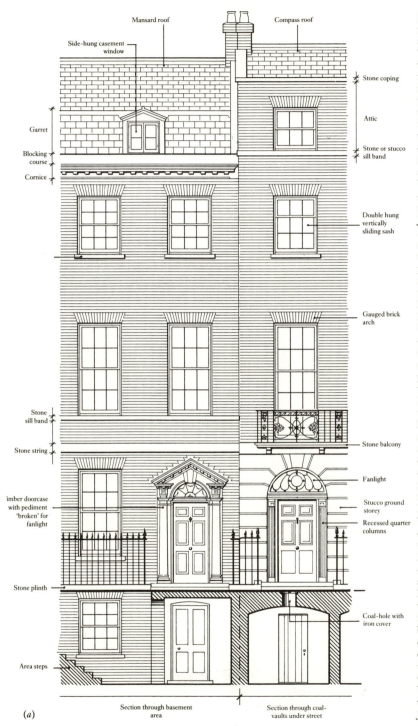

Mansard roof

Compass roof

Side-hung casement window

Stone coping

Attic

Garret

Stone or stucco sill band

Blocking course

Cornice

Double hung vertically sliding sash

Stone sill band

Gauged brick arch

Stone string

Stone balcony

Timber doorcase with pediment 'broken' for fanlight

Fanlight

Stucco ground storey

Recessed quarter columns

Stone plinth

Coal-hole with iron cover

Area steps

(a)

Section through basement area

Section through coal-vaults under street

[129] GEORGIAN (*a*) Elevations of typical Georgian terrace houses, with sections through the basement areas. The house on the left has a doorcase with broken-based pediment to permit the fanlight to rise, and the *piano nobile* is denoted by the string-course. Note the garret under the Mansard roof. On the right the ground floor has a stucco-faced front, and the fanlight is of a wider, 'teardrop' type. The balcony is carried on brackets cantilevered out from the wall, and the balcony rails are of cast iron with Greek patterns. Windows have gauged brick arches over them. Above the sill band at the top is the Attic storey. (*b*) Houses by J. Booth of 1819–23 in Clerkenwell, London, on the Lloyd-Baker Estate, showing the Greek Revival influence in the flattened pediments and wide proportions of the windows (with margin-panes). Although actually terraces, these houses are designed to look like semi-detached pairs, or even linked units. (*c*) The Church of St Chad, Shrewsbury, by George Steuart, completed 1793. This very original Georgian church has an elegant three-stage tower and a circular nave. The portico is a severe Roman Doric Order with unfluted columns, while the paired Ionic pilasters used elsewhere are uncommonly elongated. The tower has a square base, an octagonal stage above enriched with Ionic pilasters, and a crowning drum with a peristyle of Corinthian columns carrying the entablature and dome. (*d*) Double-fronted shop of two bow-windows flanking a door with fanlight over. Note the consoles and enrichment. This is a fine example in York of a type of shop-front that was common in Georgian times. (*e*) A corner of Myddleton Square, Clerkenwell, designed by William Chadwell Mylne, and built in the 1820s. This is a typical late-Georgian type of development, with a basement, a rendered ground floor, the *piano nobile* level emphasized by means of the blind arches and the cast-iron balcony railings, with cantilevered balconies, and plain upper storeys. (*f*) Simple country Georgian farmhouse near Waringstown, Co. Down, with lime-washed walls and thatched roof. (*a*, *JJS; b–f, JSC*)

(b)

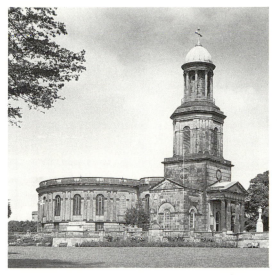

(c)

(d)

(e)

(f)

and trees are grown, and used for pleasure or study. There are also *herb gardens* and *vegetable gardens* called *kitchen gardens*. A *garden city* is a town built in the countryside consisting of houses with gardens and all amenities, and with shops, industries, etc. It was based on the ideas of Ebenezer Howard, and the first examples were Letchworth and Welwyn. The concept was to provide healthy towns in which the benefits of town *and* country could be enjoyed. These were based upon the early experiments of building model villages, such as Saltaire, Port Sunlight, and Bournville. A *garden suburb* was an early nineteenth-century invention with its roots in the ▷Romantic English ▷Picturesque landscape tradition, and its earliest prototypes were the designs for the Eyre Estate, Blaise Hamlet, the Ladbroke Estate in Kensington, and Nash's work in the Regent's Park area. The finest garden suburbs are Bedford Park (from 1875) and Hampstead Garden Suburb (from 1906). A *garden-house* is a summerhouse in a garden. For *garden wall* ▷*bond*, ▷brick. Gardening has inspired many decorative schemes showing ▷fruit, flowers, implements, the ▷seasons, and crops. Picturesque gardens were designed to look like paintings, and included deliberately ▷rural buildings such as the *cottage orné* (▷cot). Special garden ▷furniture, such as seats, were made in quantity, especially from the eighteenth century.

Garderobe A ▷wardrobe or a small room. Also a ▷closet for defaecation, etc. in a mediaeval building.

Garetta, garretta A ▷turret on the ▷battlements to provide shelter for the guard.

Gargoyle, gurgoyle. A ▷projecting ▷spout to throw the water from a ▷gutter away from a ▷wall. Sometimes they are plain, but often are carved with representations of figures or animals, frequently bizarre in treatment, and spewing out evil away from the House of God. Gargoyles are also found as features of mouldings (▷mould) unassociated with waterspouts (▷[198]). ▷Classical waterspouts were often ▷lions' ▷masks.

Garland ▷Ornaments of flowers, ▷fruits, and ▷leaves, usually found in ▷friezes; ▷festoon.

Garnet A T-shaped ▷hinge, also called a *cross-garnet*.

Garret The upper part of a house, wholly or partially within the ▷roof structure, with sloping sides, usually for the accommodation of servants. ▷Attic.

Garreting ▷Gallet.

Garretta ▷Garetta.

Garrison house A type of house made of logs of timber, with the first ▷floor ▷jettied out, and often associated with a stockade.

Garth The open space or ▷court of a ▷cloister.

Gaskin The jointing of socketed ▷vitrified clay ▷pipes with a ring of rope and ▷cement.

Gate A large ▷door, of wood or metal: the word is used to describe an entrance to a space rather than to a building. A *gate-house* is a building erected over a gateway to a ▷castle, fortified ▷manor-house, or a town. A ▷*gate-pier* is a hanging-▷post for a gate, also called *gate-post*, or *hanging-pier* or *-post*. A *gate-*▷*tower* is a fortified structure containing a gate and protecting it. A *gateway* is an opening in a ▷wall, ▷fence, or enclosure, a ▷frame or ▷arch in which a gate is hung, or a building at an entrance of some architectural significance, or for defence.

Gauge The length of a ▷slate or ▷tile below the ▷lap and equal to the spacing of the ▷battens. For *gauged arch*, ▷arch. *Gauged* implies precise brickwork, or ▷brick rubbers (▷rubbed). *Gauged* ▷*lime* ▷*mortar* is a mixture in specified proportions of sand and lime to which ordinary ▷Portland ▷cement is added.

Gault Gault clays are heavy and tough, but contain enough chalk to make the ▷bricks pale yellow or white when burnt. Gault bricks are often perforated or have ▷frogs to reduce their weight.

Gavel A ▷gable.

Gazebo Properly, a small ▷apartment on a ▷roof with a view, also called a ▷*belvedere*. A *summer-house* or any ▷ornamental structure commanding a view.

Geison A ▷raked ▷cornice, as on a ▷pediment.

Gemel Also ▷*chymol*, *gemmel*, *gymmer*, *jimmer*. Two elements in a construction, or a pair. A ▷hinge. A *gemel* ▷*window* is a two-▷light window. *Geminated* means ▷*coupled* or *paired*.

Genii Winged infants, ▷cherubs, or wingless ▷*putti*.

Genlese, gentese ▷Cusps or ▷featherings.

Geometry The science concerned with the properties and relations of magnitudes in space, as lines, surfaces, and solids. A practical art of measuring and planning, mainly associated with ▷architecture. Geometrical elements occur in architecture: ▷brick patterns, the ways in which ▷masonry is laid, ▷floor patterns, and inlay all depend on geometry, which is an essential part of ▷ornament and of the disposition of parts. The *Geometrical style* of ▷Gothic is characterized by ▷tracery consisting almost entirely of geometrical forms such as circles and multifoils, and dates from the first part of the *Second-▷Pointed* or ▷*Decorated* style of the early fourteenth century (▷Gothic, ▷tracery). A *geometrical staircase* is one in which the ▷flight of stone ▷stairs is supported by the ▷wall at one end of each ▷step, each step resting on the next. There are no ▷newels.

Georgian [129] ▷Architecture of the period of the first four Georges (1714–1830), but the term is usually applied to a very simple form of stripped ▷Classical domestic architecture featuring plain ▷window-openings with ▷sashes, doorcases that vary from the elaborate treatment with ▷consoles, ▷pediments, ▷columns and ▷pilasters, to plain openings with ▷fanlights. During the Georgian period ▷Rococo, *Chinoiserie* (▷Chinese), and Gothick (▷Gothic) influences occurred, often in interior decoration or in ▷ornamental buildings. The early Georgian period saw the rise of ▷Palladianism under the ▷aegis of Lord Burlington and his circle, but the latter half of the century witnessed the elegant and varied styles of Robert Adam, with ▷Pompeian and other influences, becoming fashionable, then giving way to ▷Neoclassicism.

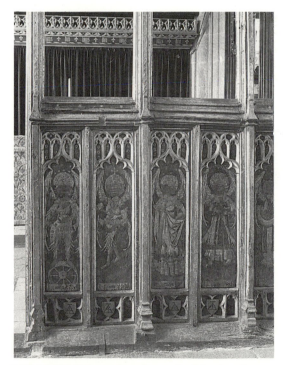

[130] GESSO Gesso-work on the panels of the chancel-screen of *c.* 1500 in the Church of St Edmund, King and Martyr, Southwold, Suffolk. (*JSC*)

German Order ▷Britannic Order.

Gesso [130] A prepared surface of ▷gypsum ▷plaster, ▷glue, and ▷whiting, to create a plane area or to give ▷relief to a painting.

Giant Order [131] An Order that rises through more than one ▷storey, also known as a ▷Colossal Order.

Gib A *gib* or *jib* ▷*door* is one ▷flush with its surroundings and concealed. A *gib* is also a metal packing-piece which holds together the pieces of a *cottered* joint, as in the ▷king-post ▷truss.

Gibbonwork Elaborate naturalistic limewood carving in the manner of Grinling Gibbons (1648–1721), and featuring ▷fruit, flowers (▷floral ornament), ▷garlands, and ▷trophies.

Gibbs surround [132] A surround of a ▷door, ▷window, or ▷niche consisting of large ▷blocks of stone interrupting the ▷architrave, usually with a triple keystone at the top set under a ▷pediment. It is named after the architect James Gibbs (1682–1754).

Giblet A *giblet-▷check* or *check* is a rebate (▷rabbet) in stone for a ▷door or a ▷shutter, where there is no wooden ▷frame.

Gigantic Order The ▷Tuscan Order, so named by Scamozzi.

Gilding ▷Gold ▷leaf applied as a surface finish, or the finish itself.

Gin palace [133] An ornate public-house developed in the 1830s after the passing of a law to encourage the drinking of beer in alehouses licensed for the sale of beer only. The large breweries and owners of public ▷taverns saw independent beer-shops as a threat, and began buying up licensed houses where spirits could be sold. ▷Plate-▷glass, newly available in large sizes (engraved and acid-etched), gaslight, coloured ▷tiles, and advertisement-mirrors were all part of the gin-palace ▷décor, designed to attract custom from the drab streets. The first gin palace appears to have been Thompson & Fearon's establishment of 1829–31 in London. The gin palace was the result and not the cause of the gin-drinking habit.

Gingerbread Elaborate carved woodwork applied to late ▷Gothic ▷Revival houses.

Giraffe A nineteenth-century ▷ornamental device.

Girandole A large branched candlestick.

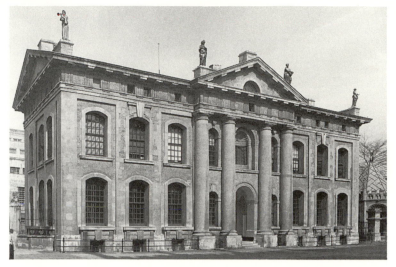

[131] GIANT ORDER The Clarendon Building, Oxford, erected 1711–15 to designs by Hawksmoor. The Giant Order of engaged Tuscan columns carries the central pediment. (*JSC*)

Girder The main ▷beam carrying the ▷joists of a ▷floor, or any main structural beam.

Girdle A horizontal ▷band or ▷fillet surrounding the ▷shaft of a ▷column.

Girt, girth A horizontal member in a ▷frame between ▷columns or ▷posts supporting a ▷floor.

Glacis In fortification, sloping ground falling from the ▷base of a ▷wall allowing the ground to be raked by fire, or the inclined surface of a ▷cornice or ▷parapet top.

Gladiatorial mask A feature of a ▷trophy or ▷panoply used as a crowning feature in ▷Renaissance and ▷Baroque ▷architecture.

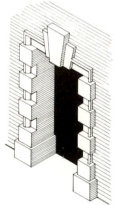

[132] GIBBS SURROUND(*JJS*)

[133] GIN PALACE Etching by Cruikshank in the series *The Drunkard's Children*, showing an early gin-palace interior, with gas flares in the large plate-glass window. (*Guildhall Library, City of London*)

Glasgow School A group of artists and ▷architects including C. R. Mackintosh (1868–1928) and Margaret Macdonald (1865–1933) who worked in Glasgow from the 1890s, and who were influenced by Continental ▷Art Nouveau and by the English ▷Arts-and-Crafts Movement. Mackintosh later developed an elongated type of design with sparse linear forms.

Glass, glazing During the Middle Ages the use of coloured ▷glass set in ▷lead was common in churches, and surviving examples are among the glories of mediaeval art. Stained and painted mediaeval glass is a major subject. ▷Windows contained brilliant colours, and told vivid stories in ▷symbol and in stylized form. Although glass was extensively used by the Romans, the material was not widely used for windows until the ▷Romanesque period when the art of glazing revived, reaching its zenith during the rise of ▷Gothic. Much glass was destroyed at the time of the Reformation, and the craft of stained-glass manufacture fell into decline. Glass was used in small ▷panes because of the difficulties of manufacturing it, and was either fixed in lead ▷cames or in small ▷panels secured by glazing-▷bars. In domestic buildings glass was too expensive, except for the very rich, and as late as 1500 linen impregnated with beeswax was more usual because of the cost. From the end of the Middle Ages until the 1830s most clear glass used for domestic glazing was ▷*crown glass*, made from molten blown glass spun so that the glass was spread into a large disc, the outer sections of which were thin and clear, but the centre of which was a hub of thick glass called the ▷*bottle*, ▷*bull's eye*, or *bullion*, which was not used. It is one of the oddities of taste that bottle-glass, or imitations of it, are used to suggest authenticity of an old building, even though it is nothing of the sort. Crown glass was preferred to *muff* or *broad* glass because of its clarity and lustre. The critical invention in 1832–39 was by Chance Bros., of Stourbridge, who improved broad glass, and then devised a method of polishing the surfaces of thin sheets to give a finish as good as crown glass, at reduced cost and without the size restrictions. This enabled glazing-bars to be removed from ▷sashes, thus altering the ▷proportions of windows. The ▷Victorians developed techniques of acid-etching, sand-blasting, etc. which created a rich field of decorative possibilities. The revival of ▷Gothic also brought about a revival of the art of stained-glass manufacture. *Glaze* is a ▷ceramic coating formed on the surface of ▷earthenware, and is commonly found on ▷bricks or ▷faience. It is burnt on in a second firing.

Globe A ▷symbol of navigation and exploration, and an ▷attribute of ▷Geometry and Astronomy in iconographical schemes featuring the ▷Liberal Arts. It also signifies universality, and, topped by a ▷cross, is a symbol of sovereignty.

Glory ▷Aureole.

Glue *Animal glue*, or *Scotch glue*, is made from the skins and bones of animals. The skins are steeped in liquid ▷lime for three weeks, washed, dried, and boiled to extract the glutin or glue. The bones are ground, placed in benzol or other solvents to remove the fat, then boiled to extract the glue, and finally purified by heating with alum (sulphate of aluminium and potassium in water). Animal glue is softened in cold water and then melted in water-jacket glue-pots. It is very strong and is used in ▷joinery, but is neither water- nor heat-resistant. *Casein glue* is derived from milk: rennet, or acids such as hydrochloric, is added to skimmed milk to precipitate the curd which is then washed, pressed, dried, and ground. Borax is then added, and the glue is sold in powdered form. It is mixed with cold water and applied cold: it is obtained either in liquid form or as a powder to be dissolved in alcohol. Resin adhesives are waterproof, fire resistant, and strong. Other traditional glues are ▷*fish glue*, *soya bean* or *oil-seed residue glue*, *vegetable glue*, and *blood-albumen glue*.

Glyph A sunken ▷channel, usually vertical: the perpendicular channels cut in the ▷projecting tablets of a ▷Doric ▷frieze (which are called ▷triglyphs from their having three vertical channels, or, more correctly, two whole channels with a half-channel at each side of the tablet) are called *glyphs*.

Glyptotheca A building for the display of ▷sculpture.

Gnomon A rod or other object which serves to indicate the time by casting its shadow on a marked surface: the pin or triangular plate on a sundial. A ▷column employed in order to observe the meridian altitude of the sun. A *gnomonic column* is a cylinder on which the hour of day is indicated by the shadow cast by a fixed or moveable stylus. An ▷obelisk.

Gobbet A ▷block of stone.

Godroon ▷Gadroon.

God's acre A churchyard.

Going The horizontal distance between two successive ▷nosings is the going of a ▷tread in a ▷stair.

Gola, gula An ▷ogee, or the cymatium (▷cyma).

Gold *Gold* ▷*leaf* is thin sheet gold used for ▷enriching ▷ornament. *Gold* ▷*size* is a sticky ▷varnish by which gold leaf is applied to a surface.

Golden section A ▷proportion defined as a line cut

through in such a way that the smaller ▷section is to the larger as the larger is to the whole.

Golgotha A place of interment, a graveyard, or a ▷charnel-house. The *golgotha* of a ▷rood is the base-▷beam into which the three figures are set. This beam was carved to represent skulls and bones set among rocks and grasses (▷[211]).

Golosniki Acoustic jars.

Gomphi ▷Curb-stones placed in a line of *umbones*, or raised curb-stones, and bigger than an ▷*umbo*, to protect pedestrians from wheeled traffic in ▷Antiquity.

Goose-neck A curved handrail on top of a ▷newel. A ▷scrolled open ▷pediment. Also called ▷*swan-neck*.

Gophus A wedge-shaped element driven between two members to force them closer to their contiguous members. Also a large wedge-shaped, round-headed stone placed between ▷curb-stones of a ▷Roman ▷pavement to protect pedestrians, also called ▷*gomphi*.

Gore A ▷crescent-shape, a half-moon, or a semi-circular object.

Gorge A ▷cavetto moulding (▷mould) or throating (▷throat), less recessed than a ▷scotia, and chiefly used in ▷frames. It is also used for the ▷cyma recta or to denote the ▷neck of a ▷column. A ▷fillet or narrow ▷band around the ▷shaft at its top and bottom. Also a narrow entrance into a ▷bastion. A *gorge* ▷*cornice* is a large cavetto or ▷Egyptian cornice. *Gorged* is encirclement of a throat in heraldry.

Gorgerin The small ▷frieze at the top of a ▷Roman ▷Doric ▷capital between the ▷astragal at the top of the ▷shaft and the ▷annulets. It is also called the ▷*neck*, or a ▷*collarino*, while Vitruvius calls it ▷*hypotrachelium*.

Gorgon A mythological female with hair of rearing ▷serpents, and with ▷wings, ▷claws, and flesh-tearing teeth. In ▷architecture only the gorgon's ▷mask (also called ▷*Medusa head*) is used. *Gorgoneia* are keystones or other elements carved with representations of the heads of Gorgons.

Gospel side The side of the ▷altar on the north.

Gothic [134] The term refers to the style of ▷architecture prevalent in Europe from the latter part of the twelfth until the sixteenth century, and, in certain locations (such as Oxford) even continuing into the seventeenth century. It is characterized by the ▷pointed arch, by ▷piers and ▷columns that owe their ▷proportions and detail only distantly to ▷Classicism,

by clustered ▷shafts, by ribbed ▷vaults, by elaborately traceried ▷windows, and by an essentially vertical emphasis. Classical architecture is *columnar* and *trabeated* in its essentials, while Gothic is ▷*arcuated*, springing upwards, striving for the heavens. Openings became large, and ▷walls were supported by ▷buttresses. Some features of Gothic were developed in ▷Romanesque architecture, but it was not until the pointed arch came into general use that the style really evolved, first in France. *First-Pointed* (known in Britain as ▷*Early English*) *Gothic* (▷[107]) had windows that were long, tall, and pointed, called ▷lancets, and were essentially holes in the wall, without ▷tracery, placed singly or grouped in walls. Mouldings (▷mould) were deeply cut and bold, while ▷enrichments, such as ▷nail-head and ▷dog-tooth were frequently employed. ▷Capitals were of the foliate or ▷bell type. Buttresses were no longer Romanesque ▷pilaster strips, but deep and narrow, clearly taking the thrust of stone-vaulted ceilings. The use of the pointed or 'hinged' arch enabled ▷rib-vaults over rectangular spaces to be constructed without the problems incurred using the semicircular arch for the same purpose. By First-Pointed is meant the period from the end of the twelfth century (although the ▷chevet and ▷narthex of the Basilica of St Denis near Paris, erected by the Abbot Suger, dates from the 1140s) to the end of the thirteenth. During the *Second-Pointed* (known in Britain as ▷*Decorated*, ▷[98]) period of the fourteenth century, tracery was developed, first ▷plate tracery, then ▷bar tracery in geometrical patterns. Nail-head and dog-tooth gave way to ▷fleuron and ▷ball-flower ▷enrichment, while ▷crockets and other ornament became profuse. The later phase of Second-Pointed Gothic saw the use of ▷curvilinear tracery, the widespread exploitation of the ▷ogee arch, the appearance of ▷mouchette or ▷dagger-forms in tracery, and the adoption of ▷reticulated patterns. Windows became very large, and the flame-like forms gave the name ▷*Flamboyant* to later elaborate Gothic. In the ▷*Perpendicular* (▷[192]) period, which started in the 1350s (although the Perpendicular choir at Gloucester dates from *c.* 1337) and continued until the seventeenth century (and is known only in England), the flowing lines were generally replaced by ▷panel-like forms with very flat ▷depressed arches. The use of ▷hood mouldings, the flattening of roofs and the adoption of ▷crenellated ▷parapets, and the elaboration of ▷lierne vaulting and then ▷fan vaulting gave Perpendicular or *Third-Pointed* its chief ▷motifs. The Gothic style did not die with the ▷Tudors, but continued into the seventeenth century. The term *Gothic Survival* denotes the survival of Gothic forms in the seventeenth century, especially in provincial traditional buildings. The *Gothic* ▷*Revival* (▷[136]) as ▷architect-designed buildings, can probably be said to overlap with Gothic Survival, for Wren used Gothic for some of his City churches, as well as for Tom Tower in Oxford. Hawksmoor also used a variety of Gothic at All Souls' College, Oxford, and his western towers of Westminster Abbey are also Gothic (although their mouldings are Classical). The Gothic Revival is generally held to have begun in the eighteenth century, largely as a result of a growing interest in romantic ▷ruins, antiquities, and irrationalism, as opposed to the Apollonian clarity of the Enlightenment. Fashionable *Gothick* really began with Sanderson Miller's (1716–80) works in Warwickshire of 1743–52, and with Horace Walpole's (1717–97) Strawberry Hill (1750–70), although the latter owed little to period precedent, and was perhaps more ▷Rococo than Gothic in spirit. Gothick (▷[135]) was associated with the ▷Picturesque, and particularly with Batty Langley's *Gothic Architecture* of 1742 which was a pattern-book of Gothick including Five 'Orders'. Although the book owed very little to real Gothic, it created a fashion for ▷Georgian Gothick that looked anything but mediaeval. Gothick was frivolous, and was essentially pretty, as Rococo or *Chinoiserie* (▷Chinese) were pretty, and it was used in interior decoration, for garden ▷follies, and for sham ruins. It was associated with Gothick horror stories and with a taste for ghosts, gloomy ruins, and the irrational. In the early nineteenth century many 'Gothic' ▷churches were built that were in reality Georgian preaching-boxes with simplified Perpendicular or Early English fenestration. True Gothic Revival, based upon a scholarly study of the mediaeval buildings, began with Rickman and Pugin. From the 1840s onwards many fine ▷Victorian churches were built in a correct Gothic manner with fittings and ▷glass to match, largely as a result of the activities of the Ecclesiological Society. Gothic Revival started with Perpendicular, settled for a while with Second-Pointed of the geometrical variety, then gradually worked its way back through First-Pointed (English first, then Continental, especially Burgundian) to a more 'primitive' source of Gothic. Interest was awakened by Street, Ruskin, and others in ▷Italian Gothic and in the use of structural ▷polychromy, so that the Gothic Revival of the 1850s and early 1860s was often very colourful, glowing with polished ▷granites, polychrome brickwork, and the like. Continental Gothic was revived for many buildings, including the Midland Grand Hotel at St Pancras by Scott, and Manchester Town Hall by Waterhouse. Towards the end of the Revival, under the influence of architects such as Bodley, interest in English Second-Pointed revived, and even Perpendicular returned to favour at the end. Gothic architecture includes lancets, ▷foils, ▷cusps, tracery, buttresses, complex vaulting, ▷pinnacles, and ▷crockets. A *Gothic* ▷*cornice* is an eighteenth-century open-work series of ▷pendants arranged as ▷interlacing Gothic arches.

Gouache Paint made of pigment mixed with gum and thinned with water.

Goufing ▷Underpinning with wedges.

Graces Three female figures, supposedly called Aglaïa, Thalia, and Euphrosyne, usually depicted holding each other's hands.

Gradation Rising by ▷steps or degrees, as in a ▷theatre. Also a barely discernible change of colour.

Gradetto An ▷annulet.

Gradine A ▷step, or a raised ▷shelf above and behind an ▷altar. A ▷platform or ▷*predella* on which an ▷altar rests.

Graffito A word, ▷inscription, or doodle on a ▷wall, not to be confused with *sgraffito* (▷scraped). Several mediaeval examples survive, at Ashwell in Hertfordshire, and in King's College Chapel, Cambridge.

Graining Imitation wood-grain or textures achieved by paint worked over with a comb, and subsequently ▷varnished.

Granary A building for storing corn.

Grange A farm, usually attached to a ▷monastery.

Granite An extremely hard, crystalline, granular rock containing felspar, quartz, and mica, with sometimes horneblende and augite in place of or as well as the mica, and with a wide variation of colour and texture. Many granites are capable of taking a high polish, and can be cut thinly, so they are ideal ▷cladding materials for use in polluted atmospheres. Joints between stones can be extremely fine, and so granites are useful for flooring, decorations, covering ▷walls, cladding ▷plinths, and for ▷monumental art. The commonest types of British granites used over the last two centuries are the Aberdeenshires such as Corrennie (salmon-red), Peterhead (brilliant red), Kemnay (silvery grey speckled with black), Lower Persley (light bluish grey), Rubislaw (bluish grey), and Sclattie (light bluish grey); Creetown (white when rough and bluish white when polished); Cornish such as De Lank Silver Grey (greenish grey), Tor Brake, and Tor Down (both silvery grey); and Shap (greyish pink and reddish brown). Irish granites are found in Counties Down, Dublin, Wexford, and Wicklow. Norwegian granites are grey, and Swedish granites are grey, red, and black, the latter being particularly dense and capable of taking a very high polish.

Granny-bonnet A type of ▷hip-▷tile in the form of a section of a cone.

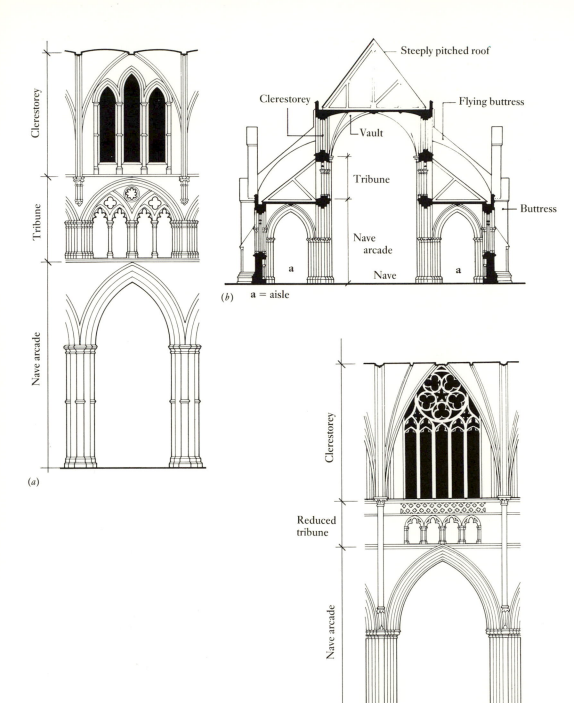

(a)

(b) a = aisle

Steeply pitched roof

Clerestorey

Vault

Flying buttress

Tribune

Nave arcade

Buttress

Nave

a

a

Clerestorey

Tribune

Nave arcade

Reduced tribune

Clerestorey

Nave arcade

(c)

[134]GOTHIC ARCHITECTURE (*a*) Typical internal bay of the First-Pointed or Early English style from Salisbury Cathedral. The piers supporting the nave arcade have become slender, and the extra shafts increase the impression of verticality. The tribune has four openings with quatrefoils over, and the clerestorey consists of three lancets. Note the cusping in the tribune openings, and the fact that the vaulting springs from corbels. (*b*) Section through Lichfield Cathedral showing Second-Pointed or Decorated Gothic. The roof of the clerestoreyed nave is still steeply pitched but the vertical emphasis is greater that ever because of the elaboration of shafts. Note also how the thrusts of the vault are taken by the flying buttresses and conveyed to the ground by means of massive buttresses. (*c*) Typical internal bay of the nave of Exeter Cathedral. An example of Second-Pointed or Decorated Gothic. Note the very large clerestorey windows with elaborate tracery combining the ogee arch and geometrical forms. The tribune has become less significant. (*d*) Section through St George's Chapel, Windsor, showing a typical Perpendicular or Third-Pointed arrangement. Note that the nave is wide and covered with a fan-vault. The roof is almost flat and is concealed behind parapets. The clerestory windows are extremely large, and admit as much light as possible. Aisles (**a**) have large windows, and have low pitched roofs over them, also concealed by the parapets. The load from the fan vaulting is taken to the ground by means of flying buttresses. (*e*) The Third-Pointed or Perpendicular recasing of the Romanesque nave of Winchester Cathedral. The tribune has become vestigial, and the panel-like effects are predominant.(*JJS*)

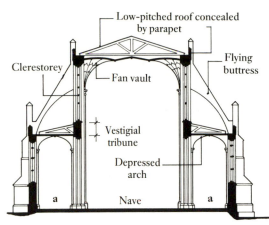

(*d*)

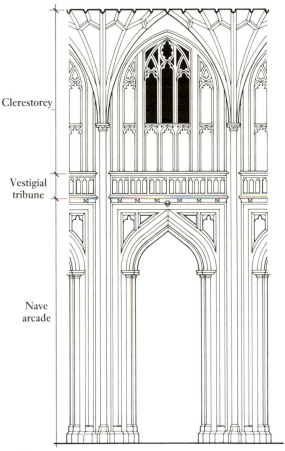

(*e*)

161

(a)

(b)

(c)

[135] GOTHICK (a)House-tomb in Calton Hill Cemetery, Edinburgh, based on a pattern published by Batty Langley. (b) Garden-front of Castle Ward, Co. Down, which is Palladian on the front and Gothick on the rear (c. 1762). This is a delightful example of Gothick in which the pointed arch and various 'Gothick' details are applied to a Classical façade. (c) The gallery of Strawberry Hill, Twickenham, designed by Chute and Thomas Pitt, of 1761–63, with *papier-mâché* fan vault based on the stone vaults of the Lady chapel at Westminster Abbey (Henry VII's chapel). This is an example of Rococo Gothick at its most enchanting. (*JSC*)

162

Granolithic A hard-wearing surface made of a mixture of one part ▷cement, one part sand, and two to three parts crushed ▷granite or whinstone.

Grapevine A very ancient decorative form, often occurring on ▷Bacchic ornament. In Christian iconography the ▷vine is Christ, the branches are His followers, and the grapes are the Eucharistic wine. It occurs as a continuous ▷ornament on mediaeval ▷screens.

Grate A surface with openings to support a fuel bed and allow air to pas through the fuel. It may be fixed or removable, and may be of iron. A *grating* is an openwork barrier, usually of metal, used to cover an opening: it is usually ▷perforated to allow air to enter or water to flow through into a drain below. A ▷grille.

Grave A place of burial, or an excavation for the reception of a corpse. The term is sometimes given loosely to any place where a body is laid, such as a ▷mausoleum or a ▷*loculus* in a ▷catacomb. A *grave-▷board* is a wooden board supported by uprights at the head and foot of the grave, and painted or inscribed with the name of the deceased. A *grave-brass* is an inlaid ▷panel of incised ▷brass or ▷latten on a *grave-▷slab* or *grave-cover*. A *grave-mound* is a hillock indicating a burial. A *grave-▷rail* is a railing around a grave. A *gravestone* is an upright slab of stone carrying an ▷inscription, usually at the ▷head of the grave, so called a *headstone*. A *graveyard* is a plot of ground containing graves.

Greek Greek ▷architecture was essentially columnar and trabeated, and this fact was expressed in its ▷Orders, the ▷Doric, ▷Ionic, and ▷Corinthian, each of which is distinct from ▷Roman versions (▷Orders). The Greeks refined the systems of the Orders, and arrived at works of architecture of rare beauty (▷temple). A *Greek ▷cross* is one with all arms of equal length. A *Greek ▷Key* (▷[137]) is a *labyrinthine ▷fret* used in ▷bands, often on ▷string-▷courses, and sometimes on ▷friezes. The *Greek ▷Revival* (▷[138]) was that phase of ▷Neoclassicism that involved using archaeologically correct elements from Ancient Greek architecture following the publication of a number of accurate surveys, notably Stuart and Revett's *The Antiquities of Athens*, which appeared from 1762. The adoption of Greek architecture involved considerable ingenuity on the part of designers: ▷towers and ▷spires involving pile-ups of Greek ▷motifs, and ▷churches with ▷galleries are but two examples where the style had to be used in highly original ways.

Green An open space or public park, or a bowling-green. The term also means unseasoned, as in timber. A *Green Man* is a *masque feuillu*, or *tête de feuilles*, featuring a human face surrounded by ▷foliage, with ▷leaves sprouting from its mouth and nostrils.

Greenheart A strong and durable ▷hardwood with pale yellow sapwood and olive-green heartwood used for ▷stair-▷treads, dock-▷gates, ▷piers, and ▷piles, and heavy construction.

Greenhouse A glasshouse for sheltering plants which would not survive outside.

Grees ▷Steps or a staircase.

Grey stocks ▷Bricks of the third quality of ▷malm bricks.

Greywood A yellowish-brown ▷hardwood with dark markings used for ▷panelling and ▷veneers.

Grid Any regular system, such as a *columnar* and *trabeated* construction at regular centres. An arrangement of parallel ▷bars with openings between; a grating. *Grid ▷tracery* is found in large ▷windows of the late-▷Gothic and early-▷Renaissance periods, and consists of a grid of ▷mullions and ▷transoms, so is a simplified version of ▷Perpendicular tracery.

Griffon Also *griffin* or *gryphon*. A mythical animal with the head, ▷wings, and ▷claws of an ▷eagle, the body of a ▷lion, and the beard of a goat. It is found in heraldry, in mediaeval ▷church ▷sculptures, and in ▷Classical, ▷Renaissance, and ▷Neoclassical designs. It occurs in ▷friezes, and because it is associated with ▷Apollo, is often found on candelabra and ▷*torchères*. It is a recurring theme in ▷Adam-style decorations.

Grille A grating or an open-work screen, usually of metal, and used to decorate or protect an opening. Decorative ▷wrought-iron grilles over ▷windows are a feature of ▷Gothic and ▷Renaissance architecture. Such designs are called *grillework*.

Grisaille A style of decorative painting done in grey tints to imitate *bas-▷relief*. Grisaille stained ▷glass also occurs in which the tones are grey-green and very subtle. In the later Middle Ages colours were covered during Lent, so the reverse of the ▷leaves of painted ▷triptych altarpieces were painted in grisaille and folded over the coloured centrepiece. Grisaille decorations were often used in ▷Neoclassical work to imitate ▷Classical ▷sculptures and decorations, notably ▷cameos.

Gritstone Strong, hard, and durable ▷sandstone such as the Millstone Grits of Berristall (creamy with free working), Bramley Fall (grey to buff, hard to work), Crosland Hill (creamy-brown with good

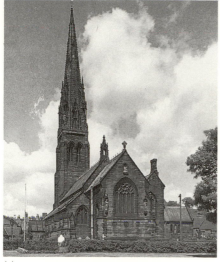

(a)

(b)

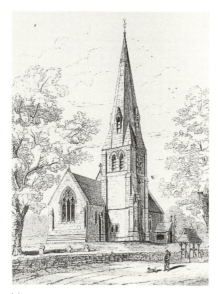

(c)

(d)

(e)

(f)

(g)

(h)

(i)

(j)

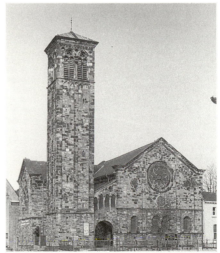

(k)

(l)

[136g–l]

(n)

(m)

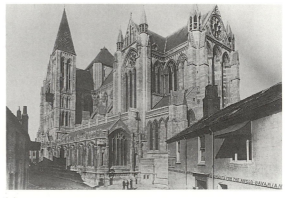

(p)

(o)

(q)

(r)

166

(*s*)

[136] GOTHIC REVIVAL (*pages* 164–167) (*a*) Church of St Giles, Cheadle, Staffordshire, by Pugin. A scholarly exercise in Second-Pointed Gothic built 1841–47. Note the chancel roof, the *sancte-cote* over the chancel-gable, the tracery, and the crocketed spire. (*RCHME AA56/8125*) (*b*) Church of St Stephen, Rochester Row, Westminster, of 1846–50, by Benjamin Ferrey. A Second-Pointed work. The illustration gives an impression of hardness, crispness, sharp details, and smooth surfaces, and anticipates later interiors which could never be confused with mediaeval buildings. (*Eastlake*) (*c*) Church of St Michael, Chetwynd, Shropshire, by Benjamin Ferrey of 1865–67. The tower with broach spire is based on precedents from Rutland, and the style is Early English or First-Pointed in general, while some of the larger windows have Geometrical tracery, although many other windows are lancets. (*Eastlake*) (*d*) View from the south-east of the church, clergy-house, and choir-school of All Saints', Margaret Street, London, of 1849–59, by William Butterfield. This was the Ecclesiologists' Model Church, an urban citadel of faith, built of brick and hard-wearing materials so that the polychromy was structural, and could withstand the polluted atmosphere. (*RCHME BB65/4481*) (*e*) Milton Ernest Hall, Bedfordshire, of 1853–56, by William Butterfield. Elements of the design look forward to the work of Norman Shaw and Philip Webb: the sash-windows are pre-echoes of the Queen Anne style, while the fenestration is very freely treated, expressing different functions within. (*RCHME AA78/6827*) (*f*) Quar Wood, Gloucestershire, by J.L. Pearson, of 1857, a house much influenced by the mediaeval Architecture of Burgundy. (*Eastlake*) (*g*) Interior of the Church of St James the Less, Westminster, of 1859, by G. E. Street, identified by Eastlake as marking a departure from English Gothic. Note the structural polychromy of the brickwork, the Continental apsidal arrangement, the plate tracery, and the bold vigour of the detailing. (*RCHME BB88/4066*) (*h*) Church of Sts Philip and James, Oxford, by G. E. Street, of 1860–66, an essay in thirteenth-century First-Pointed Gothic, with a pronounced Burgundian influence. Note the very French apse with plate tracery, and the tough tower with broach spire and massive lucarnes. (*Eastlake*) (*i*) Kelham Hall, Nottinghamshire, by Sir George Gilbert Scott, of 1858–62. The design responds to Pugin's demands for 'True Picturesque' composition, and quotes elements culled from Venetian Gothic prototypes. (*RCHME A45/1074*) (*j*) The former warehouse of Richardson Sons & Owden, Belfast, of 1867–69, by Lanyon, Lynn, and Lanyon. A fine example of Gothic Revival with a pronounced Italian flavour, probably influenced by the writings of Ruskin. (*JSC*) (*k*) Clarence Place Hall, May Street, Belfast, of 1865–66, by Lanyon, Lynn, and Lanyon. It is in the Italian Gothic style, faced in polychrome brickwork with stone dressings. (*JSC*) (*l*) Sinclair Seamen's Presbyterian church, Corporation Square, Belfast, by Lanyon and Lynn, of 1856–57, a remarkable essay in Lombardic Italian Gothic, much influenced by the writings of Ruskin. (*JSC*) (*m*) Church of St Andrew, Plaistow, Essex, by James Brooks, of 1867–70, a tough essay in French First-Pointed Gothic Revival. Note the apsidal east end, the continuous arcade of the clerestorey (with some blind arches), and the simple yet massive dignity of the roof structure. (*Eastlake*) (*n*) Church of St Columba, Haggerston, London, by James Brooks of 1865–74, showing how the Gothic Revival turned to primitive First-Pointed Continental Gothic. Note the plate tracery and the fortress-like character, implying a citadel of faith. (*Eastlake*) (*o*) The new buildings at Balliol College, Oxford, by Alfred Waterhouse, of 1867, showing the freedom of fenestration made possible by the Gothic Revival, and unthinkable in Classical architecture. (*Eastlake*) (*p*) View from the south-east in 1895 of Truro Cathedral, Cornwall, by J. L. Pearson, designed 1880. Early English merges with northern French Gothic of the thirteenth century. The low aisle on the left is the south aisle of the former Parish Church of St Mary, dating from 1504–18, an example of Third-Pointed or Perpendicular work which Pearson retained. The large, traceried windows of the sixteenth-century real Gothic contrasts with Pearson's revival of thirteenth-century First-Pointed, with its typical lancets, wheel windows, and soaring verticality. The main influence in terms of precedent is Coutances Cathedral. (*RCHME BB69/1119*) (*q*) Interior of the Church of the Holy Angels at Hoar Cross, Staffordshire, showing the sumptuous refinement of the work in a late Decorated or Second-Pointed style. (*RCHME BB69/2244*) (*r*) Exterior of the Church of the Holy Trinity, Sloane Street, London, by J. D. Sedding, commenced in 1888. It eschews Continental references, returning to English precedent, and mixes Decorated elements such as the tracery with Perpendicular forms. (*RCHME BB88/1866*) (*s*) Prudential Assurance Building in Holborn, London, by Alfred Waterhouse, of 1878–1906. A Gothic Revival building of harsh red terracotta and brick. Note the stepped gables and strongly Continental flavour of the whole. (*RCHME BB88/18220*)

[137] GREEK KEY OR FRET (*JJS*)

working), Dungeons (pink and workable), Dunn House (light brown with very free working), Earnock (white and grey with good working), and many others.

Groin The ▷intersection of two simple ▷vaults, crossing each other at the same height, and forming an ▷arris or edge (▷[245]). A *groin* ▷*arch* is one arched division of a ▷cross-vault, or an arch created by the intersection of two vaults (i.e. the arch of the groin).

Grotesque Light and fanciful ▷Classical ▷ornament consisting of ▷foliage, figures, and animal forms, fantastically combined and interwoven. The term seems to have originated from the fact that much ▷Antique ornament of this type was found in underground ▷apartments, and such underground spaces are called ▷*grottoes*. A *Grotesque* ornament, containing human and animal forms, must not be confused with ▷*Arabesque* ornament, which has none. Grotesques were common in ▷Renaissance and ▷Mannerist schemes of decoration.

Grotto An artificial cave, usually decorated with ▷shells and often incorporating a water cascade and ▷fountain. Grottoes were sometimes built in houses, and were fashionable in the eighteenth century. More often, however, they were ▷garden buildings, often adorned with *rustick* elements (▷rural architecture) on the outside. Grotto ▷ornament includes rough, rocky, ▷stalactite, and icicle or ▷frosted rustication (▷rustic).

Ground A piece of wood or other material fixed to ▷masonry to provide a means of attaching the backing for finishes. A *ground-*▷*beam* is a horizontal timber laid on a low ▷plinth from which a ▷timber-framed building rises, also called a *ground-*▷*sill*, *ground-*▷*plate*, *mud-sill*, or ▷*sole-plate*: it distributes the load. The *ground coat* is a first or preparation coat of paint. A *ground* ▷*course* is a ▷base course of ▷bricks or masonry immediately above the ground, often of waterproof material: a plinth. *Ground cover* is both planting to cover ground and a ▷damp-proof membrane. The *ground* ▷*floor* is the ▷storey of a building at ground level, often containing important rooms: it is not always the lowest floor, and can be set over a ▷basement, in which case it will be reached by a few ▷steps. The best rooms are often found on the first floor, or elevated, as a ▷*piano nobile* level over the ground floor. *Ground* ▷*glass* is obscured glass with a matt surface. *Ground-*▷*table stones* comprise the ▷projecting course of stones above the surface of the ground, known as the *plinth*, *ground table*, *earth table*, or *grass table*: it is the lowest course visible above the ground. *Groundings* are ▷battens or firrings, the same, basically, as grounds.

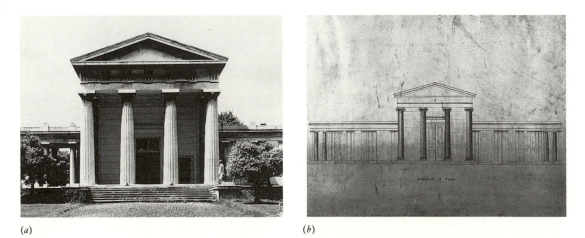

(*a*)

(*b*)

[138] GREEK REVIVAL (*a*) Prostyle tetrastyle portico of the Anglican chapel at the General Cemetery of All Souls, Kensal Green, London, by John Griffith of Finsbury, 1837. The style is Greek Doric. Note the smaller Order for the wings. (*JSC*) (*b*) Original drawing of the Dissenters' Chapel at the General Cemetery of All Souls, Kensal Green, by John Griffith of Finsbury, 1834. The Order for the prostyle tetrastyle portico is Greek Ionic, and the colonnaded wings have smaller Doric columns at the ends, with the general Order for the colonnades based on the square antae and column of the Choragic Monument of Thrasyllus in Athens. (*General Cemetery Company*)

Grouped columns More than two ▷columns grouped together on one ▷base or ▷pedestal. When only two columns are used they are called ▷*coupled columns*.

Grout A semi-liquid ▷mortar poured or forced into joints of ▷masonry or ▷rubble to consolidate the material.

Guard bar Any ▷bar for protection, as a ▷window bar. Used with other bars they form ▷grilles or guard-bars. A *guard-*▷*bead* or *guide-bead* is a ▷sash-stop. A *guard-*▷*board* is a *toe-board*. A *guard-*▷*rail* is a handrail or safety railing.

Gudgeon A ▷pin used to hold two ▷blocks or ▷slabs together: a ▷dowel, or a ▷gate-hook.

Guest-hall An ▷apartment for the reception and entertainment of strangers, as in an ▷abbey.

Guglia A tall ▷finial.

Guild A fraternity associated with a craft concerned with the interests of the brethren, and particularly involved with the keeping of guild-▷chapels or ▷altars so that masses could be said for the souls of departed guildsmen.

Guilloche [139] A ▷Classical ▷ornament in the form of two or more ▷bands or ▷strings twisting over each other so as to repeat the same figure in a continuous series, leaving circles in the centres. The term is also loosely applied to the ▷fret or ▷Greek ▷key pattern, which is really an angular ▷guilloche. Also called a ▷*plait-band*.

Gula The *cymatium* (▷cyma).

[139] GUILLOCHE Two forms of guilloche. (*JJS*)

Gun-metal An alloy of ▷copper and ▷tin or copper and ▷zinc: a type of ▷bronze.

Gunstock stile ▷Diminishing.

Gusset In metal roofing a *gusset-piece* is metal soldered over an external corner between two ▷intersecting upright surfaces and the ▷roof, as in a ▷chimney. A *gusset-*▷*plate* is a piece of wood or metal fixed to two timbers in a trussed ▷rafter to secure the timbers at an ▷angle: it is roughly triangular.

Guttae ▷Ornaments like the *frustum* of a cone hanging from the ▷soffites of the ▷mutules and ▷regulus on the ▷architrave of the ▷Doric ▷Order. Sometimes guttae are cylindrical, like ▷dowels. There are generally eighteen of them under the mutules, set in three rows, each row parallel to the front, and six under the regulus. In the case of the ▷*Roman Doric Order* the number of guttae under the soffite of the ▷cornice varies. They are sometimes called *lachrymae*, or *tears*, sometimes *campanulae*, meaning ▷bells, and sometimes ▷*drops, droplets,* ▷*nails*, or ▷*trunnels*. A *guttae*▷*band* is the *regulus*. In the ▷Choragic Monument of Thrasyllus the guttae were arranged as a continuous band under the ▷taenia, with no regulus bands: this ▷motif was used by Schinkel at the *Neue Wache* in Berlin of 1816–18.

Gutter Any open water-course or drain. A ▷channel between the ▷parapet and the lower part of a ▷roof to collect water, or a channel fixed to catch water from the roof at the ▷eaves.

Gymnasium A meeting-place for athletic practice, usually consisting of several ▷porticoes and rooms around an open space: it often had a type of ▷cloistered ▷colonnade around it. It is also known as a ▷*palaestra*, but must not be confused with a ▷*stadium* (race-course for humans), or ▷*hippodrome* (race-course for horses).

Gynaeceum, gynaeconitis The women's quarters in a ▷Greek house, or part of a ▷church reserved for women.

Gypsum Calcium sulphate, the raw material for ▷plaster. ▷Alabaster.

Gyronny A version of a ▷chequer pattern consisting of triangular ▷tiles instead of squares.

H

Habitacle   A ▷niche or a dwelling.

Hacking   In ▷rubble walling, the interruption of a ▷course by introducing another course on a different level because of a shortage of stones of the right height. A course of stones, of one, then two, then one to the height of the course. Roughening of a surface to create a surface to which ▷rendering can adhere.

Haffet   A ▷spandrel or triangular ▷bracket.

Haffit   A ▷frame, or the sides of a ▷box or opening.

Hagioscope   A ▷squint or opening in a ▷wall, usually obliquely cut, to allow the ▷high altar to be viewed from ▷transepts, ▷chapels, or ▷aisles, possibly for security reasons as much as anything.

Ha-ha   A trench, consisting of a vertical or slightly ▷battered side contained by a ▷retaining wall or ▷revetment of stone or ▷brick on the side nearest the point from which a landscape is viewed, and with the other side of the trench sloping and grassed. It prevented livestock from straying to the area contained within it, but, being invisible from the vantage-point, did not interrupt the view with a ▷fence, wall, or hedge.

Hair   Hair from cattle or goats was used in ▷plaster ▷undercoats for ▷coarse stuff as reinforcement in the proportion 1 kilogram hair to 150 litres coarse stuff: it prevented the surface from crazing.

Half   A term with wide meanings. A *half-▷baluster* is an ▷engaged baluster, ▷projecting half its diameter. A *half-▷bat* is a snapped header (▷head). A *half-checked joint* is a double-rebate joint, or a *halved joint*. A *half-▷column* is an engaged column. A *halflet* is ▷pew-end. A *half-▷newel* is half the plan section of a normal newel, and is usually placed against a ▷wall to terminate a balustrade and a ▷landing. A *halfpace* is a *half-space landing* or one at the junction of two ▷flights which changes the direction of the flight, usually 180°. A *halfpace* is also a raised ▷floor in a ▷bay ▷window, a ▷dais, or a raised fireplace ▷platform, also called a *halpace* or a *hautepace*. A *half-▷principal* is a ▷rafter that is supported at the top end by a ▷purlin, and does not reach the ▷ridge. A *half-round* is a semicircular moulding (▷mould), either a ▷bead or a ▷torus. *Half-timbering* refers to a structure formed of timber, with ▷sills, ▷lintels, ▷struts, ▷ties, ▷braces, etc. sometimes filled in with brickwork or ▷lathing, and ▷plastered. *Halving* is a method of jointing timbers by letting them into each other. A *half-figure* is the upper half of a human or animal: below the waist it becomes a ▷scroll or an inverted ▷obelisk, and is called a *term*.

Hall   The principal room of a house in the Middle Ages. Also the first room on entering a house. The public room of a corporate body. A court of justice, or any assembly-room. A building for a corporate body, such as a town hall, or a livery company hall. A *hall-▷church* is one in which the ▷nave and ▷aisles are the same height.

Hallan   A ▷biss, or a division ▷wall, boundary, or ▷stall wall, constructed by large ▷slabs of stone, such as Caithness.

Hallyngs   Hangings (▷hang), such as ▷tapestries, of a ▷hall.

Halo   A ▷nimbus or disc of radiance around a head.

Ham   A house, street, or village.

Hammer A tool with a steel head to which the handle is fixed at right-angles: one end of the steel is flat for driving ▷nails, and the other, called the *peen*, is hemispherical, wedge-shaped, or in the form of a curved ▷claw for taking out nails. A *hammer-*▷*beam* is used in the ▷principals of mediaeval ▷roofs, acting as a support at the base of the principal ▷rafter. Each principal has two horizontal hammer-beams which occupy the situation of a ▷tie-beam, but they do not extend across the width of the space, and indeed are basically ▷brackets carried on ▷braces. The ends of hammer-beams are often decorated with angels holding ▷shields (▷[212]). *Double hammer-beam roofs* have one set of hammer-beams carrying a second set on which the principals rest, used for very large spans. A *hammer-brace* is the supporting member carrying the end of the hammer-beam. A *hammer-*▷*post* is the vertical member set against the ▷wall, usually supported on a ▷corbel, on the top of which one of the ends of the hammer-beam rests, and from which the brace carrying the outer end of the hammer-beam springs, so it acts as an ▷impost and support. *Hammer-*▷*dressed* stone is roughly faced with a hammer at the quarry. A hammer is an ▷attribute of Vulcan and of work, especially ▷metalwork.

Hance The small ▷arch joining a ▷lintel to a ▷jamb, or a ▷haunch. The curve of shortest radius of a four-centred or similar arch.

Hand A single hand denotes the Hand of God. Clasped hands indicate a bond beyond the ▷grave, or friendship. Two hands with a ▷heart indicate the care taken of ▷love. A hand with a flower in funerary ▷ornament indicates death. Hands also appear as door-knockers, bell-pulls, and other artefacts. A *Red Hand* ▷*Dexter couped at the wrist affrontée gules* is the badge of the O'Neills of Ulster: the Red Hand appears on the ▷escutcheon of every Baronet, for the Noble Order of Baronets was instituted in 1611 to raise capital for the settlement of Ulster, but the hand on the ▷shields of baronets is ▷Sinister, probably in error. *Hand-*▷*float* refers to the wooden tool used by a plasterer, so hand-floated ▷plaster is finished with such a tool. A *hand-hole* is an inspection ▷chamber. A *handrail* is a ▷rail on ▷posts, or ▷balusters, to protect a ▷stair-▷well, and to assist ascent and descent. *Handed* is a mirror-image.

Hang To fit a ▷door or a ▷window on ▷hinges. A *hanger* is any member from which other parts are hung, such as a ceiling-joist or a ▷binder. A *hang-over* describes the condition of a ▷wall when the top projects beyond the bottom. *Hangings* are ▷linings of rooms, including ▷tapestry, paper, etc. A *hanging* ▷*buttress* is a vertical ▷rib supported from a wall by a ▷corbel. A *hanging-*▷*post*, otherwise ▷*gate-post*, ▷*hinge-post*, *swinging-post*, is one from which a gate is hung. *Hanging*

▷*steps* are steps built into a wall at one end and ▷cantilevered out, possibly resting on the step below. A *hanging* ▷*stile* is one to which the hinges are attached (▷[104]).

Hanse A ▷*haunch*, *basket-handled*, or *four-centred* ▷*arch*, or any arch with its ▷crown of a different curvature from that of the haunches.

Hardcore ▷Rubble used as ▷foundation material under roads and ▷floors.

Hardware Architectural ▷ironmongery.

Hardwood Timber from broad-leaved, usually deciduous trees. Hardwoods are not always 'hard', though most British types are.

Harling A render (▷rendering) on a ▷wall, with a rough texture.

Harmonic division, harmonic proportion When, in a series of quantities, any three adjoining lengths are taken and the difference between the first and second is to the difference between the second and third as the first is to the third, it is called *harmonic proportion*. The reciprocals of a series of numbers in arithmetical progression are in harmonic proportion.

Harmony An agreement, balance, or repose between all the parts of a building, having connections with ▷symmetry, serenity, ▷proportion, and colour.

Harmus A ▷tile covering the joint between two ▷common tiles.

Harp This musical instrument is found in the hands of carved or painted angels, and is an ▷attribute of David. It is the badge of Ireland, and its shape appears in chair-backs and in schemes of ▷Neoclassical decoration.

Harpy A mythical beast with the head and breasts of a woman and the ▷wings and ▷claws of a bird, sometimes very similar to ▷Roman sphinxes, and often appearing in ▷Grotesque ornament.

Hart's tongue A ▷water-leaf or ▷lily leaf in early ▷Gothic ▷ornament, usually in ▷capitals.

Hasp A slotted flap that fits over a ▷staple.

Hassack ▷Kentish ragstone.

Hatched moulding A notched moulding (▷mould), or one produced by notching the edges of a ▷band. A *hatchet* ▷*door* is one in two ▷leaves, one above the other, like a ▷*Dutch door*.

Hatchment An ▷Achievement of Arms painted in a square ▷panel hung diagonally. It was hung in the ▷church with which the deceased was associated.

Hathor-headed A ▷column with a ▷capital featuring the ▷Egyptian goddess Hathor.

Haunch The *haunch of an* ▷*arch* is that part between the ▷crown and the springing (▷[21]). The haunch of a ▷door, or *hance*, is an arched piece of timber placed under the ▷lintel proper. A *haunched* ▷*beam* is one deeper at each end.

Hawksbeak A crowning moulding (▷mould) of the ▷Greek ▷Doric ▷Order, like a ▷*cyma recta*, but with the upper concave curve concealed by a ▷beak-like overhang. A ▷beak moulding. A hawk is a ▷mortarboard, a small pinewood square with a handle below for carrying mortar.

Head A top member. The head of a ▷door, or a ▷window-head. A ▷tile used in the first ▷course at the ▷eaves. A stone with a ▷dressed end which will be exposed. *Head-nailing* is the nailing of ▷slates near the head so that each ▷nail is covered by two slates, but this method is not advisable on exposed or windy sites. A *header* is a ▷brick or stone of which the longest dimension is at right-angles to the face of the ▷wall, or a *bonder*: it is also any brick with its end exposed in the wall (▷brick). It is a framing member which supports the ends of ▷rafters or ▷joists and transfers the loads to other members below. A *header-*▷*joist* is a *trimmer*, used to ▷frame an opening and support the cut-off members. A *head* ▷*mould* is a ▷drip-stone, ▷hood mould, or ▷weather-moulding carried over the head of an opening. A *head-stock* is a ▷beam carrying a ▷bell. A *headstone* is a main stone in a ▷foundation, or a cornerstone, or a keystone: it is also an upright inscribed stone at the head of a ▷grave. *Headwork* suggests ▷ornament on a keystone, especially if a humanoid face.

Healing The perimeter of a ▷roof or its ▷eaves-layer. A *healing stone* is a ▷slate or a roofing-▷tile.

Hearse, herse [140] A metal framework set over a ▷coffin to carry the pall. Permanent metal ▷frames over funerary ▷effigies are also known as hearses, so the term appears to mean any grid-▷frame, ▷canopy, or ▷trellis. A funeral hearse was a canopy over the ▷bier, capable of carrying an immense number of wax candles. A ▷portcullis, fashioned like a harrow, on which lighted candles were placed during ▷church ceremonials and at funerals.

Heart Symbol of sacred and profane ▷love. A bleeding heart represents the sorrows of Mary and of Christ, and the Sacred Heart, pierced by ▷nails and ringed with a ▷Crown of Thorns, signifies the ▷Crucifixion. A heart crowned with thorns is the ▷emblem of the Society of Jesus. A *heart* ▷*brass* shows only a heart, sometimes held in hands, and it commemorates the burial of a heart when the whole body could not be brought back for interment. In the mediaeval period, hearts, viscera, and bodies were often buried in different places so that the deceased would benefit from different prayers. A *heart* is also an ▷ornament resembling a ▷spade.

Heart-and-dart ▷Leaf-and-dart or ▷egg-and-dart.

Heart bond ▷Masonry in which a stone lies over two other headers that join in the middle of the wall.

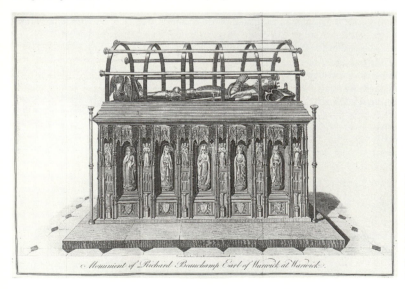

Monument of Richard Beauchamp Earl of Warwick at Warwick.

[140] HEARSE Tomb of Richard Beauchamp, Earl of Warwick, in the Church of St Mary, Warwick, drawn by Carter and engraved by Basire. Note the tomb-chest with canopied niches containing weepers of latten. The tomb-chest has the original hearse of latten over which the pall was placed. (*JSC Collection*)

Hearth The ▷floor of a fireplace and the uprights of fire-resistant material. *Hearthstone* is either one large stone ▷slab forming the floor of a fireplace or the fire-resisting materials used to construct a hearth.

Heather thatch ▷Thatch made of heather.

Hecatompedon A building 100 ▷Attic feet long or wide (101.341 English feet = 150 Attic feet). The Attic foot is based on studies of the ▷Parthenon, thought to be the ideal expression of ▷Doric ▷architecture. A *hecatonstylon* is a building with a hundred ▷columns.

Heck A ▷latticed ▷door or ▷gate, or a ▷Dutch door.

Hectastyle ▷Hexastyle, with six ▷columns in a row.

Heel The end of something. A *heel-*▷*post* is one at the end of a ▷partition of a ▷stall, or the part with the ▷hinges of a ▷gate. The *heel of a* ▷*rafter* is the foot that rests on the ▷wall-▷plate. A *heel-stone* is a stone at the ▷base of a gate-▷pier in which the bottom hinge-▷pin is fixed. A *heel-*▷*strap* is a U-shaped strip bolted to the ▷tie-beam of a ▷truss near the wall-plate and passing over the ▷back of the ▷principal ▷rafter to join it to the tie-beam.

Height of an arch ▷Arch.

Helical stair A ▷spiral stair.

Helioscene An exterior ▷louvred ▷blind which protects the interior of the room from the sun yet permits a clear view from the inside.

Helix A spiral ▷ornament or ▷volute: the term is especially applied to the sixteen volutes under the ▷abacus of the ▷Corinthian ▷capital, also called ▷*urillae*. There are two *helices* at each ▷angle, and two in the centre of each ▷face, branching from the *caulicoli* or ▷stalks that rise between the ▷acanthus ▷leaves. Vitruvius called the inner spirals only *helices*, calling the outer spirals *volutes*. The volute of an ▷Ionic capital or of a ▷modillion or ▷console. The helical line of a handrail is the spiral line, twisting, representing the form of the handrail.

Hellenic Associated with mainland ▷Greek ▷architecture and art from the fifth century BC to the end of the fourth century and the death of Alexander the Great.

Hellenistic Styles of ▷Greek ▷architecture and art after the death of Alexander, and particularly associated with Greek colonies in Asia Minor. It is characterized by a wider ▷intercolumniation and a greater elaboration, elegance, and richness in decoration. ▷Doric

became more slender and decorative, and ▷Ionic became extremely refined. ▷Roman ▷architects absorbed many aspects of Hellenistic work.

Helm roof A type of steep spired ▷roof rising from a ▷tower each face of which terminates in a ▷gable (▷[212c]).

Helmet An important element, also called a *helm*, in schemes of martial decoration. It is associated with Wisdom, Benevolence, Civilization, Learning, and the Arts (▷Minerva). With a ▷shield it represents ▷War. It is common in ▷Renaissance, ▷Baroque, and ▷Neo-classical ▷ornament.

Hem The spiral ▷projecting part of an ▷Ionic ▷capital.

Hemi This signifies half. A *hemicycle* is a semicircular ▷arena, room, or part of a room, or a recess semicircular on plan. Hemicycles occurred in ▷Roman towns and ▷gardens, and were used for seating and debate: they were larger than ▷*exedrae*. A *hemiglyph* is a half-▷channel on each side of a ▷triglyph ▷block. A *hemisphaerium* is a ▷dome. A *hemitriglyph* is half a triglyph block, or a part of a triglyph occurring in the return internal ▷angle of a ▷frieze.

Hence The narrow side of a ▷chimney-stack.

Hennebique François Hennebique (1842–1921) was a pioneer of ▷reinforced concrete as early as 1879. His ▷bridge at Viggen is one of the earliest examples of a reinforced-concrete bridge, and his system of what he described as *Ferro-concrete* (concrete mixed with iron) bears his name.

Henri II The second phase of ▷French ▷Renaissance from 1547 to 1559 after the death of François I. During this period ▷Italian Renaissance elements virtually supplanted all trace of late ▷Gothic ornament. It is particularly associated with Philibert de l'Orme, and enjoyed a nineteenth-century ▷revival.

Henri Quatre The style of ▷architecture preceding the ▷Classical styles of Louis XIII: the *Place des Vosges* in Paris of 1605–12 is a splendid example, with its tall roofs, ▷brick ▷walls, stone ▷dressings, and ▷arcaded ground ▷floors. Like the style Henri II, it too enjoyed a nineteenth-century ▷revival.

Heptastyle With seven ▷columns in a line in a ▷portico.

Heraldic Decoration based on ▷heraldic devices, and found in ▷floor-▷tiles, carving, ▷door-cases, and the like.

173

Herculean Decoration based on the story of Hercules or Herakles, and found in arms, armour, and military ▷trophies. Herculean figures sometimes occur as supports, as ▷Atlantes.

Herm A ▷pedestal, square on plan, terminating in a head of Hermes or some other figure. The pedestal has the generalized proportions of the human body, and may be tapered downwards, like an inverted ▷obelisk. A herm, unlike a ▷*term*, does not include the torso and waist, but is only the head, although feet may appear at the bottom of the pedestal. Herms are armless, but occasionally ▷volutes may sprout from the shoulders. Hermes (▷Mercury) was the messenger of the gods, so he is associated with travel and commerce: his head appears on ▷door-▷posts, gateways, and keystones. His ▷attributes are the *petasus* (broad-brimmed, winged hat), winged sandals, and the ▷*caduceus*. He is associated with ▷lyres, astronomy, and mathematics.

Hermaphrodite A figure combining male and female sexual characteristics.

Hermitage A small hut or dwelling in a secluded spot, usually built in a park or woodland as a resting-place or ▷gazebo, and constructed in the *Rustick* style, often associated with a ▷grotto, moss-hut, or *cottage orné* (▷cot, ▷rural architecture).

Heroum A ▷shrine or enclosure dedicated to a deified or heroic dead person.

Herringbone *Herringbone matching* is when ▷veneers from the same ▷flitch are alternated face-up and face-down so that a symmetrical pattern is achieved about the joint. A *herringbone pattern* is when anything, be it ▷masonry, ▷brick, ▷tile, or wood, is laid aslant instead of being bedded flat, and found in paving, nogging, and even in ▷walls (▷[53]).

Herse ▷Hearse.

Hertfordshire spike A short ▷needle-▷spire or ▷*flèche* set behind a ▷parapet, found on many Hertfordshire ▷church ▷towers.

Hewing Hand-working of stone.

Hexastyle With six ▷columns in a line in a ▷portico.

Hibernacula ▷Apartments used for winter use.

Hiberno-Romanesque [141] A type of ▷architecture and decoration developed in Ireland, often with elaborate carving, round ▷towers, and other characteristic forms. It was revived in the nineteenth and twentieth centuries as part of the ▷Celtic ▷Revival.

[141] HIBERNO-ROMANESQUE The Church of St Patrick, Jordanstown, Co. Antrim, by Lanyon, Lynn, and Lanyon, 1866. (*JSC*)

Hick-joint pointing After joints are raked out, superior ▷mortar is inserted between ▷courses, and made smooth.

Hieroglyph A design representing a meaning, a word, or a sound, and especially related to Ancient ▷Egyptian hieroglyphs. Bogus hieroglyphs were used as ▷Renaissance and ▷Neoclassical ▷ornament before *echt*-Egyptian hieroglyphs were deciphered in the nineteenth century.

Hieron The sacred enclosure of a ▷Classical ▷temple or ▷shrine.

High altar The principal ▷altar at the east end of the ▷sanctuary or ▷choir of a ▷church.

High cross A tall stone ▷cross, elaborately carved, with the cross at the top, usually of the ▷Celtic type. They stood in sacred ground, and proclaimed the doctrines of the Church. The best examples are in Ireland and Scotland.

High Gothic *Second-▷Pointed*. High ▷Victorian ▷Gothic was associated with the hard, gritty, polychromatic buildings of the 1850s, 1860s, and early 1870s, and was strongly influenced by Continental Gothic.

High relief Also called ▷*alto rilievo*, it is ▷sculpture in which the figures project more than half their volume.

High Renaissance ▷*Cinquecento*, or sixteenth-century, ▷architecture and decoration in Italy.

Hiling The covering of a ▷roof or of a building.

Hindoo A nineteenth-century term for the ▷Indian style, which became fashionable from the latter part of the eighteenth century. George Dance's front of Guildhall in the City of London is an early example. Sezincote (early 1800s) in Gloucestershire is an example of a later phase.

Hinge The joints on which ▷doors, ▷gates, etc. turn. ▷Gothic hinges are often elaborate, and are ▷ornamented with ▷scrolls. A hinge consists of two ▷plates joined by a ▷pin. A *hinge-stone* is one in which a gate pivot is set in the ground, or a large upright ▷post from which a gate is hung.

Hip The external ▷angle formed by the meeting of two sloping sides or ▷skirts of a ▷roof, or the ▷rafter under it. A *hip-*▷*knob* is a ▷finial at the end of the ▷ridge-piece of a roof, against which the hips abut. A *hip-*▷*roll* is a rounded strip of wood, finishing the hip of a roof, over which the metal is laid. A *hip-roof* is one sloping upwards on all sides to hips, rather than with ▷gables. A *hip-*▷*tile* is one covering the hips of a roof.

Hippocamp A creature with the head and forelegs of a horse, and the rest of the body the tail of a ▷fish, often associated with ▷marine ▷ornament and with ▷Neptune.

Hippodrome A race-course for horses, as opposed to a ▷stadium, or a place for equestrian exercises.

Hispano-Moresque A style derived from ▷Moorish architecture in Spain from the eighth to the fifteenth century. The Alhambra in Granada is the most celebrated example. The style was revived in the nineteenth and twentieth centuries.

Historicism A term meaning the use of past styles in ▷architecture, especially the ▷Greek, ▷Gothic, ▷Early Christian, ▷Romanesque, ▷Renaissance, ▷Elizabethan, and ▷Jacobean ▷Revivals. Historicism aimed to work in the spirit of a style, observing not only its rules, but the detail of its ▷ornament, and it was encouraged by the large number of accurate publications showing detailed drawings based on measured surveys.

Hoard Also *hoarding*, a temporary wooden structure around a building in the course of erection. Also a covered wooden ▷gallery to shelter the defenders of a mediaeval fortress.

Hog-back A ▷monumental stone placed horizontally over a ▷grave, looking like a crouching animal, and carved with scale-like backs. Good examples can be found in Penrith and Govan.

Hogging A convex curve. Unwashed freshly dug gravel.

Holdfast A metal spike driven into a joint of brickwork with a flattened eyed piece on the outside to which ▷joinery can be fixed.

Hollington stone A white-and-salmon coloured, durable, fine-textured ▷sandstone from Staffordshire, freely workable.

Hollow A *hollow* ▷*chamfer* is concave; a *hollow* ▷*gorge* is a ▷cavetto or ▷Egyptian gorge; a *hollow moulding* (▷mould) or ▷*trochilus* is a concave moulding, a cavetto, or a ▷scotia; a *hollow* ▷*newel* is an opening in the centre of a winding ▷stair, or an open ▷well, or a hollow cylinder in the middle of a circular stair; a *hollow* ▷*relief*, is a sunken relief; a *hollow square moulding* is a ▷Romanesque pattern of bands of sunken ▷pyramids, like inverted ▷nail-head mouldings. For hollow walls, ▷brick.

Holy loft A ▷rood-loft or ▷-beam.

Holy-water stone Also called a *stock*, it is the ▷stoup or other receptacle for holy water.

Homestead A piece of land capable of supporting one family, or a farm dwelling with outhouses.

Honeycomb A hexagonal structure or a pattern. A *honeycomb* ▷*vault*, or ▷*stalactite work*, is a type of ceiling based on ▷Islamic vaulting, used in nineteenth-century Oriental ▷revivals. A *honeycomb* ▷*wall* is a ▷brick wall with openings between bricks to permit air to flow freely, especially when used to support timber ground ▷floors: bricks are therefore laid with gaps, giving a honeycomb effect.

Honeysuckle The ▷anthemion ▷ornament or variants on it.

Hood A cover over an opening, as a fireplace-hood, or some other hood to gather smoke or odours into a ▷flue. A ▷canopy over a ▷door or ▷window. A ▷projecting moulding (▷mould) over the ▷heads of ▷arches, known as the ▷*drip-stone* or ▷*label* (▷[172a]). Labels are carried down on either side, terminating in decorative features called *label-*▷*stops*.

Hoof foot Also called ▷*cloven foot* or ▷*pied-de-biche*, it was used to terminate ▷cabriole legs in furniture. Sometimes legs with hooves have a ▷ram's head or a ▷satyr ▷mask at the top.

Hoop-iron Flat ▷wrought-iron ▷bars, tarred, and laid in the horizontal joints of brickwork as a reinforcement.

Hop From the seventeenth century a decorative ▷motif twining across ceilings or down ▷walls.

Hopton Wood A limestone (▷lime), usually referred to as a ▷marble, from Derbyshire. There is *light Hopton Wood* (cream with brown), suitable for interior and exterior use; *dark Hopton Wood* (with darker patches); *Black bird's-eye* (black with coloured fossils, only suitable for internal work); *Grey bird's-eye* (similar to the last); and *Derbyshire fossil* (deep grey with many fossils, again only suitable for internal work).

Horizontal cornice The lower ▷cornice of a ▷pediment.

Horn The ▷Ionic ▷volute. Also the side of an ▷altar. A ▷cornucopia or horn of plenty. An ▷attribute of fertility or of the wind. A horn of a ▷sash-▷window (▷[217]).

Hornwork An outwork of half-▷bastions joined by ▷wings to the main fortress.

Horreum A ▷Roman store for grain, implements, or wine.

Horse Four horses pulling a chariot, known as a ▷*quadriga*, are ▷symbols of victory, and are often on ▷triumphal arches. Winged horses and ▷centaurs are also found in ▷Classical ▷ornament.

Horse block A ▷platform set near a ▷door on which a rider could step before mounting a horse.

Horseshoe arch An ▷arch with a diameter wider than the opening below (▷[21]).

Hortus A ▷garden. The *hortus conclusus*, or garden enclosed, was a ▷symbol of the Virgin Mary.

Hospice A lodging for travellers, with a place of entertainment.

Hospital A building for the care of the sick, infirm, aged, and poor. In the Middle Ages it would have had a ▷chapel and communal ▷hall. *Hospitalium* was a guest ▷chamber. An *hospitium* was an ▷inn for strangers, or a *hostry*, *hostrie*, *hostel*, or *hotel*. An ▷*hôtel-dieu* was a hospital. A hospital door is a ▷flush door.

Hôtel particulier A town-house in France, normally with a ▷court towards the street closed by a ▷wall, and a ▷*corps-de-logis* at the rear of the court with a ▷garden

at the back. *Hôtel de ville* is a ▷town hall, and an *hôtel-dieu* is a ▷hospital. In modern usage an *hotel* is a building for the accommodation of strangers, and often contains dining-rooms, bars, and other facilities.

Hot-house A building constructed with glazing-bars and much ▷glass for raising plants, and heated. A ▷conservatory, ▷palm-house, ▷orangery, or ▷greenhouse.

Houff A shelter or latrine.

Hour-glass stand A ▷bracket or ▷frame for the hour-glass found in post-Reformation times in ▷churches near the ▷pulpit. An hour-glass implied passing ▷time and ▷death: with ▷wings it was a feature of funerary ▷monuments.

Housing A ▷tabernacle or ▷niche. An excavation for the insertion of some part of the extremity of another element.

Hovel An open ▷shed for cattle. A canopied ▷niche or ▷tabernacle. A badly built and wretched dwelling.

Hunt Hunting scenes were often used as decoration, especially in hunting-▷lodges, and include ▷fish, game, guns, hounds, whips, rods, etc.

Husk [45] The ▷*bellflower*, popular in the eighteenth century, used in ▷strings or ▷festoons on ▷furniture, ▷walls, and ▷frames. A *husk-▷garland* is a festoon of nut-shells ▷diminishing at the ends.

Hut ▷Primitive hut.

Hydraulic Relating to the science of hydrodynamics, conveying water, or operated by water. ▷Lime which sets and hardens under water because of the aluminium silicate or burnt clay content. Hydraulic limes should not be mixed with ▷Portland ▷cement. Non-hydraulic limes (pure calcium oxide) are most workable, or 'fat', in plasterers' parlance, but slow to dry.

Hymn board A notice-board on which the numbers of hymns and psalms are posted.

Hypaethral A building open or partly open to the air. The *hypaethron* describes the part that is roofless. An *hypaethrum* is an ▷Antique form of fanlight (▷fan), or ▷lattice over a ▷door, but held within the ▷architrave.

Hyperbolic paraboloid A double-curved ▷shell, the ▷geometry dictated by straight lines: it consists of a continuous element derived from a ▷parabolic ▷arch in one direction to an inverted parabola in the other and resembles a butterfly in elevation.

Hyperthyrum The ▷cornice over the ▷architrave of a ▷door or ▷window, or a ▷lintel, or the ▷entablature over an opening.

Hypobasis A lower ▷base or a lowest division of a base.

Hypocaust A ▷duct for heating by means of convected hot air.

Hypodromus A shady walk.

Hypogaeum, hypogeum An underground ▷chamber or ▷vault, especially one used for burial. It would have been used by one family or group, as opposed to a public underground ▷cemetery or ▷catacomb.

Hypophyge A curved depression under an element such as the recessed moulding (▷mould) beneath archaic ▷Greek ▷Doric ▷capitals.

Hypopodium ▷Hypobasis.

Hypostyle A covered ▷colonnade. A *hypostyle* ▷*hall* is a large structure with the ▷roof carried on massive ▷columns of more than one height, often including a ▷clerestorey. It is characteristic of Ancient ▷Egyptian ▷temples.

Hypotrachelium The lower part of the ▷Tuscan, ▷Greek ▷Doric, ▷Roman ▷Doric, and some ▷Ionic ▷capitals between the moulding (▷mould) at the top of the ▷shaft and the ▷fillet or ▷annulets under the ▷ovolo. The ▷frieze of the capital, or the part of the shaft below the capital, or the ▷neck. The ▷*trachelium* in the Greek Doric ▷Order is the part of the shaft between the horizontal groove or grooves circumscribing the column (known as the *hypotrachelium*) and the annulets under the ▷echinus. Thus the *hypotrachelium* has a slightly different meaning for each ▷Order, but the term seems properly to apply to the *lower* part of the neck. It is the space between the two neck-mouldings at the top of the shaft and the bottom of the capital proper. It is also called the ▷*gorgerin*.

I

I The Roman symbol for 1; II = 2; VI = 6.

Ice house An ▷insulated structure, partly underground, for the preservation of ice for use during warmer weather. The best examples were constructed during the eighteenth and early nineteenth centuries. The ▷walls were usually in double ▷leaves, sometimes insulated with sawdust, and the ▷chamber for the ice was often constructed in the form of a cone, or on ▷vaulted principles, with a drain to carry off water. *Icicles* appear in *rustication* (▷rustic), and represent flowing water: this type of rustication is called ▷*congelation* and is found in ▷grottoes, ▷fountains, rockwork, and even in ▷Rococo ▷ornament.

Ichnographia A ground-plan.

Iconostasis A ▷screen separating the ▷chancel from the ▷nave, pierced with three ▷doors, in Orthodox ▷churches. An *icon* is a stylized image of Christ or of a saint.

IHS *Jesus Hominum Salvator*, or *In Hoc Signo*, or *In Hac Salus* (Jesus Saviour of Man, In this Sign [thou shalt conquer], or In this [Cross] is Salvation). ▷Chrismon.

Image A painting or statue representing the figure or features of a person, especially a saint, deity, etc. Images of saints, Our Lord, and Our Lady were destroyed in numbers during and after the Reformation.

Imagines Roman portrait-busts or ▷masks of deceased persons, often made of painted wax.

Imbow To ▷arch over or to ▷vault with an *imbowment*, which is simply an arch or vault.

Imbrex A convex, usually semicircular-sectioned ▷tile covering two adjacent concave tiles: it is an element in ▷ornamental as well as roofing *imbrication* or *ribbing*. *Imbricated* ▷*tracery* is a pattern formed like the tiles of a ▷roof. An *imbrex supinus* is a ▷gutter made of ▷ridge-tiles laid upside down to form a ▷channel. To *imbricate* is to overlap in order, and *imbrication* is a pattern resembling roofing, or a weatherproof roof of overlapping tiles.

Immissarium A basin or ▷cistern for water to serve the immediate vicinity.

Impages The ▷door-▷rail between the ▷stiles, or the ▷border around a door-▷panel.

Impaled Two ▷coats of arms on one ▷shield separated down the middle.

Impasto The thick laying-on of paint.

Imperfect arch A ▷diminished ▷arch.

Impetus The ▷span of anything.

Impluvium The ▷cistern in an ▷atrium, or the atrium itself, to collect water from the *compluvium*, or opening in the ▷roof.

Impost The ▷capital, ▷bracket, ▷entablature, or ▷pier from which an ▷arch springs. An *impost* ▷*block* is one between the capital and the springing of an arch, also called a ▷*dosseret* or *supercapital*. The impost and the ▷abutment are closely associated (▷[20], ▷[21]), but the impost is held to be the actual point from which the springing occurs. The term *impost* is also given to the vertical element separating the two ▷lights of a ▷gemel or double ▷window.

Impresa An ▷emblem (with ▷motto) suggesting a personage, such as the ▷crescent ▷moon for Diane de Poitiers.

In-and-out A ▷bond, using headers (▷head) and ▷stretchers alternately, especially as ▷quoins. Any quoin with its length built into the ▷return of the ▷wall or ▷reveal, or with its greatest length built into the depth of the wall, is called *inban* or *inband*. An *inband* ▷*rybat* is a header-stone in a ▷jamb. *Inbond* is a header on a reveal or return. An *inbond jambstone* is a bondstone laid in the joint of an ▷aperture.

In antis Between ▷*antae*. ▷Temple.

In cavetto Design *impressed*, the opposite of ▷*relief*, and not quite the same as ▷*intaglio*, which implies ▷incised carving rather than moulding. An *incavo* is the hollow or incised part of such a design.

Incertum ▷Opus.

Incised slab A ▷memorial carved with ▷effigies, lettering, heraldry, etc., sometimes ▷inlaid with coloured ▷mastic in the incisions, and sometimes inlaid with ▷brass or ▷*latten*. The chiselled shaped hollow for the brass is called an *indent*.

Income A ▷jamb.

Indian A female head with feathered headdress: ▷*espagnolette* ornament. Such heads first appear in ▷Renaissance ▷emblem-books. Half-naked figures of Indians were introduced to ▷Rococo decorative schemes as an alternative to ▷Chinese figures. With the cult of the 'noble savage' in the eighteenth century, 'Indian' figures suggesting the inhabitants of the Americas, of Asia, and of Polynesia became popular. Indian (in terms of the Subcontinent) influences on Western ▷architecture became overt in the seventeenth century with some exotic ▷lodges, etc., but the ▷Hindoo style of the eighteenth century, incorporating both Hindu and Moghul architectural detail, was part of the ▷Picturesque. ▷Hindoo.

Industrialized buildings Mass-produced building parts were available to ▷Georgian and ▷Victorian house-builders, while the iron-foundries produced a huge variety of artefacts used in all sorts of buildings. Nash, for example, used repetitive cast-iron ▷Greek ▷Doric ▷columns at Carlton House Terrace. The ▷Crystal Palace erected for the Great Exhibition of 1851 was a spectacularly successful example of an industrialized building using repeated elements put together within a geometrical system. Standardized timber sizes, mouldings (▷mould), ▷bricks, ▷cast components, and many other elements have been avail-able for many years. Since 1945, however, much has changed: craftsmanship has declined, and 'industrialized components' have become more readily available, including entire mechanized ▷prefabricated systems of construction. The problems of industrialized buildings have included a lack of flexibility, poor design in the first place, a sameness, and, of course, a dependence on more and more production: for, like all mass-produced products, the system depends on a constant demand. The retreat from systems is due to a failure of design and construction, and to the recognition of the intractible problems carried by a mindless application of systems for their value only. As 'cheap' solutions they have proved expensive, not least in the destruction of craftsmanship and of individual caring for quality.

Infirmary A public building for the reception of infirm persons: a ▷hospital. In mediaeval times it was an aisled building with ▷cubicles in the ▷aisles, and had a ▷chapel.

Inflected Inverted, as in ▷arch.

In-glaze ▷Ceramic decoration applied on the surface of unfired glaze and then fired and matured.

Inglenook A recess for a seat built in the ▷chimney-breast, or adjacent to a fireplace.

Ingoing A ▷reveal.

Inlaid work When the surface of one material is cut away to a minimum depth in patterns, and metal, stone, ▷cement, wood, ivory, or some other substance is inserted to fill the hollows, and finished to a ▷flush surface, the result is called *inlaid work*. *Boule* or ▷*buhl* work, and ▷*marquetry* are examples. If metal is inlaid in metal it is called ▷*damascening*. ▷Mosaic inlay of wood is called ▷*intarsia*. One colour of clay embedded in a pattern in a ▷tile of a different colour is referred to as ▷*encaustic*.

Inn [142] Any house used as a hostel or lodging-house and providing food and drink. A ▷tavern. Formerly, inns were lodgings for scholars or law students, as at Oxford or the Inns of Court. Many old inns, in the sense that they are taverns, restaurants, and ▷hotels, still exist, and mediaeval examples survive (but only partially) in Glastonbury and Grantham.

Inosculating A ▷clustered column.

INRI *Jesus Nazarenus Rex Iudaeorum* (Jesus of Nazareth King of the Jews), or *In Nobis Regnat Jesus* (Jesus reigns in us), or *Igne Natura Renovatur Integra* (nature is regenerated by fire, referring to the spirit and to redemption).

[142] INN The George and Pilgrims Inn, Glastonbury, Somerset
A late-mediaeval front of stone, set in a grid of vertical panelling
with horizontal string-courses. Probably early sixteenth century.
(*JSC*)

Inscription Monumental ▷Roman ▷Architecture
was frequently ▷embellished with inscriptions such as
on the ▷Attic ▷storey of a ▷triumphal arch, or on the
▷friezes of buildings. Inscriptions were often an
essential part of mediaeval funerary art, especially
along the ▷margins of ▷slabs, in ▷incised work, and in
monumental ▷brasses. ▷Heraldic ▷mottoes were
used in late sixteenth- and early seventeenth-century
▷parapets, frontispieces, and balustrades, as at Castle
Ashby, Northamptonshire. Elaborate inscriptions
appear on ▷Baroque and ▷Neoclassical funerary
▷monuments, and are particularly interesting associated with ▷cartouches. Nineteenth-century public
buildings frequently have inscriptions saying what they
are, and public monuments often contain inscribed
information.

Insects These often occur in decorations at various
times, and enjoyed a vogue in the sixteenth and
seventeenth centuries. They occur in much ▷Art-
Nouveau work. ▷Bees and ▷scarabs are frequently
found.

Inserted column An ▷engaged ▷column, one set in
a ▷reveal, or let into a ▷wall.

Instruments of the Passion The thirty pieces of
silver, scourge with thongs, column and cord, sceptre
of reeds, crown of thorns, nails, robe, dice, lance,
ladder, sponge, and shroud, carried by angels, or
placed on a shield (*arma Christi*).

Insula A ▷block of buildings surrounded by streets.

Insulated ▷Detached. An insulated ▷column stands
free from a ▷wall: thus the columns of ▷peripteral
▷temples were said to be *insulated*. To *insulate* something is also to cut off from connection or communication, to prevent the passing of heat or sound, or to
separate.

Intaglio ▷Sculpture where the design is hollowed out
or ▷incised (▷in cavetto). *Intaglios* also means the
carved work of an ▷Order, or carving on any part of an
edifice. *Intaglio rilevato* is ▷relief which does not project
in front of the ▷naked of the surface in which it is cut.

Intarsia A wooden ▷mosaic made up of different
coloured woods (▷inlaid work).

Intavolta A cymatium (▷cyma).

Integral mullion An ▷impost or vertical element
separating the two ▷lights of a ▷gemel or double
▷window.

Interaxial *Interaxial* measurements are those from
centre to centre, say, of adjacent ▷columns, as opposed
to *intercolumnar* measurements (▷intercolumniation).

Intercolumniation The distance between ▷columns
measured from the lower parts of the ▷shafts in
multiples of the diameter of a column as measured
at the ▷base of the shaft. ▷Greek ▷Doric intercolumniation was generally that of the ▷monotriglyph
(i.e. having one ▷triglyph between the centre-lines
of two columns), but ▷Hellenistic taste favoured a
wider arrangement of two or sometimes three triglyphs
between the centre-lines. At the corners of Greek
Doric buildings, on account of the triglyphs being
placed at the ▷angles and touching at the corners,
the extreme intercolumniation is less than that of
the intermediate columns. The main types of intercolumniation as defined by Vitruvius, where *d* is the
diameter, are *Pycnostyle* ($1\frac{1}{2}d$), *Systyle* ($2d$), *Eustyle*
($2\frac{1}{4}d$), *Diastyle* ($3d$), and *Araeostyle* (more than $3d$).
Eustyle is the most commonly used intercolumniation,

although the Doric Order intercolumniation is controlled by the triglyph/▷metope relationship as triglyphs are centred on columns of ▷Roman Doric at all times (including the corners of a building), but in Greek Doric, as described above, the angle-triglyphs are not on the centre-lines of the corner columns.

Intercupola The space between two ▷cupolas, or the space between the inner and outer surfaces of a cupola. Also *interdome*.

Interdentils The spaces between ▷dentils: in ▷Roman work the dentils are set closer together than in ▷Greek.

Interfenestration The space between ▷window-openings.

Interglyph The space between the ▷channels of a ▷triglyph.

Interlace Also called ▷*entrelacs*, it is an ▷ornament of ▷bands intertwined, as in ▷knots. For *interlacing arches*, ▷arch, ▷[143]. An *interlacement band* is a ▷guilloche.

Intermediate An *intermediate* ▷*rafter* is a ▷common rafter or ▷spar. An *intermediate* ▷*rib* is one in ▷vaulting subordinate to the main ribs. In ▷sexpartite vaulting it

[143] INTERLACING ARCHES Blind interlacing arches on the north wall of Much Wenlock Priory, Shropshire. These are spectacular Romanesque examples of the twelfth century. Note the chevron motif. (*Shropshire County Council Record Office SRO 770/ Small Box 1 No. 8*)

is the ▷transverse rib in the centre of the ▷bay.

Intermodillion The space between ▷modillions, often ▷coffered and ▷ornamented.

Internal dormer A vertical ▷window on a sloping ▷roof but not covered by a pitched roof running into the slope: it is set below the slope so there is a recess in the roof.

International exhibitions Although trade fairs are of some antiquity, and there were national fairs in the eighteenth century, the first major international exhibition of the works of all nations was in London at the ▷Crystal Palace in 1851, where the flavour of he exhibits was eclectic, based on examples from history, with a strong whiff of mass-production. Many such exhibitions followed, in many countries, and many had a profound influence on taste. The 1893 Exposition in Chicago promoted a revival of ▷Neoclassicism and of ▷Baroque, while the London Exhibition of 1862 promoted ▷Arts-and-Crafts taste and a growing interest in Japanese (▷Japonaiserie) artefacts. The 1900 *Exposition* in Paris gave prominence to ▷Art Nouveau, and the *Exposition des Art Décoratifs* in Paris of 1925, coming so soon after the discovery of the tomb of Tutankhamun, created a taste for aspects of design in which ▷Egyptian, Egyptianizing, ▷Aztec, and other elements fused in the style known as ▷Art Deco.

International style The style of ▷architecture that evolved from the First World War onwards, pioneered by Gropius and his associates in Germany, and then became widely accepted in certain circles throughout Europe and America from the later 1920s. It is characterized by smooth surfaces, large areas of ▷glass, usually in horizontal ▷bands in steel ▷frames, asymmetry, cubic forms, no mouldings, and a generally trimmed appearance. ▷Roofs were 'flat'. It was regarded as progressive, left-wing, and 'democratic'. It was the style used in the Fascist headquarters at Como, for example, and it enjoyed a vogue in the Soviet Union in the 1920s. Buildings in the International Modern style were difficult to maintain, expensive to construct, wasteful of energy through heat loss and ▷insulation difficulties, and were divorced from tradition and from the decorative aspects of craftsmanship, being allegedly based on a machine aesthetic and on the forms of industrial buildings, ocean-going liners, and aeroplanes. For the first time in the history of the world, a type of architecture in which architectural ▷enrichment had no place had evolved, with the result that many traditional skills were lost.

Interpensivae ▷Cantilevers formed by the ends of ▷joists.

Interpilaster The space between ▷pilasters.

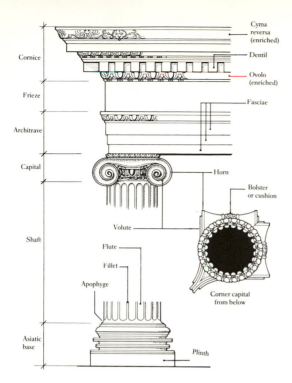

(*a*)

Cyma reversa (enriched)

Dentil

Ovolo (enriched)

Fasciae

Horn

Bolster or cushion

Cornice

Frieze

Architrave

Capital

Volute

Shaft

Flute

Fillet

Apophyge

Asiatic base

Plinth

Corner capital from below

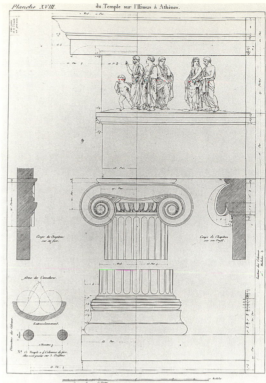

(*b*)

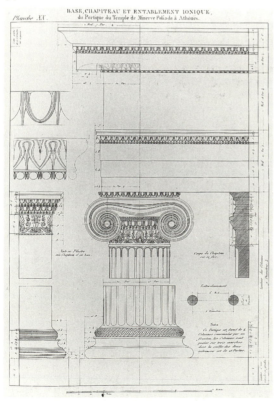

(*c*)

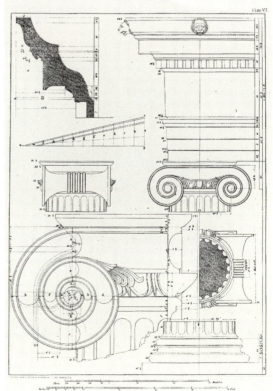

(*d*)

PIEDESTAL, BASE, CHAPITEAU ET ENTABLEMENT IONIQUE,
Planche XXVII. d'André Palladio.

THE IONIC ORDER OF VIGNOLA

Plate IX

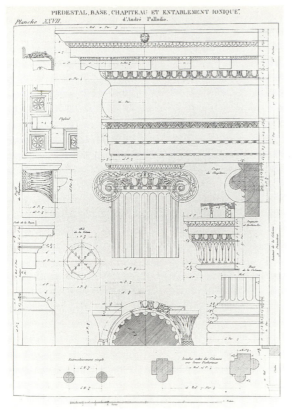

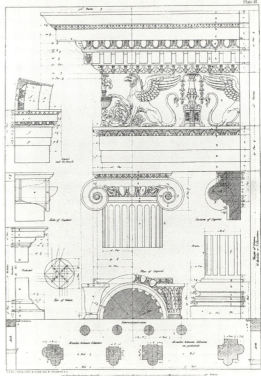

(e)

(f)

[144] IONIC ORDER (*a*) Ionic Order with Asiatic base and corner capital. Note the volutes and the entablature consisting of three distinct parts. (*JJS*) (*b*) Greek Ionic Order from the temple on the Ilissus in Athens. Note the flutes with fillets, the elaborate base, the sculptured continuous frieze and the elegance of the capital with volutes, and egg-and-dart on the echinus. (*Normand*) (*c*) Greek Ionic Order from the Erechtheion in Athens. Note the enriched Attic base, and the neck under the capital with its band of anthemion and palmette ornament. Note also that the anta capital and base differ from those of the main Order. The architrave is divided into three fasciae, and there are elegant enrichments of bead-and-reel and egg-and-dart on the entablature. (*Normand*) (*d*) Details of the Greek Ionic Order at Eleusis. Note the sections through the volute, and the elevation and plan of the pulvinus or cushion joining the volutes. (*Spiers*) (*e*) Roman Ionic Order after Palladio. Note the Attic base, the elaborate capital with volutes somewhat smaller than in Greek versions of this Order, the profusion of enrichment (bead-and-reel, egg-and-dart, etc.), the plain modillions, and the pulvinated frieze. (*Normand*) (*f*) Ionic Order after Vignola. Note the rich frieze, and the fact that there is no dentil at the corner: instead there is a pendent ornament like a pine-cone. (*Spiers*) (*g*) Ionic Order based on that of the Temple of Apollo Epicurius at Bassae, used by C. R. Cockerell at the Ashmolean Museum in Oxford of 1841–45. Note the treatment of the pulvinated frieze, that of the volutes whereby a 'special' at the corner is not necessary, and the way in which the dentils turn the corner. (*JSC*)

(g)

183

Interrupted Anything omitted, as in a ▷broken or an ▷open ▷pediment. An *interrupted arched moulding* (▷mould) is a series of ▷interlacing ▷arches, alternately interrupted, found in ▷Romanesque ▷ornament.

Intersecting ▷Interlace. ▷Arches resting on alternate supports in a row, the arches meeting and crossing each other. *Intersecting* ▷*tracery* is formed by the curving upwards, forking, and continuation of the ▷mullion ▷bars: these forks spring from the mullion bars, and intersect, creating ▷Y-forms.

Intersectio The gap between ▷dentils, also described as μετόπη (▷metope) by the Ancients, but *metope* is never used in this sense today. *Metopon* is used to describe a piece of ▷wall between ▷doors or ▷windows, a ▷Classical ▷*trumeau* or ▷mullion.

Intersticium The space between the ▷nave and ▷choir of a cruciform ▷church, where the ▷transepts cross the body. The ▷crossing. Also *interstitium*.

Intertie A horizontal connecting piece of timber placed between ▷beams or ▷posts to bind them together.

Intertignium The spaces between the *tigna* (▷tignum) or ▷tie-▷beams resting on the ▷architrave of a ▷Classical building.

Intertriglyph A ▷metope.

Intonaco A fine finishing ▷plaster coat made with ▷marble dust: it was a suitable finish for ▷fresco painting.

Intrados ▷Arch.

Inverted ▷Arch.

Involute A curve made by the end of a thread as it is unwound from a fixed ▷dowel. A spiral curve or ▷volute.

Inwrought Intricately ▷enriched.

Ionic Order [144] The second of the ▷Orders used by the ▷Greeks, and the third used by the ▷Romans. The distinguishing feature is the ▷capital, which is ▷ornamented with spiral projections known as ▷volutes. The proportions of the ▷column are more slender than in the ▷Doric Order, and the Order has a ▷base. The ▷shaft is generally ▷fluted, with ▷fillets between flutes. Ionic ▷entablatures do not have ▷triglyphs or ▷metopes, and the ▷frieze can be plain or ▷enriched. In some variations of the Order there is no frieze, but the ▷architrave is usually divided

into three ▷*fasciae*. ▷Abaci are moulded, often enriched, and much smaller than the Doric abacus. ▷Cornice mouldings are often elaborate, and include ▷dentils. The ▷echinus, ▷astragal, and fillet are common to both ▷Greek and ▷Roman capitals, and the echinus is uniformly cut into eggs surrounded with angular-sectioned ▷borders, and with ▷tongues between the borders. Astragals are rows of ▷bead-and-reel ▷ornament. When columns are used in the ▷flanks of buildings as well as in the 'front', the capitals of each ▷angular column are made to face both the contiguous sides of the buildings, with the two adjacent volutes at the corner bending in a concave curve towards the angle. Roman capitals often face the four sides of the abacus alike on each side, so that the volutes project diagonally on all four corners of the abacus, and no corner special capital is required. The Order used at the ▷Erechtheion in Athens has a frieze of ▷anthemion ▷motifs around the ▷necks of the columns below the astragal of the capital proper, giving it an especially rich flavour, especially as the abacus below the neck is also enriched with beads. Both the ▷Asiatic and ▷Attic bases are found used with the Greek Ionic Order, but the Attic is invariably used with the Roman Order; ▷Ammonite Order. The Greek Ionic Order is especially elegant and beautiful.

Ipswich window [145] A type of seventeenth-century ▷oriel, of which the best surviving examples are those of Sparrowe's House in the Buttermarket,

[145] IPSWICH WINDOW Sparrowe's House, Buttermarket, Ipswich, with pargetting decorations of *c.* 1670. Note the coat of arms with strapwork, the festoons, and the figure of Asia under the window itself. (*JSC*)

Ipswich: it has an arched centre-▷light, square-headed sides, and glazing over the top of the arched centre. Variations on this ▷motif were employed by Richard Norman Shaw on many of his buildings, notably at New Zealand Chambers of 1871–73.

Iris With the ▷lily and the ▷rose, a ▷symbol of the Virgin Mary, and of chastity. Reconciliation between Man and God.

Ironmongery Metal fixings, such as ▷bolts, ▷locks, ▷hinges and other fastenings, etc.

Ironwork [146] Some very fine mediaeval ▷wrought ironwork survives, notably in the ▷ornamental ▷door-▷hinges, ▷scrolls, decorative ▷nail-heads, and handles of ▷church ▷doors. ▷Monuments were frequently crowned with iron ▷filigree work, and some good examples survive in Westminster Abbey. A fine wrought-iron *herse* (▷hearse) over the ▷effigy, with ▷prickets, can be found in the Church of St Nicholas, West Tanfield, near Ripon, in Yorkshire. Iron ▷screens and railings survive in many grander churches, usually around ▷tombs, and iron ▷gates and railings from the seventeenth and eighteenth centuries survive in quantity. By far the biggest heritage of ironwork is ▷Victorian. Nineteenth-century manufacturers catered for a vast range of items, including ▷pipes, crestings (▷cress), ▷balusters, railings (▷rail), pissoirs, ▷stalls, ▷hot-houses, ▷lamp-posts, ▷grave-stones, ▷manhole covers, notices, name-plates, etc., and these are mostly of cast iron.

Irregular coursed rubble ▷Rubble ▷masonry in which the ▷courses are irregular, i.e. of different heights, and in which the stones vary in size.

Islamic architecture This term describes ▷architecture and ▷ornament from the Muslim world, as it developed from the seventh century onwards. The Koran forbids the representation of human or animal forms, so Islamic decoration is composed of geometrical and abstract patterning. Islamic architecture undoubtedly absorbed Persian, ▷Greek, ▷Roman, ▷Early Christian, and ▷Byzantine elements. ▷Domes, ▷horseshoe arches, low, wide, pointed ▷arches, ▷minarets, patterned ▷lattice-work, elaborate ▷vaulting (including the ▷stalactite type), and ornament (including brilliantly coloured ▷ceramics, floor patterns, and ▷damascening) are characteristic. Islamic architecture can be found in China, the former Soviet Union, India, the Middle East, North Africa, and in Spain, where the beautiful ▷Hispano-Moresque style can be admired, notably at the Alhambra, Granada. The eighteenth-century taste for the exotic encouraged the ▷Arabian, ▷Saracenic, or *Moresque*

(▷Moorish architecture) style, which reached its zenith during the nineteenth century in western Europe.

Isocephalic A ▷frieze of ▷Classical bas-▷relief, where the heads of the figures are almost on the same horizontal line.

Isodomum ▷Masonry with ▷courses of equal thickness with the vertical joint placed centrally on the ▷block under.

Isometric projection A system of drawing objects similar to ▷axonometric, but in which the plan is distorted to produce an illusion of ▷perspective (▷[202c]). The ▷plane of projection is equally inclined to the three principal ▷axes of the object, so that all dimensions parallel to these axes are represented in their actual ▷proportions.

Italian This refers to the styles introduced by the ▷architects of Italy at the end of the fifteenth century. Based on the art and ▷architecture of ▷Antiquity, the ▷Renaissance came to England during the reign of Henry VIII, but generally filtered through northern Europe, especially Flanders and France. Gradually, through the writings of Serlio, Alberti, and others, it superseded the mediaeval styles. Renaissance influences were all-powerful in England until a growing interest in Antiquarianism favoured ▷Neoclassicism from the middle of the eighteenth century. The *Italianate* style (▷[147]) began with Barry's clubs in the 1820s and 1830s, which were interpretations of astylar ▷*palazzi* with a massive *cornicione* (▷cornice) over a ▷façade in which the ▷windows were aediculated (▷aedicule). The *Italian* ▷*villa* style characterized by low-pitched ▷roofs with bracketed ▷eaves, asymmetrical plans, square ▷towers, and windows of the aediculated type and round-▷arched (▷*Rundbogenstil*), was fashionable from the 1840s. An *Italian roof* is a hipped roof of low ▷pitch, while *Italian tiling* is of the ▷pan-and-roll type. Italianate architectural ▷ornament, ▷cornices, etc. became *de rigueur* in the ▷stucco-fronted domestic buildings of Bayswater and Kensington.

Ivy Part of ▷Bacchic ornament. It also symbolizes fidelity and immortality, and so is used in funerary ▷sculpture. It occurs in ▷Gothic decoration, and was a popular ▷Victorian ▷motif, especially in ▷garden ▷furniture.

Iznik ▷Ottoman decoration on ▷ceramics featuring long serrated ▷leaves and stylized flowers, ▷palmettes, ▷Arabesques, and thin trailing stems. Colours were strong, and included cobalt blue, green, black, turquoise, purple, and dark, rich red. It was the inspiration for some ▷Arts-and-Crafts designs, notably those of William de Morgan.

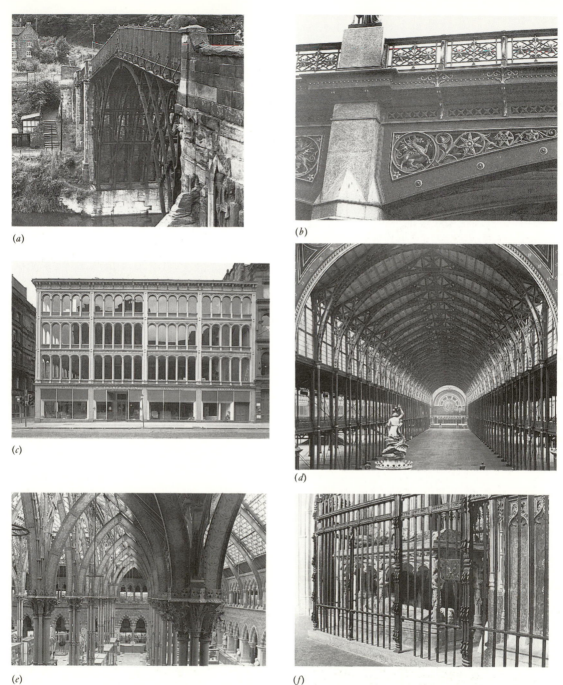

(a)

(b)

(c)

(d)

(e)

(f)

[146] IRONWORK (a) Iron bridge over the Severn at Ironbridge, designed by Abraham Darby, and cast in 1778 by his Coalbrookdale Company. (*JSC*) (b) Spandrel and balustrade of cast iron at Holborn Viaduct, 1863, by William Haywood. (*JSC*) (c) 36 Jamaica Street, Glasgow: Gardner's Warehouse of 1855–56 designed by John Baird. Virtually the entire front is of cast iron. (*RCAHMS A62019*) (d) The nave of the London Exhibition Building of the Works of All Nations of 1862 by Captain Fowke. An elegant prefabricated structure of iron and glass. (*V&A Library Collection 41225, 4577*) (e) Interior of the University Museum, Oxford, 1854–60, by Deane and Woodward, a structure of cast and wrought iron, with timber and glass. (*R. C. Roach*) (f) Tomb of Bishop Beckington (Beckynton) in Wells Cathedral. It is mid-fifteenth century in date, has an effigy on top and a cadaver in winding-sheet below. The exquisite wrought-iron railing is contemporary, and has much Gothic ornament including crenellations and quatrefoils. (*JSC*)

186

(a)

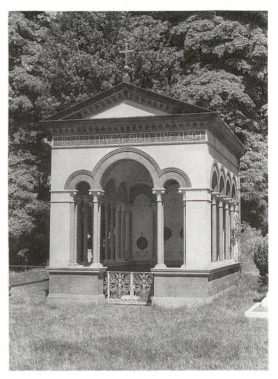

(b)

(c)

[147] ITALIANATE (a) The Reform Club, Pall Mall, London, by Sir Charles Barry, of 1837–41, a sumptuous essay in the Italian *palazzo* style (note the *cornicione*), with, on the left, Barry's Travellers' Club of 1829–32 and the Athenaeum by Decimus Burton of 1828–30 on the far left. (*JSC*) (b) The Drake mausoleum at Brookwood Cemetery, near Woking, Surrey, in an Italian Romanesque style. (*JSC*) (c) The London terminus of the Brighton and Dover Railroads, by Henry Roberts, of 1841–44. The Italianate style used for a London railway terminus. (*Guildhall Library, City of London*)

J

Jack ▷Arch. A *jack-*▷*rafter* is short, such as one fixed to the ▷hip of a ▷roof. A *jack-*▷*rib* is one in a ▷vault, ▷dome, or ▷arch, shorter than other ribs. A *jack-in-the-green* or ▷*Green Man* is a figure or face peering out of ▷foliage, often used in carvings in a mediaeval ▷church, and representing the spirit of vegetation or the tree-spirit, a pre-Christian idea.

Jacobean [148] This refers to the ▷architecture and decoration of the reign of King James I and VI (1603–25), but that style also continued in the reign of Charles I (1625–49). Although Inigo Jones introduced ▷Palladian ▷Classicism in Jacobean times, the term applies to a coarser English ▷Renaissance style, where ▷French, ▷Italian, and ▷Flemish motifs were inter-mingled. ▷Flemish Mannerist themes were strongly represented. ▷Jewelled ▷strapwork, superimposed ▷Orders, ▷herms, ▷obelisks, and ▷heraldic, ▷military, and emblematic elements were ubiquitous. ▷Dutch and curved ▷gables, and fancy ▷chimneys were also common. There was a *Jacobean* ▷*Revival* in the nineteenth century in which ▷mullioned and ▷transomed ▷windows, curved gables, and elaborate ▷brick chimneys were prominent: it was used on a number of country houses (notably by Henry Roberts [1803–76]), and subsequently was mixed with elements of the ▷Queen Anne style, an example being R. Norman Shaw's New Zealand Chambers in London of the 1870s. A further revival, incorporating ▷timber-framed gabling and ▷Elizabethan and Jacobean themes, occurred in the 1920s and 1930s, notably in housing and in public-house design.

Jagging Notching or indenting, as of ▷beams or the ▷arrises of ▷arches, giving a rasping effect.

Jam nuts ▷Lock-nuts.

Jamb The side of a ▷window- or ▷door-opening properly bearing the superincumbent load of the ▷wall, by way of the ▷lintel, but more often simply referring to the vertical ▷lining of the opening. The ▷*antepagmentum* supports the lintel or *supercilium*. Jambs are essentially the outer parts, the portion inside a window- or door-opening being the ▷reveal. A *jamb-*▷*post* is an upright timber fixed to the side of an opening, while a *jamb-*▷*shaft* is a ▷colonnette placed against or forming part of the jamb of a doorway or window-opening. A *jambstone* is one forming a jamb of a door. A *jamb-stove* is a cast-iron ▷stove set in a fireplace and ▷projecting into the room behind the fireplace.

Janua The ▷door of a ▷Roman house or any roofed structure which opened to the street, also called an ▷*anticum* or a *ianua*. It was usually framed with ▷pilasters and had an ▷entablature over, giving it an architectural presence.

Janus A two-faced ▷Roman deity, the deity of the rising and setting of the sun.

Japan A ▷varnish of exceptional hardness. *Black Japan* is a ▷varnish made by cooking asphaltum with linseed oil. *Japan* is the term given to varnish made from ▷shellac, linseed oil, and turpentine. To treat with such hard varnish is called *japanning. Japanese lacquer* is a glossy finish obtained from the sap of *Rhus Vernicifera* or *Sumach*.

Japanese pie An ▷ornament, also called *kikumon*, consisting of a stylized chrysanthemum with sixteen ▷petals and a ▷calyx on japan-patterned ware, imitated in late nineteenth- and twentieth-century architectural decorations, such as ▷friezes or fireplaces.

(a)

(b)

(c)

[148] JACOBEAN (a) Gatehouse to Stanway House, Gloucestershire, c. 1630. Note the three shaped gables, the canted bay windows with mullions, and the archway flanked by fluted Roman Doric columns on pedestals. These columns carry an entablature above which is an open-topped segmental pediment. (b) Canopied pew of post-Jacobean date, but still in the style of the Jacobean period, in the Church of St John the Baptist, Stokesay, Shropshire. (c) Superimposed Order on the frontispiece of the Schools Quadrangle in Oxford of 1613–24, based on Italo-French precedents. The first stage is Tuscan, then slim Doric paired columns sitting on a broad band of mixed strapwork and foliage motifs continuing around the pedestals, while the lower parts of the shafts are also enriched with carving. The next stage is Ionic, with elaborately carved pedestals. Above is a Corinthian Order, and on top a Composite Order. Note the strapwork cresting. This frontispiece is applied to a building that is otherwise entirely Gothic in design, with crenellations, crocketed pinnacles, and windows divided into lights with mullions. (JSC)

189

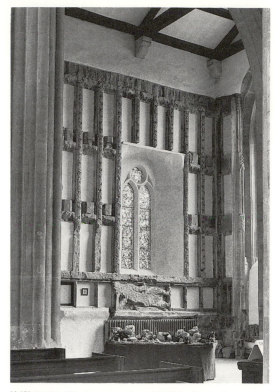

[149] JESSE The Jesse reredos of 1470 in the south transept of the Church of St Cuthbert, Wells, Somerset. The figure of Jesse is at the bottom, while in the niches above were his descendants, including Our Lord. The figures were separated by strips of carved foliage on the verticals. The whole was made by John Stowell, but it was severely damaged by iconoclasts. (*JSC*)

Japonaiserie A style derived from Japanese ▷motifs that became popular from the 1870s, associated first with the ▷Arts-and-crafts Movement and then with ▷Art Nouveau.

Jaspé ▷Marbled and coloured to resemble stone, as on a ▷dado.

Jasper An opaque quartz, red, yellow, brown or green in colour.

Jasperware A fine, hard, coloured porcelain.

Jawe piece ▷Jope.

Jerkinhead A ▷clipped or hipped (▷hip) ▷gable, or a ▷shreadhead in which the gable rises about half its height (where the ▷collar-▷beam would be), and the ▷roof is hipped back from that point.

Jerusalem A *Jerusalem* ▷*cross* is a ▷Greek cross with each arm terminating in a T and with a small Greek cross in each of the four spaces between the arms. It is also called a *Crusader's cross*. A *Jerusalem* was also the centre of a ▷maze used for symbolic pilgrimages in the Middle Ages.

Jesse, Tree of Jesse [149] A representation of the genealogy of Christ in which the persons forming the descent are placed on ▷scrolls of ▷foliage (usually ▷vine) branching out of each other. It was often represented in ▷sculpture, painting, ▷stained-glass, and embroidery. It is found in a spectacular form in the ▷tracery of the north ▷window of the ▷choir at the ▷Abbey of Sts Peter and Paul at Dorchester in Oxfordshire of *c.* 1340, and in the ▷reredos of the south ▷wall in the south ▷aisle of St Cuthbert's Church in Wells. Jesses are also found in the form of branched candlesticks.

Jesting beam An ornamental ▷beam with no function.

Jetty, jettie, jutty A part of a building that projects beyond the rest, and overhangs the ▷wall below. It is applied to the projecting ▷floor-▷joists that carry the overhang of a ▷timber-framed building. A ▷storey that projects in this way is said to be *jettied* (▷[237]). Also a ▷pier, in the sense of a construction built out into water as a landing-stage, or a wharf.

Jewelled A type of ▷strapwork in which elaborate ▷straps or ▷bands were ▷ornamented with ▷studs or ▷lozenges faceted to represent jewels (also called ▷*prismatic ornament*). It enjoyed a ▷revival from the 1830s.

Jib ▷Gib.

Joggle A notch or a ▷projection in a member fitted into a notch or projection in another to enable sound joins to be effected. The term is used in ▷masonry to signify the indentation made in one stone to receive the projection in another. What a carpenter would call a ▷*rabbet* is called a *joggle* in masonry. A *joggle-piece* is a ▷truss-▷post in a ▷roof ▷shouldered to receive a ▷brace or a ▷strut with a joggle: it is also called a *joggle-post* or ▷*king-post* A joggle-post is also a post made of two pieces of timber joggled together. *Joggle-work* is masonry with joggles.

Joinery Framing or jointing of wood for finishings, including the making of ▷doors and all better-class woodwork.

Jointing The finishes of ▷mortar-joints to create neat joints before the mortar has set, as opposed to raking the joints out and pointing (▷pointed) them.

Joist Horizontal timbers laid parallel to each other on which flooring is laid and to which a ceiling is fixed. Joists rest on ▷walls or on ▷girders and sometimes on both (▷bridging).

Jope, jopy A ▷strut or ▷brace in a ▷roof: a ▷jawe-piece or a ▷collar-▷beam.

Jube, jubé The ▷screen separating the ▷choir from the ▷nave, but more properly the ▷rood-▷loft or ▷gallery over the entrance to the choir.

Judas A spy-hole or small ▷window.

Judaic A type of decoration featuring the seven-branched candelabrum, the gabled Ark, the ram's horn, the incense shovel, and the ▷palm. Much Jewish ▷architecture in western Europe for synagogues, schools, and public buildings uses these themes and ▷symbols of the twelve tribes of Israel. Many synagogues avoided both ▷Classical and ▷Gothic ▷motifs because of their associations with the Diaspora and with Christianity, so an orientalizing architecture, vaguely ▷*Rundbogenstil* or

Byzantine, was chosen instead.

Jugendstil The 'youth style', or German ▷Art Nouveau, called after the journal *Jugend*.

Jump An abrupt rise in a level ▷course of brickwork or ▷masonry. A *jumper* or ▷*riser* in ▷rubble is a large stone (generally a *bonder* or *through-stone*) used in combination with two thinner stones known as ▷*levellers*, and a small stone called a ▷*sneck*, to form square uncoursed rubble-walling.

Jupiter Personified by an ▷eagle, by ▷fire, by ▷flames, and by a ▷thunderbolt: the latter is sometimes shown gripped in the ▷talons of an eagle.

Justice A female figure (one of the ▷Virtues) holding a ▷sword and ▷scales, often standing on a ▷globe, and frequently blindfolded.

Jutting As ▷jetty.

Jyméwe A ▷hinge.

K

Kage, cage A ▷chantry-▷chapel enclosed by means of ▷screens, ▷lattices, or ▷tracery.

Kamptulicon An elastic ▷floor-covering that had a brief vogue in ▷Victorian times.

Keel A ▷fillet, raised edge, or sharp ▷arris formed on ▷roll mouldings, by which the heaviness of the roll was relieved, and the ▷profile became two ▷ogees like the keel of a ship. A *keel* ▷*arch* is the same as an ogee arch. A *keel-moulding* (▷[150]) is the ▷ridge or edge.

Keene's cement Also known as ▷*Parian cement* (or *plaster*) or *hard-burnt plaster*, it is an anhydrous ▷gypsum plaster, giving a smooth, fine finish. It is slow-setting, and is laid on a coarse ▷rendering.

Keep The chief ▷tower or ▷donjon of a ▷castle, and the place of residence. A *keeping-room* was a combined ▷kitchen, ▷workshop, and living-room. A *keeper* is a striking-▷plate for a ▷staple or a ▷lock, or a metal ▷loop over the ▷fall-▷bar of a thumb-▷latch to confine its swing.

[150] KEEL MOULDING (*JJS*)

Kentish *Kentish* ▷*rag* is hard limestone (▷lime) much used as an external building material: many early-▷Victorian town ▷churches were clad in ragstone, which proved to be unsuitable as it weathered badly in the polluted atmosphere. *Kentish* ▷*tracery* is a type of ▷Gothic tracery featuring ▷foils separated by spikes or lobed ▷cusps, usually framed in elaborate ▷quatrefoil form, and interrupting the general flow of the tracery.

Kep A ▷door-▷stop.

Kerb A stone at the edge of a footway in a street which divides it from the carriageway: also *kirb*, *kurb*, or ▷*curb*.

Kernel As ▷crenel.

Key The roughness of a surface to enable ▷plaster or ▷stucco to stick. A ▷hardwood slip let into a joint to strengthen it. A pointing-tool for making a keyed joint. Anything that completes or holds together the parts of the ▷fabric, such as the strutting-pieces between ▷joists. A key is also a piece of wood let into another against its grain to prevent warping. The instrument to drive back the ▷bolt of a ▷lock, so a *key-drop* is an ▷escutcheon cover. A *key-*▷*block* is a keystone or ▷*sagitta* (▷arch). A *key-*▷*brick* is a wedge-shaped ▷voussoir. A *key* ▷*console* is a keystone of an arch which also acts as a console, supporting something above. A *key-*▷*course* is a course of keystones in a very deep arch where one keystone would not be enough, or used in the ▷crown of a ▷barrel-vault. A *key pattern* is a labyrinthine (▷labyrinth) ▷fret or ▷Greek key (▷[137]). A *keyed* ▷*dado* has wood laid across its grain to prevent warping.

Kicking plate A metal ▷plate fixed to the bottom ▷rail of a ▷door.

Kikumon ▷Japanese pie.

Killesse, coulisse, cullis A ▷gutter, groove, or ▷channel. A *dormer* ▷*window* (▷dormant) is sometimes called a ▷*killesse window* while a *hipped* (▷hip) ▷*roof* is sometimes called a *killessed roof.*

Kiln A building for the accumulation and retention of heat to dry or burn materials, such as timber, clay, or lime.

Kilt ▷Weathering to ▷steps of stone. A *kilt-*▷*fillet* is a tilting) (▷filt) fillet.

King-bolt A ▷tie-rod, king-rod, or long-▷bolt used in place of a ▷king-post, hanging from the ▷ridge to the tie-▷beam.

King-closer A three-quarter ▷brick used as a closer with a diagonal piece cut off one corner by a vertical cut running from the middle of one end to the centre of one long side.

King-post The centre ▷post of a ▷roof-▷truss which hangs from the ▷ridge and supports the ▷tie-▷beam of the truss by a cottered joint. Its foot is ▷shouldered or ▷joggled to carry two ▷struts which support the ▷principal ▷rafters. Where two posts are used set at equal distances from the centre, they are termed ▷queen-posts, but formerly all such posts were called *kings,* ▷*crowns,* or ▷*pricks* (▷[212]).

King table A mediaeval ▷string-▷course under ▷parapets, ▷ornamented with ▷ball-flower decorations.

Kiosk An open ▷pavilion or summer-house with a ▷colonnade. A bandstand or small, free-standing shop.

Kirb As ▷kerb or ▷curb.

Kirk A ▷church.

Kirnel As ▷crenel.

Kitchen [151] A room where food is prepared and cooked.

Kite winder The central of three ▷winders turning a ▷stair through 90° because it resembles a kite on plan.

Knapped Split, as in ▷flint, to expose the black surfaces. ▷Flush.

Knee A ▷crook or a bent piece of wood, usually fixed as a ▷corbel or ▷bracket under the ends of ▷beams. Part of the ▷back of a handrail with a convex upper

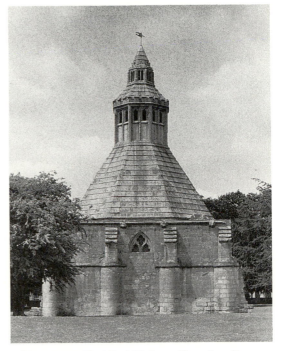

[151] KITCHEN The Abbot's Kitchen at Glastonbury, Somerset, of the second half of the fourteenth century, probably the best preserved mediaeval kitchen in Europe. It is a square building with fireplaces at the corners resulting in an octagonal interior, with an octagonal pitched roof surmounted by a tall lantern or femerell. It was the model for the laboratories of the University Museum, Oxford. (*JSC*)

surface, the reverse of a ▷ramp, which is the back of a handrail of concave form. A termination of a ▷drip-stone, ▷hood ▷mould, or ▷label, or its return at the springing of an ▷arch. The projection of ▷architrave mouldings at the ends of the ▷lintel in the ▷dressings of a ▷Classical ▷aperture, also called ▷*ear.* Any sharp right-angled bend. A *knee-piece* or *knee-rafter* is a crook ▷rafter in the principal ▷truss of a ▷roof, crooked downwards to rest firmly on the ▷walls. A *knee-timber* is a bent piece of timber formed out of a tree that has grown crookedly so that the fibres follow the curve.

Kneeler Also called a *keystone,* ▷*skew, skew-*▷*table,* or ▷*gable-springer,* it is a large stone in a gable coping (▷cope), sloped on top and flat at the bottom, supporting the ▷raked coping on a gable, which otherwise would slide off. It is also the stone that provides the ▷skew set into a ▷masonry ▷wall from which an ▷arch or a ▷vault begins its spring.

Knob A spherical handle, or a ▷finial. ▷Knot.

Knocker A hinged hammer, usually ▷ornamented,

fixed to a ▷door to attract the attention of those within. The part the hammer strikes is called a *door-nail.*

Knop   A swelling, ▷knob, or ▷finial.

Knot   Also ▷*knob, knoppe,* or *knotte.* A ▷boss. A bunch of ▷leaves or flowers or foliate ▷ornament found in ▷capitals, ▷labels, or ▷the bosses of ▷ribs. An ornamental design looking like tied ▷ropes, often with symbolic connotations. A whorl of timber formed where there was a junction with a branch. A *knotted* ▷*shaft* is a type of ▷Romanesque column carved with a knot on it. *Knotting* is the preliminary process of painting to seal knots to prevent resins bleeding into and discolouring the finished paintwork: traditionally, knots were covered with red lead, then white lead and oil, and lastly with a coat of gold ▷size, but ▷shellac dissolved in methylated spirits was also used. *Knotwork* is intricate carving looking like ▷interlacing cords, found in ▷Saxon, ▷Celtic, and Romanesque work.

Knuckle   The joint of a ▷hinge.

Knulling, knurling   A very flat ▷bead-and-reel moulding, or an ▷enriched convex moulding of very small ▷projection, a form of ▷gadrooning. A *knurl, knulled, Spanish,* or *whorl* ▷*foot* is a foot formed like an inward-turning ▷scroll and looking like a fist resting on the knuckles. *Knurled* ▷*ornament* is strips of linked beads or beads and reels.

Kufic   An Islamic script used for formal decorative ▷inscriptions found on buildings.

Kurb   As ▷kerb or ▷curb.

Kynges table   A ▷table moulding, but the exact meaning is obscure.

L

L   The Roman symbol for 50.

Labarum   The ▷Roman Imperial ▷standard used in ▷Neoclassical decoration.

Label   A ▷*drip* or ▷*hood* ▷*mould* over an ▷aperture, usually returned square and terminating in *label-*▷*stops* or ornamental ▷bosses at the ends of a hood-mould or label (▷[172]). A label-stop can be a simple turning of the label horizontally away from the opening. It is a feature of late ▷Gothic ▷Perpendicular, ▷Tudor, and Tudor ▷Revival ▷architecture. A *label* is also a rectangular framed ▷panel, often with wedge-shaped ends, used by the ▷Romans as a base for ▷inscriptions, and revived during the ▷Renaissance and ▷Neoclassical periods.

Labyrinth   A subterranean series of winding and interconnected ▷passages. A ▷maze. A ▷*mandala*, symbolic of the Grail or pilgrimage, found ▷inlaid in ▷cathedral ▷floors (as at Chartres) or cut in turf (as at Wing in Rutland). A *labyrinthine* ▷*fret* is a fret with many maze-like turnings, similar to a ▷key pattern, ▷*meander*, or a ▷Greek key. The centre of a cathedral maze was called ▷*Jerusalem* or ▷*Paradise*.

Laced   A *laced* ▷*valley* is one formed of ▷tiles or ▷slates without a valley-▷gutter: the slates or tiles are laid on a valley-▷board, and the two slopes intersect at an ▷angle, as opposed to a ▷*swept valley*. *Laced* ▷*windows* are window-openings set above each other and flanked by strips of ▷brick of a different colour (usually rubbers) from that of the ▷wall.

Laceria   Intricate geometrical patterns formed by ▷intersecting straight lines, especially mouldings, in ▷Islamic and Islamic-style ▷architecture.

Lacertine   A type of ▷Celtic and ▷Viking ▷ornament featuring a creature with snout and tail, flowing into ▷scrolls and ▷interlacing patterns, like a lizard or dragon.

Lacework   Decoration resembling lace.

Lacing course   A ▷course of ▷bricks or ▷tiles in a ▷rubble ▷wall for bonding and levelling. It is especially useful in a ▷flint wall where a continuous course of long thin stones, bricks, or tiles is used at regular vertical intervals with ▷piers every two metres or so.

Laconicum   An apsidal (▷apse) end of the ▷*caldarium* of a ▷Roman ▷bath, or the sweat-room.

Lacquer   A solution of ▷shellac in alcohol, sometimes coloured, to give a hard, glossy finish.

Lactarium   A ▷dairy-house.

Lacuna   A cavity or hole, or a ▷coffer in the ▷soffite of a ceiling or of a ▷cornice or ▷entablature. *Lacunars* are therefore the sunken ▷panels of a soffite. Where there are wide ▷bands between the coffers (or *lacunars* or *lacunae*) the soffite is termed *laquear*. The term *lacunaria* is given to the ceiling and soffite of an entablature of the ▷ambulatory around the ▷cella of a ▷temple, presumably because of the coffering.

Lady   A size of ▷slate 16 × 8 inches.

Lady chapel [152]   A ▷chapel for the veneration of Our Blessed Lady, usually placed to the east of the ▷high altar, but sometimes in other positions.

Lag and feather   A form of ▷fluting with ▷husks painted rather then modelled.

[152] LADY CHAPEL The Lady chapel of Hereford Cathedral, a remarkably pure example of the Early English or First-Pointed style of Gothic architecture dating from *c.* 1220–40. Note the dog-tooth mouldings around the lancet windows. The Decorated-style reredos by Cottingham has since been removed. (*Hereford City Library 4621*)

Lageolum A ▷lectern.

Lagging The ▷planks on the ▷centring of an ▷arch on which the ▷voussoirs are laid during construction. ▷Insulation around pipework to prevent heat loss or to protect it from frost.

Laird's loft A private ▷gallery in a ▷church for a Scots laird and family.

Lamb A ▷symbol of Christ. With a ▷flag it represents John the Baptist. On a hill with four streams it is the Church and Gospels.

Lambrequin ▷Ornament consisting of overlapping ▷aprons with looped lower edges fringed or ▷tasselled. They were an important element of a ▷Grotesque ▷orn-amentation, and were revived in the eighteenth century.

Lamb's tongue An end of a handrail turned down resembling a ▷tongue. A moulding (▷mould) of two ▷ovolos separated by a ▷fillet, especially for Regency glazing-bars.

Lamp Enlightenment. Immortality (on ▷tombs). Lamps appear as ▷finials on ▷urns.

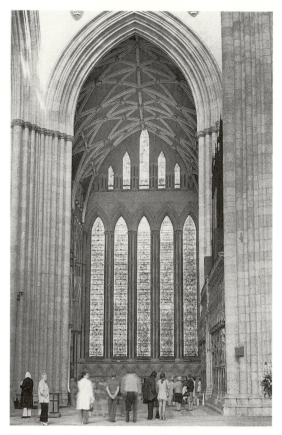

[153] LANCET The north transept of York Minster, showing the celebrated Five Sisters, or five lancets of equal height, with stepped lancets above. The date is around 1253. The wooden ribbed vaulting is later, of about 1400, much restored. (*JSC*)

Lanai A living area partly or wholly open to the outside.

Lancet [153] A tall narrow ▷window with a sharply pointed arched ▷head (▷[21q]). A lancet window was a common feature of *First-*▷*Pointed* or ▷*Early English* ▷*Gothic* from the end of the twelfth to the middle of the thirteenth century. *Lancet* ▷*architecture* is an archaic term for *First-Pointed*. *Lanciform* means having a sharp point.

Land gutter A ▷valley ▷gutter.

Landing The ▷platform at the end of a flight of ▷steps. An *angle-*▷*newel* or *landing-newel* is one located on a ▷stair-▷landing or where stairs change direction.

Landmark A ▷monument or a marker of a boundary. A building or structure of cultural importance through its character, qualities, or size.

Langley Batty Langley (1696–1751) was the author of many ▷pattern-books, and inventor of Langley Gothick, an unscholarly type of ▷pointed ▷architecture in which he attempted to create ▷Gothic 'Orders', but in fact invented a type of Rococoesque and fanciful Gothick known as *Langleyesque, Sham,* or *Carpenter's Gothick.*

Languet A U-shaped repeating pattern, or tongue, on ▷friezes in ▷Classical and ▷Neoclassical schemes.

Lantern A small structure on top of a ▷dome for the admission of light, for ventilation, or for ▷ornament. In ▷Gothic ▷architecture the term is applied to ▷louvres on the ▷roofs of ▷halls, etc. but it usually means a ▷tower, open from below, commonly found over the ▷crossings of ▷churches, as for example, at Ely Cathedral. A *lantern* also means the open structure at the tops of some towers, usually square, circular, or polygonal on plan. Any windowed ▷superstructure crowning a roof. A *lantern cross* is one with a lantern-shaped top, often enriched with ▷sculpture. A ▷*death lantern* or *lanterne des morts* is a structure with an ▷aperture through which light shone, built in grave-yards.

Laordose The ▷screen behind an ▷altar, probably a corruption of ▷*reredos.*

Lap Part of a body lying over another, such as ▷slates.

Lapis A ▷Roman milestone.

Lap-siding ▷Clap-boarding.

Lappet A repeating ▷pendant ▷motif like the ▷lambrequin used for ▷borders.

Laquear ▷Lacuna.

Lararium An ▷apartment in a ▷Roman house where the household gods were placed. A room in the ▷Neoclassical period for the display of ▷Antique cult-statues.

Larder Properly, a store for undressed meat, but now any store-room for food.

Lardos, lardose ▷Laordose.

Lares compitales ▷Shrines at the ▷intersection of two ▷Roman roads in honour of the *lares* or gods.

Larmier, lorimer The ▷corona between the cyma-tium (▷cyma) and the ▷bed moulding, or any horizontal moulding (▷mould) of similar ▷profile. Also a ▷drip or ▷roll moulding.

Last Judgement A representation, either in carved ▷relief on a ▷tympanum, or in painted form, usually on a ▷chancel-▷arch, showing Christ in majesty consigning those on His left to damnation, and those on His right to Heaven. It often includes St Michael with ▷sword and ▷scales. It was also referred to as a ▷*doom.*

Last Supper Representations are found on ▷altar-pieces, frequently in painted and carved form, on the ▷reredos.

Latch A hinged piece which drops into a ▷catch to secure a ▷door. A *latchet* is a fixing-▷welt.

Later ▷Brick, either sun-dried or burnt. *Later coctus* or *testaceus* is properly the burnt version, while *later crudus* is sun-dried. *Burned bricks or* ▷*tiles* used as facings in ▷Roman ▷concrete are called ▷*tegulae. Laterculus* is a small brick. ▷*Opus lateritum* refers to brickwork.

Lath A strip of timber to which ▷tiles, ▷slates, or ▷plaster are fixed. A *lath-*▷*brick* is a large brick. *Lath-floated and set fair* means three-coat plasterer's work: the first is ▷*pricking-up,* the second is *floating* (▷float), and the third, done with ▷*fine stuff,* is the ▷*setting coat. Lath-laid-and-set* is two-coat work, the first of which is termed *laying,* and the second may be coloured.

Latin cross A ▷cross with the head and arms short (usually of equal length), and the lower arm or tail long.

Latrina A ▷bath, wash-room, or *latrine* (water-closet).

Latrobe A ▷stove to heat a room by means of radiation, but also other rooms as well by means of convected hot air, invented by Benjamin Latrobe.

Latten An alloy resembling ▷brass used in monu-mental work.

Lattice A ▷perforated ▷panel or a network of strips or rods used as a ▷screen, particularly associated with *Chinoiserie* (▷Chinese). Metal lattices with small roset-tes (▷rose) at each junction are often found in ▷Regency ironwork. A ▷reticulated ▷window with ▷laths and openings instead of ▷glass to admit light and air. A *lattice window* is a term also applied to a window with ▷lozenge-shaped ▷leaded lights, or small pieces of glass set in a diagonal network of lead ▷cames, or, less accurately, to any hinged ▷casement light. A *lattice moulding* is one resembling lattice-work, which means any reticulated pattern, usually diagonal. A *lattice* ▷*girder* is a structural member diagonally or triangularly braced.

Laub und Bandelwerk ▷Baroque ▷ornament of

▷bands or ▷ribbons ▷interlacing with foliate and stylized floral designs.

Laudian rails Early seventeenth-century Communion- or ▷altar-▷rails, usually of turned ▷oak, erected during the archbishopric of William Laud (1573–1645) in the reign of King Charles I.

Laundry A room or place where clothing is washed, mangled, dried, steamed, and ironed.

Laurel The ▷bay or true laurel, often found on ▷wreaths and ▷garlands as a ▷symbol of immortality. The laurel is found in ▷festoons and garlands, and, as ▷bay-leaf garland, on the ▷torus moulding and on pulvinated ▷friezes.

Lavabo A stone or metal basin from which water flowed through several holes to enable ablutions to take place. A *lavacrum* was a place for washing, or where a *lavabo* was situated. A *lavatory* was a ▷cistern or trough for washing purposes: it was provided in ▷cloisters of monastic establishments. The term was also given to a ▷*piscina* in a ▷church, or to the stone basin with a drain beneath in which a priest could wash his hands, but is now given to any ▷closet or room fitted up with basins and other apparatus for washing, urinating, or defaecating.

Lavra A collection of monastic ▷cells around a ▷church and common-rooms.

Layer A ▷course of anything. A *layer-▷board* is part of ▷gutter-boarding.

Laying In plastering, the first coat on ▷lath of two-coat work. If laid on brickwork or on stone it is called ▷*rendering*.

Laylight A ceiling ▷light, or a glazed opening in a ceiling to admit light from a source above the ceiling.

Lazar-house, lazaret, lazarette, lazaretto A ▷hospital for the poor, and especially for those with unpleasant conditions, particularly leprosy, or highly infectious diseases. A segregated area or place in which infected persons were quarantined.

Lead A heavy, soft, blue-grey metal used extensively for roofing, ▷flashings, and decorative work. It is malleable and easily worked, and is used in ▷plumbing.

Leaded lights ▷Windows where the ▷glass is held in ▷cames of ▷lead, often but not always in ▷lozenge-shaped ▷panes.

Leaf One hinged side of a ▷door or ▷shutter, or a

[154] LEAF-AND-DART (*JJS*)

removable ▷panel. *Leaf-and-dart* (▷[154]) is a moulding similar to ▷egg-and-dart, but with a leaf carved on the oval shape, or substituted for the egg. A representation in carving of a lateral organ growing from the stem of a plant, or any homologous structure, such as a scale or a ▷petal. A thin shaving of something, such as a wood ▷veneer or ▷gold leaf.

Leaning-place A ▷sill-▷wall under a ▷window.

Lean-to A building the ▷roof of which pitches against or leans on another, bigger, building or ▷wall. It is also called a ▷*to-fall*, or *too-fall*, and is usually a ▷shed with a single-slope roof falling away from the adjacent building. A *pentice* (▷appentice or ▷penthouse). A ▷*lean-to* ▷*aisle* is a normal arrangement of a ▷basilican form.

Lear board The ▷plank on the feet of the ▷rafters to carry the side-piece of the ▷lead of a ▷gutter under the bottom ▷courses of the ▷slating or ▷tiling.

Leaves ▷Ornaments based on natural leaves, such as the ▷laurel, ▷palm, ▷bay, ▷olive, ▷acanthus, or other plants. The leaves of a ▷door or ▷shutter, or the leaves of a ▷cavity wall.

Learning ▷Personified by the ▷Muses, the Four ▷Evangelists, the ▷Doctors of the Church, and the ▷Liberal Arts.

Lectern The reading-desk in a ▷church. It is occasionally of stone or ▷marble, but more usually of wood or of ▷brass. The *lectorium*, *lectrinum*, or *lectricium* was the place where Scripture (usually the *Epistle*) was read.

Ledge The horizontal ▷plank of a common ▷door to which the ▷battens or planks are nailed: a surface or ▷shelf to support an object. A *ledgement* is a ▷string-▷course or any horizontal ▷band of mouldings (▷mould). A *ledgement* ▷*table* is the moulding at the top of a ▷Gothic ▷plinth.

Ledger A flat stone laid over a ▷tomb. Horizontal timbers parallel to the ▷walls are also termed *ledgers*.

Ledgement ▷Ledge.

Lenten veil A cloth or veil hung over statuary or images during Lent.

Leontarium A pool of water in the ▷atrium before a ▷basilica intended as a ▷symbol of purity, often fed by spouts from the mouths of ▷lions.

Leper's squint An opening or ▷window, also called a *low-side window* or an *offertory window*, situated on the south side of the ▷chancel near its west end so that the ▷altar can be seen from the churchyard. It was lower than other windows, and was probably a means of communication between a priest and a person outside. It was always ▷shuttered rather than glazed, and there was usually a seat outside. It was sometimes called a *lychnoscope* on the assumption that here lepers could see the service from the churchyard and presumably confess to a priest within.

Lesbian cymatium What Vitruvius called *cymatium Lesbium* seems to refer to the ▷*cyma reversa* moulding, that is with a convex shape at the top and a concave below. A *Lesbian leaf* is a ▷water-leaf with a prominent ▷rib in the middle.

Lesche A public ▷portico or meeting-room in ▷Antiquity.

Lesene A ▷pilaster strip, i.e. a pilaster with no ▷base or ▷capital, found in ▷Anglo-Saxon and ▷Romanesque ▷architecture.

Letter plate A metal ▷frame with hinged sprung flap set into either the ▷middle or bottom ▷rail of a ▷door so that letters can be delivered. It came into general use after 1840 with the introduction of the Penny Post.

Levecel A ▷penthouse or projecting ▷roof over a ▷door or ▷window: an open ▷shed, ▷appentice, or *pentice.*

Leveller A small stone in ▷rubble work bigger than a ▷sneck and smaller than a ▷riser or jumper (▷jump).

Lever board A ▷board fastened in an ▷aperture, capable of being turned to admit light and air: a ▷louvre.

Lewis A metal device which is set into a ▷dovetailed hole in a ▷block of stone and opens out when lifted so that the stone can be hoisted into position, also called a *lifting* ▷*pin.*

Liberal Arts Grammar (with two pupils or shown watering plants), Logic (with ▷serpent, scorpion, lizard, ▷scales, flowers, or nest of vipers), Rhetoric (with ▷sword, ▷shield, and ▷scroll), Geometry (with ▷compasses, ▷globe, ▷square, and ▷scale), Arithmetic (with abacus [counting-frame], ▷tablet, and ▷scale), Astronomy (with celestial ▷globe, compasses, and sextant), and Music (with organ, viol, lute, and swan).

Liberty A type of ▷Art Nouveau in Italy. A female figure with ▷Phrygian cap and flaming ▷torch.

Library A room, suite of rooms, or building for the keeping and reading of books.

Lichaven A structure of two upright stones and a flat stone spanning them, like a ▷dolmen with only two uprights.

Lich-gate A ▷roof over the entrance to a churchyard beneath which bearers paused when bringing a corpse for interment, also *lych-gate.* A *lich- or lych-stone* was a large stone at the entrance to a graveyard on which the ▷coffin could be rested.

Lierne [155] A ▷rib in a ▷vault that does not arise from an ▷impost and is not a ▷ridge-rib, but crosses from one ▷intersection of the main ribs to another. A vault with such ribs is called a *lierne-vault* (▷[245m]).

Lift A ▷platform or ▷box for carrying goods and passengers from one level to another. The ▷concrete placed between two consecutive horizontal construction joints

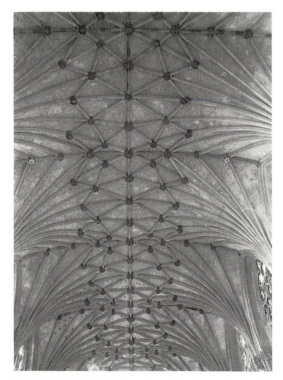

[155] LIERNE VAULT The ceiling of the Lady chapel at Ely Cathedral, *c.* 1350, and therefore in the Middle-Pointed style of Gothic. Note the fan-shaped elements that were the antecedents of the fan-vault. (*JSC*)

in *in situ* work, i.e. placed in a single pour, or any amount of ▷grout placed at one time in a structure.

Ligger A long ▷pole along the ▷ridge of a thatched ▷roof. Another term for a ▷ledger.

Light An opening through which light is admitted: the area or a compartment of a ▷window, such as an opening framed by ▷mullions and ▷transoms, also called a ▷*day*. A ▷pane of ▷glass or a window.

Lightning conductor A ▷copper ▷conductor connected to earth by which lightning is passed safely to the ground.

Lily The Marian ▷symbol, often found on funerary ▷monuments. The ▷*fleur-de-lys*. The lily leaf is also called ▷*water-leaf.*

Lime Chalk and other types of calcium carbonate, such as limestone, when burnt in a ▷kiln are called ▷*quicklime* (calcium oxide, CaO) which, when water is added, becomes *hydrated lime* or *slaked lime* (calcium hydroxide, $Ca(OH)_2$). When more water still is added, it does not combine with the lime, but reduces it to a paste called *lime* ▷*putty* which, on exposure to air, sets and forms carbonate of lime. Lime putty is used in fine-gauged rubbed brickwork, and in such cases linseed oil was very occasionally added to the putty. Lime putty, however, is usually wet hydrated lime soaked overnight to increase its plasticity. *Lime-*▷*mortar* is slaked lime mixed with an ▷aggregate such as pit or quarry sand, river sand, crushed stone, and ashes. Old broken crushed ▷bricks are also used. *Limewash* or *limewhiting* is quicklime soaked in excess water, sometimes bound with ▷size. *Lime* ▷*stucco* is ▷rendering of lime and sand, often with the addition of something such as brick-dust, burnt crushed clay nodules, stone dust, or similar. *Limestone* consists of particles of carbonate of lime connected together by a similar material, and varying in colour from white to a dark yellow-brown: it is easily worked.

Limen A ▷threshold or ▷door-▷sill (*limen inferior*) or a ▷lintel (*limen superior, limen superum*, or *supercilium*). A boundary marker.

Line and pins Two steel ▷pins with a line between used to maintain the correct alignment of a course in ▷masonry or brickwork (▷brick).

Linenfold [156] ▷Panelling of the ▷Tudor period ▷ornamented with a representation of folded linen, also called *parchemin plié* (▷parchemin).

Lining The covering of the surface of part of a

[156] LINENFOLD (*JJS*)

building with another substance, such as ▷panelling or a ▷door-▷case.

Lining paper Paper pasted to a ▷wall as a ▷base for wallpaper or the application of paint.

Linseed-oil putty Linseed oil is obtained from flax seeds. The ▷putty is made of ▷whiting (crushed chalk) mixed with the oil, and used by glaziers.

Lintel, lintol A horizontal ▷beam over an opening to support the ▷wall over it. A *lintel* ▷*course* is a horizontal course of stone the same height as a lintel and continuous with it.

Lion Courage, majesty, victory, strength, and pride. It is often associated with the Resurrection and with the sun, and is a ▷symbol of vigilance. An ▷emblem of St Mark, it is often linked with thrones, ▷lecterns, ▷fonts, etc. Lions occur as ▷ornaments on ▷cornices, as water-spouts, as ▷bosses, and elsewhere in ▷architecture. Lions' ▷paws are used in ▷furniture, especially for ▷*monopodia*. Lions recur on bosses, ▷gargoyles, ▷corbels, and keystones.

Lip moulding A ▷projecting moulding (▷mould) resembling an overhanging lip, found in Third-▷Pointed work, especially in the ▷cappings of ▷buttresses and in ▷base mouldings.

Lisena As ▷Lesene.

List, listel, listella A ▷fillet or an ▷annulet.

Listing The cutting of the sapwood from both edges of a ▷board. ▷Slates built into and ▷projecting beyond a ▷chimney-stack above ▷roof level to prevent water penetrating the junction between the roof-covering and the stack.

Listatum ▷*Opus listatum* was a ▷Roman ▷wall built of alternating ▷courses of stone and ▷brick.

Lithostrotum ▷*Opus lithostrotum* was ornamental paving such as ▷mosaic.

Litre A ▷band in a mediaeval building on which the ▷Achievements of founders were painted.

Lobby A small room communicating with one or more ▷apartments.

Lobe A ▷foil of a ▷Gothic opening. A *lobed* ▷*arch* means one with lobes and ▷cusps. *Lobed decoration* is ▷gadrooning.

Lock A piece of mechanism for fastening a ▷door, drawer, ▷chest, etc. Those on outer doors are *stock locks*; those on chamber-doors are *spring locks* or ▷*rim locks*; and those hidden in the door are ▷*mortise locks*. Locks are operated by ▷keys which move a ▷*dead-bolt*. The *lock* ▷*rail* of a door is the middle, horizontal rail to which the lock is fixed. A *lockband* is a ▷course of bonding stones. A *locker* is an ▷aumbry, or any ▷cupboard fitted with a secure door.

Loculus A recess for a body, ▷coffin, ▷sarcophagus, or ash-▷chest, as in a ▷catacomb.

Locutory A place in a ▷monastery where talking was allowed.

Lodge A small house at the ▷gate of an estate (often paired with a similar structure to provide ▷symmetry) or any small house in a park. The quarters of masons working on a mediaeval building, hence ▷Freemasons' lodges.

Loft An upper ▷platform, or the ▷gallery in a ▷church, the ▷rood-loft, organ-loft, or choir-loft. In modern parlance it is the space under the ▷rafters of a building and above the ceiling of the upper ▷floor.

Logan A rocking-stone, or upright stone capable of being rocked to and fro.

Logeion, logeum A ▷platform in an ▷Antique ▷theatre, corresponding to a ▷stage.

Loggia A ▷lodge, but more usually part of a building where one or more sides are open to the air, the opening being ▷colonnaded or ▷arcaded. It can be a separate building, but it is more often an open ▷gallery or an arcaded or colonnaded large recess at ground-floor or ▷*piano nobile* level.

Lombard style [157] ▷Architecture of the ▷Romanesque period found in northern Italy, and revived during the nineteenth century. It is based on ▷Early Christian architecture, and is mostly of ▷brick.

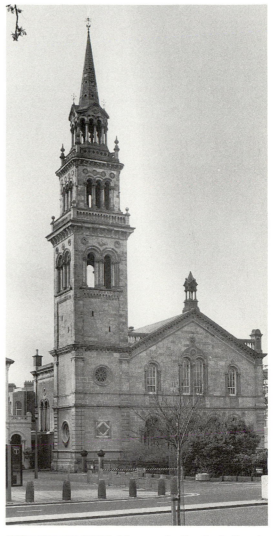

[157] LOMBARD STYLE A fine example of Lombardo-Venetian Romanesque Revival. Elmwood Presbyterian Church, Belfast, by John Corry, 1859–62. (*JSC*)

London stock A coarse-textured, yellowish ▷brick, often with red and dark pigmentation, produced in London and its environs, and commonly used throughout the capital.

Long-and-short ▷Anglo-Saxon ▷freestone ▷quoins consisting of tall uprights and short horizontals, laid alternately. The method gave good ▷bonds as the short quoins extended well into the thickness of the ▷wall.

Long gallery A very long, high-ceilinged room, often extending the full length of a grander ▷Elizabethan or

▷Jacobean house, used as a ▷gallery, ▷promenade, and multi-purpose space.

Long-stone swings Stone ▷lintels.

Lookout A *lookout* ▷*rafter*, also called a ▷*tail* or a *tail-piece*, is a rafter or ▷bracket projecting beyond the building and supporting an overhanging piece of the ▷roof. A *lookout* ▷*tower* is a ▷belvedere.

Lookum, leucomb A ▷projection on the upper ▷floor of a warehouse or ▷mill to cover a wheel and fall, or pulley-crane, with a trap-door.

Loop [158] Also *arrowloop, loop* ▷*window*, or *loophole*, it is a small, narrow slit in a ▷wall, used in fortifications, or in ▷parapets, through which missiles and arrows could be discharged. They often had circular enlargements in the middle or at the ends, and were frequently in the form of a ▷cross (▷[29]). The term *loophole* is also applied to a vertical series of ▷doors in a warehouse through which goods can be delivered by crane.

Loricula A ▷squint or ▷hagioscope.

Lorymer A ▷larmier.

[158] LOOPHOLE Loophole or vertical series of doors in a warehouse in Southwark, London, through which goods could be brought or delivered by means of the crane. (*JSC*)

[159] LOTUS Fragment of necking ornament from a column at the temple of Apollo, Naukratis, featuring lotus flowers and buds. The lotus became a favourite decorative motif of the Greeks, and was often combined with the palmette, appearing alternately with it in friezes. (*JSC*)

Lotus [159] A plant much used as the inspiration for architectural ▷ornament. Formalized flowers, buds, and ▷leaves of lotiform type were used in Ancient ▷Egyptian ▷architecture as well as in ▷Greek and ▷Neoclassical ornament. *Lotus bud* and *lotus flower* ▷capitals both occur in Egyptian and in Egyptian ▷Revival work. The lotus is related to the *palmette* (▷palm).

Loudon's hollow wall A ▷wall bonded similarly to Flemish ▷bond but with the ▷stretchers two inches apart, and the header (▷head) two inches back from the inside ▷face. The face was regular in the bond, the wall at least partially hollow, and the set-back on the inside allowed a better ▷key for ▷plaster. J. C. Loudon (1783–1843) also proposed variations on Dearn's and Silverlock's hollow walls (▷brick).

Louis Treize The style of ▷Renaissance ▷architecture of the reign of Louis XIII (1610–43).

Louis Quatorze The style of ▷Baroque and ▷Classical ▷architecture of the reign of Louis XIV (1643–1715), of which Versailles is an outstanding example.

Louis Quinze The style of ▷Classical and ▷Rococo ▷architecture of the reign of Louis XV (1715–74), lighter and more elegant than that of ▷Louis Quatorze.

Louis Seize The style of ▷Neoclassical ▷architecture and design beginning in the reign of Louis XV, but especially associated with the reign of Louis XVI (1774–92). All four Louis styles were revived during the nineteenth and twentieth centuries.

Louvre A ▷turret or ▷lantern over a ▷hall to allow smoke and steam to escape, also called a ▷*femerell*. Louvres were sometimes closed with ▷boards placed horizontally and a slope at a distance apart, to allow ventilation to take place, and these boards are known as *louvres*, *luffers*, or *lever-boards*. The term today is applied to the boards only, or to ▷glass or slats used in the same way. A *louvre* ▷*window* is one with louvres, such as in a ▷belfry ▷stage of a ▷tower. The *Louvre* in Paris is the former royal palace, now used as an art gallery.

Love Frequently alluded to in its divine and conjugal forms. ▷Personified as Cupid (with ▷bow and arrows), Amor, ▷doves (lovebirds), and Hymen. ▷Hearts, ▷knots, shackles, ▷chains, and buckles all suggest love, as do ▷myrtles, ▷roses, mistletoe, forget-me-nots, convolvulus, ▷ivy, and daisies. The ▷unicorn is associated with purity.

Low relief A *bas-*▷*relief.*

Low-side window ▷Leper's squint.

Lozenge A ▷diamond-shape found in decoration, e.g. *lozenge mouldings*. A rhomboid shape. A small ▷light above two ▷lancet-lights in ▷Gothic ▷tracery. A *lozenge* ▷*fret* is a moulding of continuous lozenges, also called a *diamond fret*. Lozenges are found in ▷diaper patterns.

Lucarne, luthern A ▷window or opening standing perpendicularly above the ▷entablature and built on the ▷naked or same plane as the main ▷façade below the entablature to illuminate the space within the ▷roof. Lucarnes can be semicircular, elliptical, segmental-headed, and of other kinds, and are associated with ▷French ▷Classical ▷architecture. They are not the same as *dormers* (▷dormant), which rise vertically from the ▷rafters of a sloping roof and do not rise perpendicularly on the naked of the façade below. The term *lucarne* can be applied, however, to the ▷gabled openings on a ▷spire.

Lucullite A black ▷marble used by the ▷Romans.

Ludion A ▷tile used as a ▷brick.

Luffer ▷Louvre.

Lunette A semicircular opening framed by an ▷arch or ▷vault, or a semicircular area on a ▷wall. An opening of such a shape above a ▷door in an arch. A painting in an area with a semicircular top. A *lune* is anything shaped like a ▷crescent or a half-moon, such as a segmental ▷pediment. Two vertical ▷mullions dividing the lunette make it a ▷Diocletian window, and if glazing-bars radiate from the centre of the ▷base, it is called a *fanlight* (▷fan). Carved repetitive semicircles filled with ▷foliage are also called lunettes, and are a feature of ▷Jacobean carving.

Luthern ▷Lucarne. It is sometimes applied to a *dormer* (▷dormant), but this is not, strictly speaking, correct.

Luting ▷Caulking.

Lycaeum Also *lyceum*, a building for education, lectures, concerts, and debate.

Lych-gate ▷Lich-gate.

Lychnoscope ▷Leper's squint.

Lychnus A suspended lamp.

Lying light A ceiling- or ▷lay-light.

Lymphaea A ▷grotto, built, not natural.

Lyre A decorative ▷Classical and ▷Neoclassical ▷ornament, an ▷attribute of ▷Mercury and ▷Apollo (▷Apollonian decoration), and used to suggest ▷music or enlightenment. It is found in chair-backs and -legs in the eighteenth century, and was a commonly used decorative ▷motif.

Lysis A ▷plinth or ▷step above the ▷cornice of the ▷podium of a ▷Roman ▷temple or similar building. A ▷stylobate.

M

M The Roman symbol for 1000.

M-roof Two common ▷roofs with a ▷valley between them.

Macadam A road surface of ▷aggregates rolled into a tarry surface on ▷hardcore.

Macellum A ▷Roman covered market.

Maceria A ▷Roman ▷wall made of many materials and not ▷faced in any regular fashion. A garden-wall.

Machicolation [160] Openings at the top of a fortified ▷wall formed by setting the ▷parapet in front of the wall and carrying it on ▷corbels: the intervals between the corbels are left open so that arrows, boiling oil, and sundry unpleasant objects could be rained on any attackers below (▷[38]).

Machinery Decorative ▷motifs derived from machine parts became fashionable in the 1920s.

Maeander Also *meander*. ▷Labyrinth.

Maenads Dancing females, or *Bacchantes*, found in ▷Bacchic ornament.

Maenhir Also *menhir*, meaning a tall, upright stone set alone in open ground, sometimes rudely carved.

Maenianum A ▷balcony, for spectators, or a range of seats in a ▷theatre divided radially by the gangways or ▷steps. Also a ▷cantilevered gallery or balcony of a ▷Roman house, or a ▷jettied ▷storey. A ▷lattice.

Magazine A store for explosives, or a large department store.

Magnesian limestone A limestone (▷lime) with a high proportion of magnesium carbonate in it, such as Anston, Linby, and Park Nook, all suitable for free working.

Magi The Three Kings or Wise Men: *Balthasar* (black, with myrrh), *Caspar* (yellow, with frankincense), and *Melchior* (white, with gold), often depicted in Christian art. Their shrine is in Cologne.

[160] MACHICOLATIONS The central tower of the St Charles Hospital, North Kensington, London, by H. Saxon Snell (1879–81), containing the chimney-flues and water-tanks. The machicolations are not defensive in this instance, and are largely decorative. (*Greater London Photographic Library 70/14289*)

Magot A small portly ▷Chinese figure, also called a ▷*Pagod*, found in *Chinoiserie* (▷Chinese) schemes of decorations.

Maiden tower A ▷keep.

Maidenhead A terminal in the form of a female head or bust, also associated with the Virgin Mary.

Majolica ▷Earthenware finished with a white glaze and a coloured over-glaze, therefore a type of ▷*faïence*.

Malm bricks ▷Bricks made from a calcareous loam, considered to be very fine in quality.

Maltese cross One formed of four equal arrow-heads or pennants jointed at the pointed ends.

Maltha A variety of waterproof compound used by the ▷Romans for repairing ▷cisterns, or a bituminous substance.

Malus One of a series of ▷poles (*mali*) at the top of the ▷walls of a ▷Roman amphitheatre from which the ▷*velarium* or tent-like ▷awning was suspended.

Mandala Also *mandoral*, *mandorla*. An ▷aureole, almond-shaped, around the figure of a sacred image, such as Christ. It is a ▷symbol of the psyche in all its aspects, and is represented by circles, polygons, ▷labyrinths, squares, and other figures which have a centre. ▷Rose ▷windows are mandalas, and so is the ▷*Vesica Piscis*. The labyrinth was represented in the ▷floors of ▷cathedrals, and was a symbol of the Holy Grail, leading the pilgrim through life to ▷Paradise or ▷Jerusalem. The mandala is also found in ▷panels and in ▷tracery.

Manger A trough in the ▷stall of a ▷stable.

Manhole An opening formed for access to a ▷sewer, an underground ▷passage, or a boiler.

Mannerism [161] A style of sixteenth-century ▷architecture characterized by the use of ▷Classical ▷motifs outside their normal context, or in a wilful or illogical manner. It was the precursor of ▷Baroque, and is generally associated with ▷Italian architecture from the time of Michelangelo until the beginning of the seventeenth century. Dropped keystones or ▷triglyphs, ▷columns ▷inserted into recesses and apparently carried on ▷consoles, and distorted ▷aedicules were features of the style. Subsequently the School of ▷*Fontainebleau* and the ▷Flemish Mannerists created a lavish style of decorations with ▷strapwork and ▷Grotesquery much in evidence, with ▷swags, ▷herms, ▷cartouches, and an almost over-elaboration. In northern Europe Classical motifs were mingled with late ▷*Flamboyant* ▷Gothic.

Manor-house A house in the centre of a manor, or owned by the lord of the manor, generally unfortified, although fortified examples are known.

Mansard A *Mansard* or ▷*curb* ▷roof is one with two inclined planes, allowing a room to be placed within it, and illuminated with ▷lucarnes. The lower slope is always very steep. It is also associated with the *Second* ▷*Empire style* (▷[212g]). It was named after François Mansart (1598–1666).

Manse A ▷parsonage house, now usually applied to the dwellings of ministers of the Presbyterian Church.

Mansfield stone A ▷sandstone from Nottingham-shire, both creamy-yellow and red, and not suitable for heavily polluted atmospheres. It is fine and evenly grained.

Mansion A large house with architectural preten-sions, or a large and spacious ▷flat in a ▷block of 'mansion flats', or a ▷manor-house. A *mansion-house* is usually the official residence of a mayor.

Mantel A ▷beam or ▷arch over a fireplace: if it is a beam of timber it is called a *mantel-*▷*tree* or *mantle-tree*. A *mantelpiece* or *mantlepiece* is the decorative ▷shelf in front of the mantel-tree supported by the ▷jambs of a ▷chimney-piece, or the ▷frame surrounding a fire-place. The part with the shelf is also called a *mantel-shelf*. A *mantle* or *mantel* is also the outer covering of a ▷wall of different material from that of the wall itself.

Mantling An ▷apron-like form with looped lower edge, used as a ▷surround for ▷shields. ▷Lambrequin.

Marble A metamorphosed crystalline limestone (▷lime) available in a great variety of colour, and capable of taking a high polish. It is easily and accurately carved, and can be burned to provide quicklime. *Marbling* is a painted finish imitating marble, or a decorative ▷*trompe l'oeil* decorative technique to sug-gest ▷alabaster, *verde antiche*, or richly veined stone.

Marchioness A size of ▷slate 22 × 11 inches or 20 × 12 inches.

Margent [162] A strip of floral or ▷foliate forms hanging downwards, often from a ▷mask or a ring, derived from ▷festoons, and often found emphasizing the sides of ▷windows or ▷niches or vertical ▷panels.

Margin The part of a ▷slate uncovered by the slate above. A *margin-*▷*draft* is the plain ▷dressed ▷border on the ▷face of an ▷ashlar block, leaving the middle

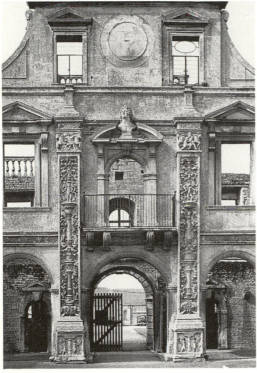

(a)

(b)

[161] MANNERISM (a) Kirby Hall, Northamptonshire. A remarkable Elizabethan House in which the Giant Order of pilasters is used for the first time in England. The date is 1570–72, although the attic storey and window-surrounds are later additions (seventeenth century). The sources for the pilaster-capitals with Pegasus features instead of volutes come from Serlio's published works, probably in the 1559 or 1566 editions. The treatment of the shafts of the pilasters comes from the frontispiece of John Shute's *The First and Chief Groundes of Architecture* of 1563: these decorations consist of candelabra and putti, and are essentially Grotesque. (b) Part of the crypt of the Roman Catholic cathedral in Liverpool by Lutyens, of 1933–40. Note the vast keystone of the arch that seems to crash down on to the transome, which bends under the weight, as though on pivots. The window is an invention based on the Diocletian type. The tapering square columns on either side of the doors are tied back to the wall with huge blocks of stone. (*JSC*)

[162] MARGENT (*JSC*)

dressed or rough: the *draft* is usually the width of a chisel. A *margin-▷light* is a *side-light* or ▷framed area of fixed ▷glass beside a ▷door- or ▷window-opening, also called a *flanking window* or a ▷*wing-light*. A margin implies an exposed flat surface, as of the ▷stiles and ▷rails forming the frames around a ▷panelled door, the surface above the ▷nosings of a ▷close ▷string, or the ▷mitred margin around a ▷hearth. A *margin strip* is the timber around a ▷floor forming a border, which can in turn be wide and elaborate.

Marigold window A circular ▷window with radiating ▷mullions, or glazing ▷bars, also called a ▷*rose window*. It is often found in ▷gables or in ▷pediments.

Marine decoration ▷Neptune with ▷trident, ▷*hippocamps*, Amphitrite, ▷dolphins, ▷Tritons, ▷mermaids, nets, ▷fish, sea-shells, etc., found in ▷Classical and ▷Rococo ▷ornament. The *columna rostrata* (▷column).

Often found in ▷grottoes, and, with ▷cables, ▷anchors, etc., used to suggest navigation.

Market cross A ▷cross set up in a market-place, sometimes consisting of a ▷shaft with a cross of stone set on ▷steps, but often an elaborate ▷arcaded cross, sometimes associated with a ▷fountain. The *market cross* or *mercat* (Scots) *cross* was intended to remind all there of the importance of the teaching of the Church.

Marmoratum A ▷Roman ▷mortar of crushed ▷marble and ▷lime-▷mortar. ▷*Opus marmoratum* was a finishing coat of calcined ▷gypsum mixed with crushed marble, and rubbed to a fine marble-like surface.

Marmoset An ▷Antic figure, often grimacing, found in ▷Gothic carving. A jester or a monkey.

Marquee A large tent, or a permanent ▷canopy over the entrance to a building.

Marquetry ▷Inlaid work of thin pieces of ivory, or coloured ▷veneers of wood glued to a ground (▷Buhl, ▷damascene).

Mars The god of ▷War found in schemes of ▷military decoration, often with ▷helmets, ▷shields, breastplates, and other military ▷trophies. ▷Mars is sometimes depicted with ▷Minerva, representing the opposite of War.

Martello A circular fortified ▷tower, two ▷storeys high, erected round the coasts of the British Isles during the Napoleonic Wars, and armed with artillery.

Martlet A swallow or martin: in heraldry, with no legs, but tufts of feathers where the legs should be.

Martyrium A part of a ▷church where the relics of saints were placed.

Mascaron A humanoid ▷mask, often ▷Grotesque or caricatured, often found on keystones.

Mask Common decorative ▷motifs on stone ▷capitals, ▷corbels, ▷label-▷stops, keystones, ▷panels, etc., found in infinite variety, and featuring ▷Grotesques, deities, ▷gorgons, etc.

Masonry [163] The craft of jointing, cutting, and laying stones for building. Some ancient masonry consisted of stones laid dry, without ▷mortar, some ▷blocks being so big that they would not subsequently shift. ▷*Cyclopean* masonry consists of large blocks of irregularly shaped stone with the interstices filled in with smaller stones. Stones laid in ▷courses represent a considerable degree of sophistication. ▷*Rubble* is masonry of undressed rough stones, *random rubble* being uncoursed. *Coursed rubble* is laid in layers. *Squared rubble* is roughly dressed. ▷*Ashlar work* is cut stone worked to even ▷faces and right-angled edges,

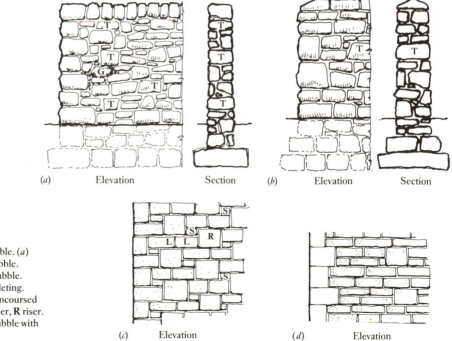

(a) Elevation Section (b) Elevation Section

[163] MASONRY Rubble. (*a*) Random, uncoursed rubble. (*b*) Random, coursed rubble. **T** through-stone, **G** galleting. (*c*) Squared, snecked, uncoursed rubble. **S** sneck, **L** leveller, **R** riser. (*d*) Squared, coursed rubble with ashlar quoins. (*JSC*)

(c) Elevation (d) Elevation

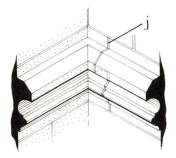

[164] MASON'S MITRE **j** joint. (*JJS*)

laid in horizontal courses with vertical joints (▷ashlar). Where the surface of stones projects beyond the joints, the finish is known as *rustication* (▷rustic), of which there are many types. Masonry of the best sort is laid with ▷lime-mortar, while ▷dry-stone walls are laid without mortar by *cowans* who were forbidden to work with lime. Hence the tool of a master-mason is the trowel. Masonic ▷emblems are commonly found, and include the square and compasses, dividers, levels, plumblines, tracing-boards, rough and squared ashlars, open Bibles, blazing sun, stars, moon, and globes, tassels, beehive, ladder, ▷Egyptian ▷motifs, twin ▷columns (Jachin and Boaz), All-Seeing Eye, and the motto *Audi, Vide, Tace*.

Mason's mitre [164] When mouldings (▷mould) of stone meet at right-angles, the diagonal mitre does not coincide with the joint: the moulding is carried through on the return ▷face, and the result is a *mason's mitre* because an acute angle in ▷masonry is fundamentally unsound and brittle. A mitre in masonry, therefore, does not have a diagonal joint.

Mass bell A *sanctus bell*, hung in a *sancte-cote* (▷sancte-bell).

Mass dial A sundial with lines radiating from the ▷gnomon the shadow of which indicates the time in relation to its position in respect of the lines. The hours for masses are indicated by means of deeper grooved lines, or by means of lines treated distinctively. A stone carved with a formal floral geometrical pattern.

Mastaba A rectangular ▷Egyptian ▷tomb with a flat ▷roof and ▷battered sides, hence a mastaba-form is any structure resembling this.

Mastic Any heavy adhesive compound, or a sealant with properties like ▷putty. *Mastic* ▷*asphalt* is a viscous mix of asphalt and some other material such as sand, which hardens on exposure to the air, used in waterproofing.

Matchboarding Boarding for ▷doors, ceilings, or ▷walls, usually with V-joints between, and ▷tongues on one side and grooves on the other.

Materiato All the timbers of a ▷Roman ▷roof.

Matroneum Part of a ▷basilica set apart for matrons.

Matting Textured surface on metalwork made by hammering with a punch, often used as a background for other decorative effects.

Mausoleum [165] A ▷monumental sepulchral building, or a roofed ▷tomb, either free-standing or attached to another building (named after the tomb of King Mausolus of Caria at Halicarnassus, a fourth-century BC ▷Hellenistic ▷monument of great size and beauty). It may contain ▷sarcophagi, ▷coffins, or cinerary ▷urns.

Mayan arch A ▷corbelled or pseudo-▷arch of triangular form, favoured in Art-Deco work, and related to Egyptianizing forms, derived from Piranesi.

Maze A ▷labyrinth cut in turf, formed of plants, or built.

Meander ▷Labyrinth. Any progressive repetitive winding ▷ornament.

Medallion A square, elliptical, circular, or oval tablet on which are figures, ▷ornaments, or busts in ▷relief. Medallions are found on ▷friezes, or are isolated architectural ▷motifs set on a wall. A *medallion-moulding* is a series of medallions, usually associated with ▷Romanesque and ▷Classical ornament.

Medicine Suggested by the rod with twined ▷serpents, lancets, leeches, eyes, and hands. The figures of ▷Asclepius and Hygeia also occur, as do pestles and mortars, flaming ▷torches, and gilt ▷knobs.

Mediaeval architecture The ▷architecture of Europe during the Middle Ages, including ▷Romanesque and ▷Gothic styles, and generally agreed to date from the end of the eighth century to the first half of the sixteenth century (▷Gothic, ▷Norman, ▷Romanesque).

Medina cement A quick-setting natural ▷cement from the Isle of Wight similar to ▷Portland cement.

Medusa ▷Gorgon. A *gorgoneion*, often found on keystones or on ▷shields.

Meeting-house A house for Non-conformist services, especially those of the Quakers or Presbyterians.

(a)   (b)

[165] MAUSOLEUM (*a*) Front elevation of the Royal Mausoleum at Frogmore, in the *Rundbogenstil* influenced by German and Italian prototypes, designed by a team led by Ludwig Grüner, and commenced in 1862. (*Windsor Royal Library*. © *1992 Her Majesty the Queen. RL19738*) (*b*) Mausoleum at Trentham Park, Staffordshire, designed by Charles Heathcote Tatham, 1807–8. Note the battered Egyptianizing elements, and the stripped, Neoclassical form. (*JSC*)

Meeting-rail In a ▷sash-▷window the horizontal members at the top of the lower and the similar member at the bottom of the upper sash. A *meeting-▷stile* is one of the stiles in a pair of ▷doors or ▷casements which join.

Megalithic Consisting or constructed of large stones.

Megaron A large room or ▷hall in a ▷Greek building, or a space in a Greek ▷temple where only the priest could enter.

Mellarium A ▷Roman ▷apiary.

Melon dome A melon-shaped ribbed ▷dome.

Memorial A structure or ▷inscription or ▷plaque commemorating persons or events. A memorial ▷arch does this: if it commemorates a victory it is called a *▷triumphal arch*. A *memorial* ▷*window* is one of etched, painted or coloured ▷glass commemorating a person, persons, or events.

Memory, The Art of A system of mnemonic devices evolved in ▷Antiquity and revived and developed in ▷Renaissance times, it was sometimes called the ▷*Phoenix*. It involved the study of a building: the student would visit the rooms in a specific order, memorizing that order and the architectural details of each room. When memorizing a speech he would revisit the building in imagination, associating the images with arguments or words which would then become the 'trigger' for the speech. The Art of Memory is fully discussed by Frances A. Yates in her book of that title (London, 1966).

Menagerie A building for housing and preserving animals: menageries were features of seventeenth- and eighteenth-century ▷gardens.

Menhir ▷Maenhir.

Menianum ▷Maenianum.

Menorah The seven-branched candelabrum.

Mensa The stone ▷slab on top of an ▷altar, or its upper surface.

Mensole A keystone (▷arch).

Mercury The messenger of the gods, associated with eloquence, speed, travel, commerce, and communications. He is shown with *petasus* (broad-brimmed winged hat), winged sandals, ▷*caduceus*, ▷lyre, numerals, ▷stars, and ▷scales. Also a silvery metallic element which is liquid at room temperature, called *quicksilver*.

Merlon The solid part of an ▷embattled ▷parapet, also called a ▷*cop*, flanked by ▷*embrasures* (▷[38]).

Mermaid Female figures with fish-tails from the waist downwards, associated with ▷marine decorations, but also found in mediaeval iconography in ▷misericords and ▷pew-ends to suggest lust, temptation, and vanity. A *merman* is a ▷*Triton*.

Meros The plain flat ▷face between the ▷channels of a ▷triglyph. Also *merus*.

Mesalorium As ▷aspaticum or aspasticum.

Mesaulae Small ▷courts or ▷passages, or ▷doors in such passages.

Messuage A house, outbuildings, and contiguous grounds.

Mestling Also *mastin*, meaning yellow metal, ▷brass, or ▷latten.

Meta A ▷column, ▷obelisk, or upright on the ▷*spina* of a ▷circus or ▷hippodrome marking a turn.

Metalwork Any construction made of metal.

Metatome The space between the ▷dentils of the ▷Ionic ▷Order, or the space between the ▷triglyphs of the ▷Doric ▷Order, also called *metoche*.

Metopa, metope, metopse The ▷panel between ▷triglyphs of the ▷Doric ▷Order, either plain or decorated. Vitruvius also states that *metope* is an equivalent of ▷*intersectio*, or the space between the ▷dentils. A *metopon* is the solid between ▷doors or ▷windows, or it is a ▷pier, square on plan, like a ▷mullion.

Mews Originally a place where hawks were kept (an onomatopoeic reference to their cat-like cries), later applied to subsidiary ranges of ▷stables or coach-houses with living-quarters above, commonly associated with grander town-houses, and situated to the rear of such houses, usually in London. The term is now commonly applied to any small-scale development off the street frontage.

Mezzanine A ▷storey of middle height between two higher ones: an ▷*entresol*, usually immediately above the ground floor.

Mezzo-rilievo Relief.

Michael A ▷chapel on a high mound or rock dedicated to the archangel, or a chapel built high in a ▷church or ▷monastery similarly dedicated, as the saint was identified with the sun.

Middle-Pointed ▷Gothic ▷architecture of the fourteenth century, also known as the ▷Decorated style.

Middle post A ▷king-post.

Middle rail The ▷rail of a ▷door to which the ▷lock or ▷bolt is fixed, also called the *lock-rail* (▷[104]).

Mid-feather A cross-▷tongue or a parting-slip.

Mid-wall column A ▷column carrying a ▷wall much thicker than its diameter, and set on the centre-line of the wall, as in Saxon belfries.

Military decoration ▷Trophies of guns, flags, armour, swords, ▷helmets, etc. used to embellish ▷arsenals, ▷barracks, etc. also found on military ▷tombs, ▷memorials, etc. ▷Laurel wreaths, ▷thunder-bolts, ▷lions, ▷eagles, ▷Fame, and ▷Victory, with ▷Mars, and Hercules, were also featured. ▷Baroque and ▷Neoclassical schemes frequently employed military decoration.

Mill A building in which corn is ground, or some material such as thread, cloth, paper, or sawn timber, is produced.

Millefleurs A background of flowers found in late mediaeval and ▷Gothic Revival work.

Milliarium A ▷Roman marker or milestone.

Minaret A tall slender circular ▷tower with one or more ▷balconies from which Muslims are called to prayer at a ▷mosque, or any form similar to it.

Minchery A ▷nunnery. A *minch-house* was an ▷inn by a roadside, often associated with a religious foundation.

Minerva Goddess of Wisdom and patron of Art and Trade, she is found in schemes balancing ▷Mars, and in decorations of ▷libraries and institutions of learning.

Minster [166] The ▷church of a ▷monastery, or to which a monastery was once attached. The name also distinguishes collegiate or conventional churches from secular or ▷parish churches, and ▷minsters were often imposing and grander than such buildings.

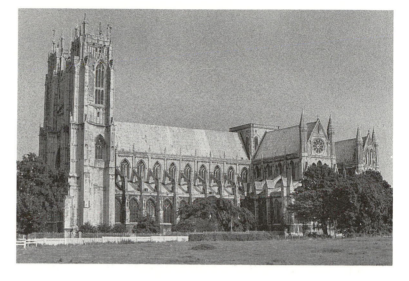

[166] MINSTER Beverley Minster, Yorkshire, from the south-west. Note the two sets of transepts. The western towers are Perpendicular (*c.* 1380–1420), the two transepts are Early English or First-Pointed (*c.* 1220–60), and the nave is mostly Second-Pointed or Decorated (*c.* 1308–49). (*JSC*)

Minstrel gallery A ▷balcony in a ▷church or ▷hall for musicians, also called *musicians' ▷gallery*

Mint A place where money is coined.

Minute A proportional measure, and a subdivision of a ▷module, such as a sixtieth part of the diameter of a ▷column at the ▷base of a ▷shaft.

Misericord [167] The ▷projecting ▷bracket or *mercy-seat* on the underside of seats in the ▷choir-▷stalls in grander ▷churches: when the hinged seats were raised, the brackets afforded a modicum of rest to someone standing or leaning upon them during the long mediaeval services. These brackets are often ▷ornamented with comic figures, allusions to ▷fables, or other ornament, and are also termed *miserere* or *subsellium*. A misericord was also a room where the monastic regulations were relaxed.

Mission tile Also called a ▷*Spanish tile*, it was a clay roofing tile, segmental in section, laid alternately convex–concave–convex.

Mitchel A 24 × 15 inches ▷Purbeck-marble stone.

Mitre The line formed by the meeting of two surfaces intercepting each other at an ▷angle. A *mitre* is also the head-dress of a bishop, consisting of a high conical cap divided by a cleft, with two ribbons hanging from the back, probably meant to suggest the head of a ▷fish. It is found in ▷church decorations, especially in wood-carvings. A *mitre-▷arch* consists of two flat ▷slabs leaning together, joined in a mitre, thus forming a triangular ▷head. A *mitre-leaf* is a moulding (▷mould) consisting of a leaf split at the base,

often found in beading, etc., as ▷*bead-and-leaf* moulding.

Mithraeum A ▷sanctuary devoted to the Graeco-Roman–Persian cult of Mithras, which flourished during the ▷Roman Empire.

Mixed arch A composite or multiple-centred ▷arch.

Mixtilinear arch An ▷arch made up of various shapes, found in *Moresque* ▷architecture (▷arch, ▷Moorish architecture).

Moat A wide ditch surrounding a town or a fortress, usually filled with water.

Moderne The ▷Art-Deco style.

Modernismo The Spanish variety of ▷Art Nouveau.

Modernist Decoration using geometrical abstract patterns based on ▷Classical ▷ornament, including ▷fluting, wave ▷scrolls, and repetitive ▷medallions. ▷Chevrons, stepped mouldings, and the use of coloured ▷glass, ▷enamel, and chrome were common, introducing an Egyptianizing element to the scheme. Modernist decoration tended to emphasize industrial processes. It was strongly influenced by ▷Art-Deco work.

Modern Movement ▷International style.

Modillion [168] A projecting ▷console ▷bracket under the ▷corona of the ▷Corinthian and ▷Composite ▷Orders, and sometimes of the ▷Roman ▷Ionic Order: it consists of a ▷scroll with ▷acanthus. If it is a plain

(a)

(b)

[167] MISERICORDS (a) The fourteenth-century choir-stalls at All Saints' Church, Hereford, showing the misericords under the raised seats. Note the elaborate canopies with ogee arches and the cresting over. (*Hereford City Library 10472*) (b) Details of misericords from the Church of St Laurence, Ludlow, Shropshire. (*JSC*)

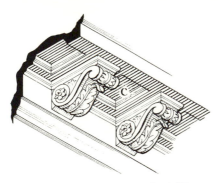

[168] MODILLIONS **c** coffer. (*JJS*)

rectangular block it is a *block modillion* or an *uncut modillion*, or even a variety of ▷*mutule*. It relates to ▷intercolumniation and the centre-lines of ▷columns. Modillions are placed with the intervention of ▷coffers or other ▷ornaments between them. They should be regularly placed so that the centre of one should always stand over the centre-line of a column or ▷pilaster. Corinthian modillions are usually more elaborate than those of the Ionic or Composite Orders. A *mutule*, which is confined to the ▷Doric and to some ▷Tuscan Orders, is always spaced in relation to the ▷triglyphs and centre-lines of columns, and is different in form compared with a modillion, although the origin is probably the same, and the function, that of enriching the ▷soffite of the corona, is identical.

Modinature The general distribution, ▷profiles, and arrangement of the mouldings (▷mould) of an ▷Order, a building, or an architectural component.

Module A measure which regulates ▷proportion by means of multiples or divisions. In ▷Classical ▷architecture it is the diameter of a ▷column, or half its diameter, at the base of the ▷shaft, and this module is divided into sixty ▷minutes. The term also refers to any system of measurement to facilitate repetitions of standard units.

Moellon Rubble used as filling between facing ▷walls.

Moenianum As maenianum.

Moghul Also ▷*Mogul* or *Mughal*. The last phase of Indian ▷Islamic architecture of the sixteenth to eighteenth century: the *Tâj Mahal* is the finest extant example. The style was copied in the nineteenth and early twentieth centuries.

Mole A construction or ▷pier in the sea to protect a haven or the shore.

Molecular A pattern or a type of structure featuring tubes and balls in crystalline forms, and associated with 'progressive' notions. The *Atomium* at Brussels of 1958 was an example of a molecular structure.

Monastery An establishment for a monastic fraternity or sisterhood (▷abbey).

Monelle A mullion.

Moneta An ▷Antique ▷mint.

Money pattern A ▷*coin moulding* or repeating pattern of overlapping discs similar to ▷guilloche.

Monial A ▷mullion.

Monkey The weight in a piling hammer, or the whole ▷pile-driving instrument. A *monkey-tail* is a vertical ▷scroll at the bottom of a handrail of a ▷stair ▷balustrade. In iconography a monkey (the animal) is associated with the ▷Devil and with the Fall, and with luxury and vanity. Monkeys appear in ▷Grotesque decoration, in ▷misericords, and in ▷Rococo ▷ornament.

Monk's Park stone A light cream-coloured limestone (▷lime) from Wiltshire, fine and even-grained, for free working.

Monochrome A system of decoration in one colour.

Monogram A ▷cypher, or initials interwoven forming a linear design, frequently reversed to give ▷symmetry. The joining of two or more letters to form one device.

Monolith An architectural member such as an ▷obelisk or a ▷column-▷shaft made from a single piece of stone. *Monolithic* means cut from one stone, made of monoliths, or something looking as though it is massive, uniform, and made of one material.

Monopodium A head and body merging with part of a disproportionately large leg, and terminating in a ▷paw, ▷claw, ▷hoof, or ▷foot, found in ▷Classical and ▷Neoclassical ▷furniture.

Monopteron A circular ▷peripteral ▷temple. *Monopteral* means a temple with no ▷walls, supported only on ▷columns, and circular in form, although Soane used the term to suggest something with columns only and no walls, whether circular or not. It appears to mean a sacred built enclosure with no ▷cell, but with a peripteral arrangement of columns, at least four in number.

Monostyle A ▷column consisting of a single ▷shaft, whether ▷monolithic or in sections, as opposed to ▷*polystyle* or made up of compound ▷shafts. The term is also given to something of one style throughout.

Monotriglyphic ▷Intercolumniation where only one ▷triglyph and two ▷metopes occur between ▷columns on the ▷frieze in the ▷Doric ▷Order.

Monoxylon Properly a boat made from one hollow piece of wood, but applied to anything made out of one piece of wood, such as a ▷coffin.

Monstrance An open or transparent vessel in which the Host is exposed or relics are displayed. It is also called an ▷*ostensory* for the Eucharistic wafer.

Montant ▷Muntin.

Months Associated with representations of the ▷seasons and with ▷Classical mythology. ▷Janus is associated with January, ▷Venus and Cupid with February, ▷Mars with March, the Bull with April, Castor and Pollux and chariot with May, Phaeton with June, Hercules with July, Triptolemus with August, ▷Ceres with September, ▷Bacchus with October, the ▷Centaur with November, and Ariadne with goat for December.

Monument An edifice or marker to commemorate a

person or an event, by its nature intended to be permanent. A marker of boundaries. Monuments were known in ▷Antiquity. Sepulchral monuments of the Middle Ages are very varied. Stone ▷coffins tapering from head to foot are common, and these often have carved lids. ▷Brasses let into ▷slabs were also numerous. ▷Altar ▷tombs and ▷canopied ▷effigies are frequently found. After the Reformation, monuments of considerable size were set up in ▷churches, including the ▷polychromatic ▷Elizabethan and ▷Jacobean examples, where ▷Renaissance and ▷Mannerist ▷motifs are used with eclectic extravagance. Many churches contain fine examples of ▷Baroque and ▷Neoclassical monuments. By far the commonest are the mural slabs and ▷cartouches of the eighteenth and nineteenth centuries. The ▷Victorians reintroduced ▷Gothic brasses and altar-tombs. Tombstones were varied and interesting throughout history, and act not only as historical records but as repositories of the history of taste. In the second half of the twentieth century, however, the design of funerary monuments has added new terrors to death.

Monyal A ▷mullion.

Moon The ▷crescent ▷moon is associated with Diana and the Blessed Virgin Mary. It is also found in decoration suggesting Turkish styles.

Moon gate A circular opening in a ▷wall.

Moorish arch A *horseshoe* ▷*arch*.

Moorish architecture The ▷Islamic architecture of North Africa and of parts of Spain occupied and settled by the Moors. *Moresque* means art and ▷architecture derived form those of the Arabs, Moors, and Saracens (▷Arabesque, ▷Arabian architecture). *Moresque* is associated with formal foliate ▷ornaments of an ▷interlacing type also known as ▷*Arabesque*.

Moot hall A public assembly-room, or a ▷town hall, especially in East Anglia.

Morning-room A private sitting-room usually facing east.

Mortar Material to bind stones and ▷bricks together: traditionally, it is composed of burnt limestone (▷lime) mixed with sand and water, sometimes with crushed ▷brick or stone added. Modern mortars usually employ ordinary ▷Portland ▷cement as a binding agent with or without the addition of lime.

Mortise In ▷carpentry and ▷joinery, a recessed cutting within a piece of timber which receives the projecting ▷tenon of another piece, or a ▷lock, or other

[169] MORT-SAFE Early nineteenth-century mort-safe at Cathcart, near Glasgow. (*JSC*)

insertion. A *mortise lock* is one that fits into a mortise in a lock-▷rail.

Mort-safe [169] A metal ▷cage over a ▷grave or ▷vault to deter body-snatchers, or a metal cage around a ▷coffin.

Mortuary A building where dead bodies are stored, or a dead-house. A *mortuary-▷chapel* (▷[170]) is one above a ▷sepulchre, usually associated with one family or personage, or a chapel in a burial-ground where bodies rest overnight until buried the next day.

Mosaic ▷Ornamental work formed by inlaying regular squares of ▷glass, stone, pottery, ▷marble, etc. into a ▷cement, ▷mortar, or ▷plaster matrix. It was used in ▷floors and in ▷walls, where the *tesserae* (▷tessella), or small pieces, formed patterns either of a geometrical or ▷naturalistic type.

Mosque A Muslim place of worship, usually characterized by a domed central form and by ▷minarets.

Motif An element in a design.

Motte [171] A steep mound on which the ▷keep stood in an eleventh- and twelfth-century ▷castle. The *motte-and-bailey* was a system of defence consisting of a ▷tower on an earth mound, enclosed by a bailey (▷bail) with palisade or ▷wall and ditch. Mottes were themselves sometimes surrounded by ditches.

[170] MORTUARY CHAPEL Mortuary chapel in the cemetery at Arbroath by Patrick Allan-Frazer, begun in 1875. It is a richly bizarre composition incorporating elements from Scottish mediaeval and early Renaissance architecture. Note the bartisans, turrets, corbels, balconies, canopied niches, machicolations, knobbly crockets on stumpy finials, and the silhouette of extraordinary vitality. (*JSC*)

Motto An ▷inscription, associated with a ▷coat of arms, an ▷*impresa*, or a ▷*rebus*.

Mouchette A fourteenth-century form like a ▷dagger found in Second-▷Pointed or ▷Decorated ▷tracery: it is pointed in a curved ▷axis and has a ▷head of ▷foils, and incorporates elliptical and ▷ogee curves.

Mould [172]   A shaped or moulded ▷brick. A *moulding* is anything with a contour or section, either projecting or inset, to give emphasis, usually to horizontal and vertical lines. It forms ▷entablatures, ▷cornices, ▷bases, ▷architraves, ▷string-▷courses, and the like, casts shadows, and defines areas. Regular mouldings in ▷Classical ▷architecture are the ▷fillet or ▷list; the ▷astragal or ▷bead; the ▷cyma recta and cyma reversa; the ▷cavetto or ▷hollow; the ▷ovolo or ▷quarter-round; the ▷scotia or ▷trochilus; and the ▷torus or ▷round. In ▷Gothic ▷architecture the diversities are great, but in ▷Romanesque work the mouldings consist almost exclusively of rounds and hollows, with some ▷splays, often very shallowly worked. Romanesque mouldings are frequently broken with zigzags, while ▷billets and ▷beak-heads are common. The First-▷Pointed styles have boldly cut mouldings, with ▷keels and fillets in abundance, and rounds and hollows prevail. Second-Pointed work is more diversified, with much ▷enrichment. ▷Perpendicular mouldings are flatter, with large elliptical hollows, and seem to owe something to ▷Classical forms ▷bolection, ▷cant, ▷chaplet, ▷dancette, ▷double-cone, ▷dovetail, ▷echinus, ▷edge roll, ▷fascia, ▷gadroon, ▷half-round, ▷nebule, ▷ogee, ▷pellet, ▷ressant, ▷running do, ▷star, ▷wave, ▷[17], [30], [39], [41], [42], [47], [48], [72], [79], [97], [102], [110], [150], [154], [176], [187], [209]. See also the figures associated with the Orders.

Mould stone   A large stone to be carved with mouldings (▷mould) usually at a ▷jamb or as part of an ▷architrave.

Mounting-steps   Steps by which a level or raised ▷block is reached, such as a ▷platform for mounting a horse.

Mourners   Statues of weeping figures around a ▷tomb or tomb-▷chest, also called ▷*weepers*.

Mouth   A ▷cavetto.

[171] MOTTE   York Castle (Clifford's Tower) of 1250–75 sited on a steep motte. The tower was originally quatrefoil on plan. (*JSC*)

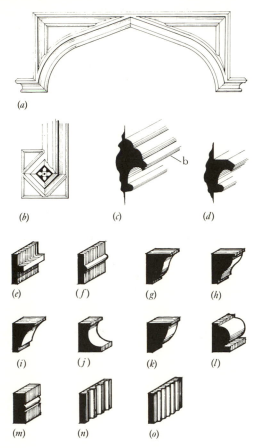

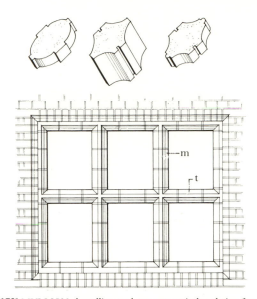

[172] MOULDINGS (*a*) Hood mould, drip-stone, or label of brick. Ranworth Old Hall, Norfolk. (*b*) Label-stop of stone. Chippenham, Wiltshire. (*c*) Detail of (*b*), **b** beak. (*d*) Detail of (*a*). (*e*) Fillet or band. (*f*) Astragal or bead. (*g*) Cyma recta or ogee. (*h*) Cyma reversa, reverse ogee, or Lesbian cymatium. (*i*) Cavetto. (*j*) Scotia. (*k*) Ovolo. (*l*) Torus. (*m*) Flush bead. (*n*) Flutes and fillets. (*o*) Reeding. (*a–d, JJS; e–o, JSC*)

Moynall Also *moynel* or *moynialle*. As ▷mullion.

Mozarabic A style of Spanish Christian ▷architecture incorporating horseshoe ▷arches and other *Moresque* elements, particularly in the ▷Romanesque period. An integration of Romanesque and ▷Islamic forms.

Mud brick Any sun-dried ▷brick or ▷adobe construction. A *mud* ▷*sill* is a ground-sill laid directly on the ground. A *mud* ▷*wall* is a ▷cob wall, or any structure made of unburnt clay.

Mudejar A style using horseshoe curves, ▷Kufic ▷inscriptions, ▷stalactite work, and ▷Arabesque decorations, found in Spanish ▷architecture, and revived in the nineteenth century.

[173] MULLION A mullion-and-transome window dating from the late sixteenth or early seventeenth century, constructed of brick. Types of mullion bricks are shown, with ovolo (left) and cavetto (centre and right) sections. **m** mullion, **t** transome. (*JJS*)

Muff ▷Glass made from a blown cylinder flattened out on a plate, also called *sheet* glass.

Mullet A five-pointed ▷star with a central hole, found in heraldry.

Mullion [173] A slender ▷pier which forms the division between the ▷lights of a ▷window or a ▷screen, often moulded. It is known as a ▷*monial*, ▷*monyal*, ▷*moynall*, *munion*, ▷*munnion*, and ▷*stanchion*.

Multicentred A figure composed of ▷arcs of differing radii disposed about a vertical ▷axis.

Multifoil An ▷arch with numerous ▷foils and ▷cusps.

Muniment-room A place where important papers are kept.

Munnion A ▷mullion or a ▷muntin.

Muntin An upright piece of timber in a ▷frame, also called a *montant*, ▷*mullion*, or *munton*. The intermediate upright ▷bar of framing in a ▷door between the outer ▷stiles, and butting into the horizontal ▷rails. Any upright framing member separating ▷panels (▷[104]).

Mural [174] Belonging to a ▷wall. A *mural* ▷*monument* is one fixed to a wall. A *mural* also means a painting on a wall.

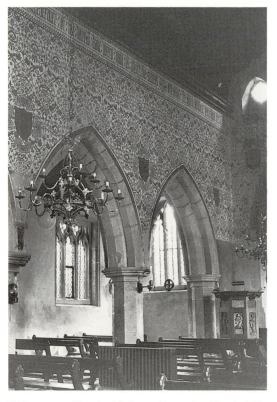

[174] MURAL Church of St James, Kinnersley, Herefordshire. The mural decorations above the nave arcade are by G. F. Bodley, and were executed by the Reverend Frederick Andrews. (*JSC*)

Muse One of the nine goddesses and companions of ▷Apollo. They were *Calliope* (books and laurel crown), associated with epic poetry; *Clio* (books, laurel crown, trumpet), representing history; *Erato* (lyre, swan, viol), representing lyric and love poetry; *Euterpe* (flute and pipe), representing music and lyrical verse; *Melpomene* (tragic mask, crown, sceptre, and a weapon), representing tragedy; *Polyhymnia* (organ and lute) representing hymns and heroism; *Terpsichore* (musical instruments), representing song and dance; *Thalia* (scroll, mask, and viol), representing comedy and pastoral verse; and *Urania* (compasses and globe), representing astronomy. They are associated with schemes of ▷Classical decoration, and during the eighteenth century became more directly associated with ▷comedy and ▷tragedy, painting and poetry, ▷fame and history, astronomy and geography, and with art and ▷architecture.

Museum A place for the reception, display, and study of natural, literary, scientific, artistic, and antiquarian objects.

Music Suggested by ▷trophies of musical instruments, Orpheus, ▷Apollo, and the appropriate ▷Muses.

Music hall [175] A ▷hall used for musical performances. A hall licensed for singing, dancing and other entertainments, often, but not always associated with a public house.

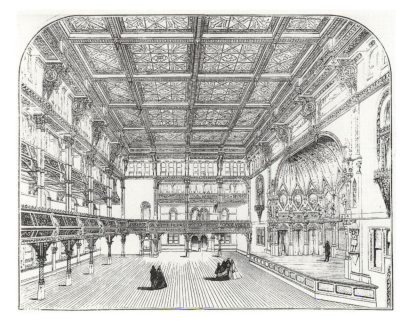

[175] MUSIC HALL The Strand Music Hall, London, by Enoch Bassett Keeling. The design exhibits all the angular spikiness of Keeling's 'Continental Gothic, freely treated'. Note the polychrome arches. (*The Building News, 1864*)

Mutilated ▷Broken or discontinued, such as a ▷cornice or a ▷pediment (▷pediment).

Mutule A sloping flat ▷block like a ▷bracket under the ▷corona of the ▷Doric ▷cornice, in the same situation as ▷modillions in the ▷Corinthian and ▷Composite ▷Orders. It may have a number of ▷guttae or ▷drops on the underside, or may be plain. Mutules are set above ▷triglyphs or on the centre-lines of ▷metopes. In the ▷Tuscan Order they can be plain brackets or blocks, and can be horizontal rather than sloping. In the grander Orders they are like ▷consoles laid on their sides and are called modillions. The term *mutule* or *mutulus* seems to imply a structural ▷beam, although in the sense it is used in connection with the ▷Doric Order it is more like a ▷rafter. Vitruvius seems to imply that in ▷Etruscan ▷temples the ▷*trabes compactiles*, ▷architraves, or ▷lintels, that were carried on the widely spaced ▷columns, supported a second set of beams at right-angles, and that these second beams were called *mutuli*, which were placed on the ▷cell walls and on the centre-lines of each column of the ▷portico, ▷projecting in ▷cantilevers forward of the line of the ▷colonnade.

Mynchery ▷Minchery.

Myrtle An attribute of marital fidelity, of ▷Venus, and of the Three ▷Graces, it is often found in funerary ▷sculpture as a ▷symbol of everlasting ▷love. It is sometimes confused with the ▷olive.

N

Nail A metal spike for fastening one piece of wood to another. *Rose nails* have square shanks; ▷*brads* are headless nails or have square heads; ▷*tacks* are short, with heads; and *cut nails* are machine-made nails. In mediaeval times heads of nails were often ▷ornamented, and were features of ▷doors, probably suggesting the *nail-head* moulding found in First-▷Pointed ▷Gothic work, consisting of bands resembling a series of pyramidal nail-heads. A *nail-head moulding* (▷[176]) is also any moulding with a centre-piece of pyramidal nail-like projections (▷mould).

Naked The unornamented plain surface of a ▷wall, ▷column, or other part of a building: the main plane of a ▷façade. A *naked* ▷*floor* is one with only one tier of ▷joists, otherwise known as a ▷*single-frame floor*, or *single-joist floor*.

Naos The ▷sanctuary of a ▷Greek ▷temple, equivalent to the ▷*cell or cella*, or the part of a temple within the ▷walls. The sanctuary of a ▷Byzantine ▷church.

Narthex Part of a ▷church, screened off from the

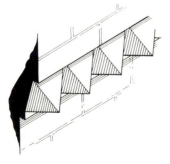

[176] NAIL. Nail-head moulding. (*JJS*)

rest, and situated near the west ▷door. An ▷antechamber or ▷vestibule at the west of the church, acting as a variety of ▷porch. It was later called a ▷*galilee* (▷[36]).

Nativity The birth of Christ, represented in paintings, carvings, and iconography.

Natte A ▷basket-weave pattern resembling matting.

Natural bed Sedimentary rocks, such as limestones (▷lime) and ▷sandstones, are stratified and laminated, usually in layers parallel to the ▷bed. It is advisable to lay the stones according to their natural beds to avoid defects, as the pressure can split the layers. ▷Walls should never be made with the stones ▷*face-bedded* (with the ▷laminae vertical and parallel to the face of the wall), for flaking will almost certainly occur. ▷Cornices and ▷projections should always be ▷edge-bedded, that is with the laminations at right-angles to the face of the wall. ▷Arches should be formed of ▷voussoirs with the natural beds parallel to the radii of the arch.

Naturalistic Any ▷ornament emulating nature, usually occurring after a period of *stylized* ornament.

Naumachia A place where mock sea-fights took place, such as a large amphitheatre.

Naval Decoration with ▷marine forms.

Nave [177] The central ▷aisle of a ▷basilican church, or the central axial ▷clerestoreyed aisle between the western ▷door and the ▷altar, but more especially that part of a church west of the ▷choir, and reserved for the laity. In most churches it consists of a tall central

[177] NAVE Nave of Hereford Cathedral looking west. Note the Romanesque nave arcades with chevron mouldings. The tribune, clerestorey, and vault are later. The west window in the Decorated or Second-Pointed style was designed by John Oldrid Scott, 1902–8. (*Hereford City Library 10339*)

division with two or more side-aisles, but can also be found without aisles. It was usually separated from the choir by a ▷screen, and many such screens survive. A ▷*nave* ▷*arcade* is an open arcade between the nave and the aisle, supporting the ▷triforium or ▷tribune and the clerestorey over (▷[36]), [66], [134], [210]).

Neat work Brickwork at the ▷base of a ▷wall above the footings.

Nebule, nebulé, nèbuly moulding An ▷ornament in ▷Romanesque ▷architecture the edge of which forms a wavy line: it is found in ▷corbel-▷tables and in ▷archivolts. Rounded ▷chevrons or ▷zigzags.

Necessarium A ▷privy.

Neck The plain part of a ▷Roman ▷Doric or ▷Tuscan ▷column between the ▷astragal at the top of the ▷shaft and the ▷fillet ▷annulets of the ▷capital. Some ▷Greek ▷Ionic columns have necks, usually enriched with ▷anthemion ▷ornament. It is also called the ▷*collarino* or ▷*hypotrachelium*. A neck moulding separates the

capital from the shaft proper. A *necking-*▷*course* is one coincident with a neck.

Necropolis Literally a city of the dead, or a large burial-place or ▷cemetery. Plural Necropoleis.

Needle A horizontal timber resting on stones or ▷posts serving as a temporary support for a weight above while the lower part of a ▷wall is being ▷underpinned. A *needle-*▷*spire* is a thin spire rising from the centre of a ▷tower and set back from a ▷parapet. *Needlework* is a ▷frame of timber with a filling of ▷plaster or ▷brick.

Nemes A type of Ancient ▷Egyptian head-dress commonly found on statues of pharaohs, with a tight band across the forehead and striped hangings at the base and sides of the head (▷Antinoüs).

Neo-Byzantine ▷Byzantine ▷Revival, or the re-use of Byzantine elements in the nineteenth and twentieth centuries [▷58].

Neoclassicism [178] A movement that had its beginnings in the rejection of ▷Baroque and ▷Rococo, and in a seeking to rediscover the ▷achitecture of ▷Classical ▷Antiquity as a less corrupted source than the architecture of the ▷Italian ▷Renaissance. An enthusiasm for the architecture of Ancient Rome was encouraged by the views of Rome by Piranesi with their exaggerated scale and ▷Sublime visual effects, but the noble simplicity and serene grandeur of ▷Greek architecture extolled by Winckelmann encouraged investigations of buildings of Classical Antiquity on a new scale. Buildings were re-examined and described, so that many Renaissance sources were rejected in favour of the archaeologically proven correctness of the ▷Antique. Neoclassicism, however, was rarely a mere copying of the works of Antiquity, although accuracy was prized in archaeologically correct ▷motifs: it was also concerned with a return to first principles, basic forms, clear uncluttered ▷geometry, and a rational approach to design, encouraged by the writings of Laugier and Lodoli. In this was an implicit faith in the superiority of *primitive* forms of stereometrical purity, which led designers such as Boullée, Ledoux, Ehrensvård, Gilly, Latrobe, and Soane to experiment with an architecture from which ▷enrichment was often eliminated. Of all the ▷Orders, ▷Greek ▷Doric began to be appreciated for its severity and *primitive* qualities, first in the surviving remains of the Greek colonies in Sicily and at Paestum, then in the systematic investigations of Greek architecture by Stuart and Revett which led to the publication of *The Antiquities of Athens* from 1762. The latter provided accurate reproductions of measured drawings of the architecture of Ancient Greece for designers, and had a profound

(a)

(b)

(c)

[178] NEOCLASSICISM (*a*) Mausoleum at Dulwich Picture Gallery, proposal by Soane 1812. Note the three severe sarcophagi on the roof, and the urns on the lantern. The Classical language of the architecture is stripped to the barest minimum. (*Trustees of Sir John Soane's Museum*) (*b*) Design for a sepulchral chapel by Soane. Note the Greek Doric porticoes, the strigillated sarcophagi above the pediments, the *couchant* lions based on Egyptian prototypes, the funerary jars around the base, and the *canephorae* in the recess. The composition mixes Graeco-Roman and Egyptianizing elements. (*Trustees of Sir John Soane's Museum*) (*c*) The Albert Dock Warehouses, Liverpool, 1843–45 by Jesse Hartley. Note the cast-iron, unfluted Greek Doric columns, deliberately stunted and made to look more powerful, the stripped-bare brickwork, massive repetitive elements, and the avoidance of ornament. This is the architecture of the Sublime. (*JSC*)

effect on taste. Two years later the publication of the *Ruins of the Palace of the Emperor Diocletian at Spalatro*, based on the measurements and drawings by Robert Adam and Charles-Louis Clérisseau, gave further impetus to an understanding of the Antique, while in the 1730s and 1740s work began on the excavation of the cities of Herculaneum and Pompeii, buried since the eighth decade of our era as a result of a catastrophic eruption of Vesuvius: the architecture, artefacts, and decorative schemes uncovered during the excavations led taste and design further towards an evocation of the Antique. Winckelmann's championship of Greek art and architecture, and the work of Stuart and Revett, prompted a Greek ▷Revival that was one of the most powerful aspects of Neoclassicism. Later, the publication of Denon's *Voyage dans la Basse et la Haute Égypte* in 1802, and of the monumental *Description de l'Égypte* by the *Commission des Monuments d'Égypte* from 1809, gave designers accurate illustrations of real Ancient ▷Egyptian buildings, and were to the Egyptian Revival what the works of Stuart and Revett had been to the Greek Revival. Egyptian architecture, with its primitive, massive character, and its simple, pure forms, such as

the ▷obelisk, ▷pylon, ▷battered ▷walls, and ▷pyramid, appealed to those Neoclassical architects who sought a stereometrical purity in their designs, and a plain, tough, masculine expression of forms. So certain Egyptian elements entered the vocabulary of Neoclassical design as though responding to the theories of Laugier and Lodoli.

Neoclassical architecture tends to be severe, stark, serious, and even rather forbidding at times. It is very controlled, and purged of much ▷enrichment, while the Orders, usually Greek, and sometimes extremely primitive interpretations of Greek (such as unfluted, simplified, stumpy Doric) were used to express structural ideas, and were rarely ▷engaged or used as mere decoration. Forms were usually starkly defined, and volumes expressed both inside and out. The ▷*Empire*

221

style of the Napoleonic era is a particularly lavish and successful phase of Neoclassicism in which a scholarly use of ▷motifs from Antiquity played no small part.

Neo-Georgian A ▷revival of ▷Georgian eighteenth-century domestic ▷architecture during the last years of Victoria's reign, but more especially in the twentieth century, often incorporating ▷brick ▷façades with rubbers (▷rubbed), ▷sashes, and simple ▷door-cases with fanlights (▷fan). ▷Colonial.

Neo-Gothic The use of ▷Gothic forms in ▷Revival styles.

Neo-Greek A style using ▷Greek forms or forms derived from ancient Greece.

Neo-Liberty ▷Art-▷Nouveau ▷Revival, especially in Italy in the second half of the twentieth century.

Neo-Romanesque ▷Romanesque ▷Revival, especially after 1820. Also Neo-▷Norman.

Neptune The sea-god, or Poseidon, often found with ▷*hippocamps*, ▷trident, rocks, ▷dolphins, ▷mermaids, etc. in ▷marine ornament.

Nereid A sea-nymph, the female counterpart of a ▷Triton, often found with ▷shells, ▷hippocamps, ▷dolphins, etc., in ▷marine ornament.

Nerve Also *nervure*, meaning a ▷rib of a ▷vault, especially one of the sides of a compartment, as opposed to the ribs which cross diagonally.

Net tracery As ▷reticulated ▷tracery. *Net* ▷*vaulting* has ribs forming ▷lozenge-shaped ▷panels.

Netherlands Grotesque Outlandish and elaborate ▷Grotesque ornament with much ▷strapwork, etc. developed by ▷Flemish Mannerists in the sixteenth century.

New Brutalism ▷Brutalism.

Newel The central ▷column, or solid, or imaginary solid, round which the steps of a circular staircase wind, often providing support. Also the principal ▷posts or ▷colonnettes at the angles and foot of a ▷stair ▷balustrade. A *newel-*▷*cap* is a terminal feature of a newel-post. A *newel-*▷*collar* is a wooden collar lengthening the base of a newel. A *newel-*▷*drop* is a terminal projection of a newel-post downwards, appearing under a ▷soffite. A *newel joint* is one between a newel-post and a handrail or between the newel-post and the ▷string. A *newel-post* is one at the ▷head or

▷foot of a stair, and supporting the ends of the balustrade. A *newel stair* is one with newels, or a ▷screw stair.

Nib A projection, as on a ▷tile, for hooking it to a ▷lath or ▷batten.

Niche A recess in a ▷wall for a statue, ▷vase, or other ▷ornament. Niches are often semicircular on plan, and are ▷arched. Some niches contain a ▷shell-▷motif, and some are treated as ▷aedicules. Others are absolutely plain, without any ▷frame. They can be extremely decorative, and surmounted by ▷canopies, ▷ogees, ▷pinnacles, and the like.

Nidged Ashlar Also *nigged* ▷ashlar, meaning ▷stone dressed on the surface with a pick or point.

Night A veiled female figure, often with ▷stars, and sometimes masked, often with two small boys (Sleep and ▷Death). Night features in bedrooms, cradles, beds, and time-pieces, often associated with the ▷crescent ▷moon, ▷owls, ▷wings, ▷masks, ▷poppies, and inverted ▷torches.

Nimbus A ▷halo around a head of an ▷image.

Nine altars ▷Retrochoirs sometimes have ▷chapels with nine ▷altars, connected with the Nine Orders or Choirs of Angels. The east end of Fountains Abbey had nine altars.

Noah The Flood and Ark are common themes in mediaeval iconography and feature animals, the Inundation, etc.

Nod An inclination of the head. A *nodding* ▷*ogee* is therefore an ogee ▷canopy-head which bows outwards as well.

Nodus A keystone or a ▷boss.

Noel A ▷newel.

Nog A *nog* is a wooden bench. *Nogging* is brickwork in a wooden ▷frame. A *nogging-piece* is a horizontal timber fixed to the uprights of a timber frame, usually to contain an infill of some sort.

Nook A small space usually with a lower ceiling opening off a larger space, often with its own ▷windows, and often with a fireplace. An ▷*inglenook*. A *nook-*▷*shaft* is a shaft or a ▷colonnette set in an ▷angle of a ▷pier, ▷wall, or corner, especially where the ▷jamb of a doorway meets the external ▷face of a wall.

Norfolk latch A lift-▷latch or thumb-latch.

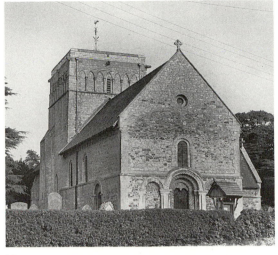

(a)

(b)

[179] NORMAN ARCHITECTURE. (a) Norman architecture is English Romanesque. The Church of St Michael and All Angels, Stewkley, Buckinghamshire, dating from the twelfth century, is an aisleless building with a large tower featuring interlacing blind arcading. (JSC) (b) The interior of the Church of St Michael and All Angels, Stewkley, Buckinghamshire, of c. 1150, showing the chancel-arch, with chevron and beak-head motifs. (JSC) (c) The Monteath Mausoleum in Glasgow Necropolis, designed by David Cousin, 1842. This circular building, with polygonal clerestorey, is loosely based on the circular Norman church in Cambridge. An example of Norman Revival. (JSC)

Norma A ▷square for setting up right-▷angles.

Norman [179] ▷Romanesque work in England or Northern France. It was a style of ▷architecture introduced to England after 1066, and was generally massive, plain, and fortress-like, with few ▷ornaments. Doorways were deeply recessed and were usually headed with semicircular ▷arches. ▷Windows were small, and had semicircular ▷heads. ▷Piers were massive, and were sometimes channelled and moulded with spirals or ▷zigzags. ▷Buttresses were broad and of small projection, like ▷pilaster-strips. ▷Vaults were simple ▷barrels, had ▷groins, or had clumsy ▷ribs without ▷bosses. ▷Apses were common, and sometimes arches had their springings well above the ▷capitals (▷Romanesque).

Norse ▷Viking ▷ornament, often incorporating ▷interlacing forms, animals, and unbroken patterns. It is often mixed with ▷Celtic and ▷Saxon ornaments, and was revived in the nineteenth and twentieth centuries, notably in Scandinavia, Ireland, Scotland, and England.

Northlight roof A ▷roof, like a ▷saw-tooth in sec-

(c)

223

tion, with glazing facing north, solid roof facing south, and ▷gutter-▷valleys between.

Nosing The prominent edge of a moulding (▷mould) or ▷drip, or the ▷projecting rounded moulding on the edge of a ▷step.

Nosocomium An ▷infirmary for the poor.

Notchboard A ▷face-▷string. *Notchings* are ▷hollows cut from one of the ▷faces of a timber or piece of stone or ▷brick. A *notched moulding* (▷mould) or ▷*ornament* is one made by notching the edges of a ▷band or a ▷fillet.

Nubilarium A ▷barn in ▷Antiquity or protecting unthreshed grain from the elements,

Nucleus The ▷base of an ▷Antique ▷floor, over which a ▷mosaic, say, would be laid.

Nulling A moulding (▷mould), usually in ▷Jacobean work, shaped like a quadrant. ▷Gadrooning.

Nunnery A ▷convent for women.

Nutmeg A *First-*▷*Pointed* ornament resembling half a nutmeg.

Nuved Knotted (▷knot).

Nymphaeum A ▷grotto, or a structure containing pools, plants, rockwork, ▷fountains, and statues, often used for relaxation and enjoyment. A cool and agreeable retreat. A *nymph* was a low-ranking female divinity: ▷*nereids* were associated with the sea, *naiads* with fresh water, *dryads* with trees, and *oreads* with mountains and grottoes. They occur in ▷Classical and ▷Neoclassical decoration.

O

Oak A light yellowish-brown to deep brown ▷hardwood of great strength, capable of being carved when ▷green, but extremely difficult to cut or work when fully seasoned. It was used for mediaeval timber ▷roofs, ▷bench-ends, ▷choir-▷stalls, ▷panelling, etc. Oak ▷leaves occur in ▷wreaths and ▷pulvinated ▷friezes, often with ▷acorns. Oak leaves and acorns are found in much decoration, while large acorns are found as terminal features on ▷gate-▷piers and ▷pedestals.

Obelisk [180] A tall tapering ▷shaft, usually square on plan, with ▷battered sides and a ▷pyramidal top. Obelisks are usually set on ▷pedestals in ▷Classical ▷architecture, and are an instance when Ancient ▷Egyptian forms entered into the language of ▷Classicism. Obelisks were often confused with pyramids, so much so that some early drawings show pyramidal forms with obelisks on top. Obelisks occur frequently in ▷Elizabethan and ▷Jacobean architecture, especially in funerary ▷monuments, and as ▷finials. Augustus brought several Egyptian obelisks to be set up in Rome: their incised ▷hieroglyphs were a source of considerable speculation throughout the ▷Renaissance period. Obelisks also occur pierced, hollowed out, or elaborated, and set on balls. They occur on ▷gables, and on ▷balustrading, and were a common feature of North European ▷Mannerist architecture.

Obices ▷Repagula.

Oblique arch As ▷skew ▷arch.

Obscured glass ▷Glass which is ground on one side, acid-etched, or moulded so that it admits light but obscures vision.

Observatory A building in which astronomical studies are carried out, using a powerful telescope. The term is also given to any place, such as an upper room, giving a wide view. A ▷belvedere.

Obtuse-angled arch ▷Arch.

[180] OBELISK Obelisk and rock-work base at Stillorgan, Co. Dublin, by Sir Edward Lovett Pearce, of *c.* 1732, intended as a mausoleum for the Allen family. (*JSC*)

225

Octastyle A building with a ▷portico of eight ▷columns in a line (▷[234 f, g]).

Octopartite Divided into eight parts, such as a ▷vault with eight ▷cells.

Oculus A ▷roundel, or circular ▷panel or ▷window, a ▷bull's-eye or ▷*oeil-de-boeuf*; or a circular opening at the top of a ▷dome. It is also the ▷disc or button in the centre of a ▷volute spiral, as in the ▷Ionic ▷capital.

Odeion, odeum A small ▷theatre in ▷Antiquity, roofed, for musical events.

Oecus It is an odd word with many meanings, including *house*, ▷*temple*, or *room*, and appears to have come to mean a large and important room in a private house in ▷Antiquity. An *oecus Aegyptus* had part of its ▷roof carried on high ▷columns to form a ▷clerestorey, leaving a flat roof-▷garden all round that clerestorey. An *oecus Corinthium* was similar to an ▷*atrium Corinthium*, except that there was a ▷vaulted roof instead of the *compluvium*, and there was no *impluvium*. An *oecus Cyzicenus* (▷Cyzicene) had ▷windows giving a view over the country. An *oecus tetrastylos* resembled the *atrium tetrastylum* without an *impluvium*, and with the centre roofed, carried on four columns (▷atrium).

Oeil-de-boeuf ▷Oculus. Properly, the ▷ox-eye ▷window should be of elliptical rather than circular form. The *oeil-de-boeuf* opening may be graced with four keystones, and it occurs in ▷*Mansard* roofs, frequently ▷ornamented.

Oeil-de-perdrix Small dotted circles enclosing white on a blue background.

Oeillet, oillet, oylett A loophole (▷loop) or opening through which arrows could be fired.

Offset The projection from the ▷faces of the different parts of a ▷wall where it increases in thickness: it is the part of a wall that is exposed upwards when the portion above is reduced in thickness. *Offsets* or *set-offs* are generally sloped in ▷Gothic ▷architecture, and have ▷projecting ▷drips, as in ▷buttresses.

Offertory window ▷Leper's squint.

Ogee [181] An S-shaped double curve, one convex and the other concave. The ▷*cyma* moulding (▷mould). It is common in both ▷Decorated (*Second-*▷*Pointed*) and ▷Perpendicular ▷Gothic ▷architecture, and is frequently found over ▷tombs, ▷shrines and ▷niches. Any moulding of ogee section is called an ogee moulding or a ▷*ressant*, *ressaunt*, or *ressaut* (▷[20], [97]). *Ogival* means with a double curve, convex and concave. ▷Nod.

[181] OGEE Ogee-headed niche with foils, flanked by crocketed pinnacles, and surmounted by a finial, in St Swithun's Church, Merton, Oxfordshire. The style is typical of fourteenth-century Decorated or Second-Pointed Gothic. (*JSC*)

Ogham A ▷Celtic system of writing. It is usually found at the ▷angles of the tall upright *Ogham stones* which appear to be sepulchral ▷monuments, often with incised Christian ▷symbols added.

Ogive A pointed ▷arch, or the diagonal ▷rib in ▷Gothic ▷vaults.

Oillet ▷Oeillet.

Old English A style in which ▷vernacular forms were revived, particularly associated with the ▷Domestic ▷Revival and the ▷Arts-and-Crafts Movement. It used patterned ▷tile-hanging, leaded ▷casements, steeply pitched ▷roofs, ▷diaper-work, ▷timber-framing, ▷ornamental ▷barge-boards, ▷jettying, ▷rubbed brickwork (▷brick), and tall ornamental ▷chimneys.

Old French The nineteenth-century and ▷Edwardian ▷Rococo ▷Revival.

Oleaginous style Also known as ▷*auricular*, *cartilaginous*, *Dutch Grotesque*, or *lobate style*, it is associated with ▷Mannerism, and with ▷ornament modelled with smooth flowing lines, folds, creases, etc., resembling ▷ears, intestines, ▷seaweed, and parts of animals and fish. It was a precursor of ▷Rococo.

Olive Often used instead of the ▷laurel or ▷bay, and similar to the ▷myrtle, occurring in ▷Classical ornament. With a ▷dove it represents ▷peace.

Ollarium A ▷niche in a ▷Roman ▷vault or ▷columbarium to hold cinerary ▷urns, usually in pairs.

Oncome The ▷corbel at the springing of an opening, or the gathering of a ▷flue.

One-centred arch An ▷arch ▷struck from one centre, such as a semicircular, segmental, or *horseshoe* arch.

One pair of stairs The first ▷storey over the ground ▷floor.

Onion dome A bulbous ▷dome resembling an onion on a ▷tower, found in central and eastern European ▷church ▷architecture.

Onyx A type of quartz allied to agate, used for decorative work and ▷cameos.

Oölite A concretionary limestone (▷lime) made up of small rounded granules, each consisting of carbonate of lime around a grain of sand. Oölitic limestones include the fine building stones from Ancaster, Bladon, Clipsham, Corsham Down, Hornton, Monk's Park, Portland, St Aldelm, and Weldon.

Opa The ▷bed of a ▷roof-▷beam in a ▷Greek building, the spaces between which are called ▷metopes. *Opae* are also the cavities receiving the beams.

Opaion A ▷lantern, or part of a ▷roof pierced and raised for the admission of light. A large ▷coffer or *lacunar*. A means by which smoke can escape in a roof.

Open An *open* ▷*cornice* or *open* ▷*eaves* is an overhanging eaves in which the ▷rafters are exposed and are often treated decoratively. An *open-*▷*heart* moulding is a series of overlapping pointed shapes in the form of ▷straps laid resembling hearts or ▷spades, with the points upwards, usually associated with a ▷roll moulding, and found in ▷Romanesque work. An *open-*▷*newel*, *hollow-newel*, or *open-*▷*well* ▷stair is one around a well between the outer ▷strings, unlike the ▷dog-leg which has no well between the strings. An *open* ▷*pediment* has raking (▷rake) sides that do not meet at the ▷apex. An *open* ▷*roof*, also called an *open-timbered roof*, is one with the ▷rafters visible from below, with no flat ceiling.

Open ▷*slating*, also called *spaced slating* or *poverty slating* is a patterned surface in which gaps are left between slates in each ▷course. An *open stair* or *open-string stair* has the ends of the ▷treads visible, often treated with ▷scrolled forms below the ends. An *open-string, openstringer*, or *cut-string* is a string with the upper part notched to receive the treads and ▷risers. *Opentimbered* refers to exposed timber frames not concealed by pargetting (▷parge work). An *open-timbered roof*, is an open roof, while an *open-timbered* ▷*floor* is one with the ▷joists exposed on the underside, unconcealed by a ceiling. *Openwork* refers to ornamental ▷perforated work (as in ▷Gothic ▷gables or ▷canopies with lacy ▷tracery), to unprotected ▷parapets or fortifications.

Opisthodomus The space at the rear of the ▷cell of an ▷Antique ▷temple, or an open ▷porch, corresponding to the ▷pronaos at the other end. It is also called ▷*epinaos* (▷[234d]).

Oppidum A ▷Roman town, or the mass of buildings at the straight end of a Roman ▷circus.

Opus Building work, usually referring to types of ▷wall or wall-finishes. For *opus albarium* or *tectorium*, ▷albarium. For *opus alexandrinum*, ▷Alexandrian work. *Opus antiquum* is ▷masonry made of small ▷rubble-stones or ▷concrete or both, faced with rubble, and sometimes containing ▷bands of ▷brick or ▷tile: it is also called *opus incertum*, and the rubble is not laid in horizontal ▷courses – only the layers of bricks or tiles are. *Opus caementicium* was a type of concrete made of undressed stones bedded in a mix of sand, ▷lime, and *pozzolan*, also called *opus structile*, *structura caementicia*, or *opus caementum*. *Opus incertum* is, as described, as *opus antiquum*. *Opus interrasile* is a decorative effect produced by cutting out a pattern so that the design is formed of openings, or by cutting out the ▷ground to leave a pattern. *Opus isodomum* is the same as ▷isodomum. *Opus latericium* or *lateritium* is ▷Roman masonry of brick or tiles or of concrete faced by brick or tiles or both. For *opus lateritum*, ▷later. For *opus listatum*, ▷listatum. For *opus lithostrotum*, ▷lithostrotum. For *opus marmoratum*, ▷marmoratum. *Opus mixtum* is a wall-facing consisting of alternate courses of bricks or tiles and ▷tufa ▷blocks used in very late Roman construction from the fourth century of our era. *Opus musivum* or *museum* is ▷mosaic using small squares of coloured ▷glass or ▷enamelled pieces. *Opus pseudisodomum* is coursed ▷ashlar with courses of unequal height or courses of alternate tall and low ▷blocks. *Opus quadratum* is walling of squared stone, i.e. ashlar, laid in regular courses. *Opus reticulatum* is walling of concrete with ▷faces of squared stones set diagonally, hence the name from the similarity to a net. The squared stones are often pyramidal, with the points set in towards the centre of the wall. *Opus scalpturatum* is a ▷pavement of ▷marble with a pattern cut out of the surface and ▷inlaid with coloured marble or a coloured ▷cement or ▷stucco. *Opus sectile* is a pavement of ▷slabs or tiles of glass, marble, and stone, the pieces of two or three uniform sizes, but very much larger than mosaic *tesserae* (▷tessella), laid in geometrical patterns emphasized by the different colours of the pieces. *Opus signinum* is a flooring surface of broken tiles mixed with ▷mortar, rather like a primitive ▷*terrazzo*. *Opus spicatum* is masonry laid in ▷herringbone patterns, often with horizontal banding-courses of tile or brick. *Opus tectorium* is the same as *opus* ▷*albarium*, or stucco finished to look like marble. *Opus tessellatum* is a pavement of *tesserae* of different colours but of larger size than in ordinary ▷mosaic work. *Opus testacaeum* or *testaceum* is a concrete wall faced with tiles or broken tiles. *Opus topiarium* is a wall-painting or ▷fresco showing ▷trellis-work, ▷gardens, ▷trees, and shrubs. *Opus vermiculatum* is fine mosaic with the patterns arranged in curving, wavy, snake-like lines, often with simulated shadows to emphasize the design.

Or ▷Heraldic ▷gold.

Orangery A ▷gallery or building with large tall ▷windows on the south-facing ▷front: it was used for the cultivation of oranges and other ornamental trees. Orangeries can be ornamental buildings in ▷gardens, or can be part of a grander composition, physically attached to a house.

Oratory A small private ▷chapel or ▷closet set aside for devotions. A ▷faldstool at which a worshipper kneels. A place of prayer. Especially a religious establishment and ▷church of the Order of St Philip Neri, known as the *Oratorians*.

Orb A ▷knob of carved ▷foliage or a plain circular ▷boss at the intersection of the ▷ribs of a ▷Gothic ceiling or ▷vault. A blank ▷window or ▷panel in mediaeval ▷tracery. A ▷ball on a ▷pier or at the top of a ▷pinnacle. ▷Orbs are often surmounted by ▷crosses.

Orchestra The place occupied by the dancers and chorus between the ▷proscenium and the ▷auditorium of an ▷Antique ▷theatre, or the semicircular space between the ▷stage and the first semicircular row of seats.

Orchid A leafy form with very round ▷lobes, also called an *octopus* ▷*leaf*, found in ▷Romanesque decoration.

Order In ▷Classical ▷architecture, an assembly of parts consisting of a ▷column, with ▷base (usually) and ▷capitals, and ▷entablature, ▷proportioned and ▷embellished in consistency with one of the so-called *Five* ▷*Orders*: these are the ▷Doric (▷Greek and

▷Roman versions), ▷Tuscan, ▷Ionic (Greek and Roman), ▷Corinthian (Greek and Roman), and ▷Composite, so there are actually *eight* distinct Orders. An Order may also include a ▷pedestal, ▷plinth, or ▷podium. The Greek Doric column has no base, and the Tuscan ▷shaft is unfluted. The Ionic Order has considerable variation of base and capital (notably in the arrangement of the ▷volutes), and has an English variant in the ▷*Ammonite Order*, named from the fossil-like forms of the capital which replace the standard volutes. A ▷*Colossal Order* is one with columns or ▷pilasters rising from the ground through several ▷storeys, also called a ▷*Giant Order*. The Tuscan Order is also called the ▷*Gigantic Order*; ▷Agricultural, ▷Britannia, ▷Composite, ▷Corinthian, ▷Doric, ▷Ionic, and ▷Tuscan ▷Orders. An *order* ▷*arch* is one with a series of concentric arches set one behind the other and diminishing in size towards the opening, usually associated with ▷colonnettes.

Organ-case [182] The decorated case around the organ-pipes, often in a prominent position in ▷halls

[182] ORGAN-CASE The crossing at York Minster, showing the pulpitum by William Hyndeley of *c.* 1475–*c.* 1506. Note the ogee gable. The organ-case is of 1902–3. Vaulting is of the lierne type and is of timber, by Sir Robert and Sidney Smirke. (*JSC*)

and ▷churches. An *organ-▷loft* is a ▷gallery or loft where an organ is placed. An *organ-▷screen* is one which encloses the organ-chamber, or a former ▷rood-screen or ▷*pulpitum* supporting the organ (the positioning of the organ over the screen dividing the ▷nave from the ▷choir is a post-Reformation phenomenon).

Organic architecture A twentieth-century theory of design that held that in structure and form a building should be based on *organic* or natural forms, and should relate to its site. The term implies organization formed as if by an organic process, but it has been so misused as to be virtually meaningless. *Organic Modernism* employed asymmetrical blob-like shapes, multi-directional curves, and the like.

Oriel, oriole, oryel A large ▷bay or recessed ▷window in a ▷hall, ▷chapel, or other room that ▷projects from the ▷naked of the outer ▷façade: on plan it may be curved or polygonal, and is always on an upper ▷floor, carried on a ▷corbel or ▷bracket.

Oriental A term used to describe all Eastern-inspired design and ▷ornament including the *▷Arabian*, *Chinoiserie* (▷Chinese), *▷Hindoo*, *▷Indian*, *▷Japonaiserie*, *Moresque* (▷Moorish), *▷Ottoman*, *▷Persian*, *▷Saracenic*, and *Turkish* styles.

Orientation The placing of a building in relation to the points of the compass, especially in the case of ▷churches, where the ▷altar should be at the east end. When a church is not actually orientated with the altar and ▷chancel at the east and the main ▷door at the west, the building is described in terms of *liturgical orientation*.

Orle A ▷fillet under the ▷ovolo or ▷quarter-round of a ▷capital. When it is at the top or bottom of the ▷shaft of a ▷column it is called a ▷*cincture*. The term also means the ▷plinth or the ▷base of a column or ▷pedestal, also called an *orlo*. In heraldry it is a small ▷*bordure*, narrow ▷band, or series of small members forming a ▷border. The smooth surface between parallel ▷flutes or grooves is called an *orle*.

Ormolu ▷Gold crushed and mixed with ▷mercury. An *ormolu mount* is an ▷ornament of ▷bronze, cast and worked to a design, coated with ormolu paste, and heated to evaporate the mercury, leaving the gold on the bronze, which is then fixed to ▷furniture or to architectural ▷enrichment. Today, it is an alloy of tin, copper, and zinc, and resembles gold.

Ornament Any detail, carved, incised, moulded, shaped, coloured, or applied, that ▷enriches ▷architecture or furnishings.

Ornate Very heavily ▷ornamented.

Ornithon An ▷Antique ▷aviary.

Orthostata A vertical ▷post, or the facing of a ▷wall. *Orthostatae* were the large vertical stone ▷slabs set at the outer ▷base of a *cella* (▷cell) of a ▷temple as a ▷*revetment*, or variety of ▷dado, below the smaller ▷blocks of the usual type of wall above.

Orthostyle An arrangement of ▷columns placed in a straight line.

Os de Mouton A ram's ▷horn or ▷volute terminating a chair-arm or a balustrade ▷rail (▷baluster).

Osier A flexible twig or branch, known as a ▷*withe* or *nythe*, used to tie down ▷thatch on ▷roofs.

Osiride A ▷pier with an ▷engaged figure of Osiris in front of it: unlike a ▷Caryatide, the pier, not the figure, supports the ▷entablature. The figure of Osiris, the ▷Egyptian deity, is also found seated. The figure was commonly found in Egyptian-▷Revival work.

Ossature The ▷frame of a building, the ▷ribs of a ▷vault, or a structure of a timber ▷roof.

Ossuary A ▷bone-house or *ossuarium*: a place where the bones of the dead are stored, often arranged in patterns. Ossuaries or ▷charnel-houses enabled burial grounds to be re-used. The term *ossuary* can also be given to a large receptacle for the bones of one person.

Ostensory A ▷monstrance for the Eucharistic wafer or Host.

Ostiole A small opening or entrance, also *ostiolum*.

Ostium A ▷hall connecting the street to the ▷atrium in a ▷Roman house, or a doorway within a house. Also the ▷door in front of the ▷stalls for chariots or horses in a ▷circus.

Ottoman Late ▷Islamic architecture dating from the fourteenth century, especially Turkish work, much influenced by Byzantium. Ottoman decorations influenced European design, and included the ▷tulip, ▷Arabesques, ▷crescents, turbans, etc. The *Ottoman style* was used as an alternative to *Chinoiserie* (▷Chinese) in the eighteenth century, and there was even an Ottoman or Turkish ▷'mosque' designed by Chambers for Kew Gardens. Ottoman ▷motifs appear in William de Morgan ▷tiles, and in many ▷ornaments of the late nineteenth century. The fashion for smoking-rooms and Turkish ▷baths encouraged a widespread use of the style. An *Ottoman* was specifically a cushioned seat for several persons sitting with their backs to each other, or a low stuffed seat with no back.

Ottonian Pertaining to early ▷Romanesque ▷architecture of the Holy Roman Empire from the second half of the tenth century. (From Kaisers Otto, 919–1024.)

Oubliette A secret ▷prison ▷cell reached only by trap-door through which the prisoners were dropped, or a secret pit in the floor of a dungeon into which a prisoner could be cast and killed. From *oublier*, to forget.

Oundy, undy A wavy moulding (▷mould) like a ▷Vitruvian scroll, or a series of stylized waves.

Out-and-in bond Alternate headers (▷head) and ▷stretchers in ▷quoins and ▷jambs. *Outban* or *outband* refers to the long stone on the main ▷face, so it, or *outbound*, is a ▷masonry stretcher, as opposed to *inband*.

Outer hearth A *front* ▷*hearth*, or a part of the hearth projecting into the room.

Outer string That ▷string on the exposed edge of a ▷stair, furthest from the ▷wall.

Outlooker A member supporting the part of the ▷roof beyond the ▷face of a ▷gable, such as a ▷purlin.

Outwindow A ▷cantilevered ▷projecting ▷balcony or ▷loggia.

Ova Egg-shaped ▷ornaments.

Overdoor That part of the ▷wall above a doorcase. The ▷Attic ▷storey of a doorcase. The ▷*sopraporta*. A fanlight.

Overglaze Decoration applied and fired on the previously glazed surface of a piece of ▷ceramic ware.

Overhand Facing brickwork laid from inside a building, requiring special skills as the bricklayers cannot see the work properly. An *overhand* ▷*struck joint* reverses the slope of a normal struck joint, and should not be used as it allows water to collect on the ledge of the ▷bricks below the joint, thus endangering the bricks and joints through frost action.

Overhang The projection of a ▷storey or any part of a building beyond a storey below or in front of the ▷naked of a ▷wall. A ▷jetty or a jutting-out portion of a building. A ▷projection over a ▷base, i.e. the opposite of a ▷batter. Also called *oversail*. An *oversailing* ▷*course* is a ▷masonry course projecting beyond the ▷face of the wall, often used with other oversailing courses for ▷cornices or ▷eaves details, or for ▷corbelling.

Overmantel An ▷ornamental structure or ▷frame, often around a mirror, set on a ▷mantel-▷shelf.

Overshot A ▷jetty.

Overstorey Any upper ▷floor, or a ▷clerestorey.

Over-tile The ▷*imbrex* or covering ▷tile.

Overthrow An ornamental top above the framework of ▷wrought-iron ▷gates, like a ▷tympanum without the ▷arch.

Ovolo A ▷quarter-round or convex moulding (▷mould) much used in ▷Classical ▷architecture. ▷Greek ovolos are flatter, more like part of the section of an egg, while ▷Roman ovolos are more mechanical, usually quarter-rounds.

Owl An ▷attribute of learning and of ▷Minerva, so found associated with ▷libraries, etc. It also represents night, sleep, and Jewry (because Judaism was regarded as the antithesis of the new light of Christianity).

Ox-eye ▷*Oeil-de-boeuf*. An ox-eye moulding is concave, less deep than a ▷scotia, but deeper than a ▷cavetto.

Ox-Head The ▷*bucranium* found on ▷Classical ▷friezes.

Oxter piece A short timber between the ceiling-▷joists and the ▷rafters near the ▷eaves. A ▷*queen-post* is sometimes called an *oxter-piece* because it is approximately arm-pit height. An *oxter* is the space between the oxter-piece and the eaves. An *ashlar-piece*.

Oyelet, oylet An *eyelet*.

P

Pace A ▷dais. A stepped ▷podium around a ▷tomb. A ▷landing in a ▷stair.

Packing Small stones between larger ones in ▷rubble ▷walls. Any stuffing or seal around a joint. A *packing-piece* is a ▷block used to raise one or more members above other members.

Pad A ▷pad or pad-stone is a strong ▷block set on or in a ▷wall or ▷pier to carry, say, a ▷truss, and distribute the load. It is also called a ▷*template*. A block of stone set at the top of a wall to finish the coping (▷cope) at the end of a ▷gable, also called a ▷*knee-stone*, ▷*kneeler*, or ▷*skew* (▷knee).

Paddle A ▷sluice.

Pagod A ▷*Magot* or ▷*Poussah*, a small squat, fat ▷Chinese figure, usually seated and wearing a large hat, found in *Chinoiserie* decorations.

Pagoda A tall polygonal structure with ▷ornamental ▷roofs at each ▷storey, originally a ▷temple in Buddhist lands, but adapted as an ▷eyecatcher and ▷pavilion in the eighteenth-century *Chinoiserie* (▷Chinese) manner. It had upturned ▷eaves, fretwork ▷brackets, and often ▷bell-like ▷ornaments hanging from the eaves.

Paillasse A supporting ▷bed in ▷masonry.

Paillette Metal or gilt used to create a jewel-like effect in ▷ornament.

Painted glass [183] ▷Glass ▷ornamented with painted decorations, often fired to fix the paint and fuse it with the glass.

Palace A large dwelling with architectural pretensions for royalty, the highest aristocracy, or dignitaries of the Church.

[183] PAINTED GLASS The east window of the Church of St Alkmund, Shrewsbury, by Francis Eginton, with painted glass set in cash-iron tracery. (*JSC*)

Palaestra A wrestling-school. A building or part of a house for athletic training, usually a ▷court with ▷colonnades, ▷baths, and other rooms around it.

Palazzo A large ▷palace, public building, or private house with architectural pretensions in Italy. The *palazzo style* evolved in the nineteenth century as an ▷astylar ▷façade with *cornicione* (▷cornice) and central ▷*cortile* (▷Italian). An example is Barry's Reform Club in Pall Mall, London.

Pale A stake placed vertically. *Pale-fencing* consists of pales or palings or slats. A *palisade* is an enclosure of stakes driven into the ground for defensive purposes, as in a ▷stockade. A *pale* is an area enclosed by a palisade or palings, so refers to an area protected or under sound government. *Paly* means divided by vertical lines.

Palimpsest A ▷church ▷brass which has an earlier ▷effigy on the hidden bedded ▷face, or an over-engraving.

Palladian [184] A style of ▷Classical ▷achitecture that evolved from the work of the sixteenth-century architect Andrea Palladio (1508–80), especially through his *Quattro libri dell'architettura* of 1570, which set out his theories, illustrated his works, and advertised his practice. Inigo Jones introduced the *Palladian style* to England in the reigns of James I and VI and Charles I, but it fell from favour for many years and was supplanted by the ▷Baroque architecture first of Wren, then of Vanbrugh, Hawksmoor, and Gibbs. A ▷revival of Palladian architecture in the eighteenth century began in the area around Venice, but achieved considerable pre-eminence in Britain largely through the efforts of Lord Burlington and Colen Campbell (who also revived interest in Inigo Jones's contributions in his *Vitruvius Britannicus*), and undermined the fashion for Baroque. Under the ▷aegis of the 'Palladians', a grammar and vocabulary appropriate to the return of academic Classical architecture were evolved that exercised a veritable tyranny of taste during the reign of the first three Georges. Palladian ideals were exported to Prussia (Knobelsdorff's Opera House on the *Unter*

(a)

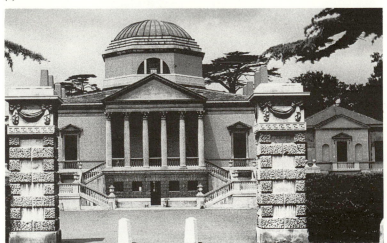

[184] PALLADIAN (*a*) The Palladian bridge of 1737 by the ninth Earl of Pembroke and Roger Morris at Wilton, Wiltshire. (*JSC*) (*b*) Chiswick Villa of 1725–29 inspired by the Villa Capra at Vicenza by Palladio. Note the octagonal cupola with Diocletian window, pedimented Corinthian portico at *piano nobile* level, and *perron* leading up to the *piano nobile* floor. The domical vault harks back to Antiquity. Note the rusticated gate-piers with swags. (*JSC*)

(b)

[185] PALM Variety of Corinthian capital from the Tower of the Winds in Athens. This unusual design has a square abacus and an upper row of palm leaves. (*JSC*)

den Linden), to Saxony (*Schloss Wörlitz*), to Russia (the work of Cameron and Quarenghi), and the British Colonies in America (the work of Jefferson). Palladian architecture was the style favoured by the Whig Oligarchy, not least because it established a link between the time of the Hanoverian succession and the Stuart reigns of James and Charles, so reinforcing the legitimacy of the Hanoverian claim to the Throne. Palladianism is associated with Anglophiles during the ▷*Aufklärung* (▷Enlightenment) in German-speaking lands. A *Palladian* ▷*window* is a ▷*serliana* or ▷*Venetian window*, and consists of an arched central opening and two narrower openings with ▷pilasters or ▷columns between them carrying two short ▷entablatures from the top of which the central ▷arch springs: it was a common feature of eighteenth-century Palladian-inspired architecture.

Palliase ▷Paillasse.

Palm [185] This ▷tree has inspired much decorative work. Palm trees were represented in ▷Egyptian ▷architecture as ▷columns with vertical banded ▷shafts and tightly-packed ▷leaves forming the ▷capital. The palm is found in ▷Rococo and *Chinoiserie* (▷Chinese) work, and recurs in ▷Neoclassical decorations. Palm leaves are used in some varieties of ▷Corinthian capitals, and are also found in ▷spandrels, frequently as ▷symbols of ▷peace, ▷victory over ▷death, the ▷crowns of martyrdom, and the surrounds of portrait-▷medallions. Flat palm fronds with curving

tips were used in eighteenth-century capitals, ▷friezes, and other mouldings (▷mould). A *palmate* capital is one resembling the leaves of a palm tree. A *palmette* is a stylized palm leaf, often used with the ▷anthemion, and recurs in ▷Classical ▷ornament and its many manifestations. It may also alternate with the ▷lotus. *Palmiform* means in the form of a palm leaf or the top of a palm tree. A *palm-house* (▷[186]) is a ▷conservatory where palms and other plants are cultivated.

Pampre An ▷ornament of ▷vine ▷leaves and grapes usually associated with ▷twisted or ▷barley-sugar ▷columns, and often used as the spiral around columns, thus suggesting the twisted form. It is also found in ▷cavettos and other continuous mouldings (▷mould), such as at the tops of ▷Perpendicular ▷screens.

Pan A square in the ▷framing of ▷timber buildings. *Pan* was also the Arcadian god of hills and woods, the protecting deity of flocks and herdsmen. He is represented with horns and shaggy goat-legs, playing a pipe. He is often represented in ▷grottoes, and his ▷attributes are the *syrinx* (pipe), a crook, a ▷garland of pine leaves, and a pine twig. He is associated with *fauns* and with ▷pastoral scenes.

Pan-and-roll Roofing-▷tiles consisting of two flat tapered under-tiles with ▷flanges and a semicircular-sectioned tapering tile laid over them to seal the joints.

Panache The triangular shape of a ▷pendentive, or its surface. A circlet of upright ▷feathers arranged in pyramidal form on a ▷helmet.

Pancarpi ▷Garlands and ▷festoons of ▷fruit, flowers, and ▷leaves for the ▷ornamentation of ▷doors, ▷windows, and ▷niches.

Pane The ▷side of any object, the ▷light of a ▷window, the space between timbers in a wooden ▷partition, etc.

[186] PALM-HOUSE Belfast Palm-House, designed by Charles Lanyon, with the two wings by Richard Turner, 1839–55. An early example of a curvilinear glass house. (*JSC*)

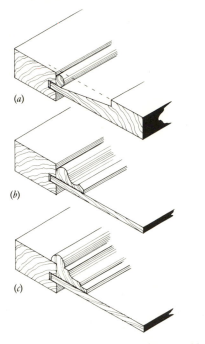

[187] PANEL MOULDINGS (*a*) Raised and fielded panel with planted bead. (*b*) Plain panel with flush mouldings. (*c*) Plain panel with bolection moulding (i.e. raised above frame). (*JJS*)

Panel A sunken compartment in a ▷wainscot, ▷door, or ceiling, etc., surrounded by a moulding (▷mould), and often ▷enriched. Panels may be treated as plain squares or rectangles, or may be ▷quatrefoils or ▷blind ▷tracery. The surfaces may be embellished with ▷linenfold, ▷heraldic devices, etc. *Panel mouldings* are the ▷beads or mouldings holding panels in place in a ▷frame, and may be ▷bolection, ▷ogee, or very simple (▷[187]). Panels may be ▷raised and ▷fielded, or enriched in other ways, such as by means of inlay. A *panel divider* is a moulding separating two panels along their common edges. *Panel tracery* is late ▷Gothic ▷Perpendicular tracery.

Panier An upright ▷corbel over a ▷pilaster and under a ▷truss. An ▷ornament resembling a ▷basket, or a *▷corbeil*.

Panoply A piled-up array of armour, uniforms, and weapons, arranged in an orderly heap, and used widely in ▷Renaissance and ▷Baroque decorations, often incorporating ▷Antique examples. ▷Trophy.

Panopticon A building with ▷corridors or ▷wings radiating from a central point, often used in the planning of ▷gaols, sometimes circular, sometimes star-shaped.

Pantheon A ▷temple dedicated to all deities, but, more especially, the great ▷rotunda in Rome consisting of a semicircular ▷coffered ▷dome on a massive circular ▷drum with an ▷octastyle ▷portico applied to the exterior, therefore any building resembling the Pantheon. A *Pantheon dome* is a simple dome resembling that of the Pantheon in Rome, with a series of concentric rings outside and coffers on the inside, sometimes with an ▷oculus in the centre.

Pantile A curved S-shaped ▷tile used for roofing.

Pantry A place in a ▷monastery where bread and other necessities were kept, hence the *pantry* in a later house. ▷Larder.

Pap A piece cast on a ▷pipe to facilitate tapping for a branch.

Paperhangings Paper fixed to ▷walls, decorated or plain.

Papier-mâché A material made of pulped paper to which ▷glue has been added: the resulting dough-like material can be moulded and finely finished.

Papyrus The paper-reed (*Cyperus papyrus*), used decoratively. *Papyriform* means in the shape of a cluster of papyrus ▷leaves and flowers. A papyrus ▷capital is found in ▷Egyptian and Egyptianizing ▷architecture.

Parabema A ▷chamber at one side of the ▷bema of a ▷basilican ▷church.

Parabolic arch An ▷arch in the form of the ▷intersection of a cone with a plane parallel to the side of the cone, so like a three-centred arch, but tending to greater verticality.

Paradise A ▷court or ▷atrium in front of a ▷church at its west end, and usually surrounded by a ▷cloister, therefore a *cloister-▷garth*. By connection, therefore, the term came to denote the west ▷porch itself, and also any upper space or room over that western porch. A monastic burial-ground. The centre of a ▷maze. A *parvise* has been said to be the room over the porch of a church, but the term is synonymous with *paradise*.

Parados Earthworks behind a fortification.

Parament Furnishings and hangings of an ▷apartment.

Parapet A low ▷wall to protect any place where there is a drop, as at the edge of a ▷roof, ▷balcony, or ▷terrace. A defensive wall. The part of a wall rising above the roof. Parapets may be plain, ▷pierced, crenellated (▷crenel), or otherwise ▷ornamented. A *parapet* ▷*gutter* is one behind a parapet wall.

Parapetasma The enclosure screening the statue of a deity in a ▷Greek ▷temple.

Parascenium A ▷wing extending forwards from each end of the *skene* of an ancient ▷theatre (▷scaena, ▷scheme).

Parastas The end of a ▷wall terminating in an ▷*anta*. A ▷pedestal wall at the end of a monumental staircase. Any flat ▷pier decorating the ▷angles of a square building. A *parastatica* is a species of ▷pilaster or an *anta*.

Parathura The rear ▷door of a ▷Greek house.

Paratorium A place on the north side of the east end of a ▷basilica for offerings. A *paratory* is any place in a ▷church for preparation, also a ▷vestry or ▷sacristy.

Parchemin A *parchment* ▷panel developed from ▷linenfold, used with ▷grapevine stems and ▷foliage in early twentieth-century ▷revivals of late-mediaeval ▷architecture. *Parchemin plié* is the same as *linenfold*.

Parclose A ▷screen separating ▷chapels or ▷tombs from the body of the ▷church, or a ▷parapet around a ▷gallery.

Paretta ▷Masonry with a surface resembling pebbles.

Parge work [188] Also *parget, pargeting, pargetting,* or *parging.* Plasterwork with ▷ornamental patterns in low

relief or indented (made with wooden ▷moulds pressed in when the ▷plaster is wet), much used on the exteriors of houses from late ▷Tudor times. ▷Vines and figures were the commonest types of decoration. *Parging* is an interior lining of a ▷chimney-▷flue to make the latter more fire-proof and to assist the passage of smoke. *Parget* is also the plaster for such lining. A *parged* ▷*verge* is the junction of ▷gable and ▷roof finished with plaster or ▷mortar, without ▷barge-boards.

Parian cement An anhydrous ▷gypsum ▷plaster with an accelerator of set, like ▷Keene's cement, but with borax instead of alum as the ▷additive.

Paries A ▷wall of a ▷Roman house. A *paries communis* was a ▷party wall. A *paries craticius* was a wall of wattles and staves covered with clay. *Paries dealbatus* was whitewashed or covered with ▷*opus albarium,* so resembled ▷marble. A *paries directus* was a ▷partition wall. *Paries formaceus* was a wall of rammed earth, or ▷*pisé* construction. *Paries fornicatus* was a ▷perforated wall (usually ▷arches). A *paries lateritius* was a ▷brick wall. *Paries solidus* was a ▷blind or blank wall. *Parietes* were the walls of rooms of Roman houses, frequently faced or painted with ▷fresco or patterns.

Parish church A ▷church of the smallest area under the jurisdiction of a rector or vicar in a division of a diocese.

Parker's cement Also called ▷*Roman cement,* patented in 1796, it was a dark-coloured ▷rendering made from powdered burnt clay nodules mixed with sand, ▷lime, and water. It set hard and fast, and was much

[188] PARGETTING An example from cottages in Suffolk. (*JSC*)

used for covering ▷façades with a representation of ▷ashlar scored into the surface like joints. ▷Pozzolan.

Parlatory A room in a ▷monastery where visitors could be received and converse.

Parlour A room for conversation in a ▷monastery, as ▷*parlatory*. The term became used to denote a ▷front or best room or comfortable ▷chamber in a house.

Parodos A side-entrance to a ▷theatre between the seats and the ▷stage.

Parotis A ▷console, ▷bracket, or ▷ancon, from a ▷Greek work associated with the ▷ear. It is also *parotides*.

Parpaing As ▷parpend.

Parpend A ▷bond-stone faced at both ends. *Parpend* ▷*ashlar* is ashlar faced on both sides.

Parpent wall A strong or substantial ▷partition ▷wall.

Parquet Polished ▷floors of ▷hardwood ▷blocks laid in patterns on a ▷base and polished, usually of a ▷herringbone type. *Parquetry* is ▷inlaid work of thin ▷veneers forming a floor-surface, also called *inlaid* or *plated parquet*. It can be of stone or wood, and can employ two or more colours. The *parquet* is also the ▷orchestra-▷stalls of a ▷theatre (*Parkett* in German).

Parrell A ▷chimney-piece, or the ▷ornaments of a chimneypiece as a whole.

Parsley ▷Foliage used in ▷ornament, often as a compromise between ▷acanthus and the ▷hart's-tongue or ▷water-leaf type.

Parsonage A building which serves as the dwelling of a priest.

Parterre A flat part of a ▷garden designed with formal beds of flowers or plants set in patterns.

Parthenon The great fifth-century BC ▷Greek ▷Doric ▷temple of Athena Parthenos on the ▷Acropolis in Athens, regarded as the most perfect example of Greek ▷Hellenic Doric ▷architecture, and the examplar for much Greek ▷Revival work.

Parting bead A beaded ▷slip in the centre of the ▷pulley-stile of a ▷sash-▷window to separate the two sash-cords and the two sashes.

Partition A ▷wall that is non-load-bearing, separating one room from another.

Party arch An ▷arch between two properties.

Party wall The fireproof ▷wall between two buildings to separate them: a ▷common wall.

Parvis, parvise ▷Paradise.

Pas-de-souris The ▷steps from a ▷moat to a ▷castle.

Passage An ▷avenue or ▷corridor leading to the ▷apartments of a building. A ▷*passage*-▷*grave* is a ▷chamber-▷tomb entered by a long passage hidden within a built mound.

Passion cross A ▷Calvary Cross set on three ▷steps, or set on a hill or in a churchyard.

Passus Five ▷Roman *pedes* (▷pes) (about 1.5 metres).

Pastas A recess off the south-facing side of the ▷peristyle of a ▷Greek house.

Pastiche A composition incorporating copies of styles, or in imitation of earlier styles, often used in a pejorative way.

Pastophorium One of two ▷apartments at the ▷sides of the ▷sanctuary of an early ▷church or temple.

Pastoral A romanticized Arcadian (▷Arcady) vision of rural life showing hunting, the worship of ▷Pan, or the tending of livestock, associated with eighteenth-century schemes of decoration. Pastoral ▷trophies included farm implements, vegetables, cheeses, and rustic musical instruments. A *pastoral* ▷*column* is one imitating a tree trunk, with bark and cut branch-stumps, associated with *rustick* retreats and the *cottage orné* (▷cot). A *pastoral staff* is a shepherd's crook, and therefore a bishop's ▷*crozier*, often found in ecclesiastical decorations, especially on funerary ▷monuments.

Patand Also *patin, patten*. The ▷base of a ▷column or ▷pier, or a base or ▷plinth carrying columns, ▷pilasters, or piers. The ▷sleeper or bottom ▷rail as the ▷foundation of a ▷wall.

Paten A dish or charger, usually circular, on which the bread is placed at the celebration of the Eucharist. Any thin circular metal plate or repetitive ▷ornament.

Patent glazing Dry puttyless glazing with metal glazing-bars used in ▷roofs and ▷walls.

Patera A circular ▷ornament, resembling a dish or ▷medallion, worked in ▷relief, often with ▷flutes.

When it is further ▷embellished to become a stylized representation of a flower, it is called a *rosette* (▷rose). It is found on ▷friezes or associated with ▷architraves, and embellishes the centres of ▷coffers. Elliptical *paterae* became fashionable in the late eighteenth century.

Paternoster A ▷bead-and-reel moulding (▷mould) resembling rosary beads. A type of passenger-lift consisting of a series of ▷platforms or cars attached to a continuous loop of chains.

Patience As *miserere*, ▷*misericord*.

Patin ▷Patand.

Patina A green encrustation of oxidization which forms on ▷bronze or ▷copper. Any stable oxide films on metal finishes. The *patina of age* is the toning down and colouration caused by ▷weathering.

Patio An outdoor ▷area beside a house, open or partly enclosed. A paved ▷terrace. An inner courtyard.

Pattée A ▷cross with the arms ending in broad flat ends joined to the arms by curves (▷cross).

Patten ▷Patand.

Pattern-books Published collections of designs intended to guide builders and craftsmen, and responsible for the dissemination of architectural taste. The eighteenth century saw the production of some of the finest pattern-books.

Paul Sts Peter and Paul are represented on either side of Christ enthroned, and their figures are shown on either side of the ▷altar. Paul is usually depicted with a sword and a book (▷symbol).

Pave To lay with paving stones, ▷bricks, or ▷tiles. *Pavé* is a paved surface, more especially one made of small ▷blocks laid in regular patterns.

Pavement A path or road laid or beaten in with stones or other materials. Pavements can be cobbled, covered with ▷rag-stone, paved in square ▷setts, laid with ▷flags, or covered with tarmacadam or ▷cement. Many other finishes are also possible. A *pavement ▷light* is formed of solid ▷glass ▷blocks cast into a reinforced ▷concrete grid, or set in a cast-iron ▷frame to illuminate a ▷basement.

Pavilion [189] A ▷turret, small building, or ▷wing of a larger structure. A detached or semi-detached building used for entertainment. A building used for specialized functions, separated from other buildings, as in a ▷hospital, for reasons of hygiene. In a large building, prominent parts, such as the centrepiece and terminating end-pieces, given especial importance by means of height, ▷enrichment, etc. A temporary structure. An ornamental or pleasure-building, such as a ▷gazebo or ▷summer-house, or a building with a ▷verandah attached to a sports ground. A *pavilion ▷roof* is one hipped equally on all sides, so pyramidal in form, or a polygonal roof.

Pavimentum A ▷pavement of crushed materials set in ▷mortar. ▷Opus.

Pavior A ▷brick used in pavements.

Pavonaceum ▷Tiles rounded at one end and laid in a way to suggest ▷scales or ▷scalloping.

Pavonazzo A ▷marble with red, blue, and yellow markings.

Paw A terminating feature of a ▷furniture leg, used

[189] PAVILION Perspective view of St Thomas's Hospital, Lambeth, London. This fine Italianate group of buildings was designed by Henry Currey, and was completed in 1870–71. The 'pavilion' principle of planning is demonstrated, where wards were separated by means of linking corridors, thus lessening the possibilities of infection, and permitting light and air to enter at the sides of the pavilions. (*RIBA British Architectural Library*)

like the ▷claw and ▷hoof; it is found supporting ▷*sarcophagi*, candelabra, and ▷*monopodia*.

Pawn A covered ▷passage, ▷gallery, or *pentice* (▷appentice).

Pax A representation of the ▷Crucifixion. A small tablet (▷table) with such an image kissed by the congregation.

Peace A female with ▷palm frond, ▷olive branch, ▷crown, ▷dove, broken ▷swords, etc., often carrying a ▷torch. Also found with Plenty (▷*cornucopia*).

Peacock A ▷symbol of immortality, often found with the ▷grapevine and ▷acanthus. It was associated with the Resurrection and with prophecy. Peacocks were especially popular during the ▷Aesthetic Movement.

Peak A point, as in ▷pointed ▷arch.

Peapod Also called the ▷*cosse de pois*, it is a seventeenth-century style of ▷ornament, partly ▷Arabesque and partly ▷naturalistic floral, mixed with sprays of ▷dots like peas.

Pear-drop A ▷pendant shaped like a pear. A term for a ▷Gothic ▷cornice because of the series of pendent forms. A support for a minor ▷arch, such as a pear-shaped ▷corbel. A pendent handle for a drawer or ▷cupboard in seventeenth-century ▷furniture.

Pearl A moulding (▷mould) of continuous pearl-like beads, called *pearling* or *beading*.

Pebble A ▷wall built of pebbles or uncut ▷flints bedded in ▷mortar, or a wall faced with pebbles. *Pebbledash* is an external finish of small pebbles thrown on a second coat of ▷rendering before it is dry.

Pectinated Having teeth in a continuous line, like ▷dentils.

Pedes ▷Roman feet. A ▷*pes* was about 29.6 cm or just under 12 inches.

Pedestal [190] A substructure placed under some ▷columns in ▷Classical ▷architecture. It consists of a ▷base or ▷plinth, a ▷dado or ▷die, and a ▷cornice. It may support a statue, ▷vase, ▷obelisk, or some other element. It is also found as a part of a balustrade (▷baluster). A continuous pedestal outside is a ▷podium, and inside it is equivalent to the ▷chair-rail and ▷dado.

Pediment [191] In ▷Classical ▷architecture, a low-pitched ▷gable crowning a ▷portico or a ▷façade, and

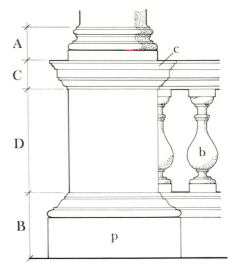

[190] PEDESTAL WITH BALUSTRADE **A** Attic base, **C** cornice, **D** dado or die, **B** base, **p** plinth, **c** cymatium or cyma reversa, **b** baluster. (*JJS*)

often containing ▷sculpture in its ▷tympanum. ▷Greek pediments are generally flatter in ▷pitch than ▷Roman pediments. A pediment is formed with the top part of the ▷entablature repeated on its gable, except that in ▷Doric pediments the ▷mutules are often omitted on the raking parts (see ▷rake). Pediments are found over ▷niches, ▷doors, ▷windows, and other features, in which case they are called *frontons* because they crown subsidiary architectural elements. While *triangular pediments* are the most common, *segmental pediments* were introduced during the Roman Empire, associated with the cults of Isis and Diana of Ephesus because of the shape of the ▷crescent ▷moon and the bow-shape of the huntress's weapon. Some Isiac ▷temples built by the Romans had segmental pediments. An *open pediment* has sloping sides that stop short of the ▷apex, also called an *open-topped* or ▷*broken-apex pediment*. If a pediment has a triangular or segmental top, but the bottom has a gap, it is called an *open-bed* or a *broken-*▷*base pediment*. A true *broken pediment* has an incomplete bottom ▷cornice and no apex or top (if segmental). Pediments often occur in eighteenth-century door-cases where the horizontal cornice is interrupted by a fanlight (▷fan), so they would be *open-bed* or *broken-base* pediments. A *scrolled pediment* (▷scroll) is an *open segmental pediment* in which the segments terminate in scrolls. A *pediment* ▷*arch* is a ▷*mitre arch* (▷[7], [234]).

Peel, pele In Scotland, Ireland, and in northern England a fortified ▷tower-house.

Pegma In ▷Antiquity, ▷boards joined together. Lifts

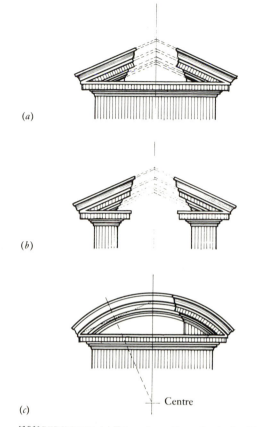

(a)

(b)

(c) ──┼── Centre

[191] PEDIMENT (a) Triangular pediment (pecked), with open-topped or broken-apex triangular pediment (solid). (b) Open-bed or broken triangular pediment (pecked), with true broken or open triangular pediment (solid). In both (a) and (b) the entablature at an angle is called the raking cornice. (c) Segmental pediment with (right) open-topped segmental pediment. The centre of the segment is obtained by drawing a line from the apex of the corona-fillet of a corresponding triangular pediment to the extremity of the fillet, bisecting the line, and drawing a line at right-angles to it. (*JSC*) For a scrolled pediment, ▷[34].

to raise animals from one level to another in an amphitheatre, or a machine to change scenery.

Peg-tile A plain ▷tile with square holes for fixing with oak pegs.

Pelasgic ▷Walls of huge stones without ▷mortar.

Pele ▷Peel.

Pelican A common ▷sculpture in ▷Gothic buildings showing the pelican vulning herself to feed her young, representing piety and the symbolism of the ▷Sacraments.

Pellet A flat ▷band on which are circular ▷discs or hemispherical projections, common in ▷Romanesque work, but recurring in nineteenth-century revivals.

Pelmet A ▷valance concealing the curtain-track or ▷blind-boxes of a ▷window. A *pelmet-*▷*board* also acts as a pelmet.

Pelta A type of wide ▷shield-like ▷cartouche used in ▷friezes, ▷trophies, and ▷Arabesques, and especially in chair-backs during the ▷*Empire* period. The sides of the shield sweep up and return as ▷eagle- or ▷rams' heads.

Pen, pen-check, pend A ▷bird's-mouth rebate in stone. A *pend* is also a vaulted ▷roof without ▷groins, or a covered ▷passage through a ▷terrace of houses. A *pentice* (▷appentice).

Pencil-rounded A slightly rounded edge, as when an ▷arris on timber is taken off by means of sandpaper.

Pencilling Painting the ▷mortar joints of brickwork with paint to emphasise the joints.

Pendant An elongated ▷boss suspended from ▷Perpendicular and later ▷vaulting. Any hanging ▷ornament on vaults or timber ▷roofs. A *pendent* ▷*frieze* is a ▷*Gothic* ▷*cornice*. A *pendant-*▷*post* is the vertical post placed against a ▷wall, the lower end on a ▷corbel or ▷capital, and the upper end fixed to a ▷beam of a ▷hammer-beam roof-▷truss.

Pendentive The portion of a domical ▷vault which descends into the corner of an angular building where a ▷dome is placed on a square ▷base. It is really a variety of concave ▷spandrel forming the junction between the corner of the square compartment and the base of a circular dome or ▷drum. Anything vaulted outwards from a ▷pier or ▷corbel. *Pendentive bracketing* is corbelling to give the rough impression of a pendentive. *Pendentive cradling* or *ribbing* is the curved ▷frame of arched and vaulted ceilings to support the ▷plaster ▷panels between them.

Pendice Related to *pentice* or ▷*penthouse* (▷appentice).

Pendiculated Supported by *pendicules*, or small ▷piers or ▷columns.

Pendill In ▷jettied or framed overhang construction, the terminating ▷pendants at the bottoms of the vertical ▷posts, often carved and ▷ornamented.

Penetralia A ▷sanctuary or an inner room of a building.

239

Pent A ▷shed ▷roof, or small sloping ▷lean-to roof. It is usually placed over a front- or side-▷door to protect a visitor, or to roof a lean-to or addition. If the pent roof is carried on all round the building or across a whole front, it is called a ▷*skirt roof.*

Pentacle A five-pointed ▷star in ▷Gothic ▷tracery with a pentagon in the middle. A *pentagram* is also a five-pointed star called a *pentalpha* because it consists of five interlocking A-figures.

Pentastyle A ▷portico of five ▷columns in a line.

Penthouse, pendice, pentice As ▷appentice. A structure occupying less than half the area of a ▷roof of a building.

Pepperpot A small circular ▷turret with a cone-shaped ▷roof, also called a *pepperbox turret.*

Perch A ▷bracket or a ▷corbel.

Perclose As ▷parclose.

Perforated A *perforated* ▷*wall* is pierced with openings, usually in decorative ▷patterns, such as the net-like forms of ▷reticulated ▷tracery.

Perget As ▷parget.

Pergola A path flanked by ▷columns carrying ▷joists, the whole to carry climbing plants. A ▷garden structure consisting of two parallel rows of columns supporting beams and ▷trellis-work. Any such ▷colonnade. A long ▷lean-to, usually open. A *pentice* (▷appentice).

Peribolus An enclosing ▷wall or colonnade around a space.

Peridrome ▷Peripteral.

Periform Pear-shaped or onion-domed.

Peripteral A building with a continuous row of ▷columns around it. The *periptery* is the row of columns around the ▷walls, and the *peridrome* is the space between a row of columns and the wall of the ▷cell or building behind. Ancient writers used the term to denote columns round an inner ▷court. The *peristasis* or *peristyle* is the range of columns surrounding a building or a court, also called the *periptery*. A *peristylium* is an inner court with columns surrounding it.

Peristalith Standing stones around something, such as a burial-mound. A *peristele* is one such stone.

Peristerium An inner ▷*ciborium.*

Peristyle ▷Peripteral.

Perithyrides ▷Ancones.

Perpend As ▷parpend. Also *perpin, perpender,* or ▷*through-stone.* A *perpend* or *perpent* ▷*wall* is a ▷pier or ▷buttress which projects from a ▷wall, or it is a wall built of perpends, all or most of which reach from one side to the other. The vertical cross-joint in ▷masonry or brickwork.

Perpendicular [192] The last of the styles of ▷Gothic ▷architecture which flourished in England, also known as *Third-*▷*Pointed* or the ▷*Rectilinear Style.* It developed in the fourteenth century, and continued well into the sixteenth, even surviving in certain instances (as at Christ Church, Oxford) well into the seventeenth century. It was therefore by far the longest-lived style of Gothic, lasting for the best part of three hundred years. It was the first style of Gothic to be revived. It is peculiarly English, and has no Continental counterpart, for in Europe the elaborate ▷*Flamboyant* styles continued until ▷Renaissance taste caused Gothic to be superseded altogether. Perpendicular is characterized by straight verticals and horizontals, especially in ▷tracery where ▷transomes are important: transomes are frequently crenellated (▷crenel), and ▷mullions rise up directly to the underside of the ▷window-▷arches, without any changes of direction. Arches became very flat, and vaulting became complex, first of the ▷lierne type, then of the (again peculiarly English) ▷fan pattern. A powerful feature of Perpendicular work is the introduction of mouldings (▷mould) framing doorways or windows, thus creating ▷spandrels which are frequently ▷ornamented, and accentuating the rigid ▷panel-like effects: such ▷hood mouldings often stop at ▷label-▷stops in the form of ▷shields or heads. The rhythm of window tracery is usually continued in ▷blind panels of stone, and some Perpendicular interiors are completely covered with blind panelling, creating a rigid, tightly controlled, logical, modular Architecture. Mouldings are generally mechanical, but there is some spectacular undercutting and very deep carving at King's College Chapel, Cambridge. Surviving ▷glass is divided into panels, and colours are generally much lighter than in ▷Decorated work, with a tendency for increased use of yellows. During the Perpendicular period, ▷roofs became almost flat, and were concealed behind tall ▷parapets, often crenellated with elaborate patterns. The ▷ogee form survived, and the ▷Tudor ▷Rose was introduced, with the ▷portcullis (itself a panelled ▷motif) (see ▷Gothic, ▷tracery). The last phase of Perpendicular is also called ▷Tudor, characterized by an increasing use of bricks ▷diaper-work, very flat arches, and pronounced hood moulds.

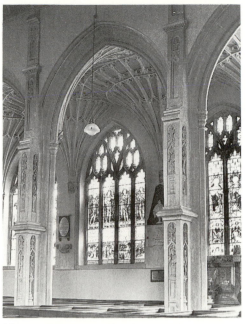

(*a*)

(*b*)

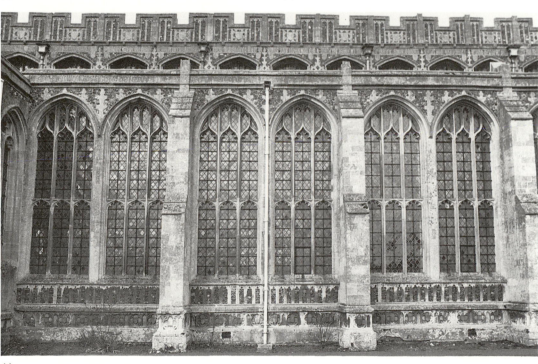

(*c*)

[192] PERPENDICULAR (*a*) The Lane aisle (1520s) in the Church of St Andrew, Cullompton, Devon, showing the fan vaulting. (*JSC*) (*b*) The Prior's House, Much Wenlock Priory, Shropshire. One of the finest surviving domestic buildings of the late fifteenth century, this façade consists of a two-storey gallery with continuous windows between buttresses, giving a typically panelled effect to the front. (*Shropshire Council Council Record Office SRO 770/Large Box 42*) (*c*) The south aisle of the Church of Holy Trinity at Long Melford, Suffolk. There is much flushwork, and the tracery with transomes is entirely Perpendicular in character. Note the panelled effects of the crenellations, and the continuous inscription over the clerestorey. The date is late fifteenth century. (*JSC*)

241

[193] PERRON The south front of Kedleston Hall, Derbyshire, by Robert Adam, of 1765. The central motif derives from the Arch of Constantine, so it is essentially a triumphal arch with four detached Corinthian columns and an attic storey. The perron, or external stair, leads up to the *piano nobile* level. Note the rusticated basement storey, and, in the foreground, the ha-ha. (*JSC*)

Perron [193] An external flight of ▷steps and a ▷landing (arranged symmetrically) giving access to the ▷*piano nobile* level of a building, usually by means of a ▷platform. It is common in ▷Palladian ▷architecture. Any formal ▷terrace or platform at a higher level than the ground.

Persian A ▷*telamon*, but one dressed as a Persian. The *Persian Style* was a term used to describe a vague range of oriental ▷motifs, and in the nineteenth century was associated with ▷Islamic and especially the ▷Arabian styles of ▷architecture and decoration.

Persic A *Persic* ▷*column* was a variety of the Persian column designs of Persepolis and Isfahan, had a ▷bell-shaped ▷capital and ▷base of the same size, and was much ▷ornamented with ▷lotus. It was an ingredient of Egyptianizing ornament of the early nineteenth century.

Persienne Outer ▷shutters with ▷louvres.

Persona A ▷mask, often of ▷Grotesque form, used as an ▷antefixa or ▷gargoyle.

Personification The encapsulation of an abstraction in a human figure. ▷Fame, the ▷Virtues, and the ▷Vices are depicted as females, and there is a vast range of sculptured figures with ▷attributes signifying the ▷Liberal Arts, commerce, justice, beauty, providence, etc. *Personification* was popularized in Cesare Ripa's influential book *Iconologia* of 1593.

Perspective A system of drawing objects that produces an image of the object to give the illusion of it in three-dimensional form, or as it would actually appear.

Pertica A ▷beam over the ▷altar of a ▷church from which ▷reliquaries were hung on special occasions.

Pes A ▷Roman foot slightly smaller than Imperial measure.

Pessulus A ▷Roman ▷door-▷bolt for fastening the ▷leaf of a door, usually placed at the top and bottom of each leaf.

Pest-house A ▷*lazar-house* or *lazaretto* for confining persons infected with contagious diseases.

Petal ▷Ornament of overlapping ▷scale-like shapes, found in roofing, ▷tile-hanging, representations of armour, and ▷diaper-work. It is sometimes pierced and used in ▷lattices. It is also called *imbrication* (▷imbrex) or *scale-pattern*.

Peter and Paul ▷Paul.

Pew An enclosed seat or any fixed wooden seat with a back in a ▷church. The ▷bench-ends of pews were usually finished with ▷finials of the ▷poppy-head type, and were elaborately carved with ▷blind ▷tracery and the like. ▷*Box-pews* were enclosed with high panelled ▷partitions, and usually date from the late seventeenth or eighteenth century where they have survived at all. A *pew-chair* was a hinged seat fixed to the face of a bench-end.

Phane A ▷vane.

Pharos An ▷Antique lighthouse (▷light) or ▷symbol of a lighthouse.

Phoenix A mythical bird which burned itself to death on a fire: three days later a young phoenix rose from the ashes. It is a ▷symbol of immortality and of the Resurrection, so appears in funerary ▷monuments and mediaeval carvings. It sometimes occurs in *Chinoiserie* decorations as the *ho-ho bird*, and is often found over ▷door-cases or mirrors (▷Chinese). *Phoenix* is also a term for the *Art of* ▷*Memory*.

Phrygian cap A conical bonnet worn as the ▷cap of ▷Liberty, shown on the figure of Liberty, or carried on a pike, associated with flags and weapons. It is found as a decorative device in France after 1789.

Piache A ▷portico, ▷porch, or partially covered ▷area.

Piano nobile The main ▷floor of a building containing the most important reception-rooms. It was higher than other ▷storeys and usually sandwiched between a ▷basement or ground floor and the upper floors: it was given an external architectural treatment to show its importance, and was frequently approached by an external staircase or ▷*perron*.

Piazza A square or rectangular open space contained by buildings. In the seventeenth and eighteenth century it came to mean any covered way or open arcaded ▷storey with buildings over it, as in the Covent Garden piazza, so *piazza* came to mean a covered way, a ▷colonnaded or ▷arcaded walk, ▷arcade, or even a *pentice* (▷appentice).

Picked ▷Masonry finished with many small pits.

Picnostyle Also ▷*pycnostyle*. ▷Colonnade, ▷intercolumniation.

Picture gallery A room or rooms for the display of paintings, drawings, etc., usually top-lit. A *pinacotheca*.

Picture rail A moulding (▷mould) for hanging pictures in a room, coincident with the bottom of a ▷frieze in ▷Classical ▷architecture.

Picturesque [194] From *pittoresco*, meaning 'in the manner of the painters', this was an eighteenth-century concept which defined a building, a building in a landscape, or a landscape that resembled a composition by Poussin, Claude, or Salvator Rosa as *Picturesque*. Asymmetrical composition, natural features (whether real or contrived), and buildings that seemed to belong to the setting were important ingredients of the Picturesque. It was a product of eighteenth-century ▷Romanticism, and featured ▷topographical decoration, ▷pastoral scenes, and the incorporation of ▷ruins (real or sham) and Gothick (▷Gothic) ▷architecture into compositions. The Picturesque movement encouraged ▷eclecticism and the association of certain architectural styles for building types.

(*a*)

[194] PICTURESQUE (*a*) Hadlow Castle, Kent, by G. L. Taylor, 1840. The Picturesque effects of asymmetry, composition, details, and verticality were not derived from necessity, and were therefore regarded by people like Pugin as shams. This is an example of the 'abbey' style of country house. (*RCHME AA51/5923*)
(*b*) Peckforton Castle, Cheshire, by Anthony Salvin, 1844–50, a fine example of a house in the style of a thirteenth-century castle. The massing derives from the plan, and so it is an example of what Pugin described as True Picturesque. (*JSC*)

(*b*)

Pie ornament The *Kikumon*, or formalized chrysanthemum, used as an ▷ornament, as a rosette (▷rose), or as a pattern.

Piecrust A type of ▷Rococo ▷scalloped and moulded ▷border around mirrors and tables, where its raised rim was an important feature.

Pied de biche A cloven ▷hoof terminating a ▷cabriole leg, often associated with a ▷ram's or goat's head, or even the head of a ▷satyr.

Piedroit A ▷pilaster with no ▷base or ▷capital, also known as a ▷*lesene*, often found in ▷Neoclassical work as a strip pilaster or part of a ▷frame.

Pien, Piend An ▷arris, ▷hip, ▷apex, or ▷ridge. A *pien* or *piend* ▷*check* is a rebate cut along the edge of a stone ▷step in a hanging ▷stair to fit into the back of the step below. A *pien joint* is that between two steps, formed of a *pien check*.

Pier Any isolated mass of construction, such as the solid between two ▷windows, or a support. Piers are much more massive than ▷columns. An ▷arch which springs from a pier is called a *pier-arch*. Piers are quite distinct from columns or ▷pillars. Mediaeval piers in nave ▷arcades vary from the massive cylinders of ▷Romanesque construction to the light and many-moulded ▷Perpendicular piers. A *pier* ▷*buttress* is a pier which counteracts the thrust of a flying buttress. Also a mass of stone, ▷metal-work, ▷concrete or timber construction built out into the sea or other water as a break-water, landing-stage, or ▷promenade: a ▷jetty or a wharf.

Pierced Any ▷wall which is ▷perforated, such as a ▷screen wall. *Pierced work* means decoration consisting of perforations in patterns.

Pierrotage Small stones mixed with ▷mortar used as nogging (▷nog) between ▷frames.

Piggery A place where pigs are kept.

Pila A free-standing ▷masonry ▷pier, square or rectangular on plan, with no mouldings (▷mould) or decorations, and not conforming to any of the ▷Orders, otherwise known as a ▷*pillar*. A baptismal ▷font on a ▷shaft. A square unmoulded ▷block over ▷columns to carry the ▷roof-timbers. A type of ▷Antique ▷mortar.

Pilaster [195] A rectangular projection attached to a ▷wall that is similar in profile to the ▷column of one of the ▷Orders, and carries an ▷entablature. It must not be confused with an ▷engaged column, which is like a column embedded in a wall. A *pilaster strip* is one with

no ▷base or ▷capital, also known as a ▷*piedroit* or a ▷*lesene*, and is frequently connected with a ▷plinth and a ▷corbel-▷table. While an ▷anta is a species of pilaster, its details differ from those of the columns of the same Order: ▷Ionic *antae*, for example, have plain capitals without ▷volutes. Pilasters, on the other hand, conform exactly to the details of columns, except that they are rectangular, ▷projecting only slightly from the wall, and are not curved: unlike antae, however, pilasters have ▷entasis. A *pilaster* ▷*face* is the front surface of a pilaster parallel to the wall. A *pilaster mass* is an engaged ▷pier to which pilasters may be attached. A *pilaster* ▷*side* is the part at right-angles to the wall. A *pilastrade* is a line of pilasters. Pilasters also acted as ▷buttresses in some ▷Mannerist ▷architecture.

Pile A large building. A ▷post of ▷concrete or timber driven into the ground to support the ▷foundations of a building.

Pile-tower ▷Peel.

Pilier cantonné A massive ▷Gothic ▷pier with four ▷colonnettes carrying the ▷nave-▷arcade, ▷aisle-▷vaults, and ▷nave-vaults.

Pillar A ▷*pila*, or ▷pier, rectangular or square on plan, with no architectural or decorative pretensions. A *pillar-stone* is a ▷corner-stone, or a stone ▷memorial. A *pillar-and-*▷*arch* is a pattern of an arch carried on an ▷entablature on two ▷columns, popular in the eighteenth century. A pillar is generally free-standing.

Pillow capital A ▷*cushion* ▷*capital*. *Pillowed* is the same as *pulvinated* (▷pulvin). *Pillow-work* is any decorative scheme with pulvinated ▷projections.

Piloti [196] One of a number of ▷piers or ▷columns raising the structure above the ground ▷floor, so that there is open space below the building.

Pin A cylindrical piece of wood used to connect two pieces of timber, in which case it is a ▷dowel, or if metal, connecting stones.

Pinacotheca A ▷picture-gallery.

Pinaculum An ▷Antique ▷roof with a ▷ridge.

Pinax A ▷panel between the ▷columns of the ▷proscenium of an ▷Antique ▷theatre.

Pineapple, pine-cone [197] A decorative ▷finial like a pineapple, but often confused with the pine-cone or ▷acorn. When the ogee forms of the pine-cone and pineapple are mixed with flowers, the pattern resembles the Indian Tree of Life. Pineapples are used on

[195] PILASTER (*a*) This example is shown without entasis, although most pilasters used with Orders have entasis to match that of the columns used. The drawing illustrates fluting and fluting with cabling, with appropriate sections. **f** flute, **c** cabling. (*JJS*) (*b*) A Giant Composite Order of pilasters at the Town Hall, Abingdon, Oxfordshire, by Christopher Kempster of Burford (one of Wren's City masons) erected 1678–82. The pilasters have no entasis, which is not correct, and they sit on high plinths. The entablature has a cornice with plain modillions. The large arched windows recall Wren's Trinity Library at Cambridge. Note the pedimented dormers. (*JSC*)

(*a*)

(*b*)

[196] PILOTI Block of flats on the Roehampton Estate, London, designed by the former London County Council Architect's Department, 1954–58, loosely based on the *Unités d'Habitation* by Le Corbusier. Note the supports below known as *pilotis*. (*JSC*)

[197] PINE-CONE Two types of pine-cone finial. The pine-cone is often confused with the acorn and pineapple, both of which are also used as finials, crowning features, substitutes for urns or statuary, and other ornament. (*JSC*)

245

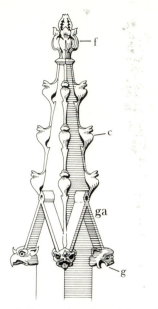

[198] PINNACLE A Decorated or Second-Pointed example. **f** finial, **c** crocket, **g** gargoyle, **ga** gablet. (*JJS*)

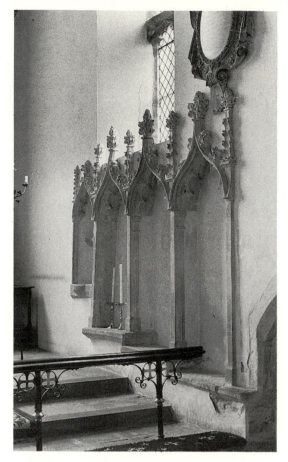

[199] PISCINA Decorated piscina and sedilia wih four cinquefoiled ogee arches with crockets and finials flanked by crocketed pinnacles in the chancel of the Church of St Swithun, Merton, Oxfordshire. (*JSC*)

▷gate-▷piers, ▷bed-▷posts, and other significant points, and it recurs in ▷Rococo ▷furniture. The pine-cone or ▷fir-cone also can be found as ▷pendants or as ▷door-▷knobs, on ▷newel-posts, mirrors, etc.

Pinnacle [198] A summit or ▷apex. The ▷crown of a ▷buttress, or a vertical ▷abutment terminating in a spirelet (▷spire), cone, or ▷pyramid, often ▷crocketed. A ▷turret-top.

Pinnings Small stones in the interstices of ▷masonry.

Pinning up Driving wedges under the upper work to bring it to bear on other work.

Pipe A conveyance for water or soil from a building, usually of metal or ▷earthenware. A *pipe-eye* is a cleaning-eye in a pipe.

Pisay As ▷*pisé.*

Piscina [199] A water-drain connected to a stone bowl within a ▷niche in the south wall of the ▷chancel. It was used to receive the water in which the priest washed his hands and which was used to rinse the chalice. Within the niche there was often a stone shelf or ▷credence-▷table for the sacred vessels. Any ▷reservoir or pond in ▷Antiquity. A pool or a basin of water. A *piscina limaria* was a tank at the end of an ▷aqueduct for depositing of sediments before the water was distributed.

Pisé A construction of rammed earth in ▷formwork, or the material itself, known as *pisé de terre*, rare in the UK. ▷*Cob* needs neither ramming nor formwork.

Pistol brick A ▷brick used for forming a coved ▷angle between a ▷wall and a ▷floor.

Pit The part on the ground ▷floor between the lower range of ▷boxes and the ▷stage of a ▷theatre. The ▷*orchestra pit* is that part occupied by the musicians, often partly under the stage.

Pitch The slope of the ▷sides or ▷skirts of a ▷roof. *Pitch* is also the residue left in the stills during the manufacture of tar: it was used with tar, sand, and pulverized chalk to make artificial ▷asphalte. It was also used for ▷caulking and as a water-proofing agent.

Pitch-faced is a term in ▷masonry meaning with all ▷arrises cut true, usually with a chiselled ▷margin, leaving the rest of the ▷face roughly ▷dressed with a pitching chisel. *Pitched stone* is a rough-faced stone with each edge of its exposed face pitched or ▷bevelled. A *pitching-piece* is the same as an ▷apron-piece, or a piece fixed into a ▷wall supporting the ends of the ▷carriage-pieces and ▷rough-strings of a ▷stair.

Pix, pixis, pyx The ▷shrine, ▷box, or vessel in which the ▷Sacrament is reserved.

Placage A shallow ▷masonry skin or ▷revetment.

Placard As *parget* (▷parge work).

Place bricks Common ▷bricks, underburnt, and therefore weak; used for ▷partition ▷walls, also called *grizzles*.

Plafond, platfond A ceiling or ▷soffite.

Plain joint A ▷butt joint.

Plain tile The ▷common, flat, roofing ▷tile of burnt clay or ▷concrete, sometimes with two ▷nibs at the ▷head and two nail- or peg-holes. Each tile overlaps two ▷courses below it, and should not be laid on ▷roofs of less than 40° pitch.

Plaisance A ▷summer-house or pleasure-▷pavilion.

Plait-band The ▷guilloche ▷ornament, so-called from its resemblance to plaits.

Planceer The ▷soffite of the ▷corona or of any projecting element, also called *plancer, plancher,* or *plancier*. A *planceer-piece* is a ▷board forming part of a planceer.

Planch A ▷plank or ▷floor-▷board, or a floor made of planks, so *planching* is flooring.

Plane tiles Flat ▷tiles.

Plank Any square-sawn flat timber 2–10 cms thick and 25 cms or more in width. A *plank-▷roof* is formed of ▷trusses made of planks cut to a curve. A *plank-house* is a building made of vertical planks.

Plantain A broad flat ▷leaf used in architectural decoration.

Planted When a moulding (▷mould) is wrought on separate material and is then fixed in place, it is said to be *planted* or *applied*. ▷Beads, etc., are usually planted, rather than cut into the solid timber.

Plaque A tablet (▷table), usually with an inscription, applied to or set into a wall, pavement, or pedestal.

Plasta An ▷antefixa.

Plaster A mixture of ▷lime, sand, water, and hair used for covering ▷walls and ceilings. Plaster of Paris is calcined sulphate of lime which, when mixed with water, rapidly hardens and expands, thus filling cracks, etc.

Platband A flat horizontal ▷fascia, ▷band, or ▷string, the ▷projection of which is much less than its height. A ▷lintel, real or decorative. The ▷fillet between two ▷flutes of a ▷column or ▷pilaster. A broad ▷step below a ▷threshold, or a ▷landing. A ▷*stria*.

Plate A general term given to all horizontal timbers laid on ▷walls or ▷posts in order to support other timbers. It could be a ▷wall-▷plate laid on walls to receive the structure of the ▷roof above. *Plate ▷glass* is glass cast in sheets and polished, of good quality, distinguished from ▷*crown-* and ▷*sheet glass*. Although plate glass was known before the nineteenth century, only in the 1830s were manufacturing techniques perfected which made plate glass widely and cheaply available. *Plated ▷parquet* has ▷inlaid pieces. A *plate-▷rail* is a narrow ▷shelf fixed to the upper part of a wall, with a groove for china plates. *Plate ▷tracery* is the earliest form of tracery, dating from the *First-▷Pointed* period, consisting of openings formed in flat stonework with no projecting mouldings: it can be likened to ▷fret-work rather than to the later more sophisticated ▷bar tracery (▷[241]).

Plateresque An ornate style of ▷architecture of Spanish origin, dating from the 1500s, incorporating ▷Gothic, *Moresque* (▷Moorish architecture), and ▷Renaissance ornament in gross profusion. Lavish architectural ornament that is quite distinct from the structure.

Platfond ▷Plafond.

Platform Timbers carrying a flat ▷roof or the roof itself. Any raised ▷dais or ▷step. Platform-boarding is that on a flat roof or dais.

Platted moulding A ▷reticulated moulding (▷mould).

Pleasance A secluded pleasure-▷garden laid out with shady walks, trees, shrubs, statuary, and ornamental water.

Plenty Associated with the ▷cornucopia, ▷symbols of fertility, and often personified as a female figure.

Plenum A system of ventilation which operates by keeping the air pressure higher than atmospheric pressure. Fresh air is introduced near the ceiling, and vitiated air is pushed out at low level close to the ▷floor. A *plenum* ▷*chamber* is one with a pressure higher than atmospheric pressure.

Plexiform Net-like or woven ▷ornament, as found in ▷Celtic and ▷Romanesque work.

Plinth Any solid ▷base. A monumental base for a statue. The base ▷courses of a building, designed to suggest a ▷platform on which the building sits. A square member forming the lower part of the base of a ▷column or ▷pilaster, or the plain ▷projecting base of a ▷wall immediately above the ground, usually ▷chamfered or moulded at the top. A *plinth* ▷*block* is the plain rectangular block at the base of an ▷architrave, ▷frame, or ▷chimney-piece which acts as a stop for the plinth, skirting (▷skirt), and architrave mouldings. A *plinth-*▷*course* is a continuous course of ▷masonry forming a plinth, or the top, chamfered course of a ▷brick plinth. A plinth is also an ▷eaves course. The plinth, or lowest member of a ▷podium, is called a ▷*quadra*. Vitruvius also calls the ▷abacus of the ▷Greek ▷Doric ▷Order *plinthus*.

Plough-and-tongue A continuous ▷mortise and ▷tenon along the edges of two ▷boards, the one with a groove and the other with a projecting ▷tongue.

Ploughshare twist The winding surface of a ▷vault between the ▷wall-▷rib and a ▷diagonal rib, which is twisted or warped like a ploughshare.

Plug A piece of timber driven into a ▷wall and sawn off so that it is ▷flush with the ▷face, used for fixings. *Plugging* is ▷dubbing out, or rough ▷rendering behind skirtings (▷skirt), or making a hole for a plug.

Plumbing The craft of casting and working ▷lead and using it in building. The term is now used to describe all pipework in a building, whether or not lead is used, as opposed to drainage, which is underground.

Plume ▷Feather.

Pluteus A ▷dwarf ▷wall or a ▷parapet, but especially a wall between the ▷columns of a ▷colonnade, usually about a third the height of the column.

Plywood Board made of an odd number of wood *veneers* (each called *ply*) glued together with the grain of each adjacent sheet at right angles to its neighbour. It is very strong and resistant to warping.

Pnyx A ▷Greek place of assembly, usually semi-circular, for orators, like the ▷Roman ▷*exedra*.

Pocket The space in the ▷pulley-stile of a ▷sash-window. A *pocket piece* is removable, enabling sash-cords to be renewed.

Podium A continuous ▷pedestal or ▷platform, such as that on which a ▷Roman ▷temple stood, usually carrying a ▷colonnade, and with mouldings (▷mould) at the top and base. A ▷*socle* or a projecting ▷base of a building. Any elevated platform.

Poecile, poekile, poikile A ▷Greek ▷*stoa* or ▷porch with the ▷walls covered with paintings.

Pointed A ▷*pointed* ▷*arch* is formed by a radius equal to the ▷span of the opening, and struck from both sides of the springing line, or any arch with a pointed head. It is characteristic of ▷Gothic ▷architecture, which is known as *First, Middle* or *Second*, and *Third Pointed* (▷[134], [241]). *Pointed* also means the rough finish of ▷masonry created by a pointed tool or pick, known as *pecking*. It also refers to the finish of ▷mortar in joints: *pointing* is such work, the material used, or the raking out of old mortar between joints and replacing it with new.

Pointel A pattern, usually in paving, of small squares arranged diagonally, or of ▷lozenge-shaped pieces.

Pole A long, slender, tapering piece of wood, circular in section. A tradesman's sign. A linear measure equivalent to 5.5 yards. A *pole-piece* is a ▷ridge-board. A *pole-*▷*plate* is fixed to the lower ends of a ▷truss to receive the ends of the ▷rafters, raising them above the ▷wall-plate.

Polis A ▷Greek city or city-state. An ▷*acropolis* is an elevated part of a Greek city containing important buildings, and fortified. A ▷*necropolis* is a city of the dead, or a ▷cemetery.

Polos A cylindrical member on the heads of ▷*caryatides*, or a ▷dowel.

Polyandrion A ▷monument to the dead of battle in Ancient Greece.

Polychromy The decoration of exteriors and interiors of buildings with several colours or tints, usually with different materials. *Structural polychrome decoration* means that the colour is not applied but is in the ▷bricks, ▷tiles, or stones used in the construction.

Polyfoil ▷Multifoil, or with many ▷foils.

Polygonal Many sided. Polygonal ▷masonry is made of stones with smooth polygonal joints between them known in ▷Antiquity as ▷*opus polygonium*. A *polygonal* ▷*apse* is the east end of a ▷church so treated, with *cants*.

Polypod With many feet. Some ▷fonts have polypod ▷bases.

Polystyle With many ▷columns.

Polytriglyphal Having more than one ▷triglyph to a single ▷intercolumniation.

Pomegranate A ▷symbol of fertility and chastity, often found in *pargetting* (▷parge work) and *carving*, and shown opened, with the seeds exposed.

Pomerium A space around a ▷Roman city wall, or a ring-road around a Roman fortress or town.

Pommel The ▷ornament on top of a ▷pinnacle, ▷finial, etc. Any globular ornament such as a ▷ball, ▷knob, ▷knot, or ▷boss.

Pompeian Pompeii was rediscovered in 1748, and when the schemes of interior decoration and details of surviving furnishings were published, the eighteenth-century concerns with authentic interpretations of ▷Antiquity made Pompeian styles a significant element in ▷Neoclassical taste. ▷Medallions, ▷grisaille figures, and delicate ▷borders, with strong colours, such as reds, blacks, yellows, and greens, became a feature of many a *Pompeian* room.

Pont-Street Dutch ▷Flemish Revival.

Pontifical altar An ▷altar set up in a central space, such as those in the ▷Roman ▷basilicas, including, of course, the great Bernini altar in St Peter's.

Poppy A common ▷Art-Nouveau ▷motif. Poppy flowers and seed-pods are found in schemes of decoration in bedrooms and ▷tombs because of their opiate powers. A *poppy-head* is the terminating feature of a carved pew-end, often in the approximate shape of the ▷fleur-de-lys, and frequently with stylized ▷foliage and figures.

Porch An exterior adjunct over a doorway, forming a covered ▷approach. If a porch has ▷columns, it is called a ▷portico, perhaps more usually if it also has a ▷pediment and resembles the front ▷elevation of an ▷Antique ▷temple. The south porches of mediaeval ▷churches were often very grand with a room over.

Poros Limestone (▷lime) coarser than ▷marble.

Porta A gateway to a ▷Roman town. A *portal* is an ▷arch over a ▷door, or the ▷frame of a ▷gate, or a small square corner in a room separated from the body of that room by ▷wainscoting. A *portal* is also an entrance-door or gate with architectural pretensions. A *portal*

[200] PORTE-COCHÈRE The Mortuary Railway Station at Regent Street, Sydney, Australia, of 1868, showing the Spiky Gothic Revival style of the *porte-cochère*. James J. Barnet, architect. (*Public Transport Commission, New South Wales*)

frame is a rigid structural frame consisting of two uprights connected at the top by a third member in such a way that it cannot move.

Portcullis A massive ▷frame or grating of iron or wood reinforced with iron and used to defend gateways. It slid up and down in a groove, and was usually kept suspended over the entrance, but was let down when danger threatened (▷yett).

Porte-cochère [200] A ▷porch big enough to admit vehicles, or a doorway large enough to allow a vehicle to pass from the street to a ▷court behind.

Portico [201] A structure forming a ▷porch in front of a building, and consisting of a roofed space open or partially enclosed at the sides, with ▷columns forming the entrance. A portico often has a ▷pediment. If the columns stand in front of the ▷face of the building, the portico is called ▷prostyle, but if the columns are recessed within the building so that they are the same plane as the front ▷wall but framed by the wall or by walls projecting from the sides, the portico is called ▷in antis because the columns are between the ▷antae of the walls. The number of columns at the front

(a)   (b)

[201] PORTICO (*a*) Roman Corinthian portico of the Congregationalist church at Saltaire, Yorkshire, designed by Lockwood and Mawson, and built 1859. (*b*) The prostyle tetrastyle Roman Doric portico at the Temple of Flora at Chatsworth, Derbyshire. Note the positions of the triglyphs at the corners, on the centre-lines of each column, and that there are two triglyphs over each intercolumniation, giving a less oppressive effect than in Greek Doric. Over the cornice is a balustrade with urns set on the pedestals. (*JSC*)

determines whether it is *tetrastyle (four) (▷tetra), ▷hexastyle* (six), ▷*octastyle* (eight), ▷*decastyle* (ten), or ▷*dodecastyle* (twelve). A projecting portico with four columns is therefore *prostyle tetrastyle*, while a recessed portico with two columns between antae would be ▷*distyle in antis*. A portico must have a ▷roof supported on at least one side by columns. A portico is a ▷colonnaded porch (▷colonnade, ▷intercolumniation, ▷[234]).

Portland *Portland* ▷*cement* is made from limestone (▷lime) and clay, and is a light grey in colour. *Portland stone* is a white limestone from Portland off the south coast of England, commonly used for public buildings after the Great Fire of London in 1666.

Portrait ▷Classical portraits in the form of heads in ▷relief, heads in ▷profile, or portrait-busts, are common features of Classical ▷architecture, and are often set in roundels. They are usually found in thematic groups, such as emperors, kings, soldiers, philosophers, musicians, poets, etc.

Post Any upright piece of timber. A *post-and-paling* ▷fence is one of posts fixed into the ground with horizontal ▷boards nailed between them. ▷Timber-framed buildings with exposed posts and with the intervals filled in with ▷plaster or ▷bricks are called *post-and-pane* work. *Post-and-*▷*beam* framing consists of horizontal members fixed to the tops of posts. *Post-and-*▷*lintel* construction is any type with uprights and horizontal beams to carry loads, also called *columnar* and *trabeated* work.

Postern A small doorway to a ▷castle, house, town, or ▷monastery, often very inconspicuous and discreet.

Postiche Added afterwards, often inappropriately, and frequently superfluous.

Posticum The ▷*epinaos, rear* ▷*porch,* ▷*opisthodomus,* or open ▷*vestibule* at the rear of the ▷*cell.* Also a back ▷door in a ▷Roman house.

Postis A ▷jamb carrying a ▷lintel.

Post-Modern A style that seems to reject the Modern Movement (▷International style), and has some ▷historicist references such as ▷pediments, ▷columns, keystones, and the like.

Pounced Decorated with ▷perforations or indentations, or the imposition of a pattern by applying a powder or a colour through a ▷stencil.

Poupée A doll's head, a ▷plaster head, or a bunch of hemp or flax used as an ▷ornament. A ▷poppy-head ▷ornament.

Powdered ▷Ornament of ▷stars, flowers, ▷crosses, etc., arranged regularly on a wall, often ▷stencilled, and associated with the ▷Gothic ▷Revival.

Poyntell ▷Pointel.

Pozzolan, pozzolona, pozzuolana A volcanic ash containing silica, alumina, ▷lime, from Pozzuoli, mixed with ▷lime and water, and producing a ▷cement-like compound. *Pozzolan cement* was commonly used in ▷Antiquity. ▷Roman. ▷Parker's cement.

Praecinctio A wide ▷passage dividing the seats of an ancient ▷theatre into two tiers.

Praetorium A residence of a Roman governor, a ▷hall of justice, or a ▷palace.

Preaching-cross A tall upright ▷cross on a ▷platform, often of three ▷steps, set up in a public place to mark where preachers would address a crowd.

Precast concrete ▷Concrete cast in ▷moulds in a factory or elsewhere before being transported to the site.

Preceptory A subsidiary manor or estate of the Knights Templars on which a ▷church and house were erected.

Predella The bottom part of an altar-piece immediately above the ▷altar, or a ▷platform on which the altar stands, or a ledge associated with the altar, or the lower ▷panels of a ▷triptych.

Prefabrication The manufacture of building components in a factory or elsewhere before transportation and erection on site.

Presbytery The part of a ▷church where the ▷altar is placed, reserved for officiating clergy. The term also means a priest's house or a ▷parsonage.

Presence-room A state-room or an audience-▷chamber in a ▷palace.

Press A ▷cupboard.

Prestressed concrete ▷Reinforced concrete, where the reinforcement is by steel cables set in ▷ducts, so that tension can be altered by tightening or loosening the cables. Prestressing induces compression of the tension area of a ▷beam *before* loading, thus making more efficient use of both steel and ▷concrete.

Prick-post A ▷queen-post, or other intermediate ▷posts in a ▷frame or ▷truss (▷[212]).

Pricket A metal spike serving as a candlestick, usually with a plate or dish to catch the wax set below.

Pricking up The first coat of ▷plaster on lathing (▷lath).

Prie-dieu A small prayer-desk.

Priest's door A ▷door at the side of a ▷chancel.

Priming The first coat for succeeding coats of paint, put on wood before ▷stopping so that the ▷undercoat will adhere.

Primitive Hut A succession of architectural theorists in France (Michel de Frémin, 1702, Jean-Louis de Cordemoy, 1706, and Marc-Antoine Laugier, 1753 and 1765) called for a return to primitive ▷Classical clarity where all superfluous ▷ornament would be eliminated, and the ▷Orders would be used functionally rather than decoratively, expressed as ▷columns with ▷entablatures, rather than as ▷engaged columns. Nature and ▷Antiquity were to be the models, and, following Vitruvius, Laugier proposed the Primitive Hut, made from four living trees with branches, as the natural origin of the Classical ▷Antique ▷temple, which should be in the forefront of the ▷architect's mind when designing new buildings. The four trees were spaced at the four corners of a perfect square, and the branches grew to form ▷gables that were equilateral triangles, a Freemasonic allusion that relates to ▷geometry and the science of ▷architecture.

Princess post A vertical ▷post in a ▷truss between a ▷queen-post and the ▷wall to give extra support.

Principal The most important member in a ▷frame. A *principal* ▷*beam* is the main beam carrying smaller beams. A *principal* ▷*brace* is one under the principal ▷rafters (▷[212]). A *principal* ▷*rafter* is the raking top member of a ▷truss carrying the ▷purlins. The *principals of a* ▷*hearse* are the ▷turrets or ▷pinnacles crowning the ▷posts and the centre of a mediaeval hearse.

Print A plaster-cast of an ▷ornament.

Priory A ▷monastery with a Prior or Prioress in charge.

Prismatic A *prismatic* ▷*billet* is a ▷Romanesque billet moulding (▷mould) in the form of a series of prisms, every other row being staggered. *Prismatic rustication* (▷rustic) is ▷masonry with pyramidal or ridge-and-hipped projections. A *prismatory* is the ▷sedilia. *Prismatic* ▷*ornament* includes ▷jewelled ▷strapwork, ▷lozenges, and ▷chamfered rustication.

Prison A building for the confining of transgressors. A ▷gaol or jail. Piranesi's imaginary prison interiors, with their vast vistas and terrifying glooms, had a powerful effect on ▷Neoclassical sensibilities, while the planning of prisons with separate ▷wings, ▷pavilions, and geometrical shapes, was a continuing development from Neoclassicism well into the present century.

Privy A *latrine* or a *necessary*. A private ▷chamber in a royal residence. A ▷presence-chamber.

Proaulion A ▷porch in front of a ▷narthex.

Pro-cathedral A ▷church used as a ▷cathedral on a temporary basis.

Procession path The ▷aisle or ▷passage behind the ▷high altar and ▷reredos in ▷cathedrals and conventual ▷churches, also known as an ▷ambulatory. A *processional way* is a monumental and formal ▷avenue for processions.

Prodomus A ▷portico standing before the ▷*naos* or ▷*cella*, also called a ▷*pronaos*. A ▷lobby in front of a house.

Profile The vertical section of anything, especially a moulding (▷mould).

Progressive ornament Continuous ▷bands of ▷guilloche or similar ornament.

Projections [202] Any parts of a structure or parts of fabric that ▷jetty out, are ▷cantilevered, or project. *Architectural projections* are drawn representations to show and explain the design, with an illusion of three dimensions.

Promenade A place for walking for pleasure or relaxation.

Pronaos The ▷portico and ▷vestibule flanked by ▷walls behind the portico in an ▷Antique ▷temple. It is partly enclosed by walls and partly by ▷columns.

Prop A support.

Proper An ▷heraldic term meaning natural colouring.

Proportion The just magnitude of each part, and of each part to another; the relationship existing between parts or elements rendering the whole harmonious in terms of balance, ▷symmetry, and repose.

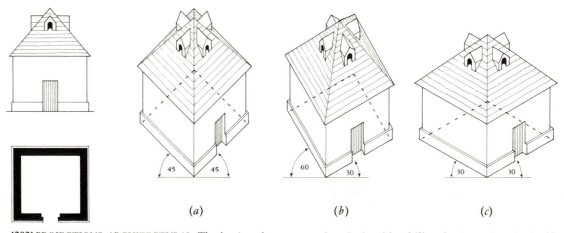

(a)   (b)   (c)

[202] PROJECTIONS, ARCHITECTURAL The drawings show axonometric projections (*a*) and (*b*), and an isometric projection (*c*), to explain the form of the building. These are projections from the elevation and plan shown on the left. (*JJS*)

[203] PROPYLAEUM The entrance-gateway and lodges at the General Cemetery of All Souls, Kensal Green, by John Griffith of Finsbury, 1834. An essay in the Greek Doric style, with an arcuated opening. Note the Attic. (*JSC*)

Propylaeum [203]   Any ▷court or ▷vestibule before a building, but more usually a formal entrance-gateway of a monumental character to such a court or enclosure.

Propylon   A monumental ▷battered gateway standing before the ▷pylons of an Ancient ▷Egyptian ▷temple.

Proscenium   The ▷stage of a ▷theatre, or the area between the curtain and the ▷pit including the ▷arch and ▷frame facing the audience. In an ▷Antique theatre the *proskenion* was a stone structure, consisting of a row of ▷columns standing on a low ▷stylobate in front of the *skene* (▷scaena) ▷wall. The ▷roof of the proskenion seems to have been the ▷platform on which the actors moved at a later stage, but originally it seems only to have been a background.

Prostas   A recessed space or ▷vestibule in a ▷Greek house, open on one side: the same as ▷*pastas*. It is also the same as *prostasis*, meaning the ▷*pronaos*, or the part of the front of the ▷temple ▷*in antis* lying between the ▷*antae.*

Prostyle   With ▷columns standing before the ▷front of the building in a line (▷[234a, c, d]).

Prothesis   A ▷chapel beside the ▷sanctuary on the north side of the ▷bema in a ▷basilican ▷church. It is also the place where the ▷Sacraments are prepared and stored.

Prothyris   A cross-▷beam.

Prothyron   The ▷porch of a ▷Greek house open to the street outside the front ▷door.

Proto   A term meaning early or primitive or first. *Proto-*▷*Doric* was a primitive Doric, and *proto-*▷*Romanesque* refers to the regional transitional styles between the fall of the ▷Roman Empire in the West and the emergence of true Romanesque, so includes ▷Carolingian, ▷Lombardic, and ▷Ottonian ▷architecture.

Protoma   A ▷projecting half-figure. *Protomai* are found on ▷capitals projecting from the ▷angles, commonly found in ▷Romanesque work.

Proudwork   Like ▷flush-work, but with the ▷freestone in greater ▷relief than the ▷flint, i.e. standing in front of the flint. It is found in ▷Tudor work.

Prow   ▷Projecting prows of ships occur as keystones, and on various parts of buildings, but are more especially associated with the ▷rostral ▷column, with ▷marine decoration, and with commerce and shipping.

Prytaneum   The headquarters of the administration of a ▷Greek city, usually containing the Perpetual Fire.

Pseudoisodomic   ▷Antique ▷masonry with low and high ▷courses alternating, sometimes with more high than low (bonding) courses.

Pseudodipteral   A building arranged to appear to be ▷dipteral (i.e. with two rows of ▷columns along the flanks), but where the inner rows are omitted, although

253

the ▷portico would suggest otherwise. The result is a very wide ▷passage around the ▷cell of the ▷temple between it and the ▷peristyle (▷[234g]).

Pseudoperipteral A ▷Classical ▷temple with ▷engaged ▷columns all the way round, or on the back and sides (▷[234h]).

Pseudoprostyle A ▷prostyle arrangement without a ▷*pronaos*, with the ▷columns placed less than an ▷intercolumniation from the ▷wall behind, or ▷engaged with that wall.

Pseudothyrum A false ▷door. Also a secret door.

Ptera The ▷colonnade around the ▷naos of a ▷Greek ▷temple.

Pteroma An ▷ambulatory or space between the ▷*cell* of a ▷temple and the ▷columns of the ▷peristyle.

Pteron An external ▷colonnade of a ▷Greek building, i.e. a ▷peripteral colonnade. A flanking colonnade.

Puddling Filling behind a ▷wall, or filling of a cavity.

Pugging A coarse ▷mortar or layer of sand on rough boarding placed between ▷joists to aid sound ▷insulation.

Pulley-stile One of the vertical side-pieces of a ▷window ▷sash-▷frame in which the pulleys and counterweights are housed.

Pulpit [204] An elevated ▷stage or desk from which sermons are delivered in ▷churches or other ecclesiastical buildings. Pulpits are of wood or stone, with some modern examples of ▷concrete or metal. They are often elaborately carved and occasionally have sounding-boards or ▷testers above to act as ▷canopies. A *three-decker pulpit* is a three-▷storeyed

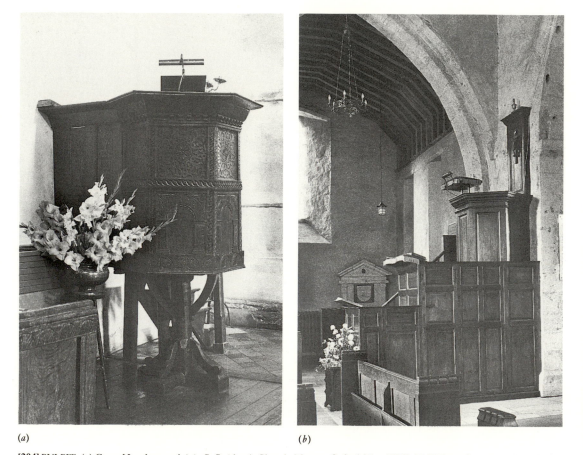

(a)   (b)

[204] PULPIT (*a*) Carved Jacobean pulpit in St Swithun's Church, Merton, Oxfordshire. (*JSC*) (*b*) Eighteenth-century three-decker pulpit in the Church of St Winfred, Branscombe, Devon. (*JSC*)

pulpit consisting of the desk for the clerk, the reading-desk, and the pulpit proper, one above the other. Pulpits should be on the north side of the ▷nave.

Pulpitum A stone ▷screen between the ▷nave and ▷choir. Also part of the stage next to the ▷orchestra in an ▷Antique ▷theatre.

Pulvin, pulvinata, pulvinus A pillow or ▷cushion, as on the sides of the ▷volutes of the ▷capital of the ▷Ionic ▷Order. Also the ▷dosseret above a capital and below an ▷arch in ▷Byzantine, ▷architecture. *Pulvinated* means with a convex ▷profile, especially a ▷frieze, looking as though it is subjected to pressure from above (▷aedicule).

Pumpkin A ▷melon-dome.

Punched, puncheoned A stone ▷face brought flat with a blunt pick, or ▷broached with broad diagonal parallel lines and with a pointed chisel.

Puncheon A short upright piece in ▷framing, or a ▷stud.

Purbeck marble A species of dark stone from the Isle of Purbeck in Dorset, very hard and capable of taking a high polish. It was widely used in ▷Gothic ▷architecture, especially in the thirteenth century, for ▷shafts or ▷colonnettes. The dark, shiny, slim shafts against the lighter limestone (▷lime) ▷walls gave a sharp effect, and ▷compound ▷piers were often surrounded with shafts of Purbeck marble, a material also widely used for ▷effigies, ▷tombs, and ▷slabs.

Purfled ▷Ornamental work in stone or other material resembling embroidery or drapery, particularly associated with Gothick (▷Gothic).

Purlin A horizontal piece of structural timber lying on the ▷principal ▷rafters of a ▷roof ▷truss to give intermediate bearing to the ▷common rafters. Purlins often span from ▷party wall to party wall in ▷terrace houses. They are also called ▷*ribs* or ▷*bridgings*, *side-wavers*, or *side-timbers* (▷roof).

Puteal A structure around a ▷well to protect the mouth. A *puteus* was an opening or ▷manhole in an ▷aqueduct, a well, or a ▷fountain.

Putlog hole A small hole left in ▷walls for the erection of ▷scaffolding, also known as a ▷*staykfald* hole. Cross-pieces of timber scaffolding are called *putlogs*. In ▷Roman work putlog-holes resembled ▷dove-holes, so Vitruvius called them ▷*columbaria*.

[205] PUTTO The monument of Humphrey Smith, designed by John Sanderson and carved by Charles Stanley, *c.* 1743, in Ely. Note the bust with asymmetrical foliage against the obelisk behind. (*JSC*)

Putto [205] A small boy or chubby male baby, often found in ▷Classical and ▷Baroque ▷sculpture, especially funerary ▷monuments. *Putti* are usually un-winged, and are found in attitudes of overt displays of grief, shedding tears, and clutching inverted ▷torches. *Putti* have a knowing air, are given to obesity, and possess a sense of retarded physical development, rendering them somewhat unwholesome.

Putty A paste of ▷whiting and linseed oil, with either white lead or ▷lamp-black added, used for fixing ▷glass in ▷frames.

Pycnostyle ▷Colonnade, ▷intercolumniation .

Pylon [206] The massive ▷battered buildings on either side of the entrance to an ▷Egyptian ▷temple. A *pylon-form* is therefore anything resembling these, with

255

battered sides crowned by a large ▷cavetto ▷cornice, and usually framed with a ▷torus moulding. Pylon-shaped ▷chimney-pots are very common. Pylon forms were used as the supports for suspension ▷bridges, and the battered section was used for ▷basements, ▷dams, and ▷retaining walls.

Pynum The coping-stones (▷cope) of a gable.

Pyramid A solid standing on a square base with four steeply ▷battered triangular sides meeting at an ▷apex, used as ▷mausolea in Ancient Egypt. Stepped pyramids occurred in both ▷Egyptian and Central American pre-Columbian ▷architecture. There were several pyramids in Ancient Rome, and the form was revived in ▷Neoclassical architecture. Pyramids were often confused with ▷obelisks, and fat obelisks with pyramids, but the two forms are quite distinct although obelisks have small flattened pyramids or *pyramidions* on top of their gently battered shafts. A *pyramidion* is therefore a small pyramid or the tip of an obelisk. A *pyramidal hipped* ▷*roof* (▷hip) is a *pavilion roof* (▷pavilion). *Pyramidal rustication* (▷rustic) is ▷*diamond-pointed rustication*.

Pyriform As ▷periform.

Pyx, pyxis ▷Pix.

[206] PYLON Isambard Kingdom Brunel's design for Clifton Suspension Bridge, near Bristol, of 1831. Note the pylon-piers, with winged globes, cavetto cornices, and sphinxes. The cables are anchored in massive sarcophagus-like blocks. The pylon form was ideal for the piers of suspension bridges, and the profile lent itself to retaining walls, dams, etc. (*City of Bristol Museum and Art Gallery*)

Q

Quadra A square ▷border or ▷frame around a ▷panel. The ▷fillets of the ▷Ionic ▷base on either side of the ▷scotia. The ▷plinth or lowest member of a ▷podium. Any small square-sectioned moulding (▷mould).

Quadrangle A figure with four angles and four sides. Any square or rectangular ▷court surrounded by buildings, a usual feature of monastic establishments and therefore of ▷colleges: those in Oxford are called *Quads*, and those in Cambridge *Courts*.

Quadratum ▷*Opus quadratum* was ▷ashlar.

Quadratura ▷*Trompe l'oeil* ▷perspective paintings of ▷architecture, often continuing the real architectural scheme, found on ▷Baroque ceilings and ▷walls.

Quadrel A square artificial stone of white material. Any square ▷tile, ▷quarrel, or quarry.

Quadrifores ▷Folding ▷doors with the ▷leaves hinged, usually with the height divided in two.

Quadrifrons Four ▷faces joined at the backs and gazing in four directions. A *tetrapylon* (▷tetra).

Quadriga A sculpture group consisting of a chariot and driver pulled by four heroic horses, usually found in ▷monuments, ▷triumphal arches, etc.

Quadripartite Divided into four compartments, as in ▷vaulting.

Quadriporticus An ▷atrium, square on plan, off which are ▷porticoes.

Quadrivium A place where four streets intersect.

Quaint A style of debased and popular ▷Art Nouveau.

Quarrel, quarry A square or ▷lozenge-shaped piece of ▷glass used in ▷leaded ▷casement ▷windows. A small square or diamond-shaped ▷floor ▷tile, or a similarly shaped opening in ▷Gothic ▷tracery. *Quarry-faced* is ▷masonry looking as though it is left rough from the quarry, so it is a type of *rustication* (▷rustic).

Quarter grain Timber grain achieved by the cutting of pieces at right-angles to the growth rings (▷felt grain).

Quarter pace A *quarter-space* ▷landing, often square on plan, between two ▷flights making a 90° turn.

Quarter round The same as ▷ovolo or ▷echinus: a moulding (▷mould) the ▷section of which is the quadrant of a circle.

Quarters The ▷posts in ▷partitions, also called ▷uprights and ▷studs. All *quartering* under five square inches in section is called ▷scantling. *Quarter* is also an obsolete term for ▷quatrefoil.

Quasi-reticulate A type of facing of ▷Roman ▷concrete formed of small regular facing-blocks set point-inwards and giving a vaguely net-like appearance.

Quatrefoil A form disposed in four arcs, with ▷cusps, in the shape of a flower with four ▷leaves. ▷Bands of quatrefoils were much used as ▷ornaments during the ▷Perpendicular period of ▷Gothic. When placed diagonally, quatrefoils are called ▷*cross-quarters*. The old term for a quatrefoil was a ▷*quarter* (▷[241a]).

Quattrocento ▷Italian ▷Renaissance art and ▷architecture of the fifteenth century.

Quay A built bank with slightly ▷battered or straight sides formed on the side of the sea or a river to enable boats to unload.

Queen A size of ▷slate 36 × 24 inches.

Queen Anne [207] A style of domestic ▷architecture evolved from the 1860s in which tall ▷sash-▷windows with ▷brick rubbers (▷rubbed) derived from late seventeenth- and early eighteenth-century brick houses of the ▷William and Mary and Queen Anne periods were used in free compositions incorporating ▷vernacular features such as ▷tile-hanging. There was also a strong ▷Dutch influence in the style. A *Queen Anne* ▷*arch* is an arch of brick rubbers over a window of the ▷Venetian or ▷Palladian type, that is with two flats on either side of a semicircular central arch.

Queen-closer A ▷brick cut in half lengthways, and used to keep the ▷bond.

Queen-post One of two ▷prick-posts or ▷side-posts placed symmetrically on a ▷tie-▷beam and forming a ▷truss with the ▷principal ▷rafters over (▷[212b]). The

upper ends of the vertical posts are connected by a ▷straining-piece across the tops.

Quetta bond A ▷bond like *rat-trap bond* with the ▷bricks laid on ▷bed rather than ▷edge, and the cavities filled with ▷grout and reinforced with steel rods. The facing bond is of the Flemish type. It is reinforced brickwork.

Quicklime ▷Lime ready for the addition of water, i.e. burned but not slaked. It is actually calcium oxide.

Quincunx An arrangement of five elements so that four are symmetrically positioned around the central object. It is often found in planting schemes.

Quire ▷Choir.

Quirk A piece taken out of the corner of a room; a re-entering ▷angle. A *quirk moulding* (▷mould) has a sharp return from its extreme projection to the re-entrant angle in a V-shape; it is an acute-angled ▷channel by which the convex parts of ▷Greek mouldings are separated from the ▷fillets. Quirks or V-shaped incisions are common in ▷Gothic work. A *quirk* is essentially a channel separating one moulding from another. A *quirk-*▷*bead* is a bead with a quirk on one

(a)   (b)

[207] QUEEN ANNE STYLE (*a*) Kinmel Park, Denbighshire, begun 1868 to designs by Eden Nesfield. It is a mixture of Queen Anne with Dutch and French Renaissance features. (*RCAHMW 860741 by kind permission of Sir John Cotterell Bt*) (*b*) 170 Queen's Gate, Kensington, by R. N. Shaw, of 1888–89. Note the mixing of eighteenth-century domestic features such as the eaves cornice, steeply pitched roof, segmental pedimented dormers, tall sash-windows, carved door-case, and brick walls with stone dressings. The Queen Anne elements and the proportions look forward to a Neocolonial Georgian manner. (*JSC*)

side as the ▷frame at the edge of a ▷panel. It is also a recessed bead ▷flush with the adjoining surfaces and separated from them by a quirk on each side, also called a *flush-bead*. A *return bead* is one at a corner with quirks on either side separating the bead from the two surfaces at right-angles to each other. A *quirked moulding* is any moulding with an abrupt return from its extreme projection, making it more defined by the quirk.

Quiver An ▷attribute of Cupid, but also found in military ▷trophies.

Quodlibet A ▷*trompe l'oeil* type of decoration featuring playing-cards, dishes, letters, scissors, and string, distributed in an apparently random fashion.

Quoin Also or *coin* or *coyn*. The external ▷angle of a building. The ▷dressed alternate header (▷head) and ▷stretcher stones at the corners of buildings, which, if raised from the surface with ▷channels between them, are called ▷*rustic quoins*, and reinforce the external corners. A *quoin header* is a header on one face and a stretcher on the other. ▷Saxon quoins are often of tall pieces secured by large stones laid horizontally, known as ▷*long-and-short* work. *Quoining* is any architectural element forming a quoin. A *quoin-*▷*post* is one to receive the ▷hinges of a ▷gate.

R

Rab-and-dab ▷Wattle-and-▷daub or ▷rad-and-dab.

Rabbet A rebate (▷rabbet) or groove, or a long ▷channel cut in one member to receive another member. A ▷window-opening with a rebate can receive the ▷frame, concealing most of the ▷sash-▷box outside, thus ensuring a watertight fit.

Race-bond A vertical joint in ▷ashlar.

Rack A case over a ▷manger where hay is placed. Any similar high-level structure of ▷bars.

Racking back The method of building a ▷brick ▷wall involves erecting the corners plumb, with brickwork stepping down to the centre of the length of wall. The graded, stepped part is called *racking back*.

Rad ▷Rab. It is mixture of clay and straw filled in between ▷laths of split ▷oak or hazel.

Radial brick A ▷voussoir.

Radial step A ▷winder.

Radiating chapels ▷Chapels projecting radially from the apsidal ▷ambulatory at the east end of a large ▷church.

Raffle leaf A ▷leaf in ornamental ▷foliage with small indentations at its edges, e.g. an ▷acanthus leaf, but treated in an asymmetrical free-flowing manner, often as S- or C-▷scrolls, and therefore an important part of ▷Rococo decoration.

Rafter An inclined timber forming the sides of a ▷roof, and meeting another rafter at the ▷ridge. A *rafter-▷plate* is the timber fixed to the bottom of rafters and supporting them.

Rag A piece of hard, coarse, rough stone, breaking up in flat thick pieces. ▷*Kentish rag* is a hard, siliceous limestone (▷lime) that is tough, but easily split, used in *close-picked* or *rough-picked* walling. *Ragwork* is generally backed with brick, and the ▷masonry is *hammer-pitched* to an irregular ▷polygonal shape and bedded in position to show the face-joints running net-like in all directions, also known as *polygonal ragwork*. A *rag ▷bolt* is one with barbs to prevent its withdrawal. *Rag ▷rubble* is rubble of small, rough stones.

Ragged end A roughened end.

Ragged staff An ▷heraldic ▷motif featuring a tree with lopped branches, leaving stumps.

Raggle Also *raglet*, it is a ▷chase or chasing for any purpose. *Raggled* means *housed* or *chased* (▷housing).

Raglet A thin groove, ▷dovetailed in stone, or in the ▷mortar-joints of brickwork, to receive ▷lead ▷flashing.

Raglin A ceiling-▷joist.

Raguly With notched or ragged edges, as though they were hacked.

Rail A horizontal piece of timber between the ▷panels of a ▷door, or ▷wainscoting, etc. Uprights are called ▷*stiles* (▷[104]). A *rail-▷bead* projects from a plane, and is not in an ▷angle or ▷reveal. A *rail-▷fence* is one in which rails are let into upright ▷posts and ▷butt against the ends of the next rail to form continuous horizontals.

Rain conductor A rainwater ▷pipe or downspout. A *rainwater head* is a box-shaped structure of cast iron or ▷lead into which rainwater is discharged from a gutter in order to convey it to the pipe below.

Rainbow roof A pitched ▷roof the slopes on each side being convex. Also called a *whaleback roof.*

Raised moulding A ▷bolection moulding (▷mould). A *raised* ▷*panel* is one with its centre higher than its edges, which are said to be ▷fielded.

Raising piece A timber, set under a ▷beam and over the ▷posts or ▷puncheons in ▷timber-framed work, carrying out the same function as a ▷wall ▷plate. Also called a *wall-plate.* A *raising-plate* supports the ▷heels of ▷rafters.

Rake The slope of a ▷roof. A *raked moulding* (▷mould) is one at an ▷angle. *Raking* means inclined. A *raking* ▷*arch* is a ▷rampant arch. A *raking coping* (▷cope) is one on an inclined surface, such as a ▷gable. A *raking* ▷*cornice* is one on the slope of a ▷pediment. A *raking* ▷*course* is one laid diagonally between two ▷faces of a ▷brick ▷wall in order to stiffen it. A *raking moulding* is one at a slant or angle such as on a pediment. *Raking cutting* is cutting not at right angles. Raking ▷flashing is let into a cut or ▷raglet parallel to a roof-slope, when *stepped flashings* would not be possible, as on an ▷ashlar ▷chimney. *Raking out* is cleaning out mortar joints before repointing. A *raking* ▷*riser* is one which is not vertical, so creating a deeper ▷tread than if the riser were set straight. A *raking* ▷*shore* is a long baulk erected to provide temporary support to a wall which is unstable, and is carried on a wooden ▷sole-▷plate at ground level.

Ram Often occurring in ▷Bacchic ornament, and as a feature of ▷friezes, in skull-form, as an alternative to the ▷*aegicrane* or ▷*bucranium.* On ▷furniture it will be associated with legs and ▷hoof-like feet. A *ram* is also a ship's beak for striking (and holding) an enemy ship. In addition, it is an ▷hydraulic ram, a device whereby the pressure-head of a moving column of water brought to rest is responsible for delivering some of the water under pressure. Also the business-end of a ▷pile-driver. ▷Column.

Rammed earth A construction of ▷wall using compacted rammed earth between ▷shuttering. With additions of ▷cement it is called ▷*pisé de terre.* Walls thus constructed must be protected at the top and at the bottom: in Hampshire, ▷thatch is often used, while ▷tile ▷roofs are often used elsewhere, and ▷plinth ▷courses of ▷brick and stone are commonly employed.

Ramp A slope to join two levels. Part of a handrail that rises more steeply at a ▷landing, or where there are ▷winders, with a concave ▷back. ▷Knee.

Rampant arch ▷Arch. A *rampant* ▷*vault* is similar, but extended as a vault.

Rampart A continuous stone or earth mound or ▷wall around a fortress or defended city, surmounted by a parapet.

Rance A ▷shore or ▷prop. *Rancing* is therefore *shoring.*

Rand A ▷border, ▷fillet, margin, or strip.

Random ashlar ▷Masonry laid without horizontal courses, also called *random* ▷*bond* or *random range.* A *random* ▷*course* is one of several horizontal masonry courses of different heights. *Random work* is stone laid in a random fashion not in regular courses.

Random tooling Also called ▷*droving*, it is the hewing of the surface of the stone by advancing a wide chisel over the face at an eighth of an inch a stroke, leaving a series of regular indentations.

Range A row or a ▷course of stone, or a row of objects in a line, as in a ▷colonnade. *Ranged* ▷*rubble* is ▷coursed rubble-work, and *ranged* ▷*masonry* is coursed ▷ashlar or *rangework.*

Raphaelesque A ▷Grotesque, because Raphael was one of the first to revive the ▷Roman Grotesque form of ▷ornament, based on ▷grotto decorations.

Ratchement A kind of flying ▷buttress springing from a corner ▷principal to meet another, forming a ▷ridged top as on a ▷hearse.

Ravelin An outwork or ▷salient constructed beyond a main ditch.

Rayonnant A type of ▷Gothic ▷architecture where ▷mullions and ▷transomes appear as rays bursting forth: a phase of Continental Middle-▷Pointed (*c.*1270–*c.*1370).

Rear arch ▷Arch. A *rear* ▷*vault* is the small vault between the ▷glass of a ▷window and the inner face of a ▷wall where the wall is thick and splayed in ▷Gothic work: it usually springs from the ▷jambs, or from ▷corbels or ▷shafts fixed against the inner edges of the jambs. These shafts are termed ▷*escoinson* shafts.

Rebate ▷Rabbet.

Rebus A non-▷heraldic badge, often suggesting the name of a person, as a falcon-head for the Falconieri, or a cock for Alcock.

Recessed arch An ▷arch set within another of the same form, but with a smaller radius. A *recessed ▷bead* is associated with a ▷quirk, and is flush with the surface.

Rectilinear Style Another term for late-▷Perpendicular ▷architecture.

Rectory The residence of a rector (the incumbent of a parish who had the right to the greater tithes of corn and wood, as well as to the lesser tithes and to the freehold of the rectory).

Redan A small ▷*ravelin* or outwork.

Redoubt An outwork separated from the main fortress.

Reed, reeding A convex moulding (▷mould), often found with several others to decorate something, such as the ▷Asiatic base of the ▷Ionic ▷Order, or some types of ▷column, so a collection of such ▷beads looks like reeds laid parallel. *Reeding* is therefore the opposite of *fluting* (▷flute). A water-plant, *Phragmites*, the tall stems of which are used for ▷thatching.

Reel ▷Bead.

Refectory The dining-hall of a ▷college, ▷convent, etc.

Régence A phase of ▷Rococo during the minority of King Louis xv in the period 1715–23.

Regency English ▷architecture during the incapacity of King George iii (1810–20). It was predominantly ▷Neoclassical, with a strong input of ▷Empire. and included Egyptianizing and ▷Oriental ▷motifs. It continued during the reign of George iv (1820–30).

Register A *damper* to alter a draught in a ▷chimney, or an outlet into a room from a ▷duct, with a damper to control the warm air. A *register-▷stove* feeds such ducts.

Reglet A flat narrow moulding (▷mould) or a ▷fillet, such as that used to cover a joint between ▷boards, also called *riglet*. The moulding of a ▷fret.

Regrating Taking off, or *skinning*, the surface of old stone to make it look fresh. It is not good practice.

Regular ▷Coursed, as in ▷rubble or ▷ashlar.

Regulus The ▷band below the ▷taenia and above the ▷guttae of a ▷Doric ▷entablature set beneath the ▷triglyphs (see the figures associated with the Doric Order).

Reignier Ornamental ▷inlaid patterns like *Boulle*-work (▷buhl).

Reind A *rind* or ▷fillet.

Reinforced concrete ▷Concrete is strong in compression and weak in tension. Steel is strong in tension. In order to strengthen concrete, steel rods are cast in where tensile strength is needed. Thus ▷beams, ▷columns, etc, may be constructed to form structural frameworks. Reinforced concrete can be readily moulded to form curved shapes which derive their strength from shape rather than mass: this attribute has been exploited to produce graceful ▷shell-roofs and ▷bridges.

Reins of a vault The ▷sides or ▷walls that carry the ▷vault.

Relief The ▷projection of any ▷sculpture or ▷ornament, known as *rilievo*. *▷Alto rilievo* stands out well from the ground; *mezzo rilievo* projects half the figures; and *basso rilievo* projects the figures less than half their true proportions. *Rilievo* is the elevation or projection of designs above the ground. To *relieve* is to lighten a colour. *Relieved work* is ornament in relief. For *relieving arch*, ▷arch. A *relieving triangle* is a triangular space over ▷lintels formed by a ▷corbelled convergence of the ▷blocks of the ▷wall.

Reliquary A casket to contain relics, made of wood, iron, stone, or costly metals, and often ▷embellished.

Renaissance Meaning literally 'rebirth', it suggests a rediscovery of the ▷architecture of Ancient Rome. In architecture it is generally held to begin with the works of Brunelleschi in Florence. Art and architecture based on ▷Italian prototypes from the early fifteenth century which dominated Europe from the middle of the sixteenth century. It evolved into ▷Mannerist and ▷Baroque phases, and then into ▷Neoclassicism with a growing interest in ▷Antiquity as the prime source rather than Italian precedents of the fifteenth and sixteenth centuries. In England, the first Renaissance work in architectural terms is found in the tomb of Henry vii by Torrigiano of Florence in Westminster Abbey. The ▷oak ▷screen of 1533–36 at King's College Chapel, Cambridge, is another early Renaissance work, while the very fine ▷stained-glass ▷windows in the same ▷chapel (1515–31) have much Renaissance architectural treatment, and are predominantly Flemish in style. English Renaissance work, therefore, was chiefly influenced by north European and French styles as well as by a survival of ▷Perpendicular ▷Gothic: the result is a curious mixture, as at Longleat, Burghley, Wollaton, and Hardwick, in which ▷mullioned and ▷transomed windows are found with the ▷Orders, ▷strapwork, etc. Isolation from the Continent after the break with Rome ensured that architecture remained peculiarly provincial, with ▷ornament and the Orders taken from ▷pattern-books. Not until Inigo Jones introduced ▷Palladian ▷Classicism at the Banqueting House, Whitehall, and the Queen's House, Greenwich, did true Italian Renaissance architecture become established, setting standards of taste for the eighteenth century to follow later. After the Civil War and the Restoration the dominant styles were a Baroque heavily influenced by French precedents, with quite a strong Netherlandish flavour in domestic architecture and in ▷brick buildings, but with the Hanoverian succession of 1714 the Palladian Revival began in earnest, although Baroque tendencies remained for some time. There was a Renaissance Revival during the nineteenth century, as a reaction in taste after the severe austerities of Neoclassicism and especially of the ▷Greek Revival.

Rendering The finishing of a surface with ▷stucco, ▷plaster, or some other finish, such as pebbledash (▷pebble). The term is also used to describe a finished drawing of a scheme, with shadow-▷projections, colour-washes, and the like. A *rendu* is an architectural drawing or rendering to solve a design problem.

Repagula Fastenings of a ▷Roman ▷door, also called *claustra* or *obices*.

Repeating ornament Any ▷ornament that can be used over an extended surface, such as ▷diaper-work or ▷chequer-board patterns.

Replum A ▷trim on one leaf of a double ▷door (against which the other leaf stops) and which conceals the ▷*commissure*. Also, erroneously, a door-▷panel.

Repoussé Raised in metal by beating on the rear side to raise the pattern in ▷relief.

Reprise The ▷return of a moulding (▷mould) in an inner ▷angle, or a seat on ▷sills for a ▷jamb or ▷mullion.

Rere arch A ▷rear ▷arch.

Reredorter A ▷privy or latrine at the back of a ▷dormitory in a ▷monastery.

Reredos [208] The ▷wall or ▷screen at the back of an ▷altar, usually much ▷ornamented with ▷niches, statues, ▷pinnacles, and the like, or having a painting, often in the form of a ▷triptych.

Reredosse An open fireplace or ▷hearth under a ▷louvred opening.

Reservoir Any artificial pond or ▷cistern for the collection of water.

[208] REREDOS Reredos in the chapel of St Catherine (north transept) of the Church of St Cuthbert, Wells. A much mutilated, but very beautiful reredos with two tiers of five niches. ▷[149]. (*JSC*)

Resonator ▷Acoustic jar.

Respond A half-▷pier attached to a ▷wall to support an ▷arch, etc., usually at the end of an ▷arcade. It may be in the form of a ▷corbel or a ▷pilaster fixed to a wall (▷[20]).

Ressant, ressault, ressaut The recess or ▷projection of a member from or before another. An ▷ogee. A ▷roll moulding (▷mould) or other ▷profiled moulding.

Rest A padstone (▷pad).

Restoration The means by which a buidling is returned, as near as can be managed, to its original design and condition, or the building itself. Restoration may be necessary in cases of severe damage, but it always involves replication. *Restoration styles* are those in Britain from the restoration of the monarchy in 1660 until the Glorious Revolution of 1688. The dominant architectural styles of the period are ▷Baroque, with plenty of ▷spiral columns, scrolled ▷pediments, and heavily moulded decoration. French and Netherlandish ▷Classical ▷architecture were the dominant influences, rather than precedents from Italy.

Retable A ▷shelf behind an ▷altar, or a carved altarpiece behind the altar and below the ▷reredos. The term is sometimes given to the ▷frame around a reredos.

Retaining wall A ▷wall built to retain a bank of earth: it is often ▷battered, and sometimes battered and arched (▷arch) with concave arched walls behind the openings to resist the thrust of the earth behind. A ▷revetment.

Reticulated Constructed like the meshes of a net. *Reticulated* ▷*masonry*, or ▷*opus reticulatum*, is constructed with diamond-shaped stones, or with square stones set diagonally. A *reticulated pattern* is a repeated ▷lozenge pattern. *Reticulated* ▷*tracery* is *Second-▷Pointed* work made up of interlocking ▷ogees forming a net-like framework (▷[241e]). A *fenestra reticulata* means a ▷window fitted with a ▷lattice of members crossing each other in net-like form.

Retrochoir The ▷chapels and other parts of a ▷church behind and about the ▷high altar. The term is sometimes given to the part of the church behind (to the east of) the high altar, but in front of (to the west of) the ▷Lady chapel and other chapels to the east.

Return The continuation of a moulding (▷mould) or a ▷projection in an opposite or different direction (usually 90°), e.g. the ▷terminations of the ▷dripstones or ▷hood moulds of a ▷window or ▷door, or the seats and desks set against the ▷screen at the west end of the ▷choir. So the terms *return-▷bead, returned end, returned moulding,* and *returned* ▷*stalls* all refer to beads or stalls similar to those in one direction, continued at an angle of 90°.

Revalé A stone moulding (▷mould) carved *in situ*.

Reveal The ▷side of an opening in a ▷wall between the framework and the outer ▷face of the wall. If cut diagonally or at an ▷angle it is called a *splayed reveal* or simply a ▷*splay*. A *reveal* ▷*lining* is any finish in a reveal or *revel*.

Reversed zigzag A jagged Z-shaped ▷chevron of one diagonal, another in the opposite direction, and a third parallel to the first, repeated on a moulding.

Revestry A ▷vestry.

Revetment ▷Retaining wall. Also any facing (▷face) of stone on a construction not intended to be seen.

Revival Any use of an earlier style, based on scholarly and archaeological investigation, such as the ▷Egyptian, ▷Gothic, or ▷Greek Revival.

Revolving door A ▷door of four ▷leaves at right-angles to each other pivoted on a central ▷post and set in a cylinder, usually glazed. It is a type of air-lock.

Revolutionary ornament Pikes, ▷*fasces*, ▷wreaths, the All-Seeing ▷Eye, equilateral triangles, the ▷square and the level, open books, cocks, cockades, and ▷cap of ▷liberty, all associated with the French and American Revolutions.

Rez-de-chaussée The ground ▷floor.

Rhone A half-round ▷gutter, or an ▷eaves-gutter.

Rib A ▷projecting ▷band on a ceiling or a ▷vault, often ▷ornamental, but structural as well. ▷Gothic ribs are ▷enriched with complex mouldings (▷mould) and have carved ▷bosses at their ▷intersections (▷vault). A *ribbed* ▷*arch* is one made up of several ribs. *Ribbed fluting* (▷flute) is fluting alternating with ▷fillets, but the term is usually given to *cabled* (▷cable) *fluting*. A *ribbed vault* is one with ribs separating the ▷panels or ▷webs. *Ribbing* is any arrangement of ribs, or the structural skeleton of anything.

Riband Any ▷ribbon-like strip.

Ribbon A ▷riband. A ▷lead ▷came in ▷stained-glass work. Ribbons are often associated with other ▷ornament, such as ▷wreaths, ▷festoons, ▷trophies, and ▷Rococo decorations. A *ribbon moulding* (▷mould) is one with a continuous ribbon-like ornament, often shown loosely entwined around a ▷stick (*ribbon-and-stick*), with reeding (▷reed), with ▷knots or ▷labels, or with rosettes (▷rose). Ribbons were often found in ▷entablatures or in ▷panelling.

Riddell A curtain around an ▷altar hung from rods suspended from *riddell-▷posts*: the latter are usually polygonal on plan, capped by angels, and there are usually four to carry the curtains around the back and sides. These posts seem to have been common in East Anglia, were widely used in the fifteenth and early sixteenth centuries, and were discarded after the Reformation. Their use was revived in the latter half of the nineteenth century, and especially through the influence of Sir Ninian Comper in the twentieth century. Also *ridel* or *riddle*.

Ridge The upper ▷angle of a ▷roof, or the internal angle of a pointed ▷vault. The term is also given to the timber against which the upper ends of the ▷rafters pitch, also called the *ridge-piece*. A *ridge-▷pole* or *ridge-▷batten* is a *ridge-▷roll* or wooden roll to take a ▷lead *ridge-cover*, but the term *ridge-▷pole* is also given to the *ridge-▷board*, *ridge-piece*, or *ridge-▷plate*. A *ridge-roll*, as well as being the wooden roll, is also the metal covering itself, or even a half-round ▷tile ridge-cover, also called a ▷*hip-roll*. A *ridge-▷beam* is a beam at the upper ends of the rafters below the ridge, also called a ▷*crown-plate*. A *ridge-▷cap* or *-capping*, or a *ridge-covering* is any cover over the ridge of a roof. A *ridge ▷course* is the topmost course of roof-▷tiles or ▷slates. A *ridge-crest* (▷cress) is an ornamental cresting of lead, iron, or tiles at the ridge of a roof. A *ridge-▷fillet* is one between two ▷channels. A *ridge-▷rib* is a horizontal rib at the crown of a ▷Gothic ▷vault. A *ridge-roof* is any pitched roof with the rafters meeting at an ▷apex or ridge, and with ▷gable-ends. For *ridge-saddle* ▷Yelm. A *ridge-tile* is a half-round tile called a *crown-tile*, *ridge-roll*, or *hip-roll*, covering a ridge or hip.

Rift sawn Timber quarter-sawn, or sawn radially, so that the growth-rings are never less than 80° to the surface.

Rim A *rim ▷latch* is a metal surface-latch fixed to the ▷shutting ▷stile of a ▷door and containing a ▷bolt turned by a ▷knob. A *rim-▷lock* has a bolt which is turned and locked by means of a ▷key.

Rinceau A continuous ▷band of undulating waving plant ▷motifs, or a ▷foliate continuous ▷ornament, like a ▷vine.

Ring course The ▷course nearest the *extrados* of an ▷arch, and several courses deep. A *ring-stone* is a ▷voussoir.

Ringed A ▷banded ▷column or ▷pilaster.

Ringhiera An open ▷loggia or ▷balcony on the ▷front of a public building in Italy, so any similar structure on an Italianate building.

Riparine ▷Ornament featuring deities of the river or water, often associated with ▷vases from which water flows, ▷naval crowns, ▷Neptune, nymphs, ▷mermaids, bullrushes, ▷swans, ▷fish, ▷dolphins, and ▷frogs.

Riprap Large boulders used for ▷foundations not regularly laid.

Riser The upright ▷face of a ▷step from ▷tread to tread. A *rising ▷arch* is a *rampant arch*. A *rising ▷hinge* is one that causes a door to rise as it opens to clear a

carpet, and has an inclination to shut itself by gravity. A stone in ▷rubble, bigger than a ▷sneck (▷jump).

Risp A ▷door rattle or -▷knocker.

Riven Split rather than sawn, as in ▷slate.

Rivet A small metal ▷bolt with a head used to secure metal ▷plates together.

Roach A ▷bed of ▷Portland stone with large numbers of cavities.

Robur An underground dungeon (▷donjon) in ▷Antiquity.

Rocaille Rock-work (▷rock-faced) of ▷pebbles, ▷shells, and stones used in the building of ▷grottoes, ▷follies, and other decorative conceits. ▷Scroll ▷ornament resembling marine plant-forms and shell-work, found in eighteenth-century ▷Rococo designs. In German, *rocaille* rock-work is called *Muschelwerk*, meaning ▷*shell-work*.

Rock-cut Excavated in solid rock.

Rock-faced The natural ▷face of ▷ashlar, or ashlar ▷dressed to look as though it is natural and straight from the quarry, with a ▷projecting rough face, also called *rock-work* or *quarry-faced work*. *Rock-work* is also a construction looking as though it is made of naturally occurring boulders or even large cliff-faces, often found in ▷garden buildings, ▷grottoes, ▷fountains, and ▷labyrinths. Rock-work featured real and artificial rocks.

Rock rash A ▷facing of assorted stones and stone shapes.

Rocking stone A ▷logan.

Rococo A light, frothy, elegant, and playful late phase of the ▷Baroque, more than ▷*rocaille*, but with much of the ▷shell-like, coral, or marine forms associated with ▷grottoes. ▷Naturalistic forms, *Chinoiserie* (▷Chinese), ▷Indian, and Gothick (▷Gothic) elements fused in this remarkable eighteenth-century art-form, which was more surface decoration than an architectural style. Its finest expressions were in France and southern Germany around the middle of the eighteenth century. Rococo decoration makes much use of the C- and S-curve, and is often asymmetrical, resembling artistically draped ▷seaweed. There was a *Rococo ▷Revival* in France after the restoration of the monarchy in 1815, and Britain, America and Germany enjoyed a revival during the 1820s. There was a further revival in the 1880s and 1890s, which probably influenced ▷Art Nouveau.

Rod of Aesculapius A ▷staff entwined with ▷serpents, often found in ▷Neoclassical ▷ornament. It resembles the ▷*caduceus*.

Rode A ▷rood.

Roll A piece of wood prepared with a rounded form for dressing ▷lead over. A *roll moulding* (▷mould, ▷[209]) is a ▷bowtell or common round, or any convex partly cylindrical form: a *roll-▷billet* moulding is a series of short billets with gaps between, set in ▷cavetto mouldings. A *roll moulding* is also a ▷drip-stone with pronounced ▷fillets and a throating (▷throat). A *roll-and-fillet* is like a roll moulding but with a ▷band or fillet giving it a hard extra line. *Roll-work* is ▷strapwork.

Roman The ▷architecture of Ancient Rome and its empire was important in its own right, but it was also an inspiration to many ▷Classical ▷revivals. The Romans used the ▷Orders, and indeed developed peculiarly Roman versions of them, adding the ▷Tuscan and ▷Composite to ▷Doric, ▷Ionic, and ▷Corinthian. Roman Doric became quite distinct from Greek, while Roman Ionic evolved an eight-▷voluted ▷capital that removed the necessity for 'specials' at the corners of a building. Roman Corinthian and Composite Orders were extremely lavish. The Romans favoured a wider ▷intercolumniation than did the ▷Hellenic Greeks, and indeed their intercolumniations derive from both ▷Etruscan and ▷Hellenistic precedents. They gave the ▷wall surface itself greater importance, often engaging the Orders with the wall, but one of the most important Roman innovations was the combination of the ▷arcuated wall with the Orders, used with wide intercolumniations, as on the Colosseum and the ▷triumphal arches. Orders were therefore often applied to walls and arcuated forms. The development of ▷brick, stone, and ▷concrete structural methods enabled the Romans to design vast arcuated, ▷domed, and ▷vaulted buildings, often of considerable geometrical complexity, in which plastic possibilities were exploited to the full. The structural and uninhibited architectural use of the ▷arch made great engineering works possible so that ▷aqueducts, ▷bridges, and efficiently organized services could be made and maintained. The Romans developed tenement blocks as well as ▷villas, and built very large public buildings, such as those around the ▷Forum. ▷Temples, civic buildings, and ▷monuments tended to be very large and grand, glorifying the divine emperors or Roman arms, as well as the deities of the Pantheon. ▷Greek monumental buildings, including the most important temples, tended to be remote edifices for ritual or ceremony, protected in an ▷acropolis or a remote site: Roman architecture paid more attention to use and to interiors, and the temples were often accessible, situated in or near places of public resort. The ▷baths and ▷basilicas were examples of very large buildings for use, while ▷theatres, amphitheatres, and ▷circuses catered for spectacle on a vast scale. The triumphalism of Roman architecture became absorbed into ▷Early Christian basilican ▷churches, while the plastic use of concrete to span very large areas enabled settings to be created for public activities. Surfaces were ▷stuccoed or clothed in ▷marble or ▷mosaic. The complexities of plan found in the Villa Adriana at Tivoli and the Golden House of Nero have an almost ▷Baroque quality, anticipating some of the geometrical ingenuities of seventeenth- and eighteenth-century design. Roman heating, services, and hygiene were models for civilized living not to be attained again until modern times. Lessons of Roman constructional techniques were kept alive by the Eastern or ▷Byzantine Empire, notably the vaults and domes, while the religious orders also retained and developed expertise in building, especially ▷masonry. A *Roman arch* is a semicircular arch made of wedge-shaped ▷voussoirs. *Roman bricks* are long thin bricks, needing up to six ▷courses per foot (30 cm). *Roman ▷bronze* was an alloy of ▷copper and ▷zinc with some ▷tin added to harden it. *Roman ▷cement*, also called ▷*Parker's cement* or a ▷*hydraulic cement*, was made from crushed calcareous clay nodules, and was brown in colour, used for ▷rendering. ▷Pozzolan. *Roman mosaic* is laid with small *tesserae* (▷tessellae) set in geometrical patterns in ▷mortar. A *Roman Order* is the *Composite Order*. A *Roman ▷tile* is a single-lap tile, consisting of a flat section with an upstand on one side and a half-round on the other, the half-round fitting over the upstand of the adjacent tile, and the *double Roman tile* has two flat ▷channels separated by a central ▷roll, with another half-round which fits over the upstand of one of the flats. *Old Roman tiling*, also called *basilican tiling* or ▷*Italian tiling*, has flat under-tiles and convex curved ▷over- or top-▷tiles, that is, a flat with upstands on either side, with a half-round laid over the upstand and the upstand of the tile adjoining.

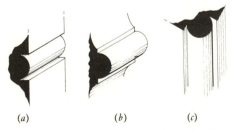

[209] ROLL MOULDINGS (*a*) Flush bead moulding. (*b*) Torus or half-round moulding. (*c*) Angle-bead or bowtell. (*JJS*)

Romanesque [210] The style of ▷architecture that dominated Western Europe from the tenth century until the end of the twelfth, characterized by the use of massive ▷walls and ▷piers, the ▷semicircular arch and

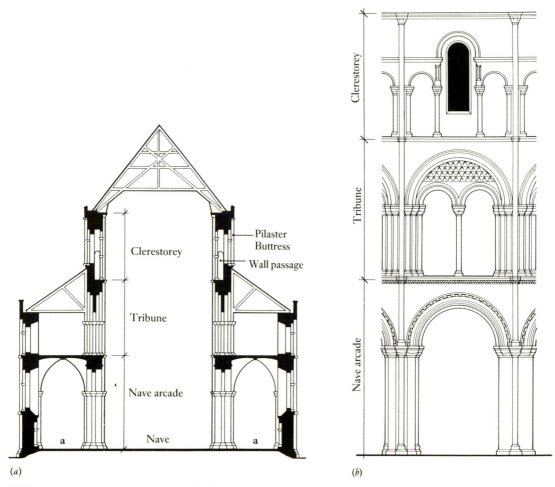

Clerestorey

Pilaster
Buttress

Wall passage

Tribune

Nave arcade

Nave

a   a

Clerestorey

Tribune

Nave arcade

(a)   (b)

[210] ROMANESQUE ARCHITECTURE (*a*) Section through Peterborough Cathedral showing the clerestoreyed nave with steeply pitched roof. Note the nave arcade, tribune and clerestorey. **a** aisle with lean-to roofs. Note that there are two storeys of windows on the side walls illuminating the aisle and the spaces over the vaulted roofs of the aisles. (*JJS*) (*b*) Elevation of interior of nave of Peterborough Cathedral showing the nave arcade, tribune, and clerestorey. (*JJS*)

▷vault, simple geometrical planning, and the use of ▷apses, often vaulted. ▷Bays in ▷churches are usually square on plan to facilitate vaulting, which became universal around AD 1000. ▷Capitals are often free adaptations of ▷Roman or ▷Byzantine forms, but are frequently much simpler, of the ▷cushion or ▷scalloped type, while mouldings (▷mould) are vigorous and very simple, often of the ▷billet, ▷chevron, or ▷beak-head type. Romanesque work is known as ▷Norman, and indeed some late ▷Anglo-Saxon architecture owed much to Continental Romanesque. Some authorities include work from the seventh century in the Continental Romanesque period, for ▷Early Christian and Byzantine influences were clear well before AD 800(▷Norman). There was a Romanesque ▷Revival associated with ▷historicism, with the ▷*Rundbogenstil*,

and with the period before the ▷Gothic Revival, notably in the work of Thomas Hopper (1776–1858), Donthorne, and Plowman. Romanesque was revived in Ireland by numerous architects, one of the best examples being St Patrick's at Jordanstown of 1866, and there was a further revival after 1922 which continued well into the 1950s in that country. ▷Hiberno-Romanesque.

Romanticism In its simplistic definition, it is the antithesis of ▷Classicism and ▷Neoclassicism, and is associated with the rediscovery of mediaeval styles, with the ▷Picturesque, and, to a certain extent, with the powerful emotions engendered by the ▷Sublime. Asymmetry, ▷Romanesque and ▷Gothic Revivals, an interest in ▷ruins and ghostly places, and the rise of the irrational are all aspects of Romanticism. If Classicism

267

is associated with the ▷Orders and with ▷symmetry, Romanticism is associated with the ivy-clad Gothic ruin in a graveyard, with the funerary ▷wreath, and with darkly mysterious places where emotion is powerful.

Romayne work ▷Profile heads framed in ▷round-els, like ▷medallions.

Rondel A circle of ▷window-glass.

Rood [211] A ▷Cross or Crucifix, often flanked by figures of St John and Our Blessed Lady. The rood was often of timber, and was set up on a *rood-▷beam* across the ▷chancel-arch, or above the *rood-▷loft* over a ▷screen separating the ▷choir from the ▷nave. The *rood-figures* in such a position were often (but not always) more than life-size, and incorporated representations of ▷Golgotha . The *rood-loft* was a ▷gallery over the screen built to carry the heavy rood, with associated figures and tapers, and with access from ▷stairs in the adjacent ▷masonry. The Reformation and subsequent iconoclasm destroyed many lofts and most roods although an interesting fragment of a Golgotha survives at Cullompton in Devon. Rood-lofts were sometimes situated above the chancel-arch, as at Northleach, Gloucestershire. A *rood-▷altar* was one standing against the screen in the nave. A *rood-arch* is the arch in a screen, not to be confused with the chancel-arch. A *rood-▷spire* or *rood-▷tower* refers to the ▷flèche, ▷spire, or ▷tower over the ▷crossing.

Roof [212] The external covering on top of a building, including its structure, sometimes of stone, but more often of wood, overlaid with ▷slates, ▷tiles, ▷lead, etc. Mediaeval *timber roofs* are very varied, and only a few examples can be mentioned here. The simplest wooden structure is a ▷*cruck*, composed of two curved timbers set on or in the ground and making a point, serving as the ▷principal frame as well as the main

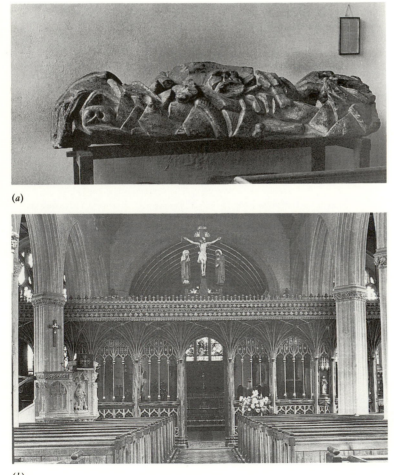

(a)

(b)

[211] ROOD (*a*) Fragment of the Golgotha scene from the base of a rood in St Andrew's Church, Cullompton, Devon. (*JSC*) (*b*) Rood and screen in the Church of St Dionysius (or Disen), Bradninch, Devon, showing the fan-vaulted coving and the cornice with strips of foliage scrollwork and cresting. (*JSC*)

▷truss (▷[94]). Roofs that are triangular in section with ▷ridges can be composed of a series of main *trusses* at certain centres resting on ▷plates, ▷piers, ▷pad-stones, or built into the ▷walls, and carrying the ▷*purlins* on which the ▷common ▷rafters rest. The commonest trusses are: the ▷*king-post*, with a central vertical ▷post, ▷tie-▷beam, ▷braces or ▷struts, and ▷principal rafters; the ▷*queen-post*, like the king-post, but with two vertical posts on either side of the centre-line of the truss; and the ▷*hammer-beam*. springing from ▷corbels carried on curved braces, and supporting hammer-beams which in turn carry arched braces that carry the principal rafters and collar-beams. The various parts of such trusses are: ▷*braces*, which are diagonally placed to stiffen the ▷frame; ▷*collar-beams*, which are timbers tying the principal rafters together at high level at a position between the ridge and the level of the wall-plates; *hammer-beams* which are horizontal ▷brackets carrying arched braces, and supported on arched braces; *king-posts* which rise from the *tie-* or *collar-beams* to the ridge; *principal rafters*, which support the ▷purlins; *purlins*, which are horizontal timbers spanning from truss to truss and which support the common rafters; *queen-posts* which rise from the tie- or collar-beams to carry the principal rafters; *struts* which are straight ▷props; *tie-beams* which are the main ties of trusses, preventing them from spreading, and which carry the king- and queen-posts; and *wall-plates*, which lie on the walls to give a fixing for the trusses and rafters. A ▷*single-framed* roof has no trusses or purlins, and consists only of ▷spars or *rafters* fixed to the ridge and wall-plate. A *common-rafter* roof has pairs of rafters, but they are not connected with collar-beams. These roofs are also called ▷*couple roofs*, and have no ▷ties or ▷collars, while a *coupled rafter* or ▷*close-couple* roof has the rafters joined with collar-beams or ceiling joists to prevent them from spreading. A *collar-roof* has the tie-beam *above* wall-plate level. A ▷*double-framed* roof has additional members called *purlins* which support the rafters, and these purlins may be carried on walls: such roofs are called *double* or *purlin roofs*. A *triple-framed* roof has three sets of members: rafters partly carried by purlins which are in turn carried on trusses, so the roof is divided into ▷bays. Other parts of timber roofs are: ▷*ashlar-pieces*, or short vertical ▷studs between ▷floor-▷joists and rafters in a roof-space, or rising from the ▷*sole-pieces* to the feet of the rafters, collectively known as *ashlaring*, or *ashlering* – they cut off the acute ▷angle formed by the slope of the rafters; *braces*, previously described, which include *arch-braces* (▷arch), *passing-braces* (long straight braces passing across other members of a truss), *scissor-braces* (a pair of braces crossing diagonally between pairs of rafters or principal rafters), and ▷*wind-braces* (short and curved, linking purlins and principals, and often decorated); ▷*crown-posts*, which stand on a tie-beam and support the principal rafters and the collar-plate, and usually

have curved braces (often four) supporting the collar-beams and collar-plate; *hammer-posts*, which are vertical timbers set on the end of a hammer-beam to carry a purlin, and are braced to a collar-beam; *principals*, which are the inclined parts of trusses, also called principal rafters; *purlins*, which are horizontal timbers spanning between trusses and carrying the common rafters, and which include collar-purlins (properly called collar-plates, which carry the collar-beams and are carried on the crown-posts), *side-purlins* (pairs set on the slope of a roof carrying the common rafters), *butt purlins* (set into the principals), *clasped purlins* (set on queen-posts or placed in the angles between principals and the collars), *laid-on purlins* (set on the principals), and *trenched purlins* (set into the ▷backs of the principals); *rafters*, which are the inclined timbers between the ridges and the wall-plates, which carry the roof-covering, and include *common rafters* (equal lengths at equal centres) and *principal rafters* (the main rafters at the tops of trusses); the *ridge*, or horizontal timber at the top of a pitched roof against which the rafters are fixed; ▷*sprockets*, which are timbers placed on rafters to form projecting ▷eaves; *struts*, which are vertical or diagonal pieces between two members to help to support them; *ties*, which are horizontal, prevent members spreading, and may even support the feet of the principals; *trusses*, which are rigid frames (usually triangular) spanning across the space to support the purlins; and the *wall-plates*, which are laid on the tops of walls to receive the ends of the rafters. For types of roof, ▷appentice, ▷Belfast truss, ▷bowstring, ▷common, ▷compass, ▷couple, ▷cradle, ▷cut, ▷double, ▷gable, ▷gambrel, ▷helm, ▷hip, ▷jerkinhead, ▷lean-to, ▷M-roof, ▷Mansard, ▷pavilion, ▷pitch, ▷saddle, ▷span, ▷wagon. A *roof-comb* is the cresting along the ridge, often decorated like a comb, also called a *roof-crest*. A *roof dormer* is the same as a *dormer* (▷dormant). A *roof* ▷*gallery* is a walkway or ▷platform on a roof, also called *widow's walk*. A *roof-plate* is a *wall-plate*. A *roof-tie* is a collar or tie. A *roof-*▷*tree* is the *ridge-board*. A *roofed ingle* is a ▷*chimney-corner* or an ▷*inglenook*.

Rope A moulding (▷mould) resembling a rope. ▷Cable. It is usually shown with twisted strands.

Rosace A *rosette* (▷rose).

Rose [213] A circular moulding (▷mould) with a carved stylized floral pattern, also called *rosace* or a *rosette*: it is used to decorate ▷strings, ▷architraves, etc. A ▷*patera*. A circular or elliptical decorative ▷plaque, or a piece fixed to a ▷wall in which a ▷balustrade ▷rail terminates. Any rosette-like ▷ornament, especially a ceiling rose, or ornamental ▷plaster in the centre of a ceiling. The rose is an ▷attribute of the Madonna, and a rose-▷garden is a ▷symbol of ▷paradise. Roses are found on confessionals (*sub rosa* implies silence or

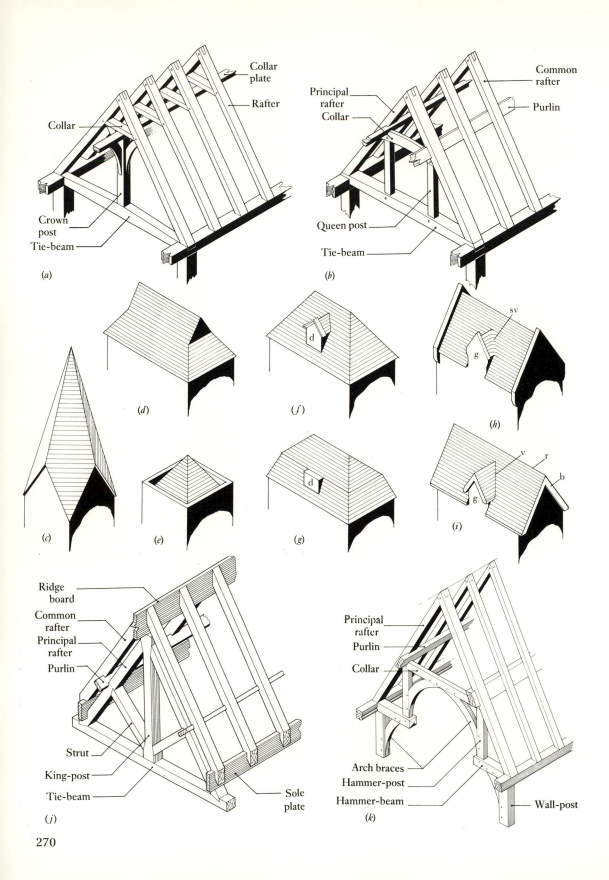

Collar
plate

Rafter

Collar

Crown
post

Tie-beam

(a)

Principal
rafter

Collar

Common
rafter

Purlin

Queen post

Tie-beam

(b)

(c)

(d)

(e)

(f)

sv

g

(h)

d

(g)

v

r

b

g

(i)

Ridge
board

Common
rafter

Principal
rafter

Purlin

Strut

King-post

Tie-beam

Sole
plate

(j)

Principal
rafter

Purlin

Collar

Arch braces

Hammer-post

Hammer-beam

Wall-post

(k)

270

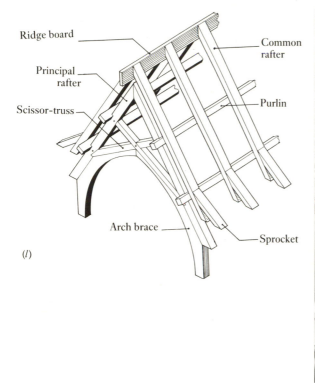

(l)

(m)

[212] ROOF (*a*) Crown-post roof. (N.B. Many early-mediaeval roofs lack the crown-post and collar-plate, and comprise paired rafters with high collars.) (*b*) Queen-post roof. (*c*) Helm roof. (*d*) Half-hipped or gambrel roof. (*e*) Pyramidal roof behind parapet. (*f*) Hipped roof with dormer, **d**. (*g*) Mansard roof with dormer, **d**. (*h*) Common pitched roof with gabled ends, swept valley, **sv**, and gablet or lucarne, **g**. (*i*) Common pitched roof continuing over the gable walls and terminating in barge-boards, **r** ridge, **v** valley, **b** barge-board, **g** gablet, lucarne, or luthern rising from the naked of the wall below. (*j*) King-post roof. (*k*) Hammer-beam roof. (*l*) Scissor-truss roof with arch bracing. (*m*) Boarded wagon-roof with angle-brackets and cross-ribs to the panels, and bosses. The rood-beam carries the Royal Arms. From the Church of St Andrew, Cullompton, Devon. (*a–l, JJS; m, JSC*)

secrecy), and occur on ▷festoons and many ornamental devices. A formalized close-petalled rose, called a *rose-ball*, was a ▷motif favoured by the ▷Glasgow School and by the Vienna Secessionists (▷Sezession). A *rose-nail* has a square ▷shank. A *rose* ▷*window* is a circular window with compartments of ▷tracery. It differs from a ▷Catherine-wheel or ▷wheel-▷window which has

[213] ROSETTE Patera in the form of a rosette. Without the floral enrichment it would be a patera. (*JSC*)

definite spoke-like ▷colonnettes set radially, and is much less overtly floral in design. ▷Catherine-wheel, ▷Marigold.

Rostral ▷Column.

Rostrum A beak-like ▷prow of a ship found in *rostral columns*. The *columna rostrata* was a ▷column on a ▷pedestal decorated with the bows of warships, celebrating naval victories. ▷Column. A rostrum is also an elevated ▷dais or ▷platform. ▷Acrostolium.

Rotunda A circular building or room, usually with a ▷dome or a domed ceiling over it. Rotundas may have ▷peristyles inside or out, or both.

Rough A *rough* ▷*arch* has ordinary rectangular ▷bricks, and the ▷mortar joints are large and wedge-

271

shaped. *Rough-▷axed* bricks are roughly shaped. *Rough* in timber means unplaned. *Roughcast* is ▷rendering of ▷mortar, with coarse ▷aggregate thrown on to a ▷wall, known (if small round stones are used) as ▷*pebble-dash*.

Round A *round* ▷*arch* is a semicircular arch. The *round-arch* style is the ▷*Rundbogenstil. Round* means circular, or part of a circle, as in *round* ▷*billet, round* ▷*church, round moulding* (▷*mould*), *round* ▷*pediment, round* ▷*ridge, round* ▷*step, round* ▷*tower*, or *round* ▷*window*.

Roundel A ▷bead or ▷astragal. A circle, circular ▷panel, or opening, such as an ▷*oculus*. A ▷bull's-eye.

Rover A moulding (▷mould) following the line of a curve.

Row house A ▷terrace house sharing a ▷party wall with its neighbours.

Rowlock A ▷brick laid on its edge with its end visible, as used in a *rowlock* ▷*arch* (i.e. one of two concentric rings of small ▷voussoirs made of bricks laid on their sides with the ends exposed).

Royal Arms When King Henry VIII broke with Rome, the Royal Arms began to be set up in ▷churches. From the Restoration of the monarchy in 1660 it became compulsory to set up the Arms of the reigning monarch in churches. The custom died out in the last century, but many fine Hanoverian examples survive.

Rubbed Joints rubbed smooth to ensure a close fit, or a surface rubbed down to make it very smooth and fine. A *rubbed* ▷*brick* or *brick rubber* is a soft, even-textured and -coloured smooth brick without a ▷frog, suitable for rubbing down to shape for fine ▷*gauged brickwork* ▷arches over ▷window- and ▷door-openings where the bricks are jointed using ▷lime-▷putty.

Rubble Rough undressed stones of various shapes and sizes. *Rubble-work* consists of ▷blocks of stone that are either undressed or comparatively roughly ▷dressed, with wide ▷mortar joints. *Random rubble* is uncoursed, and requires ingenuity in bonding and avoiding vertical joints, so requires many *bonders* (▷bond), *headers* (▷head) or ▷*throughs*. ▷*Coursed rubble* has roughly dressed stones laid in *courses*. ▷*Squared rubble*, or *square-snecked rubble* (▷sneck) is squared stones of various sizes arranged in an irregular pattern, with ▷*risers* or *jumpers* (▷jump) as through-stones, thinner stones called ▷*levellers*, and small stones called *snecks* or *checks*. Squared rubble can also be laid to *courses. Regular coursed rubble* has all the stones of one course of the same height, although each course may vary in height (▷[163].

Rudenture ▷Cabling.

Ruderatio A ▷Roman ▷pavement of pieces of ▷brick, ▷tiles, and stone.

Ruderation ▷Walls or paving of rough ▷pebbles and ▷mortar, or the process of paving or walling with pebbles and small stones in mortar.

Ruin Often depicted in ▷*capricci*, but the etchings of Piranesi created a fashion for ▷Picturesque ▷ruins. Many ▷architects drew their own buildings as imaginary ruins to compare them with ▷Antiquity. Fake ruins were built as ▷eyecatchers when Picturesque decay was fashionable.

Rule A straight-edge for working ▷plaster to a plane surface, or any other straight edge, with measures or not.

Run A fall. A *run moulding* (▷mould) is a moulding of ▷plaster formed by dragging a ▷template over the wet material.

Rundbogenstil [214] The eclectic round-arched styles, largely derived from ▷Italian ▷Early Christian, ▷Romanesque, and ▷proto-▷Renaissance ▷architecture, developed in Germany during the nineteenth century by important ▷Neoclassical ▷architects such as Schinkel, von Klenze, and Gärtner, and emulated in the mid-nineteenth century in England.

Runic cross A ▷Celtic cross, or a ▷cross carved with runic ▷inscriptions. A *runic* ▷*knot* is ▷interlaced ▷ornament of the ▷Celtic and ▷Anglo-Saxon type.

Running A progression of repetitive ▷ornaments, linked together, and leaning to the right or to the left, placed within a ▷band. A *running* ▷*dog*, for example, is a ▷Classical ornament in a ▷frieze or a ▷band, also called a *wave scroll* or a ▷*Vitruvian scroll*, with wave-like repetitive ▷motifs (▷[250]). A *running ornament* has a continuous design, intertwined, or flowing, as abstract patterns or repetitive ▷foliage with curved wavy forms. A *running* ▷*vine* is a continuous ornament of vine leaves, wavy stems, and grapes, found in ▷Perpendicular work.

Rural architecture ▷Picturesque cottage ▷architecture, or ▷rustic(k) buildings, often deliberately asymmetrical, and derived from ▷vernacular traditions, with materials such as ▷thatch, rough tree trunks as ▷columns, and a contrived attempt to appear *primitive*. The *cottage orné* (▷cot) was an example.

Rustic The term means any stones dressed with high ▷relief, or hand-▷dressed with a rough raised surface. A *rustic* ▷*arch* is a rough arch made of irregular stones.

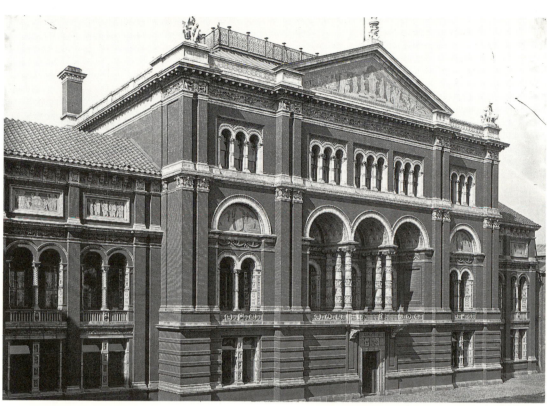

(a)

(b)

(c)

[214] RUNDBOGENSTIL (*a*) North side (1866) of the quadrangle of the South Kensington Museum, *c*. 1872, by Fowke and Sykes, an example of the round-arched Italianate style imported from Germany under the aegis of the Prince Consort and his advisers. (*V&A 9774*) (*b*) The Church of Sts Mary and Nicholas, Wilton, Wiltshire, 1840–46, by T. H. Wyatt and D. Brandon, a spectacular exercise in the Italian Romanesque basilican style, with detached campanile. (*RCHME AA51/11903*) (*c*) Church of St Mary, Wreay, Cumberland, 1840–42, by Sara Losh, mixing French and Italian Romanesque with a strong dash of Rhenish Romanesque. (*JSC*)

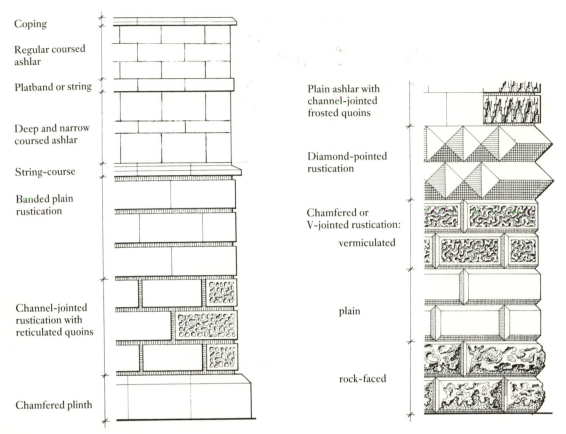

Coping

Regular coursed ashlar

Platband or string

Deep and narrow coursed ashlar

String-course

Banded plain rustication

Channel-jointed rustication with reticulated quoins

Chamfered plinth

(a)

Plain ashlar with channel-jointed frosted quoins

Diamond-pointed rustication

Chamfered or V-jointed rustication:

vermiculated

plain

rock-faced

(b)

[215] RUSTICATION (a) Examples of rustication. (JJS) (b) Fountain in Wells, Somerset, showing different types of rustication. On either side is frosted or stalactite rustication. In the centre is rock-faced work, and in the spandrels is vermiculated rustication. (JSC)

Rustication (▷[215]) is ▷ashlar-work, the joints of which are worked with grooves or ▷channels to emphasize the ▷masonry. Grooves may be moulded or plain, but the joints are emphasized, and the surface is often smooth or roughly textured. Rustication gives an emphasis to ▷plinths, ▷quoins, etc., and heavy rustication can give an impression of massiveness, impregnability, and strength. ▷*Banded* rustication has only the horizontal joints grooved or emphasized. ▷*Chamfered* rustication has V-joints. ▷*Cyclopean* rustication consists of big rough-faced ▷blocks, looking as though they were rough-hewn from the quarry (but actually carved to look like it), also called ▷*rock-faced* rustication. *Pyramidal* or *diamond-pointed* rustication has the blocks cut to resemble ▷pyramids or ▷hipped ▷roofs. ▷*Frosted* rustication has carving simulating ▷stalactites or icicles, to give a ▷grotto-like effect. ▷*Reticulated* rustication has holes in the surface carved in such a way that the pieces between the holes resemble a net. *Smooth* rustication has the joints emphasized but the faces flat. ▷*Vermiculated* rustication has irregular grooves, ▷channels, and holes all over the ▷face, like worm-tracks. A *rusticated* ▷*column* has blocks of square ▷ashlar at intervals along the ▷shaft. *Rusticating* is the applying of any texture to a face, or the act of making or carving rustication. A *rustic* ▷*brick* is a brick with a rough face. A *rustic joint* is a recessed ▷mortar joint emphasized by the channelling of the edges of the stones. A *rustic quoin* is a stone at the corner of a building which projects beyond the ▷naked of the wall. A *rustic* ▷*slate* is one of a number of slates of various thickness which, when laid, gives an irregular surface to the ▷roof or wall. *Rustic stone* is broken rough stone. *Rustic woodwork* is any construction made of timber, often with the bark still in place, used in modest structures like ▷gazebos or ▷lodges to create a primitive, rural character (▷cot).

Rybat   A ▷reveal.

S

Sabaton A broad-toed mail shoe in ▷heraldic devices or sepulchral ▷effigies.

Sabre ▷Sword.

Sacellum A small roofless enclosure. In ▷church ▷architecture the term means a screened ▷chapel within a church, usually a ▷memorial chapel, a ▷mortuary-chapel, or a ▷chantry-chapel.

Sackering bell A *sanctus bell* (▷sancte ▷bell).

Sacrament One of the rites recognized and employed by the Church in which a visible agency is employed to confer Grace. The two signs ordained by Christ (according to the Protestant view) are *Baptism* and the *Eucharist*, to which the Church has added *Confirmation, Matrimony, Penance, Orders,* and *Extreme Unction*: the Roman Catholics hold, therefore, that there are *Seven Sacraments*. A ▷font of the Seven Sacraments is designed to suggest the Sacraments.

Sacrarium A sacred ▷apartment in a ▷Roman house: a ▷shrine or family ▷chapel. The ▷*adytum* of a ▷temple, or its *cella* (▷cell). The name is now given to the part of the ▷chancel enclosed by the ▷altar-▷rails, or to any consecrated place, chapel, shrine, or ▷sacristy.

Sacring As ▷sackering or ▷sancte.

Sacristy Also *sacristry*. A ▷vestry attached to a ▷church where vestments, sacred vessels, and other ▷furniture used in worship are kept.

Saddle A ▷board of wood on the ▷floor in a doorway between the ▷jambs. A ▷threshold. A ▷ridge fixed on the top of two pitched slopes of a ▷roof, or an ▷apex-stone, or a ▷splayed coping (▷cope). A *saddle-back* is a common pitched roof with ▷gable-ends as on a ▷tower, or a coping-stone with the apex along its central ridge. *Saddle-▷bars* are iron bars set into stone to which ▷leaded ▷lights are tied. A *saddle-board* is a board at the ridge of a pitched roof covering the joint, also called a *comb-board* or a *ridge-board*. A *saddle-coping* is a saddle-backed coping of triangular section. A *saddle-stone* is any apex-stone or a stone shaped like a saddle.

Safe A ▷lead tray placed below anything (e.g. a tank) to catch any overflow, and provided with a waste-▷pipe.

Safety arch A relieving ▷arch.

Sagitta A keystone (▷arch, ▷key). Also called *saetta*.

Sagittary A ▷centaur, found on ▷Romanesque ▷fonts and carved ▷door-ways, with bows and arrows to suggest the conquest of the flesh by means of spiritual power.

Sail dome ▷Vault.

Sail-over A ▷projection.

Sail vault ▷Vault.

Saints ▷Symbol.

St Andrew's cross bond ▷English bond with the ▷stretcher-joints in alternating ▷courses displaced by half a length, giving a ▷*saltire* effect on the ▷wall.

Saint's bell A *sanctus bell* (▷sancte ▷bell).

Salamander A mythical creature like a lizard, supposedly living and breeding in fires, with the ability to put out flames. It represents enduring faith, and is found on ▷fonts. It also is an ▷emblem of fortitude, and was particularly an emblem of ▷François I, so occurs in early sixteenth-century ▷French ▷architecture and in its nineteenth-century ▷revival. It is often found on ▷grates.

Saliens A ▷fountain formed of a narrowing tube so that the water spouts under its own pressure.

Salient A ▷projection of any part of a building. A corner projecting outwards, the opposite of re-entrant. A gun-emplacement projecting outwards in a fortification, or in ▷garden designs

Sally A ▷projection. The end of a timber cut with an interior ▷angle, or ▷bird's mouth. The part of a ▷rafter projecting beyond the ▷wall-▷plate. A *sally-port* is an underground ▷passage or concealed ▷gate linking the outer and inner parts of a fortress. A ▷*postern-gate*.

Salmon The spirit of Man overcoming obstacles to return to the source from which he came, used in Christian ▷symbolism.

Salomónica Also a *Salomonic, Solomonic,* ▷*spiral*, ▷*twisted*, or ▷*barley-sugar column* or ▷*torso*. It is so-called because such twisted columns were removed to Rome from the Herodian Temple in Jerusalem in the first century AD and these were thought to be from the Temple of Solomon.

Salon, saloon A lofty or spacious room situated in the centre of a building, often ▷vaulted or ▷domed, the equivalent of two ▷storeys high, and frequently illuminated from high level by means of an ▷oculus, ▷clerestorey, or ▷lantern-▷light. A public room for a specific purpose. A ▷drawing-room. A ▷bar-room of the better class.

Saltbox A ▷timber-framed house with a pitched ▷roof and ▷gables, the rear roof sweeping over ▷ancillary accommodation to the rear, so the ▷ eaves are much nearer the ground at the rear. It is a type once common in England, especially in Essex, and the design was used in America in the eighteenth century.

Saltire A *St Andrew's* or *diagonal* ▷*cross*.

Salutatorium A ▷porch or ▷area where clergy and congregation could meet for conference in the Middle Ages.

Sample-books Collections of drawings of ▷motifs used by the masons of mediaeval Europe.

Sanatorium An establishment for the reception and medical treatment of invalids.

Sancte bell A *sanctus bell*, sounded at important moments of the Mass, usually a small hand-bell. Often a larger bell was placed in a small ▷turret or *sancte-cote* (▷bell) over the ▷chancel ▷arch above the ▷roof of the ▷church (▷[44]). It drew the attention of those not in the building to those significant moments.

Sanctuary An area around the ▷high altar of a ▷church, or a sacred ▷shrine. A ▷presbytery or eastern part of the ▷choir. A *sanctuary lamp* indicates the presence of the consecrated ▷Sacrament, or the ever-present God.

Sanctum sanctorum The Holy of Holies, or special sacred part where access is limited.

Sanctus bell ▷Sancte bell.

Sandstone A stone composed of grains or particles of sand, either mixed with other mineral substances or adhering together without visible cementing matter. It varies in colour from a rich red to dark grey-browns, with a range of warm browns between. Many sandstones are very hard, and some are suitable for carving.

Santorin A type of ▷tufa used to make ▷cement.

Saracenic As ▷Arabian or ▷Moorish. It was an exotic style favoured from the late eighteenth century, and was loosely applied to ▷Indian or ▷Arabian styles, as at Brighton Pavilion stables by Porden of 1804.

Sarcophagus [216] A stone or ▷terracotta ▷coffin, so-called from the ▷Greek, meaning flesh-eater. It was usually treated architecturally, ▷ornamented, and heroic in scale. It could have a pitched ▷roof, and ▷acroteria at the corners. It is frequently found in funerary ▷architecture, and was also used as a ▷motif in ▷Neoclassical design.

Sarking Thin ▷boards for ▷lining. Boards over the ▷rafters before ▷battening and ▷tiling. Boarding for ▷slating is also called *sarkin* in northern England and Scotland.

Sarrasine A ▷portcullis or *sarasin*.

Sash [217] A ▷frame for holding the ▷glass in a ▷window and capable of being raised and lowered in vertical grooves. Sashes are ▷single- or ▷double-▷hung, and are counterbalanced by ▷lead or iron weights in the ▷lining. The frame in which sashes are fitted is called a *sash-frame*, and the ropes on which sashes are suspended are called *sash-lines, -cords,* or -

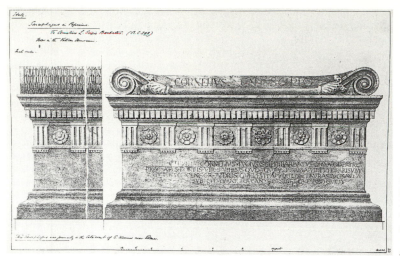

[216] SARCOPHAGUS
Sarcophagus of Cornelius Lucius
Scipio Barbatus, now in the Vatican
Museum, showing Doric triglyphs,
with paterae in the metopes, and with
a scrolled top. (*From Brindley and
Weatherley, Ancient Sepulchral
Monuments, London 1887*)

chains. Very heavy sashes in top quality work were usually suspended from chains rather than cords. Sashes began to be fashionable in England in the latter part of the seventeenth century, the type being developed from designs of the 1670s. A *Yorkshire sliding sash* has frames which slide horizontally (▷Yorkshire light).

Satan The ▷Devil, often shown in mediaeval ▷Dooms.

Satyr A creature with goat-like legs, cloven hooves, a tail, a male human torso and arms, a bearded, leering face, and horns, often garlanded with ▷ivy, and bearing ▷*cornucopiae* or pitchers of wine. Satyrs often appear from the seventeenth century as ▷masks.

Saucer dome One the height of which is much less

than its radius: a shallow ▷dome.

Saves, savers, saving-stones Stones built over a ▷lintel to distribute the load on the ▷jambs, usually in the form of a relieving ▷arch.

Sawtooth A notched jagged moulding (▷mould) like the teeth of a saw.

Saxa quadrata ▷Blocks of ▷dressed squared stone for ▷ashlar work.

Saxon ▷Anglo-Saxon buildings were often of wood, but from the ninth century the more important buildings such as ▷churches or ▷monasteries were of stone, or were ▷timber-framed structures. The Germanic tribes who settled in England from the fifth century

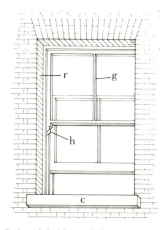

(*a*)

(*b*)

[217] SASH (*a*) Sash with hidden sash-boxes in brick window-opening with 'flat' arch of brick rubbers (skewback). **g** glazing-bar, **r** reveal, **c** cill or sill, **h** horn (horns became usual during the nineteenth century, but are not found in Georgian work). (*b*) Sash with exposed sash-boxes. (*JJS*)

had a tradition of building with timber, but with the reintroduction of Christianity, stone-building techniques were also revived. The typical Saxon church is a ▷hall rather than a ▷basilica, often very tall (with evidence of two ▷storeys), usually with a ▷chancel approached through an ▷arch. ▷Walls are of ▷rag or ▷rubble, and ▷quoins are placed alternately flat and on end, a form known as ▷*long-and-short* work. Sometimes walls are ▷ornamented externally with flat vertical ▷pilaster strips (▷*lesenes*), which are also found on ▷towers, such as those of Barnack and Earl's Barton. These strips are broken by plain horizontal ▷strings, both strings and strips projecting beyond the ▷face of the wall, indicating that the ▷panels were probably ▷rendered. Whether these ▷projections were a petrified version of timber-framed construction or a crude representation of the ▷Orders, is unclear. Walls are sometimes decorated with simple ▷blind ▷arcades of arches on vertical strips, and 'arches' are either semicircular with crudely carved curved stones (or even ▷lintels with half-circles cut from the bottom) or are triangular pseudo-arches formed of two straight stones resting against each other at the ▷apex. Walls are often made of rubble laid as ▷herringbone work. ▷Jambs, too, may be made of long-and-short work. Where there are ▷imposts they are often crude and oversized, as at Barnack and Wittering. ▷Windows are small and are often found in pairs divided by small bulbous ▷shafts or ▷colonnettes shaped like ▷balusters and encircled by ▷bands of plain mouldings (▷mould). ▷Capitals are formed of long stones, and may have rude carvings. ▷Anglo-Saxon details and methods of construction undoubtedly continued to be employed after the Conquest in 1066, and it is clear that English ▷Romanesque evolved in its own way as the cultures mixed. Anglo-Saxon ▷sculpture is often of great beauty, and many fine examples survive.

Scabellum A high ▷pedestal to support busts, ▷urns, or statues, and often isolated.

Scaena, skene The structure which faced the audience in a ▷theatre, set behind the ▷orchestra, also called *scaena frons*. The *scaena* was also the back-building of a theatre. The *scaena ductilis* was a ▷screen used as scenery.

Scaffold A temporary erection of ▷poles and ▷planks to facilitate building. A ▷*gallery* is also known as a *scaffold*. In the temporary structure sense, the upright poles are called ▷*standards*; the horizontal timbers parallel to the ▷walls are called ▷*ledgers*; and the timbers at right-angles to the walls, and fixed to them or into them, are called ▷*putlogs*, and support the planks on which operatives can stand. Any elevated ▷platform such as one for executions.

Scagliola A type of ▷plaster like ▷Keene's, or ▷stucco, with colouring pigments and material introduced so that the finished, polished material (coated with linseed oil) resembles ▷marble. Although *scagliola* was used in interior decorative schemes in ▷Classical times, it was widely used and perfected in the seventeenth and eighteenth centuries.

Scala A staircase (▷stair) or ladder. *Scalae* is a term referring to ▷steps set against a ▷wall. *Scale steps* are steps with parallel ▷nosings and equal ▷goings, while a *scale and platt* is a ▷stair with straight ▷flights and ▷landings.

Scale moulding *Imbrication* (▷imbrex), or patterns like fish-scales or overlapping shaped ▷tiles, also called ▷*petal* ▷*diaper*. It is used to suggest ▷Antique armour. Tiles are often shaped to form scale-patterns, alternating with plain and ▷lozenge-shaped patterns.

Scale steps ▷Steps with parallel ▷nosings and equal ▷goings (▷stair).

Scales ▷Symbolic of the weighing of good and evil, etc, and therefore used on Courts of Justice, in representations of logic, and as an ▷attribute of St Michael. *Imbrication* (▷imbrex) or patterns like overlapping ▷tiles.

Scallage, scallenge A lych-gate (▷lich).

Scallop An ▷ornament resembling a scallop-▷shell, often found at the ▷head of ▷niches. It is often found as a cresting (▷cress) detail (tombstones), and as an ornament on ▷cabriole legs or chair-backs. It was a badge of pilgrims in the Middle Ages who had been to the Holy Land or to the shrine of St James in Spain. One of a series of segmental curves used as a continuous decorative moulding (▷mould) like an ▷apron-edging. A *scalloped* ▷*capital* is a ▷cushion-capital with each ▷lunette cut into a series of truncated cones leaving segmental forms along the bottom edges of the vertical ▷faces (▷[60e]).

Scalpturatum ▷Inlaid work, the pattern being cut out and refilled with coloured ▷marble.

Scamilli Plain ▷blocks under ▷columns or statues, especially large blocks under ▷plinths, so forming a double plinth or stepped plinth. Unlike ▷pedestals they have no mouldings (▷mould) and are smaller in size. A *scamillus* is also a ▷bevel, curve, or the ▷apophyge between a ▷shaft and the ▷neck of a ▷column. Gwilt says that *scamilli impares* means the horizontal lines of a ▷classical building which incline almost imperceptibly from the ends to the centre to correct the optical illusion of the centre sinking.

Scamozzi Order An ▷Ionic ▷Order with eight ▷volutes radiating at the corners, so that no *special* is needed at the corner.

Scandula A ▷shingle. *Scandularis* means covered with shingles.

Scansorium ▷Scaffolding.

Scantling The dimensions of a piece of timber in breadth and thickness. The term also denotes a piece of timber under 125 square cms in area, such as ▷partition quartering, or parts of a ▷roof. In ▷masonry, *scantling* is the length, breadth, and thickness of a stone.

Scape The ▷shaft, or *scapus*, of a ▷column. The ▷*apophyge* of the shaft.

Scappling Also *scabbing* or *scapling*, it is a method of tooling the ▷face of the stone with a pick, or *scappling hammer*. The face is worked to a flat but not smooth surface.

Scarab A ▷symbol of regeneration, of good fortune, and of the sun. It was revived in Egyptianizing (▷Egyptian) design. It is a large winged beetle.

Scarcement A plain ▷band or a flat ▷set-off in a ▷wall or ▷foundation used as a ▷shelf to carry the ends of ▷joists, or for some other purpose.

Scarfing The jointing of two pieces of timber so that they appear as one continuous piece, with the ends ▷bevelled at 1 in 12, although there are many variations.

Scarp The steep banked slope below the ▷ramparts of a fortress. It was also adapted for use in ▷garden design. It is also called an ▷*escarp*, and is the inner side of a ditch.

Scene An alley (▷allée) or rural ▷portico where theatrical performances could be given. Also the same as *scena* or ▷*scaena*. A *scenic* ▷*mask* is one representing ▷*Comedy* or ▷*Tragedy*.

Scheme, skene A segmental ▷arch. The structure facing the audience in a ▷Greek ▷theatre (▷scaena).

Schola A ▷exedra or ▷alcove. An ▷apse in ▷thermae. A ▷platform or ▷ambulatory in thermae.

School A place of instruction, an institute of education, or buildings or rooms used for the teaching of special subjects.

Sciagraph An architectural ▷rendering showing shadows cast at a particular angle. *Sciagraphy* is the method of rendering shadows.

Scialbo A finishing coat of ▷plaster made of ▷marble dust capable of being painted with ▷fresco.

Scintled Laid with an uneven ▷face, as in brickwork.

Scissor-truss A cross-shaped ▷frame at intervals to support a ▷roof. It consists of four members: two ▷rafters spanning from ▷wall-▷plates to ▷ridge, and two members spanning from the wall-plates to the centres of the rafters, and fixed together where they cross (▷[2121]).

Scoinson As ▷sconcheon.

Scollop As ▷scallop.

Sconce An earthwork or fortress. A ▷screen or palisade. An ▷arch formed across the inner angles of a ▷tower, or a ▷squinch. A lamp-▷bracket for fixing to a ▷wall.

Sconcheon Also *scoinson, scontion, scuntion, scunch-eon*. The ▷return ▷face of a ▷pilaster. The portion of the ▷side of an ▷aperture from the back of the ▷jamb or ▷reveal to the interior of the ▷wall. The reveal itself. A ▷squinch or ▷sconce. A *sconcheon* ▷*arch* is one which includes all or parts of the reveals.

Scoop pattern Repeated ▷ornament of sections of vertical ▷fluting with curved closed ends set on bands or friezes.

Scotch bracketing ▷Lath fixed at an ▷angle between a ▷wall and a ceiling to form a ▷base for a ▷plaster ▷cornice.

Scotch glue Any animal ▷glue.

Scotch kiln An up-draught rectangular ▷kiln with three permanent ▷walls, one temporary wall, and no ▷roof. When the kiln is ▷charged and the ▷bricks have been dried, the top and end are filled with old bricks and ▷slaistered with clay prior to firing.

Scotia A concave moulding (▷mould, ▷figures associated with the various Orders) at the ▷base of a ▷column between the ▷fillets of the ▷torus mouldings, or under the ▷nosings of a ▷stair. It is also termed a ▷*gorge* or a ▷*trochilus*.

Scotic ▷Celtic, ▷Hiberno-Romanesque, or ▷Anglo-Saxon ▷ornament.

Scottish Baronial [218] A style evolved during the ▷Jacobean ▷Revival in England, incorporating crenellations, (▷crenel) ▷turreted ▷bartisans, and massive hewn stone. It was a regional variation of the Jacobean

[218] SCOTTISH BARONIAL STYLE Scrabo Tower, near Newtownards, Co. Down. A memorial to Lord Londonderry, of 1858. Note the machicolations, crenellations, bartisans, and conical roofs. (*JSC*)

[219] SCRAPED Scraped, sgraffito, or scratchwork. Royal College of Organists, South Kensington, London, by H. H. Cole and F. W. Moody. It incorporated seventeenth-century-style windows derived from Sparrowe's House in Ipswich (▷[145]), a type often used by Norman Shaw, with a strong Italianate manner for the façade as a whole. The front is covered with *sgraffito* decoration. (*JSC*)

and ▷Gothic Revivals, and was connected with the ▷Castle style.

Scouchon, skouchin A ▷squinch.

Scrabbled Made of ▷rubble.

Scraped [219] A finish on ▷stucco made with a steel tool while the stucco is setting, also called *sgraffito* or ▷*scratch work*. It is commonly made of a coat of coloured ▷plaster covered with a white coating which is then ▷scraped or scratched to reveal the colour underneath.

Scratch ▷Scraped. Also the first coat of ▷plaster, scratched to provide a ▷key for the second *brown* coat.

Scratchwork *Sgraffito*. ▷Scraped.

Screed A band of ▷plaster or ▷concrete applied to a surface to be covered with an applied ▷finish of the same material to act as a guide to ensure the correct depth of finish. The term is often now applied to the finish itself, e.g. a large area of ▷cement,

ususally forming the ▷base for a tiled ▷floor, or as a finish.

Screen [220] A ▷partition, enclosure, or ▷parclose, separating a portion of a room or a ▷church from the rest. It is anything which separates, protects, conceals, or secludes, but is not part of the main structure. A *screen* ▷*façade* is one that hides the form, structure, and true dimensions of a building. Screens are found in churches shutting off ▷aisles from ▷choirs, ▷chapels from aisles, ▷chancels from ▷naves, and to protect ▷tombs, etc. Many fine chancel-screens survive, usually of wood, but sometimes of stone (▷pulpitum, ▷rood, ▷golgotha). A *screens* ▷*passage* is the space at one end of a mediaeval ▷hall, usually under the ▷gallery, and situated between the ▷kitchen-▷doors and the screen (which is there to conceal).

Screwed work Work where the cutting is spiral, leaving a spiral design or pattern on the wood or stone.

Screw stair A ▷stair winding around a central ▷pier or ▷post, also called a ▷*newel-stair* or a ▷*vice-stair*.

281

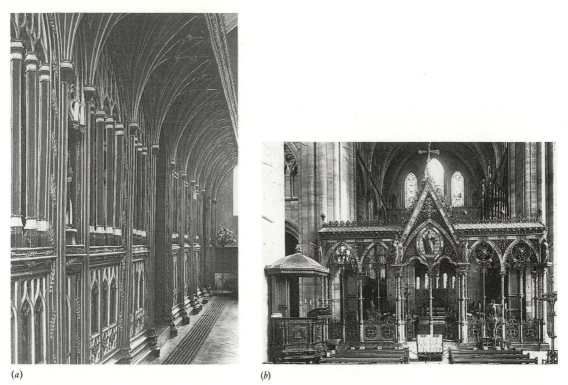

(a)   (b)

[220] SCREEN (*a*) Fifteenth-century screen in the Church of St Dionysius (or Disen) at Bradninch, Devon, showing the fan vaulting and elaborate cornice. (*JSC*) (*b*) Hereford Cathedral choir-screen before its removal. Designed by Sir George Gilbert Scott, it was made by Skidmore of Coventry in 1862, and was shown at the International Exhibition at Kensington in that year. It was made of iron, brass, and copper, and was set with about three hundred cut and polished stones. I was a masterpiece of High Victorian Gothic craftsmanship and design. Note the Vesica Piscis or mandala over the trumeau. (*Hereford City Library 6387*)

Scribbled ▷Hammer-▷dressed joints in ▷masonry with the ▷margins chiselled. *Scribbled* ▷*ornament* is lines and ▷scrolls irregularly and randomly placed over a surface as though scribbled.

Scribing Making incised lines, as in a ▷mortar-joint, with a *scriber*. A *scribed joint* is a *coped* (▷cope) joint between mouldings (▷mould) that meet at an angle. The end of one is shaped to receive the other, without mitring (▷mitre). To *scribe* is also to shape a member to fit another.

Scriptorium A writing-room or place where manuscripts were stored and copied.

Scroll A convoluted or spiral ▷ornament, either continuous or as a terminal feature. A ▷volute of an ▷Ionic, ▷Corinthian, or ▷Composite ▷capital, or a moulding (▷mould) in the form of a scroll, as on a ▷modillion or ▷console. A *scroll moulding* is a ▷projecting ▷*roll moulding* which in section has a set-back to create a hood. It occurs in ▷strings and on positions such as a ▷hood where ▷drips are required. It is also

the ▷*torsade*, or moulding like a twisted or partially unravelled scroll. A *scroll* ▷*step* is a ▷*curtail* step, the lowest in a ▷flight, with the ends or one end rounded in a scroll or spiral projecting beyond the ▷newel. *Scroll-work* is any ornament with scrolls or scroll-like forms. A scroll is based on the C-curve, and is found in many styles, including ▷Celtic, ▷Baroque, ▷Rococo, and ▷Jacobean. A *scrolled* ▷*heart* is a repeating ▷border decoration of two facing *wave scrolls*, often found in work by the Adam Brothers. A *scrolled* ▷*pediment* is also known as a ▷*swan-neck*, ▷*goose-neck*, or ▷*bonnet-scroll* pediment, and is an ▷open pediment in which the two sides are formed of S-shaped scrolls rolling inwards. *Scrolling* ▷*foliage* is repetitive scrolling ornament, often based on naturalistic forms.

Scullery, squillery A place where dishes and cooking utensils, etc. are washed, or where food is prepared. It is situated next to the ▷kitchen.

Sculpture Properly speaking, carved work. The terms *modelling*, *casting*, and *carving* are also used to denote sculptured work.

Scuncheon As ▷sconcheon.

Scupper An opening in a ▷parapet or a drain in a ▷wall to allow water to run off.

Scutcheon The ▷angle of a building or of part of a building, also called a ▷sconcheon. A ▷shield ▷charged with armorial bearings. The ▷plate on a ▷door from the centre of which the handle is suspended, or the plate over the keyhole (▷[114b]).

Scutilagium A ▷close or enclosure, especially when used as a ▷garden.

Scutula A piece of ▷marble cut in the shape of a ▷lozenge or a ▷diamond, used for paving.

Scythe With the sickle, it is an ▷attribute of ▷Time, or ▷Death, and is also found in representations of autumn, the harvest, or the ▷seasons.

Sea-dog An ▷Elizabethan ▷ornament with the head and forelegs of a ▷dog and a ▷fish-tail.

Sea-horse A scrolling animal often found in ▷Rococo work with a horse's head and forelegs, and a ▷fish-tail, also called a ▷hippocamp.

Seal-top A flat circular ▷finial, like a seal.

Seasons Often ▷personified, with ▷attributes of flowers, corn, ▷fruit, faggots, and wrappings, or suggested by ▷Classical mythology.

Seaweed Found in ▷marine▷ decoration, but seaweed forms are found in the ▷foliage and ▷crockets of *Second-▷Pointed* ▷Gothic ▷architecture. Seaweed ▷marquetry (also called ▷*endive* ▷*scroll*) is a type of *Moresque* (▷Moorish) decoration found in seventeenth-century English woodwork.

Secco Applied dry, as a painting on dry ▷plaster, unlike ▷*fresco*, which is painted on wet plaster.

Second Empire The styles associated with the reign of the Emperor Napoleon III (1852–70), or with styles derived from ▷French precedents of that period. One of the most characteristic features was the high ▷*Mansard* or ▷*French roof*, usually with ▷*dormers* (▷dormant) and especially with ▷*oeil-de-boeuf* ▷windows.

Secos A ▷shrine, *cella* (▷cell), ▷*naos* or special place with limited access for the privileged only.

Secret gutter A hidden ▷valley-▷gutter, in which the metal is covered by ▷slates or ▷tiles. It is also used occasionally at ▷eaves-level.

Secretarium ▷Sacristy.

Sectile ▷*Opus sectile* is ▷pavement formed of uniform pieces of material larger than mosaic *tesserae* (▷tessella).

Section The representation of a building or part of a building cut vertically to show the interior, or of any moulding (▷mould) cut transversely, and represented to show its ▷profile. A *plan* is a *horizontal section*. The convention is that everything beyond the line where the section is taken is shown in ▷elevation.

Sedge A coarse-leafed marsh plant, *Cladium mariscus*, used for the ▷ridge of a reed-▷thatched ▷roof, and fixed with ▷*liggers*, or hazel- or willow-sticks.

Sedilia [221] Seats recessed in the south ▷wall of the ▷sanctuary of a ▷church near the ▷high altar, and used by the officiating clergy. *Sedilia* usually comprise three ▷canopied seats, and are often associated in one composition with the ▷*piscina*. They are also known as the *prismatory*.

See A seat or ▷dais. The term refers to a diocese under the jurisdiction of a bishop.

Seed-pod ▷Pomegranates or seed-pods bursting open to show the seeds, often found in seventeenth- and eighteenth-century ▷plaster- and wood-work. It recurred in ▷Art-Nouveau design.

Seel A ▷canopy.

Segment A part cut off. A *segmental* ▷*arch* is one which consists of part of a circle, less than a semicircle. A *segmental* ▷*billet* is one of a segment of a cylinder.

Sekos As ▷*secos*.

Selenetic lime ▷Lime-▷mortar to which a quantity (about 10 per cent) of ▷plaster of Paris is added to increase hardness and improve the set.

Sell A ▷*cell* is habitation for an anchorite (▷anchorage). A ▷sill.

Sellaria, sellary A large sitting-room furnished with seats.

Semi-arch One with only half an ▷arch, as in a flying ▷buttress.

Semicircular A *semicircular* ▷*arch* is one in the form of a half circle. Thus also semicircular ▷domes and ▷vaults. A *semi-*▷*column* is a ▷*half* or ▷*engaged column*. A *semi-dome* or ▷*hemi-dome* is a quarter of a sphere used to cover an ▷apse or a ▷niche.

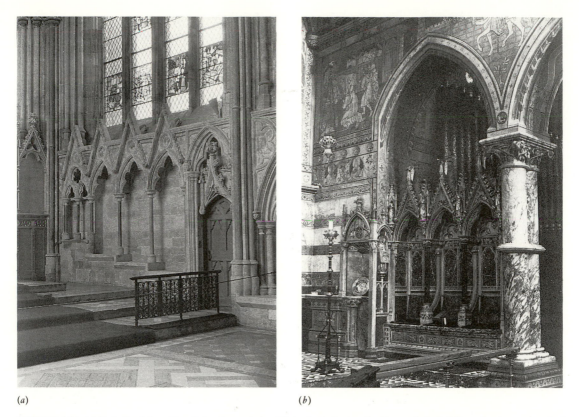

(*a*)   (*b*)

[221] SEDILIA (*a*) Early English or First-Pointed canopied sedilia in the Lady chapel at Exeter Cathedral. Note the elegant detached shafts with bell capitals. The sedilia are combined with a double piscina, also canopied, on the left. The canopy over the door on the right is an example of Decorated or Second-Pointed work. (*JSC*) (*b*) Sedilia in Beauchamp Almshouse chapel at Newland, Worcestershire, of 1862–64, by P. C. Hardwick. Note the surviving Victorian decorations and beautiful sedilia. (*JSC*)

Semielliptical arch An ▷arch with an *intrados* shaped like half an ellipse, but often a three- or five-centred arch.

Seminary A ▷school or place of education, especially for the clergy.

Senaculum A council-▷chamber in ▷Antiquity.

Senatorium Part of the ▷sanctuary of a ▷basilica placed on the opposite side to that of the ▷*matroneum*, marked off by a balustrade (▷baluster), and usually on the north side.

Sepimentum (Properly *saepimentum*.) A barrier or ▷fence. A *septum* is a low balustrade (▷baluster) which divided part of the ▷nave of a ▷basilica into a central section for the clergy and a north and south section for the laity. A *septum* is also a low ▷wall around a ▷tomb, or the ▷altar-▷rails.

Sepulchre A ▷grave, ▷tomb, place of interment or place where a body is laid. A ▷heliquary, especially the place for relics in an ▷altar. An ▷*Easter Sepulchre* is a ▷niche in the north side of the ▷chancel.

Sera A ▷bar used to fasten a ▷Roman ▷door.

Serliana [222] A ▷Venetian ▷window: any central opening with a ▷semicircular ▷arch over it flanked by two tall rectangular openings.

Serpent Found in ▷Classical ▷architecture associated with the messenger (St John, Hermes, Harpocrates, etc.). It is emblematic of healing, with wisdom, and associated with the ▷*caduceus* or wand of the messenger. When serpents are found in circular form, their tails in their mouths, they denote immortality or eternity. They are also used for handles, as binders for ▷wreaths, and simply as decorative forms. The serpent is also associated with evil and temptation in Christian iconography.

(a)

(b)

[222] SERLIANA OR VENETIAN OPENING (*a*) The west front of Christ Church, Spitalfields, by Nicholas Hawksmoor, showing a Serliana used as a portico. (*b*) Serliana or Venetian window at Heaton Park, Manchester, of 1772, by James Wyatt. (*JSC*)

Serpentine A greenish decorative stone resembling ▷marble. Snake-shaped or ▷undulating.

Serrated Notched at the ▷arris, like saw-teeth.

Setback buttress ▷Buttress.

Set-off Also ▷offset. The part of a ▷wall which is exposed upwards when the portion above it is reduced in thickness. In ▷Gothic work, the set-offs are sloped, and have a ▷projecting ▷drip or ▷throating on their lower edges, as on ▷buttresses.

Sett A squared stone used for paving.

Setting coat The finishing coat of ▷plaster.

Settlements Those parts in which failures by sinking in a building occur, and the distortions produced by unequal compression of ▷foundations. Also a human settlement, in an established village or town.

Seven Lamps These hang in front of the ▷altar, and represent the ▷sacraments, refer to the Apocalypse and the Seven Spirits of God, suggest the seven-branched candelabrum, and many other items associated with seven. The *Seven Lamps of Architecture*, according to John Ruskin (1819–1900), are those of *Sacrifice*, *Truth*, *Power*, *Beauty*, *Life*, *Memory*, and *Obedience*.

Seven Wonders of the Ancient World The ▷Pyramids at Gizeh, the ▷Mausoleum at Halicarnassus, the ▷Temple of ▷Artemis at Ephesus, the Hanging Gardens and Walls of Babylon, the Colossus of Rhodes, the Pharos at Alexandria, and the statue of Zeus at Olympia.

Severans A ▷string or a ▷cornice.

Severey, severy Also ▷civery, it is a compartment or ▷bay of a building or ▷scaffold. The term is more usually given to a bay of a ▷vault. It is sometimes used to describe a *baldacchino* (▷baldachin).

285

Sewer A large drain or ▷conduit for carrying wastes in water.

Sexfoil With six points or ▷lobes.

Sexpartite A ▷*quadripartite* ▷*vault* is a ▷bay divided into four ▷cells. A *sexpartite vault* indicates that there is a ▷rib dividing the bay into two, usually at the ▷ridge or ▷apex, so six ▷compartments are formed in a bay. A sexpartite vault can also be one where the lateral triangles are bisected by a further ▷transverse rib to make six triangles per bay.

Sextry A ▷sacristy.

Sezession When the Austro-Hungarian exponents of ▷Art Nouveau seceded from the Imperial and Royal Academy of Art in Vienna in order to exhibit their work, they gave the name *Vienna Secession* or *Sezession* to Austro-Hungarian Art Nouveau, also known as ▷*Jugendstil.*

Sgraffito ▷Scraped.

Shaft The body of a ▷column, ▷colonnette, or ▷pilaster between the ▷capital and the ▷base. In ▷Gothic work the term is given to the small columns which are clustered around ▷piers, or used in the ▷jambs of ▷doors or ▷windows. *Gothic shafts* are frequently of ▷Purbeck ▷marble, and are polished. In the *Gothic* ▷*Revival* marbles and ▷granites were used instead. The part of a ▷chimney-stack between the base and the ▷cornice is called the shaft. A *shafted* ▷*impost* is one with pier-mouldings (▷mould) differing from those of the ▷arch springing from that impost. *Shafting* is an arrangement of shafts in a pier to help to support similar outlines of mouldings above the springing. A *shaft-ring* is an ▷annulet, but more especially it is a Gothic detail of the twelfth and thirteenth centuries, and consists of a ring around a shaft, at various heights, tying it back to a ▷wall or a pier (▷band).

Shake A fissure in a timber caused by its being dried too quickly. The term is also given to a hand-split piece of ▷board or a ▷shingle cut from a radial section of a log.

Shakefork An ▷heraldic Y.

Shamble, shambles A name surviving in many streets meaning an ▷*abattoir* or place where animals are slaughtered.

Shanks Flat planes between the ▷channels of the ▷Doric ▷triglyph.

Shaped Gable A ▷gable with curved sides, often of convex and concave type. *Shaped work* is any ▷joinery involving curved work.

Sheathing Any external covering used as the ▷base for the ▷cladding. A *sheath* is found in scrolling ▷foliage to disguise the joint between the ▷acanthus ▷leaf and its ▷stalk, or it is the sheathing of a ▷*herm* between the bust and its support.

Shed A hut. A *shed-dormer* (▷dormant) is one with the ▷eaves-line parallel to the main eaves, rather than having a ▷gable, so the ▷roof is a *cat-slide*. So a *shed-roof* has only one sloping plane, as in a ▷lean-to.

Sheet glass ▷Glass blown into cylinders, opened up after slitting, and flattened, also called ▷muff-glass.

Sheet lead ▷Cast as opposed to rolled ▷lead.

Shelf A ▷board fixed to a ▷wall to carry anything.

Shell A very thin structure based on the ▷eggshell principle, made of ▷concrete, and self-supporting. A shell-▷ornament is any decoration incorporating shells, known as ▷*coquillage*, found in ▷grotto ▷ornament, ▷marine ornament, or in ▷niche-▷heads, etc.

Shellac A natural resin, soluble in alcohol, used as a sealer over knots to stop resin exuding through the paint.

Shield A ▷crescent-shaped shield is found in Graeco-Roman ▷ornament, and was revived in the ▷Neoclassical period. The triangular or ▷spade-shaped shield is common in ▷Gothic ornament. It eventually became purely decorative or ▷heraldic, was often ▷embellished with ▷strapwork, etc. and finally became the ▷*cartouche.*

Shilf Broken ▷slates.

Shingles Wooden ▷tiles used for roofing or wall-covering, also known as ▷*scandulae*. Shingles are also loose stones used for gravel or ▷concrete ▷aggregate, also known as *shivers*. *Shiver-bottoming* is ▷hard-core filling.

Shiplap A type of wooden ▷cladding in which the edges of the ▷boards are rebated (▷rabbet) so that the joints overlap.

Shoar A ▷shore.

Shoe The inclined piece at the bottom of a rainwater ▷pipe to discharge the water into a ▷gulley. A piece of timber or metal shaped to receive a ▷truss, also known as a ▷*sole-plate*. Any metal ▷base-plate for a ▷truss which is intended to resist the lateral thrust.

Shore A ▷prop to support part of a building.

Shot hole A ▷*loophole*. A *shot-*▷*tower* is a tower down which molten ▷lead was dropped into a large basin of water to form *shots* (small spherical lead pellets).

Shoulder A ▷projection, ▷ear, or ▷elbow which narrows the top of an ▷aperture, as with ▷corbelled ▷blocks. The ▷angle between a ▷bastion and the ▷side of a fortification, called a *shoulder angle*. *Shouldered*, when applied to an ▷arch, means a ▷lintel set on quarter-arches supporting a short vertical. *Shouldering* is a ▷fillet of haired ▷lime laid on the upper edge of ▷slates to prevent water from penetrating the structure. A *shoulder-piece* or *shouldering-piece* is a ▷bracket, ▷crossette, or ▷console.

Show rafter An ▷ornamental ▷rafter under a ▷cornice or ▷eaves, not structured.

Shreadhead A ▷hipped gable.

Shreddings Firrings (▷fir).

Shrine A ▷fereter or repository for relics, or any building containing such a repository. A *shrine-*▷*chapel* is an enclosed space containing a shrine. Any place or structure where worship is offered or devotions are paid to a saint or deity. An enclosure or ▷screen around an image or place associated with a saint or deity.

Shriving pew A confessional (▷confessio).

Shroud A ▷crypt of a ▷church. Also *shrowd.*

Shuttering The temporary ▷mould into which ▷concrete is poured. It is made of timber or metal.

Shutters The ▷doors or ▷frames which cover a ▷window from the outside or inside.

Shutting A *shutting-*▷*post* is one against the ▷side of a ▷gate against which the hinged part shuts. A *shutting-*▷*shoe* is a piece of metal or stone cut with a ▷shoulder and fixed in the middle of a gateway against which one ▷leaf of a double gate is stopped and secured.

Side A *side-*▷*chapel* is one on the side of an ▷aisle. A *side-*▷*light* is a framed light to the side of a ▷door or ▷window, also termed *flanking window*, ▷*margin-light*, or ▷*wing-light*. *Side-*▷*posts* are placed in pairs at an equal distance from the centre-line of a ▷truss. *Side-timbers* are ▷purlins. *Siding* is ▷weather-boarding, or a finish covering the outside of a building other than the ▷roofs. *Side* is also the broad surface of square-sawn wood, also called a ▷*face*: it is a surface or part turned in

some direction, more or less upright. *Altars* also have *sides* or ▷*horns*: they are ▷*Epistle* (south) or ▷*Gospel* (north).

Siel A ▷canopy.

Sigma A ▷portico semicircular on plan.

Signinum Flooring material made of small broken ▷tiles mixed with ▷mortar. ▷*Opus signinum* is a coating of mortar made of crushed powdered tiles used to provide a waterproof surface.

Silex ▷Flint or stone laid in polygonal patterns.

Silica bricks ▷Bricks with about 95 per cent silica (quartz, chalcedony, etc.) and 5 per cent ▷lime, pressed in powerful machines in ▷moulds, and autoclaved. They are quite brittle.

Sill, cile, cill, sole, sule The horizontal piece of timber or stone forming the bottom of a ▷window, doorway, or other opening, usually and properly designed to throw water off. The bottom member of a ▷window-▷frame. A *sill-*▷*course* is a ▷string-course or ▷band lining up with the cill.

Sima ▷*Cyma* or *cymatium.*

Simple A *simple* ▷*cornice* has a cornice only, sometimes with ▷frieze as well, but no ▷architrave. A *simple* ▷*vault* is a ▷barrel-vault, with no ribs.

Sine postico ▷Peripteral on the front and sides but not on the back. Without a rear ▷portico.

Singerie A style of decoration derived from the ▷Grotesque, but involving ▷monkeys: it was a feature of *Chinoisserie* (▷Chinese), ▷*Régence*, and ▷Rococo ▷ornament.

Singing gallery A ▷rood-▷loft or an elevated place for a ▷choir. Usually the top is fixed.

Single frame A *single-*▷*joist* or ▷*naked* ▷*floor*, with only one tier of joists.

Single-hung A ▷sash-▷window where only one sash moves.

Single-lap tile A curved or flat ▷tile which interlocks with its neighbours on either side and overlaps only a single tile in the ▷course below, holed for nails, and with ▷nibs.

Sinister The ▷heraldic left (right when viewed from the front).

Sinking A recess cut into a surface, as for fixing ▷butt-▷hinges, or to make a joint.

Siparium A ▷Roman folding ▷screen or drop in a ▷theatre.

Siren A sea-nymph with the feet and feathers of birds, but often with fish-tails like ▷mermaids.

Size A sealer for coating wood or ▷plaster to prevent paint or ▷varnish from being absorbed. ▷*Glue size* is diluted with water and applied; *varnish size* is made from oil, resin, and thinner. ▷*Gold size* is an oleo-resinous varnish: one type is used for fixing gold leaf, and the other, with more driers in it, is used in fillers.

Skeleton frame A structural ▷frame make up of timber, steel, or ▷concrete members to which is applied a non-load-bearing outer watertight skin or ▷curtain ▷wall, or ▷cladding. *Skeletons* are often found in funerary art to remind us of mortality, or as ▷personifications of ▷death.

Skene ▷*Scaena*, ▷scheme.

Skew The sloping top of a ▷buttress where it slants off into a ▷wall, or the coping (▷cope) of a ▷gable, also called a *skew-*▷*table*. A *skew-*▷*arch* is one with the ▷jambs at an ▷angle to the direction of the arch. A *skew-back* is part of an ▷abutment from which an arch springs, i.e. on which the first voussoir is laid, usually on a large ▷block: it is essentially a sloping surface of an abutment which takes the thrust of the arch, so the term is given to the stone on which the slope is formed. A *skew-block* or *skew-*▷*butt* is a ▷kneeler at the foot of a gable, i.e. which supports the thrust of the coping-stones, also known as a *skew-*▷*corbel*, ▷*summer-stone*, or ▷*springer*. A *skew-*▷*fillet* is one fixed to the junction between the ▷roof-covering and the gable upstand or coping to direct the water away from the upstand. A *skew-put* is the lowest stone of a gable. A *skew-table* is a kneeler dressed to terminate the sloping moulded section of the raked (▷rake) coping.

Skintled Laid to give an irregular ▷face.

Skirt A *skirt-*▷*roof* is one like an ▷apron around a building between the upper and lower ▷floors, thus forming a ▷verandah or similar covering. A *skirting* is a narrow ▷board placed around the ▷margin of a ▷floor at the ▷base of an internal ▷wall: it is frequently moulded (▷mould), or ▷chamfered at the top, and corresponds to a ▷plinth. The *skirts* of a roof refers to the ▷eaves.

Skull Vanity, mortality, and transitory life. The skull appears in funerary ▷architecture, and may even occur

occasionally on ▷*putto* bodies. Skulls are found with bones, hour-glasses, scythes, and the like, and can have skeletal ▷wings of ▷bats derived from winged *putti-*heads. ▷Aegicrane, ▷bucranium.

Skylight A ▷frame containing ▷glass set in a ▷roof, fixed or opening.

Skyscraper A very tall building, usually based on a steel- or ▷concrete-▷framed structure.

Sky-sign An advertisement placed so that the letters stand out against the sky.

Slab Any thin rectangular piece of stone, as a sepulchral slab over a ▷grave. The ▷hearth of a fireplace. A *slab-house* is one clad in rough-hewn ▷boards, a term which is obsolete in Britain but is still current in America (▷alley).

Slaistering A wet ▷rendering, usually suggesting ▷rough work.

Slat A thin strip of wood, such as those in ▷louvres or ▷blinds.

Slate A kind of stone capable of being split or cut in very thin regular ▷slabs and used for ▷cladding or roofing. Slate-hanging is a slate-covered ▷wall.

Sleeper A timber or ▷plate laid under the ▷ground-▷floor of a building on which ▷joists rest. The ▷walls which support ground-floor joists are called *sleeper walls*: they give intermediate support to the floor-joists. A sleeper wall may also be placed between two structural elements, such as ▷piers, in order to strengthen them and stop them shifting. The term *sleepers* may also be applied to any ▷beams carrying joists or other structural pieces, and is especially given to a long horizontal beam near ground-level which distributes the loads from the ▷posts of a ▷framed building.

Slip A narrow ▷pew or seat, or a narrow ▷passage between buildings or ▷walls. A *slip-*▷*bolt* is a ▷barrel-*bolt*. *Slips* are glazing-▷beads or ▷fillets, or ▷sprigs of ▷foliage with flowers and ▷fruit, with the stem cut diagonally. They are also very narrow strips of timber.

Sluice A ▷dam which can be raised or lowered to regulate the flow of water.

Sluing Splayed (▷splay).

Slype A covered ▷corridor in a monastic building or a narrow ▷slip between two buildings or ▷walls. A ▷passage leading from a ▷transept to another part of the ▷monastery.

Smalto A small piece of ▷vitrified coloured material used in the fine ▷mosaic-work of ▷*Cosmati* decorations.

Smithy The workshop of a worker in metals who forges with a hammer.

Snacket The ▷hasp of a ▷casement.

Snake A wavy-line moulding (▷mould). ▷Serpent.

Sneck The lifting-lever to lift the ▷latch. A *sneck-head* is a latch-▷catch. A small stone in squared ▷rubble, hence *snecked rubble*. Snecked ▷*harling* leaves certain stones in the wall unrendered.

Snow boards Horizontal wooden ▷slats with spaces between fixed to ▷bearers over a ▷box-▷gutter to allow the snow to drain away. A *snow-guard* is a ▷board or boards on edge fixed along the ▷roof slope above the gutter to prevent masses of snow from sliding off and causing damage to the gutter or ▷eaves.

Snowflake A crystalline pattern.

Soakers Small flexible metal ▷flashings, approximately the size of ▷slates, cut to interlock with ▷slates or ▷tiles, and creating watertight joints at ▷hips, ▷valleys, or ▷abutments, and bent at right-angles for use in ▷angles.

Socket Any recess receiving another piece, such as an enlarged end of a ▷pipe into which the end or spigot of another pipe is fixed. It is also the ▷mortise to receive the pivot of a pivoted ▷sash or ▷door.

Socle A plain ▷block or low ▷pedestal without mouldings (▷mould), also called *Zocle*. A ▷base ▷course for a ▷column, ▷wall, or pedestal, also called a ▷plinth.

Soffit, soffita, soffite A ceiling. The lower exposed surface of any ▷arch, ▷vault, ▷balcony, ▷corona, ▷cornice, or ▷beam. The underside of any part of a building (▷[21]). A *soffite-▷board* is one fixed to the underside of part of a building, also called *planch-piece* or *plancier-piece*.

Softwood Timber taken from conifers, such as pine.

Solar A ▷loft, ▷garret, upper ▷chamber, or ▷rood-▷loft. A *solarium* is an upper chamber or sun-▷terrace open to the sky and placed on a ▷flat ▷roof. Also a ▷*loggia* or *soler*.

Soldier A ▷brick with its long ▷face set vertically, hence *soldier ▷arch*.

Sole The ▷foundation of a building or a ▷hearth. A ▷sill or the ▷base of an ▷embrasure. A *sole-piece* is a horizontal member distributing the loads of ▷posts, or member taking the thrust of a raking ▷shore. A *sole-▷plate* is the same as a sole-piece.

Solea A raised ▷platform between an ▷ambo and the ▷bema of a ▷basilica. Also *soleiya*.

Solid A ▷struck moulding (▷mould), or one cut into a member rather than ▷planted on, also called ▷*stuck*. A *solid ▷newel* is one into which the ends of the ▷treads of a ▷spiral stair are built, so a *solid-newel stair* is one in which the tapered treads wind round and are built into the central newel-▷pier.

Solium A ▷sarcophagus, usually of ▷marble, and elaborately sculptured.

Solomonic ▷Salomónica.

Solum The area within the ▷walls of a building after the removal of the topsoil.

Sommer ▷Summer.

Sondergotik Later German ▷Gothic styles from about 1380.

Sopraporta A design of ▷sculpture or painting over a doorway. An ▷*overdoor*. The *sopraporta*, door-case, and ▷door form one composition.

Sound-boarding Short ▷boards between ▷joists, carried on ▷fillets and supporting ▷pugging, to dampen sound transmission through a ▷floor. A *sounding-board*, on the other hand, also known as a *sound-board*, is a ▷canopy or ▷tester over ▷pulpit, also known as ▷*abat-voix*.

Souse, souste A ▷corbel.

South door A small priest's ▷door in the south ▷wall of a ▷chancel.

Sowdel, sowdell A ▷saddle-▷bar.

Space frame A ▷framed ▷roof-structure of geometrical forms, usually made of lightweight tubing, and capable of covering large areas without intermediate supports.

Spade A pointed ▷shield, or a small ▷ornament in that form. As a tool, an ▷emblem of ▷death and mourning.

Spall A piece of stone fallen from a ▷face, often caused by frost or chemical action.

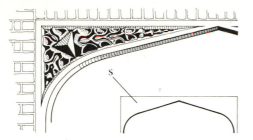

[223] SPANDREL A Tudor example with typically flat pointed arch from Honingham Hall, Norfolk. **s** spandrel. ▷[20]. (*JJS*)

Span The distance between two supports, as of a ▷lintel over ▷columns or an ▷arch between ▷imposts. A *span-piece* is a ▷collar-▷beam. A *span-▷roof* is one of two inclined sides. The ▷naves of ▷churches are usually span-roofed, while ▷aisles are often ▷shed-roofed, or ▷lean-to roofed.

Spandrel, splandrel [223] The approximately triangular space between an arched doorway and a rectangle formed by the outer mouldings (▷mould) over it, drawn from the ▷apex in a horizontal line, and from the springing in a vertical line. The surface between two ▷arches in an ▷arcade. Spandrels are sometimes called the ▷hanses or ▷haunches. They are also the ▷wall-▷panels between the tops of ▷windows and the ▷sills of the windows above in multi-▷storey ▷curtain walling, so are called *spandrel-panels*. The term is also given to the roughly triangular shape below the ▷string of a ▷stair. A *spandrel ▷step* is any solid step of approximate triangular section, the longest side of which forms part of the ▷soffite. A *spandrel wall* is one erected on the ▷extrados of an arch, so filling the spandrels.

Spanish Order A type of ▷Corinthian Order with a ▷lion's ▷mask instead of the ▷*fleuron* on the ▷abacus.

Spanish tile A segmental or semicircular roofing-▷tile, laid with the convex side alternately upwards and downwards, and overlapping, also called a ▷*mission-tile*.

Spanner A ▷cross-▷brace or ▷collar-▷beam.

Spar, sper, spur ▷Quarters, wooden ▷bars, etc., but more commonly ▷rafters. A ▷*spur* is the term given to an ▷ornamental ▷bracket supporting the ▷*breastsummer* and placed to flank a doorway. A *spar-piece* is a ▷collar-▷beam. A spar is also a ▷bar for fastening a ▷gate, a heavy timber of circular section, or a ▷brotch used for fixing ▷thatch to the structure below. *Sparred shelving* is slatted shelving.

Sparrow-picked A texture given to ▷plaster by pitting the wet surface with a stiff brush, or a texture given to ▷masonry by picking with a sharp point, like the peck-marks of a bird.

Spawled A ▷block of stone after the chips or spawls have been knocked off. To spall or spawl stone is to chip or chip off portions of the ▷face.

Speak-house A ▷parlour, or room in a ▷monastery where converse is allowed. A speaking-tube is one used to transmit messages by ▷acoustic means.

Spear Bound together like ▷fasces, or single, they were used in ▷trophies as ▷military decoration. They are commonest as spearheaded railings for ▷gates, ▷balconies, etc., probably to suggest the boundaries of property.

Specula A ▷Roman ▷watch-▷tower.

Specularia Thin sheets of ▷*lapis specularis* (mica) used instead of ▷glass in ▷windows.

Speculatorium A peep-hole in a ▷door.

Specus The ▷canal in which water flowed in ▷aqueducts.

Speer, spere, spier, spure A ▷screen across the lower end of a mediaeval ▷hall in a domestic building, marking off the *screens ▷passage* between the hall and the ▷kitchen, or any screen to prevent draughts. A *speer-* or *spere-▷truss* was a structure rising from trusses fixed to the side ▷walls of a ▷timber-framed hall which coincided with the position of the *screens passage*.

Speos A ▷temple or ▷tomb cut out of solid rock, or a ▷grotto-temple.

Speroni ▷*Anterides* or ▷buttresses, but usually interpreted as a species of ▷pilaster.

Sperver, esperver Also *sparver*. The timber ▷frame at the top of a ▷bed or ▷canopy, including a ▷tester.

Sphaeristerium A building for ball games, often attached to ▷*thermae*.

Spherical vault A hemispherical ▷dome.

Sphinx A creature with the body of a ▷lion and a humanoid head, often with the ▷Egyptian ▷*Nemes* head-dress, and often depicted as female, with breasts, although male sphinxes also recur. Egyptian sphinxes were never winged, and were usually male. Sphinxes were a popular element in ▷Neoclassical decoration.

Spica testacea Long ▷tiles usually laid in a ▷herringbone pattern for ▷Roman ▷pavements. ▷*Opus spicatum* refers to herringbone patterns.

Spier ▷Speer.

Spina The barrier in the centre of a ▷Roman ▷circus, dividing it into two long runs, at the ends of which the chariots turned. It was often decorated with ▷obelisks, statuary, ▷trophies, etc.

Spindles Timber rods of varying diameter with length, used in chair-backs, ▷galleries, and tops of desks or clocks, often found in eighteenth-century work, and revived during the ▷Arts-and-Crafts period.

Spira A ▷torus moulding (▷mould) at the base of a ▷column, or the column-base of an ▷Ionic or ▷Corinthian Order.

Spiral column A ▷*barley-sugar*, ▷*Salomónica, Solomonic*, ▷*torso, Trajan*, or ▷*twisted column*, often associated with the Temple of Solomon, and with the gates of Paradise.

Spiral stair A ▷stair, circular on plan, the flight of which winds round a central ▷newel. Spiral stairs usually ascend in a clockwise fashion. A ▷*caracole, circular*, ▷*cockle*, ▷*corkscrew*, ▷*helical*, or ▷*solid-newel stair*.

Spire [224] An acutely pointed ▷termination of ▷turrets and ▷towers forming the ▷roof, and often carried up to a great height. Spires are of stone, or of timber covered with thin ▷slabs of stone, ▷slates, ▷tiles, ▷shingles, or ▷lead. The earliest spires rose directly from the bases on which they sat, so they corresponded with the towers in terms of plan, with no ▷gutters or ▷parapets. *First-*▷*Pointed spires* were very elevated, and many were octagonal and set on square towers so that the ▷angles not covered by the spire were occupied by ▷pinnacles or by masses of ▷masonry that sloped back towards the spire. A ▷*broach-spire* is one that is octagonal, but rises from a square tower without a parapet or gutter, with the masses of masonry, or sometimes ▷slate- or ▷lead-covered *broaches*, built against the sides of the spire, and carried to points. A ▷*needle-spire* is a very thin, tall spire rising from within a parapet on a tower. A *spike* (▷Hertfordshire spike) is a short spire, spirelet, or a ▷*flèche*. The term *spire* is sometimes given to the ▷base of a ▷column, or sometimes to the ▷torus or ▷astragal, from *spira*. A *spire-*▷*light* is an opening, usually ▷gabled, in a spire, also called a ▷*lucarne*. A ▷*steeple* is the tower and spire. A ▷*splay-foot* spire is one off the straight, or one with a base that opens out with the ▷roof at a different, lower ▷pitch from that

of the spire itself, and which terminates in ▷eaves over the tower.

Spital A mediaeval ▷hospital.

Splandrel A ▷spandrel.

Splay An expansion given to an opening by slanting the sides to admit and reflect more light. Anything that is ▷bevelled or sloped. An ▷embrasure. A large ▷chamfer. A *splayed* ▷*arch* has a larger radius at one side of it than on the other. A *splayed coping* (▷cope) is one pitched one way, also called ▷*feather-edged*. A *splayed* ▷*jamb* has a face not at right angles to the ▷wall in which it is set. A *splayed* ▷*mullion* occurs in ▷canted ▷bays, between two glazed ▷windows at an ▷angle to each other. A *splayed window* has a ▷frame at an ▷angle to the ▷face of the wall in which it is set.

Split baluster An ▷engaged ▷baluster, or a baluster shape applied to decoration.

Spool-turning Turned decoration of linked spool-shapes like bobbin-turning, but less obvious, looking like cotton-reels piled up .

Spout A ▷pipe or ▷channel to convey water outwards from a ▷gutter or behind a ▷parapet. If decorated with grotesque heads it is called a ▷*gargoyle*.

Sprig A small ▷nail or ▷pin, used for fixing ▷panels or glazing.

Springer The ▷impost or point which unites an ▷arch with its support. The bottom stone of the arch on the impost is called the *springer*. The term *springer* is sometimes given to the bottom ▷cope-stone of a ▷gable. A ▷rib of a ▷vault, also called a *cross-springer* if it is the ▷transverse or ▷diagonal rib. The *spring* or *springing* is the point where an arch begins to rise from its imposts, or even the angle or curvature of the rise. A *springing* ▷*course* is where the first ▷voussoirs of an arch rest. A *spring-house* is a building erected over a spring, and therefore cool, used for storing perishables such as dairy products. The *springing line* is the horizontal plane from which an arch or vault begins to rise. A *springing* ▷*wall* is a ▷buttress. *Springed*, or sprung, indicates ▷roof-boarding or ▷sarking with ▷bevel joints. A *spring-board* is a ▷string, while a *spring-nib* is a ▷sash-fastener, also *spring-snib*.

Sprocket A wedge-shaped piece of timber, especially one fixed to the ▷foot of a ▷rafter on its upper side to raise the level of the ▷eaves, and tilt the roof slightly at the eaves. It is also called a ▷*cocking-piece*. *Sprocketed eaves* means eaves so raised.

291

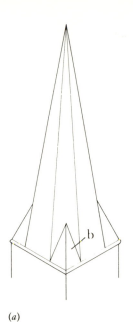

[224] SPIRE (*a*) Broach-spire. **b** broach. (*JJS*) (*b*) The three spires of Lichfield Cathedral, with their lucarnes. The west spires date from around 1325, but the central spire was largely rebuilt by Wyatt from 1788. (*JSC*) (*c*) Christ Church, Spitalfields, by Nicholas Hawksmoor, built 1714–29. Note the mightly Tuscan Order of the portico, treated like a Palladian window or a Serliana. The face of the tower appears very wide by virtue of the flanking buttresses, and the whole is crowned with a broach spire. This extraordinary composition, with its eclectic use of many motifs, has Mannerist and Baroque aspects, as well as a strong dash of mediaeval allusion in the spire. (*JSC*)

(*a*)

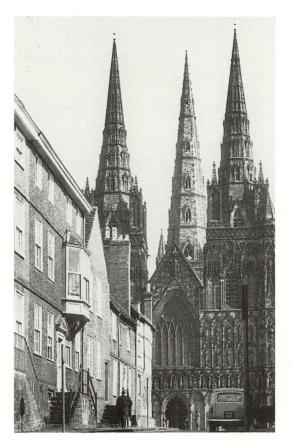

(*b*)

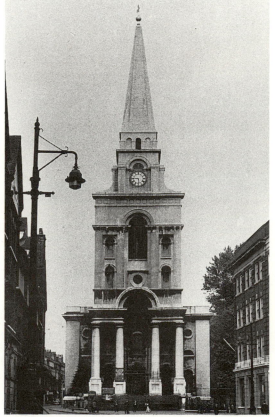

(*c*)

Sprung moulding Any curved moulding (▷mould).

Spudds and rings Rings of iron into which ▷door-▷posts are placed, with a ▷projection or *spudd* for insertion into a corresponding hole in the ▷step or ▷sill.

Spur, spure Carved timber work at a doorway supporting the *bressumer* (▷breastsummer). A short ▷strut or ▷stay set diagonally to support something. A ▷shore, a ▷prop, a sustaining ▷pier, a sloping ▷buttress. An angular outwork or ▷projection from the general ▷face of a ▷curtain or ▷wall to assist in defence. The angular edge of the ▷pier of a ▷bridge, also called a ▷cut-water. A *spur-stone* is one set at the corner of a building or on either side of a ▷carriage-entrance to prevent damage by carts. Also a decorative carving at the base of a circular pier which rests on a square ▷plinth, at the corners, often a ▷leaf-form, or as some fanciful ▷ornament: this is also called a *griffe*. A spur is also a ▷*speer* in the sense of a ▷screen preventing draughts. A *spur-beam* is a horizontal timber laid over the top of a ▷wall, fixed to the wall-▷plate, ▷rafter, and ashlering.

Square [225] A figure of four equal sides and right-angled corners. An ▷area of such form surrounded by houses, and usually paved or planted in the centre, although in this sense an urban 'square' can often be rectangular. A *square and* ▷*rabbet* is an ▷annulet. A *square* ▷*billet* is a ▷Romanesque moulding (▷mould) consisting of rows of cubes with spaces between, often in two layers. A *square* ▷*dome* is a ▷cloistered ▷arch, or a ▷vault on a square consisting of four quarter-cylinders meeting in diagonal lines. *Square headed* means an ▷aperture with parallel sides and a horizontal ▷lintel over. *Squared* ▷*rubble* is rubble-work where the stones are roughly

squared, and laid in various sizes. *Square-turned* means carved or moulded on four sides rather than circular and turned on a lathe, as in ▷balusters. A *square* is also an angle of 90° enabling exactness in construction to be achieved: it is a mason's tool, and is a ▷symbol of moral probity, hence *on the square.*

Squillery A ▷scullery.

Squinch A small ▷arch formed across an ▷angle, as when used to support the alternate sides of octagonal ▷spires. Squinches may be ▷corbelled pieces built out ▷course by course across a corner to support something above. They are also used to achieve a transition between a square compartment and a ▷dome or ▷drum. A *squinch* is also called a ▷*sconce.*

Squint [226] An opening through the ▷wall of a ▷church in an oblique direction to enable sight-lines between the ▷high altar and an ▷aisle to be established. They can occur at either side of the ▷chancel ▷arch. They are also called ▷*hagioscopes.* A *squint* ▷*brick* or ▷*quoin* is one used at an oblique corner, and therefore a special.

Stable A building for the accommodation of horses, often of considerable grandeur when part of a country-house ensemble.

Stack ▷Chimney.

Staddle A supporting framework. *Staddle-stones* are ▷battered uprights on which circular stone discs are laid with sloping tops, so looking like petrified mushrooms, used to carry ▷timber-framed barns. They not only protected the timbers from the wet ground, but prevented rats and mice from climbing up.

[225] SQUARE St James's Square (now St James's Gardens), Norland Estate, North Kensington, with the Church of St James Norlands designed by Lewis Vulliamy in a First-Pointed style, and terrace houses designed to look like paired villas by John Barnett, 1847. (*Guildhall Library, City of London*)

[226] SQUINT St Mary's Church, Charminster, Dorset. Romanesque chancel arch (twelfth century) with nail-head ornament. Note the hagioscope or squint to the left, and the doorway to the missing rood-loft. The pointed arches of the nave-arcade are Transitional of the late twelfth century. The clerestorey probably pre-dates the arcade, and is basically Romanesque with later alterations. Note the massive piers, much-scalloped capitals, and the square abaci. (*JSC*)

Stadium A place for athletics or a sports ▷arena, often shaped like an elongated ellipse. It was also a ▷Roman length of around 185 metres.

Staff ▷Ornamental ▷plaster, often moulded elsewhere, reinforced, and fixed later. A *staff*-▷*bead* is a corner- or angle-▷bead.

Staffordshire Blue A very hard, dense, blue ▷brick, often used for engineering purposes or as ▷damp-proof courses.

Stag An ▷emblem of ▷Artemis/Diana, often found in allusions to the ▷hunt. ▷Symbol, especially Sts Eustace and Hubert.

Stage A ▷floor or ▷storey. ▷Towers are always described as having ▷stages, such as the ▷*belfry stage*, rather than storeys. In a ▷theatre it is where the actors perform. The stage of a ▷buttress or a tower is the part between one splayed ▷projection or ▷string and the next. Any raised ▷dais or ▷platform for a speaker.

Stained glass ▷Glass stained or coloured through its thickness during its manufacture is called *pot metal glass*, while *white glass* coloured on the surface is called *flashed glass*. Stained and painted glass is secured in H-shaped ▷lead ▷cames and arranged in patterns.

Stair, staircase [227] That part of a building where there are ▷steps to enable persons to get from one ▷storey or level of the building to another. Parts of a staircase are as follows: ▷*apron* is the board covering the trimmer-▷joist of a ▷landing; ▷*balusters* are vertical supports for the handrail and guards for the open sides; the *balustrade* (▷baluster) consists of a handrail, ▷string, balusters, and ▷newels (*banister* is commonly used instead of *baluster*, while *banisters* is often used

where a *balustrade* would be correct); ▷*bearers* support steps; ▷*blocks* are fixed to the upper edges of bearers to give additional support to the ▷treads (blocks are also the small triangular pieces glued to the angles between treads and ▷risers on the underside); ▷*brackets* serve the same purpose as blocks; ▷*cappings* are the cover-▷mouldings (▷mould) ▷planted on the upper edges of strings; *easing* is a curved portion connecting two strings when they change direction; a ▷*flight* is a continuous set of steps from one landing to another; the ▷*going* or ▷*run of a step* is the distance measured horizontally between two risers; the *going of a flight* is therefore the horizontal distance between the face of the bottom riser and that of the topmost riser; *headroom* is the distance measured vertically from the line of the ▷nosings to the lower edge of the apron or to the ▷soffite of a flight above; a *landing* is a ▷platform between flights, or the ▷floor at the top of a stair; a *quarter-space landing* (▷quarter-pace) is one on which a quarter-turn has to be made between the end of one flight and the beginning of the next; if a landing extends for the combined width of both flights and a complete half-turn has to be made, it is known as a ▷*half-space landing*; the *line of the nosings* is a line drawn to touch the projecting edges or nosings of the treads; *newels* are vertical members placed at the ends of flights to support the strings, handrails, trimmers, and bearers; the top of a newel is called a ▷*cap*, and the lower end the ▷*drop*; a *starting newel* is the newel-post at the bottom of a stair (▷cockle or ▷spiral stair below); *nosing* is the front edge of a tread projecting beyond the face of the riser; the ▷*pitch* or *slope* is the ▷angle between the line of nosings and the floor or landing; the *riser* is the vertical part or front member of a step; the *rise of a step* is the vertical distance between the tops of two consecutive treads; the *rise of a flight* is the total height from floor to floor, or landing to landing, or floor to landing; a ▷*scotia* is the concave moulding (▷mould)

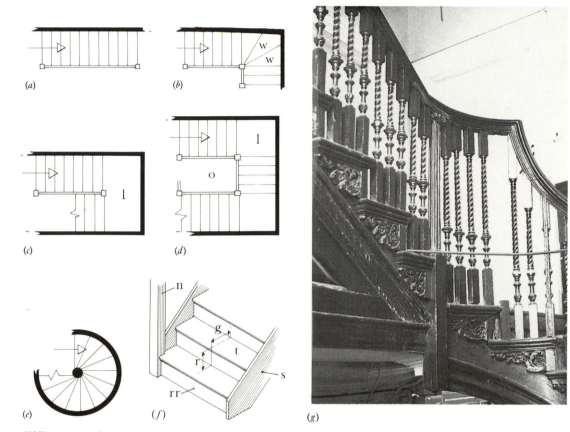

[227] STAIR (a) Straight stair or flight. (b) Quarter-turn with winders, **w**. (c) Dog-leg, i.e. without a well and with landing, **l**. (d) Open-well, **o**, stair with landings, **l**. (e) Spiral or winding stair with central newel. (f) The basic elements of a stair: **n** newel, **rr** riser, **r** rise, **g** going, **t** tread, **s** string. (*JJS*) (g) Part of the stair of 14 Fournier Street, Spitalfields, built in 1726. Note the tread ends carved with flowers and foliate scrolls. The balusters are turned and twisted, and the newels are fluted miniature columns. (*JSC*)

under the nosing; the *soffite* is the under-surface of the stair of flight; a ▷*spandrel* is a triangular surface between the outer string and the floor; *strings* or *stringers* are inclined timbers supporting the steps; *treads* are horizontal members forming the upper surfaces of steps; the ▷*well* is the space between the outer strings of the several flights of a stair; a *closed-string* stair has strings of continuous raking (▷rake) members supporting identical balusters; an ▷*open*, or ▷*cut-string*, stair has strings cut to the ▷profiles of the treads that support balusters of unequal length (in the latter case, two balusters per tread are usual in early eighteenth-century work, increasing to three by the middle of the century, and accompanied, in better-class work, by elaborately carved tread-ends). Different types of stair include: the ▷*dog-leg* (two flights parallel to each other with a landing between them and no well between the outer strings); *flying stairs* (steps ▷cantilevered from the staircase ▷wall without any

newel); *geometrical stairs* (no newels, and usually circular or elliptical on plan, with stone steps one end of which is built into the wall, and the lower front edge of which rests on the step below); *cockle, newel, spiral*, ▷*turngrece*, ▷*turnpike*, ▷*vice*, or *winding stairs* (steps wind round a central ▷pier or ▷column called a newel, and thus the narrow ends of the steps are supported by the newel); ▷*open-well stairs* (space or well between outer strings, thus differing from dog-leg); *straight-flight stairs* (meaning one flight only); and *turning stairs* (including *quarter-turn, three-quarters turn, half-turn*, and *bifurcated* [where stairs divide into two branches]). A stair that starts with one flight and returns in two is called a *double-return stair* (▷close, ▷cockle, ▷cut, ▷dancer, ▷turngrece, ▷turnpike, ▷vice, etc.). A *staircase* can refer to the building or structure in which stairs are housed. A *stair dormer* is a wide dormer (▷dormant) taking the upper part of a staircase into a roof. A *stair-*▷*tower* is a tower containing a stair, often treated with elaborate upper-works. A *stair* ▷*turret* contains a winding-stair, and often has a ▷superstructure giving access to the ▷roof.

Stalactites ▷Corbelled ▷squinches carved to resemble ▷stalactites, or ▷stucco work resembling stone, often found in ▷grottoes. Also called *muqarna*. It occurs in ▷revivals of the ▷Arabian, ▷Moorish, ▷Saracenic, and Turkish (▷Ottoman) styles.

Stalk An ▷ornament in the ▷Corinthian ▷capital from which ▷volutes and ▷helices spring.

Stall An elevated seat in the ▷chancel of a ▷church. It is a fixed seat enclosed either wholly or partly at the back and sides. In ▷cathedrals and large churches it was enclosed at the back with ▷panelling, and surmounted by overhanging ▷canopies of ▷open-work, and formed part of serried rows of ▷stalls. The open canopies were richly ▷ornamented, ▷enriched with ▷pinnacles, ▷crockets, ▷tracery, and the like. The stall-seats, if hinged, frequently had carved ▷brackets on the underside called ▷*misericords*. A ▷*theatre* seat in the front part of the ▷*parquet* or ▷*orchestra-stalls*. *Stalls* are also the divisions in ▷stables or other places. A *stall-*▷*board* is a strong ▷sill and ▷frame beneath a shop-▷window over the *stall-*▷*riser*, which is the vertical surface between the ▷pavement and the stall-▷board. A *stall-board* ▷*light* is a window in a stall-board.

Stanchion A ▷prop or vertical support. The term was also given to the upright iron ▷bars between the ▷mullions of ▷Gothic ▷windows. Mullions themselves are also known as ▷*stanchions*, as are the ▷quarters or ▷studs of a ▷partition.

Standard A massive item, not easily moved, such as a ▷chest or a candlestick, or the vertical ▷poles of a ▷scaffold. The supports for ▷shelves are called *standards*. Standards are also ▷*door-*▷*posts*, *quartering*, or *uprights* in ▷*stud-*▷*partitions*. A flag bearing ▷heraldic symbols.

Staple A loop that passes through the slot in a ▷hasp, to take a lock, or a U-shaped ▷nail with two points.

Star A pointed form of decoration. A *star moulding* (▷mould) is a decoration like a continuous ▷band of stars, often carved. A *Star of David* is a six-pointed star formed of two superimposed equilateral triangles. A *star-ribbed* ▷vault, also known as a *stellar* vault, is one with a pattern of ▷ribs forming a star-like ▷geometry. Stars occur in ▷Islamic decorations and their ▷revivals, and are common in ▷Neoclassical designs. They are also particularly associated with the Virgin Mary.

Starlings ▷Piles round the ▷piers of a ▷bridge, or the ▷cutwaters of a bridge-pier.

Statio A ▷Roman ▷castle or ▷citadel.

Stations of the Cross Fourteen representations of the progress of Christ from His Judgement to Calvary and the tomb, found in ▷churches, either as paintings or ▷sculptures.

Staunchion As ▷stanchion.

Stave An upright cylinder forming a ▷rack to contain the hay in a ▷stable. A *stave-*▷*church* is a ▷timber-framed and timber-walled church found in Scandinavia. A *stave* is one of a number of narrow ▷boards used to build up a curved surface, as in ▷*pipe-staves* or *coopering*, or is the horizontal ▷lath in ▷wattle-and-▷daub construction, or is a vertical smaller member (between widely spaced ▷studs) which helps to support the wattles. A stave is also a *caulk* (▷caulking), or a rung.

Stay A ▷brace. A *stay-*▷*bar* is a horizontal bar to support a ▷mullion or leaded ▷light. It is also a bar with holes at intervals to hold a ▷casement-light open.

Staykfald A ▷putlog hole.

Steening Brickwork (▷brick) or ▷masonry laid dry, with no ▷mortar, to form the shaft of a ▷well.

Steeple The ▷tower and ▷spire of a ▷church, housing bells.

Stele, stela An upright carved stone, often capped by an ▷anthemion, making a ▷grave in ▷Antiquity. Also a part of a ▷wall reserved for a ▷memorial.

Stell An enclosure for sheep. It is often circular on plan.

Stellar vault ▷Star, ▷vault.

Stencil A thin sheet of metal or card in which designs have been cut: when a stiff brush charged with paint is passed over the back of the sheet the pattern is applied to the surface underneath. Stencilling was often used for interior decorations in the mediaeval and Victorian periods.

Step A ▷block of any material of a height within the lift of a person's foot. A ▷stair-step consisting of a ▷riser and a ▷tread. *Stepped* means rising in steps, as a step, stepped, or ▷corbel ▷gable. A *stepped* ▷*arch* has a stepped ▷head, and can be formed of corbelled ▷courses: it was a feature of Egyptianizing (▷Egyptian) and ▷Art-Deco forms. A *stepped arch* can also be one with some of the ▷voussoirs cut square at the top so that the horizontal courses fit them easily, hence *stepped voussoirs*, giving an effect in the ▷jointing like a stepped arch. A *step* ▷*pyramid* is stepped rather than having smooth sides. *Stepped* ▷*flashing* is a flexible metal cover-flashing let into the joints of brickwork to make a watertight joint between a ▷chimney or gable-▷wall and a sloping ▷roof: it steps down from one ▷mortar-joint to the next. A *stepped skirting* occurs when an upstand joins an inclined surface of a roof.

Stereobata, stereobate The ▷stylobate or a ▷podium, or any solid mass of ▷masonry carrying a ▷colonnade or a ▷wall. The top ▷step of a *crepidoma* (▷crepido). Vitruvius defines *stereobatae* as the walls under the ▷columns above the ground, so he was thinking of the walls of ▷Roman ▷temple-podia. It is essentially the ▷platform on which a columnar temple stands.

Stereochromy A technique of painting using ▷water-glass as the binding agent between the base and the colour.

Stereotomy The art of cutting and dressing (▷dressed) of stones, especially to form ▷vaults and staircases of great technical ingenuity and beauty. It was brought to perfection between the sixteenth and eighteenth centuries in France.

Steyre A ▷flight of ▷steps.

Stiacciato A low ▷relief, not even as pronounced as bas-relief.

Stick A style of ▷timber-framed building in which the expression is very hard and angular, often with jagged, rasping elements. It became fashionable in the second part of the nineteenth century, the best examples occurring in France and America. It was also so-called from the thin slats or 'sticks' fixed to a structure to create a timber-framed image.

Stiff-leaf ▷Gothic ▷foliage of the thirteenth century (or a ▷revival of such) on ▷capitals and ▷bosses consisting of stylized ▷leaves. The term is also given to long feather-like upright leaves found in ▷Neoclassical ornament, especially on friezes.

Stile The vertical part of a ▷frame into which the ends of ▷rails are fixed with ▷mortises and ▷tenons, as in a ▷panelled ▷door. Stiles are described as *hanging* or *shutting* (▷[104]). A structure to enable a ▷wall to be crossed by means of ▷steps or ▷bars.

Stile Liberty The ▷Italian term for ▷Art Nouveau.

Stillicidium Dripping ▷eaves on ▷Doric buildings.

Still-room A room where preserves, biscuits, etc., are made and stored. A place for distilling, or a housekeeper's room.

Stilted arch An ▷arch where the springing begins above the ▷impost, giving the arch an elongated appearance, often used to elevate ▷semicircular arches to the same height as other semicircular arches of a greater span.

Stipple To alter a wet coat of paint by dabbing it with a *stippler*, or to dab on spots of a differing colour with a bristle brush.

Stoa A ▷colonnade or ▷portico, or a covered ▷hall in the ▷Byzantine style. A ▷Greek stoa was usually long, roofed, and colonnaded at the front, used as a ▷promenade and meeting-place.

Stob A ▷fence-▷post or other small upright post.

Stockade A defensive barrier of wood, or an enclosure made of logs.

Stoep A ▷verandah.

Stone state A ▷flag-stone for roofing: it is heavy and expensive. The chief types are the friable ▷limestones (▷lime) from Stonesfield or Collyweston, or the thicker ▷slabs found in Yorkshire and Lancashire.

Stoneware Clay burnt and glazed, used for drain-▷pipes, etc.

Stonework ▷Masonry.

Stooling The upper surface of the end of a stone eared ▷sill, dressed horizontal to provide a ▷bed for the ▷brick or stone over.

Stoop As ▷*stoep*, or a raised ▷verandah at the entrance to a house.

Stoothing ▷Battening of ▷walls, or ▷common ▷grounds.

Stop Anything against which a moulding (▷mould) stops, such as a ▷projecting stone or piece of wood. A moulding or rebate (▷rabbet) around a ▷door- or ▷window-▷frame against which the door or window closes and fits. A ▷bead, or a stop-bead, a narrow wooden strip against which a door or window closes. A *stop-*▷*chamfer* (▷[228]) is the decorative treatment of the transition between a chamfer and a normal square ▷arris on a ▷beam. A *stop-moulding* is a solid or ▷struck moulding which stops short of the end of the piece into which it is formed. A *stopped* ▷*flute* is where the flutes of

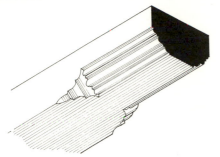

[228] STOP-CHAMFER Stop-chamfered beam of seventeenth-century type. (*JJS*)

a ▷Classical ▷column or ▷pilaster terminate, two-thirds of the way down the ▷shaft, in flat ▷bands or facets, or are partly filled with ▷cabling. A *cable flute* is also called a *stopped flute*.

Stopping Making good cracks or defects in plastering, wood, etc.

Storey One of the horizontal divisions of a building. The space between two ▷floors, or between two ▷entablatures or any other horizontal division. Storeys are described as ▷*basement*, ▷*ground*, ▷*first* (or ▷*piano nobile* if the principal rooms are on that level), *second*, *third*, etc., then ▷*Attic*, meaning above the main ▷cornice (▷[129]). ▷*Entresols* and ▷*mezzanines* are intermediate storeys. Horizontal divisions of ▷towers are called ▷*stages*. *Storey-posts* are the main upright posts carrying the ▷wall of a ▷timber-framed building.

Stoup A vessel for holding consecrated water placed near the entrance to a ▷church, usually in a simple ▷niche, or ▷cantilevered out. It is also called a ▷*holy-water stone*.

Stove An eighteenth-century cast-iron ▷*register-grate* was called a stove. The closed stove with doors was perfected by ▷Franklin in 1776, and was used as a heating and cooking apparatus. In central Europe stoves are decorative, covered in glazed ▷tiles, and are often placed in the corners of rooms. A *stove* was also a term given to a ▷greenhouse or ▷conservatory.

Straight arch A ▷lintel of ▷voussoirs based on the principle of the ▷arch, but with only a flat or slightly ▷cambered *intrados*, common in ▷Georgian ▷architecture, and often made of ▷rubbed ▷bricks or finely ▷dressed stone. It is also called a *skewback arch* (▷skew) from the steeply raked ▷abutments from which the arch springs.

Straightening ▷Plaster ▷rendering for ▷dubbing-out ▷rubble or stone ▷walls with irregular surfaces.

[229] STRAINER ARCH The remarkable fourteenth-century arches at Wells Cathedral, inserted to strengthen the piers supporting the crossing-tower. Note the rood. The nave is ten bays long, and the piers are very elaborately moulded, with fine stiff-leaf capitals, and the shafts of the piers on the diagonals are keeled. The tribune (or triforium) is treated as a continuous arcade by the placing of the corbels for the vaulting at a higher level. The date is the first part of the thirteenth century. The arches themselves have many roll mouldings, with hood mouldings terminating in head-stops. The entire ensemble, including vaulting, is the epitome of Early English, or First-Pointed Gothic, apart from the strainer arches, which are Second-Pointed or Decorated. (*JSC*)

Strainer arch [229] An ▷arch across an ▷aisle or ▷nave to prevent movement of the walls, on the principle of the flying ▷buttress.

Straining piece Also called a *straining-▷beam* or *strutting-piece*, it is a horizontal ▷strut above the ▷tie-beam, as in a ▷queen-post truss, where it occurs over the queen-posts themselves. It is any member fixed between opposing members to help to counteract their thrusts. A *straining-▷sill* is a member fixed to the top of a tie-beam to resist the thrust from the struts.

Strap An iron ▷plate for the connection of two or more timbers to which it is bolted. *Strapping* or *straps* are ▷battens, firrings (▷fir), or plugged-and-nailed ▷grounds. A *strap-▷hinge* is a *cross-▷garnet* or

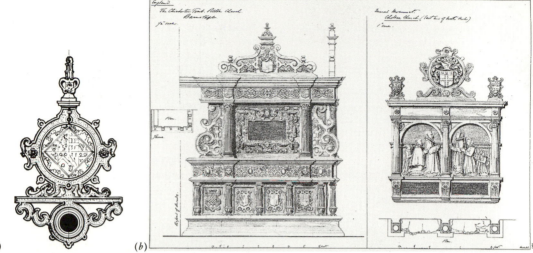

[230] STRAPWORK (*a*) (*JSC*) (*b*) (left) Monument to Sir John Chichester in the church of St Mary, Pilton, Barnstaple, Devon, of 1569. Note the bulging columns at the base with Mannerist treatment, with strapwork surrounding shields in the panels between. Virtually the whole of the rest of the monument is enriched with strapwork, including the Attic storey; (right) Monument of Thomas Larrance in Chelsea church, 1630. A typical late-Elizabethan/Jacobean arrangement with kneeling figures facing each other at prayer, and set within arcuated aedicules with Achievements over surrounded by strapwork. (*JSC Collection*)

band-and-hook hinge with two long straps of equal length. *Strap-and-jewel* is the type of ▷strapwork ▷ornament consisting of split ▷balusters and ▷bosses. A *strapped* ▷*wall* is a ▷battened wall.

Strapwork [230] A form of decoration of wood, ▷plaster, or carved ▷masonry, resembling leather ▷straps or fretwork, much used in ▷Elizabethan and ▷Jacobean times (▷[13]). It resembles narrow ▷bands folded, crossed, ▷interlaced, and cut, often further ▷embellished with ▷lozenges, etc.

Straw Stems of wheat or rye used in ▷thatch. Modern cereals are too short-stemmed, so 'long-straw' now must be specially grown. ▷Sedge may be termed *sedge-straw*.

Streamlining Design to suggest aerodynamics. It was a style involving curved shapes, parallel lines, and strips of ▷windows, associated with the 1920s and 1930s 'Modern' ▷architecture.

Stretcher A ▷brick or stone laid with its longer ▷face in the surface of the ▷wall. A stretching or stretcher-▷course is one composed of stretchers.

Stria A ▷*list* or ▷*fillet* between the ▷flutes of ▷columns or ▷pilasters. A ▷rib. *Striatura* refers to the fluting of columns, and striated means ▷*chamfered* or ▷*channelled*. *Striae* can also refer to grooves, channels, or flutes, so are confused with fillets, but the term seems to mean flutes rather than fillets.

Striga A ▷flute, so *striges* are the flutes.

Strigil [231] A type of ▷ornament on a flat ▷band, such as a ▷fascia or a ▷frieze, consisting of repeated vertical ▷flutings or ▷reedings. *Strigillation* is the curved pattern of S-shaped flutes on the sides of ▷Roman ▷sarcophagi, often used in ▷Neoclassical design.

String The sloping timbers carrying the ends of the ▷treads and ▷risers of a ▷stair, also called a *stringer* (▷stairs). A *string* or *string-*▷*course* is a horizontal ▷band or line of mouldings (▷mould) on a building. A horizontal ▷tie. *Stringing* or *banding* means thin lines of different woods ▷inlaid around the ▷borders of tables or drawer-fronts, fashionable from the eighteenth century.

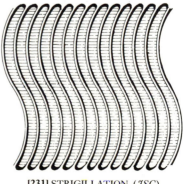

[231] STRIGILLATION (*JSC*)

299

Strix A ▷flute or *canalis*.

Strohblumenmuster *Immortelles*, or small blue flowers, as on ▷ceramic ▷tiles.

Stroked A stone surface tooled to produce a very fine surface of tiny ▷flutes.

Stroll garden One viewed from a ▷promenade, often with vantage-points.

Stronghold A fortress or ▷redoubt.

Struck A moulding (▷mould) cut into a member. A ▷mortar joint smoothed by pressing the trowel in at the upper edge to throw rain off the ▷face of the ▷brick. *Struck* also means removed, as when a temporary framework is removed after an ▷arch or ▷vault has set.

Structura ▷Antique ▷masonry. *Structura caementicia* is ▷concrete.

Strut A ▷brace. Any piece that keeps two other members apart. It is in a state of compression, unlike a ▷tie which keeps two members together, and is therefore in tension (▷[212j]).

Stuart ▷Architecture of the early seventeenth century, otherwise ▷Jacobean or ▷Carolean.

Stuc, stucco An exterior plastered finish of ▷lime, sand, ▷brick-dust, stone-dust, or powdered burnt clay nodules, mixed with water and lined to resemble ▷ashlar. Fine interior stucco is calcium carbonate mixed with marble dust, ▷glue, and hair. Stucco was often enriched and moulded (▷mould). It is also known as ▷*opus albarium* or *opus tectorium*.

Stuck ▷Struck.

Stud A ▷quarter or ▷post in wooden ▷partitions.

Studio An ▷apartment, usually with a north-▷light, for creating artwork.

Stuff Timber for ▷joinery, square-cut. ▷Plaster.

Stugged Pecked stone faced with a pointed tool.

Stump tracery Late central European ▷Gothic ▷tracery with interpenetrating ▷bars cut off like stumps.

Stupa A domed ▷sepulchre of Buddhist origin, or any form resembling a stupa, or bell.

Style 1925 ▷Art Deco.

Style Moderne ▷Art Deco.

Style Rayonnant A type of decoration radiating from centres towards rich borders. It is also associated with early Continental ▷Second-▷Pointed work.

Stylobate A continuous ▷base or substructure, consisting of the topmost ▷step of a structure of three steps called the *crepidoma* (▷crepido) on which a ▷colonnade or a building with a ▷peristyle is placed. In ▷Classical ▷architecture it has come to mean any continuous base or substructure on which a colonnade is erected but, properly, it should be distinguished from a ▷podium, which is a continuous ▷pedestal with ▷plinth and ▷cornice, while a *stylobate* is the upper of three steps (*crepidoma*) in ▷Greek ▷architecture (▷stereobata).

Sub A *sub-*▷*arch* is subsidiary or minor arch enclosed and ▷framed by a larger structural arch. A *sub-*▷*base* is the lowest part of a base with several horizontal divisions. A *sub-*▷*Order* is a secondary Order of ▷architecture, subsidiary to the main 'structural' Order. A *sub-*▷*plinth* is one under a plinth, as under a ▷column or ▷pilaster. A *subway* is any underground ▷passage for pedestrians.

Sublica A structural ▷pile in ▷Antique foundations.

Sublime An eighteenth-century ▷aesthetic concept contrasted with that of the ▷Beautiful. It is associated with terror, power, vastness, ruggedness, and the ability to stimulate imagination and the emotions. The Sublime is associated with limitlessness, storms, waterfalls, a raging sea, or mighty mountains. In ▷architecture an exaggerated scale, powerful unadorned ▷fabric, and gloomy cavernous structures would be classed as *Sublime*.

Subscus A peg or ▷dowel.

Subsellium A ▷misericord.

Sudatorium A sweating-room in ▷thermae.

Suggestus An elevated ▷platform, as in the ▷Forum or the Colosseum.

Sule A ▷sill.

Summer A ▷lintel. A horizontal ▷beam on the ends of ▷cantilevered joists and carrying the ▷posts above, also called ▷breastsummer or *bressummer*. A main beam or ▷girder in a ▷floor. Any large beam used to bear loads. A *summer-*▷*tree* or beam carrying floor-joists. A *summer-stone* is the lowest stone of a ▷gable stopping at the ▷eaves: the first stone of the tabling is set into the summer-stone, which is also called a ▷*skew-*▷*corbel*.

[232] SUNBURST (*JSC*)

Sun [232]   A representation of the Sun, associated with ▷Apollonian or ▷Louis Quatorze ▷ornament, and consisting of a male head surrounded by a *sunburst* of rods like a ▷halo. A *sunburst* is also a *fanlight*, but it is a common ▷Baroque ornament of radiating gilded rods (▷fan). A *sun-disc* is a circular disc or part of a ▷globe with ▷wings and rearing ▷*uraei*, found associated with ▷Egyptian ▷architecture, and often occurring on the ▷cavetto cornice. A *sun-light* is gas-jets under a reflector. A *sun-room* is a *solarium*. A *sunflower* became a common decorative element in nineteenth-century design. The sun and moon are found in representations of the ▷Crucifixion, with the sun on the ▷heraldic right of Christ's head and the moon on the left, suggesting the forces of good and evil.

Sunk draft   A ▷margin around a piece of ▷ashlar sunk below the ▷face of the stone. A *sunk* ▷*face* is one with a sunken ▷panel surrounded by a raised margin. A *sunk* ▷*fence* is a ▷*ha-ha*, or trench with one vertical side and one sloped and grassed. A *sunk* ▷*fillet* is a groove or rectangular ▷channel. A *sunk moulding* (▷mould) is recessed behind the prevailing surface. A *sunk panel* is set within and behind a ▷frame or carved into ▷masonry or timber. A *sunk* ▷*relief* is any relief which does not ▷project beyond the surface on which it is carved, also called ▷*cavo rilievo* or ▷*intaglio rilevato*.

Sunken garden   A secluded ▷garden set below the level of surrounding ground, and often surrounded with ▷terraces.

Super   This refers to anything above. A *super-*▷*altar* is a ▷shelf above an altar, or to the east of it, on which are placed ▷vases, etc., not to be permitted on the altar itself. A *superabacus* is an ▷impost ▷block over the ▷abacus, or a ▷dosseret, also called a *super-*▷*capital*. A *supercilium* is the ▷lintel of an opening, the ▷fillet at the top of a ▷cornice ▷cyma, the small fillet on either side of the ▷scotia of an ▷Attic base, or the top part of a ▷door or ▷window ▷architrave.

Supercolumniation   The arrangement of one ▷Order above another. When the Orders are used to define the ▷storeys of a ▷Classical ▷façade, and set one

above the other, or *superimposed*, they have a hierarchical order: ▷Doric is used at the bottom (being tough, primitive, and masculine), with ▷Ionic above, and ▷Corinthian above that. In taller buildings ▷Tuscan is used first, then ▷Roman Doric, then Ionic, then Corinthian, and finally ▷Composite.

Superstructure   Work built on the ▷foundations of a building.

Supporter   A human or animal on either side of a ▷shield in heraldry, apparently supporting it upright.

Surbase   The upper mouldings (▷mould) or ▷cornice of a ▷pedestal. The cornice over a ▷dado. A *surbased* ▷*arch* is one of less height than half its ▷span.

Surface   Applied. A surface ▷arcade is ▷blind, and a surface ▷rib is a decorative device on the ▷soffite of an ▷arch or vault.

Surmounted   An ▷arch, ▷vault, or ▷dome rising higher than half its ▷span, or a semicircular ▷stilted arch. It is also a way of stating that something is placed over part of a building: i.e. the composition is *surmounted* by a ▷sculpture of ▷*cornucopiae* and ▷*putti*.

Surround   A ▷frame, as of any architectural feature, like a ▷chimney-piece or a ▷door-surround.

Suspensura   A ▷floor carried on ▷arches, ▷piers, or ▷walls, associated with ▷Roman underfloor heating.

Sussex bond   Also called *Sussex garden-wall* ▷*bond*, it is a ▷brick bond which on each ▷course and ▷face has a sequence of three ▷stretchers and one header (▷head), repeated. The face shows a diagonal pattern.

Swag   A ▷festoon like a cloth held on two supports. The term may also be given to a pendent ▷garland, but *festoon* cannot really describe a loop of drapery. A ▷*Vandyck swag* is a loop of drapery with a scalloped lower edge, similar to the ▷lambrequin in ▷Grotesque ▷ornament and ▷strapwork.

Swallowtail   A swallowtail or dovetail moulding (▷mould) is an ▷ornament formed of running ▷bands, sometimes called a *triangular* ▷*fret, like a series of triangles alternating with bases below or above. A swallowtail* ▷*merlon* has a curved-sided V-shape notched in its top, as in Guelphic crenellations (▷Battlement).

Swan   An ▷heraldic device. An ▷attribute of ▷Apollo, found in decorations alluding to ▷music, and associated with intelligence. Swans pull the chariot of ▷Venus, so occur in themes of ▷Love. Swans were common in ▷Neoclassical and especially in ▷*Empire* design. Also associated with Zeus or ▷Jupiter and with the Leda legend.

Swan-neck A double-curved member, such as the handrail of a balustrade (▷baluster) joining the ▷newel-▷post, convex on top, and then concave, like an ▷ogee. The term is also given to the rainwater ▷pipe between the ▷gutter and the downpipe, to fit under the ▷eaves. A type of elegant drop-handle of two ogees and a straight found on ▷Georgian ▷furniture. A scrolled ▷pediment.

Swastika The ▷*fylfot* or four legs bent at the knee forming the radiating spokes. A ▷symbol of prosperity and good luck. The crooked ▷cross or *Hackenkreuz*.

Sway A small hazel or willow stick used to fix ▷thatch to the ▷roof structure.

Swelled chamfer A ▷wave moulding or ▷Vitruvian scroll.

Swept A ▷valley made of ▷shingles, ▷slates, or plain ▷tiles cut or formed to avoid a flexible-metal ▷gutter.

Swinging post A ▷post from which a ▷gate is hung.

Sword A ▷symbol of martyrdom (i.e. beheading), authority, justice, and found in schemes of ▷military decoration. It occurs in ▷Neoclassical and especially in ▷*Empire* designs.

Symbol An ▷attribute or sign accompanying a statue or picture to denote identity, common in mediaeval and ▷Baroque art. As a guide to the identity of some saints, the following ▷motifs may prove instructive:

Almond tree in a flowerpot Our Blessed Lady at the Annunciation.
Alms St Elisabeth of Hungary.
Altar: murder before altar Sts Thomas of Canterbury and Winifred.
Altar: prayer before altar Sts Clement and Canute.
Anchor Sts Clement, Felix, and Nicholas.
Angel Many saints, but notably Sts Matthew and Michael. An angel trampling a dragon especially suggests Sts George and Michael. An angel weighing souls is St Michael the Archangel.
Anvil Sts Adrian and Giles. Adrian is shown as a knight in armour, with hands on an anvil, waiting for them to be chopped off.
Apples Sts Dorothy and Nicholas.
Armour Sts George (especially), Michael (the war in Heaven, the dragon, and weighing souls), Adrian, Armil, Eustace, Pancras of Rome, and Victor.
Arms and legs amputated St Adrian.

Arrow A symbol of martyrdom or torture. Sts Christina, Cosmas and Damian, Edmund King and Martyr, Giles, and (especially) Sebastian. A crowned figure pierced by arrows is Sts Edmund King and Martyr.
Asperge Used for sprinkling holy water, and therefore a symbol of purity or holiness. Many saints, but especially Sts Benedict, Martha, Peter, and Robert of Knaresborough.
Axe Sts Boniface (axe laid to root of oak tree) and Matthias.
Bag or bag-purse Judas Iscariot and Sts Matthew and Sitha (Zita).
Ball of fire St Benedict.
Balls Usually three or six. St Nicholas.
Barn St Bridget of Kildare.
Basket Sts Dorothy, Elisabeth of Hungary, Philip, and Sitha.
Battle-axe Sts Alphege, Olaf or Olave, and Thomas of Canterbury.
Beard, on female Sts Barbara, Galla, the Blessed Virgin, and Wilgefortis.
Bed Usually of metal. St Faith.
Beehive Sts Ambrose, Bernard, and John Chrysostom.
Beggar Sts Alexis, Elisabeth of Hungary, Giles, Martin, and Medard.
Bell Sts Anthony and Benedict.
Bellows St Genevieve.
Blind, restored to seeing Sts Birinus, Magnus, Vedast, and Wulstan, and, exceptionally, Paul.
Birds Sts Blaise, Erasmus, Francis, Macentius, Paul the Hermit, and Remigius.
Boar Sts Anthony and Blaise.
Boat Sts Jude, Julian Hospitaller, and Mary Magdalene. With a boat in hand, St Vincent.
Boat-hook St Jude.
Bodkin Sts Leger and Simon of Trent.
Books Signifying that the saint was an Evangelist, a Doctor of the Church, was learned, or was in constant attendance at the services of the Church. St Hilary (with three books), otherwise Sts Catherine of Alexandria and Sitha.
Bottle and shears Sts Cosmas and Damian.
Bow St Sebastian.
Bowels Sts Erasmus and Vincent.
Box of money St Matthew.
Box of ointments Sts Cosmas and Damian, Joseph of Arimathea, and Mary Magdalene.
Boys in cauldron St Nicholas.
Branch Sts Brendan, Bridget of Kildare, and Kentigern or Mungo.
Bread Sts Cuthbert, Gertrude, Nicholas, Olave, Paul the Hermit, Philip, Roch, and Sitha .
Breast Used as altar, St Lucian; pierced or cut off, Sts Agatha and Sophia and her daughters.
Briars St Benedict.
Broom Sts Petronilla and Sitha.

Bull Sts Eustace and Polycarp.

Calves St Wulstan.

Candles Sts Beatrix, Blaise and Genevieve.

Cardinal's hat Sts Jerome and Mark.

Carpenter's tools Sts Joseph, Jude, Matthew, and Thomas.

Cart and horse St Bavo.

Casket Sts Cosmas and Damian, and Mary Magdalene.

Cattle St Cornelius.

Cauldron Sts Boniface, Cecilia, Cyprian, Cyriacus, Erasmus, Felicitas, John the Evangelist, and Lucy.

Cave Sts Benedict, Blaise, Giles, and Leonard.

Chafing dish St Agatha, whose breasts are pierced with a sword, or are on the dish, or are held in pincers or shears.

Chain Sts Bridget of Sweden, German, Ignatius, Leonard, Ninian, Peter *ad vincula*, and Radegund.

Chalice With or without the Host and paten, suggests that some saints may have been priests. Sts Barbara, Benedict, Bruno, Giles, John the Evangelist, Richard of Chichester, and Thomas. The chalice with winged serpent signifies St John the Evangelist, as the Special Messenger.

Chasuble If filled with stones, St Alphege; and if red St Thomas of Canterbury.

Chest If open, St Etheldreda; if filled with gold, St Rumold or Rumbald.

Children If three, St Nicholas.

Chrism St Remigius, often carrying the holy oils, or with a dove bringing him chrism.

Church Signifying the founder of a church or monastery, or of high rank in the Church. Sts Botolph, Helena, Martin, Osmund, Peter, Withburga, and others.

Cloak St Martin is shown dividing a cloak, and Alban with a cloak before him.

Club Sts James the Less and Simon are shown with a Fuller's club, Sts Bonifice, Fabian, and Jude with a club held in the hand, Sts Lambert, Magnus, and Valentine being beaten with clubs, and Sts Nicomede and Vitalis are depicted with clubs set with spikes.

Coals St Brice or Britius is shown with hot coals in his lap, hands, or vestments. When the figure of an acolyte is shown bearing coals in his surplice, it is St Lambert.

Cock St Peter.

Coffin In a boat, St Ouen.

Colt St Medard.

Combs St Blaise.

Cook With apron, St Evortius or Enurchus.

Corn, ears of Sts Bridget of Kildare, and Walburga.

Coronation St Edward the Confessor. The Blessed Virgin Mary is also shown crowned as Queen of Heaven.

Corpse In a coffin, St Silvester.

Cow St Perpetua is shown with a wild cow, and Sts Bridget and Morwenna with a red cow.

Cripple Clothed, represents St Elisabeth of Hungary, or St Martin.

Crocodile Under feet, St Theodore.

Cross (signifies a missionary) On the top of a wand signifies a missionary or preacher, such as Sts Alban and John the Baptist. A triple cross is any pope, and an airborne cross is St Ouen.

Crown or sceptre Signifies royal rank or sainthood.

Crown of thorns Sts Catherine of Siena, Francis of Assisi, King Louis, and William of Norwich.

Crozier or pastoral staff Significant of the dignity of a bishop or an abbot. The cross-staff signifies an archbishop.

Crucified figures, upside down Sts Peter and Philip.

Crucifix Sts Bruno, Columba, Dunstan, Francis, Thomas Aquinas, and others.

Cruets St Vincent.

Cup With dragon and serpent Sts Benedict and John the Evangelist; with dagger, Edward King and Martyr; and covered, Mary Magdalene.

Dagger (a symbol of death by assassination) Sts Agnes, Canute, Edward King and Martyr, and Olave.

Dalmatic (Roman *tunica dalmatica*, of which the alb is a variant) Sts Gervase, Protasius, Leonard, and Vincent.

Dart Sts Cosmas and Damian, and Lambert.

Deacon Sts Lawrence, Leonard, Quintin, and Vincent.

Diagonal cross or saltire St Andrew.

Dish Broken and given to the poor, St Oswald.

Distaff St Genevieve.

Does St Giles; looking up at a figure, St Withburga.

Dove The presence of the Holy Spirit or represents Christianity. Sts Bridget of Sweden, Catherine of Alexandria, Evortius, Fabian, Gregory, Hilary, Lo, Remigius, and others.

Dragon Sts Armil, George, German, Guthlac, Julian, Margaret, Martha, Michael, and Silvester, among others.

Dragon with crozier St Margaret.

Eagle Sts Augustine of Hippo, Gregory, John the Evangelist, and Medard.

Espousal to Christ Sts Catherine Martyr, and Catherine of Siena.

Ewer St Vincent.

Eyes Executioner's falling out, St Alban; carrying, St Lucy; plucked out, St Leger.

Falcon Sts Bavo, and Edward King and Martyr.

Fawn St Blaise.

Feather St Barbara.

Female figure with several small virgins St Ursula.

Ferryman St Julian Hospitaller.

Fetters Sts Egwin, German, Leonard, Ninian, and Quintin.

Fire Near him St Barnabas; passing through, St

Boniface; before him, St Patrick; extinguished by prayer, St Aidan; above the head, Sts Bridget of Kildare, Lo, and Martin; walking on, St Anthony; stabbed in, St Polycarp; in hand, St Vincent; near or over, St Bridget of Kildare; and with sword at the feet, St Agnes.

Fish Sts Andrew, Boniface, Eanswith, Egwin, John of Bridlington, Jude, Peter, Raphael Archangel, and Zeno.

Flaying knife St Bartholemew.

Flowers Sts Cecilia, Dorothy, Mary the Virgin, and Sitha.

Font Sts Patrick, Remigius and Silvester.

Footsteps in stone St Medard.

Fountain A fountain springing up represents the good results of a saintly example or of preaching but it is especially associated with the Virgin Mary as a symbol of purity. Sts Augustine of Canterbury, Bonifice, Clement, Humbert, Ives, Julitta, Leonard, Paul, Peter, and Riquier.

Franciscan habit Sts Anthony of Padua, Bonaventura, and Francis of Assisi.

Fruit Sts Anne and Dorothy.

Furnace St Victor of Marseilles.

Geese Three, St Martin; and wild, St Milburga.

Giant St Christopher.

Girdle Sts Margaret, Thomas, and Thomas Aquinas.

Globe At feet, Sts Bruno, Francis of Assisi, and Ignatius.

Goat S⁺ Anthony.

Goose By the side of a figure, St Martin; in mouth of wolf, St Vedast.

Gospel With that of St Matthew in hand, St Barnabas; with that of St John in hand, St Edward the Confessor.

Grail, Holy St Joseph of Arimathea.

Grave Stepping into, St John the Evangelist.

Gridiron Sts Cyprian, Faith, Lawrence, and Vincent.

Hair With flowing, Sts Agnes and Mary Magdalene.

Halberd Sts Matthew, Matthias, and Jude.

Hammer Sts Adrian, Eloy, and William of Norwich.

Handkerchief St Veronica.

Hands Amputated, Sts Adrian, Martha and others.

Harp Sts Cecilia and Dunstan.

Hawk Sts Edward King and Martyr and Julian Hospitaller.

Head Signifies death by decapitation. Carried in hands, on a plate or lying on the ground, Sts Alban, Clair, Decuman, Denis, Firmin, John the Baptist, Osyth, Sidwell, and Winifred, among others. St Oswald's head is usually shown being carried by St Cuthbert.

Heart Sts Augustine of Hippo, Benedict, Catherine of Siena, Clara of Rimini, Francis of Assisi, and Quintin; with the IHS motif, St Ignatius.

Hermit Very common, but especially Sts Christopher and Jerome.

Hill Preaching on, St David.

Hind Sts Giles, Withburga, and others.

Holy-water vessel and asperge St Martha.

Hook Sts Agatha, Hippolytus, Leger, and Vincent.

Horn Sts Cornelius, Hubert, and Oswald.

Horns They usually represent Moses.

Horse and cart St Bavo.

Horse leg The shoeing of, St Eligius, or Eloy.

Horses Three, pulling a figure apart, St Hippolytus.

Hunters Sts Eustace, German, and Hubert.

Idol Broken or toppling, Sts George, Philip, and Wilfred.

Infant Sts Brice and Elizabeth (who holds the infant St John, or whose child is fed by angels).

Inkhorn Sts Jerome and Matthew.

Instruments of the Passion Sts Bernard, Bridget, and Gregory.

Island of serpents St Hilary.

Jug St Vincent.

Keys Especially St Peter, but also the Blessed Virgin Mary, and Sts Dominic, Egwin, Genevieve, Hippolytus, Hubert, James the Greater, Martha, Petronilla, and Sitha, among others.

Knife Sts Bartholemew and Peter Martyr (whose head or shoulder is pierced by a knife).

Ladder Sts Alexis, Leonard, Olave, and Perpetua.

Ladle St Martha.

Lamb Sts Agnes, Catherine, Genevieve and John the Baptist.

Lamb and flag (Agnus Dei) St John the Baptist.

Lamp Sts Francis of Assisi and Lucy, but particularly associated with the Wise Virgins and with virginity.

Lance Sts Barbara, German, Hippolytus, Lambert, Matthias, Michael, Oswin, Philip, and Thomas.

Lantern Sts Gudula, or Hugh.

Letter brought by dove St Oswald.

Light, pillar of Sts Bede and Cuthbert.

Lily Especially associated with the Virgin Mary, and with purity or virginity, but also with Sts Catherine of Siena, Clare, Dominic, Gabriel, Joseph, Kenelm, and Sebastian.

Lilies among thorns Signifies confessors.

Limbs cut off St Adrian.

Lion Sts Adrian, Dorothy, Ignatius, Jerome, Mark, and Prisca. A winged lion represents Mark.

Loaf or loaves Sts Cuthbert, Gertrude, Nicholas, Olave, Paul the Hermit, Philip, Roch, and Sitha.

Lute St Cecilia.

Mallets St Denis.

Manacles St Leonard.

Mass Sts Gregory and Martin.

Medal around neck St Genevieve.

Medallion St Jude.

Milk A pan of, St Bridget of Kildare.

Millstone Sts Christina, Crispin and Crispinian, Victor of Marseilles, and Vincent.

Money Sts Martin, Matthew, and Philip. Judas Iscariot. A money-box or money-bag represents St Matthew.

Monstrance St Clare.

Nails Sts Eloy, Giles, King Louis, Quintin, and William of Norwich.

Napkin Sts Stephen and Veronica.

Neck Sts Agnes and Cecilia (pierced and wounded).

Oak being cut St Boniface.

Oar Sts Aubert, Jude, and Julian Hospitaller.

Oats, field of St Radegund.

Oil Sts Remigius, Vitus, and Walburga.

Ointment ▷*Box of ointments.*

Organ St Cecilia.

Otters St Cuthbert.

Our Lord being carried across a river St Christopher.

Ox Sts Cornelius, Frideswide, Julitta, Leonard, Lucy, Luke, Medard, Polycarp, and Silvester.

Painting St Luke.

Palm Symbol of martyrdom and victory over death. Sts Catherine of Alexandria and John the Evangelist, among others. The palm branch and a Saracen signifies St Pancras.

Peacock's feathers St Barbara.

Physicians Sts Cosmas, Damian, and Luke.

Pick-axe St Leger.

Pig Sts Anthony and Blaise.

Pile of wood Sts Agatha, Agnes, and Polycarp.

Pilgrim Sts James the Greater, Roch, and others.

Pincers Sts Agatha, Apollonia, Dunstan, and Lucy.

Pitcher St Bede.

Plague-spot or buboe St Roch.

Plough St Kentigern or Mungo.

Potsherds, bed of St Lucian.

Purses Sts Edward the Confessor and Nicholas.

Pyre ▷*Pile of wood.*

Rack St Vincent.

Rain St Swithin.

Raven Sts Adrian, Benedict, Erasmus, Oswald, Paul the Hermit, Vincent, and others.

Ring Sts Barbara, Edward the Confessor, and Peter.

Rock Sts Gregory, Martin, and Peter.

Rods Sts Benedict and Faith.

Roses A special symbol of the Blessed Virgin, but also associated with Sts Barbara, Dorothy, and Elisabeth of Hungary.

Salmon and ring St Kentigern or Mungo.

Sarum Missal St Osmund (often with a church in his hand).

Saw Sts James the Less, Simon, and others.

Scales St Michael the Archangel.

Scallop shell on hat Sts James the Greater and Roch.

Sceptre Royal saints such as Edmund King and Martyr, Edward the Confessor, Edward King and Martyr, Margaret of Scotland, Olave, and Oswald.

Scourge Signifies mortification or self-punishment.

Sts Ambrose, Boniface, Gervase and Protasius, Guthlac, and Simeon Stylites.

Scythe Sts Sidwell and Walstan of Bawburgh (or Baber).

Serpent Sts Benedict, Christina, Francis, Guthlac, Hilary, John the Evangelist, Magnus, and Patrick.

Shackles St Leonard.

Shears Sts Agatha, and Cosmas and Damian.

Sheep Sts Genevieve, Margaret, and others.

Shell ▷*Scallop shell.* A figure lying on shells is St Felix.

Ship Sts Jude, Ursula, and others.

Shoemakers Sts Crispin and Crispinian, and Theobald.

Shoeing a horse St Eloy.

Shrines Sts John of Beverley, Louis, Omer, and others.

Sick persons Sts Cosmas and Damian, and Luke.

Sieve Sts Benedict and Hippolytus.

Skin, flayed Sts Bartholomew, Crispin and Crispinian, and others martyred in this way.

Skull Suggests preparation for death, and particularly associated with Sts Jerome, Mary Magdalene, and Thomas of Canterbury.

Snakes ▷*Serpent.*

Square, carpenter's Sts Joseph, Jude, Matthew, Matthias, and Thomas.

Stabbed on horseback, in back or shoulder St Edward King and Martyr.

Staff, budding Sts Aldhelm, Christopher, Etheldreda, Joseph of Arimathea, and Ninian.

Staff and banner St James the Less; with lamb, St John the Baptist.

Staff, hat, and scallop St James.

Staff (pastoral) being struck on tomb St Wulfstan.

Staff and two doves St Joachim.

Stag Sts Aidan, Julian Hospitaller, and Kentigern or Mungo. A stag with crucifix represents Sts Eustace, and Hubert.

Star Placed on or over the head, on the breast, or in hand, Sts Bruno, Dominic, Hugh of Grenoble, Thomas Aquinas, and, around the head in numbers, the Blessed Virgin.

Stigmata Sts Catherine of Siena, and Francis of Assisi.

Stones Emblems of torture or martyrdom. Sts Alphege, Barnabas, Bavo, Matthew, Pancras of Taormina, Stephen, and Timothy. Shown beating against breasts in contrition, Sts Barnabas, and Jerome; bread turned into stones, St Olave; stones in a chasuble represent especially St Alphege.

Sunbeam St Bridget of Kildare, among others.

Swan Sts Cuthbert, Hugh of Grenoble, and Leger.

Sword Celebrates saints who died by decapitation. St Paul. Sword or swords piercing a woman's heart represents Our Blessed Lady, while a sword through the neck or throat indicates Sts Agatha, Agnes, Lucy, and many others.

Taper Sts Blaise, Bridget, Felix, and Genevieve.

T-shaped cross (Tau) Sts Anthony, and Philip.

Teeth (pulled out) St Apollonia.

Temple in the sea St Clement.

Thorn Figures lying on thorns, Sts Benedict, Dominic, and Jerome; extracted from a lion's foot, Sts Jerome, Joseph of Arimathea, and Mark.

Tiara Any pope or the Blessed Virgin Mary.

Tongs St Dunstan and others.

Tongue cut out St Leger and others.

Tooth ▷*Teeth.*

Torch Sts Aidan, Barbara, Blaise, Dorothy, and Medard.

Tower Sts Ambrose, Barbara, and others.

Trampling somebody or thing underfoot Sts Barbara, Catherine of Alexandria, Cyprian, Optatus, Pancras of Rome, and Theodore.

Tree over head of sleeping girl St Etheldreda.

Turtle doves, pair of Our Lady at Her Purification.

Vane St Leonard.

Vase Sts Cosmas and Damian, Mary Magdalene, and others.

Veil Sts Agnes, Remigius, Veronica, and others.

Vernicle St Veronica.

Vial Sts Cosmas and Damian, Walburga, and others.

Viaticum St Petronilla and others.

Violin St Cecilia.

Wallet Sts James the Greater, Jerome, and Roch.

Washing feet of poor, infirm, or diseased Sts Editha, Louis, and Thomas of Canterbury.

Well Sts Cyr, Sebastian, Sidwell, Sitha, and others.

Wheel Particularly associated with patriarchs. Sts Catherine of Alexandria, Quintin, and others.

Wild animals Sts Blaise, Columba, German, Magnus, and Radegund. A wild boar is especially associated with Sts Anthony, Blaise, and Cyr. Wild geese are emblems of Sts Martin and Milburga.

Windlass St Erasmus.

Windmill Sts James the Less and Victor of Marseilles. It is shown above St Christopher on occasion.

Wine flagon St Elisabeth of Hungary.

Wolf Sts Blaise, Columba, Edmund King and Martyr, Kentigern, Radegund, and Vedast.

Woman teaching Our Lady to read St Anne.

Wool comb St Blaise.

Wounds in the neck Sts Cecilia and Lucy.

Wreath in hands or on head St Cecilia.

Writing, by scribes St John the Divine and the Evangelists.

It may be useful to list the following saints and their ▷emblems:

Adrian, Martyr In armour, with hammer, anvil, and sword, or having his hands chopped off.

Agatha, Virgin-Martyr With sword pointing at her breasts, or stuck through them, or with breasts on a dish, or nipples held in pincers or shears. She

often has a long veil.

Agnes, Virgin-Martyr With long hair, or angels cover her with their hair. She is shown on a burning pyre, holding a sword, or with a sword in her neck, often with a lamb, and sometimes with a dove bringing her a wedding ring.

Aidan, Bishop With a stag at his feet.

Alban, Martyr With tall cross and sword, in armour, with robe and coronet, with an executioner whose eyes are dropping out. Alban's head is shown on the ground, or in a holly bush.

Alexis, Confessor A pilgrim or ragged beggar.

Alphege, Archibishop-Martyr A chasuble filled with stones, or holding a battle-axe.

Ambrose, Bishop, Doctor In episcopal vestments, with a scourge, beehive, tower, or dove.

Andrew, Apostle-Martyr An old bearded man with saltire or X-shaped cross, and often holding a fish. Sometimes he is shown with a Y-shaped cross.

Anne, mother of Mary Teaching the Virgin to read, and sometimes shown with St Joachim, or with the Infant Jesus. She has a green mantle and red dress (immortality and divine love), and holds a book.

Anselm, Archbishop With alb and mantle and green cap, near a hill, and often exorcising a monk.

Anthony the Great, Abbot-Hermit With tau-staff with bell, or bell and book, or asperge, and wild boar (often belled) at his feet. He sometimes has flames under his feet.

Anthony of Padua, Confessor In a Franciscan robe, with kneeling ass, a lily, a flowered Cross, a fish, a book, and a fire. He is sometimes shown carrying the Christ-Child.

Apollonia, Virgin-Martyr With pincers and tooth, and a fire. Also the palm.

Armil (Armagillus), Confessor In armour under chasuble, and leading a dragon.

Aubert, Bishop-Confessor Ass with panniers of bread, shovel, and book.

Augustine of Canterbury, Archbishop A fountain, and vested as archbishop with double cross.

Augustine of Hippo, Doctor In doctor's robes, and holding a heart flaming or pierced by an arrow. Also with child before him with shell or spoon, or with pen and book.

Barbara, Virgin-Martyr Holding a tower with three windows in one of which is a chalice and Host. She holds a palm, feather, or sword, and wears the crown of martyrdom. She also tramples a male figure, usually a Saracen, and her attribute is a peacock's feather.

Barnabas, Apostle-Martyr Holds the Gospel of St Matthew, and is shown with stones.

Bartholomew, Apostle-Martyr With flaying-knife, often with his skin draped over his arm.

Basil, Bishop-Doctor With pen and dove, before a fire.

Bavo of Ghent, Hermit Holds a falcon or a church, or is shown with horse and cart, with a big boulder, or as a hermit in a hollow tree.

Beatrice, Virgin-Martyr Shown strangled with ropes.

Bede, Confessor With pitcher and heavenly light.

Benedict of Cassino, Abbot Raven with cup, or cup with serpent crawling out. Shown rolling in briars, or with asperge or sieve, and a blackbird. He is shown with dove, with his index finger to his lips (silence), and with a luminous ladder.

Benedict Biscop, Abbot An Abbot with two monasteries.

Bernard, Abbot-Doctor With dog, instruments of the Passion, beehive, book, pen, demon in chains, or with a vision of the Blessed Virgin.

Birinus, Bishop Walking on the sea, carrying the Sacrament, and giving sight to the blind.

Blaise, Bishop-Martyr An iron comb, wild animals, and a lighted taper.

Boniface (or Winfred), Bishop-Martyr In episcopal robes with felled oak, or felling an oak. With scourge, or with sword piercing a book.

Botolph, Abbot With church or monastery in hand, and in Mass robes, with crozier turned outwards.

Brendan or Brandan, Abbot With branch, and preaching.

Brice or Britius, Bishop-Confessor Carrying burning coals, with infant in arms, or holding a staff in both hands.

Bridget or Bride of Kildare, Abbess Milking a cow, and near a barn, with a flame over her head, or hanging her mantle on a sunbeam. She is also shown with an altar, casting out a devil, with a branch, with bunches of corn, restoring an amputated hand to an arm, and with a pastoral staff and book.

Bridget of Sweden, Queen In nun's habit, writing, crowned, with dove overhead. A crowned Abbess with crozier, lute and chain.

Candida, Virgin-Martyr Scourged at a stake.

Cassian, Martyr Torn to pieces by his pupils wielding iron pens.

Catherine of Alexandria, Virgin-Martyr A sumptuously dressed personage of royal rank, crowned, holding a sword, trampling on Maximin, with palm of victory, dove, and book, beside a wheel set with spikes.

Catherine of Siena, Virgin With heart, crown of thorns, and lily.

Cecilia, Virgin-Martyr With harp, organ pipes, violin, and lute. Also with a wreath of red roses or white lilies, or a palm of victory. She is shown being boiled in a cauldron and with deep wounds in her neck.

Chad, Bishop A branch of a vine, and as a coped bishop holding a church.

Christina, Virgin-Martyr With an arrow, or with a tower, millstone, knife, or tongs.

Christopher, Martyr A giant fording a river and carrying a staff (frequently shown bursting into leaf), often carrying the Infant Christ: on the other bank a hermit, with hermitage, holding a lighted lantern.

Clare, Abbess A Franciscan nun with staff, closed book, and monstrance.

Clement, Pope-Martyr With anchor, papal tiara, triple cross, fountain, and lying in a marble temple by the sea.

Columba, Abbot-Confessor Taming a wild beast, kneeling with wolves, or in a bear's den. Often with fountain, sunbeams, and crucifix buds.

Cornelius, Pope-Martyr With horn, or cows, or oxen, and with tiara and cross.

Cosmas and Damian, Martyrs Attending a sick man, holding vases or phials, or pots of ointment, or surgical instruments, or medical attributes such as the rod of Asclepius or Aesculepius. They have furred robes, and are shown with arrows, swords, or crosses.

Crispin and Crispinian, Martyrs Working as shoemakers, tied to a tree and flayed, and thrown from a bridge with millstones tied to their necks.

Cuthbert, Bishop-Confessor In episcopal robes carrying the head of St Oswald. With otters, swans, loaves, or pillars of light.

Cyprian of Antioch, Martyr Burning or trampling on his books of magic. With grid-iron and sword, and shown burning in a cauldron with St Justina.

Cyprian of Carthage, Archbishop In episcopal robes, and holding a sword and a book.

Cyril, Martyr Also known as Cyriacus or Cyr, he is shown with his mother, or riding on a boar.

Cyril of Alexandria, Bishop-Confessor The Blessed Virgin Mary appears before him.

David, Bishop-Confessor On a hill which miraculously appeared for him, and with a dove on his shoulder.

Decuman, Hermit-Martyr Carrying his head to a spring to wash it.

Denis or Dionysus, Bishop-Martyr A headless bishop carrying his mitred head with the eyes closed in death.

Dominic, Confessor With lily in hand, star on head or breast, with dog and torch.

Dorothy, Virgin-Martyr Basket of flowers, or flowers and fruit from Paradise. Three roses and three apples in her hands, or with bunch or wreath of flowers and a palm.

Dunstan, Archbishop Seizing a devil with tongs, and with dove and harp. Shown hearing a voice from a crucifix, prostrate at the feet of Christ, and with a choir of angels before him.

Eanswith, Virgin-Abbess Two fishes on a half-hoop, or with crown, crozier, and book, with a fish on either side of her.

Eata, Bishop Pupil of Aidan and teacher of Cuthbert, and Abbot of Melrose. Shown with cope, mitre, and crozier at Hexham giving a benediction.

Edith of Polesworth, Queen-Abbess Dressed as an Abbess.

Edith of Wilton, Virgin In royal robes, with crozier and Wilton Church.

Edmund, King and Martyr Crowned, with sceptre, pierced by arrows, or holding arrows in his hand, with a wolf guarding his head. Unlike St Sebastian, he is fully clothed.

Edmund of Pontigny, Archbishop Making a vow before an image of the Virgin Mary. The Christ-child or St Thomas of Canterbury appears to him, and he is shown with the child at his feet. The Virgin gives him a ring, or he places a ring on Her finger.

Edward, King-Confessor Crowned and sceptred, holding up a ring, or with a purse.

Edward, King-Martyr On horseback with cup in one hand and dagger in the other, with a cup and serpent, or with a falcon. He was stabbed in the back.

Egwin, Bishop Fish with key in mouth.

Eligius or Eloy, Bishop With hammer or anvil, and a horse's leg which he cut off, shod, and put back again. He is the patron Saint of farriers.

Elisabeth of Hungary, Queen Crowned with double or triple crown giving alms, and with an apron full of roses.

Elizabeth, Mother of John the Baptist She is shown holding the infant St John, dying in the desert, with angels feeding her child, and saluting the Blessed Virgin.

Eloy ▷*Eligius.*

Enurchus or Evortius, Bishop Cook with apron, and dove on head.

Erasmus, Bishop-Martyr In episcopal robes, holding a windlass around which his bowels are wound.

Erme or Hermes, Martyr Casting the devil out of a woman or child.

Ethelbert, King-Martyr In royal robes and crowned before an altar, and trampling on a woman.

Ethelburga of Barking, Virgin-Abbess In the robes of an abbess.

Etheldreda, Queen-Abbess Crowned, with a corzier, lily, or book. Her staff blossoms to become a tree to shade her.

Euphemia, Virgin-Martyr Fire, bear, lion, palm, and a sword.

Eustace, Martyr A stag with a crucifix in its antlers. The saint is shown as a soldier on horseback, and he is accompanied by hounds. He is also depicted with a brazen bull with a fire beneath it.

Fabian, Bishop-Martyr Kneeling at a block, with sword, palm and triple crown, and on his head a dove.

Faith, Virgin-Martyr A brazen bedstead, sword, and bundle of rods.

Felicitas, Martyr A sword and seven sons, or a sword with seven male heads on the blade.

Felix, Bishop An anchor.

Firmin, Bishop Carrying a mitred head, or a sword and mitred head on the ground.

Florian, Martyr A soldier in armour, pouring water on a burning house or city, and with a millstone.

Francis of Assisi, Confessor Many attributes, but notably the skull, lily, wolf, lamb, the Crucifix, and the Stigmata.

Frideswide, Virgin-Abbess With book and abbess's staff, with an ox near by.

Gabriel, Archangel Sceptre and shield, lily in the hand, and a scroll inscribed AVE MARIA.

Genevieve, Virgin Coin stamped with a cross suspended from her neck. With a candle and a devil blowing bellows, a basket of bread, and often depicted as a shepherdess knitting or spinning.

George of Cappadocia, Martyr White banner and red cross, and often shown on horseback in armour, slaying a dragon and rescuing a woman.

German of Auxerre, Bishop A bishop among slain wild beasts, or trampling a tyrant. He is shown with fetters over his right arm, and has a closed book and staff.

Gervase and Protasius, Martyrs A scourge loaded with lead, and a sword.

Giles, Abbot In an abbot's robes, with crozier, hind, and arrow. Sometimes holding a staff with plaited interlacing bands around the shaft.

Gregory, Pope-Doctor With papal tiara, with dove at his ear. He also holds a book or writes at a lectern. He may have a tall double-barred cross. When Christ is shown descending from the altar with the instruments of the Passion, the Mass of St Gregory is suggested.

Guthlac, Hermit Scourging a devil, dragon, or serpent.

Helena, Empress With imperial crown, holding or leaning on the True Cross, with hammer and nail, or holding a model of the Church of the Holy Sepulchre in Jerusalem.

Hilary of Poitiers, Bishop-Confessor With books and treading on serpents, or with a triangle, pen, staff, or trumpet. Also a child, or a child in a cradle.

Hilda, Virgin-Martyr An abbess with crozier. A priest elevates the Host at an altar on either side, and a bird hovers near the Host.

Hippolytus, Bishop-Martyr The gaoler of St Lawrence. His attributes are keys, and he is shown being torn apart by two or three horses pulling in opposite directions.

Holy Innocents, Martyrs Herod sitting on a throne, with soldiers killing children.

Hubert, Bishop Stag with crucifix on antlers, or stag on book. Often with bishop's mitre, and hunting-horn.

Hugh of Lincoln, Bishop A dream of seven stars, with swan.

Ignatius, Bishop-Martyr Holds a heart emblazoned with IHS, and exposed to lions.

Isidore, Confessor With bowl in right hand and brushes in left. He is shown ploughing or digging for a fountain.

Ives or Ivo, Bishop A fountain flowing from his tomb.

James the Greater, Apostle A pilgrim with staff, hat, scroll, wallet, and scallop shell, or with sword, or charging Saracens on a horse.

James the Less, Apostle With a Fuller's club in hand or with palm, saw, or miniature mill.

Jerome, Confessor-Doctor Wears cardinal's robes and hat, and writes, with ink-horn, scroll, cross-staff, and lion, with skull near. He is also shown half-naked, beating his breast with a stone, or carries a church.

Joachim, father of the Virgin Mary The lamb, lilies, and doves in a basket.

John the Baptist, son of Elizabeth and Zacharias Wears tunic of camel hair, holds long reed-cross, and is associated with a lamb, or a lamb on a book. A dish on which his head lies refers to his execution.

John the Evangelist, Apostle Young and beardless, with long hair, he is seen with an eagle, or has a poisoned chalice with a serpent or dragon emerging from it. He is also shown with a palm. John the Evangelist *ante portam Latinam* is suggested by a cauldron of oil.

John of Beverley, Bishop-Confessor With shrine at his side, vested as archbishop, with cross-staff.

John of Bridlington, Confessor A canon in brown habit and blue cloak, with crozier.

Joseph of Arimathea, Confessor With a budding staff and box of ointment. Also with the Holy Grail.

Joseph of Nazareth, husband of the Virgin Mary With budded staff, dove, carpenter's plane, saw, and hatchet, and the lily.

Jude, Apostle With boat or sailing-ship, or loaves or fish, or boat-hook. Also with carpenter's square or club.

Julian, Bishop Fountain, dragon, or scourging a devil.

Julian Hospitaller, Hermit With stag, leper, angel, oar, or ferry-boat.

Julitta, Martyr With her son, Cyril, or oxen, or a fountain springing from her blood.

Just, or Justus, Martyr With swords, scourged, or drowned with lead weights around his neck. Prints of his knees are shown in a stone, and the Cross appears to him in a vision.

Kenelm, King-Martyr A king holding a lily, and trampling on his stepmother prostrate over an open book. He was stabbed from behind while drinking from a stirrup-cup, and had a falcon on his wrist.

Kentigern or Mungo, Bishop-Confessor Holding a salmon with a ring in its gills, or holding a plough drawn by two deer, or by a deer and a wolf.

Lambert, Bishop-Martyr A lancet or dart, or stabbed

with javelins. He is shown bringing hot coals in his surplice for the thurible.

Lawrence, Deacon-Martyr A deacon on or holding a grid-iron, or dish, or bag of gold, or censer, with palm.

Leger, Ledger, or Leodegarius, Bishop-Martyr Eyes plucked out and tongue cut. Shown with pickaxe, borer, or two-pronged hook.

Leonard, Deacon-Confessor Chains, fetters, manacles with a lock. He holds a crozier and a book.

Lo or Laud, Bishop-Confessor A dove or fire over his head during Mass.

Longinus, Martyr On foot at the Crucifixion, lance in hand, or on horseback, as a Roman soldier, looking up at Christ and holding his helmet in his hands.

Louis IX, King-Confessor A crown of thorns, kingly crown, sword, nails, cross, dove, lilies, and especially the fleur-de-lys.

Lucian, Bishop-Martyr Lying on potsherds, consecrating, baptizing, or carrying his own head. His body carried ashore by a dolphin.

Lucy, Virgin-Martyr Eyes in a dish or on a book. A sword, palm, or lamp. The sword is often shown through the neck or throat.

Luke, Evangelist An ox, often winged. Luke is often shown painting a picture of the Blessed Virgin, or he is depicted as a physician.

Marcellina, Virgin A small cross in her hand.

Margaret of Antioch, Virgin-Martyr Piercing a dragon with a long cross, or emerging from inside a dragon. She is often shown with a girdle, or with pearls in her hair.

Margaret of Scotland, Queen Holds a black cross, visits the sick, and prays her husband Malcolm out of Purgatory.

Mark, Evangelist Writing, with lion (winged or unwinged), near by. Dragged by the neck and strangled.

Martha, Virgin With dragon, or asperge, or with ladle and keys.

Martin, Bishop As priest or bishop, with naked beggar at his feet. In mail, he has a mitre in his hand, and a cap and cloak, which he divides to clothe the poor.

Mary Cleopas, Mother of Saints St Jude with boat, St Simon with fish, St James the Less a palm, club, or Fuller's mill, St Joseph a cup or bowl, or three stones or loaves.

Mary, Blessed Virgin Many attributes, including blue robe, lily, rose, fountain, stars, garden, etc., and holding the Christ-child.

Mary Magdalene Flowing hair, with box or vase of ointment, and boat and open book.

Matthew, Apostle-Evangelist His symbol is an angel. He is shown with table, money-bag, axe, inkhorn, carpenter's square, sword, halberd, or tall cross.

Matthias, Apostle Sword, scimitar, halbert, lance, axe, stone, or carpenter's square.

Maurice, Martyr An armoured knight with banner, often with halberd.

Maxentius, Abbot Birds flying.

Medard, Bishop A dove, or three white doves, or an eagle above. He is shown imprinting his footsteps on a stone, or holding a knife with the point upwards.

Michael, Archangel An armoured or feathered angel, unmounted, trampling or piercing a dragon or a devil, with spear, cross, or sword. He is often shown weighing souls, with the Virgin interceding for them.

Milburga, Virgin-Abbess Wild geese flying away by her order, or she holds a church in her hand.

Morwenna, Virgin-Abbess Teaching princesses to read, with a red cow beside her.

Mungo ▷Kentigern.

Neot, Confessor Preceptor of King Alfred.

Nicholas, Bishop-Confessor Three children in a tub, chest, or basket. Three balls, apples, loaves, or purses. An anchor or a ship.

Nicomede, Martyr A club set with spikes.

Ninian, Bishop With crozier, heavy chain hanging from right wrist, and a staff taking root and with a fountain gushing from its roots.

Olave or Olaf, King-Martyr Crowned king seated, with cross and battle-axe, or sceptre and sword, or dagger. Also with dream-ladder. He is also shown with a loaf or with stones.

Osmund, Bishop With church in hand, or the Book of the Sarum Use.

Oswald, King-Martyr With a big cross, or blowing a horn, or a raven bears a chrismatory or a ring. He holds a silver dish, and tramples a heathen king.

Oswin, King-Martyr With spear, or spear and sceptre.

Osyth, Sitha, or Zita, Queen-Martyr Carries her head.

Owen or Ouen, Bishop His coffin a boat, or a cross in the air.

Pancras of Rome, Martyr An armed youth, with book and palm, trampling on a Saracen.

Pancras of Taormina, Bishop-Martyr Two idols and stones.

Patrick, Bishop-Confessor In episcopal robes, trampling on or expelling serpents. He is usually shown near a font, or being held by the devil in a fire, but protected by an angel.

Paul, Apostle-Martyr Tall old man with bald forehead and long beard, holding a sword and book. The three fountains rose where his head bounced three times when cut off.

Paul, Hermit Bearded or dressed in leaves. A bird brings a loaf.

Paulinus, Archbishop Shown baptizing, vested as an archbishop and holding a staff.

Perpetua, Martyr With wild cow by her side. A ladder guarded by a dragon.

Peter, Apostle-Martyr With curly hair, short thick beard, and bald spot on the top of his head. With key or keys, and church, or book, and with tiara and double-barred cross. Also with cock, holding a fish, holding a staff, keys, and asperge.

Peter Martyr, Martyr In Dominican dress, holding cross and book. A dagger or an axe cleaving his skull.

Petronilla, Virgin With turban and key, or broom and clasped book. St Peter is shown conversing with her.

Philip, Apostle Carries a basket with loaves, or a cross with which he killed a dragon, or a column because he was martyred by being suspended from it.

Polycarp, Bishop-Martyr Stabbed and burnt to death at a stake, or on a pyre, or in an oven shaped like an ox.

Prisca, Virgin-Martyr With lions or eagle near, and holding a palm or a sword.

Radegund, Queen With royal robes, crown, and sceptre. Wolves and other wild beasts which were tame with her are near. With crozier and book. She has a white head-dress, a tunic with fleur-de-lys, mantle with castles, and a field of oats.

Remigius, or Rémy, Bishop Carries the holy oils, or a dove brings chrism. Birds feed from his hand. Clovis kneels in front of him.

Richard of Chichester, Bishop Shown ploughing, sowing, or with a chalice at his feet or before him.

Riquier, Abbot Holds two keys, and a fountain springs from under his staff.

Robert of Knaresborough, Hermit Threatens devil with asperge.

Roch, Confessor With plague-spot on thigh, with cross-keys or scallop shell on his hat. A dog also holds a loaf in its mouth. An angel sometimes touches the plague-spot.

Rumbald, or Rumold, King-Martyr A chest filled with gold.

Sampson, Bishop With cross and dove, low mitre, closed book, and staff.

Sebastian, Martyr Almost naked, he is pierced by arrows, or holds an arrow, or arrows and a bow.

Sexburga, Queen-Abbess With palm.

Sidwell, or Sativola, Virgin-Martyr Decapitated with a scythe and near a well.

Silvester, or Sylvester, Pope-Confessor Tiara and double-cross, with ox near by. He holds a chained dragon, and baptizes the Emperor Constantine.

Simon Zelotes, Apostle With fish in his hand, or on a book, with an oar, Fuller's bat, or long saw.

Sitha, or Zita, Virgin Carrying a pitcher or basket or keys. In her apron are loaves which turned to flowers. Also carries her head.

Stephen, Deacon-Martyr Holds stones in his hand, in a napkin, in his robe, or on his shoulders. He is young, tonsured, wears a *dalmatic*, and carries a palm.

310

Swithin, Bishop A shower of rain. He wears episcopal robes, carries a crozier, and a closed book.

Symphorian, Martyr Comforted by his mother on his way to Martyrdom, or trampling on an image.

Theobald, Bishop-Confessor In episcopal vestments.

Theobald, Hermit Cobbler's tools.

Thomas, Apostle-Martyr With spear or lance, or with carpenter's square. He is shown handling the Saviour's wounds, and receiving the girdle from the Virgin Mary.

Thomas of Canterbury, Archbishop-Martyr With archiepiscopal cross and pallium. The crozier has a battle-axe head. A sword is stuck in his skull, and he is shown martyred before the altar. He receives a red chasuble from the Virgin, and carries in his hand the corona, or crown of his skull.

Timothy, Bishop-Martyr With the club with which he was killed.

Titus, Bishop-Martyr A bright and beaming face.

Ursula, Virgin-Martyr Shot with arrows or holding them. Many miniature virgins peer from her mantle. She is shown with a ship and her companions.

Valentine, Bishop-Martyr Represented as a priest with a sword, holding a sun, or giving sight to a girl.

Vedast, Bishop A wolf with a goose in its mouth.

Veronica, Virgin Holding the veil or handkerchief imprinted with the face of Christ.

Victor of Marseilles, Martyr In armour, with windmill or millstone.

Vigor, Bishop In episcopal vestments, with dragon.

Vincent, Deacon-Martyr With bowels ripped out with an iron hook and body burned on spiked grid-iron. A millstone. A raven driving wild beasts from his body. He sometimes holds two cruets in his right hand.

Walstan of Bawburgh, Confessor Crowned, with ermine cape, sceptre and scythe. He died while mowing. He is seen with calves.

Werberga, Virgin-Abbess An abbess with crozier, carrying a church.

Wilfred, Archbishop In archiepiscopal vestments with pallium. Baptizing or preaching to pagans, and breaking idols.

Wilgefortis, Virgin-Martyr Bearded woman, crucified, with ropes.

William of Norwich, Martyr A child crucified, stabbed, and bleeding, with nails and hammer.

William of York, Archbishop In archiepiscopal vestments, with mitre and cross and shield with eight lozenges.

Winifred, Virgin-Martyr Beheaded before an altar, carrying her head, and often with a palm. She is pursued by a prince on a white horse, and a stream flows from a well-head.

Withburga, Virgin-Abbess With church in her hand and two does.

Wulfram, or Wolfran, Bishop A youthful king near him. He is shown baptizing.

Wulfstan, or Wolstan, Bishop Fixing his crozier in St Edward the Confessor's tomb.

Zeno, Bishop In episcopal robes, with fish suspended from crozier.

Symmetry Uniformity or balance of one part of a building and another. Equal disposition of parts and masses on either side of a centre-line.

Synagogue A place of assembly for Jewish religious observances. In iconography a blindfolded female figure.

Synthronon Benches for the clergy in an ▷Early Christian ▷church, usually in the ▷apse.

Syrian arch A series of small arches set over a series of wider arches, centred on the piers and arches below.

Syrinx A narrow rock-cut ▷passage in an ancient ▷tomb. An Arcadian nymph, or a pan-pipe.

Systyle ▷Colonnade, ▷intercolumniation.

T

Tabby A mix of ▷lime and water to which ▷shells or broken stones have been added: it is a type of ▷concrete or artificial stone.

Tabern A ▷tavern. A *taberna* was a ▷Roman shop or ▷stall. A *taberna diversoria* was a Roman ▷inn or lodging.

Tabernacle [233] The receptacle for the ▷Sacraments placed over the ▷altar, or any ▷niche or ▷canopy, especially a free-standing canopy such as a ▷*ciborium* or *baldacchino*. Sepulchral ▷monuments, ▷choir-stalls, and ▷sedilia can be surmounted by rich canopy-work known as *tabernacle-work* with ▷crockets, ▷pinnacles, cresting (▷cress), and so on. A *tabernacle* is also a large ▷church for a Protestant sect. It is also the name given to the mounting to which a flagstaff is secured at its base.

Tabia Rammed earth to which ▷lime and stones have been added.

Tablature A tablet. A pictorial representation of something over a surface, such as a ceiling or a ▷panel, possibly a ▷fresco or similar.

Table A ▷slab, ▷board, layer, or flat surface. A ▷panel or a slab. An ▷altar-frontal. A slab on supports, such as ▷colonnettes, hence *table-*▷*tomb*, meaning a flat stone carried on ▷piers or ▷columns. *Tabled* means flat-topped, or having a smooth sloping surface of ▷dressed stone. A *table* is also any horizontal moulding (▷mould), such as a ▷string-▷course, dividing one ▷storey from another, or a carved panel, as over a ▷door. A *table-stone* is the same as a table-tomb, and the term is also applied to a ▷*cromlech* or ▷*dolmen*. A *tablet* is a ▷wall-slab or a monumental tablet, regularly

shaped, framed, and carved: it is also a *coping-stone* (▷cope), set flat, and a series of such stones is called *tabling*, meaning the coping. A *tablet flower* is a variation of *Second-*▷*Pointed* ▷ballflower, resembling an open flower with four ▷petals. A *tablet-tomb* is a ▷*loculus* in a ▷catacomb in which a tablet is set to seal it.

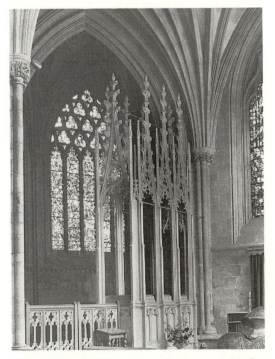

[233] TABERNACLE Tabernacle-work on a canopy of the fourteenth century in Wells Cathedral. Note the crocketed gables. (*JSC*)

Tablinum A room in a ▷Roman ▷villa with one side open to the ▷atrium, or to a ▷colonnade or ▷portico. It is also called the *tabulinum*.

Tabularium As ▷archarium.

Tabulate To reduce to the form of a ▷table, or a flattened surface, hence *tabulated*.

Tack Also called a *clip* or ▷*tingle*, it is a strip of ▷lead used to stiffen ▷flashings to stop the edges being lifted by a strong wind, or to secure loose slates.

Taenia, tenia The ▷fillet or ▷band at the top of a ▷Doric ▷architrave, separating it from the ▷frieze.

Tail As ▷lookout.

Tailloir The ▷abacus of the ▷Ionic ▷capital.

Talbot An ▷heraldic ▷dog with mastiff's body, head of a hound and ears like those of a bloodhound.

Tallboy A long slender ▷chimney-pot, often decorated. A high ▷cupboard. A hood over a chimney.

Tallet Also *tallot* or *tallut*, meaning the slope or ▷batter of a ▷wall. A *tallus wall* is therefore a *battered wall*, usually a ▷retaining ▷wall. It is also the ▷floor of a ▷loft, especially in a ▷barn or other agricultural building.

Talon An ▷ogee moulding (▷mould). A *talon and ball* is a common type of ▷foot on a leg of a piece of ▷furniture or other ▷ornament.

Tambour A ▷drum of a ▷column-▷shaft. The ▷ground or ▷bell on which the ▷leaves of a ▷Corinthian ▷capital are fixed. The ▷wall or drum of a ▷cupola, or any drum-shaped cylindrical object. A circular ▷lobby or ▷vestibule, often with revolving ▷doors.

Tanking A waterproof membrane, usually of ▷asphalte laid under a ▷basement ▷floor and up the ▷walls to prevent water penetration.

Taper A gradual ▷diminution with height as of a ▷column, ▷obelisk, or ▷spire. The taper can be upwards or downwards.

Tapestry An ornamental textile used for wall-hangings, made by weaving coloured threads among the warp-threads.

Taphos A ▷barrow or mound of earth.

Tapia ▷Adobe, or earth or clay compacted material.

Tarras Strong ▷cement or *trass* made of ▷*pozzolan*.

Tarsia Inlay. ▷Inlaid work.

Tas-de-charge The lowest ▷course of an ▷arch or ▷vault, or the lowest ▷voussoir with a horizontal ▷bed. Also the part of a group of vault-▷ribs between the springing and the point where the individual ribs separate.

Tassel Also *tassle*, *torsel* or *tossel*, it is the timber ▷plate on which ▷beams or ▷joists rest. An ornamental hanging tuft of threads, found in drapery, ▷trophies, flags, ▷standards, and ▷lambrequins, and often found on ▷architraves, etc.

Tau ▷**cross** St Anthony's Cross, the T-shaped ▷cross derived from the ▷Egyptian ▷*Ankh*.

Tauriform A ▷*bucranium* or a bull's-head ▷ornament.

Tavern A public-house for the sale of alcoholic beverages.

Teagle-post A ▷post supporting the end of a ▷tie-▷beam in ▷timber-▷framed construction.

Tease-tenon Also *teaze-tenon*. A ▷tenon cut to be fixed to two horizontal pieces of timber at right-▷angles to each other, so the tenon is L-shaped.

Tebam A ▷rostrum, ▷dais, or ▷platform, especially in a synagogue.

Tectiform In the shape of a ▷roof or like a roof.

Tectonic Associated with a construction or a structural system.

Tectorial A covering, or a ▷roof structure.

Tectorium ▷Opus.

Tee A ▷finial shaped like an ▷umbrella, associated with exotic or Eastern styles of ▷architecture.

Tegimen A ▷*baldacchino*.

Tegula A roofing-▷tile, or facing-▷brick for ▷walls.

Tegurium A ▷canopy over a ▷sarcophagus or ▷tomb-▷chest, usually pitched, and carried on ▷colonnettes.

Telamon A male figure used instead of a ▷column to carry an ▷entablature. *Telamones* are not to be confused with ▷*Atlantes*.

Telonium A custom-house in Ancient Rome.

Temenos The sacred precinct of a ▷Classical ▷temple.

Tempera A paint made from egg-white (sometimes with the yolk), ▷glue, pigments, and water. It was used for ▷murals and dried rapidly.

Tempietto A small ▷temple, especially used in post-▷Renaissance ▷gardens, and often circular.

Template, templet A short timber or ▷block of stone under a ▷girder, also called a *padstone* (▷ pad). A pattern for setting something out, or for shaping a moulding (▷mould). Also a ▷beam over a ▷door or window to carry the ▷joists and conduct the load to the ▷piers on either side.

Temple [234] A building dedicated to pagan deities. ▷Classical temples were usually rectangular, with a body or ▷cell, a ▷portico, and a ▷sanctuary. Often they were surrounded by ▷columns and had ▷gables (▷pediments) at each end. Circular temples were also known in ▷Antiquity. The various arrangements of columns are described elsewhere (▷anta, ▷colonnade, ▷intercolumniation). A ▷synagogue. A Protestant ▷church (especially in France). A building with architectural pretensions for special use. A word associated with the ▷preceptories of the Knights Templar. The Temple of Solomon, and so the term is given to Masonic ▷lodges. A *temple ▷tower* is a stepped structure, or a ▷*ziggurat*.

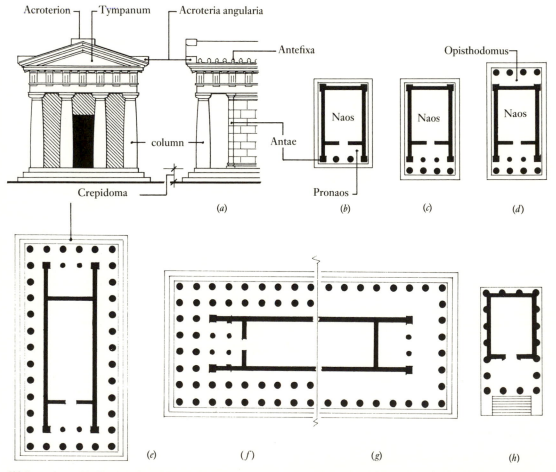

[234] TEMPLE (*a*) Front and partial side elevations of prostyle tetrastyle temple (plans (*c*) and (*d*). Note the acroterion and the acroteria angularia, the antefixae, and the antae. Note also that in Greek Doric the triglyphs always touch at the corners of the frieze, so that the rule that the triglyphs are on the centre-lines of columns or intercolumniations breaks down at the corner, and the corner columns are moved in nearer their neighbours. (*b*) Distyle *in antis*. (*c*) Prostyle tetrastyle. (*d*) Amphi-prostyle tetrastyle. (*e*) Peripteral hexastyle. (*f*) Dipteral octastyle. (*g*) Pseudodipteral octastyle. (*h*) Roman temple with prostyle tetrastyle portico and pseudoperipteral cella. (*JJS*)

Templet ▷Template.

Templon A ▷colonnade with ▷entablature enclosing the ▷*bema* of an early ▷church.

Tendril Curling forms of climbing plants occur in much ▷enrichment, notably in ▷Celtic work, ▷Art-Nouveau styles, and ▷naturalistic and stylised ▷foliage, especially the ▷grapevine (▷[17]).

Tenia ▷Taenia.

Tenon, tenant A ▷projecting rectangular piece on the end of a piece of timber to be inserted into a ▷mortise in another piece. Hence mortised-and-▷tenoned joint.

Tent ceiling A ▷camp ceiling. Tent forms are often found in late eighteenth-century ▷garden buildings and ▷Regency ▷canopies (i.e. with concave sloping ▷roofs over ▷doors or ▷balconies). The were associated with the exotic, and especially with *Chinoiserie* (▷Chinese). Tent ▷ornament with ▷spears and lances occurs in ▷*Empire* decoration.

Tepidarium A room in a ▷Roman ▷bath set at a medium-warm temperature.

Teram A ▷scroll at the end of a ▷step.

Term A ▷pedestal like an inverted ▷obelisk supporting a bust, or merging with it, also called a *terminal*. It differs from a ▷*herm*. A *terminal pedestal* is one like an inverted obelisk to carry a bust.

Termination An ▷ornament which stops a moulding (▷mould), ▷label, or other architectural element such as a ▷hood mould.

Terminus A popular word for the end of a railway-line, or its main station. A bust or the part of a human body above the waist, rising from a plain ▷block, a ▷pilaster, or a ▷console. A *terminal figure*. Also a stone used to mark a boundary, often in the form of a ▷*term*.

Terrace [235] A raised space or ▷platform adjoining a building, often paved, planted, and ▷embellished with ▷sculpture. A row of houses joined together as a unified design, *not* to be described as *terraced* houses.

Terracotta Baked clay, unglazed, used for ▷ornamental work on façades of buildings.

Terrazzo A ▷floor or ▷dado ▷finish of ▷marble-chips set in ▷cement and then ground down and polished.

Terreplein An earthen embankment with a flat top.

Tessella A small square of ▷marble, pottery, ▷brick, ▷glass, ▷tile, stone, etc., also called *tessera*, set in ▷mortar, with other *tessellae*, forming a ▷mosaic. To say something is *tessellated* means it is formed of *tessellae*. *Tessellated work* is found in ▷pavements.

Tessera A ▷tessella.

Testa A ▷brick or ▷tile, or a shard of an object made of burnt clay.

Tester A ▷canopy over a ▷pulpit, ▷tomb, ▷bed, etc.

Testudo A ▷vault over a ▷hall, or any grand arched ▷roof. *Testudinate* means roofed with a vault, but the term is also given to a ▷ridged or ▷hipped roof, with four sides converging to a point or a ridge and points, which completely covers a building.

Tetra A word preceded by *tetra* means with four. *Tetrakionion* means a ▷canopy on four ▷columns. *Tetraprostyle* means having a ▷portico of four columns standing in front of the *cella* (▷cell). *Tetrapylon* means having four gateways, or an ▷arch having four identical ▷façades, as over two intersecting ▷axes. A *tetrastoön* refers to a ▷court with ▷colonnades on each of the four sides. *Tetrastyle* means having four columns in the portico, or any colonnade of four columns (▷[234a, c, d, h]). A *tetrastyle* ▷*atrium* is one with four columns arranged around it to support the ▷roof.

Texture A quality of surface apart from its colour.

Thalamos, thalamium A ▷Greek inner ▷chamber in a house.

Thatch A ▷roof-covering of reeds, rushes, or straw, used in mediaeval times, but later favoured for the *cottage orné* (▷cot) or for *rustick* buildings.

Theatre A building with a ▷stage for the performance of drama, with seating for the audience. ▷Classical theatres were semicircular, grouped round the ▷orchestra, with the *skene* (▷scaena) behind. ▷Greek theatres were often hollowed out of rock, while ▷Roman theatres were more often built on level ground. An *amphitheatre* consists of two theatres joined together, producing a circular or elliptical structure.

Thermae Public ▷baths in ▷Roman times that contained many amenities apart from baths. *Thermae* were often of great magnificence, and their complex planning was the source for much ▷Renaissance and later ▷Classical interrelationships of rooms. Small baths were called ▷*balneae*. A *thermal window* is a

315

(a)

(b)

[235] TERRACE (a) A fine range of
early nineteenth-century terrace
houses in Eastgate Street,
Winchester. Note the chimney-pots
in the shape of Egyptian pylons, the
bracketed eaves, the lesenes or
pilaster strips, and widely
proportioned windows with margin-
panes. (*JSC*) (b) Grosvenor Terrace,
Glasgow, by J. T. Rochead, 1855.
Note the superimposed Orders
(Tuscan, Ionic, Corinthian)
combined with arcuated forms for the
windows. It is based on Venetian
precedent, the Procuratie Nuove of
1584 by Scamozzi in the Piazza San
Marco. (*Mitchell Library, Glasgow*)

▷semicircular ▷window subdivided by two ▷mullions, also called a ▷Diocletian window: it is a feature of ▷Palladian ▷architecture (▷[101]).

Thesaurus A ▷Greek ▷treasury.

Thistle Used in decorations to give a Scottish flavour, and often occurring in ▷Jacobean plasterwork after 1603. It is also used as a ▷finial, and its ▷leaves are found instead of the ▷acanthus. It also occurs in ▷Art-Nouveau work.

Thole, tholos The ▷dome of a circular building, or the building *in toto*. A domed ▷rotunda. A ▷niche where offerings were placed. A ▷knot or ▷shield at the top of a ▷vault, or hiding the junction of ▷ribs. A *tholobate* is a circular substructure for a *tholos*. A *tholos* ▷*tomb* is a ▷beehive or a ▷corbelled pseudo-domed ▷chamber under a mound and reached by a ▷*dromos*.

Three For *three-centred arch*, see ▷arch. For *three-decker pulpit*, ▷pulpit. A *three-hinged arch* is one with flexible joints at the springings and at the ▷crown: it is also called a *three-pinned arch*. A *three-light* ▷*window* is one with three distinct openings separated by ▷mullions or ▷tracery. A *three-pointed arch* is an equilateral arch, i.e. a *two-centred arch*. A *three-quarter* ▷*brick* is one cut to reduce its length by a quarter. *Three-quarter* ▷*bond* is where the bonding is three-quarters the thickness. A *three-quarter header* (▷head) is three-quarters of the thickness of the ▷wall.

Threshold A strip of wood, stone, or metal fixed to the ▷floor under a ▷door, used to cover the joint between two types of floor finish. Thresholds can also help to prevent water penetration at external doorways.

Throat A groove on the underside of a coping (▷cope) or ▷string to throw the water off. A ▷drip or drip moulding (▷mould). The ▷throat of a ▷chimney, or the narrowest part of a ▷flue.

Through A *through-stone* is on in a ▷wall the full thickness of the wall, so it is a ▷*bond-stone, parpen, parpend*, or *parpent*. Similarly, a *through-*▷*arch* is one the full width of a thick wall. A *throughstane* is a ▷table-▷tomb, i.e. a horizontal ▷slab on ▷piers or ▷colonnettes.

Thumb moulding ▷Gadroon.

Thunderbolt A spiral ▷roll, often in the ▷talons of an ▷eagle, as an ▷attribute of ▷Jupiter. It is also hown winged, or with ▷zigzag flashes of lightning. Thunderbolts are often found on the ▷soffites of ▷Classical ▷cornices, but occur in ▷*Empire* decoration and in schemes associated with the ▷Elements, or with electricity.

Thymele A small ▷altar dedicated to Dionysus, and often set in the ▷orchestra of a ₃Greek ▷theatre.

Thyroma A ▷door in an ancient house opening on the street, or a doorway in the upper part of the ▷stage of an ▷Antique ▷theatre. A *thyrorion* was a ▷passage in a Greek house leading from the street-door to the ▷peristyle around the ▷atrium.

Thyrsus A ▷staff with a pine-cone at one end, entwined with ▷ribbons, ▷ivy, or ▷grapevines. It is associated with ▷Bacchic decoration.

Tie A member tying two bodies together, such as a tie-▷rod of metal or a timber ▷beam. A *tie-beam* is that connecting a pair of principal ▷rafters (▷[212a]): it is a horizontal member fixed to the lower ends of the rafters to prevent them from spreading.

Tierceron A secondary ▷rib springing from the junction of two other ribs, or one that rises between a main diagonal and transverse ribs from the springing to the ▷ridge-rib in a ▷Gothic ▷vault (▷[2451]).

Tige The ▷shaft or a ▷column between ▷base and ▷capital.

Tiger Associated with ▷Bacchic ornament, and also with *Chinoiserie* (▷Chinese), ▷Indian, and exotic *Eastern* or *Oriental* styles.

Tignum A ▷tie-beam or a timber for building.

Tile [236] A thick ▷plate of burnt clay or other material used to cover a ▷roof or a ▷wall. Thicker tiles are used for paving. Flat tiles are ▷*plain tiles*, and curved ones are called ▷*pan-tiles*. *Tile-and-a-half tile* is a plain tile one-and-a-half times the width of that of the tiles with which it is used, placed in ▷laced and ▷swept ▷valleys, and in ▷verges. When walls are clad in tiles

[236] TILE Decorative floor-tile from Winchester Cathedral showing the type of pattern achieved with two colours of clay, one set in the other, called encaustic tile. (*JJS*)

the surface is called *tile-hanging*. For *encaustic tiles*, ▷encaustic. Glazed wall-tiles were much employed in ▷Victorian ▷architecture. *Tile-creasing* is two or more ▷courses of tiles projecting above a wall to protect it from the weather, and often found on ▷gables.

Tilt A *tilt-and-turn* ▷window is a bottom-hung inward-opening ▷casement, which can convert to a side-hung inward-opening casement to facilitate window-cleaning from inside the room. A *tilting-*▷*fillet* is a piece of timber triangular in section fixed to the ▷rafters so that the ▷pitch of the ▷roof is less steep at the ▷eaves-▷courses: it is also a triangular piece of wood to give the lowest course of tiles or slates the same tilt-angle it would have had if there had been another course below.

Timber framing [237] A building construction of timber as the main structural element, set on a ▷foundation of ▷brick or stone, with the spaces between filled with brick or ▷plaster (▷breastsummer).

Timber, tymbre The crest (▷cress) on top of a helm, or on top of a ▷femerell or ▷lantern.

Time An old man, sometimes winged, with ▷scythe and hour-glass, and occasionally with crutch, ▷scales, and ▷serpent (often with tail in mouth). Time may also be suggested by outstretched wings with an hour-glass in the centre, based on the Ancient ▷Egyptian winged globe or disc.

Tin A silvery-white, fusible, malleable metal (Sn). *Tinning of ironwork* is mediaeval decorative ironwork that was *tinned* to protect it from rust.

Tingle A strip of flexible metal to hold a replacement ▷slate in place, or to secure a piece of glass: one end is fixed and the lower end is folded around the bottom of the edge of the object to be secured.

To-gall, too-fall A ▷*lean-to* or *pentice* (▷appentice).

Tolbooth, tollbooth A ▷booth, office, or ▷stall where duty was collected. A Scottish town ▷gaol often associated with the duty-collection point. A ▷town-hall or a ▷guild-hall. A *toll-house* was a small dwelling for the keeper of a toll-bridge or highway, from which tolls were collected.

Tomb [238] A ▷sepulchre or ▷grave, including a ▷monument. A *tomb-*▷*chest* is a stone form shaped like a chest, also known as an ▷altar-tomb, set above the grave: it rarely contained the ▷coffin, which was buried or entombed beneath. Tomb-chests were plain or had ▷effigies on top, either as sculptured figures or as ▷incised designs (e.g. '▷brasses'), and often had stand-ing or kneeling figures called ▷weepers around the sides. A ▷*table-tomb* is a flat ▷slab on ▷piers or ▷colonnettes. Grander built tombs are called ▷*mausolea*. A *tomb-*▷*canopy* is one built over an altar-tomb, usually to protect the effigies. A *tombstone* is an upright or horizontal stone placed over a grave, and usually inscribed: it is a ▷memorial and a marker. A *tombstone light* is a small ▷window with ▷light or lights shaped like a tombstone, and usually set above a doorway.

Tondino A small *tondo* (circular ▷plaque or ▷medallion), or a circular moulding (▷mould) or ▷ornament.

Tongue A ▷projecting ▷feather to fit within a groove, as in *tongued-and-grooved work*, meaning ▷floor-boards so feathered-and-grooved.

Tooth ▷Ornament in the form of four-leafed flowers ▷projecting in points, or hollow pierced ▷pyramids, also known as ▷*dog-tooth* or *tooth ornament*. A *toother* is the same as dog-tooth. *Toothing stones* are projecting stones left in a ▷wall to which another building is to be joined: they are also called *tusses* or ▷*tusks*.

Top beam A ▷collar-▷beam.

Top rail The top moulding (▷mould) of wainscoting or of a ▷dado.

Topiary Trees and shrubs (usually evergreen) cut and trimmed to form ▷garden ▷ornaments, shaped forms, etc. ▷*Opus topiarium* was ▷Roman wall-painting showing gardens, ▷trellis-work, trees, and shrubs.

Topographical decoration Decoration showing real places, such as scenes of Ancient ▷Egyptian ▷architecture copied from Denon's *Voyage . . .* of 1802, or other locations.

Torch A common ▷motif in ▷Classical ▷ornament. An inverted torch on funerary ▷monuments, frequently held by a weeping ▷*putto*, represents ▷death (the extinguishing of the flame). With the flaming ▷urn and lamp, torches appear as ▷finials. *Torching* is ▷lime-▷mortar pointing to the undersides of ▷slates and tiles over the ▷heads to prevent the tails of the ▷course above from lifting, and to prevent wind-blown rain and snow from entering the building.

Torchère A support for a ▷*flambeau* or candles.

Tore As ▷torus.

Torsade A ▷cable or ▷rope moulding (▷mould), a spiral or twisted moulding, or an ornamental ▷twist.

Torso A spiral or ▷twisted column.

Tortoise Often used as a decorative foot-support. The shells of tortoises are found in ▷*Buhl*-work.

Torus A large convex moulding at the ▷base of a ▷column and set over the ▷plinth (▷orders). It can be enriched with ▷bay leaf (▷[39]) or other ornament.

Touchstone A smooth black stone used for ▷tombs, e.g. ▷Purbeck ▷marble.

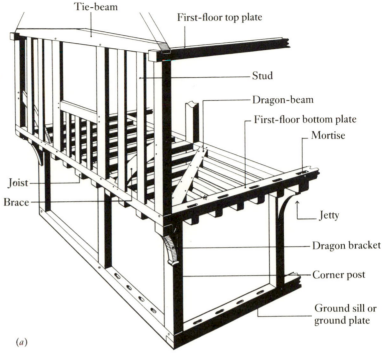

[237] TIMBER FRAME (*a*) An example of a timber-framed structure with jettied upper floor, dragon-bracket and -beam, and studding. (*JJS*) (*b*) Timber-framed houses in Broad Street, Ludlow, Shropshire. The house on the left has two bold jetties, with a dragon-beam on the corner. Next to it are jettied storeys, the upper one with gables with nineteenth-century barge-boards and finials. The ground-floors probably had some system of covered walks known as 'piazzas' or pentices. (*JSC*) (*c*) The Feathers Hotel, Ludlow. A fine, late-Elizabethan timber-framed building of 1603. Note the balcony with flat-open-work balusters, and the lozenge pattern on the first floor. On the second floor are cusped concave lozenges and canted bays with gables treated with arched motifs, barge-boards, and finials. (*JSC*)

Tie-beam

First-floor top plate

Stud

Dragon-beam

First-floor bottom plate

Mortise

Joist

Brace

Jetty

Dragon bracket

Corner post

Ground sill or ground plate

(*a*)

(*b*)

(*c*)

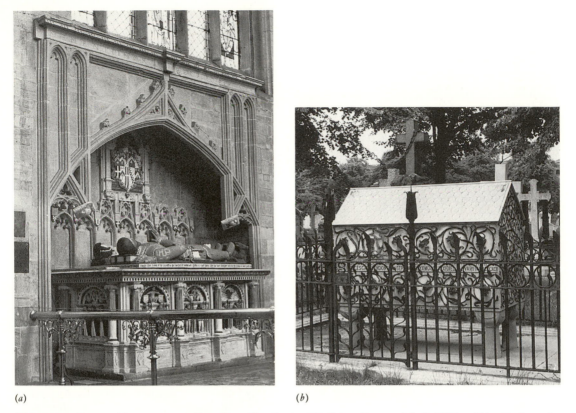

(a)   (b)

[238] TOMB Church of St Laurence, Ludlow, Shropshire. Tomb of Sir Robert Townsend (built 1581) and his wife. It consists of a tomb-chest with fluted engaged Ionic columns between which are niches with standing weepers. On top of the slab are two recumbent effigies. (*JSC*) (*b*) The exquisite tomb of F. R. Leyland in Brompton Cemetery, London, by Sir Edward Burne-Jones. A beautiful example of Arts-and-Crafts work, with Art-Nouveau and Romanesque elements. (*JSC*)

Tourelle A ▷corbelled ▷turret.

Tower [239] A tall building on a circular, square, polygonal, or rectangular plan, used for defence, as a landmark, for the placing of a clock, or for the hanging of bells, as in a ▷church tower. ▷Storeys of a tower are called ▷*stages*. A *tower-*▷*bolt* is a ▷*barrel-bolt*. A *tower-house* is a fortified house of several storeys with the main ▷chamber raised well above the ground.

Town canopy [240] A ▷sculpture like a small building used as a ▷canopy over a statue. It occurs on ▷tomb-▷slabs (especially ▷*brasses*).

Town hall A building for use as the administrative headquarters of a municipality, and which contains a large ▷hall for public meetings, concerts, etc.

Trab A ▷wall-▷plate. *Trabeation* means anything with an ▷entablature or a ▷beam on supports, as opposed to

▷*arcuated*. To say a building is *trabeated* means it is constructed on the ▷post-and-▷lintel system.

Trabes compactiles The main ▷beams or ▷architraves on the ▷columns of ▷Etruscan ▷temples.

Tracery [241] The intersection of the ▷mullions and ▷transomes of ▷windows, ▷screens, ▷panels, or ▷vaults. *Tracery* is also referred to as *forms* or ▷*form-pieces*. Early tracery is of the .073plate variety, consisting of flat panels of ▷masonry pierced with ▷lights, and often consists of two ▷lancets with the ▷spandrel above pierced by a circle, ▷quatrefoil, or simple opening. From the thirteenth century, moulded mullions and separate window-lights were formed at the ▷heads of windows to describe circular or other forms, leaving the other parts of the spandrel open. Simple ▷*bar tracery* formed patterns of a *geometrical* nature, but in the later phase of *Second-*▷*Pointed* work (fourteenth century), formed ▷*flowing* or ▷*curvilinear* tracery in

(a)

(b)

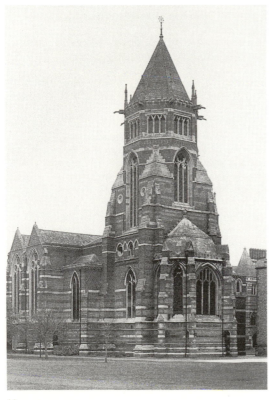

(c)

[239] TOWER (a) Church of St James, Kinnersley, Herefordshire. The west front with its blocked Romanesque door and
mighty tower of the early fourteenth century. Note the saddle-
backed roof. (JSC) (b) The Church of St George-in-the-East by
Nicholas Hawksmoor, of 1717–22, with tower passing between
the ends of open-topped pediments with scrolled ends, an almost
Mannerist device. The bizarre octagonal lantern is capped with a
series of altars in the Antique style. (JSC) (c) The massive tower
with octagonal belfry-stage and huge gargoyles at Rugby School,
by William Butter eld, of 1872. Note the polychrome brickwork.
The style is free Second-Pointed. (JSC)

321

[240] TOWN CANOPY Effigy of Edward III in Westminster Abbey, drawn by Blore, and engraved by Le Keux, showing the canopy. (*JSC Collection*)

tracery forms subdivisions within the two equal curves of the opening, and the ▷geometry of the bars and arched opening is set up from the same centres with different radii. ▷*Kentish* tracery is foiled, with barbs between the ▷foils. ▷*Panel* tracery is typical of late-▷Gothic, *Third*-▷*Pointed*, or ▷*Perpendicular* work, and has vertical straight lights: the mullions run up to the underside of the (usually flattish ▷arch), and transomes are often crenellated (▷crenel). Such panel tracery is often carried over the wall-surface, and is also called ▷*rectilinear* tracery. ▷*Reticulated* tracery is a typical form of *Second-Pointed* work, with ogees giving a net-like appearance at the top of the window. ▷*Y-tracery* is the basic type of branched mullion, developed as intersecting tracery (*c.* 1300). ▷Rayonnant, stump.

Trachelion, trachelium The ▷neck of a ▷column between the ▷*hypotrachelion* and the ▷capital proper.

Tragedy Represented by a conventional ▷mask of drama, one of the ▷attributes of the ▷Muses, in this case *Melpomene.*

Trail ▷Trayle.

Trajan column ▷Triumphal column.

Transe A ▷through-passage.

Transenna A ▷lattice-▷screen around a ▷shrine, often of ▷marble. A ▷Roman cross-▷beam.

Transept The transverse portion of a cruciform ▷church, or the arms on either side of the ▷crossing, often with ▷chapels at the east sides, and possibly with ▷aisles as well (though not always). Larger churches may also have secondary transepts, or cross-aisles. A *transept-aisle* is one at the east or west of a transept, and a *transept-chapel* is one at the east of a transept, usually set in the *aisle*, but possibly projecting from it. ▷Towers often stood over the main crossing (▷[66]).

Transition A term used to denote the passing of one style to another, especially ▷Romanesque to ▷Gothic in the twelfth century.

Transome A horizontal ▷bar dividing a ▷window into two or more ▷lights in height. A bar separating a ▷door from a fanlight (▷fan) over. Also *transom.*

Transtrum A ▷Roman ▷beam.

Transverse An ▷ornamental ▷border at the top of an opening, also called ▷*chambranle*. A *transverse* ▷*arch* is an arch dividing a compartment of a ▷vault from another, i.e. built across a ▷hall at right angles to the long ▷axis. A *transverse* ▷*rib* is therefore one

which compound ▷ogee curves, without any interruption, created ▷dagger-like or flame-like lights, hence the term ▷*Flamboyant. Geometrical* tracery employs circles and foiled circles, and was in use from around 1250 to 1300 (earlier in France), being revived in the nineteenth century. *Curvilinear* or ▷*undulating* tracery dominated the fourteenth century. ▷*Intersecting* tracery has mullions which branch out until they arrive at the heads of the windows, and thus form ▷Y-shapes: such at right angles to the long axis, dividing a vault into ▷bays.

Transyte A narrow ▷vestibule or ▷passage in mediaeval ▷architecture, also called *tresaunce, trisantia* or *tresawnte. It was near the* ▷*chapter-house.*

Trass Natural ▷*pozzolan.*

Travated Divided into ▷bays or *traves.* A *trave* or *travis* is therefore a ▷cross-▷beam or a dividing element forming bays in a ceiling. A *traviated* ceiling is the same as *travated.* A *travis* or *trevis* is also the name given to the dividing ▷walls between the ▷stalls in a ▷stable.

Traverse A ▷screen with curtains to give privacy, or a ▷gallery or ▷loft of communication.

Travertine A type of limestone (▷lime) with pronounced banding, coloured yellow-brown, with coarse cells, extensively used in the buildings of the city of Rome. It can take a polish, and is used for ▷floors or for interior facing. It is referred to as a ▷marble.

Tray ceiling A ceiling formed partly within the pitched ▷roof, with sloping sides and a flat top, also known as a ▷*camp ceiling.*

Trayle A *trail,* ▷*vignette,* or *vinette,* meaning a ▷running ▷ornament of ▷vine ▷scrolls with vine leaves and grapes, common in late ▷Gothic work as an ▷enrichment of a horizontal member, such as at the top of a ▷screen.

Tread The horizontal part of a ▷step or ▷stair.

Treasury A building or room in which precious objects are kept.

Tredyl ▷Grees.

Tree A large ▷beam, ▷lintel, or ▷gallows. A *tree-*▷*nail* or ▷*trunnel* is a long ▷dowel of ▷hardwood, or a ▷*gutta.* Tree trunks were used as the model for ▷columns in some ▷Renaissance ▷architecture, complete with lopped branches, and recur in ▷Mannerist ▷patternbooks. They were also used to suggest the ▷Primitive Hut, and so were found in *rustick* buildings. For *Tree of Jesse,* ▷Jesse. The *Tree of Life* was characteristic of some ▷Jacobean decoration, with ▷tendrils, flowers, ▷fruit (often the ▷pomegranate), birds of paradise, and ▷butterflies.

Trefid, trefoil, trifid, pied-de-biche, split-end A decorative ▷foot, also known as a *drake's foot,* in the form of a ▷tripartite ▷splay.

Trefoil A ▷Gothic ▷ornament of three ▷foils in a circle or a roughly triangular figure. A *trefoil* ▷*arch* has three ▷lobes or ▷foils.

Treillage A ▷trellis to carry ▷vines or for ▷*espalier*-work. Also *trellage,* often made with false perspective.

Trellis A ▷lattice of thin ▷bars of metal or wood used as a ▷screen or as a support for plants. A *trellis moulding* (▷mould) is an ▷ornament of the ▷Romanesque period consisting of overlapping ▷chevrons giving a trellis appearance. The ▷fillets of the trellis are secured within two horizontal framing mouldings, and are often studded. A *trellis* ▷*window* is the same as a ▷*lattice window.*

Trenail ▷Tree.

Tresaunce ▷Transyte.

Tresse Flat or convex ▷bands intertwining, also called ▷*interlacing* ▷*ornament.* A type of ▷*guilloche.*

Tressel A *trestle,* or ▷prop for a horizontal ▷plank.

Tressure A ▷border within an ▷heraldic ▷shield narrower than the ▷*orle,* generally doubled.

Trestle ▷Tressel.

Trevis ▷Travated.

Triangular arch A false ▷arch of two flat stones ▷mitred at the top spanning an opening.

Triangular fret ▷Dovetail.

Triapsidal With three ▷apses, often arranged round a curved ▷sanctuary.

Tribelon An ▷arcade connecting a ▷nave to a ▷narthex, usually with three ▷doorways.

Tribune An ▷apse, a raised ▷platform, or a ▷church ▷gallery, such as that between the ▷nave-▷arcade and the ▷clerestorey. The gallery or arcade in the ▷wall above the nave arcade in a grander church, often associated with a wall-▷passage above the arcade and under the clerestorey. ▷Triforium.

Trichila, trichilum A shady place in a ▷Roman ▷garden, often formed of ▷trellis-work. Also called *tricla* or *triclia.*

Triclinium A room in which ▷Roman feasts were held and guests were received.

(a)

(b)

(c)

(d)

[241] TRACERY (a) Plate tracery from the church of St Andrew, Peckham, by Enoch Bassett Keeling (1837–86), architect. Note the quatrefoils and simple geometrical shapes. (b) Geometrical tracery of the late thirteenth century from the chapter-house of Salisbury Cathedral. (c) Intersecting tracery of Y-pattern with cusps from North Stoke in Sussex, c.1290. (d) Elaborate curvilinear Decorated or Second-Pointed tracery from Selby Abbey in Yorkshire, a fine example of the fourteenth century flowing style. Note the mandala form in the top, the dagger-like (mouchette) forms, and the flame-like character. (e) Reticulated (net-like) tracery from Worstead, Norfolk, with cusps. Second half of the fourteenth century. (f) Perpendicular tracery from Bath Abbey, of the early sixteenth century. Note the two transomes, the survival of ogee arches, the panel-like effect of the mullions and transomes, and the fact that the mullions rise to the underside of the main arched opening. (g) The west window of York Minster, a sumptuous design of eight lights, in pairs, with a great heart-shaped mass of flowing tracery above (1338). This is a fine example of Decorated or Second-Pointed flowing or curvilinear tracery. (h) The great east window of York Minster, early fifteenth century, showing the strong panelled effect of Perpendicular, mixed with posthumous Decorated elements. The screen behind the altar is in the Perpendicular style, with crenellations, and is by Sir Robert Smirke, of the 1830s. (a–f, JJS; g, h, JSC)

324

(e)

(f)

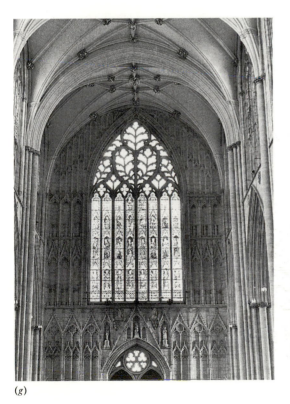

(g)

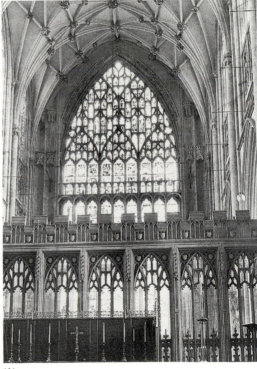

(h)

Triconch With ▷apses on three sides of a square plan.

Trident Found in a ▷marine decoration, associated with ▷Britannia, and with thunder and lightning.

Triforium The ▷gallery or ▷arcade in the ▷wall above the ▷nave arcade, often associated with a wall-▷passage above the arcade and under the ▷clerestorey, now thought to be an incorrect use for a ▷tribune (▷[134]). *Triforium* seems more properly to apply to a three-arched opening *in the tribune*.

Triga A sculptured chariot group drawn by three horses.

Triglyph The vertical ▷block in a ▷Doric ▷frieze, comprising two ▷glyphs and two half-glyphs (hence the 'three' glyphs), separating the ▷metopes. In late-▷Renaissance versions the two half-glyphs are often omitted, so the block becomes a ▷*diglyph*. Triglyph blocks occur over the centre-lines of ▷columns and centre-lines of spaces between columns. In the ▷Greek Doric ▷Order the triglyphs at the corners of the building join, so they are not over the centre-lines of the columns at the corners, and the spaces between columns at the corners of the building are smaller: in ▷Roman Doric the triglyphs are over the centre-lines of the corner columns, so that there is part of a metope at the angle of the frieze separating the triglyphs (▷[106a–g]).

Trigonum A ▷mosaic of triangular *tesserae* (▷tessella).

Trilith, trilithon Two vertical stones supporting one horizontal stone like a ▷lintel, so three stones are involved.

Trilobe With three ▷foils, i.e. ▷trefoil.

Trim A ▷frame or edging. A *trimmer* is a timber that supports the ends of ▷joists, etc. A ▷partition ▷wall would be trimmed up between ▷floor and ceiling, while the cutting of a trap-door in a floor would involve the insertion of trimmers. A *trimmer* ▷*arch* is a low segmental arch used to support a fireplace-▷hearth: it is also called a *trimmer*. A *trimming* ▷*joist* is one supporting the end of a trimmer, and parallel to the ▷common joists: it is usually of a greater section. A *trimstone* is a stone dressing (for ▷architraves, ▷quoins, etc.) where the backing material is of inferior ▷stuff.

Tringle A small ▷fillet.

Tripartite A ▷vault over a triangular plan with three distinct parts.

Tripod A ▷table or stand with three legs, usually placed on high above the crowning ▷cornice on a ▷pedestal. The legs often terminate in claws or feet.

Tripteral With three rows of ▷columns, i.e. a treble ▷*pteron*, or with three ▷wings.

Triptych A picture with folding ▷doors on either side (also painted) which close over it. When opened three pictures are revealed. A triptych usually forms a ▷reredos, and is typical of late ▷Gothic work. It is called a *Flügelaltar* (winged altar) in German.

Triquetra An ▷ornament of three almond shapes interlocked, to give a three-▷lobed shape.

Trisantia ▷Transyte.

Triskele A ▷Y-shaped sun form, often with human or animal legs, as on the Manx ▷emblem.

Tristyle With three ▷columns in a line.

Trisula A three-pointed ▷ornament.

Triton Half-man and half-fish, occurring in ▷marine decoration. A merman, often blowing a conch-shell.

Triumphal arch [242] ▷Arch. There are two main types: those with a single arch over an ▷axis (Titus, Rome, first century of our era), and those with a large central arch flanked by two smaller arches (Septimius Severus, Rome, third century of our era). In both types a rich ▷Order is applied to the ▷arcuated form with wide ▷intercolumniation, and over the ▷entablature is the ▷Attic ▷storey with dedication. The form was revived in ▷Renaissance times, not only for festive ▷architecture, but, in a variation, for building ▷façades or parts of façades. Later triumphal arches, such as the *Arc de Triomphe* in Paris by Chalgrin (1806–35) and the great Thiepval Arch by Lutyens of the 1920s, exploit more than one axis.

Triumphal column A large single ▷column on a ▷pedestal erected as a public ▷monument. The most celebrated example is that of Trajan (second century of our era) with its spiral bands of ▷sculpture and its massive ▷base that contained the ▷tomb-▷chamber of the emperor.

Trivium A junction of three ▷Roman roads.

Trochilus A ▷scotia, or concave moulding (▷mould).

Trompe A ▷vault in an external corner consisting of a quarter-sphere. A partial vault. A *trompe l'oeil*, or trick of the eye, is a creation in paint (two dimensions) to suggest

[242] TRIUMPHAL ARCH
Entrance to Canterbury Quad,
Christ Church, Oxford, designed by
James Wyatt, 1773–83. A fine essay in
Roman Doric, showing the trabeated
and arcuated forms mingled. (*JSC*)

a three-dimensional set of objects. It may also apply to techniques of *marbling*, ▷*graining*, or other illusions.

Tropaeum A ▷monument erected on the site of a military victory.

Trophy A decorative group of armour and arms, occasionally incorporating ▷wreaths, ▷garlands, and ▷festoons, as though hung on a wall. ▷Panoply.

Troubadour A variety of ▷French Gothick associated with the Napoleonic and post-Napoleonic period.

Trullo A cone-shaped, pseudo-▷vaulted (i.e. ▷corbelled) house in southern Italy, or any such structure.

Trumeau A stone ▷pier or ▷shaft in the middle of a ▷church ▷door, supporting the ▷tympanum.

Trumpet arch A ▷squinch like part of a cone. A *trumpet pattern* is one of curved trumpet-like shapes found with sinuous intertwined ▷ornament in ▷Celtic art. A *trumpet* is also an ▷attribute of ▷Fame, the ▷Winds, and the ▷Elements, and in decorations associated with ▷Music or ▷War.

Trunnel ▷Tree. A ▷*gutta*.

Truss A combination of timbers to form a ▷frame, placed at intervals, and carrying the ▷purlins. As well as a frame, of timber or metal, the term also means a ▷*projection* from the ▷face of a ▷wall, or a large ▷*console*, ▷*corbel*, ▷*crossette*, or ▷*modillion*.

Tuck pointing Lines to mark the joints in brickwork, made with ridges of ▷lime-▷putty after joints have been raked out and replaced with ▷mortar coloured to match the brickwork. It gives an impression of very fine work. *Bastard tuck-pointing* is an imitation of tuck-pointing, and is made entirely of the infilling mortar.

Tudor [243] Late ▷Perpendicular ▷Gothic associated with the Tudors, especially with the period 1485–1547. For *Tudor arch*, see ▷arch: a pointed arch of very flat appearance. A *Tudor flower* is an ▷ornament of a flat flower or ▷trefoil ▷leaf placed upright on its ▷stalk and used in cresting (▷cress) in late-Perpendicular work. A *Tudor Rose* is a stylized ▷rose with five ▷petals. The *Tudor* ▷*Revival* was associated first with the ▷Picturesque, and many examples (often houses, ▷schools, and workhouses) were erected in the

[243] TUDOR STYLE Queen's University of Belfast of 1846–49 by Sir Charles Lanyon, a fine essay in the Tudor-Gothic style, with a central tower modelled on the Founder's Tower at Magdalen College, Oxford. Tudor Gothic, featuring diapered brickwork, crenellations, and large windows with flat hood moulds, seems to have found favour for use in educational buildings, workhouses, almshouses, and the like. (*JSC*)

first half of the nineteenth century. Fine Tudor Revival work based on ▷timber-framed exemplars, was associated with the ▷Domestic Revival. A further revival occurred in the twentieth century, often associated with suburban houses and ▷taverns.

Tufa A porous cellular stone much used by the ▷Romans.

Tulip Common in sixteenth-century decoration, especially in ▷Flemish Mannerism or styles influenced by it.

Tullianum A subterranean ▷prison in the ▷Roman state ▷gaols.

Tumbling course Sloping ▷courses of brickwork at right angles to the *rake* of a ▷gable, ▷chimney, or ▷buttress, also known as *tumbling in*.

Tumulus A mound over a ▷grave. A ▷barrow.

Tun A ▷chimney-▷shaft. A ▷barrel, suggesting trade, especially in wine or beer.

Tunnel An underground ▷channel protected by a ▷vaulted ▷roof, as in a sewer or over a railway line. A *tunnel-vault* is a ▷barrel-vault.

Turkish style ▷Ottoman.

Turn button A ▷catch for a ▷cupboard ▷door consisting of a small length of material pivoted on a screw.

Turned Stone or wood pieces such as ▷balusters, turned and cut on a lathe, and circular on plan.

Turngrece A winding ▷stair.

Turning bar A metal ▷bar carrying the ▷wall over a fireplace opening, also called a ▷*chimney-bar*.

Turning piece Also called a *trimming-piece*, it is a ▷*camber*-▷*slip* used as *centring* for a *flat* ▷*arch*.

Turnpike stair A ▷spiral stair.

Turrellum A ▷turret.

Turret As ▷tourelle. A small ▷tower or large ▷pinnacle, but ▷corbelled out at a corner. A *turret-*▷*step* is a keyhole-shaped stone forming part of a ▷spiral or ▷newel-▷stair, the ends of which form the central ▷column or newel of the stair. A building with turrets is referred to as *turriculated*. *Turriform* means tower-shaped.

Turris A ▷tower in a fortified ▷wall, usually one of a series.

Turtle Associated with night, with conjugal affection and constancy, with esoteric cults, and with exoticism. A *turtle-back* was a ▷boss found in ▷Jacobean work.

Tuscan Order [244] The simplest of the ▷Orders of ▷Classical ▷architecture. The ▷shaft of the ▷column is never ▷fluted, and the ▷capital has a square ▷abacus. The ▷base consists of a square ▷plinth and a large ▷torus, and the ▷entablature is plain. In a primitive version of the Order the ▷frieze and ▷cornice are omitted, and a wide overhanging ▷eaves carried on long ▷mutules is placed directly over the ▷architrave. The Tuscan Order is essentially a plain and simplified version of ▷Roman ▷Doric. The Tuscan ▷*cavaedium*

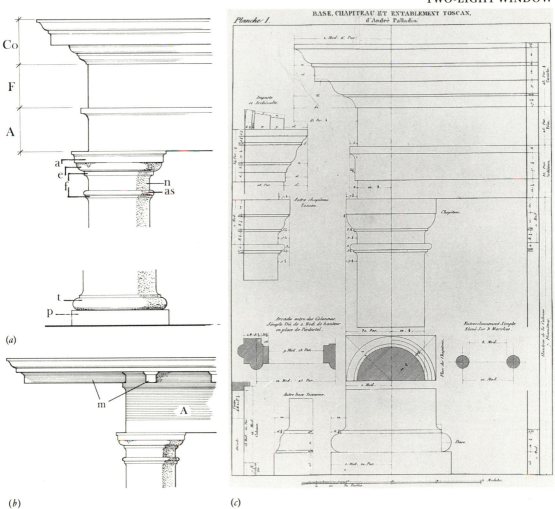

(a)

(b) (c)

[244] TUSCAN ORDER (*a*) Tuscan Order after Sir William Chambers. **Co** cornice, **F** frieze, **A** architrave, **a** abacus, **e** echinus, **f** fillets, **n** neck, **as** astragal, **t** torus, **p** plinth. (*JJS*) (*b*) Tuscan Order after Inigo Jones. **m** mutules, **A** architrave. Note there is no frieze. The capital is similar to that used in the Chambers example. (*JJS*) (*c*) Tuscan Order after Palladio. Note the simple torus moulding at the base, the way in which the shaft joins the fillet at the top and bottom by means of an apophyge, and the very plain entablature. Note also the variation to base and capital when used with arches. (*Normand*)

had an inward tilt in all four directions so that the rain drained through the *compluvium.*

Tusk, tooth, tuss A *tusk-▷tenon* is a tenon formed at the end of a *trimmer ▷joist* to fix it to the *trimming joist* (▷trim), passing through a ▷mortise, and itself mortised to take a wedge the other side of the trimming joist. A ▷projecting stone left in a ▷wall to which another building is to be joined.

Tusses ▷Tooth.

Twin arch Two ▷arched openings beside each other.

Twining stem A ▷Romanesque moulding (▷mould) formed of a ▷half-▷round with a spiral stem twisted round it, often found in a ▷cavetto. It is also called *twisted stem.*

Twist A spirally turned object, such as a ▷baluster. It was thought, incorrectly, in the nineteenth century to be peculiarly ▷Elizabethan.

Twisted column A ▷spiral column or a ▷torso.

Two-light window One with two ▷lights, i.e. divided by a ▷mullion or a ▷transome. A ▷gemel ▷window.

Tympan, Tympanum The ▷face of a ▷pediment between the level ▷fillet of the ▷corona and the ▷raked ▷cornice of the sloping sides. The space between a ▷lintel and an ▷arch over the lintel. *Tympana* are frequently ▷embellished with ▷sculpture in ▷relief.

Type An example, prototype, specimen, exemplar, or pattern. A ▷tester or sound-board. A ▷capping of a ▷turret or ▷cupola ▷roof.

U

Umbo A ▷kerb-stone in a ▷Roman street, or a ▷projection with a conical or tombstone-shape rising from a kerb, e.g. to stop wheeled vehicles mounting ▷pavements.

Umbraculum A ▷*baldacchino* or ▷umbrella.

Umbrella A stone *chattra* on a ▷*stupa*, found in ▷Indian ▷Revival ▷architecture. An *umbrella* ▷*dome* is a ▷*melon-shaped* ribbed dome, also called a *parachute* or *pumpkin* dome, more like a parachute than an umbrella, because the ▷webs curve outwards.

Uncoursed ▷Masonry laid in a random form, or *snecked* (▷sneck). ▷Rubble.

Unctuarium As ▷aleipterion.

Uncut modillion A plain unornamented ▷block-▷modillion, or a simple ▷mutule.

Undé, undée A ▷wave moulding. ▷Oundy.

Undercloak A ▷course of ▷slates, or ▷tiles laid under upper courses at ▷eaves or ▷verges changing the slope.

Undercoat A coat of paint applied after ▷priming and before the finishing, or top, coat. It contains more pigment and less varnish than the top coat.

Undercroft A ▷vault or ▷crypt under a ▷church or other building.

Undercut tenon A ▷tenon with the ▷shoulder cut off the square to give good bearing on ▷mortised timber.

Under-eaves course A ▷course or courses of ▷tiles or ▷slates under the ▷eaves to provide a surface requiring little maintenance.

Underlay A layer of building paper between two layers of building components to allow them to move. A damp-proof membrane can act as an underlay. *Underlay* can also refer to a layer of plywood or hardboard placed over a rough surface to enable ▷tiles or ▷parquet, etc., to be laid.

Underpin To bring a ▷wall up to the ▷ground-▷cill. The term also denotes the strengthening of the existing ▷foundations for a wall by new foundations which are built up to the existing base of the wall.

Underpitch An *underpitch* ▷*groin* is one formed by an *underpitch* or ▷*Welsh* ▷*vault*, that is, two vaults springing from the same level, but of different sizes and heights, joining at right angles, in a rectangular compartment.

Underthroating The ▷cove of a ▷cornice to act like a ▷drip.

Undulating An *undulating moulding* is an ▷oundy or ▷Vitruvian or ▷wave ▷scroll, also called an *undulate band*, or continuous strip of wavy mouding (▷mould). *Undulating* ▷*tracery* is ▷flowing or ▷curvilinear tracery.

Undy ▷Oundy.

Unframed A ▷door hung directly on ▷hinges, with no ▷frame. A *battened* door.

Unicorn A bearded ▷horse with a single spiral horn and a ▷lion's tail. It is a ▷symbol of purity and, especially, of the Virgin Mary.

Updraught kiln ▷Scotch kiln.

Uphers ▷Fir-▷poles used for crude roofing.

Upright A soldier, or ▷brick laid on end.

Upstart A ▷reveal-stone higher than it is long.

Uraeus The ▷snake ▷symbol on the head-dresses of Ancient ▷Egyptian pharaohs and deities, often on the ▷*Nemes* head-dress. *Uraei* are also found on either side of discs or globes, associated with winged globes.

Urillae The ▷volutes under the ▷abac s of a ▷Corinthian ▷capital, also called ▷*helices*.

Urn A ▷vase for ashes or cremated remains. It is often used as a decorative ▷motif on top of the ▷pedestals of balustrades (▷baluster), or on ▷walls, or in ▷niches, or as ▷garden ▷ornaments, in all of which positions it is not associated with the ▷furniture of ▷death. It is also used in funerary ▷architecture, either draped, plain, or with a ▷flame at the top and many have a ▷medallion of the deceased on the side. It usually has a lid, unlike a ▷vase.

Ustrinum A ▷platform on which ▷Romans were cremated. ▷Bustum.

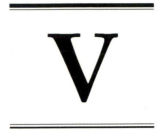

V The Roman symbol for 5. LV = 55.

Vagina The lower part or ▷pedestal of a ▷term from which the bust grows. Also a lower part of the pedestal in which a statuette or other ▷motif is inserted.

Vair ▷Heraldic fur, represented as ranged bell-shaped pieces.

Valance Hung drapery or simulated drapery round a ▷tester, the vertical ▷boards resembling such hangings on the edges of ▷canopies, or the ▷frame, board, or drapes at the top of a ▷window to hide the curtain-rails.

Valetudinarium A ▷Roman ▷infirmary.

Vallatorium A part of a building which ▷projects.

Valley The internal meeting of two slopes of a ▷roof, or the trough or ▷gutter between them. A *valley* is therefore the opposite of a ▷hip, and, with ▷thatch, plain ▷tiles, ▷slates, or stone slates, can be a gentle, gradual slope, that is without a sharp ▷angle and without a valley-gutter. A *valley-▷board* is fixed on and parallel to the *valley-▷rafter*, and supports the *valley-gutter* or the roof surface in a ▷laced or ▷swept valley. A *valley-▷jack* sits on a valley-rafter or valley-board.

Vallum A palisaded ▷rampart of a ▷Roman ▷fort.

Valva A ▷leaf of a folding ▷door.

Vaimure, vamure, vaumure, vauntmure In fortifications, any advanced ▷wall or earthwork thrown out in front of the main fortifications, or the outer wall of a fortress. The term is also used for an ▷*alura*, the walk behind the ▷parapet.

Vandyck swag A loop of drapery with ▷scalloped lower edge, like a ▷lambrequin or the collars in portraits by Sir Anthony van Dyck (1599–1641). It is often found in ▷strapwork.

Vane A metal ▷banner fixed to the top of a ▷tower, and swivelling to show the direction of the wind: it is also called a ▷weather-cock, and may show the north, south, east, and west signs.

Variegated Irregularly marked or coloured.

Varnish A resin dissolved in oil or spirit which dries to give a shiny, transparent, waterproof film.

Vas As ▷aenum.

Vase An ▷ornamental vessel, often used to decorate ▷niches, or as a ▷garden feature. Vases occur in considerable variety in ▷Classical design. Also the ▷bell of a ▷Corinthian ▷capital. ▷Urn.

Vault [245] An ▷arched structure over a room or a space, constructed of stone or ▷brick, and occasionally of wood or ▷plaster in imitation of stone or brick. The simplest vault is the ▷*barrel-*, ▷*cylindrical-*, ▷*tunnel-*, or ▷*wagon-vault* that springs from opposite parallel ▷walls: it is a continuous arch of semicircular or segmental section which requires thick walls to support it. It presents a uniform concave surface throughout its length. If a *tunnel-vault* is divided into ▷bays by means of arches carried on ▷piers then the arches are called ▷*transverse*, and are at right angles to the walls. Two identical barrel-vaults intersecting at right angles form ▷*groins* (▷arrises) at the junctions between the concave surfaces, and result in a *groin-* or *cross-vault*. A *domical vault* (▷dome) has a square or polygonal base, and the

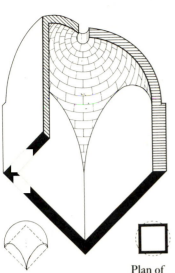

Form of sail dome

Plan of
sail dome

Plan of dome
on pendentives

Form of dome
on pendentives

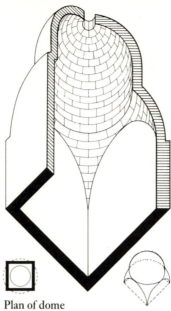

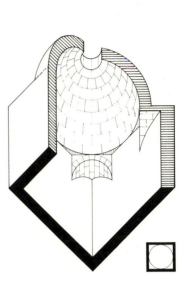

(a)

(b)

(c)

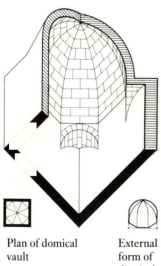

Plan of domical
vault

External
form of
domical
vault

(d)

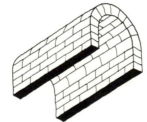

(e)

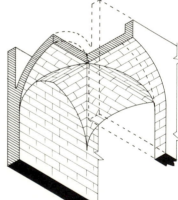

(g)

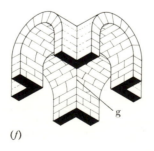

g

(f)

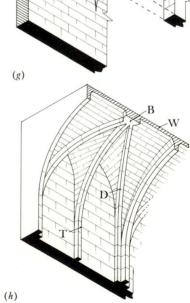

B

W

D

T

(h)

334

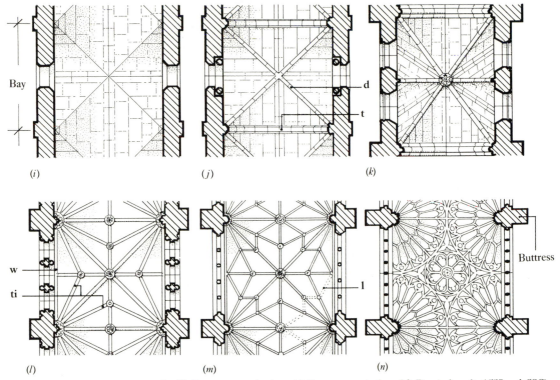

Bay

(*i*)   (*j*)   (*k*)

w

ti

Buttress

(*l*)   (*m*)   (*n*)

[245] VAULT (*a*) Sail-dome or -vault. (*b*) Dome on pendentives. (*c*) Dome on squinches. (*d*) Domical vault. (*JJS* and *JSC*) (*e*) Barrel vault. (*JSC*) (*f*) Intersecting barrel-vaults, **g** groin. (*JJS*) (*g*) Quadripartite groin-vault. (*JJS*) (*h*) Sexpartite rib-vault (halved): **B** boss, **W** web, **D** diagonal rib, **T** transverse rib. (*JJS*) Plans showing the development of vaulting. Note that as vaults become more elaborate the size of the windows and depth of the buttresses increases. (*i*) Groin-vault (intersecting barrel vault). (*j*) Quadripartite rib-vault: **d** diagonal rib, **t** transverse rib. (*k*) Sexpartite rib-vault. (*l*) Tierceron rib-vault: **w** wall rib or formeret, **ti** tierceron. (*m*) Lierne-vault: **l** lierne. (*n*) Fan-vault. (*JJS*)

curved vaults (called ▷*cells*, ▷*severies*, or ▷*webs*) rise directly from the walls, the curved surfaces meeting at groins. A *domical vault* or ▷*cloister-vault* is not a true dome, which is a vault with a segmental, semicircular, bulbous, or pointed section rising from a circular base. A *sail-dome* or *-vault* is constructed on a square base with the diagonal of the square being the diameter of the sail-dome: thus the dome form actually begins in the corners of the compartment to be covered, rising as on ▷pendentives, but the curve continues smoothly. The term *sail* derives from the resemblance to a sail, with the corners fixed, billowing in a strong wind. Sail-domes are also called *handkerchief vaults*. A dome on a square plan-base involves the construction of members between the square plan and the circular plan of the dome proper: these members can be ▷squinches (or arches) at 45° between the sides of the square, or pendentives, which are triangular elements on curved planes. In the cases of pendentives and squinches the diameter of the dome is the same as the dimension of a side of the square, but the diameters of the

pendentives are the same as the diagonal of the square base.

Domes of segmental section placed directly on the circle formed by the pendentives (or the bodged circle formed by the squinches) are called ▷*saucer-domes*, but if the section is semicircular, it is called a ▷*calotte*. A ▷drum placed between the circle formed by the pendentive or squinch-supports over which a saucer-dome or a dome of different section is placed enables ▷windows, ▷peristyles, and other architectural treatment and elaboration to be included. A squinch can be formed of several layers of arches, each with a greater diameter than that behind it, so that the corners of a square compartment are filled with diagonals: the resulting octagonal form can carry either a domical vault with groins, or, by ▷corbelling out over the angles of the octagon, or 'fudging' these corners, a circular base for the dome over can be created. It should be noted that a dome on pendentives or squinches rises from a distinct circular or polygonal base, but that a sail-dome does not possess that distinct circular base

335

because the concave surfaces beginning in each corner of the square compartment merge smoothly with the dome proper, as the diagonal dimension of the square compartment is the same as the diameter of the form of the sail-vault or dome. A *melon-, parachute-, pumpkin-,* or *umbrella-dome* also sits on a circular base, but its form is broken into webs that are segmental on plan, and rise up to a point in a curve with groins between each segmental web, so it is like an umbrella with the fabric billowing convexly from each rib rather than concavely as is the case with a real umbrella, hence the name *parachute-dome*. Another term for a vault is a ▷*voussure*. A vault is, strictly speaking, so contrived that the stones or other materials of which it is composed support and keep each other in their places. When vaults are more than a semicircle in section they are called ▷*surmounted vaults*, and when less than a semi-circle (i.e. segmental) in section, they are termed ▷*surbased*. A vault is also a burial-▷*chamber*, from the form, but the term can also be applied to a burial-chamber roofed with flat ▷slabs. A ▷*fan-vault* is formed of concave-sided cones or funnel-shapes with their rims meeting at the ▷apex of the vault, with flat areas between them. The entire surface of the ceiling is decorated with ▷panels, giving a thoroughly organized appearance. Where the cones fan out from the ▷im-posts, they rise from five ▷ribs on the piers. *Fan vaulting* is characteristic of ▷Perpendicular work, and is not known on the Continent. A ▷*lierne-vault* is a ribbed vault with *liernes*, or tertiary ribs, i.e. ribs not springing either from the central ▷boss or from the main ▷springers, but which spring from rib to rib. A *net vault* is one formed of a net-like series of ▷lozenges. A *ploughshare-vault* or a *stilted vault* has wall-ribs spring-ing from higher points than those of the diagonal ribs in order to gain height to let more light in from the ▷clerestorey. A ▷*quadripartite vault* is divided into four webs or cells by diagonal and transverse ribs. A *rampant vault* is a tunnel-vault with ▷abutments at different heights. A *rib-vault* has arched ribs framing the cells and covering the groins. A ▷*ridge-rib* is the rib along the ridge of the vault. A ▷*sexpartite vault* is like a quad-ripartite vault, but with an extra ▷transverse rib creating six compartments, webs, or cells. This effect of sexpartite vault-cells is also created by the addition of a ridge-rib. A *shell-vault* is a thin membrane based on the principle of an eggshell, on frame members, i.e. stressed-skin construction. A *stellar vault* has ribs, but also lierne-ribs and ▷tiercerons forming a star-shaped pattern on plan. A ▷*tierceron* is a rib that springs from the main springing-points to a boss on the ridge-rib. A *transverse arch* separates one bay from another, and springs from the wall and pier at right angles to the longitudinal axis. A *vaulting* ▷*shaft* is a shaft, ▷column, pier, or cluster of shafts supporting the ribs of a vault at their springing: such shafts sometimes rise from a point near the ▷floor, or from ▷corbels (▷diaphragm,

▷dome, ▷groin, ▷rear, ▷underpitch vault, ▷Welsh). A *vault-bay* is defined by the transverse ribs, also called a ▷*severy. Vaulted* means so constructed, or covered or closed by means of a vault. *Vaulting* means vaults collectively. A *vaulting* ▷*capital* is that of a ▷pier to support a vault.

Vegetables These often occur in ▷naturalistic ▷orna-ment in mediaeval work, but recur in ▷Renaissance and late designs, notably in ▷Grotesques, ▷festoons, ▷cornucopiae, or ▷trophies representing gardening or agriculture.

Velarium The ▷awning over an amphitheatre or ▷theatre, also called *velum*.

Vellar cupola A ▷dome over large staircases and ▷salons (saloons) or ▷rotundas, that is, over a compart-ment more than two ▷storeys high.

Veneer A thin ▷leaf of wood of superior quality to cover a wood of a commoner variety, often finely ▷figured. A *veneered* ▷*wall* is one with a facing fixed to a backing, but incapable itself of sustaining a load.

Venetian [246], [247] A type of ▷terrazzo with larger chips of ▷marble than usual. A *Venetian* ▷*arch* is a form of arched opening consisting of a pointed or semi-circular arch within which are two semicircular-headed ▷lights separated by a ▷colonnette. Above the colonnette is a ▷roundel or foiled opening (▷[21]). A Venetian ▷blind is composed of horizontal slats adjust-able to admit or keep out light. A *Venetian* ▷*dentil* is a moulding consisting of a ▷fillet with its sides cut alter-nately into notches which reach the middle of the face, giving the effect of a double row of ▷dentils. A *Venetian* ▷*door* or ▷*window* is an arched central opening flanked by narrower flat-topped openings: over the flanking openings is an ▷entablature from which the central arch springs. The entablatures are carried on ▷columns or ▷pilasters which sit on the ▷sill, usually designed with a full ▷base, ▷pedestal, or other ▷Classical devices. The central arch has an ▷archivolt and keystone. It is also called a ▷*Serliana* or ▷*Palladian window* because it was first illustrated in Sebastiano Serlio's (1475–1554) *L'Architettura* of 1537–51, and was much used by Andrea Palladio. It was also used by the Palladian Revivalists during the eighteenth century. *Venetian* ▷*mosaic* is ▷terrazzo. *Venetian red* is red iron oxide. *Venetian* ▷*Gothic* (▷[246]) was revived during the nine-teenth century, expecially after John Ruskin's *Stones of Venice* appeared in the 1850s, and is associated with structural ▷polychromy. *Venetian* ▷*Saracenic* refers to ▷Arabesque and ▷Damascening work.

Vent A ▷flue or funnel of a ▷chimney. Any ▷con-duit for carrying off fumes. A *ventilation* ▷*eyebrow*

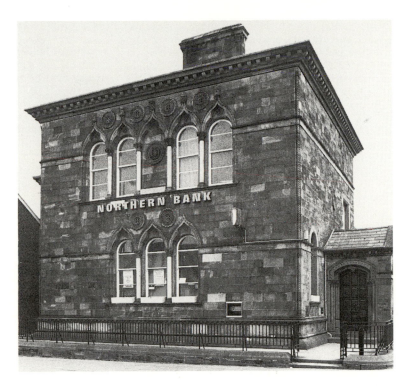

[246] VENETIAN GOTHIC
Former Belfast Banking Company's
premises at Newtownards, Co.
Down, by W. H. Lynn, 1850s. (*JSC*)

[247] VENETIAN RENAISSANCE
REVIVAL The Army and Navy Club,
Pall Mall, London, of 1848–51, by
C. O. Parnell and Alfred Smith,
incorporating elements from
Sansovino's St Mark's Library in
Venice on the upper floor, and
elements from the Palazzo Corner
della Ca' Grande on the Lower.
(*RCHME BL21670*)

is a bottom-hinged inward-opening semicircular ▷window or ▷lunette, or a low dormer (▷dormant) on a ▷roof-slope, with no sides, the roof being curved over it like an eyebrow. A *ventilator* is an opening ▷light, or an outlet for air and water vapour: it is also a glazier's term for a cracked pane of ▷glass.

Venus Aphrodite, the goddess of Love in ▷Antiquity, associated with the ▷scallop shell, the ▷dolphin and ▷marine decoration. She may be shown with the Three ▷Graces, Cupid, ▷doves, ▷Mars, ▷swans, ▷hearts, and ▷*flambeaux*.

Veranda, verandah An open ▷gallery with a ▷roof or ▷canopy on light ▷columns or ▷posts, also called a ▷*stoep*. It is usually placed before the principal rooms to shelter them from the sun, and extends along the outside of the building. It may be closed to form a ▷conservatory. Verandahs were fashionable from the ▷Regency period onwards.

Verdigris A light-green deposit on ▷copper forming a protective and attractive ▷patina on ▷domes, etc.

Verge The ▷shaft of a ▷column, or a very small shaft of a ▷colonnette in ▷Gothic ▷architecture. The edge where a pitched ▷roof joins the ▷gable and projects slightly over the ▷naked of the ▷wall: in such a case the verge is finished with broken ▷tiles, ▷mortar, tumbled (▷tumbling course) brickwork, or other details. If the verge is finished with mortar to make the junction water-tight, it is called a *parged verge* (▷parge work). If the roof is extended over the naked of the wall and finished with a ▷barge-board, that ▷board is also called a *verge-board*. A *verge-▷fillet* is a strip fixed to the roof ▷battens over a gable to cover the upper parts of the gable.

Vermiculated ▷Rustic work having the appearance of being eaten by worms, i.e. with irregular shallow ▷channels over the surface. Anything with irregular wavy lines, such as in certain ▷mosaic patterns.

Vermiculite A lightweight insulating material made from mica, used in ▷screeds.

Vermilion A brilliant orange-red pigment.

Vernacular A term to describe local regional traditional building forms and types using indigenous materials, and without grand architectural pretensions, such as farm buildings and country cottages. Vernacular forms were the precedents for the ▷Domestic ▷Revival of the nineteenth and early twentieth centuries.

Versurae ▷Wings of the ▷stage of a ▷Roman ▷theatre, connecting the straight walls of the *cavea*

(▷auditorium) with the ▷*scaena*.

Vertebrate band A ▷band of ▷ornament with a spine to which the decorations are attached, such as a straight stem, or even an animal's vertebrae.

Vertical *Vertical grain* is the edge-grain of quarter-sawn wood. *Vertical shingling* or *weather-shingling* is a covering of ▷shingles on a ▷wall, like ▷tile-hanging, which provides a decorative and weatherproof covering to a vertical surface (also called *vertical tile-hanging*). A *vertical sliding-▷sash* is a term used to differentiate between the normal vertical sashes, and the horizontal sliding windows, also termed ▷*Yorkshire lights*.

Vesica Piscis [248] A vertical almond-shaped form contained by means of the interpenetration of two equal ▷arcs of a circle: it is a common form of the almond, ▷*aureole*, ▷*mandala*, or *glory* surrounding representations of the Trinity, Christ, etc. The design is a ▷symbol representing the ▷fish, which contains the ▷Greek letters of the name and title of Our Lord (▷Chrismon). It is the eye of the needle through which it is difficult to pass, and the gateway to Paradise. It is commonly found in ▷Gothic ▷panels, ▷tracery, and especially in the ▷tympanum above a doorway, where it usually encloses Christ in Majesty as the Judge. The *Vesica Piscis* contains the basic form of the ▷pointed ▷arch (▷mandala).

Vestiary A room for storing vestments or other clothes.

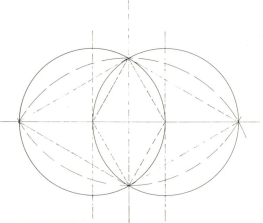

[248] VESICA PISCIS If two circles overlap, their circumference passing through the centres of each other, an almond-shaped *mandala* form is created in the middle. The overlapping circles also produce pointed arches, and associated are two equilateral triangles and a larger almond shape with its axis lying horizontally. The figure has considerable significance in terms of geometry and metaphysics, and contains within it the essence of mediaeval constructional and decorative forms. The 'hinged' pointed arch enabled it to be used for vaulting spaces rectangular on plan, keeping the tops at the same level. (*JSC*)

Vestibule A room which serves as a communication-▷lobby between rooms, or as an entrance-lobby or ▷hall. It is essentially an anteroom leading to a bigger space. A *vestibulum* was a ▷court in front of a ▷Roman house with access to the street on one side.

Vestry, revestry A room adjacent to the ▷chancel of a ▷church, sometimes called a ▷*sacristy*, in which sacred vessels and vestments were kept.

Vethym Six feet, or a ▷fathom.

Via A paved ▷Roman road, often with raised footway. A *via munita* was paved with polygonal blocks of stone, while a *via terrena* was any way with a level surface of earth. *Viae* are also spaces between ▷mutules.

Viaduct A long ▷bridge carrying a road or railway, often on a series of ▷arches.

Vicarage The residence of a vicar.

Vice, vis, vyse A ▷spiral staircase around a central ▷pier. A *vice* is also a blemish or fault, ▷personified as Pride, Lust, Envy, and so on (▷Virtues and Vices).

Victorian Anything dating from 1837 to 1901, i.e. the reign of Queen Victoria.

Victory A winged female figure with ▷laurel ▷wreaths and ▷palm, often associated with arms and armour, and found in the ▷spandrels of ▷triumphal arches. She is often associated with ▷Fame, captured

weapons, and the globe. A *victory* ▷*column* was a single ▷shaft, used to commemorate some great event.

Vicus A ▷Roman house or group of houses.

Vienna Secession ▷Sezession.

Vignette A ▷running ▷ornament of ▷leaves and ▷tendrils in ▷cavetto mouldings (▷mould) in ▷Gothic work, also called a ▷*vinette*. A metal ▷rail on a ▷balcony, often with elaborate ends and centrepiece. A picture or portrait with the edges softened or shaded off, leaving only the central part, i.e. with gradual opacity from the centre outwards. An ornamental or decorative design occupying a small proportion of the space. Any ▷embellishment, illustration, or picture enclosed in a ▷border, or having its edges shading off. A portrait showing only head and shoulders, with the edges fading off.

Viking A style of ▷ornament with ▷interlacing and animal ▷motifs in unbroken patterns, associated with Hiberno-▷Saxon-▷Celtic art.

Villa [249] A country house, often with outbuildings, as the headquarters of a farm and estate. Later villas were set in a ▷garden, such as the *Villa Capra* near Vicenza, or Lord Burlington's villa at Chiswick. In the nineteenth century it came to mean a detached house on the outskirts of a town, essentially a suburban dwelling. The ▷Roman *villa rustica* had rooms for the steward and the workers, stores, and ▷stalls for the animals, as well as rooms for the family. The *villa*

[249] VILLA Late-Victorian villa at Mistley, Essex, showing the influence of the Gothic Revival and of polychrome in the structure. The disposition is entirely asymmetrical. (*JSC*)

urbana was more a pleasure-house set in a landscape, and designed to exploit a view or views: it had separate summer and winter quarters, and had facilities for leisure.

Vine   A ▷grapevine, trail (▷trayle), or ▷vine-▷scroll.

Vinette   As trail, ▷trayle, or ▷vignette in the sense of a ▷scroll of vines.

Virgin Mary   ▷Symbols, ▷Lady chapel.

Virtues and Vices   ▷Personifications of the *Christian Virtues* (Faith, Hope, Charity) and the ▷*Cardinal Virtues* (Justice, Fortitude, Prudence, and Temperance): Pride and Humility, Vice and Virtue, Lust and Chastity, and so on, are often shown in opposition in iconographical and decorative schemes. About twelve *Virtues* were in common use in the mediaeval and ▷Renaissance periods, with their opposing *Vices*.

Vis   ▷Vice.

Viscountess   A size of ▷slate 18 × 9 inches.

Vitrified   Glazed, as ▷bricks with a surface glaze caused by the beginnings of melting in intense heat. Vitrified clayware is fired through and needs no surface glaze.

Vitrum   ▷Glass used in ▷mosaics, or as a ▷wall- or ceiling-covering, or as flooring.

Vitruvian opening   An opening, such as a doorway or a ▷window, with ▷battered sides, like an ▷Egyptian ▷pylon. It is found in ▷Neoclassical ▷architecture, usually that with ▷Greek and Egyptian influences. It is so-called because it was described by Vitruvius (Marcus Vitruvius Pollio) who flourished in the days of Julius Caesar and Augustus, and was the author of *De Architectura*, the only surviving architectural text from ▷Antiquity.

[250] VITRUVIAN SCROLL Also known as running dog or a wave scroll. (*JJS*)

Vitruvian scroll [250]   A continuous ▷band of ▷ornament like a series of waves, found in ▷Classical ▷architecture: it is also called a ▷*running dog* or a ▷*wave scroll*, and is found on ▷string-▷courses, ▷friezes, ▷dados, etc.

Vivarium   A place for breeding animals and studying them.

Vivo   A ▷shaft of a ▷column.

V-joint   A ▷V-shaped ▷channel in ▷match-boarding formed of two adjacent ▷chamfers at the joint. Also a small horizontal joint in ▷mortar made with a pointed tool. A V-▷roof is one with two ▷lean-to roofs meeting in a ▷valley.

Volsura   A ▷voussoir.

Volute   A spiral ▷scroll forming the distinguishing feature of the ▷Ionic ▷capital: it is also found in the ▷Composite ▷capital, and, in a smaller form, in the ▷Corinthian. It is also called a ▷*helix*, and occurs in ▷consoles, ▷ancones, and ▷modillions (▷figures associated with the individual Orders). Also a ▷stair handrail detail.

Vomitory   An exit from a ▷Roman ▷theatre or amphitheatre, often one of a series in a bank of seats.

Votive   Something given or erected as a result of a vow, such as a ▷cross or ▷altar.

Voussoir   A wedge-shaped stone or ▷brick forming part of an ▷arch or ▷vault, with its radiating sides coinciding with the radii of that arch. It is also known as a *cuneus* (▷[21]).

Voussure   A ▷vault.

Voutain   The jointing of the parts of the ▷web or ▷cell of a stone ▷vault.

Vulcanizing   Treatment of rubber, etc., with sulphur compounds to improve properties of wearing, etc.

Vulne window   A low-side window or lychnoscope (▷leper's squint).

Vyse   ▷Vice.

W

Wagon A *wagon-ceiling* or *wagon-*▷*vault* is a ceiling or vault over a rectangular space, and consists of a simple half-cylinder. It is also called a ▷*barrel-vault*, a *wagon-head vault*, or a *wagon-roof (*▷*vault). A wagon-*▷*chamfer* is one with a series of small scoops taken out of a rectangular section, commonly found in ▷Arts-and-Crafts ▷panelling. A *wagon-*▷*roof*, or ▷*cradle-roof*, is formed of closely spaced ▷rafters with arched ▷braces, looking like the covering of a wagon: such roofs can be plastered or panelled.

Wagtail A ▷parting-▷slip.

Wainscot A timber lining to ▷walls, or timber ▷panelling, fixed to the lower part of an internal wall or ▷partition. Panelling of ▷box-▷pews. A ▷dado.

Waling Shoring (▷shore), usually given in the plural.

Wall Any structure of ▷brick, stone, timber, etc. erected for security, or to enclose a space, a room, a ▷fort, etc. A ▷*wall-*▷*anchor* is a ▷beam-anchor. A *wall-*▷*arcade* is a ▷blind arcade. A *wall-*▷*base* is a ▷socle or a ▷plinth. A *wall-*▷*column* is an ▷engaged column. A *wall-garden* is a wall with plants set in its joints or in ▷sockets. A *wall-piece* is a wall-▷plate, or timber laid horizontally on a wall, to which ▷joists, ▷rafters, and ▷roof-▷trusses are fixed: it is also a ▷board set vertically to a wall against which shoring (▷shove) is fixed. A *wall-*▷*press* is a built-in ▷cupboard. A *wall-*▷*rib* is a rib against the outside wall of a ▷vault compartment. A *wall-*▷*shaft* is a ▷colonnette on a ▷corbel supporting vaulting. A *wall-*▷*string* is one on the side of the ▷stair next the wall.

Wane Bark or the round surface under the bark on sawn timber, hence *waney edge*, meaning a defective edge or corner.

War Suggested by ▷Mars, ▷military decoration, or ▷trophies featuring weapons, ▷helmets, and armour.

Ward A ▷court in a ▷castle, surrounding the ▷keep, also called a *bailey* (▷bail). An administrative division in a town. A department in a ▷prison or ▷hospital.

Wardrobe A room or ▷cupboard for storing clothes. A ▷*garderobe* means the same thing, but is more usually applied to a ▷privy or a private room.

Warp Distortion in timber, such as a twist.

Watch A *watching* ▷*loft* is a lookout in a ▷tower or high place, or a ▷gallery in a ▷church where a watch was made over a ▷shrine, or from where persons called the monks to their devotions: such a gallery was called ▷*excubitorium*. A *watch-tower* was any high tower from which watch could be kept, as in a ▷bartizan.

Water ▷Classical decorations include water flowing from ▷vases, often used in ▷grottoes and ▷fountains, or in depictions of the rivers, or schemes of the four ▷Elements, or in ▷marine decoration. It is found with icicle *rustication* (▷rustic).

Water-bar A steel ▷bar bedded on edge in a groove on a sill to fit a groove under the sill of the fixed wooden ▷frame and on top of a door-sill and under a ▷door to prevent water penetration.

Water-glass A viscous solution of sodium or potassium silicate in water, used as an adhesive or as a protective covering.

Water-leaf A carved ▷leaf found in twelfth-century ▷Transitional or Early ▷Gothic work: it was used in

341

▷capitals, with a large leaf flowing out and returning at each angle, curving up towards the ▷abacus and the inwards. In ▷Antique ▷Classical ▷ornament a water-leaf was a type of ▷lotus leaf, sometimes with a ▷rib, called a *Lesbian leaf*: it is a strap-like, feather-shaped leaf, also known as ▷*stiff leaf*. *Water-leaf* is also known as ▷*hart's tongue* or ▷*lily leaf*. A *water lily*, *lily-pad*, or *lotus*.

Water ramp A ▷ramp down which water flows, or a series of basins from which water flows to the basins below.

Water-shot Dry walling of stones laid to a slope so that water pours outwards, common in the Lake District.

Water table A horizontal ▷offset in a ▷wall, sloped or ▷chamfered on the top. A *barge*, or projecting ▷ledge at the base of a ▷chimney.

Wattle A light ▷frame of reeds or sticks, interwoven, and fixed to the structural frame. *Wattle-and-*▷*daub* (▷[251]) is mud or clay placed on a basketwork of wattle to fill the framework of ▷timber-framed buildings instead of ▷brick-nogging (▷nog). It is also called ▷*reed-and-daub*. A *wattle-groove* is a rebate (▷rabbet) in the side of wooden ▷posts or ▷plates or ▷staves into which wattles are sprung.

Wave moulding A moulding (▷mould) like a continuous repetitive run of S-shaped waves, also called a ▷*Vitruvian scroll* or ▷*running-*▷*dog*. ▷Oundy, ▷undé. S-shaped ▷flutes on the sides of ▷*sarcophagi* are known as *strigillation* (▷strigil), and appear to indicate waves (▷[231], [250]).

Weapons Used in ▷military decoration, ▷panoplies, and ▷trophies to suggest ▷victory or ▷war.

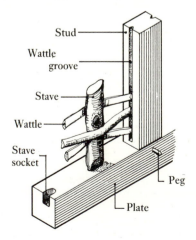

Stud
Wattle groove
Stave
Wattle
Stave socket
Peg
Plate

[251] WATTLE-AND-DAUB (*JJS*)

Weather-boarding An external ▷cladding of timber ▷boards, also called ▷*clap-boarding* or *siding*, with a ▷lap to prevent water penetration, and laid horizontally.

Weather-cock A ▷vane.

Weathered Exposed to the elements, and worn. Also as ▷weathering, i.e. with an inclined top.

Weathering An inclination given to horizontal surfaces to throw off water.

Weather-moulding A ▷hood ▷mould, or ▷projecting moulding (▷mould) with a ▷weathered top, as on the bottom ▷rail of a ▷door, with a drip.

Weather-struck A ▷mortar-joint set at an angle so that the water is thrown or drained outwards to the ▷face of the ▷brick.

Weather-tiling ▷Walls clad in ▷tiles. Weather-slating means clad with ▷slates, or *slate-hung*.

Weather-vane A ▷vane or ▷weather-cock.

Web Infilling between the ▷ribs of a ▷Gothic ▷vault, i.e. one of the compartments of a rib-vault, also known as a ▷*severy* or a ▷*cell* (▷vault).

Wedge-coping A feather-edged coping (▷cope). ▷Feather.

Weeper A statue in an attitude of mourning (▷mourners) placed in the ▷niche of a ▷tomb-▷chest, usually one of a series. A *weeping-*▷*cross* was set up by a wayside where penitents could pray. A *weep-hole* is a small drainage hole for water to escape.

Weeping willow An ▷attribute of mourning, often found on funerary ▷monuments, and also associated with *Chinoiserie* (▷Chinese).

Weights of a sash Two weights on either side of a ▷sash by which it is suspended on cords or chains over pulleys.

Weldon stone A pink-brown limestone (▷lime) from Weldon, Northamptonshire.

Well A deep shaft sunk to allow water to seep in from the soil. In a flight of ▷stairs it is the space left beyond the ends of the ▷steps or ▷strings.

Well kerb An upstand around the top of a ▷well, often associated with a ▷canopy and lifting device on pulleys.

Welsh For ▷Welsh (or Welch) arch, ▷arch. A *Welsh ▷groin* is one formed by the intersection of two cylindrical ▷vaults, one of which is higher than the other (i.e. an ▷*underpitch* or *Welsh vault*).

Welt A seam in any flexible roof-covering. A *welted ▷drip* is turned down at the ▷eaves or ▷verge to make a drip, folded back on the ▷roof, and sealed.

Westmorland A grey-green ▷slate from the Lake District.

Wheat A ▷symbol of fertility and of the harvest, used in agricultural decoration, and associated with Demeter/▷Ceres, the ▷seasons, and the Eucharist. Wheatsheafs are found on corn exchanges.

Wheel An ▷attribute of time, fortune, the sun, and St Catherine. A *wheel▷window* or *wheel▷tracery* is a circular window with radiating spokes formed of ▷colonnettes, loosely (but inaccurately) called a ▷*rose window*. A *wheeler* is a ▷*winder*, as is a *wheel ▷step*. *Wheelers* and ▷*kneelers* are crenellations (▷crenel) or ▷battlements. A *Wheel-head ▷cross* is a typically ▷Celtic type.

Whiplash A whip-like flowing, sinuous curve, which is a dominant form in ▷*Art-Nouveau* decoration.

Whitbed A seam in limestone (▷lime), especially ▷Portland stone, immediately above the base-▷bed, producing the best quality stone.

Whiting Pure chalk, used in ▷size.

Whitening A streaky white grain in varnished or polished woods, with a coarse texture.

Whitewash ▷*Whiting* or ▷*lime-wash* made with ▷quicklime in an excess of water, sometimes with alum, casein, ▷size, or other binders.

Wicket A small ▷door set in a larger one.

Wigwam A circular or elliptical plan on which is a structure of bent ▷poles over which is a covering of bark or skins: it was a dwelling of the American Indians, and inspired *rustick* types of hut in Europe in the eighteenth and early nineteenth centuries.

Wild man A ▷*woodwose* or human figure covered with hair, with a wooden club, a ▷symbol of aggression and lust. It is also known as ▷*wodehouse*.

William and Mary ▷Architecture and style of the period 1688–1702 in England, much influenced by the Netherlands, by French Huguenots, and by a taste for the exotic, notably *Chinoiserie* (▷Chinese). It comes midway between the ▷Baroque of the ▷Restoration and the ▷Queen Anne period.

Willow pattern A standard blue-and-white *Chinoiserie* (▷Chinese) design featuring water, a ▷bridge, boat, island, ▷pagoda, willow trees, fishermen, and birds, surrounded by a ▷fret ▷frame, reputedly invented in the 1780s.

Wind ▷Personified by the north wind, *Boreas* (▷Triton's horn), the south wind, *Notus* (pouring rain from a ▷vase), the east wind, *Eurus* (with ▷fruit and flowers), and the west wind, *Zephyrus* (with spring flowers). The most celebrated personifications were on the Athenian Tower of the Winds, published and copied by James Stuart in the second half of the eighteenth century. Puffed-out cheeks and bellows are commonly associated with the winds.

Wind beam A ▷collar-▷beam.

Wind brace A ▷brace strengthening a timber structure such as a ▷truss against the wind, especially a diagonal brace or an arched brace (▷[237]).

Winders ▷Steps radiating from a centre, usually wedge-shaped, used in a winding or screw ▷stair.

Wind-filling ▷Beam-filling or nogging (▷nog) between ▷floor- or ceiling-▷joists at their supports to strengthen the joists and create a fire-stop.

Window An ▷aperture in a ▷wall to admit light and air. If the aperture is subdivided, each part is known as a ▷*light*. ▷Classical windows are usually vertical rectangular openings, sometimes framed by moulded ▷architraves, and sometimes crowned with an ▷entablature with or without a ▷pediment. If the opening has ▷columns or ▷pilasters on either side supporting an entablature, pediment, ▷gable, ▷lintel, or ▷plaque, it is said to be ▷*aediculated*.

Window-▷frames in Classical ▷architecture are of two basic types: the ▷*casement* and the ▷*sash*, the former hinged and the latter sliding in a frame (*chassis*). In the seventeenth century the casement frame was often ▷cruciform, with ▷quarries of ▷glass in ▷lead ▷cames supported by ▷saddle-bars, and the opening lights (often of iron) were hinged at the sides, opening in or out. In 1685 the frames of the ▷Palladian Banqueting House in Whitehall were replaced by wooden sash-windows, one frame of which slid vertically in grooves in front of the other. The sashes were suspended on cords over pulleys and counterbalanced by means of weights held in the surrounding frames within the ▷jambs, an English invention of the 1670s, known as *double-hung sashes*. This type of sash-window rapidly gained in popularity from that time, and replaced the casement types in all the better-class work. ▷*Crown glass* was generally used, but the sashes were subdivided by means of glazing-bars which were generally thick and clumsy. During the eighteenth century the glazing-bars became finer, with elegant mouldings (▷mould), and the ▷panes became bigger. In the nineteenth century in the first decades, the wider proportions of windows fashionable with the ▷Neoclassical styles produced the need to have narrow bands of glazing around the larger panes of glass: these are called ▷*margin-panes*, and were sometimes coloured. From around 1830 larger panes of ▷sheet-glass became available at economical rates, and it became fashionable to remove glazing-bars from sashes: this altered the vertical emphasis of windows and the proportional relationship of the window-openings and the ▷façade in its entirety. The repeal of taxes in England on glass in 1845 and on windows in 1851 gave windows greater prominence in ▷elevations from those dates. Other types of window associated with Classical architecture include ▷*bay* and ▷*bow-windows*, canted, segmental, or semicircular on plan, and were found in eighteenth- and nineteenth- century domestic architecture. The term *bay* is usually applied to the canted form on plan, while *bow* suggests the *segmental* or *semicircular* type: both bays and bows rise from the ground. A bow may also be a projection of the window-frame only rather than part of the structure itself. ▷*French* or ▷*croisée windows* are casements carried down to the floor-level, and open like ▷doors to ▷gardens, ▷verandahs, or ▷terraces: they are so-called from their use in the 1680s at Versailles. *Dormer* (▷dormant) windows are set on the slope of a ▷roof and are independently roofed themselves: they are named from the fact that they usually illuminated and ventilated sleeping-quarters within the roof. A dormer should not be confused with a ▷*lucarne* or *luthern* (▷dormant). A *Palladian window* is also called a ▷*Venetian window* or a ▷*Serliana*: it became a commonly used feature in English Palladian architecture, and consists of two, tall, flat-topped windows (framed by ▷columns or ▷pilasters carrying ▷entablatures) on either side of a ▷semicircular-headed wider central window, the ▷arch of which springs from the two entablatures. A ▷*Wyatt window* is like a *Serliana* except that the central window is flat-topped instead of arched. The ▷*Diocletian* or *thermal* window, named after its use in the ▷Thermae of Diocletian, was also used by Palladio, and was employed in Palladian architecture in England: it is a semicircular window divided into three lights by means of two ▷mullions. The Classical language also allowed arched windows, or circular windows.

▷*Anglo-Saxon* windows were small, often with large ▷splays, and were often arched, or headed with lintels into which semicircular holes were cut on the undersides: in ▷towers the openings are usually of two lights divided by small, squat, turned ▷baluster-▷colonnettes. Anglo-Saxon window-heads were often triangular. ▷*Romanesque* windows were often of considerable size, frequently were splayed, and were usually with semicircular arched heads, sometimes ▷enriched with ▷chevron or ▷billet mouldings. Romanesque openings were sometimes paired, divided by ▷shafts, and placed within a larger semicircular opening, while circular windows were not unusual. In *First-*▷*Pointed Gothic*, windows were first of all pointed, narrow, long holes in the walls, called ▷*lancets*, and occur singly or in groups. ▷*Plate* ▷*tracery* is found dating from this period, while circles, ▷quatrefoils, and other figures are common. Then, in early *Second-Pointed* fenestration, comes *geometrical* ▷*bar tracery* and ▷*Y-tracery*. With *later Second-Pointed* work (▷*Decorated*) comes ▷intersecting, ▷reticulated, ▷curvilinear, or ▷flowing tracery, all with lights separated by mullions which flow into the ornate tracery in the upper part of the window. ▷*Perpendicular* or *Third-Pointed* windows have mullions and ▷transomes dividing the area into great numbers of lights, mullions rise up to the (often very ▷depressed) window ▷heads, and transomes are often crenellated (▷crenel). ▷Tudor-Gothic windows often have four-centred heads, with rectangular ▷hood ▷moulds framing the opening so that decorative ▷spandrels are created. ▷*Oriel windows* are ▷projections, usually from an upper ▷storey, containing lights, and supported on ▷corbelling or on ▷brackets. A *picture window* is a large window in a frame with a single undivided pane of ▷glass. A *Chicago window* is the width of a structural ▷bay, has a large fixed central window and narrow vertical sashes on each side. A *fanlight* (▷fan) is a window over a door, whether in the shape of a ▷fan or not. For *Ipswich window*, ▷Ipswich. ▷Bay, ▷Catherine-wheel, ▷clerestorey, ▷compass, ▷cross, ▷Diocletian, ▷dormant, ▷fan, ▷French, ▷laced, ▷lancet, ▷lattice ▷low-side, ▷leper's squint, ▷lucarne, ▷oculus, ▷oeil-de-boeuf, ▷oriel, ▷rose, ▷sash, ▷Serliana, ▷skylight, ▷tracery, ▷Venetian, ▷wheel, ▷Wyatt, ▷Yorkshire light. *Window-bossing* is a recess under a window. A *window-head* is the upper cross-member or bottom of the lintel, or the decorative work over a window. A *window seat* is a seat built into the base of the interior of a window within the thickness of the wall, and under the sill.

Wine cellar A room in a ▷basement for the storage of wines at a cool, stable temperature, often fitted with stone, ▷slate, or wooden ▷bins.

Wing The side portion of a main ▷façade, subordinate to the principal and central ▷front, or one of two smaller buildings flanking the main ▷block. The *wing of a moulding* (▷mould) is a ▷fillet. A *winged disc* or *globe*, usually with rearing ▷*uraei*, is the same as a ▷sun disc. A *wing-*▷*light* is a ▷side-light. A *winged* ▷*horse* is

Pegasus, and is also associated with the swift passing of life. *Wing* is also therefore the feathered limb by which a creature flies, or its representation.

Wire-cut ▷Bricks shaped by extrusion under pressure through a die, and cut to size with wires.

Wired glass ▷Glass cast with wire-mesh so that if the glass cracks it will not fall. It is used in ▷doors, ▷windows, and ▷roof-▷lights.

Withe The ▷partition between two ▷flues in a ▷chimney-stack. Also a flexible *mythe* or ▷*osier* used to fix the ▷thatching to roof-structures.

Wivern, wyvern A mythical beast with the forelegs of an ▷eagle, the ▷wings of a ▷dragon, and a scaly tail with a spear-like end. The head is birdlike, with a hooked beak. It represents ▷war and pestilence.

Wodehouse ▷Wild man.

Wood brick A timber the same size as a ▷brick built into a ▷wall to facilitate fixings.

Wood ▷**mosaic** ▷Marquetry or parquetry (▷parquet).

Woodwose ▷Wild man.

Woolton stone A red, fine-grained ▷sandstone with good working properties from Woolton, Liverpool.

Workshop A room or place where work is done and artefacts are made or repaired.

Worthies There are nine: David, Joshua, Judas Maccabaeus, Alexander the Great, King Arthur, Charlemagne, Godfrey de Bouillon, Hector of Troy, and Julius Caesar.

Wreath The curved part of a ▷string or handrail in a geometrical ▷stair. Also a circular or elliptical ▷chaplet or ▷garland of flowers or ▷leaves used in decoration, to suggest immortality, sovereignty, or commemoration. A *wreathed* ▷*column* is a ▷barley-sugar, or contorted ▷twisted column, or a column ▷festooned with a spiral of ▷vines or other leaves or ▷tendrils, including ▷ivy. A *wreathed* ▷*stair* is a geometrical stair. A *wreathed* ▷*string* is the circular portion of a stair-string where there is a ▷well or hollow ▷newel. A *wreath-piece* is a curved section of a stair-string or handrail.

Wrenaissance A style of the 1880s derived from the ▷Queen Anne ▷Revival, leading to ▷Edwardian ▷Baroque. It evolved from a study of the works of Wren (1632–1723), and its chief practitioners were John Belcher and Mervyn Macartney.

Wrought iron Malleable iron that is *forged* or *rolled*, rather than cast, or brittle, iron: it is hammered into shape while hot. A *wrought* ▷*nail* is a hand-made nail, often with a decorative head.

Wyatt window A ▷*Serliana* without the arched centre, named after its inventor James Wyatt (1746–1813).

Wye As the letter Y in the alphabet.

Wythe ▷Withe.

Wyvern ▷Wivern.

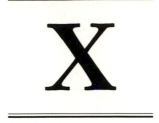

X The symbol denoting 10 in the Roman system; XX = 20. It is also an abbreviation for Christ, representing the first letter of *XPICTOC*. *XP* are the first two letters, hence *chi–rho*, or ☧ (▷Chrismon).

Xenodochium A room or building for the reception of strangers, or a hostel, or guest-house.

Xiphoid Sword-shaped.

Xiphopagus A twin monster joined by the band extending down from the xiphoid cartilage.

Xystus A spacious ▷portico, usually attached to a ▷gymnasium, where athletes exercised in inclement weather. In ▷Roman ▷architecture it was a long covered or open ▷colonnade around a ▷garden or ▷court. An ▷*hypaethral* walk.

Y

Y-tracery ▷Tracery with the ▷mullions dividing to form Y shapes.

Yard A paved ▷area, generally at the back of a house. An enclosed utilitarian area surrounded by ▷walls or outbuildings. A long piece of timber. A measure equivalent to three feet.

Yealm ▷Yelm.

Year ring An annual growth-ring in timber.

Yelm A prepared bundle of reeds or straw for ▷thatch, approximately 250 mm wide and 150 mm thick used in roofing for either ▷coatwork or *ridge-saddles* in long straw, or combed reed.

Yett A grated ▷door or ▷portcullis made of iron, and distinguished by the horizontals passing alternately through the thickness of the verticals and vice versa.

Ymage An ▷image or statue.

Yoke A horizontal ▷board in the ▷frame of a ▷sash-▷window against which the sashes stop at the top.

York stone A term given to ▷sandstones from Yorkshire which are very hard and durable, often used for ▷steps, copings (▷cope), flagstones (▷flag), etc.

Yorkshire bond *Monk bond*, i.e. *Flemish bond*, but with two ▷stretchers and a header (▷head) repeating on each ▷course.

Yorkshire light A ▷mullioned ▷window containing two ▷lights, one fixed, and the other a sliding ▷sash moving horizontally.

Yorky A ▷slate with a curved surface where split.

Yurt A tent-like portable dwelling on a ▷frame.

Z

Zeta A small ▷chamber or a room over the ▷porch of an ▷Early Christian ▷church.

Ziggurat Properly, a series of ▷platforms, or a ▷temple ▷tower, consisting of ▷stages, each smaller in area than the one below. It is a form found in Ancient Mesopotamia, but the name has been applied to stepped ▷pyramidal forms, as often found in ▷Classical designs.

Zigzag A ▷Romanesque decoration consisting of mouldings (▷mould) running in zigzag lines, known as a ▷*chevron* or ▷*dancette*. They can project outwards, can be a continuous line as on a ▷string, or can be placed around an ▷arch with the points of the chevrons vertical rather than projecting horizontally.

Zinc A flexible metal used as a ▷roof-covering, or as a protective coat on ▷galvanized iron.

Zocco, zoccolo, zocle As ▷socle or ▷plinth.

Zodiac signs Twelve signs: *Aries* (ram), *Taurus* (bull), *Gemini* (twins), *Cancer* (crab), *Leo* (lion), *Virgo* (virgin), *Libra* (scales), *Scorpio* (scorpion), *Sagittarius* (archer), *Capricorn* (goat), *Aquarius* (water-bearer), and *Pisces* (fish). They occur in ▷Classical, ▷Romanesque, and ▷Gothic work, and are asso-ciated with the Apostles. They are also used in decorations of clocks, maps, and interior ▷orna-ment.

Zoomorphic ▷Ornament featuring stylized animal forms, especially in ▷Celtic, ▷Romanesque, and ▷Art-Nouveau work.

Zoophorus, zophorus A ▷frieze decorated with ▷reliefs featuring animals, such as the ▷Ionic frieze when sculpted with reliefs.

Zopfstil A style of decoration featuring children and animals in silhouette in contemporary dress, in eighteenth-century German decorations.

Zotheca A small room or ▷alcove, especially a ▷niche for a statue or ▷urn in a ▷sepulchre.

Zwiebelmuster An onion-pattern of blue-and-white *Chinoiserie* (▷Chinese), actually stylized peaches or figs, but thought to be onions.

Zwinger A ▷bailey or outer ▷court. A bear-pit or tournament place, or formal area for display, as at the *Zwinger* in Dresden.

Zystos A long ▷portico. As ▷xystus.

Select Bibliography

In a compilation of this sort many sources have been consulted, especially *The Oxford English Dictionary*, Clarendon Press, Oxford, 1933, *The Oxford Latin Dictionary*, Clarendon Press, Oxford, 1982, and many other standard works. The brief list set out below has to be very select, otherwise the bibliography would rival the book itself in length. The main sources, however, are Bond, Chambers, Dinsmoor, Gwilt, Loudon, McKay, Nicholson, Normand, Parker, Rickman, Robertson, and Vitruvius, details of which are given below. The basis of the book is derived from my own *English Architecture: an Illustrated Glossary*, first published in 1977.

ADAMS, HENRY, *Cassell's Building Construction*, Cassell, London, 1912.

ALBERTI, LEON BATTISTA, *De Re Aedificatoria*, Lorenzo Alamani, Florence, 1486. See the version entitled *On the Art of Building in Ten Books*, translated by Joseph Rykwert, Neil Leach, and Robert Tavernor, MIT Press, Cambridge, Mass., and London, 1988.

ALBERTI, LEON BATTISTA, *L'Architettura*, edited by Giovanni Orlandi and Paola Portoghesi, Il Polifilo, Milan, 1966.

ALDRICH, HENRY, *The Elements of Civil Architecture, according to Vitruvius and Other Ancients, and the most approved Practice of Modern Authors, especially Palladio*, Prince and Cooke, Oxford, and Payne et al., London, 1789.

ARNOLD-FOSTER, FRANCES, *Studies in Church Dedications or England's Patron Saints*, Skeffington, London, 1899.

AVILER, AUGUSTIN CHARLES D', *Cours d'Architecture qui comprend les ordres de Vignole, avec des commentaires, les figures & descriptions de ses plus beaux bâtimens & de ceux de Michel-Ange . . .*, etc., Langlois, Paris, 1696.

BARING-GOULD, S., *The Lives of the Saints*, John Grant, Edinburgh, 1914.

BARON, HANS, *The Crisis of the Early Italian Renaissance*, Princeton University Press, Princeton, 1966.

BILLINGTON, JOHN, *The Architectural Director*, Henry G. Bohn, London, 1848.

BLONDEL, FRANÇOIS, *Cours d'Architecture, enseigné dans l'Académie Royale d'Architecture . . .*, Mortier, Paris, 1698.

BLUM, HANS, *Quinque Columnarum exacta descriptio atque deliniatio cum symmetrica earum distributione . . .*, Froschouerum, Zürich, 1550. See also *The Booke of Five Collumnes of Architecture . . . Gathered . . . by H. Bloome out of Antiquities*, Stafford, London, 1608.

BOLGAR, R. R., *The Classical Heritage and Its Beneficiaries*, Cambridge University Press, 1963.

BOND, FRANCIS, *The Chancel in English Churches*, Humphrey Milford, Oxford University Press, 1916.

BOND, FRANCIS, *Dedications and Patron Saints of English Churches*, Humphrey Milford, Oxford University Press, 1914.

BOND, FRANCIS, *Fonts and Font Covers*, Henry Frowde, Oxford University Press, 1908.

BOND, FRANCIS, *An Introduction to English Church Architecture from the Eleventh to the Sixteenth Century*, Humphrey Milford, Oxford University Press, 1913.

BOND, FRANCIS, *Screens and Galleries in English Churches*, Henry Frowde, Oxford University Press, 1908.

BURCKHARDT, JACOB. *The Architecture of the Renaissance in Italy*, Secker & Warburg, London, 1984.

BURCKHARDT, JACOB, *The Civilization of the Renaissance in Italy*, Phaidon, Vienna, and Allen & Unwin, London, n.d.

CAMPBELL, COLEN, *Vitruvius Britannicus or the British Architect*, vols 1, 2 and 3, with an Introduction by John Harris. First published in three volumes, London, 1715–25. Reissued in one volume (vol. 1 of the three-volume facsimile edition), Benjamin Blom, New York, 1967.

See also Badeslade *et al.*, *Vitruvius Britannicus or the British Architect*, the hitherto unpublished vol. 4 by J. Badeslade and J. Rocque, and vols 5 and 6 by John Woolfe and James Gandon, first published 1767–71. Reissued in one volume (vol. 2 of the three-volume facsimile edition), Benjamin Blom, New York, 1967.

See also Richardson, George, *The New Vitruvius Britannicus . . .*, first published in two volumes, 1802–1808. Reissued in one volume (vol. 3 of the three-volume facsimile edition), Benjamin Blom, New York, 1970.

See also Breman, Paul and Addis, Denise, *Guide to Vitruvius Britannicus . . .*, (vol. 4 to *Vitruvius Britannicus*), Benjamin Blom, New York, 1972.

CHAMBERS, SIR WILLIAM, *A Treatise on Civil Architecture, in which the Principles of that Art are laid down; and illustrated by a Great Number of Plates, accurately designed, and elegantly engraved by the best hands*, Haberkorn, London, 1759. The third edition of 1791 was augmented and published as *A Treatise on the Decorative Part of Civil Architecture*. See also *A Treatise on the Decorative Part of Civil Architecture, by Sir William Chambers . . ., with Illustrations, Notes, and An Examination of Grecian Architecture, by Joseph Gwilt*, Priestley & Weale, London, 1825. See also a further version with an essay by John B. Papworth and nine new plates, J. Taylor, London, 1826. Chamber's great book is of considerable importance in refining and classifying the Classical Language of architecture.

CHITHAM, ROBERT, *The Classical Orders of Architecture*, Architectural Press, London, 1985.

CLARKE, BASIL FULFORD LOWTHER, *Church Builders of the Nineteenth Century. A Study of the Gothic Revival in England*, David & Charles, Newton Abbot, 1969.

COLVIN, HOWARD, *A Biographical Dictionary of British Architects 1600–1840*, John Murray, London, 1978.

CORDEMOY, J. L. DE, *Nouveau Traité de Toute L'Architecture, ou L'Art de bastir; utile aux entrepreneurs et aux ouvriers . . . Avec un Dictionnaire des Termes d'Architecture . . .*, J.-B. Coignard, Paris, 1714.

CROOK, J. MORDAUNT, *The Dilemma of Style. Architectural Ideas from the Picturesque to the Post-Modern*, John Murray, London, 1987.

CROOK, J. MORDAUNT, *The Greek Revival: neo-classical attitudes in British architecture, 1760–1870*, John Murray, London, 1972.

CURL, JAMES STEVENS, *The Art and Architecture of Freemasonry*, Batsford, London, 1991.

CURL, JAMES STEVENS, *Victorian Architecture*, David & Charles, Newton Abbot, 1990.

DIETTERLIN, WENDEL, *Architectura Von Ausztheilung. Symmetria und Proportion der Fünff Seulen, und aller darausz folgender Kunst Arbeit, von Fenstern, Caminen, Thürgerichten, Portalen, Bronnen und Epitaphien. Wie dieselbige ausz jedweder Art der Fünff Seulen, grund, aufzureissen, zuzurichten, und ins Werck zubringen seyen, allen solcher Kunst Liebhabenden, zu einem beständigen, und ring ergreiffenden underricht, erfunden, in zwey-hundert Stuck gebracht, Geetzt, und an tag gegeben*. In five books: B. Caymor, Nürnberg, 1598. Another edition was published in Nürnberg by Pauluss Fürst in 1655, again in five books with a portrait. A French version was published in 1861–62.

DINSMOOR, WILLIAM BELL, *The Architecture of Ancient Greece*, Batsford, London, 1950.

DURAND, JEAN-NICHOLAS-LOUIS, *Essai sur l'Histoire Générale de l'Architecture . . . pour servir de texte explicatif au recueil et parallèle des édifices de tout genre, anciens et modernes, remarquables par leur beauté, leur grandeur, ou leur singularité . . .*, L.-C. Soyer, Paris, 1809.

DURAND, JEAN-NICHOLAS-LOUIS, *Précis des Leçons d'Architecture données à l'École Polytechnique*, Durand, Paris, 1802–09.

EASTLAKE, CHARLES L., *A History of the Gothic Revival*, Longmans Green, London, 1872.

FRÉART DE CHAMBRAY, ROLAND, *Parallèle de l'Architecture Antique et de la Moderne, avec un recueil des dix principaux autheurs qui ont écrit des cinq ordres; sçavoir Palladio et Scamozzi, Serlio et Vignola, D. Barbaro et Cataneo, L. B. Alberti et Viola Bullant et De Lorme, comparez entre eux . . .*, Martin, Paris, 1650. This appeared in a translation by John Evelyn as *A Parallel of the Antient Architecture with the Modern*, Roycroft & Place, London, 1664.

FYFE, THEODORE, *Hellenistic Architecture: An Introductory Study*, Cambridge University Press, 1936.

GADOL, JOAN, *Leon Battista Alberti, Universal Man of the Early Renaissance*, University of Chicago Press, 1969.

GERSON H., and TER KUILE, E. H., *Art and Architecture in Belgium 1600 to 1800*, Penguin, Harmondsworth, 1960.

GIBBS, JAMES, *A Book of Architecture, Containing Designs of Buildings and Ornaments*, n.p., London, 1728.

GIBBS, JAMES, *Rules for Drawing the Several Parts of Architecture, in a More Exact and Easy Manner than has been heretofore practised, by which all fractions, in dividing the principal members and their parts, are avoided*, Bowyer, London, 1732.

GRAFTON, ANTHONY, *Joseph Scaliger: A Study in the History of Classical Scholarship*, Oxford University Press, 1983.

GRAY, A. STUART, *Edwardian Architecture. A Biographical Dictionary*, Duckworth, London, 1985.

GUNNIS, RUPERT, *Dictionary of British Sculptors 1660–1851*, Abbey Library, London, 1968.

GWILT, JOSEPH, *An Encyclopaedia of Architecture*, Longmans, Green, London, 1903 (revised by Wyatt Papworth).

HARRIS, CYRIL M., *Dictionary of Architecture and Construction*, McGraw-Hill, New York, 1975.

KALNEIN, WEND GRAF, and LEVEY, MICHAEL, *Art and Architecture of the Eighteenth Century in France*, Penguin, Harmondsworth, 1972.

LANGLEY, BATTY, *The City and Country Builder's and Workman's Treasury of Designs: Or the Art of Drawing and Working the Ornamental Parts of Architecture*, S. Harding, London, 1745.

LAUGIER, ABBÉ MARC-ANTOINE, *Essai sur l'Architecture*, Duchesne, Paris, 1753. Another edition, augmented with a dictionary of terms and plates to explain the terms was published in Paris in 1755.

LAWRENCE, A. W., *Greek Architecture*, Penguin, Harmondsworth, 1962.

LEWIS, PHILIPPA, and DARLEY, GILLIAN, *Dictionary of Ornament*, Macmillan, London, 1986.

LOUDON, JOHN CLAUDIUS, *An Encyclopaedia of Cottage, Farm, and Villa Architecture and Furniture . . .*, Longman, Rees, Orme, Brown, Green & Longman, London, 1834.

MacGIBBON, DAVID, and ROSS, THOMAS, *The Castellated and Domestic Architecture of Scotland from the Twelfth to the Eighteenth Century*, David Douglas, Edinburgh, 1887.

MARTIN, THOMAS, *The Circle of the Mechanical Arts: Containing Practical Treatises on the Various Manual Arts, Trades, & Manufactures*, Bumpus, Sherwood, Neely, and Jones, London, 1818.

McKAY, W. B., *Building Construction*, Longmans, Green, London, 1957.

NICHOLSON, PETER, *An Architectural and Engineering Dictionary*, John Weale, London, 1835. Also *A New Improved Edition of Nicholson's Dictionary*, edited by Edward Lomax and Thomas Gunyon, Peter Jackson, London, 1852.

NICHOLSON, PETER, *The New Practical Builder, and Workman's Companion: Containing a Full Display and Elucidation Of the most recent and skilful Methods, pursued by Architects and Artificers . . .*, Thomas Kelly, London, 1823.

NORMAND, CHARLES, *Nouveau Parallèle des Ordres d'Architecture des Grecs, des Romains et des Autres Modernes*, Normand Aîné and Carilian, Paris, 1852.

ORME, PHILIBERT DE L', (sometimes given as DELORME) *Architecture*, F. Morel, Paris, 1567.

PALEY, F. A., *Illustrations of Baptismal Fonts*, John van Voorst, London, 1844.

PALLADIO, ANDREA, *I Quattro Libri dell'Architettura*, D. de'Franceschi, Venice, 1570. See also *The Architecture of A. Palladio in four books . . . to which are added several notes and observations made by Inigo Jones . . .*, Leoni, London, 1715.

PARKER, JOHN HENRY, *A Glossary of Terms used in Grecian, Roman, Italian, and Gothic Architecture*, John Henry Parker, Oxford, and David Bogue, London, 1850.

PERRAULT, CLAUDE, *Ordonnance des Cinq Espèces de Colonnes Selon La Méthode des Anciens . . .*, Coignard, Paris, 1683. This was translated by John James and published as *A Treatise of the Five Orders of Columns*, printed by Motte and sold by Sturt, London, 1708.

RICHARDSON, A. E., *Monumental Classic Architecture in Great Britain and Ireland during the Eighteenth and Nineteenth Centuries*, Batsford, London, 1914.

RICKMAN, THOMAS, *An Attempt to Discriminate the Styles of Architecture in England from the Conquest to the Reformation*, John Henry Parker, London and Oxford, 1848.

ROBERTSON, D. S., *A Handbook of Greek and Roman Architecture*, Cambridge University Press, 1945.

RUSKIN, JOHN, *Works*, Longmans Green, London, 1903–12.

SALMON, WILLIAM, *Palladio Londoniensis*, Ward & Wickstead, London, 1734.

SCAMOZZI, VINCENZO, *L'Idea dell'Architettura Universale*, printed at the expense of Scamozzi by Giorgio Valentino, Venice, 1615.

SCAMOZZI, VINCENZO, *The Mirror of Architecture . . . Reviewed and Inlarged . . . By Joachim Schuym . . . Translated out of the Dutch . . .*, Fisher, London, 1687.

SCOTT, JOHN S., *The Penguin Dictionary of Building*, Penguin Books, London, 1984.

SERLIO, SEBASTIANO, *The Booke of Architecture*, E. Stafford, London, 1611.

SERLIO, SEBASTIANO, *Architettura di S. Serlio Bolognese, in sei libri divisa . . .*, Gio. Giacomo Hertz, Venice, 1663.

SEYFFERT, OSKAR, *A Dictionary of Classical Antiquities*, revised by Henry Nettleship and J. E. Sandys, Swan Sonnenschein, London, 1899.

SHUTE, JOHN, *The First and Chief Groundes of Architecture*, Thomas Marshe, London, 1563.

SMITH, WILLIAM (Ed.), *Dictionary of Greek and Roman Antiquities*, Taylor, Walton, & Maberly, and John Murray, London, 1848.

SMITH, WILLIAM (Ed.), *Dictionary of Greek and Roman Geography*, James Walton John Murray, London, 1870.

SPIERS, R. PHENÉ, *The Orders of Architecture, Greek, Roman, and Italian Selected from Normand's Parallel and other Authorities*, Batsford, London, 1893.

STRATTON, ARTHUR, *Elements of Form and Design in Classic Architecture Shown in Exterior and Interior Motives Collated from Fine Buildings of All Time on One Hundred Plates*, Batsford, London, 1925.

SUMMERSON, JOHN, *The Classical Language of Architecture*, Thames & Hudson, London, 1980.

VIGNOLA, GIACOMO BAROZZI DA, *Regola delli Cinque Ordini d'Architettura*, Porro, Venice, 1596. See also *The Five Orders of Architecture according to Vignola*, arranged by Pierre Esquié and edited by Arthur Stratton, Tiranti, London, 1926.

VITRUVIUS POLLIO, MARCUS, *Architettura*, edited by Ferri, Palombi, Rome, 1960.

VITRUVIUS POLLIO, MARCUS, *De Architectura*. The edition published in Venice in 1567 has plates by Palladio. See also the Frank Granger translation (Heinemann, London, and Harvard University Press, Cambridge, Mass., 1944–56).

VRIES, PAULUS VREDEMAN DE, *L'Architecture ... avec quelques belles ordonnances d'Architecture, mises en perspective per J. Vredman Frison* (and P. V. de V.), Jean Janson, Amsterdam, 1651. Many versions were published following the first Antwerp edition of 1577 entitled *Architecture ...*

VRIES, PAULUS VREDEMAN DE, *Les cinq rangs de l'Architecture, a sçavoir, Tuscane, Dorique, Ionique, Corinthique, et Composée, – avec l'instruction fondamentale faicte par H. H.* [Henrik Hondius the Younger]. *Avec ... quelques belles ordonnances d'architecture, mises en perspective, inventées par J. Vredeman Frison et son fils*, Jean Janson, Amsterdam, 1617.

WARE, ISAAC, *The Complete Body of Architecture. Adorned with Plans and Elevations, from Original Designs*, Osborne and Shipton, Hodges, Davis, Ward and Baldwin, London, 1756. One of the greatest works of the whole Palladian style.

WATKIN, DAVID, *English Architecture, A Concise History*, Thames & Hudson, London, 1979.

WATKIN, DAVID, *A History of Western Architecture*, Barrie & Jenkins, London, 1986.

WIEBENSON, DORA, *Sources of Greek Revival Architecture*, Zwemmer, London, 1969.

WITTKOWER, RUDOLF, *Architectural Principles in the Age of Humanism*, Tiranti, London, 1952.

WITTKOWER, RUDOLF, *Palladio and English Palladianism*, Thames & Hudson, London, 1974.

WOOD, JOHN, *Dissertation upon the Orders of Columns*, Bettenham & Leake, London, 1750.

WREN SOCIETY, *Publications*, vols I–XX, Oxford University Press, 1924–43.

YARWOOD, DOREEN, Encyclopaedia of Architecture, Batsford, London, 1985.